THE
GUN
CONTROL
DEBATE

Contemporary Issues

Series Editors: Robert M. Baird
Stuart E. Rosenbaum

Other titles in this series:

SECOND EDITION

THE GUN CONTROL DEBATE

YOU DECIDE

EDITED BY

LEE NISBET

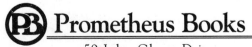 Prometheus Books

59 John Glenn Drive
Amherst, New York 14228-2197

Published 2001 by Prometheus Books

Inquiries should be addressed to
Prometheus Books
59 John Glenn Drive
Amherst, New York 14228–2197
VOICE: 716–691–0133, ext. 207
FAX: 716–564–2711
WWW.PROMETHEUSBOOKS.COM

05 04 03 02 01   5 4 3 2 1

Library of Congress Cataloging-in-Publication Data

The gun control debate : you decide / edited by Lee Nisbet.—2nd ed.
        p. cm. — (Contemporary issues series)
    Includes bibliographical references.
    ISBN 1–57392–861–5 (alk. paper)
    1. Gun control—United States. I. Nisbet, Lee. II. Contemporary issues
(Amherst, N.Y.)

HV7436 .G866 2000
363.3'3'0973—dc21   00–062576

To my wife, Lynette, and son, Jeffrey,
for your unconditional support and patience
despite my preoccupation and unconscionable piles of papers
around the house.

CONTENTS

ACKNOWLEDGMENTS

I would like to acknowledge the following people:

Lynette Herron, for a magnificent job deciphering my miserable handwriting, her patience with endless additions and the polish of the final manuscript.

The members of the Theodore Roosevelt Academic Affairs Steering Committee for their helpful comments on my ideas.

The librarians of Medaille College for their research assistance.

Steven, L. Mitchell, editor in chief of Prometheus Books for his continued encouragement to produce the second edition of *The Gun Control Debate: You Decide*.

My father, Arthur M. Nisbet for his taping of gun control discussions and his supportive lunches.

My late mother, Dr. Dorothea E. Nisbet for her love of ideas and intellectual controversy.

My editor, Art Merchant, for superb editorial work on a complex manuscript.

INTRODUCTION

In 1993 39,595 Americans were killed with guns. Seventy-one percent of these gun deaths (27,726) were committed with handguns. Suicides constituted 48 percent of the firearm toll, homicides 47 percent, gun accidents 4 percent and police killings and executions 1 percent. In addition 104,390 people sought medical treatment for gunshot wounds. The year 1993 represents the highest peacetime gun toll in U.S. history.[1]

However, by 1997 a startling three-year decline in recorded firearm violence had taken place. Total gun deaths had dropped by 21 percent (32,436) and non-fatal medically treated gun wounds had dropped 41 percent (64,207). During this period there was a matching 21 percent drop in violent crime overall and a 25 percent drop in students reporting carrying guns to school.[2]

The declines in reported violence continued. In 1999 the FBI reported the U.S. murder rate had dropped to a 31 year low. The firearm homicide rate had dropped to 64.9 percent (from 71 percent in 1993 and 67.8 percent in 1997).[3]

Also, in 1999, Education Department Secretary Richard Riley citing figures from the Gun Free School Act Report claimed that there had been a 31 percent drop (from 5,724 to 3,930) in gun related expulsions from 1997 through 1998. The secretary pointed out these figures were consistent with the Center for Disease Control and Prevention report issued the week before declaring a significant decline in teen violence in and out of school since the 1990s.[4]

What factors explain these dramatic statistical declines in both gun violence and violent crime? Was it the implementation of the Brady Act (February 1994), which required both a background check and a five-day waiting period between purchase and delivery of a handgun? Was it the 1994 federal ban on possession, manufacture, and sale of nineteen models of assault weapons? Was it the Instant Record Check System (November 1998) which replaced the Brady Act? Was it more rigorous enforcement of existing gun laws or targeting likely looking suspects in urban settings for street searches with penalties accruing for carrying illegal weapons? Was it mandatory add-on penalties for carrying weapons while committing crimes? Was the drop in violent crime due to thirty-one states (by 1999) allowing tens of thousands of law-abiding citizens to carry concealed weapons through a mandatory issue permit system? Or, was it all these measures in combination, or did none of these measures singly, or in combination, cause violent crime and gun crime rates to drop? Was it rather an aging population, longer prison sentences for violent offenders, and a drop in crack cocaine usage? Or, were these decreases in reported violence merely a *statistical* phenomena— extreme variables tending to be followed by less extreme variables (regression to the mean)? How effective are gun control measures anyway? Do citizens "packing heat" really cause violent crime to drop? How can we find out?

And here is another enigma, why despite all these encouraging trends in gun mortality, injuries and gun related school expulsions did the gun control debate reignite in 1999 with ever renewed fervor? Giants of the print media (major newspapers, newsweeklies, and magazines) and the visual media (major broadcast and cable network nightly news and news programs made gun control a dominant issue the first eight months of the year. NBC ran news segments entitled "Americas War on Guns." An episode of the popular series *Law and Order* (NBC) featured a conscience-driven prosecutor fighting to bring a renegade gun manufacturer to justice. The legislative process, he announced, had failed due to the unprincipled efforts of an unnamed "special interest" group. The courts were the only hope. Not coincidently extensive media coverage was being given to a coalition of cities and counties waging novel class action lawsuits against gun manufacturers. The lawsuits sought damages for the costs of deaths and injuries inflicted by guns. The litigations' aim was to force manufacturers to tighten regulation of distribution of guns to retail outlets. President Clinton threatened also to sue the gun industry on behalf of 3,200 violence plagued public housing units (more guns, more violence). Pro–gun control politicians along with media sources predicted that restrictive or even prohibitionist gun control measures would become major even decisive issues in the November 2000 Presidential election. A host of gun control proposals were resurrected, debated and advocated including confiscating all handguns and "assault weapons," mandatory licensing, severe penalties for gun owners whose weapons were stolen and criminally misused, mandatory background checks for all gun show gun purchases, the development of "smart gun" technology, and mandatory trigger locks for handguns. The National Rifle Association opposed all of the above, claiming what was needed was better enforcement of existing gun laws (criminal control, not gun control). The organization was ridiculed by TV talk show hosts, cartoonists, and editorialists for obstruction of sane, sensible and necessary gun controls. Its demise was confidently predicted. The NRA featuring this media treatment in its membership drives, announced its ranks had hit the three million mark.*

To repeat, why, when the statistical risks of gun deaths through homicides, suicides, and accidents, had declined so significantly along with gun carrying in schools would gun control be so featured by the media and politicians?

This updated and revised volume is dedicated to answering these and even more fundamental questions at the core of the gun control debates. As in the earlier volume, published one decade ago, the often conflicting views of historians, criminologists, sociologists, economists, medical experts, and constitutional scholars provide in-depth analysis of the key issues in the gun debate. Their analysis in many cases is radically at odds with the popular media's portrayal of the gun control issue. In other cases the reader is presented with the very studies and data that drive the mass media's presentation of issues. In sum, the materials contained here are not only crucial to understanding what the gun control debate is about but vital for evaluating the strengths, weaknesses, and accuracy of the opposing points of view.

In addition, this new volume goes further in challenging the reader to reach decisions on contentious issues using principles of inquiry. The section introductions, together with selections focusing on methods of analysis, will draw the reader's attention to how (and how well) conclusions are drawn and supported. An entire section deals with ways to evaluate the mass media's treatment of gun control. Readers will also be given strategies to scrutinize both the accuracy and objectivity of their own decision making processes regarding gun issues.

ASSUMPTIONS, QUESTIONS, AND ORGANIZATION

Understanding what America's gun control debate is about requires that we first come to know what it is *not* about. The gun control debate is *not* about whether the government, at any level, has the legal authority and ethical obligation to *regulate* the sale, possession, and use of firearms. All contending parties in the debate recognize the government's legitimate power to so do. The fact that there are presently over 20,000 federal, state, and local laws to accomplish such regulation would make a debate on this score irrelevant in any case. The debate is also *not* about whether government has the legal power to prohibit certain categories of people, such as felons and mental incompetents, from owning firearms or to legislate additional penalties for criminal activities involving firearms. Even the National Rifle Association (NRA), for example, supports government efforts

---

*The exact number was 3.6 million following the intensive media coverage of the "Million Man March" in Washington, D.C., on Mother's Day, May 14, 2000. The protesters demanded gun registration, mandatory licensing, and so on.

in this direction; in fact, it promotes mandatory licensing* for the carrying of concealed weapons as well as mandatory sentencing and additional penalties for criminal misuse of firearms. In short, everyone, involved in the gun control debate agrees that since firearms can be used wittingly or witlessly as lethal weapons, it is both legally and ethically essential to regulate and hence restrict firearm possession and use.

If there is so much agreement about regulating guns, what *is* the debate about? It's about *how much* regulation and *what kinds* of regulations there ought to be. Specifically, the gun control controversy concerns proposals and arguments whose assumptions and evidence would seriously restrict or prohibit mentally competent adult noncriminals from owning firearms that are presently legally obtainable. The controversy focuses on proposals that would markedly restrict access to, or legally ban and confiscate, whole classes of firearms such as handguns, assault weapons, and Saturday night specials. In short, the controversy centers on proposals that would require many Americans to give up freedoms— believed by many to be constitutionally guaranteed—that they now enjoy. Criminologists, using figures on the numbers of guns manufactured, imported and exported, as well as surveys estimate that approximately 80 million Americans own between 170 and 230 million firearms (1994). Handguns comprise up to 80 million of this total. Up to 50 percent of all American households contain guns and 25 percent contain handguns. Women now constitute 11 to 17 percent of the gun owning population, with self-defense an important motivation for many.[5] America has more guns per capita than any of the world's nations.

The political, legal, ethical, and economic implications and consequences of such restrictive gun control proposals are therefore enormous. The burden of demonstrating that further restrictions (or complete prohibition) are both necessary and feasible relative to public safety and order lies squarely on gun control advocates; it's a challenge that the proponents of gun control readily acknowledge.

Now, as the reader may suspect, it is not merely the number of people affected by these proposals that explains the virulence of the gun control debate or the importance attached to its outcome. Like many volatile social controversies, whole systems of values—political, social, personal, and aesthetic—are in conflict. Firearms *mean* different things to different groups of Americans, hence they are valued in radically different ways by these groups. Therefore, proposals that appear to have as their aim severely restricting or prohibiting access to firearms that are at present legally obtainable will be perceived by many to strike at the very heart of a constitutionally guaranteed freedom, one that is personally cherished and revered. On the other hand, such proposals are perceived by equally caring and dedicated people as necessary and eminently sensible approaches to eliminating a dire threat to public and personal safety. Succinctly put, millions of Americans are fearful and contemptuous of exactly what millions

---

*Mandatory licensing systems provide specific criteria for screening applicants which, if met, *legally require* the issuing of a permit to carry a concealed weapon.

of other Americans love and cherish. The fierceness of the debate over every gun control proposal, however innocuous it may appear, is explained both by perceived prohibitionist agendas and by these deeply conflicting meanings and valuations of "the gun."

Millions of Americans not only own firearms, they *love* them. The gun is a treasured source of recreation, a cherished instrument of sport, and a valued source of security in a crime-ridden world. Furthermore, for many of these enthusiasts, the gun is a venerated aesthetic object to be collected and traded as well as written and read about for its impact on history, politics, and warfare. Books devoted to the development and historical impact of a specific firearm become collector's items in their own right. Beyond their utility and history, a great many Americans own and collect firearms for purely aesthetic reasons: the beautiful integration of form, substance, and function. Others are attracted to the power of firearms—the sounds and results of shooting. Millions of Americans consume the many monthly publications devoted to every conceivable aspect of firearm use and lore. Many experienced hunters and target shooters "hand load"—that is, assemble—their own ammunition as a special hobby. They learn the theory and mathematics of ballistics and purchase expensive electronic equipment to monitor and improve the results of the ammunition they fabricate. These devotees maintain memberships in shooting clubs, write and exchange newsletters, "talk guns" at gun shops, and attend local and national gun shows. They are the people who have made big-game hunting with handguns one of the fastest growing types of hunting activity. Handguns chambered for such powerful cartridges as the .44 Magnum and the .454 Casull and equipped with scopes put even more challenge into hunting deer and grizzly.

These are the enthusiasts: guns are an integral part of their lives; in fact, firearms here constitute a way of life. They are gas station attendants and corporate executives, presidents of sportsmen's clubs, and leaders of some of the most important conservation organizations in the country. They constitute what some have referred to as the "gun culture."

It was the nineteenth-century members of this gun culture who, in 1871, formed the National Rifle Association to promote shooting proficiency and safety. It is the contemporary members of this culture who, while retaining the NRA's traditional functions, transformed it during the 1960s and 1970s into a vehicle for political action in response to prohibitionist gun control proposals that followed in the wake of political assassinations and highly publicized gun violence. Such proposals were perceived by many firearm enthusiasts as nothing more than attempts to eliminate their constitutionally guaranteed freedom to own firearms on grounds that were both factually unsubstantiated and politically suspect. In short, as long as gun control remains cast in restrictivist or prohibitionist terms, gun enthusiasts will continue to respond by forming an ever-expanding and unyielding political counterforce to protect their collective interests. At the forefront of this political struggle is the NRA, the "gun lobby." Today 4 million strong, the NRA is arguably the most potent single-issue lobbying organization is the history of American democracy. It is no coincidence, therefore, that in the age of radical gun control, not only were Presidents Reagan and Bush members of the NRA, so, too, were Nixon, Eisenhower, and Kennedy.

On the other side of the gun control debate stands a large group of politically active and socially concerned Americans who perceive criminal and negligent use of firearms in this country to be a problem of major dimensions. They believe large-scale public ownership and access to firearms, especially handguns and "assault"-style semiautomatic guns, to be both a social anachronism and a major public safety menace. All available evidence suggests that this sector of the population is well educated and urban. They are supported in their views by the giants of the American media: national news magazines, nearly all metropolitan newspapers, and the major television networks promote additional and sometimes far-reaching restrictions on ownership of these classes of firearms. Such restrictions are advocated as the only effective means of keeping lethal weapons out of the hands of criminals, lunatics, political assassins, and especially gun owners who, in times of emotional distress, kill spouses, relatives, acquaintances, and/or themselves and whose negligence often allows guns to kill their children. Supporters of restrictive gun control emphasize the claim that firearm ownership, especially of handguns, constitutes a much greater menace to family safety and home security than do intruders and burglars.

Responding to the public safety issue and the success of the "gun lobby" (most notably the NRA), the proponents of gun control have formed their own political action organizations. These groups advocate a prohibitionist or restrictivist approach to gun control and emphasize the view that there is no constitutional guarantee for individual citizens to own firearms, especially handguns. The most effective of these organizations, Handgun Control Inc., has a membership of one half million. It was founded in the 1970s by Pete Shields after his son was killed by a pistol-wielding black terrorist. The present leader of the organization is Sarah Brady, whose husband, James, was permanently disabled in the attempted handgun assassination of Ronald Reagan.

It is in this emotionally charged and politically and culturally polarized atmosphere that gun control proposals and the evidence on their behalf are debated in the popular media and fought over on the political battlefields of federal, state, and local government. The polarized nature of the gun control debate has important consequences. Highly organized and financially powerful advocacy groups are able to gain media attention and, in so doing, define the debate in terms of contrary propositions: far-reaching restrictions on firearms are both constitutional and necessary versus the view that such restrictions are unconstitutional and unworkable. Each side marshals arguments and makes selective use of studies that support its position, while large segments of the public support the view most in agreement with their attitudes, values, and interests. Further, the organized advocacy groups, assisted by the popular media, have successfully made each other the issue. For many, the gun control debate reduces to a hostile attitude toward either the "gun lobby" or the "antigunners."

By presenting some of the most important contemporary studies and the most persuasive arguments developed by experts on both sides of the issue, this volume avoids as much as possible the selectivity that polarization engenders. It is noteworthy that none of the authors represented are connected with the major organized advocacy groups. The sources and impact of political and cultural polarization cannot be ignored, however, for they rule the gun control debate as it is popularly engaged in and significantly influence the form it assumes in academic circles. Selections are provided that explain not only *why* the debate has taken its present course but also the consequences of this course for identifying and resolving actual problems. At the same time, the selections included here identify key questions as well as the controversies they generate; both are empirically independent of social and political agendas and must be resolved before any "solution" to firearm-related problems can be entertained.

Specifically, what problems do gun control proposals seek to remedy? What is the magnitude and significance of these problems and to what extent can gun control resolve them? In sum, after reading this volume, you, the reader, will have the opportunity to form your own judgments on the relative merits of the gun control proposals, based upon your assessment of the often conflicting answers given by experts to the following key questions:

- Does the present freedom to own firearms constitute a threat to political and social stability?
- Is the debate over gun control influenced by political, cultural, and sociological factors?
- Does mass media coverage of gun-violence events and issues accurately reflect and present the range of scholarship on the subject?
- Is mass media coverage of gun control issues biased? If so, in what direction, and exactly how and why and with what consequences?
- Are the gun control policies and experiences of other countries relevant to the problems we face in the United States?
- Is contemporary research at odds with the findings and conclusions of earlier scholarship on the necessity for and workability of gun control?
- What are the sources of information used to support proposed gun control policies? How reliable is this information?
- Do sources of cognitive and motivational bias make it difficult for us to make objective decisions on gun control issues?
- Would further restrictions on public access to handguns, or the banning of them altogether, prevent more criminals and mentally unstable people from obtaining these weapons?
- Would banning handguns lead criminals to use more or less lethal weapons?
- Is the present availability of guns to the general public causally related to rates of violence? If so, how?
- Does gun ownership deter such crimes as murder, mugging, burglary, and rape?

- Are firearms in the hands of ordinary citizens an effective or ineffective, widely or seldomly used, means of self-and home defense?
- Does possession of firearms by ordinary law-abiding citizens place them and/or their relatives, acquaintances, and children at significant risk?
- Should Saturday night specials and assault weapons be banned?
- Would mandating additional jail terms for crimes involving firearms deter their use in crime, and is this approach politically and economically feasible?
- What gun control measures are likely to be effective and why?
- What are the prospects for significantly more restrictive gun control in the United States and what would be its costs as well as benefits?
- Do individual Americans have a constitutional right to own firearms?
- Has scholarship on the Second Amendment been influenced by political and social concerns?

To both raise and provide answers to these crucial questions, the volume is organized in the following format:

Part One: *Gun Control as Kulturkampf*

Selections from historians, sociologists, and criminologists illustrate and explore the cultural and political agendas that influence, polarize and bias past and current discussions.

Part Two: *Gun Control in the Age of (Mis)Information*

Selections provide specific examples of mass media treatment of gun massacres. The section introduction and selections from experts in critical thinking suggest ways to evaluate both the significance mass-media sources attribute to these events and the policy lessons drawn. The reader is invited to apply these methods and questions to selections throughout the book. Further, the reader is challenged to use these methods and questions, to evaluate the reliability of their own judgments concerning the debate. Revisiting these media selections after completing the book is recommended.

Part Three: *Gun Availability and Violence*

Social scientists and criminologists raise and debate key questions. Does the present level of gun availability in the United States influence levels , patterns, and concentrations of violent crime? If so, how, and with what policy implications? Issues of methodology involved in both raising, exploring and answering these questions develop and reinforce critical thinking issues raised in the previous chapter.

Part Four: *The Armed Citizen: More Violence or Less*

Experts in public health, economics and criminology explore the most contentious questions in the gun debate: Do armed citizens constitute a menace to family (especially children) relatives and acquaintances? Or, has the utility of arms for civilian defense against crime been clearly demonstrated on both an individual and social level? Exactly how often do Americans employ guns defensively? What are the policy implications of these defensive uses for gun control measures?

Part Five: *The Second Amendment: The Culture Wars Revisted*

Two distinguished historians present very different views on the right to bear arms. Political, social, and cultural agendas re-emerge that infuse all levels of this volitile debate.

NOTES

1. National Safety Council, 1996; U.S. Bureau of Justice Statistics, 1996; Uniform Crime Reports, 1994; and Centers for Disease Control and Prevention 1999. See also Gary Kleck, *Targeting Guns* (Hawthorne, N.Y.: Aldine de Gruyter, 1997).

2. Centers for Disease Control and Prevention as reported in the *Journal of the American Medical Association* VC.238 (January 5, 2000): 47.

3. Associated Press, 18 October 1999 (*Buffalo News*).

4. *Washington Post*, 11 August 1999.

5. See Gary Kleck, "Guns and Violence: An Interpretive Review of the Field," p. 274 in this volume.

PART ONE

GUN CONTROL
AS <u>KULTURKAMPF</u>

Underlying the gun control struggle is a fundamental division in our nation. The intensity of passion on this issue suggests to me we are experiencing a sort of low grade war going on between two alternative views of what America is and ought to be.

B. Bruce-Briggs, "The Great American Gun War"

"The assault weapons ban (proposed legislation to ban 19 types of 'assault weapons') will have no ultimate effect on the crime rate or on personal security. Nevertheless, it is a good idea. . . . Ultimately a civilized country must disarm its citizenry if it is to have a modicum of domestic tranquility of the kind enjoyed in sister democracies like Canada and Britain. . . . Passing a law like the assault weapons ban is a symbolic—purely symbolic—move in that direction. Its only real justification is not to reduce crime but to desensitize the public to regulation of weapons in preparation for their ultimate confiscation."[1]

Is this another skirmish in the liberal (democrats) versus conservative (republicans) political wars? Yes, but with a twist—the syndicated columnist is not liberal. He is a contemporary conservative. Charles Krauthammer uses a strong gun control stance to chide liberals (democrats) for their supposed "soft on criminals" approach to crime control. "Yes, Sarah Brady is doing God's work. Yes, in the end America must follow the way of other democracies and disarm. But there is not the slightest chance that it will occur until liberals join in the other fight to reduce the incidence of and increase the penalties for crime." Krauthammer acknowledges the role of guns in the current crime wave ("True,

23

part of the reason for the high crime rate is the ubiquity, of guns . . .") but returns to his thesis that "so long as crime is ubiquitous, so long as Americans cannot trust their personal safety to the authorities, they will never agree to disarm." Therefore, being tough on criminals, in Krauthammer's view, is the key to getting rid of guns in America.

Now, this argument is confounding in several respects. True, a conservative is using gun control to bash liberals, but it is a bashing by a conservative who passionately shares the supposedly liberal gun control rationale. Is Krauthammer an anomaly or do some people who disagree with contemporary liberals on many issues share their views on gun control (and conversely, might we find people who are political liberals passionately against gun control)? And even more confusing, why on the gun control issue, as the reader will discover, do political conservatives and liberals *tend* to adopt the very positions they deride on other crime control and civil liberties issues? In short, does casting gun control as simply one part of a larger liberal versus conservative political struggle ignore other variables more predictive of people attitudes?

And second, where does Mr. Krauthammer get his information concerning the "ubiquity" of crime? Statistical information that introduced this volume shows clearly that crime rates, especially violent and violent gun crime rates were rapidly falling by 1996. If Mr. Krauthammer is correct that Americans are heavily armed because they believe they are at high risk from criminal activity, where do they get their (mis)information (see Part Two)? Some historical background concerning the origins and nature of the gun control debate might be helpful in considering these questions.

The gun control movement in America has been a twentieth-century response to the problems of urban crime and domestic violence. The movement's traditional target was, and continues to be, the readily concealed weapon—the handgun. The fact that it can be easily carried and concealed has made the handgun the "weapon of choice" for those who use firearms for illicit purposes. In urban areas, these same qualities have also made the handgun the preferred weapon for those who desire a means to defend themselves against criminals. In such settings the effective distances at which deadly encounters take place are short. The long barrels of shotguns (unless shortened or "sawed off") and rifles are a disadvantage in these encounters, and the fact that they cannot be easily concealed eliminates the advantage of surprise.

Technical factors alone, however, do not explain why the handgun has become so controversial in contemporary American urban areas, unlike their European counterparts. One difference is the availability of such weapons. There are roughly 80 million handguns in the United States at the present time: the ratio of existing handguns to the total population has remained relatively constant over the last century.[2] Availability, of course, is in part a function of demand. But why do large numbers of Americans—honest citizens comprising 99 percent of handgun owners—feel the need to own these weapons?

One reason is heritage: as noted historian Richard Hofstadter documents, the early frontier experience, the role (actual and idealized) of the citizen-soldier in the Revolutionary War, the continued wars against Indian tribes and bandits while settling the nation's frontier with America's hunting tradition, gave the gun an honored place in our culture. Hofstadter and other historians who analyze the role of firearms in American life agree, however, that this heritage alone does not explain why Americans remained heavily armed after the frontier was closed and especially after millions of people settled in large eastern cities. One hypothesis of particularly contemporary relevance centers on nineteenth-century urban crime, social unrest, and the public's perception that the police could not effectively protect citizens from criminals. Historians Lee Kenneth and James Anderson, in their classic volume *The Gun in America: The Origins of a National Dilemma*, point out that the gun habits of nineteenth-century *urban* Americans (like their twentieth-century counterparts) had more to do with crime than frontier nostalgia:

> The general tendency to keep arms or carry them on the person may well be linked to the "urban explosion" that transformed American cities in the period 1820–1860. Its mechanism of everyday law enforcement did not keep pace with its growth so that the inhabitant felt an increased need to fend for himself. . . . This sense of personal insecurity in the face of crime probably did more to hasten the trend toward personal armament than anything else. . . .[3]

It should be noted that most police forces in eastern and midwestern urban areas were not permitted to carry weapons until the latter part of the nineteenth century. Throughout the 1800s, Americans distrusted a standing armed police force as much as eighteenth-century Americans distrusted a standing or professional army. This mistrust, when combined with America's individualistic "self-help" ethic, the availability of weapons, and most of all the existence of chronic, violent urban criminal activity, contributed both to the ideal and the fact of an armed citizenry. In sum, the tradition of citizens being armed, which permeated nineteenth-century America, together with the continued explosive growth of cities, violent gun-related urban crime, and social unrest, set the stage for both the contemporary gun control movement and the debate it has fostered.

The debate began, not surprisingly, in New York City during the turn of the century. At this time in our nation's history, the fact that citizens carried handguns was both commonplace and noncontroversial in urban areas throughout the country. In 1911, however, the Sullivan Law—passed in New York State.* How did this extraordinary legislation come to pass?

---

*The Gun Control Act of 1968, a *federal* act, is the most important legislation regulating firearms passed to date. The act prohibited the importation of surplus military weapons and small, short-barrelled, cheap foreign handguns popularly referred to as Saturday night specials. Most importantly, however, it outlawed the interstate retailing of all firearms. The last provision aimed at preventing criminals and assassins like Lee Harvey Oswald from ordering firearms through the mail under assumed names. Earlier federal acts in 1934 and 1938 effectively prohibited the possession of machine guns, assault rifles, sawed-off shotguns, and silencers. This legislation also required the licensing of firearms manufacturers and dealers.

Prominent political, civic, religious, and financial leaders in New York City mobilized newspaper support for a campaign that portrayed handgun control as vital in fighting the city's growing criminal and domestic violence. Newspapers inundated the public with feature stories on gun accidents and incidents of gun violence. In addition, as Kennett and Anderson note, gun control was promoted by the press, prominent citizens, and civic groups as a statement affirming America's resolve to become a sane, civilized, cosmopolitan nation, no longer to be embarrassed by its crude and violent frontier past.

The ideal of the citizen armed for self-defense in an age of a modern police force was ridiculed as a dangerous anachronism, a throwback to those bygone days of the old frontier. Gun control was also advocated as a way to disarm what was regarded as a suspect new wave of immigrants. Taking a stand against gun control was condemned as advocating crime, barbarism, and ethnic violence. Through the efforts of New York City's major newspapers, the Sullivan Law passed the state legislature with little opposition. The law was significant for the future of gun control debate for several reasons:

1. For the first time a state had made a serious legislative commitment to regulate the handgun. A permit was now required to purchase, own, and possess such a weapon. Carrying an unlicenced handgun became a felony. The permit was issued at a local authority's discretion and could be denied or revoked for criminal behavior or suspect character.*

2. The rationale for such regulation firmly linked handgun control to crime control and the civilizing process. The handgun lost its traditional place of honor and was now officially regarded as a potential menace, with citizens being required to prove their fitness and need for ownership.

3. Despite the law, the handgun violence in New York City continued to rise, which encouraged both critics and advocates of the statute. Critics argued that the law served only to disarm the law-abiding public while doing nothing to keep handguns out of criminal hands. Criminals, it was observed, were not likely to apply for handgun permits. Supporters countered that the Sullivan Law's failure to stem gun violence only proved the need for stricter controls in neighboring states or, better yet, federal controls.

4. All of the arguments for and against the Sullivan Law would be echoed from the 1960s on into the 1990s as the movement grew for stricter regulation, if not the outright banning of handguns.

---

*Discretionary licensing, as opposed to mandatory licensing (supported by the NRA), does not presume that an applicant has a right to a license unless there is a specified cause for denial. The applicant must prove that he/she has a "reasonable need" to own and carry a concealed handgun. The issuing authority alone decides if the applicant has made his/her case. In New York City, for example, the discretionary permit system is used effectively to preclude the average citizen from owning and carrying a handgun.

Most importantly, the Sullivan Law, along with its advocates and critics, marked the emergence of the firearm as a symbol of a much larger ongoing political, social, and cultural struggle—*kulturkampf*—to define the kind of nation America should be. Specifically, gun control might be viewed as a weapon in an ongoing struggle between groups who consistently despise each other's values on a number of issues. However, the special meanings of "the gun" sometimes involves some very estranged groups in fascinating dalliances (gun toting feminists and the NRA, for example). The conflict of values theory will provide important insights into the nature, course, and meaning of "gun control." Knowledge of the political and social agendas involved in this controversy will help us to understand why the "facts of the case" mean different things to different people depending upon the specific issue: gun-crime control, self-defense, or the meaning of the Second Amendment. The readings in Part One, therefore, have been selected not only to acquaint readers with the classic positions for and against strict gun control, but also to demonstrate how political and social agendas sometimes influence the debate.

Historian Richard Hofstadter presents the classic procontrol position, mustering historical, political, and social evidence to make his case for strict gun control, especially as that view was advanced in the 1970s in response to political assassinations, social unrest, and increasing rates of criminal and domestic violence involving handguns.

B. Bruce-Brigg's work is another classic from the 1970s. Here, however, for the first time, a social scientist takes a skeptical look at the various arguments advanced to support restrictive gun control policies. He wonders how such definitive policy recommendations can be made when, in his view, no credible social science research had ever been done on the subject. Bruce-Briggs's challenge touched off the movement in the decade of the 1980s and 1990s to do the needed research. His work reinforces the hypothesis that the gun control debate is symptomatic of a much wider cultural skirmish.

Social scientist William R. Tonso takes aim at Hofstadter's historically based recommendations for gun control. More importantly, Tonso broadens the context of the gun control debate by focusing on the impact of political and social agendas influencing both research and policy recommendations on gun control issues.

Selections from criminologist Gary Kleck are especially useful in debunking the idea that gun control is simply the clash of conservative and liberal politics. Kleck finds besides the fact that some conservatives and liberals sometimes hold unexpected views on gun control, each side tends to shift to the position of the other concerning police power issues and crime control strategies. Conservatives when guns are at issue become ardent civil libertarians. While liberals became champions of police search and seizure powers, racial profiling (e.g., Project Exile) mandatory and draconian prison terms for gun crimes and celebrate the virtues of prohibition of a popular but dangerous vice.

Kleck also finds that support for gun control measures is not based upon confidence that they will substantially inhibit violent crime. What then on the political and popular level is the volitile gun control debate about? Kleck's answer might explain why this century-old debate has become so polarized, propagandistic, and seemingly irresolvable. Further, this selection has particular relevance to the newsweekly coverage of gun control issues included in Part Two, "Gun Control in the Age of (Mis)Information."

NOTES

1. Charles Krauthammer, *Washington Post* (*Buffalo News*, 8 April 1996).

2. See Gary Kleck, "Guns and Violence: An Interpretive Review of the Field," p. 274 in this volume.

3. Lee Kenneth and James Anderson, The Gun in America: The Origin of a National Dilemma (Westport, Conn.: Greenwood Press, 1975), p. 148.

1

AMERICA AS A GUN CULTURE

RICHARD HOFSTADTER

Senator Joseph Tydings of Maryland, appealing in the summer of 1968 for an effective gun control law, lamented: "It is just tragic that in all of Western civilization the United States is the one country with an insane gun policy." In one respect this was an understatement: Western or otherwise, the United States is the only modern industrial urban nation that persists in maintaining a gun culture. It is the only industrial nation in which the possession of rifles, shotguns, and handguns is lawfully prevalent among large numbers of its population. It is the only such nation that has been impelled in recent years to agonize at length about its own disposition toward violence and to set up a commission to examine it, the only nation so attached to the supposed "right" to bear arms that its laws abet assassins, professional criminals, berserk murderers, and political terrorists at the expense of the orderly population—and yet it remains, and is apparently determined to remain, the most passive of all major countries in the matter of gun control. Many otherwise intelligent Americans cling with pathetic stubbornness to the notion that the people's right to bear arms is the greatest protection of their individual rights and a firm safeguard of democracy—without being in the slightest perturbed by the fact that no other democracy in the world observes any such "right" and that in some democracies in which citizens' rights are rather better protected than in ours, such as England and the Scandinavian countries, our arms control policies would be considered laughable.

From *American Violence: A Documentary History*, ed. Richard Hofstadter and Michael Wallace (New York: Knopf, 1970). Copyright © 1970 by Alfred A. Knopf, Inc. Reprinted by permission of Alfred A. Knopf, a Division of Random House, Inc.

Laughable, however, they are not, when one begins to contemplate the costs. Since strict gun controls clearly could not entirely prevent homicides, suicides, armed robberies, or gun accidents, there is no simple way of estimating the direct human cost, much less the important indirect political costs, of having lax gun laws. But a somewhat incomplete total of firearms fatalities in the United States as of 1964 shows that in the twentieth century alone we have suffered more than 740,000 deaths from firearms, embracing over 265,000 homicides, over 330,000 suicides, and over 139,000 gun accidents. This figure is considerably higher than all the battle deaths (that is, deaths sustained under arms but excluding those from disease) suffered by American forces in all the wars in our history. It can, of course, be argued that such fatalities have been brought about less by the prevalence of guns than by some intangible factor, such as the wildness and carelessness of the American national temperament, or by particular social problems, such as the intensity of our ethnic and racial mixture. But such arguments cut both ways, since it can be held that a nation with such a temperament or such social problems needs stricter, not looser, gun controls.

One can only make a rough guess at the price Americans pay for their inability to arrive at satisfactory controls for guns. But it can be suggested in this way: there are several American cities that annually have more gun murders than all of England and Wales. In Britain, where no one may carry a firearm at night, where anyone who wants a long gun for hunting must get a certificate from the local police chief before he can buy it, and where gun dealers must verify a buyer's certificate, register all transactions in guns and ammunition, and take the serial number of each weapon and report it to the police, there are annually about .05 gun homicides per 100,000 population. In the United States there are 2.7. What this means in actual casualties may be suggested by the figures for 1963, when there were 5,126 gun murders in the United States, twenty-four in England and Wales, and three in Scotland. This country shows up about as badly in comparative gun accidents and, to a lesser degree, in suicides. There is not a single major country in the world that approaches our record in this respect.

Americans nowadays complain bitterly about the rising rate of violent crime. The gun is, of course, a major accessory of serious premeditated crime. Appealing for stronger gun controls in 1968, President Johnson pointed out that in the previous year there had been committed, with the use of guns, 7,700 murders, 55,000 aggravated assaults, and more than 71,000 robberies. Plainly, stronger gun controls could not end crime, but they would greatly enhance enforcement of the law (as New York's Sullivan Law does) and would reduce fatalities. Out of every one hundred assaults with guns, twenty-one led to death, as compared with only three out of every one hundred assaults committed by other means. In five states with relatively strong gun laws the total homicide rate per 100,000 population—that is, homicides from all causes—runs between 2.4 and 4.8. In the five states with the weakest gun laws this rate varies from 6.1 to 10.6.

In 1968, after the assassinations of Robert F. Kennedy and Martin Luther King Jr., there was an almost touching national revulsion against our own gun culture, and for once the protesting correspondence on the subject reaching senators and representatives outweighed letters stirred up by the extraordinarily efficient lobby of the National Rifle Association. And yet all that came out of this moment of acute concern was a feeble measure, immensely disappointing to advocates of serious gun control, restricting the mail-order sales of guns. It seems clear now that the strategic moment for gun controls has passed and that the United States will continue to endure an armed populace, at least until there is a major political disaster involving the use of guns.

Today the urban population of the nation is probably more heavily armed than at any time in history, largely because the close of World War II left the participating countries with a huge surplus of militarily obsolescent but still quite usable guns. These could be sold nowhere in the world but in the United States, since no other country large enough and wealthy enough to provide a good market would have them. More weapons became available again in the 1950s, when NATO forces switched to a uniform cartridge and abandoned a stock of outmoded rifles. These again flooded the United States, including about 100,000 Italian Carcanos of the type with which John F. Kennedy was killed. Imported very cheaply, sometimes at less than a dollar apiece, these weapons could be sold at enormous profit but still inexpensively—the one that killed Kennedy cost $12.78.

It has been estimated that between five and seven million foreign weapons were imported into the United States between 1959 and 1963. Between 1965 and 1968 handgun imports rose from 346,000 to 1,155,000. Domestic industries that make cheap handguns are approaching an annual production of 500,000 pistols a year. Thus, a nation in the midst of a serious political crisis, which has frequently provoked violence, is afloat with weapons—perhaps as many as fifty million of them—in civilian hands. An Opinion Research poll of September, 1968, showed that 34 percent of a national sample of white families and 24 percent of blacks admitted to having guns. With groups like the Black Panthers and right-wing cranks like the Minute Men, not to speak of numerous white vigilante groups, well armed for trouble, the United States finds itself in a situation faced by no other nation. One must ask: What are the historical forces that have led a supposedly well-governed nation into such a dangerous position?

It is very easy, in interpreting American history, to give the credit and the blame for almost everything to the frontier, and certainly this temptation is particularly strong where guns are concerned. After all, for the first 250 years of their history Americans were an agricultural people with a continuing history of frontier expansion. At the very beginning the wild continent abounded with edible game, and a colonizing people still struggling to control the wilderness and still living very close to the subsistence level found wild game an important supplement to their diet. Moreover, there were no enforceable feudal inhibitions against poaching by the common man, who was free to roam where he could and shoot what he could and who ate better when he shot better. Furthermore, all farmers, but especially farmers in a lightly settled agricultural country, needed guns for the control of wild vermin and predators. The wolf, as we still say, has to be kept from the door.

Finally, and no less imperatively, there were the Indians, who were all too often regarded by American frontiersmen as another breed of wild animal. The situation of the Indians, constantly under new pressures from white encroachments, naturally commands modern sympathy. But they were in fact, partly from the very desperation of their case, often formidable, especially in the early days when they were an important force in the international rivalries of England, France, and Spain in North America. Like the white man they had guns, and like him they committed massacres. Modern critics of our culture who, like Susan Sontag, seem to know nothing of American history, who regard the white race as a "cancer" and assert that the United States was "founded on a genocide," may fantasize that the Indians fought according to the rules of the Geneva Convention. But in the tragic conflict of which they were to be the chief victims, they were capable of striking terrible blows. In King Philip's War (1675–76) they damaged half the towns of New England, destroyed a dozen, and killed an estimated one out of every sixteen males of military age among the settlers. Later the Deerfield and other frontier massacres left powerful scars on the frontier memory, and in the formative days of the colonial period wariness of sudden Indian raids and semimilitary preparations to combat them were common on the western borders of settlements. Men and women, young and old, were all safer if they could command a rifle. "A well grown boy," remembered the Reverend Joseph Doddridge of his years on the Virginia frontier, "at the age of twelve or thirteen years, was furnished with a small rifle and shotpouch. He then became a fort soldier, and had his port-hole assigned him. Hunting squirrels, turkeys, and raccoons, soon made him expert in the use of his gun."

That familiarity with the rifle, which was so generally inculcated on the frontier, had a good deal to do with such successes as Americans had in the battles of the Revolution. The Pennsylvania rifle, developed by German immigrants, was far superior to Brown Bess, the regulation military musket used by British troops. This blunt musket, an inaccurate weapon at any considerable distance, was used chiefly to gain the effect of mass firepower in open field maneuvers at relatively close range. The long, slender Pennsylvania rifle, which had a bored barrel that gave the bullet a spin, had a flatter and more direct trajectory, and in skilled hands it became a precision instrument. More quickly loaded and effective at a considerable distance, it was singularly well adapted not only to the shooting of squirrels but to the woodsman's shoot-and-hide warfare. It struck such terror into the hearts of British regulars as to cause George Washington to ask that as many of his troops as possible be dressed in the frontiersman's hunting shirt, since the British thought "every such person a complete Marksman." The rifle went a long way to make up for the military inconsistencies and indifferent discipline of American militiamen, and its successes helped to instill in the American mind a conviction of the complete superiority of the armed yeoman to the military professionals of Europe.

What began as a necessity of agriculture and the frontier took hold as a sport and as an ingredient in the American imagination. Before the days of spectator sports, when competitive athletics became a basic part of popular culture, hunting and fishing probably were the chief American sports, sometimes wantonly pursued, as in the decimation of the bison. But for millions of American boys, learning to shoot and above all graduating from toy guns and receiving the first real rifle of their own were milestones of life, veritable rites of passage that certified their arrival at manhood. (It is still argued by some defenders of our gun culture, and indeed conceded by some of its critics, that the gun cannot and will not be given up because it is a basic symbol of masculinity. But the trouble with all such glib Freudian generalities is that they do not explain cultural variations: they do not tell us why men elsewhere have not found the gun essential to their masculinity.)

What was so decisive in the winning of the West and the conquest of the Indian became a standard ingredient in popular entertainment. In the penny-dreadful Western and then in films and on television, the western man, quick on the draw, was soon an acceptable hero of violence. He found his successors in the private eye, the FBI agent, and in the gangster himself, who so often provides a semi-legitimate object of hero worship, a man with loyalties, courage, and a code of his own—even in films purporting to show that crime does not pay. All mass cultures have their stereotyped heroes, and none are quite free of violence; but the United States has shown an unusual penchant for the isolated, wholly individualistic detective, sheriff, or villain, and its entertainment portrays the solution of melodramatic conflicts much more commonly than, say, the English, as arising not out of ratiocination or some scheme of moral order but out of ready and ingenious violence. Every Walter Mitty has had his moment when he is Gary Cooper, stalking the streets in High Noon with his gun at the ready. D. H. Lawrence may have had something, after all, when he made his characteristically bold, impressionistic, and unflattering judgment that "the essential American soul is hard, isolate, stoic, and a killer." It was the notion cherished also by Hemingway in his long romance with war and hunting and with the other sports that end in death.

However, when the frontier and its ramifications are given their due, they fall far short of explaining the persistence of the American gun culture. Why is the gun still so prevalent in a culture in which only about 4 percent of the country's workers now make their living from farming, a culture that for the last century and a half has had only a tiny fragment of its population actually in contact with a frontier, that, in fact, has not known a true frontier for three generations? Why did the United States alone among industrial societies cling to the idea that a substantially unregulated supply of guns among its city populations is a safe and acceptable thing? This is, after all, not the only nation with a frontier history. Canada and Australia have had theirs, and yet their gun control measures are far more satisfactory than ours. Their own gun homicide rates, as compared with our 2.7, range around .56, and their gun suicide and accident rates are also much lower. Again, Japan, with no frontier but with an ancient tradition of feudal and military violence, has adopted, along with its modernization, such rigorous gun laws that its gun homicide rate at .04 is one of the world's lowest. (The land of hara-kiri also has one of the lowest gun suicide rates about one-fiftieth of ours.) In sum, other societies, in the course of industrial and urban development, have succeeded in modifying their old gun habits, and we have not.

One factor that could not be left out of any adequate explanation of the tenacity of our gun culture is the existence of an early American political creed that has had a surprisingly long life, albeit much of it now is in an underground popular form. It has to do with the antimilitaristic traditions of radical English Whiggery, which were taken over and intensified in colonial America, especially during the generation preceding the American Revolution, and which became an integral part of the American political tradition. The popular possession of the gun was a central point in a political doctrine that became all but sacrosanct in the Revolution: a doctrine that rested upon faith in the civic virtue and military prowess of the yeoman; belief in the degeneration of England and in the sharp decline of "the liberties of Englishmen" on their original home soil; and a great fear of a standing army as one of the key dangers to this body of ancient liberties. The American answer to civic and military decadence, real or imagined, was the armed yeoman.

By the same reasoning the answer to militarism and standing armies was the militia system. It had long been the contention of those radical Whig writers whose works did so much to set the background of American thought, that liberty and standing armies were incompatible. Caesar and Cromwell were commonly cited as the prime historical examples of the destructive effects of political generals on the liberties of the people. The Americans became confident that their alternative device, an armed people, was the only possible solution to the perennial conflict between militarism and freedom. Their concern over the evils of repeated wars and institutionalized armies was heightened by the eighteenth-century European wars in which they were inevitably involved. Blaming the decay that they imagined to be sweeping over England in good part on the increasing role of the military in the mother country, they found their worst fears confirmed by the quartering of troops before the Revolution. John Adams saw in the Boston Massacre "the strongest proof of the danger of standing armies." The Virginian George Mason, surveying the history of the nations of the world, remarked: "What havoc, desolation and destruction, have been perpetrated by standing armies!" The only remedy, he thought, reverting to one of the genial fictions of this school of thought, was the ancient Saxon militia, "the natural strength and only stable security of a free government." Jefferson reverted to the idea of a popular Saxon militia by providing in his first draft of the Virginia Constitution of 1776 that "no freeman shall ever be debarred the use of arms."

Washington, who had to command militiamen, had no illusions about them. He had seen not a single instance, he once wrote, that would justify "an opinion of Militia or raw Troops being fit for the real business of fighting. I have found them useful as light Parties to skirmish in the woods, but incapable of making or sustaining a serious attack." Despite the poor record of militia troops in the Revolution, as compared with the courage and persistence of Washington's small and fluctuating Continental Army, the myth persisted that the freedom of America had been won by the armed yeoman and the militia system, and the old fear of a standing army was in no way diminished now that it was not to be under the command of an English aristocracy but of native American generals. In the mid-1780s, when the Americans had won their independence and were living under the Articles of Confederation, Secretary of War Henry Knox found himself the administrator of an army of about seven hundred men. In the 1790s, when it was proposed under the Constitution to add only about five hundred more, Pennsylvania Democrat Senator William Maclay anxiously observed that the government seemed to be "laying the foundation of a standing army"! Only the disastrous performance of militiamen in the War of 1812 persuaded many American leaders that the militia was a slender reed upon which to rest the security of the nation.

In the meantime the passion for a popular militia as against a professional army had found its permanent embodiment in the Second Amendment to the Constitution: "A well regulated Militia, being necessary to the security of a free State, the right of the people to keep and bear Arms, shall not be infringed." By its inclusion in the Bill of Rights, the right to bear arms thus gained permanent sanction in the nation, but it came to be regarded as an item on the basic list of guarantees of *individual* liberties. Plainly it was not meant as such. The right to bear arms was a *collective*, not an individual right, closely linked to the civic need (especially keen in the absence of a sufficient national army) for "a well regulated Militia." It was, in effect, a promise that Congress would not be able to bar the states from maintaining well-regulated militias.*

The Supreme Court has more than once decided that the Second Amendment does not bar certain state or federal gun controls. In 1886 it upheld an Illinois satute forbidding bodies of men to associate in military organizations or to drill or parade with arms in cities or towns. When Congress passed the National Firearms Act of 1934 forbidding the transportation in interstate commerce of unregistered shotguns, an attempt to invoke the Second Amendment against the law was rejected by the Court in what is now the leading case on the subject, *United States* v. *Miller* (1939). In this case the Court, ruling on the prosecution of two men who had been convicted of violating the National Firearms Act by taking an unregistered sawed-off shotgun across state lines, concluded that the sawed-off shotgun had no "reasonable relationship to the prevention, preservation, or efficiency of a well-regulated militia." The Court ruled that since the gun in question was not part of ordinary military equipment, its use was unrelated to the common defense. The Court further found that the clear purpose of the Second Amendment was to implement the constitutional provision for "calling forth the Militia to execute the Laws of the Union, suppress insurrec-

---

*For a more detailed discussion of issues related to the Second Amendment, see Part Five of this volume.—Ed.

tions and repel invasions" and declared that the Second Amendment "must be interpreted and applied with that end in view."

While the notion that "the right to bear arms" or federal gun regulation is largely confined to the obstinate lobbyists of the National Rifle Association, another belief of American gun enthusiasts enjoys a very wide currency in the United States, extending to a good many liberals, civil libertarians, and even radicals. It is the idea that popular access to arms is an important counterpoise to tyranny. A historian, recently remonstrating against our gun policies, was asked by a sympathetic liberal listener whether it was not true, for example, that one of the first acts of the Nazis had been to make it impossible for the nonparty, nonmilitary citizen to have a gun—the assumption being that the German people had thus lost their last barrier to tyranny. In fact Nazi gun policies were of no basic consequence: the democratic game had been lost long before, when legitimate authorities under the Weimar Republic would not or could not stop uniformed groups of Nazi terrorists from intimidating other citizens on the streets and in their meetings and when the courts and the Reich Ministry of Justice did not act firmly and consistently to punish the makers of any Nazi Putsch according to law. It is not strong and firm governments but weak ones, incapable of exerting their regulatory and punitive powers, that are overthrown by tyrannies. Nonetheless, the American historical mythology about the protective value of guns has survived the modern technological era in all the glory of its naïveté, and it has been taken over from the whites by some young blacks, notably the Panthers, whose accumulations of arms have thus far proved more lethal to themselves than to anyone else. In all societies the presence of small groups of uncontrolled and unauthorized men in unregulated possession of arms is recognized to be dangerous. A query therefore must ring in our heads: Why is it that in all other modern democratic societies those endangered ask to have such men disarmed, while in the United States alone they insist on arming themselves?

A further point is of more than symptomatic interest: the most gun-addicted sections of the United States are the South and the Southwest. In 1968, when the House voted for a mild bill to restrict the mail-order sale of rifles, shotguns, and ammunition, all but a few of the 118 votes against it came from these regions. This no doubt had something to do with the rural character of these regions, but it also stems from another consideration: in the historic system of the South, having a gun was a white prerogative. From the days of colonial slavery, when white indentured servants were permitted, and under some circumstances, encouraged, to have guns, blacks, whether slave or free, were denied the right. The gun, though it had a natural place in the South's outdoor culture, as well as a necessary place in the work of slave patrols, was also an important symbol of white male status. Students in the Old South took guns to college as a matter of course. In 1840 an undergraduate at the University of Virginia killed a professor during a night of revelry that was frequently punctuated by gunfire. Thomas Hart Benton, later to be a distinguished Missouri senator, became involved, during his freshman year at the University of North Carolina, in a brawl in which he drew a pistol on another student, and was spared serious trouble only when a professor disarmed him. He was sixteen years old at the time. In the light of the long white effort to maintain a gun monopoly, it is hardly surprising, though it may be discouraging, to see militant young blacks borrowing the white man's mystique and accepting the gun as their instrument. "A gun is status—that's why they call it an equalizer," said a young Chicago black a few years ago. "What's happening today is that everybody's getting more and more equal because everybody's got one."

But perhaps more than anything else the state of American gun controls is evidence of one of the failures of federalism: the purchase and possession of guns in the United States is controlled by a chaotic jumble of twenty thousand state and local laws that collectively are wholly inadequate to the protection of the people and that operate in such a way that areas with poor controls undermine those with better ones. No such chaos would be tolerated, say, in the field of automobile registration. The automobile, like the gun, is a lethal instrument, and the states have recognized it as such by requiring that each driver as well as each car must be registered and that each driver must meet certain specified qualifications. It is mildly inconvenient to conform, but no one seriously objects to the general principle, as gun lobbyists do to gun registration. However, as the United States became industrial and urban, the personnel of its national and state legislatures remained to a very considerable degree small town and rural, and under the seniority system that prevails in Congress, key posts on committees have long been staffed by aging members from small-town districts-worse still, from small-town districts in regions where there is little or no party competition and hence little turnover in personnel. Many social reforms have been held back long after their time was ripe by this rural-seniority political culture. Gun control is another such reform: American legislators have been inordinately responsive to the tremendous lobby maintained by the National Rifle Association, in tandem with gunmakers and importers, military sympathizers, and far-right organizations. A nation that could not devise a system of gun control after its experiences of the 1960s, and at a moment of profound popular revulsion against guns, is not likely to get such a system in the calculable future. One must wonder how grave a domestic gun catastrophe would have to be in order to persuade us. How far must things go?

2

SOCIAL PROBLEMS
AND SAGECRAFT

GUN CONTROL AS A CASE IN POINT

WILLIAM R. TONSO

T his essay is not about the gun control issue per se. It is about the way the issue has typically been dealt with by those social scientists who, in one social scientific capacity or another, have had occasion to be concerned with it. Or, more accurately, this essay focuses on the more publicized social scientific treatments of the gun control issue—those passed on to college students through social problems texts, anthologies, and monographs, and to the general public through magazine articles and the published findings of various social science assisted federal commissions on crime, violence, and civil disturbances. The objective is to point out some of the shortcomings of what will be referred to as the conventional social scientific approach to controversial social issues and social problems.

While the controversial issue examined here is gun control, other examples could conceivably have been used to make the same points: issues such as school busing, pornography, or the legalization of marijuana, or social problems such as discrimination, pollution, poverty, unemployment, or crime. There is a missionary aspect to the conventional approach to such issues and problems in that it often goes beyond analysis to lend, subtly or otherwise, supposedly scientifically based support to one means or other of coping with these phenomena. This support is disseminated through textbooks, commission findings, and so forth, and being "scientifically" based can be ignored only at the risk of one's being

38

considered unenlightened. It will be argued, therefore, that the conventional social scientific treatments of controversial social phenomena often have much more in common with the work of those to whom Florian Znaniecki referred as "sages" than they have with social science, and consequently that such treatments obscure more than they reveal about the issues or problems with which they are dealing. The first part of the essay describes the conventional social scientific treatment of the gun issue, places this treatment into social cultural context, and finally links it to Znaniecki's comments on the social role of the sage. The second part points out, through a critique of the conventional treatment of the gun issue, how the concerns of the sage affect the social scientific enterprise, here defined broadly enough to include social history.[1]

SOCIAL SCIENCE OR SAGECRAFT?

It seems to be generally accepted that the civilian possession of firearms in the United States is widespread, but whether or not this state of affairs is desirable has been the subject of much controversy since the early part of the twentieth century.[2] The side of this controversy that has received the most publicity through the media, however, maintains that this widespread possession constitutes, if not a social problem unto itself, a major contributing factor to other social problems such as crime, violence, and civil disorder. It is hardly surprising, then, that efforts to bring the civilian possession of firearms under strict control and to reduce the number of firearms in civilian hands have also received a great deal of publicity through the media.

A perusal of the *Reader's Guide to Periodical Literature's* "Firearms Laws and Regulations" section can give one some indication of the magnitude of this media support for gun controls. Since the latest major push for controls began in the early 1960s, articles on the subject in such news and general interest magazines as *Life, Time, Newsweek*, the *Saturday Evening Post, Reader's Digest, Harper's, Saturday Review*, the *Nation*, and the *New Republic* have been almost unanimous in their strong support of gun controls, with only the outdoor, gun, and libertarian magazines consistently taking an anticontrol stand. The national television networks have also been almost unanimous in their support of controls through various documentaries on the subject as well as through [popular] television [dramas and sitcoms]. The leading urban newspapers have all editorialized in favor of controls, the *Washington Post* once doing so for seventy-seven straight days,[3] as have many medium- and small-town newspapers and the syndicated columnists and political cartoonists appearing in them—Ann Landers, Art Buchwald, Jack Anderson, and Herblock, among others. Newspapers and magazines have also helped publicize the works of such procontrol authors as Carl Bakal and Robert Sherrill.[4] And even comic strips, such as "Goosemyer," "Tank McNamara," and "Doonesbury," have supported gun controls by ridiculing the anticontrol position.

While those responsible for the various newspaper editorials, columns, magazine articles, and TV documentaries that have over the years argued for controls have often looked to the "experts" on man and society—psychiatrists, psychologists, and sociologists—for assistance, by the middle 1960s the social sciences were starting to get more directly involved in the controversy. In response to the political assassinations and civil disturbances of the period, a number of federal commissions aimed at discovering and eradicating the causes of crime, violence, and civil disturbances were established, and these commissions were invariably assisted by social scientists. The commissions also invariably ended up recommending that strict gun controls be enacted as one means of reducing the amount of crime, violence, and civil disorder.[5]

Beginning with the federal commissions, the social scientific involvement with the gun control issue has extended increasingly to monographs, textbooks, and anthologies which deal with various social problems and are aimed at the college market. Based on commission reports and the treatment that the gun issue has received in the various texts, and so forth, that have dealt with it, the sentiments concerning civilian firearms possession and gun control that have been transmitted through these, various social science sources can be summarized as follows:

1. When the United States was being transformed from a raw wilderness to a modern, urban, industrial nation, passing through a rural, agricultural stage along the way, private citizens often had use for firearms if they were to provide themselves with food and/or protection.[6]

2. The United States no longer has a frontier, and in fact, it is now primarily urban and industrial rather than rural and agricultural. Consequently, the large number of firearms that have gotten and continue to get into civilian hands no longer serve any useful purpose and are more trouble than what they are worth. They no longer contribute to the establishment of law and order but actually undermine efforts to establish order, as the high rate of firearms-related crime shows.[7]

3. The United States is the only modern, urban, industrial nation that does not strictly regulate the civilian possession of firearms. The effectiveness of such controls is demonstrated by the fact that other modern, urban, industrial nations, all of which have them, have violent crime rates far lower than those of the United States.[8]

4. It is obvious, therefore, that the United States is badly in need of strict gun controls that at a minimum would require the registration of all privately owned firearms, and licenses and identification cards for all firearms owners, plus a drastic reduction of the number of privately owned handguns.[9]

5. The pollsters have shown that considerably more than half of the populace supports all of these measures and that as many as three-fourths support some of them.[10]

6. The only reason that such regulations have not been enacted into law is

that the domestic firearms industry and the National Rifle Association have, through well-organized lobbying efforts, been able to take advantage of the weaknesses of the federal system of government to block such legislation.[11]

7. This opposition to obviously needed firearms regulations, though thus far effective, is self-serving, irresponsible, irrational, unenlightened, reactionary, uninformed, etc.[12]

The impression given by the foregoing is that through historical research, crosscultural comparisons of crime rates, and the scientific analysis of public opinion, social scientists have been able to establish definitely that the United States would benefit significantly from gun controls, that the majority of Americans want such controls, and consequently, that opposition to such controls is self-serving or unreasonable. But there are things about the conventional social scientific analysis of the gun control issue that make one wonder about the impartiality of those engaged in it. First, it should be noted that the conventional social science position on gun control summarized earlier is identical to the position that procontrollers have taken for years without social scientific assistance. In fact, it is not uncommon for nonsocial scientific, nonscholarly, procontrol, antigun polemics such as *The Right to Bear Arms*, by irate citizen Carl Bakal, and *Saturday Night Special*, by "investigative reporter" Robert Sherrill, to be cited in social science textbook analyses of the gun issue.[13] And when such sources are cited, no mention is made of the acknowledged procontrol, antigun sentiments of their authors.

A second interesting aspect of the conventional social scientific treatment of the gun issue is that qualification of the material presented on the subject is rare to nonexistent. Poll findings are accepted at face value, although there is good social scientific cause to do otherwise.[14] Similarly, crosscultural comparisons of firearms-related crime rates are made with no consideration given to factors having little or nothing to do with gun controls that might help account for crosscultural differences between such rates.[15]

Finally, it is worthy of consideration that the conventional social scientific treatment of the gun issue makes no attempt to put the control controversy into social, cultural, and historical perspective in order to foster nonjudgmental understanding of the sentiments and vested interests of both those who support controls and those who oppose them. Occasional attempts are made to present the anticontrol position along with the procontrol position,[16] but no effort is made to uncover the vested interests of the people who subscribe to these conflicting views of control, and one is seldom left in doubt concerning which position is the most sophisticated, informed, and logical. Similarly, the gun's place in American history is sometimes examined by conventional social scientists,[17] but its survival is obviously viewed as unfortunate and is explained in terms of cultural lag.

In other words, the conventional social scientific treatment of gun control leaves much to be desired if its goal is the scientific illumination of this controversial issue. Why? To answer this question it is helpful to put both the issue and those studying it into social, cultural, and historical context, as the conventional have been so reluctant to do; a very unconventional work by social historians Lee Kennett and James LaVerne Anderson provides a starting point for such an effort. In *The Gun in America: The Origins of a National Dilemma*, Kennett and Anderson make no policy recommendations or insinuations. They simply fit the gun into American history, demonstrating along the way how the pro- and anti-control factions evolved and came into conflict with each other as the United States became ever more urban and industrial, and less rural and agricultural. They conclude that the trends are against the gun, but they do not hint that American society will be either better or worse off if this is the case.

While Kennett and Anderson make no attempt to delineate the role that the social sciences have played in the gun control controversy, their treatment of the phenomenon in terms of culture conflict is quite suggestive along these lines. Taking their lead from a *Wall Street Journal* article dealing with gun control, they argue that the controversy is best seen "as a skirmish in the larger battle over the nation's cultural values, a battle in which 'cosmopolitan America' is pitted against 'bedrock America.'"[18] Expanding on the differences between the worldviews of these two Americas and commenting on the appropriateness of the labels applied to them, Kennett and Anderson continue:

> The terms are apt; they could be used to describe the protagonists when the Sullivan Law was debated fifty years ago. Progun spokesmen have long been addicted to those assaults on the liberal establishment in which Spiro Agnew excelled, and those in the other camp have not always concealed their contempt for the "shirtsleeve crowd." Cosmopolitan America foresees a new age when guns and the need for them will disappear; bedrock America conceives of it as 1984. Cosmopolitan America has always been concerned about its international image; bedrock America has always been nativist. Shortly after Robert Kennedy's assassination, Gunnar Myrdal reportedly said that if the Constitution allowed such indiscriminate ownership of guns, "then to hell with the Constitution." Cosmopolitan America would have found this food for sober reflection; bedrock America, without reflection, would have said: "To hell with Gunnar Myrdal."[19]

If, as Kennett and Anderson argue, the gun controversy is "a skirmish in the larger battle over the nation's cultural values," a battle pitting cosmopolitan America's lifestyles, worldviews, and ways of interpreting reality against those of bedrock America, it is hardly surprising that the conventional social scientific treatment of the control issue amounts to an unquestioning scientific stamp of approval of the media-supported procontrol stand. Kennett and Anderson make no claim that the "cultural battle lines" between the two Americas are rigidly fixed. In fact, they claim that "sophisticated America and shirtsteeve America war in all of us."[20]

While the two Americas may war in many of us—all is surely an exaggeration—one gets the impression that the purest cosmopolitanism is likely to be found in the urban, highly educated (degreed might be more appropriate), philosophically and politically liberal, upper-middle class; the purest bedrockism is likely to be found in the rural and small-town, less degreed, philosophically and politically conservative, lower-middle and working classes.[21] If this is the case, at the very cosmopolitan-sophisticated core of cosmopolitan-sophisticated America, along with those who control the nation's media—or at least the national television networks, large circulation metropolitan newspapers, general interest periodicals, and major publishing houses—are the American intellectual elite. And of course, the American intellectual elite includes not only the nation's "top" writers, journalists, and other such literary folk, but its "top" educators, scholars, and scientists, social and otherwise, as well. Cosmopolitan America, therefore, is not only generally more adept at articulating its views than is bedrock America; it also possesses the means to place its views before bedrock as well as cosmopolitan America; *Reader's Digest* and TV for the former; *New Republic* and college social science courses for the latter. Through its scholarly and scientific connections, cosmopolitan America can also coat these views with a thick veneer of what passes for impartial scientific authority: consider the gun control issue and the conventional social scientific treatment of it as a case in point.

That the media, the scholarly-intellectual community, and even the social scientific subcommunity of the latter are, for the most part, part of what the *Wall Street Journal* and Kennett and Anderson have referred to as cosmopolitan America, rather than impartial observers and interpreters of and reporters on the passing scene, has been noted by a number of maverick social scientists. Sociologist, Roman Catholic priest, and columnist Andrew Greeley, himself a strong supporter of strict gun controls, has claimed that the intellectual community—social scientists not excluded—has all the characteristics of an ethnic group, including divisive factions and an ethnocentrism that encourages it to look down upon rather than attempt to understand the nonintellectual "masses."[22] Michael Lerner, while a graduate student in political science and psychology at Yale, claimed in an even more scathing polemic that the "upper classes" are extremely prejudiced against the lower-middle class and that "one of the strongest supports for this upper-class, 'respectable' bigotry lies in the academic field of psychology."[23] Clearly including social scientists, sociologist Stanislav Andrzejewski has noted that liberal intellectuals are not as tolerant as they think they are when it comes to dealing with those who do not subscribe to their Liberal-Humanitarian religion or participate in their "supranational culture."[24] And sociologist Peter Berger has written about the rising "New Class" of knowledge producers, symbol- rather than thing-manipulators, who have class vested interests of their own. According to Berger, "institutionally, prestige universities and other centers of knowledge production (such as think tanks) are centers of New Class power, while publishing houses, periodicals, and foundations serve as distributing agencies."[25] He goes on to point out that the New Class has a vested interest in government intervention because the greater part of its livelihood is derived "from public-sector employment. . . . Because government interventions have to be legitimated in terms of social ills, the New Class has a vested interest in portraying American society as a whole, and specific aspects of that society, in negative terms."[26]

In other words, to these critics and analysts of the knowledge-producing and disseminating class to which they themselves belong, knowledge producers and disseminators in general tend to be so bound up with the worldviews, lifestyles, values, and vested interests of their own urban, upper-middle class, degreed, liberal, sophisticated, cosmopolitan lives that their analyses of various controversial social issues and problems might be expected to be somewhat one-sided and aimed at promoting their own cosmopolitan interests. If this is the case, such knowledge producers and disseminators are involved in what might be called "sagecraft" in behalf of the cosmopolitan America of which they are not only an integral but a central part. "The original status of the sage lies within his party," according to Florian Znaniecki, "and his original function consists in rationalizing and justifying intellectually the collective tendencies of his party. It is his duty to 'prove' by 'scientific' arguments that his party is right and its opponents are wrong."[27]

In order to perform his duty, the sage must demonstrate that his party's position is right because it is based on truth, and that the opposition's stand is wrong because it is based on error. "There is no doubt but that he can perform this task to the satisfaction of himself and his adherents," says Znaniecki, "for in the vast multiplicity of diverse cultural data it is always possible to find facts which, 'properly' interpreted, prove that the generalizations he accepts as true are true and that those he rejects as false are false."[28] Of course, the sage is likely to be opposed by the sages of the other side. Unless opposition sages can be silenced, the sage must call their reasoning and/or facts into question.

If the knowledge producers and disseminators form the core of cosmopolitan America, as suggested in the aforementioned, it is hardly surprising that the social scientific treatment of the gun issue that has been publicized through federal commissions and college social problems books is identical to the procontrol stand almost unanimously supported by the media. Neither is it surprising that such treatments do not critically examine poll findings, crosscultural comparisons of crime rates, and so forth, that can be used to support controls; nor that they invariably fail to put the control controversy into social, cultural, and historical context examining the vested interests of the pro- as well as the anticontrol factions. That sagecraft, purposeful or the inadvertent product of cosmopolitan ethnocentrism, helps account for such oversights is suggested by statements made by two prominent sociologists associated with a federal commission headed by Milton Eisenhower. In spite of the fact that his own research ten years earlier had found no correlation between the availability of guns and the incidence of gun crime, one of these, Marvin E. Wolfgang, stated in a letter to the editor of *Time* magazine: "My personal choice for legislation is to remove all guns from private possession. I would favor statutory provisions that require all guns to be turned in to public authorities."[29] The other, Morris Janowitz, is in complete agreement: "I see no reason . . . why anyone in a democracy should own a weapon."[30]

Inadvertent or otherwise, a sage orientation results in social scientific analysis that is social scientific in name only. The social scientist who is primarily concerned with "rationalizing and justifying intellectually the collective tendencies of his party," rather than with shedding as much light as possible on a complex social phenomenon is quite limited. He or she is not likely to consider personal position as part of the phenomenon being studied, or to recognize how one's ideological position restricts one's vision.

SAGECRAFT AND THE SOCIAL SCIENTIFIC ENTERPRISE

While it is being suggested that those social scientists responsible for the conventional social scientific treatment of the gun control issue are acting as sages in behalf of a cosmopolitan America that is generally antigun, no claim is made that they are, in most cases at least, consciously doing so. It would not be surprising to find that most of those social scientists assisting federal commissions or passing information concerning the phenomenon to students through textbooks actually feel that they are letting the facts—crime rates, poll results, and so forth—speak for themselves. The point being made is that such social scientists have been inclined to take too much for granted about the gun issue, possibly due to their own cosmopolitan worldviews, lifestyles, values, and vested interests, and in doing so they have provided "scientific" support-sage fashion-for the cosmopolitan tendencies that they not only share but help to create. A few examples should suffice to demonstrate how such cosmopolitan ethnocentrism and the sage orientation it encourages can affect the social scientific enterprise.

Consider the late Richard Hofstadter's attempt to explain the widespread civilian possession of firearms in the United States. Along the way, as he attempted to discredit the "frontier past" explanation for a state of affairs that he clearly considered to be deplorable, Hofstadter noted that the American frontier experience could not account for the persistence of what he referred to as the American gun culture, since the frontier faded away several generations ago. "Why," Hofstadter asked, "did the United States alone among industrial societies cling to the idea that a substantially unregulated supply of guns among its city populations is a safe and acceptable thing?"[31] Canada and Australia have had frontiers, and Japan has had a violent past, he reminds us, yet the gun homicide, suicide, and accident rates for these nations are far lower than those for the United States. Hofstadter credits the "rigorous gun laws" that Japan (the land of hara-kiri) has adopted as it has modernized with producing that country's extremely low gun homicide and suicide rates. "In sum," he states, "other societies, in the course of industrial and urban development, have succeeded in modifying their old gun habits, and we have not."[32]

The preceding is typical of the conventional social scientific use of crosscultural comparisons to support gun controls. The facts have apparently been allowed to speak for themselves. But interestingly enough, the conventional never tell us anything about the "old gun habits" of other nations that gun controls have supposedly modified. In fact, the conventional not only do not tell us anything about these "old gun habits," but they show no sign that they are familiar with them or that they have made any attempt to become so. Hofstadter, for example, simply assumed that Japan's "old gun habits" were similar to ours because of that nation's tradition of feudal and military violence, and that Australia's and Canada's were similar to ours because both nations have had frontiers. Such assumptions certainly amount to convenient lapses of scholarly curiosity, since the works of various scholars who have not involved themselves with the gun control controversy—firearms historians, students of Japanese history, and those who have compared frontiers—give us no reason to believe that the "old gun habits" of these nations were anything like ours.

With respect to Japan, if we are to accept what other scholars have written on the subject, firearms were used extensively in the feudal wars after having been brought to Japan by the Portuguese toward the middle of the sixteenth century, but the populace as a whole never seemed to have become familiar with them.[33] The sword remained the most respected weapon through the 250 years of relatively peaceful Tokugawa rule down to rather recent times. During this period, partly due to traditional concerns and partly due to official policy, little or no effort was made to improve firearms, and when Perry "reopened" Japan to the rest of the world in the middle of the nineteenth century, the Japanese were still using matchlock guns of the same basic variety as those to which they had been introduced by the Portuguese 300 years earlier. What "old gun habits" did the Japanese have to modify as they became urban and industrial? Why should "rigorous gun laws" that came with "modernization" be credited with producing a low gun-related homicide rate when, prior to "modernization," Japan had relegated the gun to the status of plaything of the wealthy and had shown little or no concern for developing it as a weapon? Similarly, how can such laws be credited with producing a low gun-related suicide rate in a tradition-bound land where the honored way to commit hara-kiri was with a knife?

With regard to Canada and Australia, scholars who have compared them have found many differences between the Canadian and Australian frontiers and our own-differences that may account for dissimilar patterns of firearms usage between those of our frontiers and the others. Except for the trouble that the French experienced with the Iroquois Confederacy in eastern Canada during the eighteenth century, for instance, neither Canadian nor Australian frontiersmen encountered the formidable aboriginal opposition that Americans encountered on the fringes of settlement for some 250 years of "recurring pioneering experience."[34] In fact, neither the Canadian nor the Australian frontier experience could even be described as recurring. Part of the Canadian cast was simply transported west after the railroads penetrated the Laurentian Shield in the late nineteenth century; in Australia, pioneer expansion was stopped short in the mid-nineteenth century by the uninhabitable interior deserts.[35] Centralized police forces, for another example, were reasonably effective in Canada[36] and Australia, though hardly popular in the latter,[37] while "law and order" was often brought to American frontier communities through vigilante action,[38] a phenomenon hardly known on the other two frontiers. In short, it would seem that American frontiersmen over a period of 250 or so years were required to rely more heavily on their firearms for their own protection than were their Canadian and Australian counterparts.

But Hofstadter not only was not aware of, or conveniently overlooked, differences between frontiers that might have produced dissimilar "old gun habits" in these various ex-frontier nations; he also overlooked differences that developed behind the frontiers in these nations—differences that also might have had some bearing on the forms these "habits" took and on their preservation. To compare modern firearms-related crime rates of formerly frontier nations without considering the differences in the magnitude of the transformations that these nations have experienced is to "stack the deck" sagefashion in favor of one's own cause rather than to attempt to foster understanding. When one considers that the United States, 3,615,122 square miles in area to Canada's 3,851,809 and Australia's 2,967,909, has almost five times the population and over eight times the Gross National Product of Canada and Australia combined, it is obvious that much more has occurred behind the frontier here than in either of the other nations. And it seems generally agreed that this American transformation generated much more social disruption and civil strife than has resulted from the lesser transformations in Canada and Australia. What were the Canadian or Australian equivalents of our Revolutionary and Civil Wars, for example-conflicts that set neighbor against neighbor and lasted at that level long after the battlefields had grown silent? When did either Canada or Australia have racial, ethnic, or labor wars to approach those that Americans have waged against each other behind the frontier?

In other words, the passing of the frontier in the United States did not appreciably reduce the risk to life and limb that Americans have created for each other, so, given the political nature of law enforcement that conflict theorists take such delight in exploring, why is it surprising that many Americans continue to look to the gun for protection as well as for recreation? How can Canadian and Australian gun laws be credited with producing lower gun-related crime rates than ours by modifying "old gun habits" assumed to have been similar to ours, when there seems to be good reason to believe that neither their frontiers nor what came afterward actually produced "old gun habits" like ours?

Hofstadter's comments on the modified "old gun habits" of other nations appeared in an *American Heritage* article entitled "America as a Gun Culture" [reprinted in this collection—Ed.]. This article developed a theme first mentioned in Hofstadter's introduction to an anthology he and Michael Wallace edited, entitled *American Violence: A Documentary History.*[39] If his assumptions concerning the "old gun habits" of other nations have been challenged in the scholarly literature on the gun issue published to date, such challenges have received little publicity.

Another example of the selective perception that scholarly supporters of gun controls carry into their crosscultural comparisons of crime rates is provided by a social science assisted staff report submitted to the National Commission on the Causes and Prevention of Violence, headed by Milton Eisenhower. This report, directed by George D. Newton and Franklin E. Zimring, pointed out that of the four homicides per 100,000 persons recorded in England and Wales in 1967, only one out of each four involved the use of a firearm.[40] In the United States during the same period, sixty-one crimes of this sort were recorded per 100,000 persons, with thirty-eight of each sixty-one involving the use of firearms. Similarly, in England and Wales, ninety-seven robberies per 100,000 persons were recorded, with only six of each ninety-seven involving firearms, while in the United States 1,020 robberies per 100,000 persons were recorded, with 372 out of each 1,020 involving the use of firearms.

To the extent that one is inclined to take statistics at face value, these figures are interesting. Suppose that no American citizen had possessed a firearm in 1967, and let us assume that none of the crimes in which firearms were used that year would have been committed if a firearm had not been available, a questionable assumption to say the least. Subtracting the firearms-related crimes from the others, we find that the United States still would have led England and Wales in homicides 23 to 4 per 100,000 (5.8 to 1) and in robberies 648 to 97 per 100,000 (6.7 to 1). A scholar interested in shedding light on a complex issue might wonder, then, if it is English gun laws or the differences between English and American societies that are responsible for the lower rate of firearms-related crime in England and Wales. Newton and Zimring acknowledge this possibility but do not dwell on it, since they are building the case for controls. A scholar might also point out that the passing of the frontier has not, according to these figures, removed the sorts of threats that humans create for one another from the United States (and these threatening conditions have continued not simply because of the absence of strong firearms regulations). A procontrol sage, of course, would hardly be expected to consider seriously either of these issues, but Newton and Zimring and the social scientists who assisted them were supposedly searching for "truths" upon which to base policy recommendations.[41] It should be mentioned that Marvin Wolfgang, whose strong procontrol sentiments have been mentioned, was one of the social scientists associated with the report.

As the conventional have been inclined to take too much for granted about firearms use, past and present, in other parts of the world, they have also been inclined to accept uncritically and pass on Gallup and Harris poll results that invariably show that there is a great deal of public support for various gun control measures. Sociologist Rodney Stark, for example, wrote the following in his college-level social problems text: "The failure of national, state, and local governments to enact strict gun-control legislation offers considerable insight into the American political process. For decades a dedicated minority has had its will over an apathetic majority. What does the majority believe?"[42] Looking to the public opinion polls for the answer to his question, Stark noted that 84 percent of those polled on gun control by Gallup in 1938 believed that " 'all owners of pistols and revolvers should be required to register with the Government, that 75 percent of those polled in 1959 "(and 65 percent of gun owners) believed no one should be permitted to buy a gun without a police permit," and that "no poll conducted in the United States has ever found that more than a third of those polled opposed tough gun controls."[43] This same message, as has been noted, can be found in other social problems texts and anthology readings, always presented in a matter-of-fact manner as if the poll findings are indisputable. But poll findings are not indisputable, as anyone familiar with the measurement and interpretation problems encountered by survey researchers is likely to be aware.

To claim that the "apathetic majority" believes that we should have "tough gun controls" of some type or other implies that we know that the people concerned have seriously considered the issue, taken a stand in favor of controls, but been unwilling to put forth the effort required to get them enacted. But might we not just as easily conclude that the majority is inactive because most of those who are a part of it have seldom given any consideration at all to the issue and are really not particularly committed to controls? The apparent overwhelming pro-control support reported by the polls does not preclude this interpretation. The appearance of support might be the product of one or both of the following:

1. Even if an individual has given little or no consideration to the gun control issue, and consequently is not committed to either a pro- or anticontrol stand, once he has decided to cooperate with the pollsters, he or she must make some effort to answer their questions. And, given the situation, it would hardly be surprising for the responses to support tough gun laws. Though not committed, the individual may quite understandably feel that this is the response expected. Survey researchers are familiar with the measurement problems posed by "social desirability" responses,[44] and with the overwhelming media support for controls, the possibility that such responses may have inflated the procontrol column of the polls can scarcely be dismissed. The way the questions are posed, the demeanor of the interviewer, and recent news events may also tend to make the procontrol response seem to be the expected response. Who but the most dedicated opponent of controls could tell an urbane interviewer that he or she was against tough gun controls after a presidential assassination involving the use of a firearm?

2. Apart from the social desirability response issue, the way that single questions or a series of questions are posed can, inadvertently or otherwise, elicit the responses desired by those commissioning the polls. Thus the Harris and Gallup polls, commissioned by the procontrol. media, ask whether the respondent is for tough gun controls and invariably find that most Americans want the controls that the media support. On the other hand, the less-publicized survey conducted for the anticontrol National Rifle Association by Decision/Making/Information (DMI), a California-based opinion measuring firm, asking simply "What should

be done to reduce crime?" When only 11 percent suggested that gun laws were needed, DMI reported that "the lack of gun control laws is not spontaneously mentioned as either a national problem or a local problem by a significant number of citizens. Their attention had to be called to the issue before they expressed an opinion."[45] Once their attention was called to the issue, 73 percent answered that they did not believe that even firearms confiscation would reduce crime, and 68 percent answered that they felt that most gun owners would not turn in their guns if the federal government demanded that they do so. Not surprisingly, the bias built into the DMI poll satisfied the NRA. When NBC made the mistake of asking similar questions, they found that 59 percent of those polled answered that a handgun ban would not reduce crime and 11 percent answered that it would increase crime.[46] Certainly this was a tactical error in the war between the sages.

Even if we assume that the interviewer's questions have tapped the "true feelings" of the American public on a given issue, however, we are still faced with the problem of interpretation. It may be that the majority of Americans, after carefully thinking over the issue, support tougher gun controls. It may also be, given what appears to be an American, or at least a bedrock, tendency to view crime in terms of "us good guys" against "those bad guys,"[47] that many such supporters, particularly those who are firearms owners, do not consider the possibility that they themselves may be adversely affected by such laws. After all, the police would never deny them permission to acquire or possess the firearm of their choice—only the "bad guys" would be affected. This assumption may shed light on the apparent paradox noted by Kennett and Anderson: according to the polls, most Americans support gun controls at the same time that most would use their guns against urban rioters.[48] What response would Gallup and Harris receive if they asked those being interviewed if they would support firearms regulations even though there was a good chance that those regulations would restrict their own possession and usage of firearms?

Many social scientists are aware of the problems associated with polls and survey research in general, and in fact, the preceding commentary is largely based on Armand L. Mauss and Milton Rokeach's critique of a 1976 Gallup poll. The purpose these two sociologists give for their critique is as follows: "We would like to suggest a number of considerations that should be kept in mind by the intelligent and sophisticated reader in assessing the significance of survey results like these, and then offer a few opinions of our own about their meanings."[49] This objective could certainly be considered praiseworthy, an example of the scientific, inquiring mind at its best, taking for granted no more than necessary, and helping others to examine that which they might have overlooked. The poll findings being critiqued, however, had nothing to do with gun control. Significantly, the poll chosen for critical examination dealt with religious beliefs and had found, among other things, "that 94 percent of Americans still believe in God," and that "69 percent believe in immortality." Bedrock America, of course, might be expected to revel in these findings, but ultra-cosmopolitan

America would probably find them disconcerting. And also significantly, the critique appeared in the *Humanist*, the journal of the ultra-cosmopolitan secular humanists. When poll findings indicating that the majority of Americans favor strong gun controls are cited in texts and commission reports, they are not accompanied by "considerations that should be kept in mind by the intelligent and sophisticated reader in assessing the significance of survey results."

As the conventional have been inclined to take too much for granted about the use of firearms past and present in other parts of the world, and to accept uncritically and pass on Gallup and Harris poll findings, so have they been reluctant to treat the gun issue as some of their number have treated other controversial social issues. Edwin M. Schur, for example, has claimed that categories of victimless crimes have been created through the outlawing of abortion, homosexuality, and the use of certain drugs. He has argued that such laws are unenforceable, and that they may have unwelcome side effects—the establishment of "the economic basis for black-market operations," or the production of "situations in which police efficiency is impaired and police corruption encouraged."[50] While bedrock America might find such an argument hard to accept, cosmopolitan America would probably tend to agree with it.

If the argument holds for laws against the use of certain drugs, and so forth, does it not also hold for attempts to regulate firearms possession? Those who do not register their guns when registration is required, or who do not turn in their handguns when handgun possession is banned become classifiable as criminal even though they have not misused firearms or committed other acts classifiable as serious crimes. How would gun control affect police efficiency? The more difficult it becomes to acquire firearms legally, the more valuable supposedly confidential firearms registration and owner registration lists become to professional burglars who wish to locate firearms for illegal sale; hence, more temptation is placed in the way of those officials charged with guarding such records. If an attempt is made to disarm the populace, the guns that the police are able to confiscate become valuable items. How many will be filtered back into private hands via the black market? How could gun controls not foster official and police corruption? When laws are difficult to enforce, as attorney Don B. Kates Jr., has noted, "enforcement becomes progressively more haphazard until at last the laws are used only against those who are unpopular with the police."[51] How could gun control not lead to selective enforcement and discrimination against minorities and the poor? It would seem that Schur, of all people, would be in a position to recognize that if this argument concerning the creation of victimless crime categories and their side effects holds for any attempts to regulate behavior, it holds as well for gun control. But not surprisingly, the recognition seems to have escaped him, as it has other social scientists, and he has even indicated that he believes gun controls could play a significant part in reducing violence and civil disorder.[52] Need more be said concerning the restricted vision that cosmopolitan ethnocentrism and sagecraft can impose on the social scientific enterprise?

NOTES

1. While the tone of this essay might seem polemical in places, its aim is not to argue against gun control. Though the author does personally oppose such controls, whether or not they are necessary or desirable is a political issue to him, rather than a social scientific issue. The essay's polemics are not aimed at gun control, therefore, but at one-sided social science, which in this case is pro-gun control.

2. Lee Kennett and James Laverne Anderson, *The Gun in America: The Origins of a National Dilemma* (Westport, Conn.: Greenwood Press, 1975), chap. 7.

3. Ibid., pp. 239, 312.

4. Carl Bakal, *The Right to Bear Arms* (New York: McGraw-Hill, 1966), Robert Sherrill, *The Saturday Night Special* (New York: Charter House, 1973).

5. See George D. Newton and Franklin E. Zimring, *Firearms and Violence in American Life*, a staff report to the National Commission on the Causes and Prevention of Violence (Washington, D.C.: U.S. Government Printing Office, 1969), pp. 151–62. This work is a prime example of such commission reports, and it includes a summary of several others.

6. See Richard Hofstadter, "America as a Gun Culture," *American Heritage* (October 1970): 7, 10; Richard Hofstadter and Michael Wallace, eds., *American Violence: A Documentary History* (New York: Vintage Books, 1970), p. 24; Eugene W. Holton, *Frontier Violence: Another Look* (New York: Oxford University Press, 1974), pp. 121–22; Charles H. McCaghy, *Deviant Behavior: Crime, Conflict, and Interest Groups* (New York: Macmillan, 1976), p. 125; Joseph Buskin, "The Essential American Soul: Violent," in *Issues in American Society*, ed. Joseph Buskin (Encino, Calif.: Glencoe, 1978), p. 43; Daniel Glazer, *Crime in Our Changing Society* (New York: Holt, Rinehart and Winston, 1978), p. 201; Charles E. Silberman, *Criminal Violence, Criminal Justice* (New York: Vintage Books, 1978), pp. 48–49; and Newton and Zimring, *Firearms and Violence in American Life*.

7. See Kenneth Westhues, *First Sociology* (New York: McGraw-Hill, 1982), pp. 457, 460–62; Newton and Zimring, *Firearms and Violence in American Life*; Hofstadter, "America as a Gun Culture"; Hofstadter and Wallace, *American Violence*, pp. 25–26; Holton, *Frontier Violence*, pp. 121–22; McCaghy, *Deviant Behavior*, p. 125; Buskin, "The Essential American Soul," p. 48; Glazer, *Crime in Our Changing Society*, p. 260; and Silberman, *Criminal Violence*, pp, 80–81.

8. See Amitai Etzioni, "Violence," in *Contemporary Social Problems*, eds. Robert K. Merton and Robert Nisbet (New York: Harcourt Brace Jovanovich, 1971), p. 740; Lamar Empey, "American Society and Criminal Justice Reform," in *Current Perspectives on Criminal Behavior: Original Essays in Criminology*, ed. Abraham S. Blumberg (New York: Oxford University Press, 1974), pp. 295–96; Arthur S. Shostak, ed., *Modern Social Reforms: Solving Today's Social Problems* (New York: Macmillan, 1974), p. 291; Rodney Stark, *Social Problems* (New York: Random House, 1975), p. 226; Martin R. Haskell and Lewis Yablonsky, *Crime and Delinquency* (Chicago: Rand McNally, 1978), pp. 340–41; Michael S. Bassis, Richard J. Gelles, and Ann Levine, *Social Problems* (New York: Harcourt Brace Jovanovich, 1982), p. 477; Donald Light Jr. and Suzanne Keller, *Sociology*, 3d ed. (New York: Alfred A. Knopf, 1982), p. 254; Newton mid Zimring, *Firearms and Violence in American Life*, pp. 119–28; Hofstadter, "America as a Gun Culture," p. 82, Hofstadter and Wallace, *American Violence*, p. 26; and Holton, *Frontier Violence*, p. 122.

9. See Joseph Julian, *Social Problems* (New York: Appleton-Century-Croft, 1973), pp. 481–82; Marvin E. Wolfgang, "Violent Behavior," in *Current Perspectives on Criminal Behavior: Original Essays on Criminology*, ed. Abraham S. Blumberg (New York: Oxford University Press, 1974), p. 246; Frank Scarpitti, *Social Problems* (New York: Holt, Rinehart and Winston, 1974), p. 431; President's Commission on Law Enforcement and the Administration of Justice, "Control of Firearms," in *Contemporary Social Issues: A Reader*, ed. Rose Giallombardo (Santa Barbara, Calif.: Hamilton, 1975), pp. 176–77; Hugh Barlow, *Introduction to Criminology* (Boston: Little, Brown and Company, 1978), p. 116; Jeffrey H. Reiman, *The Rich Get Richer and the Poor Get Prison: Ideology, Class, and Criminal Justice* (New York: John Wiley and Sons, 1979), pp. 192–93; Newton and Zimring, *Firearms and Violence in American Life*, pp. 139–48; Hofstadter, "America as a Gun Cul-

ture"; Hofstadter and Wallace, *American Violence*, pp. 25–26; Etzioni, "Violence," p. 740; Empey, "Criminal Justic Reform," p. 296; Stark, *Social Problems*, pp. 226–27; McCaghy, *Deviant Behavior*, p. 126; Buskin, "The Essential American Sour," p. 48; Glazer, *Crime in Our Changing Society*, pp. 260–64; Haskell and Yablonsky, *Crime and Delinquency*, p. 752; and Bassis, Gelles, and Levine, *Social Problems*, p. 477.

10. See Michael J. Harrington, "The Politics of Gun Control," in *Readings in Sociology Contemporary Perspectives*, ed. Phillip Whitten (New York: Harper and Row, 1979), p. 257; Newton and Zimring, *Firearms and Violence in American Society*, p. 152; Shostak, *Modern Social Reforms*, p. 292; President's Commission, "Control of Firearms," p. 174; Stark, *Social Problems*, p. 227; McCaghy, *Deviant Behavior*, p. 126; and Glazer, *Crime in Our Changing Society*, p. 262.

11. See Hofstadter, "America as a Gun Culture," p. 85; Etzioni, "Violence," pp. 739–44; Julian, *Social Problems*, p. 481; Scarpitti, *Social Problems*, p. 431; President's Commission, "Control of Firearms," pp. 174–75; Stark, *Social Problems*, p. 227; McCaghy, *Deviant Behavior*, pp. 127–29; Barlow, *Introduction to Criminology*, p. 115; Glazer, *Crime in Our Changing Society*, p. 262; Haskell and Yablonsky, *Crime and Delinquency*, p. 341; and Harrington, "The Politics of Gun Control."

12. See Newton and Zimring, *Firearms and Violence in American Life*, pp. 195–99; Hofstadter, "America as a Gun Culture"; Hofstadter and Wallace, *American Violence*, p. 25; Etzioni, "Violence," pp. 739–40; Julian, *Social Problems*, p. 481; Shostak, *Modern Social Reforms*, pp. 278–92; President's Commission, "Control of Firearms," pp. 174–75; Stark, *Social Problems*, p. 227; McCaghy, *Deviant Behavior*, pp. 127–29; Barlow, *Introduction to Criminology*, p. 115; Haskell and Yablonsky, *Crime and Delinquency*, p. 341; and Harrington, "The Politics of Gun Control."

13. See Hofstadter and Wallace, *American Violence*, p. 26: Barlow, *Introduction to Criminology*, p. 143; Glazer, Crime in our Changing Society, pp. 213, 261, 262, 263; Haskell and Yablonsky, *Crime and Delinquency*, p. 340; and Joseph F. Sheley, *Understanding Crime: Concepts, Issues, Decisions* (Belmont, Calif.: Wadsworth, 1979), p. 229.

14. See President's Commission, "Control of Firearms," p. 174; Glazer, *Crime in Our Changing Society*, pp. 261–62; Shostak, *Modern Social Reforms*, p. 292; McCaghy, *Deviant Behavior*, p. 126; and Harrington, "The Politics of Gun Control," p. 257.

15. See Newton and Zimring, *Firearms and Violence in American Life*, pp. 119–28; Hofstaclter, "America as a Gun Culture," p. 82; Hofstadter and Wallace, *American Violence*, p. 26; Etzioni, "Violence," p. 740; Empey, "American Society," pp. 95–96; Hollon, *Frontier Violence*, p. 122; Stark, *Social Problems*, p. 226; Haskell and Yablonsky, *Crime and Delinquency*, pp. 340–41.

16. See Shostak, *Modern Social Reforms*, pp. 287–92; and McCaghy, *Deviant Behavior*, pp. 124–29. McCaghy handles the gun control issue in a more evenhanded manner in a recent textbook, *Crime in American Society* (New York: Macmillan, 1980), pp. 112–15. Though he still accepts much that is questionable about public opinion polls, handgun usage, and so forth, in this book McCaghy does question the practicality and effectiveness of gun controls.

17. See Hofstadter, "America as a Gun Culture," and Hollon, *Frontier Violence*, pp. 106–23.

18. Kennett and Anderson, *The Gun in America*, p. 254.

19. Ibid., pp. 254–55.

20. Ibid., p. 255.

21. Ibid., p. 254; and American Rifleman Staff, "Pro-gun Poll Comes as Revelation," *The American Rifleman* (February 1976): 16–17.

22. Andrew M. Greeley, *Why Can't They Be Like Us?* (New York: Dutton, 1970), chap. 10.

23. Michael Lerner, "Respectable Bigotry," *The American Scholar* (Autumn 1969): 608.

24. Stanislav Andrzejewski, *Military Organizations and Society* (London: Routledge and Kegan Paul, 1954), pp. 13–14.

25. Peter L. Berger, "Ethnics and the Present Class Struggle," *World View* (April 1978): 7.

26. Ibid., p. 10.

27. Florian Znaniecki, *The Social Role of the Man of Knowledge* (New York: Harper & Row, 1968), pp. 72–73.

28. Ibid., p. 74.

29. Marvin E. Wolfgang, "Letters to the Editor," *Time* (July 5, 1968): 6.

30. See "The Gun Under Fire," *Time* (June 21, 1968): 17.

31. Hofstadter, "America as a Gun Culture," p. 82 [see p. 29 in this volume].

32. Ibid.

33. See Noel Perrin, *Giving Up the Gun: Japan's Reversion to the Sword, 1543–1879* (Boston: Godine, 1979). See also Georges Sansom, *Japan: A Short Cultural History* (New York: D. Appleton-Century, 1936), pp. 412–13; and *A History of Japan 1334–1615*, vol. 2 (Stanford, Calif.: Stanford University Press, 1961), pp. 263–64.

34. Ray Allen Billingion, "Frontiers," in C. Vann Woodward, ed., *The Comparative Approach to American History* (New York: Basic Books, 1968), p. 79. See also Richard A. Preston and Sydney F. Wise, *Men in Arms: A History of Warfare and Its Interrelationships with Western Society* (New York: Praeger Publishers, 1970), pp. 165–66.

35. Billington, "Frontiers," p. 79.

36. See Seymour Martin Lipset, "The 'Newness' of the New Nations," in *The Comparative Approach to American History*, ed., C. Vann Woodward (New York: Basic Books, 1968), p. 70; and Paul F. Sharp, *Whoop-Up Country: The Canadian American West, 1865–1885* (Minneapolis: University of Minnesota Press, 1955), p. 110.

37. See H. C. Allen, *Bush and Backwoods: A Comparison of the Frontier in Australia and the United States* (Sydney: Angus and Robertson, 1959), p. 103; and Russel Ward, *The Australian Legend* (New York: Oxford University Press. 1958), p. 144.

38. See Richard Maxwell Brown, *Strains of Violence: Historical Studies of American Violence and Vigilantism* (New York: Oxford University Press, 1975).

39. Hofstadter and Wallace, *American Violence*, pp. 5, 25–27.

40. Newton and Zimring, *Firearms and Violence in American Life*, p. 124.

41. Ibid., p. iii.

42. Stark, *Social Problems*, p. 227.

43. Ibid.

44. See Derek L. Phillips, *Abandoning Method: Sociological Studies in Methodology* (San Francisco: Jossey-Bass, 1973), pp. 38–59.

45. A American Rifleman Staff, "Pro-gun Poll," p. 16.

46. NBC Special, "Violence in America," 1977.

47. Kennett and Anderson, *The Gun in America*, p. 252.

48. Ibid., p. 255.

49. Armand Mauss and Milton Rokeach, "Pollsters as Prophets," *The Humanist* (May–June 1977): 48–51.

50. Edwin M. Schur, *Crimes Without Victims: Deviant Behavior and Public Policy-Abortion, Homosexuality, Drug Addiction* (Englewood Cliffs, N.J.: PrenticeHall, 1965), p. 6.

51. Don B. Kates Jr., "Handgun Control: Prohibition Revisited," *Inquiry* (December 5. 1977): 21.

52. Edwin M. Schur, *Our Criminal Society: The Sociological and Legal Sources of Crime in America* (Englewood Cliffs, N.J.: Prentice-Hall, 1969), pp. 143, 237.

3

THE GREAT AMERICAN GUN WAR

B. BRUCE-BRIGGS

For over a decade there has been a powerful and vocal push for stricter government regulation of the private possession and use of firearms in the United States—for "gun control." The reader cannot help being aware of the vigorous, often vociferous debate on this issue. Indeed, judging from the amount of energy devoted to the gun issue—Congress has spent more time on the subject than on all other crime-related measures combined—one might conclude that gun control is the key to the crime problem. Yet it is startling to note that no policy research worthy of the name has been done on the issue of gun control. The few attempts at serious work are of marginal competence at best, and tainted by obvious bias. Indeed, the gun control debate has been conducted at a level of propaganda more appropriate to social warfare than to democratic discourse.

No one disagrees that there is a real problem: Firearms are too often used for nefarious purposes in America. In 1974, according to the FBI's Uniform Crime Reports, 10,000 people were illegally put to death with guns, firearms were reportedly used in 200,000 robberies and 120,000 assaults, as well as in a small number of rapes, prison escapes, and other crimes. There is universal agreement that it would be desirable, to say the least, that these numbers be substantially reduced. So everybody favors gun control. But there is widespread disagreement about how it can be achieved. Two principal strategies are promoted. To use the military terminology now creeping into criminology, they can be called "interdiction" and "deterrence."

Advocates of deterrence recommend the establishment of stricter penalties

From the *Public Interest*, no. 45 (fall 1976): 37–62.

to discourage individuals from using firearms in crimes. But "gun control" is usually identified with interdiction—that is, the reduction of the criminal use of firearms by controlling the access of all citizens to firearms. The interdictionist position is promoted by a growing lobby, supported by an impressive alliance of reputable organizations, and sympathetically publicized by most of the national media. Every commission or major study of crime and violence has advocated much stricter gun control laws. The only reason that this pressure has failed to produce much tighter controls of firearms is a powerful and well-organized lobby of gun owners, most notably the National Rifle Association (NRA), which has maintained that improved interdiction will have no effect on crime, but will merely strip away the rights and privileges of Americans—and perhaps even irreparably damage the Republic. The organized gun owners advocate reliance on deterrence.

The debate between the "gun controllers" (as the interdictionists are generally identified) and the "gun lobby" (as the organized gun owners have been labeled by a hostile media) has been incredibly virulent. In addition to the usual political charges of self-interest and stupidity, participants in the gun control struggle have resorted to implications or downright accusations of mental illness, moral turpitude, and sedition. The level of the debate has been so debased that even the most elementary methods of cost-benefit analysis have not been employed. One expects advocates to disregard the costs of their programs, but in this case they have even failed to calculate the benefits. . . .

GUN OWNERS VERSUS INTERDICTION

Why do people feel it necessary to obtain firearms to defend themselves? The rising crime rates would suggest it is not lunacy. But the data are improperly understood. Despite the high crime rates, there is a very small chance of being attacked or robbed in one's home, or even during any given excursion into the highest crime area. But the average citizen does not make such calculations and certainly would not have much faith in them if he did. He is scared. The gun, if it does nothing else, gives the citizen reassurance.

This last is a reason for large numbers of guns being owned—not quite defense, but insurance. Many people have weapons tucked away with no explicit idea of how they might be used except "you never know when you might need one." No violent intent is implied, any more than a purchaser of life insurance intends to die that year. It is pure contingency.

Apparently most owners care little about their firearms per se, considering them as mere tools, to be properly cared for—and, because they are potentially deadly, to be handled with caution. Yet within the ranks of the gun owners is a hard core of "gun nuts" (they sometimes call themselves "gunnies") for whom firearms are a fanatic hobby. To them, the possession, handling, and use of guns are a central part of life. They not only accumulate guns, but also read books and magazines about firearms and socialize with kindred spirits in gun clubs and gun stores. Many such people combine business with pleasure as gun dealers, gunsmiths, soldiers, policemen, and officials of gun owners' organizations. All this is symptomatic of the earnest devotees of any hobby—there are similar ski nuts, car nuts, boat nuts, radio nuts, dog nuts, even book nuts. In this case, however, the "nuts" have political importance because they are the core of the organized gun owners, easily aroused and mobilized to thwart the enemies of their passion.

Polls are unreliable on this point, because internal inconsistencies in the data and common sense suggest that many respondents won't admit to gun ownership, but it appears that at least one half of all American households are armed. They own guns for recreation or self-protection. The principal form of recreation, hunting, has deep cultural roots. In rural areas and small towns, a boy's introduction to guns and hunting is an important rite of passage. The first gun at puberty is the bar mitzvah of the rural WASP. Possession of a gun for self-protection is based upon a perception of a real or potential threat to personal, family, or home security that is beyond the control of the police. Very rarely is there criminal or seditious intent. Yet these people are told by the interdictionists that their possession of weapons is a threat to public safety and order, that they must obtain permits, fill out forms, pay taxes and fees, and keep and bear arms only by leave of the state. Inevitably, some of them have organized themselves against such interdiction. With a million members [in 1976], the NRA is the largest and most effective consumer lobby in America. It maintains its morale and membership by broadcasting the statements in favor of "domestic disarmament" by extreme and loosemouthed interdictionists and by publicizing the legislative attempts to restrict gun ownership as merely part of a fabian strategy— to use the interdictionists' code words, a "step in the right direction"—toward liquidating the private ownership and use of firearms in America.

The interdictionist position rests on the self-evident proposition that if there were no guns, there would be no crimes committed with guns. But few are sanguine about achieving that situation. Instead, their argument is that if there were fewer guns and/or if gun ownership were better controlled by the government, there would be fewer crimes with guns.

Can interdiction work? Let us examine what is proposed. Guns and control are subdivided in several ways. Usually there is an attempt to distinguish between mere possession and use. Furthermore, different controls are suggested for different types of weapons—"heavy stuff" (machine guns and cannon); long guns (rifles and shotguns); handguns (revolvers and pistols); and "Saturday Night Specials" (cheap handguns). The levels of possible control can be roughly ranked by degree of severity: market restrictions, registration, permissive licensing, restrictive licensing, prohibition.

"Market restrictions" seek to limit the number of manufacturers, importers, or retailers of firearms, in order to keep better track of them. As in all areas of economic regulation, a principal effect is to promote the interests of the favored outlets, at the cost of the consumer. They do not deny anyone access to guns, but push up the cost—both the money cost and the personal inconvenience—thereby presumably discouraging some marginal purchasers, but surely few criminals, lunatics, and terrorists.

"Registration" is widely discussed, but no one is really advocating it. To register is merely to enroll, as a birth is registered. Merely to enroll weapons would be costly, to little or no purpose. What goes by the label of registration is actually "permissive licensing" whereby anyone may obtain a firearm except certain designated classes: minors, convicted criminals, certified lunatics.

"Restrictive licensing," such as New York's Sullivan Law, permits only people with a legitimate purpose to own a firearm. Police, security guards, hunters, target shooters, and collectors are obliged to demonstrate their bona fides to the licensing authorities. Typically, personal or home defense is not ordinarily considered a legitimate purpose for gaining a license.

"Prohibition" is self-defined. If there were no or few firearms already in circulation, a simple ban would be sufficient. But with tens of millions out there, prohibition would require buying or collecting existing weapons or some more complicated policy intended to make them useless.

The preferred program of most interdictionists today contains four elements, most of which have been attempted one way or another in one jurisdiction or another: (1) continuing and tightening all existing laws, (2) permissive licensing for long guns, (3) restrictive licensing for all handguns, and (4) prohibition of cheap handguns, the so-called Saturday night specials.

The third element is currently considered most important. Because the great majority of gun crimes are committed with handguns, control of them would presumably promote domestic tranquility. Concentration on handguns is also politically useful. Relatively few of them are used for recreation, so this would seem to outflank the objection of sportsmen to restrictions.*

EXISTING GUN CONTROL

There are reportedly some 20,000 gun control ordinances in the various jurisdictions of the United States. Most are prohibitions against discharging a weapon in urban areas or against children carrying weapons, and are trivial, reasonable, and uncontroversial. Most states and large cities have laws against carrying concealed weapons, the rationale being that no person has a legitimate reason to do so. In a few large cities and states, particularly in the Northeast, a license is required to buy or possess a handgun, and in a very few but growing number of Northeastern cities and states a permit or license is required to possess any sort of firearm.

At first sight, licensing seems eminently reasonable. Dangerous criminals should not have weapons, nor should the mentally disturbed. But the adminis-

---

*In the 1980s handguns, due to improved cartridge technologies, became extremely popular as long-range target and hunting arms. Their popularity for such purposes continues in the 1990s.—Ed.

trative "details" of licensing become incredibly difficult. It is fairly easy to check out an applicant for a criminal record, which can be a legitimate reason for denying a license. But many criminals, judging from the comparison between reported crime and conviction rates, are not convicted of crimes, especially violent crimes, so the difficulty exists of whether to deny people the privilege of purchasing weapons if they have merely been arrested, but then set free or acquitted. Civil libertarians should be taken aback by this prospect. The question of mental competence is even nastier to handle. Is someone to be denied a firearm because he sought psychiatric help when his wife died?

From the point of view of the organized gun owners, licensing is intolerable because of the way that it has been enforced in the past. One of the peculiarities of most local licensing is the lack of reciprocity; unlike marriage licensing, what is recognized in one jurisdiction is not in another. In the Eastern states it is nearly impossible to travel with a firearm without committing a felony (not, of course, that this troubles many people). Also many police agencies, particularly in the Northeastern states with restrictive licensing, have engaged in some extremely annoying practices. Not only do they load up questionnaires with many superfluous personal questions, but they also require character witnesses to provide intimate information. When the police wish to restrict privately owned firearms, they resort to all manner of subterfuge. In a test of the local licensing procedure some years ago, the Hudson Institute sent several female staff members to try to make the necessary application. The forms were not available and the people responsible for the forms were absent.

Even when the applications are submitted, the waiting period is often deliberately and inordinately long. I have a friend on Long Island who spent three years getting a pistol permit for target shooting. Influence is useful, but even it is not necessarily sufficient. A staff aide to a leading New York politician who has frequently been threatened applied for a permit to carry a handgun as his boss's bodyguard. Even a letter to the police commissioner of New York City on the gentleman's stationery was inadequate; a personal phone call had to be made-and that has not speeded up the process very much. The system is not much better with long guns and sympathetic police. Immediately after New Jersey required the licensing of rifles, I happened to be in a police station in a suburb of Philadelphia when a young man came in to get his license. The process had taken six weeks. He commented bitterly, "It's a good thing that I planned well in advance for my Maine hunting trip." (By the way, if he had lost or damaged his weapon during a hunting trip, the Federal Gun Control Act of 1968 would have made it extremely difficult for him to get a replacement out of state.)

This sort of anecdotal evidence can be continued almost indefinitely. It suggests to the organized gun owners that licensing systems are a screen not against criminals but against honest citizens, and that licensing authorities are not to be trusted with any sort of discretionary power. It is certainly an inefficient system that dribbles out gun permits and refuses to recognize self-defense as a legitimate reason for owning a gun, while muggers operate with impunity, illicit pistols are exchanged openly on the streets, and penalties for gun-law violations—even by people with criminal records—are very rarely imposed.[2]

Among the most unproductive local gun control measures are the moratoria permitting individuals to surrender their firearms without fear of prosecution. The police will then investigate such people to make sure they are not wanted by some other agency, and they are then entered in police files. (Obviously, if you really wish to dispose of an illegal weapon, you merely disassemble it and throw the parts from a bridge.) The number of weapons delivered under such programs is infinitesimal. An extension of such programs is the buying of weapons by police departments. This was attempted in Baltimore and obtained a substantial number of guns. But the total collected is a matter of simple economics: Large numbers of guns worth much less than the price offered will be obtained. Few valuable weapons will be turned in—and it is perhaps needless to note that there has been no perceptible effect on the crime rate.

The latest innovation in local gun control is a sort of interdiction through deterrence. Massachusetts recently passed a law mandating a minimum jail term of one year for possession of an unlicensed weapon. This reflects an interesting set of social values, because there are no such mandated sentences for burglary, armed robbery, rape, or even murder in Massachusetts. Every hunter who passes through the state on the way to Maine is risking a year in prison. What is happening is predictable: The law is not enforced.

The Massachusetts experience is both a caution to the interdictionists and a reassurance to the organized gun owners. If restrictive gun legislation is passed, the police will be hesitant to arrest ordinary citizens, prosecutors will be loathe to prosecute, juries will be unwilling to convict, and judges will devise ingenious loopholes.

Most of the existing interdiction laws have been in effect for many years, yet it is not possible to make any sort of estimate as to whether they do any good in reducing crime. Attempts have been made to correlate gun ownership and/or gun control laws with gun-related crimes, but they are singularly unconvincing for the very simple reason that the data are so miserable—we have no firm estimate even of the number of guns available nationwide, much less in any given community, and it seems that the gun laws now on the books are rarely enforced. Some ingenious attempts to use regression analyses are easy to demolish.

In any event, no serious student of the subject would disagree that regional, racial, and cultural factors completely swamp the effects of gun control laws. It is true that places with gun control laws tend to have lower violent crime rates, but it happens that these are Northern communities with a long tradition of relative nonviolence, and the existence of gun control laws on the statute books is merely evidence of the same relative peaceableness that is also reflected in the low rates of violent crime. The gun-toting states are also the gun-using states and the violent states, mostly in the South. And where Southerners or ex-Southerners are in the North, there are high violence rates regardless of laws. In recent years a few Northern states have imposed stricter licensing and use laws, with no perceptible effect on the crime rate. As with so many things, the laws on the books don't matter as much as their application. People in these states claim that any effects of their laws are spoiled by the spillover of easily available weapons from outside the state, which certainly sounds eminently reasonable. But if the economists are right, the gun control laws should at least increase the cost or the inconvenience of getting guns, and therefore discourage their use. Retail handgun price differentials between open sources in the South and the black market in New York prove that the Sullivan Law does pass the cost of a less efficient transportation system onto the consumer. But we have no idea of the effect of these increased costs upon the demand for guns. Presumably, those who want to buy guns for illicit purposes are not likely to be much affected by an extra $25 or $100 on the price tag.

The spillover effect has led many public officials in the gun controlling states to advocate essentially the extension of their systems of licensing to the entire nation. It is easy to sneer at this approach as the characteristic reflex of failed government programs—X didn't work, so let's try 10X. But the thesis seems plausible. If one could cut off the supply of guns from, say, South Carolina, they would be more difficult to obtain in, say, New York; that is, they would be more difficult to obtain casually. So the principal interest of gun controllers is in national legislation.

FEDERAL FIREARMS CONTROL

National firearms control legislation is a relative innovation. The first important law passed was the Federal Firearms Act of 1934, which was allegedly a response to the wave of gangsterism that swept the country in the depths of the Depression. Originally the Roosevelt administration attempted to require national licensing of all weapons, but it was thwarted by a previously quiescent organization, the NRA. The watered-down version that passed Congress effectively prohibited (through punitive taxes) the private possession of submachine guns, silencers, sawed-off rifles and shotguns, and other weapons presumably of use only to gangsters. While there appears to be no information whatever on the effectiveness of this law, it seems to have been reasonably successful. Submachine guns are rarely used in crimes. That success, however, may simply reflect the fact that very few such weapons were in circulation, and their rarity gives them too much value to be risked in crime. (We know, of course, that there certainly are tens of thousands of unregistered automatic weapons in the United States, largely war souvenirs. Vietnam veterans brought back thousands of M-16s and Kalashnikov assault rifles in their duffel bags. But most of these gun owners have no criminal intent or any intention of selling such weapons to criminals.) Sawed-off shotguns and rifles may be made illegal, but they are impossible to prohibit; all that is needed is a hacksaw and a few minutes' time.

The second federal effort was the National Firearms Act of 1938. Again, this took the form of a revenue measure, requiring the licensing of firearms manu-facturers and dealers. The law requires the firearms trade to keep records of the purchasers of weapons, and prohibits sales to known criminals. But only a simple declaration on the part of the buyer is required. These records are useful for tracing firearms. If a weapon needs checking, it is merely necessary to go back to the original manufacturer or importer and trace it through the serial number to the dealer. Although these records are not yet centralized, in effect there has been registration of every new weapon sold in the United States since 1938. How many crimes have been solved through this means, or how it has otherwise been effective to law enforcement, is by no means clear. It would not be diffi-cult to find out, but no one has really tried to. Presumably, such registration is of some help to the police—though it seems to have had no effect on the crime rate or the conviction rates.

The most important national measure is the Gun Control Act of 1968, the immediate result of the disturbances in the 1960s and the assassinations of Robert Kennedy and Martin Luther King Jr. The act raised taxes on firearms dealers, added cannon to the list of weapons subject to punitive taxes, prohib-ited the importation of surplus military firearms and Saturday night specials, and prohibited the interstate retailing of all firearms. The last provision is the most important. The purpose was to prevent individuals like Lee Harvey Oswald from ordering weapons by mail under phony names. But it also has more annoying side effects. For example, if you live in Kansas City, Kansas, and wish to give your brother, who lives in Kansas City, Missouri, a .22 caliber rifle for his birthday, it is illegal for you to do so. If you are traveling in another state and see a weapon you wish to buy, you must go through the rigamarole of having it sent to a dealer in your own state. So far as one can determine, the law has had no per-ceptible effect in slowing down the interstate sale of arms.

Enforcement of federal firearms laws was given to what is now the Bureau of Alcohol, Tobacco, and Firearms (BATF) of the Department of the Treasury. These are the famous "revenuers" whose most important function was stamping out moonshining. But for economic and social reasons, the illicit liquor trade is fading and the BATF needs other things to do than break up stills. Since 1968 they have rapidly expanded their funding and activity in firearms control and now devote about half their personnel and budget to that function. BATF seems to be a crude and unsophisticated police agency, more like the Bureau of Nar-cotics and Dangerous Drugs or the Border Patrol than the FBI or the Secret Ser-vice. For example, it says it has no idea how many of the 250,000 licensed Title 11 firearms (i.e., machine guns, cannon, etc.) are held by police or other public agencies and how many by private citizens; nor has it any information on how many unlicensed Title 11 firearms were used for criminal purposes. Some of its methods of operating have been irritating to legitimate gun owners.[3] The Gun Control Act of 1968 says that BATF shall have access to the premises of a gun dealer during normal business hours, which BATV interprets to mean that there must be a business premises separate from, for example, a private residence, and that there shall be ordinary posted business hours. BATF also took upon itself the enforcement of local zoning laws. This problem arises because many gun owners have taken advantage of simple and cheap licensing procedures to obtain dealer licenses so they can buy firearms wholesale. The majority of the nearly 150,000 dealers operate from their homes.

The organized gun owners see the activities of the BATF as a plot against them, not realizing that its habits and state of mind are not much different from other regulatory agencies. Once an activity has been licensed, it becomes a privilege; a citizen is obliged meekly to petition the regulator for the boon and to modify his behavior to suit the needs of the bureaucracy. At the present time, the Department of the Treasury is asking for a large increase in the licensing fee of gun dealers in order to reduce the number of license holders—not for any public benefit but because it will make the job of regulation easier for BATF.*

SATURDAY NIGHT SPECIALS

The Saturday night special is the latest target of the interdictionist. It is identified as a cheap, unreliable, inaccurate, and easily concealed handgun, allegedly employed for large numbers of "street crimes." Because it is impossible to define a Saturday night special precisely, the NRA claims that the concept is fraudulent—but any definition in practice or law is necessarily arbitrary. Concentration on the Saturday night special has definite political advantages. Firearms enthusiasts scorn it as sleazy junk quite unsuited for serious work. Nevertheless, the organized gun owners are making an effective fight against banning the Saturday night special. They were unable to block prohibition of its importation in 1968, but have resisted attempts to ban domestic manufacture and the assembly of imported parts.

It has been said against the Saturday night special that it is employed to commit a disproportionately large number of street crimes, and that getting rid of it would cut substantially into those crimes. A BATF study claimed that 65 percent of "crime guns" used for street crime in sixteen major cities were cheap Saturday night specials. Unfortunately, the text of the report reveals that these weapons were not those used in crimes but all those handguns collected by police, and anyone who knows anything about how reliable the police are in handling contraband knows that the chances of a quality firearm like a good Smith and Wesson finding its way into the reporting system are infinitesimal. Because the principal sanction against the illegal carrying of guns is on-the-spot seizure by the police, it stands to reason that individuals would pack the cheapest effective gun.

But even if Saturday night special are used for some half of crimes with handguns, their elimination is hardly likely to reduce handgun crime by that much. People buy them because they are cheap. If people want a weapon, and

*The Department of Treasury is still seeking such licensing increases.—Ed.

if their demand for handguns is highly inelastic, this only means that whatever guns fell outside of whatever arbitrary definition of a Saturday night special that was adopted would sell more. Perhaps this is recognized by the proponents of banning the Saturday night special, because they have written bills to give the Secretary of the Treasury sufficient discretion to ban all handguns.

Actually, neither side cares much about the Saturday night special one way or another. The interdictionists advocate its regulation as a stepping stone toward tight licensing of handguns or the licensing of all guns, while the organized gun owners fear it as a camel's nose in the tent. It is difficult to escape the conclusion that the Saturday night special is emphasized because it is cheap and is being sold to a particular class of people. The name is sufficient evidence—the reference is to "nigger-town Saturday night."

CRACKPOT SCHEMES

Some other suggestions for gun control are simply silly. One idea is to have all weapons locked up in armories of various sorts, to be drawn by hunters or target shooters when they are needed. But most hunters and gun owners perform ordinary maintenance on their own weapons, so that a storage facility would have to provide room for that. The most overwhelming drawback against the idea is the enormous cost of providing such facilities—no one has calculated how much, and they would, of course, be targets for anyone who wished to obtain illicit firearms.

Another crackpot scheme is to record the ballistics of all weapons, rather like fingerprints. This would not be enormously expensive, costing only a few million a year for new weapons only. But it is physically impossible. The pattern that the rifling of a barrel imprints on a bullet is not consistent and can be simply modified by changing the barrel. Ballistics is excellent at a one-to-one comparison between bullets, but cannot be employed for a general identification search.

Perhaps the most peculiar gun control proposal to date was made by the Department of Justice in 1975. It recommended that, when the "Violent crime rate has reached the critical level," possession of handguns outside the home or place of business be banned altogether. This assumes that those areas where law enforcement is least efficient could enforce a handgun ban, and that where the forces of public order are weakest citizens should be denied the means to defend themselves. In almost all high-crime areas the carrying—or at least the concealed carrying—of handguns is already illegal. (Hard data are necessarily spotty, but it now appears likely that the widespread private ownership of handguns for self-protection among crime-liable populations leads to some transfer to criminals, principally by theft. If this is true, it would not seem unreasonable to dry up the demand for guns by providing security to these people.)

THE LIMITS TO INTERDICTION

So the utility of interdiction has not and perhaps cannot be demonstrated. While the lack of evidence that a policy can be effective should make prudent men wary of promoting it, that does not mean the policy is necessarily without merit. Nevertheless, in the case of gun control it is possible to identify some weaknesses in the principles behind the policy.

To begin with, gun control as a general anticrime strategy is flawed because most crimes, including many of the crimes most feared, are not committed with guns. Firearms are rarely employed for rape, home burglary, or street muggings. On the other hand, a good portion of the most heinous crime, murder, is not a serious source of social fear. The majority of murders are the result of passionate argument, and although personal tragedies, are not a social concern—ditto for crimes committed by criminals against one another. Furthermore, the worst crimes, involving the most dangerous and vicious criminals, will not be affected by gun control. No serious person believes that an interdiction program will be effective enough to keep guns out of the hands of organized crime, professional criminals, or well-connected terrorists and assassins. And almost all the widely publicized mass murderers were eligible for licensed guns.

Gun control advocates grant this, and emphasize the need to limit spontaneous murders among "family and friends" that are made possible by the availability of firearms. But the commonly used phrase "family and friends" is misleading. The FBI's Uniform Crime Reports classify relationships between murderers and victims as "relative killings," "lovers' quarrels," and "other arguments." The last can be among criminal associates, as can the others. Nor can we necessarily conclude that such murders are spontaneous. The legal distinction between premeditated and nonpremeditated murder prompts killers (and their lawyers) to present murders as unplanned.

The very nature of interdiction suggests other weaknesses. It is a military term used to describe attempts, usually by aerial bombing, to impede, not halt, the flow of enemy supplies to the battlefield. Interdiction has been the principal strategy used in drug control; it works only when pressure is being applied at the street level at the same time that imports and production are being squeezed. If there are 140 million privately owned firearms in the United States and guns can last centuries with minimum maintenance, merely cutting off the supply will have little or no effect for generations, and if the supply is not cut off entirely (which no serious person believes it can be), an interdiction policy is hardly likely to have a major effect even over the very long run. To my knowledge, no interdiction advocate has given a plausible answer to the very simple question of how to get 140 million firearms out of the hands of the American people.

Even more to the point, is it cost-effective to try to deal with 140 million weapons when you are presumably concerned with a maximum at the outside of 350,000 weapons used in violent crimes? The odds of any gun being criminally used are roughly on the order of one in 400. For handguns the rate is considerably higher; for rifles and shotguns considerably lower. I estimate that in 1974, roughly one of every 4,000 handguns was employed in a homicide, compared with one in 30,000 shotguns and one in 40,000 rifles. There are probably more privately owned guns in America than there are privately owned cars, and with the obvious exception of murder, the rate of criminal use of firearms is almost certainly less than the rate of criminal use of automobiles. How are we to control the 400 guns to prevent the one being used for crime? And if we decide the only way is to reduce the 400, to what must we reduce it? It must be assumed that the one gun used for crime will be the 400th.

Moreover, interdiction is a countermeasure against crime. Countermeasures provoke counter-countermeasures: Substitution is the most obvious strategy. If guns cannot be bought legally, they can be obtained illegally—organized crime is ready to cater to any illicit demand. If cheap handguns are unobtainable, expensive handguns will be used. If snub-nosed pistols and revolvers are banned, long-barreled weapons will be cut down. If the 40-million-odd handguns disappear, sawed-off rifles and shotguns are excellent substitutes. If all domestic production is halted, we will fall back on our tradition of smuggling. If all manufactured weapons vanish, anyone with a lathe and a hacksaw can make a serviceable firearm. In the 1950s, city punks produced zip guns from automobile aerials. A shotgun is easily made from a piece of pipe, a block of wood, several rubber bands, and a nail.

A more promising variation is to go after the ammunition rather than the gun. Whereas firearms are easily manufactured and last indefinitely, modern ammunition requires sophisticated manufacturing facilities and has a shorter shelf life. Recently the interdictionists attempted to get the Consumer Product Safety Commission (CPSC) to prohibit the sale of handguns on the basis of their being inherently unsafe. This was certainly the most intelligent gun control tactic attempted so far; yet it failed because Congress explicitly prohibited CPSC from meddling in firearm matters. But a strategy directed against ammunition is also flawed. Hundreds of thousands of Americans "hand load" ammunition at home from commercially purchased shells, powder, and bullets in order to obtain substantial cost savings and to get precisely the sort of load they desire. Shell cartridges last forever and there are untold billions in circulation. Lead and steel bullets can be made by anyone with a stove or a file. So it would be necessary to close off powder sales as well. Smokeless powder would be extremely difficult to make at home, but the old-style black powder that fired weapons for 500 years can be manufactured by any kid with a chemistry set. Besides, any ammunition cutoff would be preceded by a long debate and bitter fight—during which time everyone would stock up. Also, thefts from the military, National Guard, and police would continue to be a major source of ammunition.

THE COSTS OF INTERDICTION

Against the unconvincing or unsupported benefits of any interdiction law, one must count the costs; practically no attention has been paid to them. BATF is now [1976] expending $50 million per annum on enforcement of federal laws. Local police, court, and corrections expenditures are buried in budgets. The only serious accounting of costs was prepared for the Violence Commission of 1968 and was downplayed in the final report. New York's Sullivan Law licensing cost about $75 per permit in 1968; double that for current levels of expenditure; assume that a maximum of half the households in the country will register their weapons; the cost is therefore in excess of $5 billion—or more than one-third of the present cost of the entire criminal justice system, from police to prisons. Simple "registration" on the model of auto registration would cost proportionately less, but the numbers are always in the hundreds of millions of dollars.

The financial costs do not exhaust the potential expense of gun control laws. It is too much to expect government to count as a cost the time and trouble to a citizen of registering a gun, but we might look at the price of diverting police and other law enforcement officials from potentially more rewarding activities.

But the worst cost is that of widespread flouting of the law. Existing gun controls are now being disobeyed by millions. More severe restrictions will be widely disregarded by tens of millions, including a huge group of stalwart citizens whose loyalty and lawfulness we now take for granted. Needless to say, the organized gun owners cite the Prohibition experience.

THE LIMITS TO DETERRENCE

Organized gun owners, on the other side of the issue, advocate enforcing the existing gun control laws. I suggest that they do not take this recommendation seriously; the existing laws are not enforceable. Another suggestion would appear to be more credible at first glance—to employ deterrence by having add-on sentences for the use of guns in crime. But such laws are on the books in several states and are not enforced, for a fairly obvious reason: Americans are not concerned with the use of a gun in a crime, but with the crime itself. The murder or armed robbery is objectionable, not the gun. *Illegal gun ownership is a victimless crime.*

Several practical problems make a deterrence strategy extremely difficult. There is trouble putting anyone away these days, and enforcement of existing gun laws or of new laws would add to the overload of an already jammed criminal justice system. Perhaps most important of all, when the effective sentence for premeditated murder is seven or eight years in a penitentiary,[4] how much leeway is there to add to sentences for lesser crimes? Given the advantages of a firearm to a robber, a few more weeks or months of jail is hardly likely to deter him from using it.*

---

*See Parts Three and Four for the latest research findings on this issue.—Ed.

The organized gun owners also claim that the widespread possession of firearms in itself deters crime; criminals are likely to be restrained by an armed citizenry. Perhaps but consideration of criminal tactics suggests the idea is limited in application. Take burglars—by definition they prefer stealth, choosing unoccupied houses. If the owner is at home it is unlikely that he will awaken. A noise that arouses him will also alert the burglar. Should the householder awake, the burglar will probably hear him—especially if he is fumbling for a gun that is, as it should be, secured. In a confrontation, the burglar is alert, while the householder is sleepy-eyed. It is far more likely that a gun will be stolen than that it could be used against a burglar.

In store robberies, the robber also has the advantage. Guns are clearly not a deterrent, since the armed stores are those most often hit—because to use Willie Sutton's phrase, "that's where the money is." Arming stores will certainly dissuade nongun robberies, obliging robbers to escalate to firearms. Street robberies offer a similar tactical imbalance: the mugger has the initiative. It is not unknown for even police to be disarmed by criminals.* It is true that areas with high gun ownership tend to have less crime against property, but this is probably largely the result of cultural factors. In any event the low quality of data on crime rates and gun ownership makes rigorous examination impossible.

INTERNATIONAL EXPERIENCE

Many peripheral arguments used in the gun control debate have little relevance to the issue, but must be addressed. Both sides will deploy the testimony of police chiefs on the desirability or futility of gun control laws. Liberal interdictionists often cite the testimony of those gentlemen who have most illiberal views on most other law enforcement matters. Most, but not all, big-city chiefs favor interdiction, while small-town chiefs generally oppose it, both nicely reflecting the views of their political superiors. But, for what it is worth, one can cite the sheriff of Los Angeles County staunchly demanding stricter gun control laws and the chief of police of Los Angeles City saying that public order has broken down so far that only a fool would not arm himself. The gun owners gained strong reinforcement when the Superintendent of Scotland Yard recently pointed out that the number of guns available in America makes an interdiction strategy impossible.

A surprising amount of attention has been paid in the gun control debate to international experience. In the world of gun control there seem to be only three foreign countries: Great Britain, Japan, and Switzerland. British gun control is taken by the interdictionists as the model of a desirable system. Guns are tightly regulated in the United Kingdom, violent crime is trivial by United States standards, and even the police are unarmed. But, as James Q. Wilson recently

---

*See Parts Three and Four for the latest research findings on this issue.—Ed.

pointed out in this journal, the English situation is slowly eroding. The key to the low rates of personal violence in England is not in rigorous gun control laws (which only date from 1920), but in the generally deferential and docile character of the populace. Perhaps it is significant that interdictionists point to "Great Britain" as their model; gun control laws are even stricter in the other part of the United Kingdom, Northern Ireland.

Japan is an even more gun-free country. Not only does it restrict the ownership of weapons, but it has prohibited the ownership of handguns altogether, and the rates of violent crime are so low as to be hardly credible to Americans. To which the organized gun owners reply that Japanese-Americans have even lower rates of violence than Japanese in Japan.

The third international comparison is used by the organized gun owners. Switzerland has a militia system: 600,000 assault rifles with two magazines of ammo each are sitting at this moment in Swiss homes. Yet Switzerland's murder rate is 15 percent of ours. To which the interdictionists respond that the Swiss have strict licensing of weapons, though this would seem to have very little to do with the thesis that the mere availability of weapons provokes murder and other crimes with guns. It is not entirely clear what these very different countries—with very different histories, political systems, and national character—have to do with the United States. Those interdictionists who defend civil liberties would be appalled at the suggestion that even the English system of justice be applied to the United States, much less the Swiss civil law or the authoritarian Japanese judicial system—none of which provides the criminal with the rights and privileges he has in the United States.

But let me muddy these waters by introducing two other countries of great interest. Israel is mostly inhabited by a people who have no tradition whatever of using firearms in self-defense and whose compatriots in America are for the most part unarmed and have little taste for hunting. But the objective political conditions of Israel have required them to arm in self-defense and the country bristles with public and private weapons. In addition to the armed forces, soldiers on pass or in casual transit in border areas carry their small arms with them. There is a civil guard in the tens of thousands. Every settlement has an arsenal, and individual Israelis are armed. The government requires registration of all weapons, but the system is very lenient on handguns (for Jews, of course; considerably tighter for Arabs) and very tough on rifles and shotguns, which might be used for military purposes. Israeli gun control policy is directed toward internal security, not against crime. But despite these restrictions, the Israelis have accumulated huge numbers of privately owned military weapons, including automatics, in various wars and raids. These are held "just in case" they may be needed. But strangely, hunting is on the increase in Israel, as are target shooting and gun collecting, and there is talk of forming an Israeli national rifle association. Needless to say, the crime rate in Israel is much lower than in the United States.

The special conditions of Israel are too obvious to note, but Canada is closer to home, and it is odd that so little attention has been paid it. Since the early

1920s, Canada has registered all pistols on what is essentially the same basis as New York's Sullivan Law. Rifles and shotguns are sold freely, even through mail order. Canada's crime rate is much lower than the United States'. Here, too, cultural factors seem to predominate. It is not usually observed that without the South and Southerners (black and white) transplanted to the North, the United States would have crime rates comparable to other industrial nations. In fact, there is no appreciable difference in murder rates for "Yankee" whites in states and provinces on either side of the 49th parallel.

The best point of the interdictionists is that America is an exception to the international system of strict restrictive licensing. To which the "gunnies" reply that our ancestors came here to free themselves and us from the tyrannies of the Old World.*

THE SECOND AMENDMENT

One reason the organized gun owners have had bad public relations is that they take an absolutist position regarding the Constitution, relying on the Second Amendment of the Bill of Rights: "A well regulated Militia, being necessary to the security of a free State, the right of the people to keep and bear Arms, shall not be infringed."

To the NRA and other organizations this is an unqualified right, like the freedom of the press, not to be compromised on any grounds. To the interdictionists, the amendment merely guarantees the right of the states to maintain what is now called the National Guard. Actually, the status and meaning of the Second Amendment can be the subject of debate among reasonable men. It is certainly true that the original intention of the Second Amendment was that there be an armed citizenry. A "militia" as understood in the eighteenth century was indeed the people armed with their own weapons, and the inclusion of the Second Amendment in the Bill of Rights was meant to protect the independence of the states and the people against the threat of the central government's employing the standard instrument of baroque tyranny, the standing army. However, there was no intention of the Founding Fathers to guarantee the use of firearms for recreation, nor for self-defense against criminals (although of the thirty-eight states that have similar "right to bear arms" provisions in their constitutions, eighteen specifically provide for personal defense, and one, New Mexico, for recreation).

The supreme arbiter of the Constitution has never ruled directly on the matter. The four cases that have come before the Supreme Court have been decided on narrow technical issues. Three nineteenth-century cases seem to support the view that states have the right to regulate firearms, and the one twentieth-century case, which rose out of the Federal Firearms Act of 1934, was

---

*See Part Three for further discussion of international comparisons. See also Tonso, "Social Problems and Sagecraft.—Ed.

decided on the very narrow ground of whether a sawed-off shotgun was a weapon suitable for a well-regulated militia.*

Gun-owning lawyers claim that the doctrine of "incorporation" to the states of Bill-of-Rights restraints protect gun owners from state controls. This is reasonable on the face of it. However, the Supreme Court, as it was intended to do, applies the standards of an enlightened public opinion to the law. If the dominant elements in the country favor gun control, it is to be expected that the courts will rule accordingly.

The organized gun owners also see the armed citizenry as a last line of defense against insurrection. This idea has roots in the disturbances of the 1960s. While many Americans viewed the urban riots as the inevitable outcome of centuries of repression, many more merely saw police standing aside while looters cleaned out stores and homes, then envisioned the same happening to their stores and homes, and armed themselves. They did not understand that the looting was permitted only so long as it was contained to black neighborhoods; any attempted "breakout" would have roused the forces of public order from their lethargy. Indeed, the contingency plans have been prepared.

The gun owners claim that any registration lists would be used by a conqueror or tyrant to disarm the potential resistance. A minor debate has grown up over what the Nazis did in occupied Europe, especially in Norway. A source in the Norwegian Defense Ministry says the Nazis did not make use of registration lists but rather offered to shoot anyone who failed to turn in his weapons.

But there are examples of the use of registration lists to disarm the public. All handguns were called in following the assassination of the governor of Bermuda a few years ago. And the late, unlamented regime of the Greek colonels ordered the registration of all hunting weapons, followed by their confiscation, in order to disarm the royalists. Although the guns were later returned by the colonels, the present republican regime is continuing the control apparatus, presumably "just in case." When the IRA† began its offensive in Ulster earlier in the decade, the Irish Republic used registration lists to confiscate all privately owned firearms in the South.

PHALLIC NARCISSISM

A common assertion in the dispute is that gun owners are somehow mentally disturbed. The weapon is said to be a phallic symbol substituting for real masculinity, for "machismo." The historian Arthur Schlesinger Jr. has written of "the psychotic suspicion that men doubtful of their own virility cling to the gun as a symbolic phallus and unconsciously fear gun control as the equivalent of castration." When queried about the source of this suspicion, he responded that he thought it was a "cliché." Such statements never cite sources because there are

---

*See Part Five for an extended discussion of Second Amendment issues.—Ed.
†The Irish Republican Army.—Ed.

no sources. Every mention of the phallic-narcissist theory assumes it is well known, but there is no study or even credible psychoanalytical theory making the point. The germ of the idea derives from the tenth lecture in Sigmund Freud's *General Introduction to Psychoanalysis*, where he maintains that guns can symbolize the penis in dreams—as can sticks, umbrellas, trees, knives, sabers, water faucets, pencils, nail files, hammers, snakes, reptiles, fishes, hats and cloaks, hands, feet, balloons, aeroplanes, and Zeppelins. In other words, any long object can represent a phallus in a dream. Gun owners laugh at the thesis, or are infuriated. One said to me, "Anybody who associates the discharge of a deadly weapon with ejaculation has a real sexual problem."

Studies of hunters reveal that they are not much interested in guns or in killing but in the package of skills and camaraderie involved in the hunt. No one has studied the psychology of gun owners or even hardcore gun nuts, nor are there studies of gun phobia. Fortunately, there is a reasonable amount of sociological data available, in the form of public opinion polls, which are believable because they give support to ordinary observation. Gun ownership is more prevalent among men, rural and small-town residents, Southerners, veterans, and whites. Except for the lowest income groups (who may not be willing to admit ownership), guns are fairly evenly distributed by income. Education, occupation, and politics make little difference. Protestants are more likely to be armed than other religious groups. When asked why they own guns, most people respond that they hunt or target shoot. But most handgun owners have them for self-defense, and longgun owners admit to defense as a secondary purpose of their firearms.

Two generations of good data show that substantial majorities of the populace support gun registration, and this is cited fervently by individuals who prefer not to cite similar data favoring, e.g., maintaining prohibitions on marijuana, having courts get tougher with criminals, and restoring capital punishment. Of course, questions on "registration" are considerably misleading, because no one is advocating the mere registration of weapons, but rather licensing. Most people live in places where there is no licensing and have no idea of the difficulty and expense this would impose upon public authorities and gun owners if the standards of New York or Connecticut were applied nationwide. Gun owners and people with knowledge of existing gun control laws are considerably less enthusiastic for registration. Supporters of interdiction are more likely to be young, single, prosperous, well-educated, liberal, New England nongun owners with little knowledge of existing gun control laws.

THE REAL ISSUES

The main point that emerges from any serious analysis is that the gun control issue, under conditions that exist in the United States today, has practically nothing to do with crime control. I think that there are other issues at stake.

In 1967, armed robbers with pistols killed two policemen in London. There was a wide outcry to "bring back the noose." The Labour government, opposed to capital punishment, responded by extending strict licensing requirements to small-bore shotguns used in rural areas for shooting birds and rodents. In Canada in 1974, there were two incidents of boys running amok with rifles in schools. There was wide agitation to restore capital punishment. The Liberal government, opposed to capital punishment, proposed a far-reaching program to eliminate registered pistols in private ownership and to register all rifles and shotguns. It is possible that gun control is, at least in part, a strategy to divert the mob away from the issue of capital punishment.

Political factors are clearly important. The assassinations of the 1960s and 1970s rather unnerved the politicians. But the wide social unrest of the 1960s probably had more impact. In 1939, George Orwell noted, "When I was a kid you could walk into a bicycle shop or ironmonger's [hardware store] and buy any firearm you pleased, short of a field gun, and it did not occur to most people that the Russian revolution and the Irish civil war would bring this state of affairs to an end." There is a remarkable coincidence between gun control agitation and periods of social upheaval. English and Canadian gun laws date from the "red scare" following the First World War, and the original United States national controls are the product of the violent days of the New Deal.

But underlying the gun control struggle is a fundamental division in our nation. The intensity of passion on this issue suggests to me that we are experiencing a sort of low-grade war going on between two alternative views of what America is and ought to be. On the one side are those who take bourgeois Europe as a model of a civilized society: a society just, equitable, and democratic; but well ordered, with the lines of responsibility and authority clearly drawn, and with decisions made rationally and correctly by intelligent men for the entire nation. To such people, hunting is atavistic, personal violence is shameful, and uncontrolled gun ownership is a blot upon civilization.

On the other side is a group of people who do not tend to be especially articulate or literate, and whose worldview is rarely expressed in print. Their model is that of the independent frontiersman who takes care of himself and his family with no interference from the state. They are "conservative" in the sense that they cling to America's unique premodern tradition—a nonfeudal society with a sort of medieval liberty writ large for every man. To these people, "sociological" is an epithet. Life is tough and competitive. Manhood means responsibility and caring for your own.

This hardcore group is probably very small, not more than a few million people, but it is a dangerous group to cross. From the point of view of a right-wing threat to internal security, these are perhaps the people who should be disarmed first, but in practice they will be the last. As they say, to a man, "I'll bury my guns in the wall first." They ask, because they do not understand the other side, "Why do these people want to disarm us?" They consider themselves no threat to anyone; they are not criminals, not revolutionaries. But, slowly, as they become politicized, they find an analysis that fits the phenomenon they experience: Someone fears their having guns, someone is afraid of their defending their families, property, and liberty. Nasty things may happen if these people begin to feel that they are cornered.

It would be useful, therefore, if some of the mindless passion, on both sides, could be drained out of the gun control issue. Gun control is no solution to the crime problem, to the assassination problem, to the terrorist problem. Reasonable licensing laws, reasonably applied, might be marginally useful in preventing some individuals, on some occasions, from doing violent harm to others and to themselves. But so long as the issue is kept at white heat, with everyone having some ground to suspect everyone else's ultimate intentions, the rule of reasonableness has little chance to assert itself.

NOTES

1. One obvious reason for the growing gun sales is that the prices of firearms, like most mass-produced goods, have not risen as fast as incomes. The classic deer rifle, the Winchester 94, in production since 1894, cost 250 percent of an average worker's weekly take-home salary in 1900, 91 percent in 1960, and 75 percent in 1970. The relationship to annual median family income has been even more favorable—from 2.8 percent in 1900 to 1.4 percent in 1960 and 1.0 percent in 1970. More important, increased competition during the past decade has lowered the absolute price of handguns.

2. The Police Foundation is currently engaged in a study of the details of local handgun-law enforcement. Unfortunately, because its head is known as a vocal interdictionist, the credibility of its results will necessarily be somewhat compromised.

3. The BATF also made the grave error of providing the organized gun owners with their first martyr. In Maryland, in 1971, a local pillar of the community—a Boy Scout leader, volunteer fireman, and gun collector—was in his bathtub when a group of armed men in beards and rough clothes—BATF agents—broke through the door. Understandably, he reached for a handy antique cap-and-ball pistol and was shot four times and left on the floor while his wife, still in her underwear, was dragged screaming from the apartment. What had happened was that a local boy reported a hand grenade in the apartment. There was, but it was only the shell of a hand grenade. A simple records check would have been adequate to establish the resident's bona fides, and if there was an interest in following up the matter, someone might have come and knocked on his door. He is now crippled for life.

4. The assassin of George Lincoln Rockwell was released from prison last year.

4

IDEOLOGY, POLITICS, AND PROPAGANDA

GARY KLECK

IDEOLOGICAL IRONIES AND CROSSCURRENTS*

One of the ironies of the gun control struggle is how traditional political positions often become reversed when the issue is guns. Although twentieth-century liberals have usually supported expanding the state's power to regulate business, they have generally opposed expanding its authority to regulate the behavior of individuals. They have commonly opposed restrictions on free speech, public demonstrations, political associations, sexual behavior, abortion, drug use, and pornography. More specific to criminal justice matters, they have usually opposed the expansion of the power and authority of police and prose-cutors to search homes, interrogate suspects, gain confessions, and seize contra-band. And although conservatives have opposed expanding the state's power to regulate business, they generally have supported expanding the state's authority and power to regulate private behavior of which they disapprove, and to enforce laws that concern behaviors mainly engaged in by lower class persons, including so-called street crime. Liberals usually give a broad reading to the Bill of Rights regarding individuals rights of criminal suspects, privacy, and limits on govern-mental power in general, whereas conservatives give it a narrow one, especially regarding the rights of criminal suspects and dissenters. Liberals generally

*Reprinted with permission from Gary Kleck, *Point Blank: Guns and Violence in America* (Hawthorne, N.Y.: Aldine de Gruytner, 1991), pp. 3–15. Copyright © 1991 by Walter de Gruyter, Inc., New York.

oppose increasing the scope and severity of penalties for typically lower-class forms of criminal behavior, whereas law-and-order conservatives support the death penalty, mandatory sentencing, and more severe punishment of crime. More generally, liberals oppose expanding the scope of the criminal law to include more "victimless crimes," i.e., prohibited categories of behavior that involve no unwilling victim, such as illegal drug use or gambling (Stinchcombe et al. 1980).

When the issue is gun control, liberals and conservatives switch places. Many liberals support gun laws that confer broad power on government to regulate individual behavior, especially in private places, whereas conservatives oppose them. Some liberals dismiss the Second Amendment to the Constitution as an outmoded historical curiosity that never really guaranteed an individual right to keep and bear arms, whereas conservatives defend a view of this amendment that is every bit as broad as the American Civil Liberties Union's (ACLU) view of the First Amendment regarding free speech or the Fourth, Fifth, and Sixth Amendments as they pertain to suspects' rights.

Some liberals seek to pass gun control laws that create and expand a category of victimless crime (gun possession), whereas some conservatives oppose the effort, citing all the arguments liberals use to oppose laws restricting drug use, gambling, pornography, and sexual conduct: the laws create black markets, criminalize and stigmatize otherwise noncriminal people, encourage discriminatory law enforcement, are impossible to effectively enforce, invite police corruption and abuse of authority, and divert law enforcement resources from areas in which they are more effectively deployed (Kessler 1980). Although murder and robbery with a gun are not victimless crimes, laws banning the mere possession, acquisition, sale, or carrying of firearms clearly encompass "victimless" behaviors. An especially noteworthy example of this particular reversal can be found in the work of Edwin Schur, the principal popularizer of the "victimless crime" concept (Schur 1965). Schur is also a strong supporter of gun control, who shows no apparent awareness of any possible contradiction—"Effective general gun control . . . is one of the few public policy measures directly aimed at controlling crime that could really have a beneficial impact" (Schur 1974, p. 237). Other proponents of the victimless crime perspective have been more intellectually consistent in applying it to gun law violations as well as to the behaviors traditionally discussed under that heading, drugs, gambling, prostitution, and so on (Kaplan 1979; Kessler 1980; Kates 1984a).

It is a mildly amusing pastime to read virulently anticontrol propaganda written by obviously ultraconservative authors, who rail against improper warrantless searches of gun owners' homes and gun dealers' business premises, sounding for all the world like spokesmen for the ACLU (e.g., the March/April and September/October 1987 issues of the *Gun Owners*, newsletter of Gun Owners of America). On the other hand, the writings of otherwise liberal proponents of gun control are frequently most remarkable for what they leave out—any discussion of the search-and-seizure issues that make effective enforcement of many gun laws so problematic or of evidence of discriminatory enforcement (Kates 1986). Even when these concerns are confronted, however superficially, they are commonly dismissed as minor (e.g., Drinan 1976). At one point the city attorney of Berkeley, California, which had what was arguably the most liberal city government in the United States, was even researching the legality of establishing the nation's first neighborhood "weapons checkpoints," allowing random police searches of cars for weapons (Levine 1987).

The current ideological lineup on gun control has shallow historical roots. Before 1963, gun control was not a salient issue for most Americans. Only two Gallup polls from the 1930s up to 1959 asked even a single question on the issue (Crocker 1982). Support for gun control was not a major tenet of liberalism before that time. Indeed, in the nineteenth and early twentieth century, gun control laws were most often targeted at blacks in the South and the foreignborn in the North, and were supported by persons who would clearly not be recognized today as liberals. The stated motives behind support were often overtly racist and xenophobic, revolving around a desire to control "dangerous populations," including not only racial and ethnic minorities, but also radicals, anarchists, union organizers, and other "troublemakers." Southern gun laws during the antebellum and immediate postwar years were explicitly limited to blacks. And although those during and after Reconstruction were written in race-neutral language, they, too, were aimed at, and largely enforced against, blacks (Kennett and Anderson 1975, pp. 50–51, 81, 153–55, 167; Kates 1979a, pp. 12–22; Kessler 1984, pp. 476–78). In the North, legislative activity on guns were most intense during the period of rapid immigration from about 1890 to World War I, and proponents often justified their proposals with references to the dangers of violent foreigners, anarchists, and other radicals, rather than just the "criminal classes" (Kennett and Anderson 1975, pp. 163, 167, 174, 177–78, 183, 213; Kates 1979a, pp. 15–22).

Between World War I and the assassination of President John Kennedy in 1963, there was still little clear conservative liberal lineup on gun control, and limited legislative activity (Kennett and Anderson 1975, pp. 187–215). John Kennedy was himself a gun owner and life member of the National Rifle Association. Ownership and even carrying of firearms were common among prominent liberals of earlier eras, such as Theodore Roosevelt, Eleanor Roosevelt, and columnist Drew Pearson (Kennett and Anderson 1975, p. 235; Kates 1986). However, since 1963, liberalism and support for gun control have become closely linked in the public mind. Surveys have documented a rough association between gun control support and a wide variety of other opinions conventionally associated with liberalism. Interestingly, it turns out that this link is solely due to higher gun ownership among conservatives-gun-owning liberals are no more likely to support gun control than gun-owning conservatives.

Further, not all liberals take a procontrol stance. A book published in 1979 was titled *Restricting Handguns: The Liberal Skeptics Speak Out* (Kates 1979a). Its editor was a former law clerk to radical lawyer William Kunstler and had helped draft civil rights legislation for the U.S. House of Representatives. Its preface was written by U.S. Senator and leading Vietnam War opponent Frank Church, and its contributors included the cofounder of American Amnesty International, the vice president of the Southern California ACLU, various civil rights activists, and a former legal aid lawyer who worked for Cezar Chavez' United Farm Workers and who took part in the earliest Freedom Rides of the civil rights movement. All expressed concerns, rooted in liberal principles, about the wisdom of gun control in its more restrictive forms. The book's chapters documented the antiblack and anti-immigrant origins of many gun control laws, reinstated the Second Amendment as an important part of the Bill of Rights, and argued the importance of gun ownership for deterring government oppression. The contributors asserted that guns provided the only effective means of defense for minorities and dissidents deprived of legal protection by hostile authorities, and argued from a feminist position that guns are vital "equalizers" for women with a need to protect themselves from violent, physically stronger men.

It is interesting in this connection that support for gun control is often one of the few "liberal" positions taken by otherwise dyed-in-the wool conservatives, including William F. Buckley Jr., who once flirted with a procontrol position, former Du Pont executive and self-described conservative Pete Shields, chairman of Handgun Control, Inc., and dozens of law-and-order big city police chiefs (Shields 1981; Alviani and Drake 1975, p. 52). Taking a procontrol stand allows such individuals to thereby display their open-mindedness and ability to rise above rigid ideological categories, by endorsing a position that has a liberal reputation, but is not really all that alien to the rest of their generally conservative beliefs.

Radical scholars such as Raymond Kessler (1984) have asserted that gun laws are fundamentally conservative or even reactionary, having in times and places served a variety of conservative political functions beyond simple crime control, including (1) increasing citizen dependence on the state for protection, (2) facilitating repressive action by governments, (3) reducing popular pressures for more fundamental reforms that might reduce crime, and (4) enabling selective enforcement against dissident political groups and racial and ethnic minorities. In sum, it is by no means clear that the intellectually natural position for liberals is support for restrictive gun controls or that the natural position of conservatives is opposition.

THE APPEARANCE OF REASON— FALLACIES IN GUN CONTROL REASONING*

By disposing of some of the more specious arguments for and against gun control, the air can be cleared so as to focus with fewer distractions on the more valid arguments. . . .

---

*Reprinted with permission from Gary Kleck, *Point Blank: Guns and Violence in America* (Hawthorne, N.Y.: Aldine de Gruytner, 1991), pp. 338–44. Copyright © 1991 by Walter de Gruyter, Inc., New York.

FALLACIES IN ANTICONTROL ARGUMENTATION

The Overmotivated Criminal

Gun control opponents argue that criminals cannot be disarmed or prevented from committing crimes through gun control because they will always be willing and able to either get a gun or to commit the crime without a gun. There is certainly some merit to this argument, as even proponents will concede. It is, however, an exaggeration, one that is based on a conception of criminal motivation that sees every criminal as powerfully motivated and driven to commit crime regardless of the obstacles. Like noncriminals, however, criminals do many things that are casually or only weakly motivated. Indeed, much crime is impulsive or opportunistic, with criminals committing some crimes only if it requires little effort and entails little risk (Feeney 1986). Certainly, gun control is unlikely to have much effect on crime committed by criminals with the strongest and most persistent motivation to commit crimes, such as drug dealers, emotionally disturbed mass murderers, professional hit men, terrorists, or political assassins. However, it is not al all impossible for crime preventive effects to be achieved among the more weakly or temporarily motivated criminals who may make up the majority of the active offender population. Note also that if conservative opponents of gun control really believed this argument, they would not support proposals to prevent crime through deterrence produced by more severe penalties. Offenders as strongly motivated as they allege most criminals to be would not be deterred by any penalty, no matter how severe.

ANYTHING SHORT OF TOTAL SUCCESS IS UTTER FAILURE

Opponents of gun laws, like opponents of any law, like to point to the failures of the laws—how many crimes are committed even in places with strict gun laws, how many criminals have guns despite the laws, and so on. This argument, however, is a non sequitur; it does not follow that gun laws are ineffective. All laws are violated and thus less than completely effective, and most important criminal laws are violated frequently, as a glance at criminal statistics indicates. Even some laws widely supported by the population have been violated by a majority of the population, as self-report surveys of the population have long shown (e.g., Wallerstein and Wyle 1947). Yet no one concludes that the thousands of homicides committed each year mean that laws prohibiting murder are ineffective and should be repealed. It is unreasonable to oppose a law merely because some people will violate it.

A more sensible standard to apply is to ask whether the benefits of the law exceed its costs, i.e., whether the world will, on balance, be a better place after the law is in effect. It is impossible to directly count the number of successes, i.e., the number of crimes deterred or otherwise prevented by the existence of laws prohibiting the acts, since one can never count the number of events that do not occur. And no matter how many failures there are, it is always possible that there are still more successes. The only way one can assess the relative balance of successes and failures is to compare jurisdictions having a law with those lacking the law, or to compare jurisdictions before and after they adopt a law, to see if there is, on balance, less crime with the law than without it. just counting failures settles nothing.

Criminals Will Ignore the Law

A corollary to the previous fallacy is the assertion that many criminals will ignore gun laws and get guns anyway. This is indisputably true, but not especially decisive regarding the desirability of gun control, since it does not address the number of successes of gun control. There is no clearly established minimum level of compliance that must be achieved before a law is to be judged a success. And if there were such a standard, it certainly could not reasonably be 100 percent, and would not necessarily be even 50 percent or any other similarly high level. It is even conceivable that if just 1 or 2 percent of potentially violent persons could be denied a gun, the resulting benefits might exceed the costs of whatever measure produced this modest level of compliance.

As it happens, there appears to be some compliance with gun laws even among the "hard-core" felons incarcerated in the nation's prisons. A survey of over 1800 felons in 11 state prisons found that 25 percent of felon gun owners reported having registered a firearm and 15 percent reported having applied for a permit to purchase or carry a gun, percentages that would have been higher had felons in states without such legal requirements been excluded from the computations (Wright and Rossi 1986, p. 84). Although the self-reported compliance levels were low, as one would expect in a sample of felons, they were also not zero. Among potentially violent persons not in prison, who are probably less persistently and seriously involved in law-breaking, compliance levels would presumably be even higher.

One Thing Leads to Another

Gun control supporters often wonder how the National Rifle Association (NRA) and other gun owner organizations can possibly oppose some of the more modest and apparently inoffensive regulations. Opponents reply that today's controls, no matter how limited and sensible, will just make it that much easier to take the next, more drastic step tomorrow, and then the next step, and the next, until finally total prohibition of private possession of firearms is achieved. They argue that gun control is a "slippery slope" on which it is hard to stop halfway, and that many proponents do not want to stop with just the more limited restrictions.

This fear is not completely unreasonable, as bills calling for a national ban on private possession of handguns have been introduced in Congress (Aviani and Drake 1975, pp. 55, 57) and much of the general public does favor prohibitions. In national opinion polls, about 40 percent of Americans say they support bans on the private possession of handguns, and one in six even support a ban on possession of *any* guns. Since about 75 percent of all Americans favor registering gun purchases and about 70 percent favor requiring police permits to buy a gun, this means that *most* supporters of these moderate controls also favor a total ban on private handgun possession. If this is so among ordinary nonactivist supporters of gun control, it almost certainly is true of activists and leaders of gun control advocacy groups.

There have always been enough prominent prohibitionists willing to air their views in a highly visible way to lend credence to fears about a movement toward total prohibition. For example, criminologist Marvin Wolfgang, in a letter to the editor of *Time* magazine, advocated a total national ban on possession of all firearms (July 5, 1968, p. 6), a sentiment echoed by noted sociologist Morris Janowitz (*Time*, 6-21-68).

Most leaders of gun control advocacy groups eventually became cautious about publicly describing their prohibitionist intentions, but earlier in the debate some were quite open about them. In 1969, one of the leading gun control advocacy groups was the National Council for a Responsible Firearms Policy (NCRFP). Its secretary, and a member of its Board of Directors, was J. Elliott Corbett. Responding to a letter writer who evidently had complained that the NCRFP's support for a moderate handgun control bill did not go far enough, Corbett wrote: "I personally believe handguns should be outlawed. . . . Our organization will probably officially take this stand in time but we are not anxious to rouse the opposition before we get the other legislation passed. It would be difficult to outlaw all rifles and shotguns because of the hunting sport. But there should be stiff regulations. . . . We thought the handgun bill was a step in the right direction. But, as you can see, our movement will be towards increasingly stiff controls" (reproduced in the *Congressional Record*, 3-4-69). Other advocates have expressed similar support for a one-step-at-a-time or incrementalist strategy. In a 1990 television documentary, a reporter asked the mayor of Stockton, California why she suported restrictions on so-called assault rifles while leaving much more powerful hunting rifles unregulated. She replied "I think you have to do it one step at a time . . . banning semi-assault [*sic*] military weapons . . . is the first step" (ABC-TV documentary, *Guns*, broadcast 1-24-90).

Leaders of procontrol advocacy groups such as Handgun Control and the Coalition to Stop Gun Violence (previously the National Coalition to Ban Handguns) used to assure audiences that they were interested only in regulating handguns, so hunters and sport shooters who used rifles and shotguns had nothing to fear from them (e.g., Fields 1979; Shields 1981, p. 124). Yet, once "assault rifles" became a highly publicized issue, leaders of these groups immediately pushed for strict controls on semiautomatic rifles. This kind of policy shift undercuts their credibility regarding their ultimate intentions, and feeds the worst paranoia of anticontrol extremists. In Don Kates's words, this sort of "extremism poisons the well," making it all the harder to get people to seriously consider more reasonable alternatives (1984b, p. 533).

It would be unfair to generalize from such cases to all supporters of moderate controls. Undoubtedly, many of those who insist they are not interested in further controls are sincere. Unfortunately, it is impossible for gun owners to know for sure which gun control supporters are sincere, how numerous they are, whether they will continue in the future to adhere to their commitment to limited controls, and whether they will dominate the gun control movement in the future. There are uncomfortable historical parallels between the gun control movement and the Temperance movement. The latter movement was originally directed toward regulating alcohol and encouraging, as its name suggested, moderation in drinking and a reduction in alcoholism. Yet it eventually evolved into the national Prohibition movement, which completely banned the production and sale of alcohol, and thereby criminalized millions of Americans (Gusfield 1963, esp. pp. 74, 96–110).

The political advantages of an incrementalist strategy are obvious. If one imagines a hypothetical scale of gun control restrictiveness going from, say, one (least restrictive) to ten, it is easier to move incrementally from level one to level two, then from two to three, and so on, up to level ten, than it is to jump straight from level one to level ten. Each single step looks less radical than a leap of several steps.

However, this is true about all solutions to any social problem. The fact that such escalation *could* happen says nothing about whether it *will* happen. The belief that "one thing inevitably leads to another" would preclude action of almost any kind, since a minor dose of any given solution to any problem could always lead to an overdose. It might be argued that use of the death penalty for murder or long mandatory prison sentences for serious violent crimes might lead to applying them to petty theft, then to minor traffic violations, and eventually to spitting on the sidewalk or speaking an unkind word to one's neighbor. Yet one never hears conservative gun control opponents applying this line of reasoning to their preferred solutions to crime. If such thinking is unreasonable in those examples, it is equally unreasonable to apply it to gun control, in the absence of any evidence showing the gun issue to be significantly different in this respect.

The fact remains that although most Americans support moderate gun controls such as requiring a permit to buy a gun, decades of lawmaking and propaganda have not persuaded a majority of them to support a general ban even on private possession of handguns, never mind all guns. The efforts of gun prohibitionists notwithstanding, the historical record does not support the view that public support for gun control has increased inexorably over the years; indeed it has remained fairly stable regarding most moderate controls, and even declined slightly with regard to handgun bans. Nor does the record support the view that gun law has inevitably gotten more restrictive. Indeed, the gun lobby's victories in passing state preemption laws, the 1986 amendments weakening the federal 1968 Gun Control Act, and recent liberalization of state gun carrying laws (Blackman 1985, p. 13 suggest an opposite trend in restrictiveness. A few minor procontrol factories notwithstanding, so far, at least, one thing has not lead to another. Regardless of their prohibitionist intentions, the more extreme gun control advocates have not, with few exceptions, been successful in moving very far toward banning guns. Opponents frequently cite New York City as an example of a place where originally moderate laws evolved, through gradual amendment and exploitation of administrative discretion, into virtual prohibition. There is merit to this claim as it pertains to New York City, but opponents can cite very few other examples, leading to the conclusion that such an evolution has been the exception rather than the rule with gun controls.

To Reduce Crime, We Should Get Tough with Criminals, Not Gun Owners

It may surprise some readers to learn that gun owner groups do support some kinds of gun control—severe, mandatory penalties for persons who commit crimes with firearms. However, this sort of "get tough with criminals" approach is usually regarded as an alternative to the measures most people have in mind when the term "gun control" is used, rather than being gun control itself. That is, opponents recommend "criminal control" as an alternative to gun control. However, proponents point out that to regard these as forced-choice alternatives is an error, since there is nothing to prevent governments from doing both (Shields 1981, pp. 123–24). Indeed, this is precisely what most governments do. The same legislators who support gun control proposals are often quick to point out also how "tough on criminals" they are, and the same is even true of some leaders of procontrol groups (e.g., Shields 1981, p. 156).

Nevertheless, both proponents and opponents who consider this an effective approach to crime reduction, as distinguished from a cynical but effective propaganda strategy, are on empirically weak ground. A long series of "get tough" strategies have been tried, carefully evaluated, and found to be either ineffective in producing significant crime reductions or hopelessly expensive. These failed strategies include longer prison terms mandatory prison terms, use of capital punishment, "selective incapacitation" of career criminals, increasing police manpower, and reducing procedural restraints on police and prosecutors (see the excellent book-length assessment by Walker 1989). While there are many promising alternatives to gun control for reducing violence, the "get-tough" approach is not one of them.

FALLACIES IN PROCONTROL ARGUMENTATION

The Undermotivated Offender

Just as opponents of gun control envision the typical criminal to be so strongly motivated that no gun law could possibly restrain him, proponents envision the opposite: weakly motivated offenders who could be prevented from committing crimes merely by placing procedural obstacles or delays in their way, making the acquisition of a gun marginally more expensive or difficult. The truth, of course, lies somewhere between these extremes. At least a few murderers are weakly or only temporarily motivated to kill their victims, and some are ambivalent or unclear in their intentions. Proponents exaggerate this image, however, by suggesting that killers rarely intend to kill, that the fatal outcome of their assaults was largely the product of weapon availability and chance. They argue that this implies that some criminals can be prevented from getting guns, and that many killers will *not* do whatever it takes to kill and will not kill using other means if they are denied guns (e.g., Zimring 1968). There is little direct empirical support for this idea and the evidence presented to support it usually has little clear bearing on the issue. Most homicides are unpremeditated, most develop out of arguments, and many involve combatants who knew one another, but none of these facts imply anything about how strongly killers wanted to kill or how angry they were at the time of the attack. Consequently, they imply nothing about whether most assaulters still would have killed had they not had a gun, or about whether they could have been prevented from getting a gun by gun control laws (see Wright et al. 1983, pp. 189–206).

It is necessary, however, for this imagery to be maintained if proponents are to argue that gun control can reduce crime. They must believe in the existence of a substantial number of persons who are willing and able to break serious laws such as those prohibiting murder, assault, and robbery, yet who are not willing or able to break gun control laws. If someone lacks the first attribute, preventing them from getting guns would be pointless for crime control; if they lacked the second, it would be impossible.

Guns That Are Good for Just One Thing—Murder (Targeting the "Bad" Types of Guns)

In the face of a U.S. civilian stock of over 200 million guns (half of U.S. households have at least one firearm), many gun law proponents have narrowed their political efforts, targeting specific types of guns, which they argue are "good for only one thing—to kill" (Shields 1981, pp. 38, 46). These proponents in effect differentiate "good" (or at least not-so-bad) types of guns, like the old family deer rifle, from "bad" types of guns. At various times, the especially dangerous, "bad" subcategory has been (1) handguns, (2) the cheap, small handguns known as Saturday night specials, (3) so-called assault rifles, (4) machine guns, and (5) plastic guns. Proponents argue that these weapons are mily useful for committing crimes, and sometimes even imply that they are never used for any other purposes (Fields 1979; Shields 1981). Because the guns have no legitimate purposes, it is argued, there can be no valid objection to outlawing them.

The logical problem with this position is that whatever technical attributes guns have that make them suitable for committing crimes necessarily also make them useful for a variety of lawful applications.

Gun Control Is Worthwhile Even if Just One Life Can Be Saved

This argument is convenient for gun control proponents since it relieves them of the need to establish just why they consider a gun-linked problem to be serious or to demonstrate that their proposals will save a large number of lives. Advocates will at times cite data documenting the large number of lives supposedly lost due to guns, yet at other times (usually after doubt has been cast on their figures) hint that the number of lives lost due to guns is not really an important matter because every human life is infinitely valuable. Almost any plausible gun control measure is bound to save at least one life, somewhere, sometime in the future. Therefore, it is implied, only a cold-hearted monster could deny the wisdom of a policy that could save that life.

There are two problems with this argument. First, it ignores the costs of gun control, in particular the possibility that gun control could cost lives by denying effective defensive weaponry to at least a few people who need and could successfully use guns in self-defense—almost any control that saved lives could also cost at least one life. Second, most major social problems have multiple possible solutions, each costing something, and each having some potential for reducing the problem. However, since resources are limited, choices inevitably must be made as to which strategies the resources should be invested in. More resources devoted to some strategies means less available for others. Consequently, the adherents of one particular strategy are obliged to at least roughly assess the potential benefits that strategy would produce rather than merely arguing that it does not matter whether a proposed policy would save one life or a 1,000 lives. It is unlikely that many people would seriously argue that a problem resulting in 1,000 deaths is no more important than one resulting in one death, so numbers do matter. In any case, it is doubtful if advocates really believe to the contrary—most invoke the "one life" argument only when one of their numerical claims regarding the harms of guns is challenged as being inflated.

Procontrol propagandists sometimes avoid making meaningful assessment of the seriousness of a particular gun-related problem if the effort would not yield a supportive result. They frequently note that more than three-fifths of homicides are committed with guns, but when targeting assault rifles or machine guns are silent on how many crimes are committed with these weapons, and do not cite any meaningful standard by which one could judge criminal use of these guns to constitute a serious problem. Proponents do note that gun suicides outnumber suicides by any other means, a meaningful comparison, but do not indicate what standard should be used to judge gun accidents to be an important source of mortality among children (e.g., Schetky 1985). Or sometimes they use a standard of comparison that is uninformative or misleading, as when proponents state that fatal gun accidents are the fourth leading cause of *accidental* death among children aged 14 and under (Center to Prevent Handgun Violence 1989). Although approximately accurate (they are the fifth leading cause rather than the fourth), the ranking is not very enlightening, since it conceals the fact that only the first of the leading accidental causes, motor vehicle accidents, is responsible for a large number of child deaths. Out of more than 20,000 deaths, from all causes, of children age 1 to 14 in 1987, over 4,000 were due to motor vehicle accidents, compared to about 250 due to gun accidents (National Safety Council 1989). If gun accidents are responsible for only 1 percent of child deaths, then the only standard by which this call be regarded as a major source of child mortality is the one which states that every human life is infinitely valuable and that all causes of death therefore are "major." But by this standard, comparisons arnong causes of death are pointless.

COMMON PROBLEMS OF PERSUASION

Members of advocacy groups on both sides of the great American gun debate share some rhetorical difficulties in common. Each side is committed to overstating the problem it addresses. For the procontrol forces, that problem is the contribution of guns to violence and crime, while for the anticontrol forces that problem is the procontrol forces. Each side faces a delicate dilemma in their propaganda efforts, one familiar to fund raisers everywhere—they must convey the enormity of the problem, yet also instill confidence in their own effectiveness by pointing to their victories and the progress they have achieved. Thus the NRA must simultaneously convince its current and potential members and contributors that it is facing a powerful gun control movement that is a serious threat to gun owners' rights if not checked, but also convince them that the NRA has beaten the enemy in the past and can do so again in the future, if they are just given the support they need. Likewise Handgun Control, Incorporated (HCI) and the Coalition to Stop Gun Violence (CSGV) overstate the connection between guns and violence, and speak darkly of the NRA's vast political power, seemingly unlimited funds (largely derived, it is inaccurately hinted, from economically self-interested gun manufacturers), and their victories over majority public opinion, while also boasting of their own organization's growing membership and recent legislative victories (e.g., Handgun Control Incorporated 1989; National Coalition to Ban Handguns 1988). To believe both sides, one would have to believe that both parties to the conflict are simultaneously weak and strong, triumphantly victorious and headed toward ignominious defeat. Each set of advocacy groups serves as the demon with which the other side can rally the troops, raising morale and money. The public is not enlightened by this war of words because neither set of advocates has any stake in merely presenting the plain unvarnished truth, even to the extent that flawed and biased human minds can understand it. Quite the contrary—to tell the truth and nothing but the truth would place one side at a distinct disadvantage if the other side did not also lay down their propaganda weapons. As a consequence, the intended audience for these propaganda efforts is inundated with an avalanche of misinformation, half-truths, irrelevancies, trivialities, and outright falsehoods. And this bad information drives out the good, either displacing it because there is only so much attention that can be paid to any given issue, or rendering accurate information useless because it cannot be recognized as such, being so thoroughly intermixed with the disinformation that only the most diligent and unusually well informed readers and viewers can and will separate the two.

THE NONUTILITARIAN NATURE OF MUCH GUN CONTROL SUPPORT*

Why do people support gun control? The obvious answer is that they want to reduce violence and believe that gun control will help accomplish this goal. Unfortunately, this appealingly simple utilitarian explanation is inadequate for explaining the positions of many, and possibly most, gun control supporters.

Both Wright (1981; Wright et al. 1983) and Crocker (1982) have noted that although a majority of Americans favor a variety of moderate gun control measures, large majorities also believe that handgun control will not keep criminals from getting guns, that gun controls cannot prevent assassinations, and (on most questions) that gun laws will not reduce crime or violence. When asked about existing gun laws, most Americans believe they are ineffective in reducing violent crime. In a December 1993 survey for CBS News, 64 percent endorsed the view that "gun control laws . . . do not reduce violent crime" (DIALOG 1995). Further, about half of Americans do not see much potential for reducing violence even if gun laws were made stricter in the future. A December 1993 survey for Time/CNN found that 49 percent of Americans believed that stricter gun laws will not reduce violence (DIALOG 1995).

It is quite common for Americans to simultaneously hold to two views: (1) they favor many moderate gun control laws, yet (2) they do not believe that the laws will reduce crime or violence. For example, although 87 percent of Americans favored the Brady Act's provisions of a five-day wait and a background check to buy a handgun (1993 Yankelovich survey, table 10.2), after the law was passed, 61 percent of Americans also thought that the Brady Act did not make it harder for people with criminal records to get a gun (February 1995 CBS

*Reprinted with permission from Gary Kleck, *Point Blank: Guns and Violence in America* (Hawthorne, N.Y.: Aldine de Gruytner, 1991), pp. 338–44. Copyright © 1991 by Walter de Gruyter, Inc., New York.

News/New York Times poll; DIALOG 1995). Since this was the mechanism by which the Brady measure was supposed to reduce violence, this would seem to imply that most Americans believed the law would have no impact on violence.

This seemingly odd combination of views—support for controls and the belief that they will not work—is not peculiar to gun control. The American public holds many such apparently "nonutilitarian" opinions on measures alleged to control crime. For example, although half of the population believes that prison sentences do not discourage crime, 69 percent nevertheless approve of building more prisons so longer sentences can be given to criminals (U.S. Bureau of justice Statistics 1984:260, 270). Similarly, when a 1981 survey asked death penalty supporters why they favored capital punishment, only 35 percent gave answers indicating they thought it was a deterrent to killers (U.S. Bureau of Justice Statistics 1981:278). Most commonly the death penalty was favored for reasons of retribution. Thus, many crime control measures are favored for moralistic or symbolic reasons with no necessary connection with crime control.

Interpreting gun control opinion polls, Wright concluded that "many people support such measures for reasons other than their assumed effects on the crime rate" (1981:35). He summarized public opinion as follows:

> Just as licensing and registration of automobiles seem to have very little effect on reducing automobile accidents, so too do most people anticipate that stricter weapons controls would have little or no effect on crime. This, however, does not stop them from favoring at least some stricter gun control measures. The underlying concept here seems to be that weapons, as automobiles, are intrinsically dangerous objects that governments ought to keep track of for that reason alone. (ibid.:39)

Nevertheless, despite rather pessimistic views on the effectiveness of gun control in general, clear majorities of Americans do believe that at least some specific moderate controls will be effective in fighting crime at least to some degree, even if others are viewed as ineffective (see 1978 DMI survey results in Crocker 1982:258).

A 1990 national survey indicated that, among people who thought that more gun control laws were needed, 46 percent also believed that if there were more laws, crime would either stay the same or even increase (Mauser 1990). Thus, nearly half supported more gun laws even though they believed the laws would not reduce crime, even slightly. One generally procontrol commentator concluded that "gun owners believe (rightly in my view) that the gun controllers would be willing to sacrifice their interests even if the crime control benefits were tiny" (Moore 1983: 187–88).

Much support for gun control, then, rests on grounds other than a utilitarian belief that it will reduce crime. What those grounds might be is not clear from the results of individual survey questions. Perhaps some hints can be derived from detailed analysis of the patterns of support for gun control. Knowing who supports gun control may indirectly shed light on why they support it.

WHO SUPPORTS GUN CONTROL?

There is a tremendous variety of types of gun control, but analyzing opinion patterns on all of these would be impractical. Instead the results pertaining to one specific, moderate gun control measure are presented here: gun purchase permits. Since more polls have asked identically worded questions about police purchase permits than any other measure, this would seem to be an appropriate measure to examine in more detail.

Close examination of exactly which segments of the population are most likely to favor purchase permits can be used to get a rough idea as to who is most likely to favor gun controls in general. Although levels of support vary sharply across different control measures, patterns of support by respondents tend to be very similar. Thus, the same groups that are most likely to support one measure are generally the ones most likely to support others. . . . (U.S. Bureau of Justice Statistics 1989:172–75). Thus, variables predicting support for police purchase permits relate in virtually identical ways to support for handgun bans, except that blacks were less likely than whites to support handgun bans [Brennan, Lizotte, and McDowall (1993:301–302); these authors' results regarding registration are not comparable to their other results because they pertain to perceptions of likely compliance levels and effectiveness rather than just support or opposition].

[In] the General Social Surveys, the exact question wording used to measure support for gun control was: "Would you favor or oppose a law which would require a person to obtain a police permit before he or she could buy a gun?" The strongest bivariate associations are as follows: Females are significantly more supportive of a permit than are males, urban dwellers are more supportive than are rural inhabitants and small-town residents, those not from the South are more supportive than are southerners, nonhunters are more supportive than hunters, and non-gun owners are more supportive than those who own guns. There are other weaker relationships that are statistically significant only because the sample was so large. These bivariate associations could be misleading, of course, since they may reflect the confounding effects of other variables, especially gun ownership itself. Indeed, some variables were found to be unrelated to public opinion on permits, once gun ownership was controlled in a multivariate analysis. There was no significant association between conservatism and opinions on permits, once gun ownership and hunting were controlled. Apart from the very small indirect effect it has through gun ownership and hunting, being a conservative does not appear to decrease the likelihood of support for permits; conversely, liberalism does not directly increase support. In fact, persons who think the courts are not harsh enough on criminals (surely a conservative attitude) are actually slightly more likely to favor a permit law, other things being equal. Thus, it may be misleading to discuss gun control opinion as if it clearly divided along ideological lines. Liberals are also not substantially more supportive of gun control when a stricter control measure is involved. A follow-up survey conducted after the Massachusetts referendum to ban handgun possession found that although 66 percent of conservatives voted against the measure, so did a nearly identical 64 percent of liberals (Holmberg and Clancy 1977:83).

Being afraid to walk in one's neighborhood and prior victimization in a burglary also were unrelated to permit opinion once multivariate controls were introduced. The positive bivariate association between fear and permit support may have been a spurious one due to the correlation of fear with income: low-income Americans are more likely to be fearful and more likely to support gun control. It had been the hope of gun control activists that increasing victimization and rising fear of crime and violence would eventually motivate more Americans to support gun control (Shields 1981). However, support did not increase significantly during 1963–1974, when crime rates were rapidly increasing. The present results explain why: apparently fear and prior victimization do not motivate support for gun control. Indeed, indirectly they may tend to have the opposite effect. Results indicated that prior burglary victimization and higher crime rates may motivate acquisition of handguns, while other findings indicate that gun ownership in turn strongly discourages support for permits.

There also was no bivariate association between prior victimization and support for a purchase permit. However, where more stringent controls are at stake, victimization may discourage support for gun control. A statewide survey was conducted during the fight over Maryland's referendum to ban Saturday night specials. [Respondents] were asked whether they or a family member had ever been a victim of handgun crime. Although half of the nonvictims supported the ban, only a third of the victims did (*Washington Post*, 27 October 1988, p. A9). One reasonable generalization from these results would be that if there seems to be a possibility that a measure would take guns away from people who feel they might need them for self-defense, crime victims are less likely to support the measure than nonvictims. Purchase permits, in contrast, would not disarm most crime victims. Consistent with this interpretation, Brennan and her colleagues (1993:30) found that while nonwhites were more supportive of purchase permit laws, they were less likely than whites to support a ban on handgun ownership.

CULTURE CONFLICT AND THE WAR OVER GUNS

. . . It is possible that some people support gun control as a way of stigmatizing another, disliked group and its culture, using the criminal law to declare that some kinds of activities, such as owning guns, are shameful and morally objectionable, and should be limited for this reason alone. Some gun control support, therefore, would be unrelated to either the specifics of the particular measure asked about, or to concerns about reducing crime. Recall that about half of gun control supporters support more gun laws even though they believe they will not reduce crime. Don Kates has noted the indifference that gun ban advocates show for practical issues such as enforceability, and has interpreted this as indicating that "the antigun crusader's concern is of symbolic rather than pragmatic value," and concluding that "antigun crusaders view a ban on guns as an official or symbolic endorsement of their moral superiority and as a simultaneous condemnation of guns and gun owners" (Kates 1990:10).

Some people who do not own guns stereotype gun owners as "gun nuts" and "rednecks," who are thought to be violent, anti-intellectual, racist, reactionary, and dangerous (Kaplan 1979:6). Gun control, then, may be viewed by some supporters not merely as a form of violence control, but as redneck and reactionary control as well. The debate over gun control is merely one reflection of larger status conflicts involving the tactics of the "stigma contest." Guns are merely symbolic of associated people and cultures, such as Southerners and Southern culture, that are disliked, largely for reasons not directly related to gun ownership (Hawley 1977). Thus, Northerners are more likely to support gun control than Southerners, despite widespread skepticism about whether controls reduce violence (Brennan et al. 1993). Some observers see in the gun control struggle a conflict between the older, more traditional culture of "bedrock America," and the newer, more urban one of "cosmopolitan America" (*Wall Street Journal*, 7 June 1972, p. 14). Others have emphasized the regional dimensions of the conflict, seeing the antigun movement as reflecting hostility to Southern culture (Hawley 1977). Still others have stressed a class dimension, interpreting the conflict as one in which predominantly upper-middle-class and upper-class supporters such as the late Pete Shields (a former executive in the Du Pont corporation and longtime chairman of HCI) attempt to impose their views on working-class people exposed to the realities of street crime (Kates 1979a).

Finally, still others have stressed a racial dimension. For example, liberal investigative reporter Robert Sherrill flatly concluded that "the Gun Control Act of 1968 was passed not to control guns but to control blacks" (1975:280). Sherrill argued that the ghetto riots of 1967 and 1968 impelled Congress to ban imports of cheap handguns, which they associated with ghetto blacks, while leaving more expensive handguns, along with rifles and shotguns, relatively untouched. Tonso quoted the founder of the National Black Sportsman's Association as asserting, "Gun control is really race control. . . . All gun laws have been enacted to control certain classes of people, mainly black people, but the same laws used to control blacks are being used to disarm white people as well" (1985:23).

Kates's (1979a; also 1986) review of the early history of gun control supports these views in regard to the origins of gun laws. Nevertheless, it should be stressed that however much the impact of gun laws may disproportionately fall on minorities and poor people, this does not necessarily imply anything about the motives of those who support gun laws. It is difficult to distinguish a person who uses a concern about violence control as a mere rationalization for supporting gun controls from one whose support is genuinely based on concerns about the role of guns in violence. Nevertheless, given the nonutilitarian nature of much gun control support, it is likely that some of the drive for gun laws relies as much on concern about controlling despised or feared "dangerous classes" as on a desire to control crime. If this perspective is accurate, gun control support should have little association with variables related to crime, but be strongly associated with membership in groups likely to be hostile to guns and gun ownership. Likewise, support for gun control may reflect hostility to culturally defined groups associated with gun ownership.

These hypotheses were empirically tested with an analysis that combined national survey data about individuals with crime data describing the cities in which the individuals lived (Kleck 1996a). That analysis indicated that support for a law requiring a police permit to purchase a gun was unrelated to violent crime rates of the cities in which people resided or to their own prior experience of crime victimization, and was related to their stated fear of crime only among white females. Higher burglary rates even appeared to *decrease* gun control support. In contrast, support for permits was significantly related, controlling for gun ownership, to membership in social groups thought to be hostile to guns and gunowners: persons with more formal education, those with higher income, political liberals, blacks, Jews, and those who do not hunt. On the other hand, contrary to some prior research (Brennan et al. 1993), there was no evidence of an effect of southernness on permit support. In other respects, however, support for gun control was generally associated with membership in groups likely to be hostile to gun ownership, but was unrelated to exposure to high crime rates, experience as a crime victim, or (except among white females) fear of crime.

While some gun control supporters believe gun control might reduce crime, they apparently are rarely impelled to support controls as a result of personal experiences with crime, or exposure to higher crime rates. Thus, there is no empirical support for the idea that rising crime rates will increase support for gun control, or that falling rates will decrease it.

REFERENCES

Alviani, Jospeh D., and William R. Drake. 1975. *Handgun Control . . . Issues and Alternatives.* Washington, D.C.: U.S. Conference of Mayors.

Brennan, Pauline Gasdow, Alan J. Lizotte, and David McDowall. 1993. "Guns, Southernness, and gun control." *Journal of Quantitative Criminology* 9:289–307.

Center to Prevent Handgun Violence. 1988. "Child's Play." Pamphlet. Washington, D.C.: CPHV (education and research affiliate of Handgun Control, Inc.).

———. 1989. "The Killing Seasons." Pamphlet. Washington, D.C.: CPHV (education and research affiliate of Handgun Control, Inc.).

———. 1993. "Kids Carrying Guns." Pamphlet. Washington, D.C.: CPHV (education and research affiliate of Handgun Control, Inc.).

———. 1996a. "Firearm Facts." Propaganda sheet. Washington, D.C.: CPHV (education and research affiliate of Handgun Control, Inc.).

———. 1996b. "Children and Guns." Propaganda sheet. Washington, D.C.: CPHV (education and research affiliate of Handgun Control, Inc.).

Crocker, Royce. 1982. "Attitudes toward gun control: A survey." In *Federal Regulation of Firearms.* Edited by Harry L. Hogan. Washington. D.C.: U.S. Government Printing Office, pp. 229–67.

Fields, Sam. 1979. "Handgun prohibition and social necessity." *St. Louis University Law Journal* 23:35–61.

DIALOG. 1990. Computer search of DIALOG database, File 468, Public Opinion Online (POLL) file of public opinion survey results. Palo Alto, CA.: DIALOG Information Services, Inc.

———. 1995. Computer search of DIALOG database, File 468, Public Opinion Online (POLL) file of public opinion survey results. Mountain View, CA.: Knight-Ridder Information, Inc.

———. 1997. Computer search of DIALOG database, File 468, Public Opinion Online (POLL) file of public opinion survey results, January 1997. Mountain View, CA.: Knight-Ridder Information, Inc.

Hawley, Fred. 1977. "The gun control debate: Stigma contest, social science, and cultural conflict." Unpublished paper. Department of Criminal Justice, Louisiana State University, Shreveport.

Homberg, Judith Vandell, and Michael Clancy. 1977. *People* vs. *Handguns*. Washington, D.C.: U.S. Conference of Mayors.

Kaplan, John. 1979. "Controlling firearms." *Cleveland State Law Review* 28:1–28.

Kates, Don. B., Jr. 1979a. "Toward a history of handgun prohibition in the United States." In *Restricting Handguns: The Liberal Skeptics Speak Out*. Edited by Don. B. Kates Jr. Croton-on-Hudson, N.Y.: North River, pp. 7–30.

———. 1979b. "Some remarks on the prohibition of handguns." *St. Louis University Law Journal* 23:11–34.

———. 1982. *Why Handgun Bans Can't Work*. Bellevue, Wash.: Second Amendment Foundation.

———. 1983. "Handgun prohibition and the original meaning of the Second Amendment." *Michigan Law Review* 82:204–73.

———. 1984a. "Handgun banning in light of the prohibition experience." In *Firearms and Violence: Issues of Public Policy*. Edited by Don B. Kates Jr. Cambridge, Mass.: Ballinger, pp. 139–65.

———. 1984b. "Conclusion." In *Firearms and Violence: Issues of Public Policy*. Edited by Don B. Kates Jr. Cambridge, Mass.: Ballinger, pp. 523–37.

———. 1984c. *Firearms and Violence: Issues of Public Policy*, Cambridge, Mass.: Ballinger.

———. 1986b. "Criminological perspectives on gun control and gun prohibition legislation." In *Why Handgun Bans Can't Work*. Edited by Don B. Kates Jr. Bellevue, Wash.: Second Amendment Foundation, pp. 3–76.

———. 1990. *Guns, Murders, and the Constitution*. Policy Briefing, Pacific Research Institute for Public Policy, San Francisco.

———. 1979. "Handgun prohibition and homicide." In *Restricting Handguns*. Edited by Don B. Kates Jr. Croton-on-Hudson, N.Y.: North River, pp. 91–118.

Kennett, Lee, and James LaVerne Anderson. 1975. *The Gun in America: The Origins of a National Dilemma*. Westport, Conn.: Greenwood.

Kleck, Gary. 1996a. "Crime, culture conflict and sources of support for gun control: A multi-level application of the General Social Surveys." *American Behavioral Scientist* 39(4):387–404.

Mauser, Gary A., and Michael Margolis. 1990. "The politics of gun control." Paper presented at the annual meetings of the American Political Science Association, San Francisco.

National Safety Council. 1981. *Accident Facts*, 1981 edition. Chicago: Author.

———. 1988. *Accident Facts*, 1988 edition. Chicago: Author.

———. 1995. *Accident Facts*, 1995 edition. Itasca, Illinois: Author.

———. 1996. *Accident Facts*, 1996 edition. Itasca, Illinois: Author.

Schetky, Diane H. 1985. "Children and handguns." *American Journal of Diseases of Children* 139:229–31.

Sherrill, Robert. 1973. *The Saturday Night Special*. New York:Charterhouse.

———. 1975. *The Saturday Night Special*. New York: Penguin.

Shields, Pete. 1981. *Guns Don't Die—People Do*. New York: Arbor House.

Tonso, William R. 1983. "Social problems and sagecraft in the debate over gun control." *Law & Policy Quarterly* 5:325–44.

———. 1985. "Gun control: White man's law." *Reason* (December):22–25.

Wallerstein, James S., and Clement J. Wyle. 1947. "Our law-abiding law-breakers." *Probation* 25:107–12.

Wright, James D. 1981. "Public opinion and gun control." *Annals* 455:24–39.

———. 1984. "The ownership of firearms for reasons of self-defense." In *Firearms and Violence* Edited by Don B. Kates Jr. Cambridge, Mass.: Ballinger, pp. 301–27.

———. 1989. "Guns and sputter." *Reason* (July):46–47.

———. 1990. "In the heat of the moment." *Reason* (August/September):44–45.

Wright, James D., and Peter H. Rossi. 1985. *The Armed Criminal in America: A Survey of Incarcerated Felons.* National Institute of Justice Research Report. Washington, D.C.: U.S. Goverment Printing Office.

———. 1986. *Armed and Considered Dangerous: A Survey of Felons and Their Firearms.* Hawthorne, N.Y.: Aldine de Gruyter.

Wright, James D., Peter H. Rossi, and Kathleen Daly. 1983. *Under the Gun: Weapons, Crime, and Violence in America.* Hawthorne, N.Y.: Aldine de Gruyter.

PART TWO

GUN CONTROL IN THE AGE OF (MIS)INFORMATION

We are predisposed to see order, pattern and meaning in the world, and we find randomness, chaos and meaninglessness unsatisfying.... As a conse-quence we tend to "see" order where there is none, and we spot meaningful pat-terns where only the vagaries of chance are operating.

... Once a person has (mis)identified a random pattern as a "real" phe-nomenon ... it is quickly integrated into a person's preexisting theories and beliefs ... which then serve to bias the person's evaluation of new informa-tion. ...

Thomas Gilovich, *How We Know What Isn't So*

In November of 1999, figures from the Centers for Disease Control and Pre-vention were encouraging. The Associated Press quoting these statistics reported that from 1993 to 1997 gun deaths had dropped by 21 percent and firearm caused injuries by 41 percent. AP had reported in October that FBI figures showed the U.S. murder rate had hit a thirty-one-year low and the gun homicide rate was down 7 percent from 1993. The *Washington Post* in August, 1999 published fig-ures from a U.S. Department of Education study showing a 31 percent drop over the last two years in gun expulsions from public schools. Dr. Barry Glassner, a risk assessment expert, claimed in a *Wall Street Journal* article that statistically a child is far more likely to be hit by lightning on a playground than shot in a classroom.

Statistically, then, the nation and the schools were significantly safer regarding gun violence then they had been in last seven years. Regarding vio-lence, and gun violence, in particular, America was moving in the right direction.

However, from April 1999 through September of 1999, gun violence and gun control issues dominated the U.S. media. From September 1999 into the presidential election year 2000, newspapers and magazines featured not only gun violence incidents but politicians advocating highly publicized gun control schemes. Also a number of opinion pieces dealt with the perception that "No one or no place is safe any more." In the American media coexisting statistics and coverage of issues regarding gun violence risks, seemed widely at variance. What was going on here? What happened?

On April 20, 1999, two high school students in Littleton, Colorado, shot and murdered thirteen fellow students and killed themselves. The massacre was carefully planned. The *Wall Street Journal* reported (October 21, 1999): "Television bombarded viewers with round the clock coverage. The telephones of Handgun Control Inc. jammed solid with calls. And President Clinton proposed what he called 'the most comprehensive gun crime legislation any administration has put forth in a generation.' Coming after a series of school shootings elsewhere in the country (one in 1997, three in 1998), the carefully planned rampage by Columbine High School students Eric Harris and Dylan Klebold seemed precisely the sort of lurid evidence that gun foes needed to enact new national gun control laws and put the (gun) industry further on the defensive."*

"We hadn't seen a public reaction like this before," says Robert Walker, president of Handgun Control in Washington, the country's largest gun control advocacy organization. "We perceived a historic opportunity."

This "historic opportunity" was soon to be enhanced. Another highly publicized school shooting, in Arkansas (five killed), and then on July 29th a bloody gun rampage by an Atlanta stockbroker in which nine people were murdered. Gun control and gun violence again became dominant issues in the mass media, especially among the newsweeklies.

Business Week (August 16, 1999), spurred on by these events ("with each new massacre, America's outrage about gun violence flames higher") produced a six-page cover story on gun violence, gun control, gun litigation and the gun industry. Included was a full-page commentary entitled "Guns Are Wounding Americas Image Abroad." The author argued "permissive U.S. gun laws that allow deranged individuals to kill innocents were negatively affecting our image abroad." He concluded that how the present gun debate goes "will have a strong effect on the American image abroad." *Business Week* was not done with guns. An editorial (included in this volume) called for gun registration and the banning and further restrictions on owners of classes of presently legal weapons ("It's time for serious gun control").

Time magazine in its competing issue (August 9) focused on the "Atlanta massacre." It also featured a two-page opinion piece entitled "Get Rid of the Damned Things" (included in this volume).

---

*In fact, school shootings are not a new phenomena. From 1974 to 2000, there have been 37 shooting incidents involving 41 students. U.S. Secret Service, "U.S.S.S. Safe School Initiative," October 2000, www.ustreas.gov/usss/home.htm

On August 10, another shooting! A middle-aged neo-Nazi walked into a Jewish community center in Granda Hills, California, and wounded, with a semiautomatic pistol, two adults and three children.

Newsweek devoted the core of its August 23 issue to gun control and gun violence. The magazine introduced the topic with a three-page editorial entitled in bold print "Guns in America: What Must Be Done" (included in this volume) which established the media gun control agenda for the November 2000 presidential elections. A multipaged "Special Report" followed "The Gun War Comes Home." The report opened by emphasizing the middle-class dimensions of the shootings and attendant political implications: "The shooting victims of today's headlines are not distant leaders but school children and office workers. Political emotions are rising, and for the first time, the debate over firearms may become a central part of the presidential campaign." Gun violence had broken out of the ghetto into the social mainstream. Guns were now an issue for the class that puts presidents into office.

The "Special Report" was laced with highlighted findings of a telephone poll commissioned by the magazine on August 12 and 13.

"In the Newsweek Poll, *74 percent* support registration for all handgun owners and *93 percent* favor a mandatory waiting period for people who want to buy handguns."

Seventy-eight percent think gun control will be an important issue in next years election. By a margin of 34 percent to 26 percent they agree more with the Democrats on the issue.

Only *21 percent* of gun owners favor an outright ban on nonpolice handguns. But *50 percent* of the people who didn't own firearms are in favor of such a ban.

Sixty-eight percent say military-style assault gun should be outlawed, and *51 percent* want to ban gun shows where weapons are bought and sold with little regulation. (The poll questions asked were not included. There was no discussion of whether the recent concentrated coverage of gun violence was affecting the results.)

Besides an interview with a NRA official this "Special Report" contained an article entitled "The New Age of Anxiety" with "Anxiety" printed in large bold, blood red letters. Centered in the page is a dramatic picture of a sobbing student being led away from an apparent shooting. The author reaches the conclusion that "No one is safe anymore." (as proven by the Columbine Massacre) while at the same time acknowledging "schools are among the safest places children can be . . . only a tiny fraction of all homicides involving school age children occur in and around schools, according to the federal Centers for Disease Control and Prevention" (article included in Part Two). *Newsweek*'s treatment of gun issues concluded with an essay by psychiatrist Robert Jay Lipton ("The Psyche of a Gunocracy") which opens with the neo-Nazi gunman who attacked the Jewish community center and concludes with reflections about ordinary Americans "caught up in the cult of the gun. . . . Americans have shown signs of a change in their feelings about guns, seeing them increasingly as more dangerous than sacred. This kind of collective psychological shift is necessary if we are ever to transcend the crippling fraternity of the gun."

There would be other shootings that received considerable and vivid print and electronic media coverage. On September 15, a gunman killed seven worshipers at a church prayer meeting and then killed himself. On December 6, a thirteen-year-old student, wounded four students with a semiautomatic handgun in Fort Gibson, Oklahoma.

These shootings provoked articles on fear and risk. A nationally syndicated article[1] that appeared in January 2000 is illustrative. It's title read in black bold print: "*A Scar on America's Psyche*: Mass Shootings at School, Church, Work Have Left People Feeling: 'No place is safe anymore.' "

This article recapitulates the publicized gun violent gun massacres of 1999 and counts a total of nine school shootings since 1997. One conclusion reached "as the tragedies have dominated the news, including more cities and towns across America, public comfort levels have plummeted" ("Media fueled images have been seared into the public consciousness forever; panicked students streaming out of Columbine High School").

The author, however, while acknowledging the impact of "media fueled images" has to wrestle with the same problem found in the *Newsweek* article, the apparent conflict of sensational anecdote and expert opinion: "Although indications are that few people actually fear for their own personal safety when they go to church or work or school—and the knowledge of these shootings apparently has not curtailed public outings—more people seem to consider the possibilities of getting caught in such gunfire." She quotes the anxieties of a dry-cleaning shop operator living in a suburb of Birmingham, Alabama, where a workplace shooting took place one week after the "Atlanta Massacre"; "I always thought this area was so nice and quiet and safe, and no place is safe anymore." However, the author also quotes Alan Lipman, a professor of clinical and criminal psychology at Georgetown: "There is no reason to believe in terms of large numbers that this society as a whole is beginning to fear going out . . . I don't think it's denial, there's no question that most of our schools are safe, most of our workplaces are safe, and while we should become more sensitized to the possibility of violence happening, its critically important not to go overboard." If Professor Lipman is correct, the article's subheadline in bold "Mass shootings at school, church, work have left people feeling 'no place is safe anymore,' " is false. And, if the statistical data cited earlier is correct, Professor Lipman's claim that America's schools and work places in general are less threatened by gun fire than ever, is true.

But these *Newsweek* and *Washington Post* writers were not alone in seeking meanings, connections, and patterns. Literally dozens of syndicated articles and countless editorials sought to "explain" these violent events by linking them to a myriad of supposedly violence inducing agents: violent music, violent videos, violent computer games, violent TV programming, violent movies, violent child rearing, violent jocks, violent "goths," violence obsessed media, violence against the unborn and of course, America as a "violent society." All of these commentators in the print and electronic media agreed that no matter what the specific form, no matter that violence in general was ebbing, that violence itself, was, begetting this "rash" of new violence.

Are these extraordinarily bloody, vividly covered events in 1999 (or 1997 and 1998) connected? If so, how do media commentators know? Are they, by looking backward, through retrospective analysis, able both to detect and document underlying patterns, causal connections? Are they able to prove through retrospective analysis that violence-infused events are making apparent clusters of violent events happen?

To initially address these questions let's consider the mass media's record concerning other events throughout the 1990s. First, let's consider AIDS. The last decade began with assurances from the Center for Disease Control enthusiastically transmitted by the mass media of a coming AIDS epidemic that would soon engulf white, heterosexual America. It wasn't just gays, and intravenous drug users concentrated in minority population who were at risk.

We were now "*all* at risk."

On the basis this new knowledge public health programs aimed their messages—and money at the largest at-risk population—white middle-class heterosexuals. Programs aimed at smaller groups of gays and intravenous drug users concentrated among minorities received less attention—and money.

Meanwhile a new medical disaster would begin to supplant AIDS in terms of media attention. Leaking silicone breast implants were allegedly destroying the immune systems of tens of thousands of American women. How did the media know? Anecdotal example after example as well as statistics were supplied by advocacy groups and lawyers pursuing class action lawsuits against the silicone implant industry. Out-of-court settlements in the billions put that industry out of business.

AIDS and breast implants however, were not the only crises to be stalking Americans. The media began to supply example after example of satanic cults that had infiltrated teen culture. Reports of ritual killings of animals and humans swept across America.

And worse, pederastic cults, composed of ostensibly respectable citizens and day care workers were raping and sodomizing disturbing numbers of children and further, "repressed memory" specialists not only uncovered these pederasts but also dozens of cases of female victims of parental sexual abuse that had happened decades before.

And thousands of children were being abducted by strangers and adults by sex-crazed space aliens and hundreds of black churches were being burned by right-wing white racists and tens of thousands of ethnic Albanians were being systematical slaughtered by organized Serbian death squads. Hence, only a NATO air war could overt genocide.

Enough! This recesitation of media complicity in dubious "scares" is obviously biased.

Didn't the information industry ever get it right? Yes, they did. Various media sources *eventually* got all the above scares sorted out (well, maybe not space aliens). The *Wall Street Journal* in 1996, for example, investigated and documented the Centers for Disease Control's 1987 campaign to falsely convince the media and Americans that the misleading generalization "we are all at risk" was true ("AIDS Fight Is Skewed by Federal Campaign Exaggerating Risks," *Wall Street Journal*, 1 May 1996).

Dorothy Rabinowicz of that paper both during and after the "repressed memory" sexual abuse scares crusaded and crusades on behalf of the unfairly accused and convicted.

Both the print and television media gave extensive coverage to the subsequent scientific debunking of the breast implant scare. Print and electronic media after the successful NATO air war against the Serbians publicized the findings of United Nations investigators which found no evidence of mass, systematic genocide carried on in Kosovo against ethnic Albanians.

In short, various media sources eventually acknowledged that events or patterns to events that they thought were there, weren't. But why was it easier for me (and maybe you) to remember and focus on media failures and ignore eventual media successes? Part of the answer may lie in the findings of cognitive and motivational psychologists such as Thomas Gilovich. Investigators have documented both motivational (our goals, preferences, dislikes) and cognitive (ways we process information and arrive at conclusions) sources of bias. If people are basically skeptical toward the mass media there will be a tendency for them to look for all the relevant information that will confirm their skepticism. They will gravitate toward experts who will share and reinforce that skepticism. Also, preferences "influence not only the *kind* of information they consider, but also the *amount* they examine. When the initial evidence supports our preferences, we are generally satisfied and terminate our search; when the initial evidence is hostile, however, we dig deeper . . . (we keep) our investigative engines running until we uncover information that permits a conclusion that we find comforting."[2] In short, motivational factors bias us toward seeking confirmations and against disconfirmations by subjecting discrepant data to much harsher inspections than confirmatory data

> for propositions we want to believe, we ask only that the evidence not force us to believe otherwise—a rather easy standard to meet, given the equivocal nature of much information. For the propositions we want to resist, however, we ask whether the evidence *compels* such a distasteful conclusion—a much more difficult standard to achieve. . . . By framing the question in such ways, however, we can often believe what we prefer to believe, and satisfy ourselves we have an objective basis for doing so.[3]

Once these motivational sources of bias have succeeded in confirming our beliefs and discrediting contrary evidence then we will seek the company of those who share our beloved possessions and eschew those who would besmirch or rob us of what we have worked so hard to acquire.

But how do we form these biased beliefs in the first place? Might cognitive sources of error, the way we process information and arrive at conclusions, be at work?

> We humans seem to be extremely good at generating ideas, theories, and explorations that have the ring of plausibility. We may be relatively different however, in evaluating and testing our ideas once they are formed. One of the biggest impediments to doing so is our failure to realize that when we do not precisely specify the kind of evidence that will count as support for our position we can end up "detecting" too much evidence for our preconceptions.[4]

Social scientists are very aware of the role that both motivational and cognitive bias play in producing false beliefs. To avoid motivational bias in judging the results of experiments or studies they employ whenever possible, "double blind" evaluation procedures. For example, experimenters as well as participants in human experiments are deliberately kept unaware of who received what thus helping experimenters to avoid favoring confirmations over disconfirmations. To avoid sources of cognitive error they employ statistical tools to avoid confusing random events, with "patterns"; they employ control groups and random sampling to prevent drawing misleading conclusions from insufficient or unrepresentative data. Most importantly, as Gilovich emphasizes above, experimental method is *prospective*. Hypotheses in *advance* with as much *specificity* as possible must state what evidence would count in favor of an idea and hence what evidence would count against it. In sum, science has a "two-sided" approach to belief formation, emphasizing as much and even more, specifying in advance what would count against a belief as for it (scientists became famous by overturning existing knowledge and theories, e.g., Copernicus, Darwin, Einstein).

Two-sided events in ordinary experience are those "that stand out and register as events regardless of how they turn out."[5] Sporting events, for example, on which we have bet are "two sided." We are focused on the moment which will decisively determine whether we won or lost. Defeats, because of this temporal focus will be remembered as well or better than wins.

But what explains, why, beyond motivational factors identified above, human beings focus more on confirmations than disconfirmations in maintaining beliefs. The reason, Gilovich argues is that most of our beliefs are not focused (two sided), but rather, unfocused and "one sided."

> One-sided events are those that stand out and are mentally represented as events only when they turn out one way. Consider, for example, the set of experiences that might produce and maintain the belief that "the phone always rings when I am in the shower." If the phone rings while showering it will stand out and register as an event by virtue of the conflict that arises in deciding whether to answer it. . . . In contrast, if the phone does not ring while showering, it is unlikely to register as an event. Nothing happened. Logically, such an occurrence is just as much an event as an occurrence, but phenomenally, it is not.[6]

Logically, when a belief is made *inferential* or *predictive* the *failure* of the inference or prediction to occur is a decisive event, it falsifies the belief. However, *psychologically*, if the event is "one sided," is temporally unfocused, disconfirmations are not decisive because *experientially* they never happened!

But what determines whether an event will be two sided or one sided?

"Perhaps the most common determinant if an event is one sided is the base rate frequency of different possible outcomes. When certain outcomes occur frequently enough, they become part of our experiential background and go unnoticed. Departures from normality, in contrast, can generate surprise and draw attention. The unexpected can sometimes be unusually memorable."[7]

A person we know with "incurable cancer" tries a unconventional "holistic" remedy and recovers. Using this unrepresentative example,* we generalize, "holistic cures work!" Gilovich notes, "Because we do not expect people to get better we hardly notice any time someone tries an unconventional treatment and it fails; (the base rate) when such treatments are successful, in contrast, the outcome violates our expectations, and stands out in our memory."[8]

The unexpected, the shocking, the unrepresentative, the extreme: it is these kinds of events that psychologically command attention and become prime candidates for one-sided belief formation. Their very departure from the "base rate" of everyday experience renders that experience *psychologically* noteworthy. On the other hand, the very data that would falsify an unfocused, one-sided belief based upon a extraordinary or notable experience ("holistic medicine cures"; the media *always* gets it wrong) becomes invisible (people who try holistic cures die at the same rate as people who don't; the media often does provide accurate information).

Therefore, once an unfocused belief formed on the basis of the unexpected becomes a prized, personal possession the aforementioned motivational factors involved in biased judgment come into play; we will protect, nuture, confirm, and selectively discount—and thereby reinforce the original one-sided, unfocused, belief. Every "confirmation" will reinforce the belief and every disconfirmation will go unnoticed or be confidently dismissed.

The psychological and logical issues involved in the distinctions between two-sided and one-sided beliefs, their formation, evaluation, maintenance, and extinction provides important insights into mass-media handling of the gun control issue.

Policy analysis, policy recommendations, evaluations of the significance of data, forecasts, etc. that are not to be contaminated with possible bias must be focused, "two-sided" discussions. Treating gun control as a two-sided event would mean that policy discussions, for example, would focus on *particular* problems and the effectiveness of proposed remedies relative to those specific problems (e.g., How are most criminal guns obtained?). Only then can specified

---

*Not only would this example be unrepresentative but itself an example of the post hoc fallacy—the erroneous assumption that simply because one event preceds another, it must have made the subsequent event happen.—Ed.

measurable predictions be made concerning the timing, impact, desirability (benefits versus costs to whom) and workability of proposed solutions. In short, only by treating gun control proposals as "two sided" can we specify *in advance* what evidence would count for, and more importantly would count against them. Hence, we could create measures of how well a policy is working or not working. Logical and psychological processes under these conditions would be mutually reinforcing.

However, if mass-media treatment of the gun control issue is one sided and hence contaminated with bias undetectable to those who manifest that bias *then* we should find in the previously treated media discussions of gun control and media selections the following:

1. A lack of precise definitions of the violence problems to be resolved. A lack of discussion of exactly how and with what costs and benefits specific gun control proposals would resolve problems. A lack of specific criteria which would establish and measure what data would count as evidence for and against such proposals. No discussion of exactly *when* we should expect the benefits of policies to occur.
2. A emphasis on "confirming" facts and events and disregard for discrepant data either by ignoring or discounting it or a refusal to consider its implications.
3. And finally an emphasis on extraordinary, hence random data which leads to "detecting" nonexistent patterns between random events, believing that effects must resemble their causes and the creation of theories to "explain" nonexistent connections which are creations of a one-sided approach itself.

This last predicted fact for the hypothesis that media treatment of "gun control" contains bias needs amplification.*

If it is true that we are cognitively and motivationally predisposed to seek order then we are vulnerable to imposing order on situations where there is none. Unfortunately, the misidentification of random occurrences with ordered sequences has pernicious consequences for truth seeking. If random events are psychologically noteworthy (e.g., gun massacres) then this "noteworthiness" will be accounted for by retrospective analysis that searches for some noteworthy something that is "the cause."

Psychologically "we expect effects to look like their causes, thus we are more likely to attribute a case of heartburn to spicy rather than bland food."[9] Psychologically we notice that in many attention-getting cases, that effects do resemble their causes. Big or very bright parents, do produce, an average, bigger or brighter children. It is easy, therefore, to form the one-sided belief that effects

---

*To the extent these predicted facts fail to occur then the hypothesis that media coverage of the gun control issue is biased would be unreliable or false.

inevitably resemble causes so that knowledge of the effect (violent children) tells us something about the cause (e.g., they must have had bad, violent, abusive parents). Every case that "confirms" this one-sided belief is noticed but we fail to look for, notice, or even may disregard every case in which horrible children have nice parents and vice versa (the base data).

Gilovich notes that at the root of this "fallacy of representativeness" (like goes with like) is the difficulty we have in understanding the concept of regression to the mean which explains why very bright or big parents do produce brighter or bigger children than average, but not usually as bright or big as the exceptional parents. Regression to the mean, means simply that "whenever two variables are imperfectly correlated, extreme variables of one are matched, on the average to extreme variables of the other."[10]

The belief, for example, that extremely high profits in one year "should" be followed by as strong results the next is based upon the assumption that like goes with like; that exceptional profits (the effect) therefore, imply exceptional management practices. The actual causes may have little to do with management strategies and more to do other unidentified factors. If so, next year's regression to the mean will be misinterpreted as necessarily "caused" by less effective management practices. Likewise, if falling violent crime rates are thought to *necessarily* resemble their causes, then existing crime *reducing* strategies will be credited with having "caused" the decline when in fact, it may be simply regression of extraordinarily high crime rates to historic means. Only if these causal claims are turned into hypotheses, rendered *predictive*, and then tested with controls on independent sets of data could we begin to access their effectiveness.[11]

This erroneous idea that effects must resemble causes* raises serious questions concerning the media's assumption discussed earlier (see also included media selections) that random violence must be "explained" in terms of violence resembling causes (violent technology, violent media, violent music, violent cults, violent parents, etc.) Is it possible that the causes of each violent event look nothing like violence (e.g., neuro-endocinological disorders might predispose some individuals to violent behavior and, therefore, *as a consequence* to focus on violent media, music, technologies, etc.). Hence, controlled longitudinal studies in which subjects are followed over extended periods of time to see who develops the condition, natural experiments, and even clinical trials of drugs would be necessary to test such a hypothesis. One-sided beliefs, however, assume that both the causes and the direction of causation are simply obvious.

In sum, the media assumption that violent events necessarily resemble their causes and creation of elaborate theories to explain and account for this erroneous assumption stems from the original error of confusing unconnected, coincidental events with ordered sequences. Such random events if they are psychologically noteworthy seem to demand explanation. Their "noteworthiness"

---

*The list of effects that don't resemble their causes (and vice versa) is endless, e.g., malignant tumors don't resemble viruses, offspring don't resemble sperm and eggs, cities don't resemble the agriculture which is the necessary condition for their existence, etc., etc.

causes us to one-sidedly see "clusters" which are then retrospectively accounted for by searching diligently for the noteworthy somethings that resemble the events and are identified as "the cause." When we look at the extraordinary and hence notable gun violence featured by the media in 1999 and 2000 are we required to believe connected events are occurring? Or, is the "connection" a result of the fact that the media has selected these events for special treatment because they are extraordinary, hence random, and disconnected? Has the media confused the very attention it accords these events with some causal pattern? In sum, is media coverage of these events unable to reconcile the statistical data concerning violent gun crime with their search for "the meaning" of these events simply because all their "search engines" keep uncovering is the "one-sidedness" of the coverage?

Remember the issue addressed here is the *process* by which mass media selects, presents, and interprets the significance of extraordinary hence psychologically noteworthy events. The issue here is the information and/or misinformation outcomes of this process, *not* the merits of specific proposals. The workability or effectiveness of any gun control policy proposal is independent of the defects or omissions of the rationale for that proposal. A conclusion supported by defective reasoning is not false, merely unsupported.

However, an approach that eschews allegiance to procedures and assumptions designated to safeguard against bias, whether from motivational sources (e.g., a desire to influence presidential campaign agendas) or cognitive sources (the treatment of news and policy issues as "one-sided" events) deserves careful scrutiny. Such scrutiny is especially warranted when giant, sometimes multinational, multimedia corporations monopolize the means of communication and have both the will and the means to influence both *what* and *how* issues are discussed. The political implications for democratic processes of these whats and hows are enormous.

The following selections from both the mass media and their academic critics aim to further develop both critical questions and criteria regarding mass-media treatment of gun violence issues. Some of these critics explicitly disagree on gun control issues and others do not address the issue directly. All however, raise key questions, propose explanations, and in some cases offer remedies to what they believe are errors in assumptions and methods that damage the reliability of information generated by the mass-media. The reader is thereby invited to apply these questions not only to the media selections included in Part Two, but to all mass-media treatment of gun control.

The media selections are taken from *Time*, *Newsweek*, and *Business Week* which appeared in August 1999.

The selection authored by criminologist Gary Kleck deals directly with the issue of media bias in the treatment of gun control topics. Kleck (a political and social liberal), attempts to document the specific ways by which media coverage of gun issues such as assault weapons, cop killer bullets, machine guns and the Goetz case, are contaminated by "one-sided" motivational and cognitive bias.

The selections from sociologist, Barry Glassner (also a political and social liberal), focus on the role that the mass media plays in abetting (and sometimes) debunking dubious scares. However, Glassner disagrees with Kleck on the direction of media bias. He believes bogus but widely influential media "scares" featuring "killer kids," "road rage," and so on, too often obscure the true danger that gun availability constitutes to the safety of Americans. His analysis not only of how "scares" are created but *why* certain "dangers" are selected over others has special relevance to the mass media, culture conflict view of the gun debate no matter what position is taken on specific gun issues.

The selection authored by social psychologist John Ruscio deals with why the mass media chooses certain events as newsworthy, the impact of this criteria on the way stories are delivered and the consequences of this process for the accuracy of information remembered by the consumer.

When reading or viewing media stories concerning issues that feature an anecdotal approach, here is an incomplete list of critical questions I believe are relevant:

1. Why were the anecdotes chosen as newsworthy? Were they selected for their dramatic impact?
2. If they are extraordinary, how often do things like this happen to people I know? How often *doesn't* it happen to people I know?
3. Are these anecdotes used to arrive at generalizations about the subject and serve as evidence for policy decisions? If so, do they engage primarily in one-sided retrospective analysis which uses primarily confirmative examples and ignores or discounts discrepant data or views?
4. Are the anecdotes delivered in an authoritative manner by the commentator? Is the commentator an expert in that subject or an expert in commentating?
5. If the commentator cites experts are they representative of expert opinion in that field?
6. Does the commentator eschew statistics and recognized experts and depend on vivid testimonials from people the audience can identify with?
7. If the commentator cites anecdotes that are fearsome, how is the degree of risk established? Does the vividness or bloodiness of the anecdotes alone serve as proof of risk?
8. If statistics concerning risk are introduced, are the sources identified? Are the statistics and the anecdotes mutually supportive or inconsistent?
9. If the activities' risk is deemed statistically large, how is the risk established? Is it "relative" (e.g., 3 times more [which is meaningless]) or actual (e.g., how many people have access to guns in a year, how many and what kind are killed or wounded? How many and what kind aren't?) As far as *my risk*—how many people do I know who have access to firearms are shot? How many aren't?
10. If the commentator claims that the anecdotes cited are evidence of

causally linked "patterns" or "trends" what evidence is cited? Is the evidence simply the fact that these events happened, that they resemble each other, therefore, the prior events must have influenced the subsequent event (violent effects must have violent causes—fallacy of representativeness, one event was prior to the other, hence it is the cause of the other—post hoc fallacy).

I invite the reader to further refine and develop the list of relevant questions. In doing so, the reader establishes a formidable criteria for evaluating the anecdotal media treatment of gun violence issues.

NOTES

1. Sue Anne Pressley, "A Scar on America's Psyche: Mass Shootings at School, Church, Work Have Left People Feeling: 'No Place Is Safe Anymore,' " *Buffalo News*, 9 January 2000.

2. Thomas Gilovich, *How We Know What Isn't So* (New York: Free Press, 1991).

3. Ibid.

4. Ibid, p. 58.

5. Ibid, p. 82.

6. Ibid, p. 63.

7. Ibid, p. 70.

8. Ibid, p. 7.

9. Ibid, p. 18.

10. Ibid, p. 24.

11. Ibid, pp. 24–26.

GET RID OF THE DAMNED THINGS

ROGER ROSENBLATT

As terrible as last week's shooting in Atlanta was, as terrible as all the gun killings of the past few months have been, one has the almost satisfying feeling that the country is going through the literal death throes of a barbaric era and that mercifully soon, one of these monstrous episodes will be the last. High time. My guess, in fact, is that the hour has come and gone—that the great majority of Americans are saying they favor gun control when they really mean gun banishment. Trigger locks, waiting periods, purchase limitations, which may seem important corrections at the moment, will soon be seen as mere tinkering with a machine that is as good as obsolete. Marshall McLuhan said that by the time one notices a cultural phenomenon, it has already happened. I think the country has long been ready to restrict the use of guns, except for hunting rifles and shotguns, and now I think we're prepared to get rid of the damned things entirely—the handguns, the semis, and the automatics.

Those who claim otherwise tend to cite America's enduring love affair with guns, but there never was one. The image of shoot-'em-up America was mainly the invention of gunmaker Samuel Colt, who managed to convince a malleable nineteenth-century public that no household was complete without a firearm— "an armed society is a peaceful society." This ludicrous aphorism, says historian Michael Bellesiles of Emory University, turned 200 years of Western tradition on its ear. Until 1850, fewer than 10 percent of U.S. citizens had guns. Only 15 percent of violent deaths between 1800 and 1845 were caused by guns. Reput-

From *Time*, 9 August 1999, pp. 38–39. Reprinted with permission.

edly wide-open Western towns, such as Dodge City and Tombstone, had strict gun control laws; guns were confiscated at the Dodge City limits.

If the myth of a gun-loving America is merely the product of gun salesmen, dime-store novels, movies, and the National Rifle Association (NRA)—which, incidentally, was not opposed to gun control until the 1960s, when gun buying sharply increased—it would seem that creating a gun-free society would be fairly easy. But the culture itself has retarded such progress by creating and embellishing an absurd though appealing connection among guns, personal power, freedom, and beauty. The old western novels established a cowboy corollary to the Declaration of Independence by depicting the cowboy as a moral loner who preserves the peace and his own honor by shooting faster and surer than the competition. The old gangster movies gave us opposite versions of the same character. Little Caesar is simply an illegal Lone Ranger, with the added element of success in the free market. In more recent movies, guns are displayed as art objects, people die in balletic slow motion, and right prevails if you own "the most powerful handgun in the world." I doubt that any of this nonsense causes violence, but after decades of repetition, it does invoke boredom. And while I can't prove it, I would bet that gun-violence entertainment will soon pass, too, because people have had too much of it and because it is patently false.

Before one celebrates the prospect of disarmament, it should be acknowledged that gun control is one of those issues that are simultaneously both simpler and more complicated than it appears. Advocates usually point to Britain, Australia, and Japan as their models, where guns are restricted and crime is reduced. They do not point to Switzerland, where there is a gun in every home and crime is practically nonexistent. Nor do they cite as sources criminology professor Gary Kleck of Florida State University, whose studies have shown that gun ownership reduces crime when gun owners defend themselves, or Professor John R. Lott Jr. of the University of Chicago Law School, whose research has indicated that gun regulation actually encourages crime.

The constitutional questions raised by gun control are serious as well. In a way, the antigun movement mirrors the humanitarian movement in international politics. Bosnia, Kosovo, and Rwanda have suggested that the West, the United States in particular, is heading toward a politics of human rights that supersedes the politics of established frontiers and, in some cases, laws. Substitute private property for frontiers and the Second Amendment for laws, and one begins to see that the politics of humanitarianism requires a trade-off involving the essential underpinnings of American life. To tell Americans what they can or cannot own and do in their homes is always a tricky business. As for the Second Amendment, it may pose an inconvenience for gun control advocates, but no more an inconvenience than the First Amendment offers those who blame violence on movies and television.

Gun control forces also ought not to make reform an implicit or explicit attack on people who like and own guns. Urban liberals ought to be especially alert to the cultural bigotry that categorizes such people as hicks, racists, psychotics, and so forth. For one thing, a false moral superiority is impractical and incites a backlash among people otherwise sympathetic to sensible gun control, much like the backlash the proabortion rights forces incurred once their years of political suasion had ebbed. And the demonizing of gun owners or even the NRA is simply wrong. The majority of gun owners are as dutiful, responsible, and sophisticated as most of their taunters.

That said, I am pleased to report that the likelihood of sweeping and lasting changes in the matter of America and guns has never been higher. There comes a time in every civilization when people have had enough of a bad thing, and the difference between this moment and previous spasms of reform is that it springs from the grass roots and is not driven by politicians or legal institutions. Gun control sentiment is everywhere in the country these days—in the White House, the presidential campaigns, the legislatures, the law courts and the gun industry itself. But it seems nowhere more conspicuous than in the villages, the houses of worship and the consensus of the kitchen.

Not surprisingly, the national legislature has done the least to represent the nation on this issue. After the passage of the 1994 crime bill and its ban on assault weapons, the Republican Congress of 1994 nearly overturned the assault weapons provision of the bill. Until Columbine the issue remained moribund, and after Columbine, moribund began to look good to the gun lobby. Thanks to an alliance of House Republicans and a prominent Democrat, Michigan's John Dingell, the most modest of gun control measures, which had barely limped wounded into the House from the Senate, was killed. "Guns have little or nothing to do with juvenile violence," said Tom Delay of Texas. Compared with his other assertions—that shootings are the product of day care, birth control and the teaching of evolution—that sounded almost persuasive.

A more representative representative of public feeling on this issue is New York's Carolyn McCarthy, whom gun violence brought into politics when her husband was killed and her son grievously wounded by a crazed shooter on a Long Island Rail Road train in 1993. McCarthy made an emotional, sensible and ultimately ineffectual speech in the House in an effort to get a stronger measure passed.

"When I gave that speech," she says, "I was talking more to the American people than to my colleagues. I could see that most of my colleagues had already made up their minds. I saw games being played. But this was not a game with me. I looked up in the balcony, and I saw people who had been with me all along on this issue. Victims and families of victims. We're the ones who know what it's like. We're the ones who know the pain."

Following upon Columbine, the most dramatic grass-roots effort has been the Bell Campaign. Modeled on Mothers Against Drunk Driving, the campaign plans to designate one day a year to toll bells all over the country for every victim of guns during the previous year. The aim of the Bell Campaign is to get guns off the streets and out of the hands of just about everyone except law officers and hunters. Andrew McGuire, executive director, whose cousin was killed by gunfire many years ago, wants gun owners to register and reregister every year. "I used to say that we'd get rid of most of the guns in 50 years," he tells me. "Now I say 25. And the reason for my optimism is that until now, we've had no grassroots opposition to the NRA."

One must remember, however, that the NRA, too, is a grassroots organization. A great deal of money and the face and voice of its president, Charlton Heston, may make it seem like something more grand and monumental, but its true effectiveness exists in small local communities where one or two thousand votes can swing an election. People who own guns and who ordinarily might never vote at all become convinced that their freedoms, their very being, will be jeopardized if they do not vote Smith in and Jones out. Once convinced, these folks in effect become the NRA in the shadows. They are the defense-oriented "little guys" of the American people, beset by Big Government, big laws, and rich liberals who want to take away the only power they have.

They are convinced, I believe, of something wholly untrue—that the possession of weapons gives them stature, makes them more American. This idea, too, was a Colt-manufactured myth, indeed, an ad slogan: "God may have made men, but Samuel Colt made them equal." The notion of guns as instruments of equality ought to seem self-evidently crazy, but for a long time Hollywood—and thus we all—lived by it. Cultural historian Richard Slotkin of Wesleyan University debunks it forever in a recent essay, "Equalizer: The Cult of the Colt." "If we as individuals have to depend on our guns as equalizers," says Slotkin, "then what we will have is not a government of laws but a government of men—armed men."

Lasting social change usually occurs when people decide to do something they know they ought to have done long ago but have kept the knowledge private. This, I believe, is what happened with civil rights, and it is happening with guns. I doubt that it will be twenty-five years before we're rid of the things. In ten years, even five, we could be looking back on the past three decades of gun violence in America the way one once looked back upon eighteenth-century madhouses. I think we are already doing so but not saying so. Before Atlanta, before Columbine, at some quiet, unspecified moment in the past few years, America decided it was time to advance the civilization and do right by the ones who know what the killing and wounding are like, and who know the pain.

6

GUNS IN AMERICA
WHAT MUST BE DONE

NEWSWEEK

After it was over, after the SWAT teams had swept in and the suspect had fled, after the screams and the tears, a little boy too young to know his letters wanted to thank the men who rescued him from the shooter. Handing a green crayon and a piece of blue construction paper, four-and-a-half-year-old Nathan Powers started dictating. "Thank you policemen," Nathan said, "for saving us from the gun because you're our friend."

For saving us from the gun. Nathan had been in day care at the North Valley Jewish Community Center in Granada Hills, an outlying Los Angeles community, last Tuesday morning, when Buford O. Furrow Jr.—loner, hater, white supremacist—came through the front door. Armed, authorities say, with an Uzi (he had four other assault weapons back in his van), Furrow opened fire, spraying the day-care center's lobby with seventy rounds. Five were wounded; as the gunman escaped, he used a Glock 9mm pistol to kill a letter carrier, thirty-nine-year-old Joseph Ileto. Once again, the nation asked why—why an armed man had brought sudden death to a place that ought to be safe.

At the end of the century ancient forces (hate, heartbreak, reversals of fortune, inexplicable demons) and newer ones (busy and broken families, Hollywood, the Internet, videogames, and music) can, alone or in concert, produce explosions of violence. Few terrible acts like Furrow's can be traced to a single cause, and as the body count mounts and the country tunes in to a depressing series of shootings-of-the-week, there is plenty of blame to go around. In the *Newsweek* Poll, majorities blame poor parenting (57 percent) and violence in the media (52 percent). Seventy-two percent believe intense media coverage makes people feel more endangered than they really are. But from Littleton, Colorado, to Atlanta to Granada Hills, there has been one common link in the chain of violence: firearms, which are growing ever more lethal.

Madmen will always do mad things; we can never legislate evil out of existence; people kill people with broomsticks and bombs and their bare hands. Yet the facts are inescapable: there are more than 200 million guns in circulation in the United States, and more than a third of American households have one. Though our gun-related death rate has been mercifillly falling overall, we still lose an average of eighty-seven people a day to firearms. We lead the industrialized world in the rate at which children die from guns. Three years from now, gunfire may surpass cars to become the leading cause of nonnatural death in the United States.

The debate over firearms has been polarized for too long. Millions of law-abiding people own and enjoy guns. But criminals and the disturbed and even confused kids often use firearms, too, to tragic and devastating effect. Reflexive liberals tend to want to ban all guns, and portray their owners as rednecks who don't seem to care that gangbangers and hatemongers can get their hands on firepower. At the other extreme, entrenched gun lobbyists appear to believe that virtually any regulation is a threat to their constitutional rights. They fear, they say, an eventual "knock at the door" that will bring a government confiscation of their weapons.

America, or at least the sensible center where most of us stand, has had enough of this senseless violence, and of this circular debate. For more than a generation, we've watched as the great and the pedestrian have died in the line of fire. Though it won't do to act as though, in the emotional aftermath of yet another shooting, a sweeping ban or a single bill will keep more tragedies from happening, it also won't do to shrug off the deadly role guns play.

So what must be done? It is time, as Franklin Roosevelt said long ago, to try something. The antigun movement must accept that the United States realistically will not, and should not have to, abolish handguns or any reasonable sporting weapon. At the same time, the progun forces ought to acknowledge that the Second Amendment is not unconditional and be open to reasonable restrictions. If the warring camps can make that tentative peace, there may be a path out of this bewildering debate.

We must slow the flow of guns into a market that too often seems to serve criminals, who shouldn't get guns, rather than hunters and hobbyists, who should. Those who cherish their firearms might consider judging every possible regulation by the following standard: is a loss of convenience, of privacy, or of a category of gun worth the price if the reform has a chance of keeping a firearm away from somebody—a criminal, or maybe a kid—who shouldn't have it?

It will be a difficult argument to win; guns are in our blood. For millions of us the whiff of cordite is intermingled with the smells of home and family: of hunting dove, ducks, or deer. For others a pistol seems to offer security in a dangerous world. The roots of the culture run deep, back to the Bill of Rights. The Founders believed that the right to bear arms and to form grass-roots militias was a safeguard against another tyrannical government. Hence the Second Amendment. . . . It was the beginning of an undeniably romantic mythology. Militiamen and minutemen threw off the British yoke; the pioneers settled the frontier with long rifles, and the West was home to towering, gun-toting cowboys.

The truth, however, is more complicated. Emory University historian Michael Bellesiles has shown that from the Revolution to about 1850, no more than a tenth of the population owned guns. So how did guns seep into the culture? Samuel Colt and the Civil War. Colt was an impresario, targeting his company's firearms at middle-class anxieties about self-defense by giving his guns names like "Equalizer." Then came the real boom: Fort Sumter. Between 1861 and 1865, guns went into mass production, and both Union and Confederate soldiers kept their weapons after Appomattox. Suddenly there was widespread ownership, and an industry to feed a growing market. If we separate legend from history, guns can be seen not just as inviolate relics of the Revolution but as what they are: products.

And products are something we often need to regulate, be they cars, lawn mowers, or pharmaceuticals. It's time to apply consumer-product safety standards to firearms (Saturday night specials, for example, ought to have to meet minimum safety requirements). We should always be wary of relying on government, but it's reasonable to weigh the Second Amendment against the common good and risk more bureaucracy; even property owners have to submit to zoning. "No federal appellate court or the Supreme Court has ever ruled you can't put some limits on the Second Amendment," says Tom Diaz, a senior policy analyst at the Violence Policy Center. Here are proposals that ought to be part of the debate. They are not exhaustive. But each has a reasonable chance of slowing the flow of guns from the law-abiding to the potentially dangerous.

Require background checks on all sales and transfers. The Brady Bill requires an instant background check when someone purchases a firearm from a licensed dealer. The law has kept hundreds of thousands of felons and other prohibited purchasers (fugitives, those who were committed to a mental institution by a court, the military's dishonorably discharged, those with a record of domestic abuse) from buying guns at a legitimate source. More can be done: the country needs to build a reliable database that won't let felons slip through the system. It's especially important to pay attention to the "secondary market," that largely unregulated universe of private sales and gun shows, where, in many cases guns change hands without a record. By some estimates 40 percent of American firearms in transfers take place in the secondary market, and in virtually every state anyone can sell firearms at gun shows or flea markets without conducting a background check on the buyer. (The Glock Furrow used to kill the postal worker, for example, came from this netherworld.) All sales and transfers of guns should require a check. Will that keep one guy from swapping or selling with someone else off the books? No. But this would make it harder for the nefarious to obtain guns openly.

Enforce what's on the books. Credit the National Rifle Association for pushing this common-sense solution. Born in Richmond, Virginia, Project Exile encourages police and prosecutors to strictly enforce federal gun laws. Among other things, it's illegal to carry a gun when you're in possession of drugs. But for years, authorities didn't make such gun cases a priority. In Richmond, prosecutors started using these statutes, cracking down on people who are likely to use guns in a crime. It's worked: Richmond has seized 512 guns and sent 215 violators to jail. Meanwhile, the homicide and robbery rates have fallen about 30 percent each.

Ban assault weapons—for real. We've been here before, and the lessons from that battle shed light on the tricky terrain ahead. The Uzi Furrow probably used in Granada Hills can no longer be legally imported to the United States, but was obviously available. Gun control wouldn't have stopped him. Still, assault weapons have few sporting purposes. With their folding stocks and pistol grips, they resemble their military ancestors, which were designed to lay down a lot of ammunition very quickly over a small field of fire. In 1994, when the federal ban on assault weapons passed, many manufacturers slightly modified their models to get around the law and went back to market. Gun enthusiasts argue that this is cosmetic debate, that we want to ban guns that look sinister when all semiautomatics are deadly in the wrong hands. One answer is to follow California and ban the sale, manufacture, and import of semiautomatics with the capacity to hold more than ten rounds, and prohibit features—like high-capacity magazines, flash suppressors, bayonet lug nuts—that attract the criminal and the irresponsible.

License owners and register all guns. To ears unaccustomed to the nuances of the gun debate, this could sound innocuous, or at worst bureaucratic. But proposals to establish a gun registry, either state by state or nationally, raise gun owners' most fundamental fears. Still, licensing could operate along the same lines as the DMV: to drive a car, you need to pass a minimal test. There are potential perils; authorities might be distant, or abusive, or inattentive. But licensing could improve gun safety, particularly for beginners.

Registration pushes the most buttons. The gun lobby says the government shouldn't know who owns a firearm, and on Second Amendment grounds it has a point. Bill Clinton isn't likely to confiscate guns, but some president in the distant future might. Still, all rights have to be balanced with the need for public order, and registration is one surefire way of shutting off a line of supply to criminals. Why? If all sales of firearms have to be logged in a registry, then the typical gun owner who gets his firearm legitimately knows the government has a record of his acquisition. He may then be much more careful about what happens to that gun for fear that crimes committed with it would bring the police to his door. Would it stop underground gun traffic altogether? No, and the NRA says the measure would create "massive civil disobedience." But registration could help keep guns from slipping through a careless private sale or swap, into a criminal's grasp.

On the morning after the shootings in Granada Hills, parents of children at the day camp arrived early, determined not to flinch in the face of hate, or of guns. "We're not going to let anyone scare us," one father said. Bringing sanity to the gun wars, and safety to our schools and public places, will take the same flinty courage. The road will be rough and long, the battles pitched and confusing, the compromises difficult and costly. But let us begin.

7

THE NEW AGE OF ANXIETY

BARBARA KANTROWITZ

It is indeed an anxious season—nowhere more than in Littleton, Colorado, where students return this week to Columbine High School. Some, like junior Lance Kirklin, whose face was shattered by a bullet in the massacre last spring, bear physical scars of the tragedy. Others carry wounds in their hearts. Parents in Littleton say they are determined to protect their children. "We're trying very hard to make it as normal as possible," insists the mother of junior Diana Cohen. But will things ever be "normal" again, in Littleton or anywhere else?

Columbine—and Paducah and Granada Hills—sounded the alarm for parents around the country. Whether they live in the inner city or the most serene suburb, they now know that their kids are not immune from the threat of guns. "The places you used to think were safe have been violated by these random acts of violence," says Kathy Thomas, a mother of three from Thousand Oaks, California, "I certainly don't want my kids to live in fear." Parents worry about how schools will protect their children and aren't sure how to begin the uncomfortable but essential dialogue with their kids about the risks of guns. In that task they face "a terrible dilemma," says Neil Guterman, a professor of social work at Columbia University and an expert on children and violence. "They have to convey a sense of safety and security to their children and, at the same time, not hide the truth."

Although 81 percent of those surveyed in the *Newsweek* poll think there has been an increase in gun-related incidents at schools lately, violence in the classroom has actually declined dramatically in this decade. Schools are among the safest places children can be. The National School Safety Center reports that last year there were just twenty-five violent deaths (including fifteen at Columbine), compared with an average of fifty in the early 1990s. Only a tiny fraction of all homicides involving school-age children occur in or around schools, according to the federal Centers for Disease Control and Prevention.

But it's also true that guns are a serious threat to kids. "People are too worried about school," says Kevin Dwyer, president of the National Association of School Psychologists. "I think they need to be more worried about the avalanche of guns in the community." According to government statistics, 4,223 children were killed by firearms in 1997, many of them in accidents while playing at friends' homes in their own neighborhoods. Thousands more were injured by guns. Some experts predict that firearm-related injuries could soon replace car crashes as the leading cause of death for young children.

More and more people seem to be getting that message. In the *Newsweek* poll, 64 percent of parents of kids under eighteen were somewhat or very concerned that their children might get hurt or into trouble while visiting the homes of friends who own guns. "I lived in New York City for fourteen years and felt safer there because nobody had a gun in the house, but here people have rifles" says Debra Leonard, a physician who lives in rural Bethel Township, Pennsylvania. "I tell my kids nobody can protect themselves from a gun if it's not locked up in a cabinet, so they should leave the [friend's] house and call me to pick them up if anyone ever handles a gun."

Unlike some parents, Leonard did allow her two sons to play with toy guns. "Our children have water guns and cowboy guns," she says. "If you don't give them guns, they build them. My younger boy was a Lego maniac, and he built guns out of Legos." In fact, there's no evidence that playing with toy guns turns kids into killers. Many studies confirm Leonard's experience, that children—particularly boys—will turn anything available (a carrot, even a piece of spaghetti) into a weapon. "Toy guns are a minor issue," says Kathleen Heide, a criminologist at the University of South Florida. "The real concern should be helping kids deal with negative feelings and resolving conflicts." But the problem is that younger children often think real guns are toys. Parents should make sure their kids understand the distinction between play guns and weapons that kill.

Staying alert is the best defense. Karen Kaul, the mother of a third grader in suburban Wilmette, Ill., took quick action recently when she overheard the younger brother of one of her daughter's playmates say he was going to get a gun from his house. Although it turned out to be a BB gun, "I called the parents, and they talked to the kids about it Kaul says.

Experts advise tailoring information about guns and violence to the age of the child. Youngsters under six may have heard news about shootings on TV and worry that they are directly in the line of fire. "Adults should be saying very emphatically that they are doing everything they can to keep kids safe," advises

Betsy McAlister Groves, director of the Child Witness to Violence Program at Boston Medical Center. And, she says, limit their exposure to violent images on television and in the movies. Slightly older kids, from about six to ten, "may sound more sophisticated than they actually are," McAlister Groves says. "Talk to them, reassure them." Young adolescents, from about eleven up, are more able to understand real risks and statistics.

At all ages, McAlister Groves says, "allowing kids to voice their worries is very important." The worst thing a parent can do is fail to provide an opportunity for children to talk. "We tend to think that if they don't talk about it, it will get better, but that's not the right message," she says. "They might think it's something that frightens us" and that would only increase their own fears.

The wave of gun violence has irrevocably altered the national self-image and should be a wake-up call to parents. "People had their confidence shaken and their complacency dispelled this past year," says Cornell University's James Garbarino, who has studied children and violence for years. "There is a growing recognition that the epidemic of youth violence has now reached a point where virtually every school contains boys who are troubled, angry, and violent enough, who have access to weapons and violent scenarios and images, to become the next tragedy. I think people are now understanding that in their hearts-and minds."

No one is safe anymore. That's the lesson Lance Kirklin learned last April at Columbine High School. One bullet dug a crater in his cheek, and he faces four more operations. Still, he says he's not worried that such a cataclysmic tragedy will strike Littleton twice. Should people in the rest of the country be scared? "Yes," he says. "It will definitely happen again." Parents everywhere can only hope that he's wrong.

8

SAY YES TO SERIOUS GUN CONTROL

BUSINESS WEEK EDITORIAL

W hen it comes to gun ownership in America, personal liberty has long been defined in terms equal to anarchy—no rules, no regulation, no nothing. Extremists on the fringe of society have all too effectively manipulated symbols of American culture to propagate a myth of the individual standing alone against bandits, "foreign" enemies, and the government itself. A culture of violence has replaced common sense, and the moderate voices of responsible hunters and sport shooters have been silenced. Congress, cowed by the lobbying power of the National Rifle Association, cannot even bring itself to put real guns under the same consumer safety regulation applied to toy guns. Something must be done.

It appears that the American people are finally about to act. Polls show that an overwhelming majority want much tougher restrictions on handguns. In the wake of the bloody shootings by an unhinged day trader in Atlanta and by schoolchildren in Colorado and Arkansas, most Americans say they are more likely to vote for a presidential candidate in 2000 favoring stricter gun control.

The obvious answer is to limit ownership and require registration of all guns and licensing of all gun owners. In Switzerland and Israel, where most citizens serve in the military and remain in the reserves, nearly all households have weapons. But each rifle and pistol is registered with the government, and each user undergoes months of training. In the United States, licensing is already a way of life for hunters who must buy permits from local authorities to shoot a limited number of deer and ducks each season. A few states and localities already require registration of guns. Extending this kind of local regulation throughout the nation and ensuring that people know how to maintain their weapons responsibly is the best way to cut gun violence. Democratic presidential contender Bill Bradley has come out in favor of full registration. He's right.

It is also vital to crack down on the handful of gun dealers who time and again provide weapons to criminals. Statistics from the Bureau of Alcohol, Tobacco and Firearms show that most weapons used in crimes come from the same group of dealers. The ATF should shut them down. At the same time, buyers at gun shows and flea markets should be subjected to the same criminal background checks as those purchasing directly from dealers. The ludicrous loophole in the 1993 Brady bill that allows any private gun owner to sell his weapon to anyone anywhere has to be closed.

The gun industry itself is beginning to split under the political pressure. There are companies in the Southwest that produce cheap Saturday night specials and powerful automatic weapons that skirt the law. These "Ring of Fire" companies play to the apocalyptic fears of survivalists and anarchists who want to get "off the grid" of normal life and oppose any form of government. Then there are the more established Connecticut Valley companies that make more expensive, quality handguns and hunting rifles. They and their customers are increasingly open to the kind of sensible gun regulation that the police support in every town and city in the United States.

Sometimes the obvious must be stated. There is no rational reason for any individual to own assault weapons. There is no reason most people, especially those with children, should own handguns. There is no reason extremists should determine government gun policies that threaten the lives of innocent people. It's time for serious gun control.

9

MEDIA BIAS

GUN CONTROL, ASSAULT WEAPONS, COP-KILLER BULLETS, THE GOETZ CASE, AND OTHER ALARMS IN THE NIGHT

GARY KLECK

Most Americans receive the bulk of their information about crime and violence through the mass media rather than from direct personal experience. Does this information, as it pertains to guns and violence, neutrally reflect reality, or has it been shaped or managed to encourage some conclusions and discourage others? The premise [here] is that the nation's most important news sources do indeed shape information on gun issues in a way that encourages procontrol conclusions. [My] purpose is to identify and illustrate the forms that this information shaping can take.

This assertion should not be viewed as being part of a broad accusation of liberal bias in the press or mass media generally. Survey evidence does indicate that reporters and editors are somewhat more liberal than the general public (*Los Angeles Times* 8-11-85), but newspapers, magazines, and television and radio stations and networks are owned by wealthy businessmen, and most wealthy businessmen are not liberals. It seems unlikely that these wealthy owners would consistently permit their property to be used to promote a liberal ideology they personally oppose.

Instead of procontrol bias being but one part of a general liberal bias on the part of news workers, bias on the gun issue is a thing apart, whose persistence may be possible partly because it does not conflict with any strongly held elements of the ideology of the owners of media corporations. Consequently, the

Original paper presented at the annual meetings of the American Society of Criminology, San Francisco, November 20–23, 1991.

gun issue may provide a fairly rare situation where purportedly "liberal" ideas can be repeatedly favored by reporters without provoking intervention from management.

It should also be stressed that it is not being argued that there is a consciously calculated or coordinated campaign to lie about or distort the gun issue. Rather, a variety of information management techniques may be used to produce impressions that news managers honestly believe to be accurate. It is thus not the sincerity of news workers that is in question. The content of news stories is what is at issue in this [essay], not the intentions of the stories' authors. Most news people probably sincerely believe that guns are a major cause of the nation's high rates of violence and that there would be less violence if there were more gun control and fewer guns. Therefore, to be procontrol or antigun is merely to be in accord with the facts, "biased" only in favor of the truth. From this viewpoint, news sources are merely accurately informing the public of a genuinely one-sided issue rather than slanting the news to create a one-sided picture of what is actually a multisided issue.

There are occasional outrageous and obvious "smoking gun" examples of antigun/procontrol bias, but these are exceptions to the general rule of more subtle information manipulation. For example, there was the presumably unusual case of a newspaper firing a staff writer for publicly expressing support for positions taken by the National Rifle Association (*Brown Deer [Wisconsin] Herald* 3-23-89). Sophisticated information management does not rely primarily on lies or crude censorship but rather on less obviously illegitimate or sloppy techniques.

First and foremost, news stories can shape the audience's views through the omission of accurate, relevant information that would tend to undercut the theme of the story. Biased exclusion of information is both more important and more effective in shaping public opinion than inclusion of inaccurate information. Lies do not further the interests of propagandists in a democracy in the long run, because they are vulnerable to exposure and threaten the future credibility (and possibly the profits) of the news outlet. Information that contradicts a news story's thesis can be excluded from a story either by a reporter or by an editor or producer. All news stories necessarily must exclude information in the interests of brevity, but exclusions are biased when they are patterned to consistently weed out information contradicting a theme or message favored by the producers of the news. The practice is especially pernicious because, unlike inaccurate or biased statements that are included in a story, excluded facts are generally invisible to the ordinary reader or viewer. Further, there rarely can be any "smoking gun" proving propagandistic intent because, ordinarily, no one could prove that a reporter was aware of the information in the first place.

Second, in deciding which bits of information to include, and, if included in the story, whether to treat information as factual, different levels of skepticism, and different standards for assessing importance, can be applied to information supporting the preferred view and to information contradicting it. Information contrary to the preferred view can be subjected to intense and searching scrutiny, or downplayed as unimportant or self-serving, while information supporting the preferred view is spared any comparable scrutiny and is presented to the audience without comment, or even with comments suggesting the information is credible and of great importance.

Third, differing amounts of "play" can be given to stories with pro- or anti-control implications. Stories with implications supporting the preferred view can be given coverage that is prominent (front page vs. inside page), extended (15 column inches vs. 6), and prolonged (coverage on multiple days rather than just one), whereas stories with contrary implications can be given little play or ignored altogether.

Fourth, procontrol editorial positions prevail among the nation's major daily press outlets, and such positions can lend credibility and legitimacy to a procontrol stance as the preferred position of responsible and educated persons (see Cohen and Young 1981; Bagdikian 1987; Herman and Chomsky 1988 for general discussions of media influence on public opinion).

SINS OF OMISSION–EXCLUSION BIAS

Examples of biased exclusion of information are not hard to find in news stories on guns. It should be stressed that in each of the following examples, the omitted information was critical to judging the main theme of the story and could have been included in the story in a single sentence. Therefore, it cannot be argued that the omissions were due to either the information being irrelevant or unimportant or to space limitations making it impossible to include the information.

The major gun-related story of 1989–1991 was the alleged proliferation and criminal use of so-called assault rifles (ARs) or, more broadly, assault weapons (AWs), a vague category that encompassed handguns and shotguns as well as rifles. AWs are semiautomatic firearms with a "military-style" appearance. AWs were presented in the press as especially threatening to public safety mainly because they allegedly (1) were more lethal than their ordinary counterparts (especially ARs compared with civilian rifles), (2) had rapid rates of fire, and (3) had large ammunition capacities. The first claim was false, the second either false or barely true to a trivial degree, whereas the third was sometimes true but of limited significance for most incidents of violence, which rarely involve large numbers of rounds fired (Kleck 1991, pp. 70–82). News stories that addressed the rate-of-fire issue commonly hinted or stated that AWs either fired as rapidly as machine guns or that they might as well do so as they could easily be converted to fire like machine guns (e.g., *Newsweek* 10-14-85, pp. 48–49). The convertability claim was inaccurate and was apparently repeated by news sources simply because they did not, as the *New York Times* eventually did (4-3-89), check with the relevant authorities to see if it was true (but see also the contradictory editorial in the *New York Times*, 8-2-88). The implication that AWs could fire like machine guns was hinted at through descriptions of shootings in which the gunman allegedly "sprayed" an area with bullets from his AW. Without making the claim explicit, this wording strongly hinted that ARs were capable of fully automatic fire, that is, sending out a virtually continuous stream of bullets as long as the trigger was held down and ammunition remained. In fact, AWs can fire only in semiautomatic mode, that is, one shot is fired for each trigger pull, the same as is done with ordinary revolvers (Kleck 1991). Television network news programs also hinted at the same idea by overlaying reporters speaking about semiautomatic AWs with film of fully automatic weapons being shown on the screen.

Failing to make this distinction explicit could leave the average reader or viewer with the erroneous impression that AWs were machine guns, and that therefore machine guns were being legally sold without significant restrictions. In 1989, most news stories about AWs omitted this critical piece of information. A content analysis of a random national sample of 115 newspaper stories on guns and gun control indicated that nearly 80 percent of the 65 stories on ARs failed to distinguish fully automatic fire from semiautomatic fire, or to in any way indicate that ARs could not fire like machine guns (Etten 1991).

In 1985 and 1986, one of the major gun-related stories concerned armor-piercing ammunition. Numerous examples of biased exclusion of relevant information can be found in stories on these "cop-killer" bullets, projectiles capable of penetrating the body armor worn by police officers. Two facts were consistently omitted from stories on this issue: (1) supporters of restrictions had never documented a single case in which this ammunition actually killed a police officer by penetrating his body armor, and (2) many common types of rifle ammunition had always been capable of penetrating police body armor and had been commonly available for years. Leaving aside whether restrictions on this ammunition were advisable, these facts were obviously relevant to informed public debate about the issue, yet somehow they did not make it into print in the nation's leading newspapers (e.g., *New York Times* 7-20-85, p. 22; 9-27-85, p. A30; 3-7-86, p. A15; *Chicago Tribune* 3-7-86, pp. 1–3; *Los Angeles Times* 12-19-85, pp. 11–16; 3-7-86, pp. 1–15; 8-15-86, pp. 1–2; 8-29-86, pp. 1–4). There was at least one exception-the *Los Angeles Times* did mention, in one article, that no police officer had ever been killed by the bullets. The diligent reader could find it on page 20, in the middle of the twelfth paragraph of a fourteen-paragraph story (*Los Angeles Times* 8-29-86). Marginalizing the information in this way is only slightly better than omitting it altogether. Can it seriously be argued that it is not relevant and important that the "cop-killer" bullet had never killed a cop?

At the very least, the repeated use of an inflammatory and inaccurate term like "cop-killer bullet" was dubious journalistic practice. News sources uncritically accepted a label invented by procontrol activists for propaganda purposes. One presumed justification would be that this term had become the commonly used label for the ammunition in question. This is something of a circular justification as it became the commonly used term at least partly because news workers had chosen to accept and disseminate it. Although the ammunition certainly is capable of killing a police officer (or civilian for that matter), the term nevertheless is not very descriptive because the same is also true of any other firearms ammunition. The desire for a pithy, hard-hitting label apparently won out over a commitment to accuracy.

One of the difficulties in documenting specific instances of "sins of omission" is that it is usually impossible to be sure that the reporter knew about the information; therefore, one cannot be certain that the information had been deliberately excluded. Usually, one can only be sure that the reporter either did not make an effort to acquire the information or someone excluded it. There are, however, occasional exceptions.

I have given hundreds of interviews about gun issues, sometimes talking for as long as two hours at a time with reporters. Occasionally I have read the stories that print reporters prepared on the basis of interviews with me and others. It was often apparent that reporters had been assigned a story with a preset theme and charged with gathering relevant information. The nature of the theme sometimes became apparent during the course of an interview, and when it was inconsistent with what I knew, I would convey the contrary information to the reporter. Again and again I have had the experience of providing information that flatly contradicted a procontrol theme of the story as finally published, yet the contradictory information was neither rebutted nor mentioned in the story. Space (or time) limitations can account for omission of information that is marginal or irrelevant to a story, or whose accuracy has been put in doubt, but it cannot account for exclusion of unrebutted information that directly contradicts the principal claims or themes of the story.

The following examples are illustrative. On June 14, 1989, I was interviewed by a reporter from *USA Today*. The story concerned child gun accidents and had been stimulated by five gun accidents involving children in Florida, all occurring within a week of each other. I told the reporter that unconnected accidents, and rare events in general, occasionally cluster together in time, that this is bound to happen somewhere, sometime, and that such short-term clusterings were not a sound basis for concluding that there was a significant trend developing. I then told her what the actual national trends had been in recent years—the number of fatal gun accidents involving children (under age 10) had dropped sharply, from 227 in 1974 to about 92 in 1987, the latest year for which data were available. (The same was true of accidents in all age groups.) When the story appeared the next day (*USA Today* 6-15-89, p. 3A), it was a fairly long article (or as long as they get in *USA Today*—50 square inches including photo and charts), but evidently not long enough to have room for either these facts or any others I provided the reporter. The theme of the article was the supposedly large number of recent child gun accidents, the article's headline being "Spate of shootings spurs Florida to act." The article had room for a statistic provided by a procontrol advocacy group, to the effect that gunshot wounds to children had increased by 300 percent (!) since 1986, in certain unspecified "large urban areas." It did not, however, have room for the only relevant national data available to the reporters and editors that bore directly on the frequency of child gun accidents, data that indicated that fatal gun accidents were sharply declining and had been doing so for many years.

One might be tempted to dismiss this sort of selectivity on this issue as characteristic only of a news outlet with a less-than-lofty journalistic reputation. However, CBS News, the organization that Edward R. Murrow built, broadcast a story with the exact same misleading theme, presented even more bluntly. On the CBS evening news for October 11, 1989, anchorman Dan Rather read a story on child gun accidents, describing the problem as "an epidemic that shows every sign of worsening." In fact, the only data reliable for judging national trends in such accidents, mortality statistics, had long indicated precisely the opposite. However, in this case it is impossible to know whether CBS knew about, or made any effort to discover, these figures.

In December of 1989 I gave an interview lasting about an hour to a reporter from the National Public Radio (NPR) affiliate in St. Paul, Minnesota. The interview was done as part of national effort by NPR affiliates to explore the gun issue, and the resulting reports were distributed to NPR member stations. The bulk of my remarks concerned the considerable evidence indicating the utility of guns for self-defense, as well as evidence indicating that most existing gun laws appear to be ineffective in reducing violence. I also very briefly (for a minute or two) noted the risks of keeping guns for defense in homes with children, and remarked that most crime victimizations occurred in circumstances that do not permit effective defensive use of a gun. When WETA-FM, the NPR affiliate in Washington, D.C., broadcast an excerpt of about thirty seconds from my interview, it was entirely taken from my brief remarks noting the limits and risks of keeping guns for self-defense. None of my extensive (and unrebutted) remarks noting the defensive effectiveness of guns were included. Further, the brief excerpts were placed in a section of the broadcast devoted to arguing a proposition—that keeping a gun for defensive purposes was irrational—which was clearly contradicted by both the bulk of my remarks and by the overwhelming weight of scholarly evidence (broadcast 12-17-89, as part of the "All Things Considered" program; compare with Kleck 1991, chapter 4).

In June of 1989 I gave a series of interviews lasting over two hours to a reporter from *Time* magazine, in which I noted, among other things, that gun violence had been decreasing since the early 1980s. The magazine's story briefly noted, in the text, the decrease in gun deaths in the 1980s (p. 31), but this was undercut by their twice referring in large type to the "epidemic" of gun violence (pp. 3, 30). If "epidemic" does not mean an increasing or spreading problem, exactly what does it mean?

One section of this article pertained to suicides. Without mentioning any evidence rebutting that which I had discussed with the reporter, the article asserted that "most people who attempt to kill themselves do not really wish to die." I had told the reporter that although this claim was true of suicide attempters in general, there was good reason to believe it was not true of those who use guns. The article noted that only 1 in 20 suicide attempts results in death, whereas, according to one study, 92 percent of gun attempts are fatal. I had told the reporter that the fatality rate in suicide attempts with guns was indeed very high but that the rate was nearly as high in attempts using such likely substitutes for shooting as hanging, carbon monoxide poisoning, and drowning.

The article described a gun suicide in which the absence of a gun allegedly could have made a difference as to whether the attempter eventually survived. I had told the reporter that one reason few suicides could be prevented by removing guns was that the people who use guns in suicide typically have a more serious and persistent desire to kill themselves than suicide attempters using other methods. If denied guns, some or all of this group would substitute other methods and kill themselves anyway. The case the article cited seemed to provide the perfect illustration of my point, since the woman had suffered from "recurring depression" and had made at least three suicide attempts. Yet the article implied that the woman died only because she had found a "swift and certain" method of suicide and that her depression could have been cured before the next attempt had she not obtained a gun (*Time* 7-17-89, pp. 30–61).

In this thirty-one-page article, as finally published, no experts on gun violence were quoted or explicitly cited, with the exception of a single remark by James Wright (p. 61). I have no idea how many other experts were consulted and provided Time reporters with information contrary to their preferred views, and I can only be sure that they excluded the information I provided. Professor Wright, however, was interviewed and was quoted in a context that inverted his remarks' original meaning. Wright was quoted as saying that "everyone knows that if you put a loaded .38 in your ear and pull the trigger, you won't survive." His intended meaning was that ambiguously motivated people intending only to make a "cry for help" do not make such attempts with guns. Only people who truly want to die use guns to attempt suicide, and these highly motivated persons would just use other means to kill themselves if guns were not available. Professor Wright has confirmed to me in a letter that this was indeed his meaning (Wright 1991a; see also Wright 1991b, p. 446 for his published views on this point). However, the remark was quoted in a context that suggested precisely the opposite, that gun victims would have survived had guns not been available, because guns are a uniquely lethal method of suicide.

This story illustrates another noteworthy pattern. Recent news stories that give very extended coverage of gun issues (e.g., feature-length newspaper or magazine stories or hour-long broadcast stories) usually make virtually no use of expert commentary. This raises the possibility that reporters did seek out expert information but could not find any acknowledged experts who would confirm the preset themes of the story. By defining the experts' unsupportive remarks as irrelevant or unimportant, reporters would be able to exclude them from the final story on grounds the reporters considered to be legitimate. This must necessarily remain a speculation, however, because news stories never report which experts were consulted but ignored.

A SPECULATION ABOUT HOW
EXCLUSION BIAS WORKS

Reporters and editors do not decide to exclude certain pieces of information from stories because they know them to be false but rather because they consider them to be suspect, trivial, or irrelevant to their stories. They are especially likely to arrive at such an assessment, however, when the data do not fit into their general worldview as it pertains to guns and gun control. Such information does not seem to jive with the rest of the information in their possession, leading to the suspicion on the reporter's part that the information may be inaccurate or tainted by the source's personal biases. The information is suspect because it deviates from the accepted orthodoxy, even if the reporter does not know of any solid facts that directly contradict the suspect claims.

Further, since the suspect information would be hard to integrate with the rest of the information in their story, the easiest way for the reporter to handle such anomalous data is simply to drop them from the story, a decision that also comports nicely with the general pressure to conserve print space or air time. This sort of decision to exclude can be done in good faith, for who can criticize excluding suspect information?

This process largely works on an individual, ad hoc basis, reporter by reporter, and story by story. However, if reporters for the major national news outlets generally share the same worldview on guns and gun control, they will also tend to reject the same kinds of troublesome information, without any coordinated conspiracy being needed to achieve this result. The result, nevertheless, is exactly the same as it would be if there *were* a calculated conspiracy.

Unfortunately, this phenomenon sets up a vicious circle. Because reporters are themselves consumers of news, they read other reporters' stories on guns, which, of course, excluded the same sorts of suspect information as their own stories did. This reinforces their skewed worldview, which then encourages their subsequent decisions to exclude the anomalous information.

UNBALANCED SKEPTICISM APPLIED
TO PRO AND CON INFORMATION

Media bias often results from what might be termed "sloppiness in the service of bias." Because the people who produce and manage the news are operating under deadlines, and under limits on print space, air time, and resources of all kinds, a certain amount of sloppiness and imperfection in news coverage is unavoidable. Therefore, inevitable there are limits to the thoroughness with which reporters can evaluate debatable claims. However, it is illegitimate bias when reporters selectively direct their reportorial skepticism predominantly toward those advocating ideas with which they disagree, and devote the bulk of their limited resources to debunking such positions, while directing little skepticism at those who espouse more congenial views, and devoting little or no time to checking out the factual basis for those views.

Sloppiness in checking out technical claims made about guns is a chronic problem. Consider the case of a newspaper that published a mislabeled photograph to support their claim that a particular "assault rifle" was an unusually powerful and lethal rifle. On January 23,1989, the *Los Angeles Herald-Examiner* (pp. A1, A6 ff.) printed a news story that focused on the "AK-47" (actually a semiautomatic civilian adaptation of the AK-47), the type of gun used in the 1989 Stockton, California, schoolyard killing of five children. The story was accompanied by a photo showing a melon being blown apart by a bullet supposedly fired from the "AK-47." The text made a number of perfectly accurate comments about the high penetrating power of the ammunition used in this gun, although it failed to note other attributes of the ammunition that tended to make it less lethal than other rifle rounds (see Fackler et al. 1990).

Unfortunately, the shot that had so dramatically blown up the melon had not come from the "assault rifle" in question, or indeed from any kind of rifle. A member of the Los Angeles County Sheriff's Department had initially been asked by a reporter to fire an "AK-47" round through the melon, which he did, using the fully jacketed, military-style 7.62 x 39 mm ammunition type used in the Stockton shootings. Because the ammunition in question does not in fact create an unusually large wound cavity (Fackler et al. 1990), it failed to blow up the melon, creating a small hole and merely cracking the melon instead. For comparative purposes, the deputy sheriff was also asked to fire a police handgun round (a 9 mm 115 grain jacketed hollow point) from a Beretta Model 92 pistol, which he did, causing the melon to blow up (Van Horn 1989).

That the rifle ammunition in question does not blow up melons as portrayed was substantiated by tests conducted by *Gun Week*, a weekly firearms newspaper (5-5-89, p. 1), and later in an ABC-TV documentary (*Peter Jennings Reporting: Guns*, broadcast 1-24-90). Consequently, it was evidently a photograph of the effects of the police handgun round that was published in the newspaper and described in the picture's caption as portraying "the power of an AK-47." Apparently, the photographer or an editor mislabeled the photo of the melon being blown up by the handgun round, identifying it instead as portraying the effects of an AK-47 round. The reporter present at the scene could not be sure whether this was what had happened (Askari 1989), and the photographer never returned my phone calls. The *Los Angeles Herald-Examiner* has since gone out of business.

After the *Herald-Examiner* published this story, local television stations, including the Los Angeles ABC affiliate, KABC-TV, broadcast filmed demonstrations showing melons being blown up, supposedly by an "AK-47." Finally, one year after the Stockton shooting, the ABC-TV network broadcast an accurate demonstration in which the "AK-47" round merely put a small split in a melon, while ordinary civilian hunting rifle ammunition caused one to explode (*Peter Jennings Reporting: Guns*, broadcast 1-24-90).

The KABC broadcasts become more understandable in the context of the station's editorial stance. Bill Press, News Commentator for KABC-TV, testified to the U.S. Senate that his station's reports on AWs stemmed from a conscious decision on the part of the station to influence the public: "We have involved the public in this issue through our daily commentary. We are working every day with the Los Angeles Police Department. Every time there is an incident using a semiautomatic rifle in the city of Los Angeles, we report it on the news and we ask people to write to the State legislature to ban these weapons" (U.S. Congressional Research Service 1992, pp. 38–39).

Numerous other allegations about a variety of guns and ammunition have been made in various news stories, could easily have been checked out, but were not. The following claims (stated or implied) all had clear procontrol (or antigun) implications, all were false, and all could have been disconfirmed with a single phone call: (1) AWs are readily convertible to fully automatic fire like a machine gun, (2) ARs are more lethal than ordinary civilian-style hunting rifles, (3) AWs are the preferred weapon of criminals in general, or of drug dealers or youth gangs in particular, (4) large numbers of police officers have been killed with AWs, and (5) large numbers of police officers have been killed with "cop-killer" bullets. (See Kleck 1991, chapter 3, for documentation of the assertion that these claims are all inaccurate.)

AMOUNT OF "PLAY"— EXTENT AND PROMINENCE OF COVERAGE

Bias can also be evident in the amount of "play" gun stories are given depending on whether their implications are pro- or anticontrol, that is, the amount of space or air time devoted to a story and the prominence given it—front page versus inside page, lead story in a broadcast, or a later one. Major victories for the anticontrol forces are sometimes downplayed, whereas procontrol victories are given disproportionately prominent coverage. Trivial procontrol victories such as the banning of nonexistent "plastic" guns, outlawing of "cop killer" bullets, and temporary federal import bans on "assault rifles" have been given front-page treatment, whereas more far-reaching anticontrol victories such as the passage of state preemption bills have been virtually ignored.

A state preemption measure establishes that only the state may regulate guns, wiping out local gun controls and preventing local governments from passing further restrictions. The significance of these measures derives partly from the fact that rather than merely eliminating just one form of control, they commonly void entire broad categories of controls, usually virtually all forms of gun control. Further, this does not affect just a single local jurisdiction but hundreds of local jurisdictions in a given state. Finally, typical preemption measures not only strike down existing controls but also make local enactment of future controls impossible. All this is of special significance in light of the fact that the nation's strongest gun controls have all been imposed by local governments

(Kleck 1991, chapter 8). The NRA and other anticontrol forces have gained state preemption laws in at least thirty-four states, with at least twenty-three being passed or strengthened in the period from 1982 to 1987 (*U.S. News & World Report*, 4-25-88; NRA 1987). These victories were largely ignored by the national news media, usually being covered only within each affected state.

In sharp contrast, a minor bill allowing a commission to ban certain types of cheap handguns, passed in Maryland in 1988, was given front-page coverage in papers across the nation. (The low frequency of involvement of cheap handguns in crime is documented in Kleck 1991, chapter 3.) To establish the national newsworthiness of what seemed to be, disregarding the amount of news coverage itself, a minor local story in Maryland, news sources falsely claimed that this was "the first state law to outlaw the cheap handguns called Saturday Night Specials" (e.g., *Chicago Sun Times*, 5-29-88; see also *Washington Post*, 4-12-88). In fact, at least four other states already had similar statutes on the books: Illinois, Hawaii, Minnesota, and South Carolina. The first three banned both sale and manufacture of the guns, and the last banned only sale. The Hawaii statute was even stronger than the Maryland measure, banning most possession of the guns as well as sale and manufacture (Hawaii 1980, pp. 70–71). One major newspaper even made this "first in the nation" claim while directly contradicting itself in another story on the same page, by the same author, noting the existence of these "similar statutes" (*Chicago Sun Times* 5-29-88)! The only novel element of the Maryland law was the technical details of how authorities would determine which handguns would be prohibited.

EDITORIAL STANCES AND OTHER NEWSPAPER POLICIES

According to historians Kennett and Anderson, "three quarters of the nation's newspapers, and most of the periodical press" support gun control (1975, p. 237). These authors described the media as "mostly unsympathetic" to the progun forces, stating that, in the 1960s, "large urban dailies with mass circulation—the *New York Times, Washington Post, Los Angeles Times,* and *Christian Science Monitor*—issued continual calls for new and tougher laws. With few exceptions the popular magazines followed suit." They noted that the Washington Post, in what may be a record, once published procontrol editorials on the gun issue for 77 consecutive days (pp. 239, 312). Perhaps the *Post* had moderated their views by 1988 when the Maryland handgun referendum was voted on—they published strongly worded proreferendum editorials for only nine consecutive days before the vote (*Washington Post* 10-30-88 to 11-7-88).

News organizations regularly insist on the independence of their news coverage and their editorial stances, but media scholar Ben Bagdikian has stated that "studies throughout the years have shown that any bias in the news tends to follow a paper's editorial opinions" (1987, p. 100). This claim received support regarding the gun control issue in Etten's (1991) study of daily newspaper stories—papers with procontrol editorial policies were more likely to show procontrol bias in their new stories.

The general public apparently is sensitive to a pro-control slant in news stories about gun control. In a 1985 national *Los Angeles Times* poll, people were asked how they thought their daily newspapers felt about stricter gun laws. Among those who thought they knew their paper's stance, 62 percent felt that stance was procontrol. Further, among those who thought they knew their paper's stance, most said they knew this because of the way their paper covered *news stories* on gun control rather than from editorials (DIALOG 1990). Apparently, bias in news coverage of gun issues is sufficiently obvious to convey newspapers' gun control preferences even to large numbers of ordinary readers. Media bias is not exclusively exercised in the newsroom. Advertising industry publications have reported that the advertising departments of national publications, including *Newsweek*, *Time*, the *Christian Science Monitor*, and *Reader's Digest* magazines, as well as the NBC and CBS television networks, have refused to accept paid advertisements from the National Rifle Association (Adweek 6-26-89, p. 4). Consequently, gun owner groups are often in the position of not being able to even buy the opportunity to counter the claims of the news media.

OTHER FORMS OF BIAS

Antigun bias can take even more subtle, sometimes subliminal, forms. In recent years, local television stations have taken to displaying a stylized handgun "insert" or "super" to introduce crime stories, including those not involving handguns. This is done even though less than 1 percent of all crimes, and only 13 percent of violent crimes involve handguns (Rand 1994). Thus, "crime" and "handgun" are repeatedly paired in the minds of viewers, even though handguns are neither a predominant nor even a very common element of crime. A practice that reinforces an association between handguns and violence is not questioned, perhaps because the contribution of handguns to violence, and the high frequency of their use in violent acts, are taken for granted as unquestioned facts, fixed elements of the "consensual paradigm" under which news workers operate (Young 1981).

A CASE STUDY—A CBS TELEVISION DOCUMENTARY

Close examination of a particular case will illustrate some common forms of news media bias as they pertain to gun issues. On March 16, 1989, the CBS television network broadcast an episode of its *48 Hours* news magazine program titled "Armed and Deadly." The program's purported topic was "assault rifles," defined in the documentary as military-style semiautomatic rifles. However, the focus often wandered to both fully automatic machine guns and to the broader category of "assault weapons," which includes handguns and shotguns.

Although no written analysis can fully convey the emotional and visual impact of a television documentary, the following description covers in some detail all of the major segments of the program, in their original sequence. The subheadings of paragraphs convey what seemed to be the main theme of each segment. I will usually refer to assertions being made by CBS, rather than by particular reporters, to emphasize that the documentary was a collaborative product. (All assertions about what is actually true about ARs and AWs are documented in Kleck 1991, chapter 3.)

Vivid images of "assault weapon" violence. The documentary opened with dramatic footage of a trauma center helicopter flying a gunshot victim to a Washington, D.C., hospital. Viewers heard a medical technician speaking to hospital staff over the helicopter's radio, saying the victim was shot five times with a "high caliber automatic pistol." As it turned out, this was inaccurate; the weapon was evidently an ordinary nine millimeter (9 mm) semiautomatic pistol, that is, one that is neither automatic in fire nor large in caliber. Thus, in a documentary supposedly focusing on "assault rifles," the opening footage did not even pertain to a recent "assault rifle" killing, almost certainly because such events are so rare in any one city, even one as large as Washington, that CBS would have had to wait for months before they could have gotten footage an such a crime.

Perhaps to establish the relevance of footage on a handgun killing, rather than an "assault rifle" killing, a District of Columbia homicide detective was filmed at the hospital claiming that a 9 mm semiautomatic pistol is "just as dangerous as any assault rifle," because it can carry twelve to seventeen rounds at a time. CBS did not explicitly vouch for the validity of this claim, but simply broadcast the claim without criticism or commentary from gun or medical experts on the lethality of different types of firearms. The statement was incorrect regardless of how one might define dangerousness. The higher lethality of rifles in general (including "assault rifles") compared to handguns (including 9 mm handguns) is one of the few traits that truly does make at least some assault rifles more dangerous than other guns. A 9 mm pistol has neither the muzzle velocity nor maximum magazine capacity assault rifles commonly have. Thus, CBS conveyed both the message that "assault rifles" are especially dangerous guns, and the message that they are no more dangerous than very common semiautomatic handguns, with no evident awareness of the contradiction.

Persuading viewers the problem affects them, too. Next, the head of the hospital's trauma unit was interviewed, and he alluded to "this epidemic of violence," implying that criminal gun violence was rapidly increasing. Although this was true in the District of Columbia at that moment, it was not true nationally or in most local areas—the number and rate of gun homicides had been fairly stable for years. CBS neither noted this fact nor denied it but simply presented an unrebutted statement that surely would lead at least some viewers to draw the seemingly obvious, but erroneous, conclusion that the nation, and perhaps their own community, was also undergoing an "epidemic" of gun violence. In fact, the U.S. homicide rate (the most accurately measured violent crime rate) had fluctuated, without any consistent trend, within a narrow range between 7.9 and 8.6 from 1983 through 1988, and had declined sharply from its peak of 10.2 in 1980. Likewise, the share of homicides involving guns fluctuated very slightly between 58 and 61 percent from 1983 through 1988, down from the peak of 68 percent in 1974 (U.S. FBI 1990, p. 48).

A physician was then interviewed, and he argued that the ordinary medical patient might face a shortage of blood or might have important surgery delayed because of the heavy hospital gunshot caseload, and implied that trauma centers are closing down and are unavailable to treat automobile accident victims because of the increasing burden of gunshot cases. CBS anchorman Dan Rather asked the doctor whether some trauma centers have "been forced to close" because of "these new pressures," that is, the allegedly increasing numbers of gunshot wounds. The doctor replied "They have," citing unnamed trauma centers in Chicago, Los Angeles, the District of Columbia, and South Florida, which refused to "open their doors to the care of the injured." Note that this response did not actually answer Rather's question, since the doctor did not cite any specific cases of trauma centers closing but only some that restricted their services, nor did he explicitly claim that gunshot wounds were the sole or even the principal reason for even these limited restrictions. Rather did not inquire whether the well-known increases in medical malpractice insurance costs, the increasing difficulties of recouping payment from low-income patients, or troubles in finding physicians willing to work in urban emergency rooms might have been more important factors, and moved on to the next segment. Rather's hinted claim that gunshot wounds were responsible for the closing of urban trauma centers was highly implausible. Washington, D.C., had the highest homicide rate of any large U.S. city at the time, yet the hospital that treated 30 to 40 percent of the city's adult gunshot patients in the 1980s admitted only about four such patients a week even during the peak violence years of 1983-1990 (Webster et al. 1992, pp. 694, 695).

This is a new crisis, not the same old thing. Rather stated that only about 4,000 "military-style assault weapons" were imported into the United States in 1986, compared to the first few months of 1989, when over 100,000 importation applications had been submitted. The documentary never claimed that the mechanically identical civilian-appearing semiautomatic rifles are any less dangerous than their military-style counterparts or that imported "assault weapons" are more dangerous than domestically manufactured ones. (In fact, Rather later asserted that three out of four ARs in the United States were domestically made.) Therefore, it is unclear what the viewer was to learn from trends only in imports of the military-style weapons.

An "assault rifle" is basically a semiautomatic centerfire rifle. It was not mentioned that nonmilitary-style semiautomatic rifles had already been commonplace in the United States for decades, a fact anyone in the firearms industry could have told CBS. No basis was provided for believing that relative increases in the total sales of all semiautomatic centerfire rifles were anywhere as large as was implied by the import figures. In fact, it is not clear that the trend in total sales of these rifles was upward at all. In 1972, well before the popularity of "military-style" ARs began, 360,000 centerfire semiautomatic rifles were produced for civilian sale by domestic U.S. manufacturers, compared to only 149,000 in 1987, well after the increase in AR sales was supposed to have begun. Even taking into account the increase in rifle imports, total sales in semiautomatic centerfire rifles may well have declined between 1972 and 1987 (Kleck 1991, table 3.1). Although imports of military-style semiautomatic rifles did grow in the 1980s, there was little technically different in these few weapons from the much larger number of ordinary nonmilitary-style semiautomatic rifles that had already been common, and nothing at all of criminological significance in the fact that the weapons were imported. Citing the import figures appears to have served no other purpose than to impress the viewer with the contrast between the very large 100,000 figure and the very small 4,000 figure. In any case, this supposed trend was the synthetic product of an apples-and-oranges comparison between the number of guns actually imported in one period versus the number for which import applications had been filed. Because it costs an importer no more to apply for the importation of many guns than it does for few guns, the import application figures commonly are much higher than the numbers actually imported.

In the next segment, at a D.C. police firing range, an officer was shown firing first a bolt-action rifle, firing four shots in about nine seconds, and then an AR, firing five rounds in about five seconds, to demonstrate the higher rate of fire of ARs. Because bolt-action rifles are the slowest firing major type of multishot firearm, virtually any gun will fire more rapidly. Therefore, this exercise did not demonstrate any unique superiority peculiar to ARs. Then a policewoman was shown firing about sixteen or seventeen rounds from an AR in about eight seconds. No comparison was made with ordinary revolvers, which are the most common type of gun used by criminals, perhaps because such a comparison would have revealed little or no difference in rate of fire.

The police officer erroneously claimed on camera that "when you talk about semiautomatic weapons, you always talk about a large, a lot of, uh, a large capacity hold [*sic*] ammunition," holding up a magazine that appeared to be capable of holding about 30 rounds (she later referred to "32 rounds"). In fact, ARs are commonly sold with magazines holding only about five rounds; a 32-round magazine would be the largest magazine commonly sold with an AR, not the typical one (Warner 1988, pp. 293–302). Certainly ARs are not "always" sold or used with large magazines, and CBS cited no evidence they are even typically sold or used with large magazines. Again, CBS did not explicitly endorse the policewoman's claim; they merely presented it to viewers and allowed it to stand unquestioned.

"Assault rifles" are machine guns waiting to be converted. In the next segment, reporter David Martin related how he found, in two hours, a gunsmith willing and able to convert an AR into a fully automatic weapon. He did not say how he located him, or whether the ordinary violent criminal would be able to locate such a person. The unnamed "gunsmith" was shown, in a series of seven camera shots

lasting a total of fifteen seconds of air time, allegedly converting the gun. The editing of the sequence was rapid and unlike that in the rest of the program, evidently intended to convey the rapidity of the conversion. "Nine minutes later, he had turned it into an automatic rifle," said reporter Martin. Although Martin did not say one way or the other whether the man used any unusual, expensive, or specialized machine shop tools, the gunsmith was shown on camera using no tool more exotic than a pair of pliers. In most shots, he was shown using only his hands—he even held the rifle between his legs while working on it rather than using a vise. Likewise, there was no mention of the need for any additional, hard-to-obtain (or illegal) parts. The viewer was left with the distinct impression that the conversion could be done quickly, without special tools or parts.

According to Ed Owen, chief of the Bureau of Alcohol, Tobacco, and Firearms (BATF) Firearms Technology Branch, it is unlawful to buy or otherwise transfer any guns that are readily convertible to automatic fire, since such guns are defined by BATF as machine guns. Thus, the semiautomatic guns legally on the market at the time of the documentary could not be "readily converted" to fully automatic fire, according to BATF standards. Owens' branch of BATF is charged with, among other things, determining whether guns are convertible to automatic fire. Owen had been supplied with a videotape of the CBS "conversion" sequence by an anti–gun control group, Gun Owners of America. After viewing the brief tape frame-by-frame, Owen said that although he could not conclusively say that a nine-minute conversion was impossible or whether it had in fact occurred, he "was not aware that a conversion could be done in the manner shown." Thus, one of the nation's leading authorities on conversions had never seen a conversion done in the manner supposedly performed in nine minutes by a gunsmith CBS was able to locate in under two hours (Owen 1989).

This becomes more interesting in light of the fact that no one was shown demonstrating the allegedly converted weapon's ability to fire in fully automatic mode. Casual viewers might be forgiven if they thought they had seen the weapon fired this way, since the documentary cut directly from the gunsmith segment to footage of Martin firing "an automatic rifle" at a firing range. If viewers were not paying very close attention, they would not have noticed that the gun fired was different from the rifle supposedly converted. Thus, juxtaposition of the sequences probably left some viewers with the impression that it was the converted weapon's fully automatic capabilities being demonstrated, without CBS actually saying so. The documentary never did say whether anyone checked to see if the "conversion" was successful. It is worth noting that if the conversion did indeed occur, CBS induced the gunsmith to commit a federal crime, assuming he was not licensed to manufacture machine guns (U.S. Bureau of Alcohol, Tobacco, and Firearms [BATF] 1988, pp. 14–16).

Assault rifles are especially dangerous firearms. In this sequence at the police firing range, reporter Martin fired a fully automatic rifle, noting that he could not fire the gun accurately, and then switched over to semiautomatic fire. He did not note the implication that this difficulty in controlling fire would presumably make the gun less useful for killing people, instead commenting only that "semi-automatic was all the firepower I needed." At this point, it became hard to understand what the purpose of the conversion sequence had been. If fully automatic fire does not provide any additional capability for harming people, what purpose was served by attempting to establish how easily ARs can be converted to fully automatic fire?

Martin and a police officer then examined the damage done to a wrecked car at which Martin had fired. The officer pointed to a hole in a side door of the car, saying "look at that—straight through the car." Neither he nor Martin noted that the same result could also have been achieved with most medium or large caliber bolt- or lever-action rifles, shotguns loaded with rifled slugs, or even a magnum revolver. The impression left with at least some viewers, but never explicitly stated by anyone, was that ARs have unique or unusually high penetrating or hitting power. In fact, ballistics data on the ammunition most commonly fired from ARs, the .223 round, indicate that it is smaller than average for a rifle round and imparts less energy than the average rifle round. Further, one of the principal military advantages of this ammunition is that it usually does not kill but rather wounds, thereby not only removing the wounded soldier from combat but also diverting enemy resources to evacuate and treat the wounded soldier.

The procontrol forces are winning. In the next segment, Dan Rather noted that many people had been urging President George Bush to do something about getting ARs "off the streets." At that point, CBS had not actually established that there were large numbers of ARs on the streets, but treated it as a given. In fact, even in areas supposedly heavily afflicted by ARs, such as Los Angeles, these guns are almost never used by criminals and are only a tiny fraction of firearms seized by police or linked to homicides. Dan Rather then discussed Bush's decision to temporarily ban importation of ARs.

Next, Rather reported the results of a CBS *48 Hours* poll—73 percent of the 663 respondents (Rs) supported a "total ban on military-style assault weapons," with 22 percent opposed, and 5 percent missing. The significance of these findings is impossible to gauge in the absence of any evidence indicating that Rs knew what interviewers meant by the term "assault weapons." It is likely that many, perhaps most, of the Rs believed that the guns referred to were capable of fully automatic fire; indeed, true military assault rifles do have this capability. The weapons available to civilians, however, do not. The contrary view was also encouraged by the aforementioned news stories that repeatedly blurred the distinction between automatic and semiautomatic fire and that inaccurately insisted that weapons currently on the market can be readily converted to fire like a machine gun. With this background, it would not be surprising that a large majority of Americans favor a ban on private possession of machine guns, especially since this is already the law of the land (U.S. BATF 1988). It was not clear whether Rs opposed weapons that have a military appearance, opposed semiautomatic weapons, understood what "semiautomatic" meant, or even knew that the weapons referred to in the question were semiautomatic. Given that even news sources were confused about the relevant distinctions, it cannot be assumed that the survey Rs understood what they were being asked about.

The *48 Hours* documentary itself wandered back and forth between machine guns, "assault weapons," "assault rifles," "military-style assault rifles" and even commonplace semiautomatic pistols. Like CBS, other prominent news sources also have asserted that semiautomatic weapons are little more than fully automatic machine guns waiting to be converted. For example, even though federal law bans guns readily converted to fully automatic fire and no weapons available for sale to the public had this property, the *New York Times* (8-2-88) insisted in an editorial that "many semiautomatics can be made fully automatic with a screwdriver, even a paperclip," a claim that their own reporters then contradicted just eight months later (4-3-89).

Survey researchers know that most respondents are reluctant to admit they do not know what a surveyor is asking about and will generally provide a response, however meaningless, to an opinion question. They will even "express an opinion about an issue they could not possibly know anything about, simply because they do not wish to appear empty-headed or uninformed." For instance, they will respond to questions asking about prejudice against imaginary ethnic groups or about nonexistent government officials invented by the surveyors (Lewis and Schneider 1982, p. 42). CBS presented the results without commentary, letting viewers draw the apparently obvious conclusion about the popularity of the restrictions in question.

The violence problem is an assault rifle problem. The next segment was devoted to anecdotal information about the prevalence of ARs "on the streets" and among crime weapons. Two Boston police officers were shown on patrol; they offered the opinion that there were a lot of ARs "out there." Then a police detective was shown in a Fort Lauderdale police property room against a backdrop of dozens or hundreds of confiscated guns. CBS did not report what fraction of these seized guns were ARs. At least thirty-six reports on the prevalence of assault weapons among crime guns recovered by police, from at least thirty jurisdictions, indicate that less than 1 percent are "assault rifles" and only about 2 percent fall into the more broadly defined "assault weapons" category (Kleck 1996).

The detective described how he thought local drug gangs typically killed people—"they'll spray the area, just an indiscriminate shooting. . . . If they hit innocent bystanders along the way, no big deal." CBS did not ask how many times innocent bystanders had been killed in indiscriminate drug relating shootings, did not ask the officer to relate even one such incident, and did not confirm that it had actually happened, even once. Fortunately, such incidents are in fact extremely rare. (Note again that the word "spray" could suggest, without anyone explicitly saying so, that the guns were capable of fully automatic fire.)

Late in the documentary, in a segment largely devoted to showing machine gun scenes from commercial films, the first and only scholarly expert of any kind to appear or even be cited on the program was interviewed. Professor David Malamud was questioned about the effect of media violence on real-life violence.

None of the research he cited bore specifically on the significance of media portrayals of either weapons generally, or automatic (or semiautomatic) weapons specifically. No gun violence researchers of any kind were interviewed or cited in the program in connection with any of the issues addressed.

A live studio discussion followed, involving two persons: Larry Pratt, spokesman for Gun Owners of America, an organization even more strongly opposed to gun controls than the National Rifle Association, and a man named Joseph McNamara. Pratt was clearly identified as being a spokesman for an anti-control group, but McNamara was described only as chief of the San Jose police department. Some viewers might assume that McNamara had arrived at his views purely on the basis of his experience as a police officer familiar with violent crime. In fact, he is a gun control activist, a board member of The Handgun Information Center, a tax-exempt branch of Handgun Control, Inc., has frequently testified in favor of gun control before legislative bodies, and holds views arguably as extreme in support of AR restrictions as Pratt's are in opposition (*New York Times* 6-8-86, p. A26).

No police administrator was shown expressing skepticism about the likely efficacy of AR restrictions or the frequency of their involvement in crime. CBS did not overtly describe McNamara as a disinterested or representative spokesman for responsible law enforcement opinion; they merely presented his views without mentioning his affiliation with gun control lobbying groups and without any opposing law enforcement views. Because of his affiliation, Pratt's opinions could be easily dismissed by the viewer as the biased views of a mouthpiece for the gun lobby. But a spokesman clearly affiliated with the "gun lobby" was not "balanced off" by identifying the spokesman for Handgun Control as such. It is unlikely that spokespersons affiliated with advocacy groups and those not so affiliated would be perceived by viewers as equal credible.

The final sequence concerned the critical event that stimulated the movement to restrict ARs, the January 17, 1989, Stockton, California, schoolyard massacre. Dan Rather stated that the killer, Patrick Purdy, "brought his imported AK-47 to a school playground in Stockton, California. He fired 106 bullets within 120 seconds. Five children were murdered, 29 wounded." The *Los Angeles Times* (1989) reported that 110 shots were fired, in three to four minutes. While both time estimates should be viewed skeptically, the time difference is important. The *L.A. Times* figures implied a rate of fire that was only half as rapid as that implied by the CBS figures and that was no faster than that which can be easily sustained by an ordinary revolver—about one shot every two seconds.

In this and many of the examples previously cited, there is no reason to believe CBS knew they were misinforming their audience. On the other hand, there is also little reason to doubt that the documentary was intentionally constructed to persuade viewers that ARs represented a major threat to public safety. Its producers probably believed what they were attempting to persuade their audience to believe, even though their message was largely without firm factual foundation. They did not discover this because they failed to exercise sufficient journalistic skepticism or diligence in seeking out potentially contrary information. They did not bother to check out questionable claims or to seek out expert opinion on dubious propositions, perhaps because they did not seriously entertain the possibility that the assertions were questionable or subject to dispute in the first place.

None of the information management strategies used by CBS are unique to that organization. Other television documentaries about guns have been equally unbalanced, sloppy, and manipulative of viewers. The *48 Hours* program was not an unusual or extreme case. For example, NBC TV's program, *Guns, Guns, Guns* (broadcast in June of 1988), could easily have served as an even more extreme example of shoddy coverage of the issue.

NEWSWEEK AND THE INVENTION OF A MACHINE GUN CRISIS

Magazines have also manipulated information to create a procontrol impression. The Newsweek cover story of October 14, 1985, on "machine guns" is a straightforward example. The cover headline was "MACHINE GUN U.S.A." with a subheadline claiming that "Nearly 500,000 Automatic Weapons Are Now in the Hands of Collectors and Criminals." In fact, no one had any idea how many automatic weapons were in private hands, least of all *Newsweek*. The 500,000 figure was mentioned only once in the article itself, and then it referred neither to machine guns nor to fully automatic weapons but rather to semiautomatic "military-style assault guns" or "assault weapons" (Morganthau 1985, pp. 46, 49). These weapons fire only one shot per trigger pull, the same as revolvers. But even this number as it pertained to semiautomatic "assault weapons" was nothing more than a guess supplied by the general counsel of the National Coalition to Ban Handguns. *Newsweek* apparently saw nothing improper about using a guess from a gun control lobbyist as the sole basis for a cover headline. No basis was ever provided for the claim of 500,000 machine guns.

The only numbers that did pertain to automatic weapons were the number of federally registered automatic weapons (116,000 at the time, according to BATF) and a guess by the gun control lobbyist that "perhaps 125,000" of the 500,000 "assault weapons" (a guess derived from a guess) had been converted to full automatic fire. In fact, only 40 percent of the federally registered automatic weapons were even in private hands at the time (*Los Angeles Times*, 11-16-86, p. D4), implying about 46,000 registered machine guns in private hands. There was no factual basis whatsoever for the claim that a quarter, or even 1 percent, of "assault weapons" had been converted to full automatic status. Indeed, even among the guns confiscated by police (presumably more criminally involved than other guns, and thus more likely to have undergone an illegal conversion), semiautomatic "assault weapons" converted to fully automatic fire are virtually nonexistent (U.S. Congressional Research Service 1992, p. 18 [*none* of

3,527 Washington, D.C., guns were converted]; U.S. Senate 1989, p. 379 [of over 4,000 Los Angeles guns, six had been converted]).

The article vaguely asserted that these weapons were somehow "raising the risks of criminal violence" (p. 46) yet never cited a single national or even local crime statistic to indicate that the frequency of crimes committed with either machine guns or "assault weapons" was increasing. Indeed, the authors came up with descriptions of a grand total of two fatal machine gun attacks, occurring in two different years. In lieu of any hard evidence on the prevalence of such incidents, Edward Conroy, a Miami BATF agent, was quoted as claiming that "South Florida is the mecca of illegal automatics, and machine-gun hits are almost commonplace. . . . There are even brazen attacks at stoplights, with grandma and the kiddies getting greased along with the target" (p. 48). In fact, both machine-gun killings and accidental killings of innocent bystanders in drug shootouts (at stoplights or anywhere else) were virtually nonexistent, even in Miami during the peak of its drug related homicide problem. Perhaps the sort of incident Conroy described did occur once. However, Newsweek neither bothered to confirm it nor to question the claim that it was "almost common." Even in Miami less than 1 percent of homicides in 1980 involved machine guns, and none of these involved innocent bystanders being killed (Kleck 1991, chapter 3).

The article also contained a long series of half-truths and unsupported assertions similar to those repeated four years later in the CBS *48 Hours* documentary—for instance, that assault rifles are easily converted to fully automatic fire, so the distinction between these weapons and machine guns is an "increasingly tenuous" one (pp. 48–49); that they pose a major threat to police officers (p. 50); that they are unusually lethal (p. 51); and so on. And, as with the CBS documentary, not a single expert on guns and violence, either favoring or opposing the premises of the story, was quoted or cited. Because few experts in the field could have provided evidence supporting the main propositions of the story (Kleck 1991, chapter 3), the omission of expert commentary was perhaps understandable.

THE BERNHARD GOETZ CASE

Perhaps the most heavily publicized case of a purported defensive use of a gun in recent decades was an incident in which Bernhard Goetz shot four young men in a New York subway train on December 22, 1984. As the story was handled by the national press, the following were the salient facts of the incident. The four individuals who were shot by Goetz had "asked" for money, the stories hinting that they may have merely been panhandling rather than attempting to rob Goetz. The four were "youths" who were merely acting a bit rambunctious, rather than menacing. Although the four had prior records of "brushes with the law," the offenses involved were "minor." After shooting two of the four, Goetz shot at least one, possibly two of them, in the back as they were attempting to flee. After turning himself in to police, Goetz confessed to shooting all four, then pausing, seeing one of them already wounded, and firing another shot into the helpless victim. Goetz was described as a "subway vigilante" and writers speculated that the incident would stimulate future criminal use of guns by citizens encouraged to carry guns as Goetz did. Goetz was acquitted of the most serious charges connected with the shootings, being convicted only of unlawful possession of a firearm. The press hinted that Goetz had been treated leniently by the court and reported speculations that the leniency was racially motivated, and was due to the fact that Goetz was white and the four victims were black (see, e.g., *Newsweek* 3-11-85, 4-1-85; *Time* 1-21-85).

The only problem with this account of the case was that nearly all of it was either false, misleading, or unsupported by the available facts. From the very beginning there had been no doubt that the incident began with an attempted robbery. Two of the four victims admitted to police and reporters that they had intended to rob Goetz. (Even twelve years after the incident, the *Los Angeles Times* was uncritically repeating the robbers' claim that "they were only panhandling"—see Goldman 1996.) Leaving aside its wisdom or morality, New York State law is clear that victims of robbery may use force, including deadly force, to resist robbery, regardless of whether the robbers are armed or whether the victim could safely retreat (Fletcher 1988, p. 25).

The victims were not ordinary, rambunctious children—all were eighteen or nineteen years old at the time, and all four had extensive criminal records. At the time of the incident, there were a total of nine convictions, many more arrests, plus twelve cases pending and ten bench warrants for nonappearance in court against the four. Some later news reports conceded this, but others attempted to undercut it by only acknowledging the more minor offenses (e.g., *Newsweek* 4-1-85, p. 23). In fact, the charges included rape, armed robbery, and assault with a deadly weapon. At the time of the incident Darrell Cabey was awaiting trial on charges of armed robbery with a shotgun, and six months later James Ramseur was arrested for (and later convicted of) the rape and robbery of a pregnant woman, who required forty stitches to close her wounds and had to be hospitalized for four days.

News accounts laid special emphasis on Goetz's videotaped confession in which he stated that, after wounding all four of the robbers, he paused, looked the fourth (Cabey) over, said, "You don't look too bad, here's another," and shot the already-wounded man a second time (*Newsweek* 4-1-85, p. 23). Although Goetz did tell police something like this, the confession was contradicted by seven eyewitnesses, who agreed that the shots had all been fired in rapid succession without a pause. No one saw Goetz calmly shoot a helpless man after walking over to him and delivering a speech. Even the prosecutor expressed doubts about whether Goetz spoke, at the scene, the words he later confessed to, though he nonetheless insisted that Goetz had shot one of the men a second time without justification (Lesley 1988, pp. 193–214).

The press freely used the term "vigilante" to describe Goetz, but the use was inaccurate. The word derives from "vigilance committee" and traditionally refers to members of groups who seek to punish criminals where the legally constituted authorities are unable or unwilling to do so. Scholars have noted the existence of modern vigilantes, but these are always members of anticrime groups (Brown 1969, pp. 187–93). The term "lone vigilante" is therefore an oxymoron, since vigilantism is by definition a group activity. More importantly, there was never any clear evidence Goetz set out to punish criminals or sought contact with either the four he shot or any other criminals (Lesley 1988, p. 317). Instead, whether morally justified or not, whether excessive or not, Goetz's act was believed by the jury to be an act of self-defense. Further, there is no evidence that this incident encouraged other people to commit illegal acts of self-defense. The only possible effect on criminal behavior documented so far was a pronounced decrease in subway robberies in the weeks and months following the incident (drops the New York authorities attributed to added transit police in the subways) (*New York Times* 3-99-85, p. B4; 4-18-85, p. B7).

Finally, there is no evidence Goetz was treated leniently by the court, for any reason. There was never any solid legal foundation for doubting that the four young men were attempting to rob Goetz, nor any ambiguity about whether New York State law permits use of force against robbers. Consequently, there was little legal basis for convicting Goetz for shooting the first three men, and only conflicting and inconsistent evidence sustaining the charges pertaining to the second wounding of the fourth man (Lesley 1988). Goetz was convicted of an unlawful weapons possession charge, a Class D Felony of which he was undoubtedly guilty. In 1989, of 2,308 people convicted in New York City for illegal gun possession, half received no jail time at all, including the four out of ten who received only probation (*New York Times* 1-29-90). Goetz was sentenced to one year in jail (and served over eight months), five years' probation, 280 hours of community service, a $5,000 fine or another year in jail, and was ordered to seek psychiatric help (Lesley 1988, p. 320). In short, Goetz was treated more harshly than most less-publicized defendants convicted of the same charge.

One might argue that the acquittal on the shooting-related charges was itself the product of racism. For example, Benjamin Hooks, head of the NAACP, was quoted in the press as asking: "If a white youth had been shot in similar circumstances by a black man, what would have been the outcome?" Oddly enough, a similar incident was in fact handled by the New York courts around the same time, with the races of the participants reversed. According to a newspaper account, a twenty-three-year-old black man named Austin Weeks, while riding a New York City subway train, was accosted by two white teenagers who called him a racist name. Weeks shot and killed one of them with an unlicensed pistol. A Brooklyn grand jury refused to indict Weeks, he never had to face the prolonged trial Goetz faced, and consequently Weeks received no legal punishment of any kind (Kerrison 1987). Thus, in a shooting with a more legally questionable justification (no robbery was involved, but only a verbal provocation) and a fatal outcome, a black man accused of killing a white teenager was treated more leniently than a white man accused of nonfatally shooting four black teenagers. The Weeks case was ignored by the national press.

IS IT BIAS OR JUST RANDOM SLOPPINESS?

It might be argued that these many specific examples only represent the inevitable imperfections of work done under a deadline and with limited resources. Reporters are human and make mistakes like everyone else. Although this is obviously true, it cannot account for the unbalanced, consistently procontrol character of the flaws. If these flaws were truly just innocent mistakes unrelated to biased views of guns and gun control, they would be randomly distributed and equally likely to be pro- or anticontrol in their implications. They are not.

The prevalence and direction of bias was addressed directly in former reporter Tamryn Etten's (1991) content analysis of newspaper stories on gun issues. Etten examined a nationally representative sample of 117 gun stories published in 1989 and selected from Newsbank, a database covering virtually all large circulation, and many small-to-medium circulation, daily newspapers in the United States. Each story was coded for indications of bias in the content of the story, such as unrebutted statements favoring one side or the other, use of words tending to weaken or strengthen the impact of pro- or anticontrol arguments (e.g., advocate Smith "claimed" versus "stated"), use of unattributed facts or opinions, and use of sarcasm directed at advocates or arguments on one side or the other. Using a "net bias" score that measured the excess of procontrol bias over anticontrol bias, Etten's results indicated that 71 percent of the stories contained net bias in one direction or another, and that among stories with some net bias, 81 percent were biased in favor of gun control. Thus, stories biased in favor of the procontrol side outnumbered stories favoring the anticontrol side by a margin of four to one (Etten 1991).

Perhaps the most telling evidence of the one-sided character of national news media coverage of the gun debate is the almost total absence of complaints about it from the procontrol side. Even though the gun press is filled with bitter complaints of antigun bias in the national media (e.g., Brown 1989; Blackman 1987), the writings of gun control advocates almost never even mention the issue. Either they see little national news coverage to object to, or they are remarkably forbearing in saying anything about it. One especially strong supporter of strict gun controls approvingly described early television news coverage of gun issues as "balanced" (Bakal 1966, p. 127). The Chairman of Handgun Control Inc., Pete Shields, all but acknowledged the nation's newspapers as an active ally in the gun control movement: "I would be remiss if I failed to mention the support that the handgun control movement has received from the editorial pages of papers across the nation. Some of these papers have supported the movement for its entire life. As a group, American editorial writers have done a great deal to keep the cause of handgun control before the American public" (Shields 1981, p. 89).

This sort of free media support provided more than just the intangible benefits of public goodwill and organizational legitimacy. Shields recalled the effects of interviews he gave in 1977 to *Parade* magazine and the top-rated *60 Minutes* news magazine program on CBS-TV, crediting them with providing a critical early boost to his organization's growth. "As a result of these two features, we were accorded what you might call 'instant credibility.' The phones (at Handgun Control Inc.) rang more than ever, and the mail thundered in. The huge number of contributions and letters of support showed us that . . . the American people favored some form of gun control" (1981, p. 134).

DISCUSSION AND CONCLUSIONS

Etten's content analysis results indicated that strong procontrol/antigun bias is not universal. Some major news sources have covered the gun issue in a competent and balanced fashion, notably PBS television (which produced what may be the best broadcast documentary on the issue, in its *Frontline* series), the *Wall Street Journal*, and *U.S. News & World Report*. And there are certainly many local newspapers that also cover gun control issues in a reasonably balanced way, though many of these are small-circulation outlets with strictly local impact. Nevertheless, even though the antigun bias is not universal among the major national news outlets, it is certainly widespread. Further, it is not balanced by important news sources with a progun bias. No major national news source, broadcast or print, can reasonably be described as biased in a progun or antigun control direction.

To be sure, biases in news coverage of gun control are not unique to that issue. The news industry's handling of drug issues is at least as distorted, and coverage of crime issues in general is superficial, sloppy, and uncritical of official views (Cohen and Young 1981). Nevertheless, the partiality and lack of skepticism toward one side in the dispute seem especially pronounced in connection with gun control.

Why should such bias exist? How can professional journalists, committed to an ethic of objectivity and fairness, nevertheless engage in such unbalanced coverage of an issue and apparently be so unaware of any bias? One possible explanation is that many news professionals do not believe there are two legitimate sides to the gun debate. Although there are obviously two parties to the dispute, only one is believed to have a legitimate case to make, one that goes beyond mere narrow self-interest. One possible consequence is that some members of influential news organizations set the gun issue apart, make it an exception, and do not feel bound by customary standards of objectivity and even-handedness where gun control is concerned. Consider the following unusually frank excerpt from a form letter sent from the editorial offices of *Time* magazine to a reader who had objected to one of their stories on guns:

> The July 17 (1989) cover story is the most recent in a growing number of attempts on the part of *Time* editors to keep the gun-availability issue resolutely in view. Such an editorial closing of ranks represents the exception rather than

the rule in the history of the magazine, which has always endeavored to provide a variety of opinions and comment, in addition to straightforward news reporting, as a way of engaging readers in interpreting the significance of issues and events as they arise. *But the time for opinions on the dangers of gun availability is long since gone, replaced by overwhelming evidence that it represents a growing threat to public safety.* (Hammond 1989, emphasis added)

"The time for opinions . . . is long since gone." Were the issue any other one, would any respectable journalist fail to find such a sentiment disturbing? The guns-violence issue is evidently beyond debate in the editorial offices of *Time*. In sharp contrast to the debates among experts on the subject, there were no honestly differing views among the editors on "the dangers of gun availability" or the assertion that it was "a growing threat to public safety." This was not an issue with two sides, which *Time* was obliged to cover fairly, but rather was an issue with only one valid or respectable side. The only remaining issue was how best to convey to tile readers of *Time* the indisputable truth that the editors saw so clearly.

The political implications of this imbalance are important. Few would dispute that the mass media influence public opinion and lawmaking in a democracy. Consequently, the one-sided character of much of the news reporting on the gun issue is a serious matter, although clearly not one that has been widely acknowledged among opinion leaders. Media manipulation of information in general has certainly not gone unnoticed (see, e.g., Cohen and Young [1981], concerning media treatment of crime, deviance and social problems; Bagdikian [1987] on economic and political issues in general; and Herman and Chomsky [1988] on political, especially foreign policy, issues). However, the unequal character of the propaganda struggle over guns is not as well known or as frequently addressed by scholars.

Author Roger Caras commented in 1970 on the quality of the debate over guns: "Any careful observer of the battle must be distressed at the ignorance, ill will, and dishonesty apparent on both sides" (1970, p. 122). Caras's assessment was true as far as it went, but its bland evenhandedness obscured the extremely unequal impact of "the ignorance, ill will, and dishonesty" of each side. The purveyors of misinformation are not all equally influential or well-placed to disseminate their views. The indisputably biased publications of the National Rifle Association (NRA) and the rest of the gun press have a combined circulation probably well under ten million (about 5.5 million in 1982, for the four largest circulation gun and outdoor magazines, according to Standard Rate and Data Service 1983 figures [SRDS 1983]), whereas *Time* and *Newsweek* alone reach over 7 million households every week, and the commercial television networks reach many tens of millions of households every day. The biased views of gun control proponents find a sympathetic outlet in the major print and broadcast media, whereas the equally biased views of gun control opponents are largely confined to the pages of gun and hunting magazines, where they are read almost exclusively by a comparatively small audience of the already-converted faithful.

Regardless of how successful a political lobbying organization the NRA may or may not be (see Langbein and Lotwis 1990 for evidence that NRA influence is exaggerated), this power is greatly counterbalanced by the disproportionately procontrol slant of the nation's most influential providers of news. Whereas the NRA has to purchase (when media advertising departments permit it to do so) print and broadcast advertisements in order to reach a substantial share of the general public, procontrol forces are in effect given sympathetic media dissemination of their views free of charge.

When a California referendum to limit private possession of handguns was defeated in 1982 by a 63 percent to 37 percent margin, its supporters attributed its defeat to NRA spending, specifically $5.5 to $7 million spent on print and broadcast advertisements, compared to only $1.5 to $2.6 million spent by proponents (Bordua 1983). Did the NRA's much higher media spending "buy" it the referendum? The ads and air time it bought surely helped, but the issue of media impact can also be considered from a broader perspective. David Bordua (1983) noted that CBS broadcast a fifteen-minute, strongly antihandgun segment on its highest rated program, *60 Minutes*, just nine days before the referendum vote. Bordua also noted that the referendum was preceded by no fewer than nine procontrol editorials by the *Los Angeles Times*, not to mention similar ones from much of the rest of the state's newspapers. Proponents of the referendum did not have to buy this mass media help, but it was obviously to their benefit and was certainly intended to persuade voters. Bordua estimated that fifteen minutes of CBS airtime during the *60 Minutes* program would cost about $6 million if it had been purchased as proreferendum advertising rather than being granted as a free gift, as it were, by CBS. Even if one assesses the value of the segment simply by the costs of the commercial time usually purchased during a fifteen-minute period, the segment was worth about $800,000. Depending on a variety of assumptions about the value of various forms of free media exposure, and counting in the value of newspaper editorials and free air time on local TV and radio stations available to proponents under the Fairness Doctrine (still in effect back in 1982), Bordua's analysis indicated that supporters of the referendum may actually have received greater media exposure, paid and unpaid, than opponents.

The lesson is that it is unrealistic to view the gun lobby as the only powerful player in the political struggle over guns. The most important mass media news sources are powerful, and many of the more influential among them have taken sides on the gun issue. For the battle to be portrayed by these media sources as a procontrol David against an anticontrol Goliath is not only inaccurate but also blatantly self-serving. It allows the news media to inaccurately portray themselves as neutral bystanders in a political struggle they merely report rather than one in which they play an active part. This is especially apparent in news coverage of the procontrol findings of public opinion surveys, which are reported as if public opinion was something that existed and evolved on its own and that the media merely reported, rather than something heavily shaped by the media themselves.

If the media were in fact neutral, the struggle would indeed be a very unequal one, for the NRA is undoubtedly a better funded lobbying organization than its opposite numbers on the procontrol side. However, the news establishment is not neutral on the gun issue, and so the struggle is considerably more equal than one would guess from news stories that narrowly focus on campaign spending and lobbying efforts by the advocacy groups and ignore the media's own crucial role (e.g., Kohn 1981; *New York Times* 4-12-86, p. A26; *Boston Globe* 4-3-89).

What are the effects of this slanted coverage of the gun issue? First, the public is poorly informed. With limited space and time, bad coverage drives out good coverage, and unbiased sources are drowned out by biased ones. Second, gun owners are made to feel like embattled victims of a disinformation campaign whose distortions can only be fought with further distortions in the opposite direction. Public debate gets deformed by pushing responsible moderates to the extremes and polarizing the issue. Discussion degenerates into exchanges of increasingly outrageous claims and insults (Kates 1984). Finally, the legislative process is warped by inducing lawmakers to focus on highly publicized but substantively trivial side-show issues, such as bans on assault weapons, plastic guns, "cop killer" bullets, and Saturday night specials, rather than addressing more serious, but perhaps less exciting, control measures like gun buyer background checks or improved enforcement of existing bans on criminal possession and unlawful carrying of guns. Because the news media affect public opinion, politicians can ill afford to ignore the implicit policy agenda set by the news industry when it focuses disproportionate attention on trivial or unproductive policies.

REFERENCES

Askari, Emilia. 1989. Telephone conversation, October 1989, between author and Emilia Askari, reporter for the *Los Angeles Herald Examiner.*

Bagdikian, Ben H. 1987. *The Media Monopoly.* 2d ed. Boston: Beacon Press.

Bakal, Carl. 1966. *No Right to Bear Arms.* New York: McGraw-Hill.

Blackman, Paul. 1987. "Mugged by the Media." *American Rifleman* 135 (June): 34-36, 80-81.

Bordua, David J. 1983. "Adversary Polling and the Construction of Social Meaning." *Law & Policy Quarterly* 5:345–66.

Brown, Marshall J. 1989. "Wound Ballistics Expert Exposes Media AK Fakery." *Gun Week*, 5 May 1989.

Brown, Richard Maxwell. 1969. "The American Vigilante Tradition." In *Violence in America.* Edited by Hugh Davis Graham and Ted Robert Gurr. New York: Signet, pp. 144–218.

Caras, Roger. 1970. *Death as a Way of Life.* Boston: Little, Brown.

Cohen, Stanley, and Jock Young. 1981. *The Manufacture of News: Deviance, Social Problems, and the Mass Media.* London: Constable.

DIALOG. 1990. Computer search of DIALOG database POLL file of public opinion survey results. Palo Alto, Calif.: DIALOG Information Services, Inc.

Etten, Tarnryn. 1991. "Taking Sides: A Look at Media Bias and Gun Control." Unpublished master's thesis, School of Criminology, Florida State University.

Fackler, Martin, J. A. Malinowski, S. W. Hoxie, and A. Jason. 1990. "Wounding Effects of the AK-47 Rifle Used by Patrick Purdy in the Stockton Schoolyard Shooting of 17 January 1989." *American Journal of Forensic Medicine and Pathology* 11:185–89.

Fletcher, George P. 1988. *A Crime of Self-Defense.* New York: The Free Press.

Goldman, John J. 1996. "Jury Awards Millions to Victim of Shooting by Subway Gunman." *Los Angeles Times* wire service story appearing in *Tallahassee Democrat*, April 1996, p. 1A.

Hammond, Gloria. 1989. Form letter from Gloria Hammond, Editorial Offices of *Time*, dated 1 August 1989.

Hawaii. 1980. Hawaii Revised Statutes. Section 134-32. St. Paul: West Publishing.

Herman, Edward S., and Noam Chomsky. 1988. *Manufacturing Consent.*

Kates, Don B., Jr. 1984. "Conclusion." In *Firearms and Violence.* Edited by Don B. Kates Jr. Cambridge: Ballinger, pp. 523–37.

Kennett, Lee, and James LaVerne Anderson. 1975. *The Gun in America.* Westport, Conn.: Greenwood Press.

Kerrison, Ray. 1987. "Here's Proof Goetz verdict Wasn't Racist." *New York Post*, 23 June 1987.

Kleck, Gary. 1991. *Point Blank: Guns and Violence in America.* Hawthorne, N.Y.: Aldine de Gruyter.

———. 1996. Unpublished compilation of results of reports on assault weapons prevalence.

Kohn, Howard. 1981. "Inside the Gun Lobby." *Rolling Stone*, 5-14-81, pp. 1, 19–25, 70.

Langbein, Laura I., and Mark A. Lotwis. 1990. "The Political Efficacy of Lobbying and Money: Gun Control in the U.S. House, 1986." *Legislative Studies Quarterly* 15:414–40.

Lesley, Mark. 1988. *Subway Gunman.* Latham, N.Y.: British American Publishing.

Lewis, I. A., and William Schneider. 1982. "Is the Public Lying to the Pollsters?" *Public Opinion* 5:42–47.

Morganthau, Tom. 1985. "Machine Gun U.S.A." *Newsweek*, 14 October, pp. 46–51.

National Rifle Association. 1987. "Legislative Status." Fact sheet on state gun laws. Washington, D.C.: National Rifle Association.

Owen, Ed. 1989. Telephone conversation with Ed Owen, chief of the Firearms Technology Branch of the Bureau of Alcohol, Tobacco, and Firearms.

Rand, Michael. 1994. *Guns and Crime. Crime Data Brief. Bureau of Justice Statistics.* Washington, D.C.: U.S. Government Printing Office.

Shields, Pete. 1981. *Guns Don't Die—People Do.* New York: Arbor House.

Standard Rate and Data Service (SRDS). 1983. "Consumer Magazine and Farm Publications." Rates and Data 65.

U.S. Bureau of Alcohol, Tobacco and Firearms. 1988. *Federal Firearms Regulation 1988–89.* Washington, D.C.: U.S. Government Printing Office.

U.S. Congressional Research Service. 1992. "Assault Weapons": *Military-Style Semiautomatic Firearms Facts and Issues.* Report 92-434 GOV. Washington, D.C.: Congressional Research Service.

U.S. Federal Bureau of Investigation. 1990. *Uniform Crime Reports—1989* (and earlier issues, covering 1974-1988). Washington, D.C.: U.S. Government Printing Office.

U.S. Senate. 1989. Committee on the Judiciary, Subcommittee on the Constitution. Assault Weapons. Hearings on S. 386 and S. 747. Feb. 10 and May 5,1989. Washington, D.C.: U.S. Government Printing Office.

Van Horn, Dwight. 1989. Telephone conversation with Deputy Sheriff Dwight Van Horn of the Los Angeles County Sheriff's Department, 9-12-89.

Webster, Daniel W., Howard R. Champion, Patricia S. Gainer, and Leon Sykes. 1992. "Epidemiological Changes in Gunshot Wounds in Washington, D.C., 1983–1990." *Archives of Surgery* 127:694–98.

Warner, Ken. 1988. *Gun Digest—1989.* 43rd Annual Edition. Northbrook, Ill.: DBI Books.

Wright, James D. 1991a. Letter to the author, dated 15 February 1991.

———. 1991b. "Guns and Crime." In *Criminology: A Contemporary Handbook.* Edited by Joseph H. Sheley. Belmont, Calif.: Wadsworth, pp. 441–57.

Young, Jock. 1981. "Beyond the Consensual Paradigm." In *The Manufacture of News: Deviance, Social Problems and the Mass Media.* Edited by Stanley Cohen and Jock Young. Beverly Hills: Sage, pp. 393–421.

10

WHY AMERICANS FEAR THE WRONG THINGS

BARRY GLASSNER

Why are so many fears in the air, and so many of them unfounded? Why, as crime rates plunged throughout the 1990s, did two-thirds of Americans believe they were soaring? How did it come about that by mid-decade 62 percent of us described ourselves as "truly desperate" about crime—almost twice as many as in the late 1980s, when crime rates were higher? Why, on a survey in 1997, when the crime rate had already fallen for a half dozen consecutive years, did more than half of us disagree with the statement "This country is finally beginning to make some progress in solving the crime problem"?[1]

In the late 1990s the number of drug users had decreased by half compared to a decade earlier; almost two-thirds of high school seniors had never used any illegal drugs, even marijuana. So why did a majority of adults rank drug abuse as the greatest danger to America's youth? Why did nine out of ten believe the drug problem is out of control, and only one in six believe the country was making progress?[2]

Give us a happy ending and we write a new disaster story. In the late 1990s the unemployment rate was below 5 percent for the first time in a quarter century. People who had been pounding the pavement for years could finally get work. Yet pundits warned of imminent economic disaster. They predicted inflation would take off, just as they had a few years earlier—also erroneously—when the unemployment rate dipped below 6 percent.[3]

From Barry Glassner, *The Culture of Fear: Why Americans Are Afraid of the Wrong Things* (New York: Basic Books, 1999), pp. xi–xxvii. Reprinted by permission of Basic Books, a member of Perseus Books, LLC.

We compound our worries beyond all reason. Life expectancy in the United States has doubled during the twentieth century. We are better able to cure and control diseases than any other civilization in history. Yet we hear that phenomenal numbers of us are dreadfully ill. In 1996 Bob Garfield, a magazine writer, reviewed articles about serious diseases published over the course of a year in the *Washington Post*, the *New York Times*, and *USA Today*. He learned that, in addition to 59 million Americans with heart disease, 53 million with migraines, 25 million with osteoporosis, 16 million with obesity, and 3 million with cancer, many Americans suffer from more obscure ailments such as temporomandibular joint disorders (10 million) and brain injuries (2 million). Adding up the estimates, Garfield determined that 543 million Americans are seriously sick—a shocking number in a nation of 266 million inhabitants. "Either as a society we are doomed, or someone is seriously double-dipping," he suggested.[4]

Garfield appears to have underestimated one category of patients: for psychiatric ailments his figure was 53 million. Yet when Jim Windolf, an editor of the *New York Observer*, collated estimates for maladies ranging from borderline personality disorder (10 million) and sex addiction (11 million) to less well-known conditions such as restless leg syndrome (12 million) he came up with a figure of 152 million. "But give the experts a little time," he advised. "With another new quantifiable disorder or two, everybody in the country will be officially nuts."[5]

Indeed, Windolf omitted from his estimates new-fashioned afflictions that have yet to make it into the Diagnostic and Statistical Manual of Mental Disorders of the American Psychiatric Association: ailments such as road rage, which afflicts more than half of Americans, according to a psychologist's testimony before a congressional hearing in 1997.[6]

The scope of our health fears seems limitless. Besides worrying disproportionately about legitimate ailments and prematurely about would-be diseases, we continue to fret over already refuted dangers. Some still worry, for instance, about "flesh-eating bacteria," a bug first rammed into our consciousness in 1994 when the U.S. news media picked up on a screamer headline in a British tabloid, "Killer Bug Ate My Face." The bacteria, depicted as more brutal than anything seen in modern times, was said to be spreading faster than the pack of photographers outside the home of its latest victim. In point of fact, however, we were not "terribly vulnerable" to these "superbugs," nor were they "medicine's worst nightmares," as voices in the media warned.

Group A strep, a cyclical strain that has been around for ages, had been dormant for half a century or more before making a comeback. The British pseudoepidemic had resulted in a total of about a dozen deaths in the previous year. Medical experts roundly rebutted the scares by noting that of 20 to 30 million strep infections each year in the United States fewer than 1 in 1,000 involve serious strep A complications, and only 500 to 1,500 people suffer the flesh-eating syndrome, whose proper name is necrotizing fasciitis. Still the fear persisted. Years after the initial scare, horrifying news stories continued to appear, complete with grotesque pictures of victims. A United Press International story in 1998 typical of the genre told of a child in Texas who died of the "deadly strain" of bacteria that the reporter warned "can spread at a rate of up to one inch per hour."[7]

KILLER KIDS

When we are not worrying about deadly diseases we worry about homicidal strangers. Every few months for the past several years it seems we discover a new category of people to fear: government thugs in Waco, sadistic cops on Los Angeles freeways and in Brooklyn police stations, mass-murdering youths in small towns all over the country. A single anomalous event can provide us with multiple groups of people to fear. After the 1995 explosion at the federal building in Oklahoma City first we panicked about Arabs. "Knowing that the car bomb indicates Middle Eastern terrorists at work, it's safe to assume that their goal is to promote free-floating fear and a measure of anarchy, thereby disrupting American life," a *New York Post* editorial asserted. "Whatever we are doing to destroy Mideast terrorism, the chief terrorist threat against Americans, has not been working," wrote A. M. Rosenthal in the *New York Times*.[8]

When it turned out that the bombers were young white guys from middle America, two more groups instantly became spooky: right-wing radio talk show hosts who criticize the government—depicted by President Bill Clinton as "purveyors of hatred and division"—and members of militias. No group of disgruntled men was too ragtag not to warrant big, prophetic news stories.[9]

We have managed to convince ourselves that just about every young American male is a potential mass murderer—a remarkable achievement, considering the steep downward trend in youth crime throughout the 1990s. Faced year after year with comforting statistics, we either ignore them—adult Americans estimate that people under eighteen commit about half of all violent crimes when the actual number is 13 percent—or recast them as "The Lull Before the Storm" (*Newsweek* headline). "We know we've got about six years to turn this juvenile crime thing around or our country is going to be living with chaos," Bill Clinton asserted in 1997, even while acknowledging that the youth violent crime rate had fallen 9.2 percent the previous year.[10]

The more things improve the more pessimistic we become. Violence-related deaths at the nation's schools dropped to a record low during the 1996–97 academic year (19 deaths out of 54 million children), and only one in ten public schools reported any serious crime. Yet *Time* and *U.S. News & World Report* both ran headlines in 1996 referring to "Teenage Time Bombs." In a nation of "Children Without Souls" (another *Time* headline that year), "America's beleaguered cities are about to be victimized by a paradigm shattering wave of ultra-violent, morally vacuous young people some call 'the superpredators,' " William Bennett, the former secretary of education, and John Dilulio, a criminologist, forecast in a book published in 1996.[11]

Instead of the arrival of superpredators, violence by urban youths continued to decline. So we went looking elsewhere for proof that heinous behavior by young people was "becoming increasingly more commonplace in America" (CNN). After a sixteen-year-old in Pearl, Mississippi, and a fourteen-year-old in West Paducah, Kentucky, went on shooting sprees in late 1997, killing five of their classmates and wounding twelve others, these isolated incidents were taken as evidence of "an epidemic of seemingly depraved adolescent murderers" (Geraldo Rivera). Three months later in March 1998 all sense of proportion vanished after two boys ages eleven and thirteen killed tour students and a teacher in Jonesboro, Arkansas. No longer, we learned in *Time*, was it "unusual for kids to get back at the world with live ammunition." When a child psychologist on NBC's *Today* show advised parents to reassure their children that shootings at schools are rare, reporter Ann Curry corrected him. "But this is the fourth case since October," she said.[12]

Over the next couple of months young people failed to accommodate the trend hawkers. None committed mass murder. Fear of killer kids remained very much in the air nonetheless. In stories on topics such as school safety and childhood trauma, reporters recapitulated the gory details of the killings. And the news media made a point of reporting every incident in which a child was caught at school with a gun or making a death threat. In May, when a fifteen-year-old in Springfield, Oregon, did open fire in a cafeteria filled with students, killing two and wounding twenty-three others, the event felt like a continuation of a "disturbing trend" (*New York Times*). The day after the shooting, on National Public Radio's "All Things Considered," the criminologist Vincent Schiraldi tried to explain that the recent string of incidents did not constitute a trend, that youth homicide rates had declined by 30 percent in recent years, and more than three times as many people were killed by lightning than by violence at schools. But the show's host, Robert Siegel, interrupted him. "You're saying these are just anomalous events?" he asked, audibly peeved. The criminologist reiterated that anomalous is precisely the right word to describe the events, and he called it "a grave mistake" to imagine otherwise.

Yet given what had happened in Mississippi, Kentucky, Arkansas, and Oregon, could anyone doubt that today's youths are "more likely to pull a gun than make a fist," as Katie Couric declared on the *Today* show?[13]

ROOSEVELT WAS WRONG

We had better learn to doubt our inflated fears before they destroy us. Valid fears have their place; they cue us to danger. False and overdrawn fears only cause hardship.

Even concerns about real dangers, when blown out of proportion, do demonstrable harm. Take the fear of cancer. Many Americans overestimate the prevalence of the disease, underestimate the odds of surviving it, and put themselves at greater risk as a result. Women in their forties believe they have a 1 in 10 chance of dying from breast cancer, a Dartmouth study found. Their real lifetime odds are more like 1 in 250. Women's heightened perception of risk, rather than motivating them to get checkups or seek treatment, can have the opposite effect. A study of daughters of women with breast cancer found an inverse correlation between fear and prevention: the greater a daughter's fear of the disease the less frequent her breast self-examination. Studies of the general population-both men and women-find that large numbers of people (who believe they have symptoms of cancer delay going to a doctor, often for several months. When asked why, they report they are terrified about the pain and financial ruin cancer can cause as well as poor prospects for a cure. The irony of course is that early treatment can prevent precisely those horrors they most fear.[14]

Still more ironic, if harder to measure, are the adverse consequences of public panics. Exaggerated perceptions of the risks of cancer at least produce beneficial by-products, such as bountiful funding for research and treatment of this leading cause of death. When it comes to largescale panics, however, it is difficult to see how potential victims benefit from the frenzy. Did panics a few years ago over sexual assaults on children by preschool teachers and priests leave children better off? Or did they prompt teachers and clergy to maintain excessive distance from children in their care, as social scientists and journalists who have studied the panics suggest? How well can care givers do their jobs when reg- ulatory agencies, teachers' unions, and archdioceses explicitly prohibit them from any physical contact with children, even kindhearted hugs?[15]

Was it a good thing for children and parents that male day care providers left the profession for fear of being falsely accused of sex crimes? In an article in the Journal of American Culture, sociologist Mary DeYoung has argued that day care was "refeminized" as a result of the panics. "Once again, and in the time-honored and very familiar tradition of the family, the primary responsibility for the care and socialization of young children was placed on the shoulders of low-paid women," she contends.[16]

We all pay one of the costs of panics: huge sums of money go to waste. Hysteria over the ritual abuse of children cost billions of dollars in police investigations, trials, and imprisonments. Men and women went to jail for years "on the basis of some of the most fantastic claims ever presented to an American jury," as Dorothy Rabinowitz of the *Wall Street Journal* demonstrated in a series of investigative articles for which she became a Pulitzer Prize finalist in 1996. Across the nation expensive surveillance programs were implemented to protect children from fiends who reside primarily in the imaginations of adults.[17]

The price tag for our panic about overall crime has grown so monumental that even law-and-order zealots find it hard to defend. The criminal justice system costs Americans close to $100 billion a year, most of which goes to police and prisons. In California we spend more on jails than on higher education. Yet increases in the number of police and prison cells do not correlate consistently with reductions in the number of serious crimes committed. Criminologists who study reductions in homicide rates, for instance, find little difference between cities that substantially expand their police forces and prison capacity and others that do not.' "

The turnabout in domestic public spending over the past quarter century, from child welfare and antipoverty programs to incarceration, did not even produce reductions in fear of crime. Increasing the number of cops and jails arguably has the opposite effect: it suggests that the crime problem is all the more out of control.[19]

Panic-driven public spending generates over the long term a pathology akin to one found in drug addicts. The more money and attention we fritter away on our compulsions, the less we have available for our real needs, which consequently grow larger. While fortunes are being spent to protect children from dangers that few ever encounter, approximately 11 million children lack health insurance, 12 million are malnourished, and rates of illiteracy are increasing.[20]

I do not contend, as did President Roosevelt in 1933, that "the only thing we have to fear is fear itself." My point is that we often fear the wrong things. In the 1990s middle-income and poorer Americans should have worried about unemployment insurance, which covered a smaller share of workers than twenty years earlier. Many of us have had friends or family out of work during economic downturns or as a result of corporate restructuring. Living in a nation with one of the largest income gaps of any industrialized country, where the bottom 40 percent of the population is worse off financially than their counterparts two decades earlier, we might also have worried about income inequality. Or poverty. During the midand late 1990s 5 million elderly Americans had no food in their homes, more than 20 million people used emergency food programs each year, and one in five children lived in poverty—more than a quarter million of them homeless. All told, a larger proportion of Americans were poor than three decades earlier.[21]

One of the paradoxes of a culture of fear is that serious problems remain widely ignored even though they give rise to precisely the dangers that the populace most abhors. Poverty, for example, correlates strongly with child abuse, crime, and drug abuse. Income inequality is also associated with adverse outcomes for society as a whole. The larger the gap between rich and poor in a society, the higher its overall death rates from heart disease, cancer, and murder. Some social scientists argue that extreme inequality also threatens political stability in a nation such as the United States, where we think of ourselves not as "haves and have nots" but as "haves and will haves." "Unlike the citizens of most other nations, Americans have always been united less by a shared past than by the shared dreams of a better future. If we lose that common future," the Brandeis University economist Robert Reich has suggested, "we lose the glue that holds our nation together."[22]

The combination of extreme inequality and poverty can prove explosive. In an insightful article in *U.S. News & World Report* in 1997 about militia groups reporters Mike Tharp and William Holstein noted that people's motivations for joining these groups are as much economic as ideological. The journalists argued that the disappearance of military and blue-collar jobs, along with the decline of family farming, created the conditions under which a new breed of protest groups flourished. "What distinguishes these antigovernment groups from, say, traditional conservatives who mistrust government is that their anger is fueled by direct threats to their livelihood, and they carry guns," Tharp and Holstein wrote.[23]

That last phrase alludes to a danger that by any rational calculation deserves top billing on Americans' lists of fears. So gun crazed is this nation that Burger King had to order a Baltimore franchise to stop giving away coupons from a local sporting goods store for free boxes of bullets with the purchase of guns, We have more guns stolen from their owners—about 300,000 annually—than many countries have gun owners. In Great Britain, Australia, and Japan, where gun ownership is severely restricted, no more than a few dozen people are killed each year by handguns. In the United States, where private citizens own a quarter-billion guns, around 15,000 people are killed, 18,000 commit suicide, and another 1,500 die accidentally from firearms. American children are twelve times more liked to die from gun injuries than are youngsters in other industrialized nations.[24]

Yet even after tragedies that could not have occurred except for the availability of guns, their significance is either played down or missed altogether. Had the youngsters in the celebrated schoolyard shootings of 1997–98 not had access to guns, some or all of the people they killed would be alive today. Without their firepower those boys lacked the strength, courage, and skill to commit multiple murders. Nevertheless newspapers ran editorials with titles such as "It's Not Guns, It's Killer Kids" (*Fort Worth Star-Telegram*) and "Guns Aren't the Problem" (*New York Post*), and journalists, politicians, and pundits blathered on endlessly about every imaginable cause of youthful rage, from "the psychology of violence in the South" to satanism to fights on *Jerry Springer* and simulated shooting in Nintendo games.[25]

TWO EASY EXPLANATIONS

In the following discussion I will try to answer two questions: Why are Americans so fearful lately, and why are our fears so often misplaced? To both questions the same two-word answer is commonly given by scholars and journalists: premillennial tensions. The final years of a millennium and the early years of a new millennium provoke mass anxiety and ill reasoning, the argument goes. So momentous does the calendric change seem, the populace cannot keep its wits about it.

Premillennial tensions probably do help explain some of our collective irrationality. Living in a scientific era, most of us grant the arbitrariness of reckoning time in base-ten rather than, say, base twelve, and from the birth of Christ rather than from the day Muhammad moved from Mecca. Yet even the least superstitious among us cannot quite manage to think of the year 2000 as ordinary.

Social psychologists have long recognized a human urge to convert vague uneasiness into definable concerns, real or imagined. In a classic study thirty years ago Alan Kerckhoff and Kurt Back pointed out that "the belief in a tangible threat makes it possible to explain and justify one's sense of discomfort."[26]

Some historical evidence also supports the hypothesis that people panic at the brink of centuries and millennia. Witness the "panic terror" in Europe around the year 1000 and the witch hunts in Salem in the 1690s. As a complete or dependable explanation, though, the millennium hypothesis fails. Historians emphasize that panics of equal or greater intensity occur in odd years, as demonstrated by anti-Indian hysteria in the mid 1700s and McCarthyism in the 1950s. Scholars point out, too, that calendars cannot account for why certain fears occupy people at certain times (witches then, killer kids now).[27]

Another popular explanation blames the news media. We have so many fears, many of them offbase, the argument goes, because the media bombard us with sensationalistic stories designed to increase ratings. This explanation, sometimes called the media-effects theory, is less simplistic than the millennium hypothesis and contains sizable kernels of truth. When researchers from Emory University computed the levels of coverage of various health dangers in popular magazines and newspapers they discovered an inverse relationship: much less space was devoted to several of the major causes of death than to some uncommon causes. The leading cause of death, heart disease, received approximately the same amount of coverage as the eleventh-ranked cause of death, homicide. They found a similar inverse relationship in coverage of risk factors associated with serious illness and death. The lowest-ranking risk factor, drug use, received nearly as much attention as the second-ranked risk factor, diet and exercise.[28]

Disproportionate coverage in the news media plainly has effects on readers and viewers. When Esther Madriz, a professor at Hunter College, interviewed women in New York City about their fears of crime they frequently responded with the phrase "I saw it in the news." The interviewees identified the news media as both the source of their fears and the reason they believed those fears were valid. Asked in a national poll why they believe the country has a serious crime problem, 76 percent of people cited stories they had seen in the media. Only 22 percent cited personal experience.[29]

When professors Robert Blendon and John Young of Harvard analyzed forty-seven surveys about drug abuse conducted between 1978 and 1997, they, too discovered that the news media, rather than personal experience, provide Americans with their predominant fears. Eight out of ten adults say that drug abuse has never caused problems in their family, and the vast majority report relatively little direct experience with problems related to drug abuse. Widespread concern about drug problems emanates, Blendon and Young determined, from scares in the news media, television in particular.[30]

Television news programs survive on scares. On local newscasts, where producers live by the dictum "if it bleeds, it leads," drug, crime, and disaster stories make up most of the news portion of the broadcasts. Evening newscasts on the major networks are somewhat less bloody, but between 1990 and 1998, when the nation's murder rate declined by 20 percent, the number of murder stories on network newscasts increased 600 percent (not counting stories about O. J. Simpson).[31]

After the dinnertime newscasts the networks broadcast newsmagazines, whose guiding principle seems to be that no danger is too small to magnify into a national nightmare. Some of the risks reported by such programs would be merely laughable were they not hyped with so much fanfare: "Don't miss Dateline tonight or YOU could be the next victim!" Competing for ratings with drama programs and movies during prime-time evening hours, newsmagazines feature story lines that would make a writer for *Homicide* or *ER* wince.[32]

"It can happen in a flash. Fire breaks out on the operating table. The patient is surrounded by flames," Barbara Walters exclaimed on ABC's *20/20* in 1998. The problem—oxygen from a face mask ignited by a surgical instrument— occurs "more often than you might think," she cautioned in her introduction, even though reporter Arnold Diaz would note later, during the actual report, that out of twenty-seven million surgeries each year the situation arises only about a hundred times. No matter, Diaz effectively nullified the reassuring numbers as soon as they left his mouth. To those who "may say it's too small a risk to worry about" he presented distraught victims: a woman with permanent scars on her face and a man whose son had died.[33]

The gambit is common. Producers of TV news magazines routinely let emotional accounts trump objective information. In 1994 medical authorities attempted to cut short the brouhaha over flesh-eating bacteria by publicizing the fact that an American is fifty-five times more like to be struck by lightning than die of the suddenly celebrated microbe. Yet TV journalists brushed this fact aside with remarks like, "whatever the statistics, it's devastating to the victims" (Catherine Crier on *20/20*), accompanied by stomach-turning videos of disfigured patients.[34]

Sheryl Stolberg, then a medical writer for the *Los Angeles Times*, put her finger on what makes the TV newsmagazines so cavalier: "Killer germs are perfect for prime time," she wrote. "They are invisible, uncontrollable, and, in the case of Group A strep, can invade the body in an unnervingly simple manner, through a cut or scrape." Whereas print journalists only described in words the actions of "billions of bacteria" spreading "like underground fires" throughout a person's body, TV newsmagazines made use of special effects to depict graphically how these "merciless killers" do their damage.[35]

IN PRAISE OF JOURNALISTS

Any analysis of the culture of fear that ignored the news media would be patently incomplete, and of the several institutions most culpable for creating and sustaining scares the news media are arguably first among equals. They are also the most promising candidates for positive change. Yet by the same token critiques such as Stolberg's presage a crucial shortcoming in arguments that blame the media. Reporters not only spread fears, they also debunk them and criticize one another for spooking the public. A wide array of groups, including businesses, advocacy organizations, religious sects, and political parties, promote and profit from scares. News organizations are distinguished from other fear-mongering groups because they sometimes bite the scare that feeds them.

A group that raises money for research into a particular disease is not likely to negate concerns about that disease. A company that sells alarm systems is not about to call attention to the fact that crime is down. News organizations, on the other hand, periodically allay the very fears they arouse to lure audiences. Some newspapers that ran stories about child murderers, rather than treat every incident as evidence of a shocking trend, affirmed the opposite. After the school-yard shooting in Kentucky the *New York Times* ran a sidebar alongside its feature story with the headline "Despite Recent Carnage, School Violence Is Not on Rise." Following the Jonesboro killings they ran a similar piece, this time on a recently released study showing the rarity of violent crimes in schools.[36]

Several major newspapers parted from the pack in other ways. *USA Today* and the *Washington Post*, for instance, made sure their readers knew that what should worry them is the availability of guns. *USA Today* ran news stories explaining that easy access to guns in homes accounted for increases in the number of juvenile arrests for homicide in rural areas during the 1990s. While other news outlets were respectfully quoting the mother of the thirteen-year-old Jonesboro shooter, who said she did not regret having encouraged her son to learn to fire a gun ("it's like anything else, there's some people that can drink a beer and not become an alcoholic"), *USA Today* ran an op-ed piece proposing legal parameters for gun ownership akin to those for the use of alcohol and motor vehicles. And the paper published its own editorial in support of laws that require gun owners to lock their guns or keep them in locked containers. Adopted at that time by only fifteen states, the laws had reduced the number of deaths among children in those states by 23 percent.[37]

The *Washington Post*, meanwhile, published an excellent investigative piece by reporter Sharon Walsh showing that guns increasingly were being marketed to teenagers and children. Quoting advertisements and statistics from gun man-ufacturers and the National Rifle Association, Walsh revealed that by 1998 the primary market for guns—white males—had been saturated and an effort to market to women had failed. Having come to see children as its future, the gun industry has taken to running ads like the one Walsh found in a Smith & Wesson catalog: "Seems like only yesterday that your father brought you here for the first time," reads the copy beside a photo of a child aiming a handgun, his father by his side. "Those sure were the good times—just you, dad and his Smith & Wesson."[38] . . .

MORALITY AND MARKETING

To blame the media is to oversimplify the complex role that journalists play as both proponents and doubters of popular fears. It is also to beg the same key issue that the millennium hypothesis evades: why particular anxieties take hold when they do. Why do news organizations and their audiences find themselves drawn to one hazard rather than another?

Mary Douglas, the eminent anthropologist who devoted much of her career to studying how people interpret risk, pointed out that every society has an almost infinite quantity of potential dangers from which to choose. Societies differ both in the types of dangers they select and the number. Dangers get selected for special emphasis, Douglas showed, either because they offend the basic moral principles of the society or because they enable criticism of disliked groups and institutions. In *Risk and Culture*, a book she wrote with Aaron Wildavsky, the authors give an example from fourteenth-century Europe. Impure water had been a health danger long before that time, but only after it became convenient to accuse Jews of poisoning the wells did people become preoccupied with it.

Or take a more recent institutional example. In the first half of the 1990s U.S. cities spent at least $10 billion to purge asbestos from public schools, even though removing asbestos from buildings posed a greater health hazard than leaving it in place. At a time when about one-third of the nation's schools were in need of extensive repairs the money might have been spent to renovate dilapidated buildings. But hazards posed by seeping asbestos are morally repugnant. A product that was supposed to protect children from fires might be giving them cancer. By directing our worries and dollars at asbestos we express outrage at technology and industry run afoul.[39]

From a psychological point of view extreme fear and outrage are often projections. Consider, for example, the panic over violence against children. By failing to provide adequate education, nutrition, housing, parenting, medical services, and child care over the past couple of decades we have done the nation's children immense harm. Yet we project our guilt onto a cavalcade of bogeypeople-pedophile preschool teachers, preteen mass murderers, and homicidal au pairs, to name only a few.[40]

When Debbie Nathan, a journalist, and Michael Snedeker, an attorney, researched the evidence behind publicized reports in the 1980s and early 1990s of children being ritually raped and tortured they learned that although seven out of ten Americans believed that satanic cults were committing these atrocities, few of the incidents had actually occurred. At the outset of each ritual-abuse case the children involved claimed they had not been molested. They later changed their tunes at the urging of parents and law enforcement authorities. The ghastly tales of abuse, it turns out, typically came from the parents themselves, usually the mothers, who had convinced themselves they were true. Nathan and Snedeker suggest that some of the mothers had been abused themselves and projected those horrors, which they had trouble facing directly, onto their children. Other mothers, who had not been victimized in those ways, used the figure of ritually abused children as a medium of protest against male dominance more generally. Allegations of children being raped allowed conventional wives and mothers to speak out against men and masculinity without having to fear they would seem unfernninine. "The larger culture," Nathan and Snedeker note, "still required that women's complaints about inequality and sexual violence be communicated through the innocent, mortified voice of the child."

Diverse groups used the ritual-abuse scares to diverse ends. Well-known feminists such as Gloria Steinem and Catharine MacKinnon took up the cause, depicting ritually abused children as living proof of the ravages of patriarchy and the need for fundamental social reform.[41]

This was far from the only time feminist spokeswomen have mongered fears about sinister breeds of men who exist in nowhere near the high numbers they allege. Another example occurred a few years ago when teen pregnancy was much in the news. Feminists helped popularize the frightful but erroneous statistic that two out of three teen mothers had been seduced and abandoned by adult men. The true figure is more like one in ten, but some feminists continued to cultivate the scare well after the bogus stat had been definitively debunked.[42]

Within public discourse fears proliferate through a process of exchange. It is from crosscurrents of scares and counterscares that the culture of fear swells ever larger. Even as feminists disparage large classes of men, they themselves are a staple of fear mongering by conservatives. To hear conservatives tell it, feminists are not only "antichild and antifamily" (Arianna Huffington) but through women's studies programs on college campuses they have fomented an "antiscience and antireason movement" (Christina Hoff Sommers).[43]

Conservatives also like to spread fears about liberals, who respond in kind. Among other pet scares, they accuse liberals of creating "children without consciences" by keeping prayer out of schools-to which liberals rejoin with warnings that right-wing extremists intend to turn youngsters into Christian soldiers.[44]

Samuel Taylor Coleridge was right when he claimed, "In politics, what begins in fear usually ends up in folly." Political activists are more inclined, though, to heed an observation from Richard Nixon: "People react to fear, not love. They don't teach that in Sunday school, but it's true." That principle, which guided the late president's political strategy throughout his career, is the sine qua non of contemporary political campaigning. Marketers of products and services ranging from car alarms to TV news programs have taken it to heart as well.[45]

The short answer to why Americans harbor so many misbegotten fears is that immense power and money await those who tap into our moral insecurities and supply us with symbolic substitutes.

NOTES

1. Crime data here and throughout are from reports of the Bureau of Justice Statistics unless otherwise noted. Fear of crime: Esther Madriz, *Nothing Bad Happens to Good Girls* (Berkeley: University of California Press, 1997), chap. 1; Richard Morin, "As Crime Rate Falls, Fears Persist," *Washington Post National Edition*, 16 June 1997, p. 35; David Whitman, "Believing the Good News," *U.S. News & World Report*, 5 January 1998, pp. 45–46.

2. Eva Bertram, Morris Blachman et al., *Drug War Politics* (Berkeley: University of California Press, 1996), p. 10; Mike Males, Scapegoat Generation (Monroe, Maine: Common Courage Press, 1996), chap. 6; Karen Peterson, "Survey: Teen Drug Use Declines," *USA Today*, 19 June 1998, p. A6; Robert Blendon and John Young, "The Public and the War on Illicit Drugs," *Journal of the American Medical Association* 279 (March 18, 1998): 827–32. In presenting these statistics and others I am aware of a seeming paradox: I criticize the abuse of statistics by fearmongering politicians, journalists, and others but hand down precise-sounding numbers myself. Yet to eschew all estimates because some are used inappropriately or do not withstand scrutiny would be as foolhardy as ignoring all medical advice because some doctors are quacks. Readers can be assured I have interrogated the statistics presented here as factual. As notes throughout the book make clear, I have tried to rely on research that appears in peer-reviewed scholarly journals. Where this was not possible or sufficient, I traced numbers back to their sources, investigated the research methodology utilized to produce them, or conducted searches of the popular and scientific literature for critical commentaries and conflicting findings.

3. Bob Herbert, "Bogeyman Economics," *New York Times*, 4 April 1997, p. A15; Doug Henwood, "Alarming Drop in Unemployment," *Extra*, September 1994, pp. 16–17; Christopher Shea, "Low Inflation and Low Unemployment Spur Economists to Debate 'Natural Rate' Theory," *Chronicle of Higher Education*, 24 October 1997, p. A13.

4. Bob Garfield, "Maladies by the Millions," *USA Today*, 16 December 1996, p. A15.

5. Jim Windolf, "A Nation of Nuts," *Wall Street Journal*, 22 October 1997, p. A22.

6. Andrew Ferguson, "Road Rage," *Time*, 12 January 1998, pp. 64–68; Joe Sharkey, "You're Not Bad, You're Sick. It's in the Book," *New York Times*, 28 September 1997, pp. Nl, 5.

7. Malcolm Dean, "Flesh-eating Bugs Scare," *Lancet* 343 (4 June 1994): 1418; "Flesheating Bacteria," *Science* 264 (17 June 1994): 1665; David Brown, "The Flesh-eating Bug," *Washington Post National Edition*, 19 December 1994, p. 34; Sarah Richardson, "Tabloid Strep," Discover (January 1995): 71; Liz Hunt, "What's Bugging Us," *The Independent*, 28 May 1994, p. 25; Lisa Seachrist, "The Once and Future Scourge," *Science News* 148 (October 7, 1995): 234–35. Quotes are from Bernard Dixon, "A Rampant Non-epidemic," *British Medical Journal* 308 (June 11, 1994): 1576–77; and Michael Lemonick and Leon Jaroff, "The Killers All Around," *Time*, 12 September 1994, pp. 62–69. More recent coverage: "Strep A Involved in Baby's Death," UPI, 27 February 1998; see also, e.g., Steve Carney, "Miracle Mom," *Los Angeles Times*, 4 March 1998, p. A6; KTLA, "News at Ten," 28 March 1998.

8. Jim Naureckas, "The Jihad That Wasn't," *Extra*, July 1995, pp. 6–10, 20 (contains quotes). See also Edward Said, "A Devil Theory of Islam," *Nation*, 12 August 1996, pp. 28–32.

9. Lewis Lapham, "Seen but Not Heard," *Harper's*, July 1995, pp. 29–36 (contains Clinton quote). See also Robin Wright and Ronald Ostrow, "Illusion of Immunity Is Shattered," *Los Angeles Times*, 20 April 1995, pp. A1, 18; Jack Germond and Jules Witcover, "Making the Angry White Males Angrier," column syndicated by Tribune Media Services, May 1995; and articles by James Bennet and Michael Janofsky in the *New York Times*, May 1995.

10. Tom Morganthau, "The Lull Before the Storm?" *Newsweek*, 4 December 1995, pp. 40–42; Mike Males, "Wild in Deceit," *Extra*, March 1996, pp. 7–9; *Progressive*, July 1997, p. 9 (contains Clinton quote); Robin Templeton, "First, We Kill All the 11-Year-Olds," *Salon*, 27 May 1998.

11. Statistics from "Violence and Discipline Problems in U.S. Public Schools: 1996–97," National Center on Education Statistics, U.S. Department of Education, Washington, D.C., March

1998; CNN, "Early Prime," 2 December 1997; and Tamar Lewin, "Despite Recent Carnage, School Violence Is Not on Rise," *New York Times*, 3 December 1997, p. A14. Headlines: *Time*, 15 January 1996; *U.S. News & World Report*, 25 March 1996; Margaret Carlson, "Children Without Souls," *Time*, 2 December 1996, p. 70. William J. Bennett, John J. Dilulio, and John Walters, *Body Count* (New York: Simon & Schuster, 1996).

12. CNN, *Talkback Live*, 2 December 1997; CNN, *The Geraldo Rivera Show*, 11 December 1997; Richard Lacayo, "Toward the Root of Evil," *Time*, 6 April 1998, pp. 38–39; NBC, *Today*, 25 March 1998. See also Rick Bragg, "Forgiveness, After 3 Die in Shootings in Kentucky," *New York Times*, 3 December 1997, p. A14; Maureen Downey, "Kids and Violence," 28 March 1998, *Atlanta Journal and Constitution*, p. A 12.

13. Jocelyn Stewart, "Schools Learn to Take Threats More Seriously," *Los Angeles Times*, 2 May 1998, pp. Al, 17, "Kindergarten Student Faces Gun Charges," *New York Times*, 11 May 1998, p. A11; Rick Bragg, "Jonesboro Dazed by Its Darkest Day" and "Past Victims Relive Pain as Tragedy Is Repeated," *New York Times*, 18 April 1998, p. A7, and idem, 25 May 1998, p. A8. Remaining quotes are from Tamar Lewin, "More Victims and Less Sense in Shootings," *New York Times*, 22 May 1998, p. A20; NPR, "All Things Considered," 22 May 1998, NBC, *Today*, 25 March 1998. See also Mike Males, "Who's Really Killing Our Schoolkids," *Los Angeles Times*, 31 May 1998, pp. M1, 3; Michael Sniffen, "Youth Crime Fell in 1997, Reno Says," Associated Press, 20 November 1998.

14. Overestimation of breast cancer: Willam C. Black et al., "Perceptions of Breast Cancer Risk and Screening Effectiveness in Women Younger Than 50," *Journal of the National Cancer Institute* 87 (1995): 720–31; B. Smith et al., "Perception of Breast Cancer Risk Among Women in Breast and Family History of Breast Cancer," *Surgery* 120 (1996): 297–303. Fear and avoidance: Steven Berman and Abraham Wandersman, "Fear of Cancer and Knowledge of Cancer," *Social Science and Medicine* 31 (1990): 81–90; S. Benedict et al., "Breast Cancer Detection by Daughters of Women with Breast Cancer," *Cancer Practice* 5 (1997): 213–19; M. Muir et al., "Health Promotion and Early Detection of Cancer in Older Adults," *Cancer Oncology Nursing Journal* 7 (1997): 82–89. For a conflicting finding see Kevin McCaul et al., "Breast Cancer Worry and Screening," *Health Psychology* 15 (1996): 430–33.

15. Philip Jenkins, *Pedophiles and Priests* (New York: Oxford University Press, 1996), see esp. chap. 10; Debbie Nathan and Michael Snedeker, *Satan's Silence* (New York: Basic Books, 1995), see esp. chap. 6; Jeffrey Victor, "The Danger of Moral Panics," *Skeptic* 3 (1995): 44–51. See also Noelle Oxenhandler, "The Eros of Parenthood," *Family Therapy Networker* (May 1996): 17–19.

16. Mary DeYoung, "The Devil Goes to Day Care," *Journal of American Culture* 20 (1997): 19–25.

17. Dorothy Rabinowitz, "A Darkness in Massachusetts," *Wall Street Journal*, 30 January 1995, p. A20 (contains quote); "Back in Wenatchee" (unsigned editorial), *Wall Street Journal*, 20 June 1996, p. A18; Dorothy Rabinowitz, "Justice in Massachusetts," *Wall Street Journal*, 13 May 1997, p. A19. See also Nathan and Snedeker, *Satan's Silence*; James Beaver, "The Myth of Repressed Memory," *Journal of Criminal Law and Criminology* 86 (1996): 596–607; Kathryn Lyon, *Witch Hunt* (New York: Avon, 1998); Pam Belluck, " 'Memory' Therapy Leads to a Lawsuit and Big Settlement" *New York Times*, 6 November 1997, pp. Al, 10.

18. Elliott Currie, *Crime and Punishment in America* (New York: Metropolitan, 1998); Tony Pate et al., *Reducing Fear of Crime in Houston and Newark* (Washington, D C: Police Foundation, 1986); Steven Donziger, *The Real War on Crime* (New York: HarperCollins, 1996); Christina Johns, *Power, Ideology, and the War on Drugs* (New York: Praeger, 1992); John Irwin et al., "Fanning the Flames of Fear," Crime and Delinquency 44 (1998): 32–48.

19. Steven Donziger, "Fear, Crime and Punishment in the U.S.," *Tikkun* 12 (1996): 24–27, 77.

20. Peter Budetti, "Health Insurance for Children," *New England Journal of Medicine* 338 (1998): 541–42; Eileen Smith, "Drugs Top Adult Fears for Kids' Well-being," *USA Today*, 9 December 1997, p. DI. Literacy statistic: Adult Literacy Service.

21. "The State of America's Children," report by the Children's Defense Fund, Washington,

D.C., March 1998; "Blocks to Their Future," report by the National Law Center on Homelessness and Poverty, Washington, D.C., September 1997; reports released in 1998 from the National Center for Children in Poverty, Columbia University, New York; Douglas Massey, "The Age of Extremes," *Demography* 33 (1996): 395–412; Trudy Lieberman, "Hunger in America," *Nation*, 30 March 1998, pp. 11–16; David Lynch, "Rich Poor World," *USA Today*, 20 September 1996, p. Bl; Richard Wolf, "Good Economy Hasn't Helped the Poor," *USA Today*, 10 March 1998, p. A3; Robert Reich, "Broken Faith," *Nation*, 16 February 1998, pp. 11–17

22. Inequality and mortality studies: Bruce Kennedy et al., "Income Distribution and Mortality," *British Medical Journal* 312 (1996): 100–47; Ichiro Kawachi and Bruce Kennedy, "The Relationship of Income Inequality to Mortality," *Social Science and Medicine* 45 (1997): 112–27. See also Barbara Chasin, *Inequality and Violence in the United States* (Atlantic Highlands, N.J.: Humanities Press, 1997). Political stability: John Sloan, "The Reagan Presidency, Growing Inequality, and the American Dream," *Policy Studies Journal* 25 (1997): 371–86 (contains Reich quotes and "will haves" phrase). On both topics see also Philippe Bourgois, *In Search of Respect: Selling Crack in El Barrio* (Cambridge: Cambridge University Press, 1996); William J. Wilson, *When Work Disappears* (New York: Knopf, 1996); Richard Gelles, "Family Violence," *Annual Review of Sociology* 11 (1985): 347–67; Sheldon Danziger and Peter Gottschalk, America Unequal (Cambridge, Mass.: Harvard University Press, 1995); Claude Fischer et al., Inequality by Design (Princeton, N.J.: Princeton University Press, 1996).

23. Mike Tharp and William Holstein, "Mainstreaming the Militia," *U.S. News & World Report*, 21 April 1997, pp. 24–37

24. Burger King: "Notebooks," *New Republic*, 29 April 1996, p. 8. Statistics from the FBI's Uniform Crime Reports, Centers for Disease Control Reports, and Timothy Egan, "Oregon Freeman Goes to Court," *New York Times*, 23 May 1998, pp. Al, 8.

25. Bill Thompson, "It's Not Guns, It's Killer Kids," *Fort Worth Star-Telegram*, 31 March 1998, p. 14; "Guns Aren't the Problem," *New York Post* 30 March 1998 (from *Post* Web site), "Arkansas Gov. Assails 'Culture of Violence,' " Reuters, 25 March 1998; Bo Emerson, "Violence Feeds 'Redneck,' Gun-Toting Image," *Atlanta Journal and Constitution*, 29 March 1998, p. A8; Nadya Labi, "The Hunter and the Choir Boy," *Time*, 6 April 1998, pp. 28–37; Lacayo, "Toward the Root of Evil."

26. Alan Kerckhoff and Kurt Back, *The June Bug* (New York: Appleton-Century-Crofts, 1968), see esp. pp. 160–61.

27. Stephen Jay Gould, *Questioning the Millennium* (New York: Crown, 1997); Todd Gitlin, "Millennial Mumbo Jumbo," *Los Angeles Times Book Review*, 27 April 1997, p. 8.

28. Karen Frost, Erica Frank et al., "Relative Risk in the News Media," *American Journal of Public Health* 87 (1997): 842–45. Mediaeffects theory: Nancy Signorielli and Michael Morgan, eds., Cultivation Analysis (Newbury Park, Calif.: Sage, 1990); Jennings Bryant and Dolf Zillman, eds., Media Effects (Hillsdale, N.J.: Erlbaum, 1994); Ronald Jacobs, "Producing the News, Producing the Crisis," *Media, Culture, and Society* 18 (1996): 373–97

29. Madriz, *Nothing Bad Happens to Good Girls*, see esp. pp. 111–14; David Whitman and Margaret Loftus, "Things Are Getting Better? Who Knew," *U.S. News & World Report*, 16 December 1996, pp. 30–32.

30. Blendon and Young, "War on Illicit Drugs." See also Ted Chiricos et al., "Crime, News, and Fear of Crime," *Social Problems* 44 (1997): 342–57.

31. Steven Stark, "Local News: The Biggest Scandal on TV," *Washington Monthly* (June 1997): 38–41; Barbara Bliss Osborn, "If It Bleeds, It Leads," *Extra*, September–October 1994, p. 15; Jenkins, *Pedophiles and Priests*, pp. 68–71; "It's Murder," *USA Today*, 20 April 1998, p, 132; Lawrence Grossman, "Does Local TV News Need a National Nanny?" *Columbia Journalism Review* (May 1998): 33.

32. Regarding fearmongering by news magazines, see also Elizabeth Jensen et al., "Consumer Alert," *Brill's Content* (October 1998): 130–47.

33. ABC, *20/20*, 16 March 1998.

34. Thomas Maugh, "Killer Bacteria a Rarity," *Los Angeles Times*, 3 December 1994, p. A29;

Ed Siegel, "Roll Over, Ed Murrow," *Boston Globe*, 21 August 1994, p. 14. Crier quote from ABC's *20/20*, 24 June 1994.

35. Sheryl Stolberg, "'Killer Bug' Perfect for Prime Time," *Los Angeles Times*, 15 June 1994, pp. Al, 30–31. Quotes from Brown, "Flesheating Bug"; and Michael Lemonick and Leonjaroff, "The Killers All Around," *Time*, 12 September 1994, pp. 62–69.

36. Lewin, "More Victims and Less Sense"; Tamar Lewin, "Study Finds No Big Rise in Public-School Crimes," *New York Times*, 25 March 1998, p. A18.

37. "Licensing Can Protect," *USA Today*, 7 April 1998, p. A11; Jonathan Kellerman, "Few Surprises When It Comes to Violence," *USA Today*, 27 March 1998, p. A13; Gary Fields, "Juvenile Homicide Arrest Rate on Rise in Rural USA," *USA Today*, 26 March 1998, p. A11; Karen Peterson and Glenn O'Neal, "Society More Violent, So Are Its Children," *USA Today*, 25 March 1998, p. A3; Scott Bowles, "Armed, Alienated, and Adolescent," *USA Today*, 26 March 1998, p. A9. Similar suggestions about guns appear in Jonathan Alter, "Harnessing the Hysteria," *Newsweek* 6 April 1998, p. 27.

38. Sharon Walsh, "Gun Sellers Look to Future-Children," *Washington Post*, 28 March 1998, pp. A1, 2.

39. Mary Douglas and Aaron Wildavsky, *Risk and Culture* (Berkeley: University of California Press, 1982), see esp. pp. 6–9; Mary Douglas, *Risk and Blame* (London: Routledge, 1992). See also Mary Douglas, Purity and Danger (New York: Praeger, 1966). Asbestos and schools: Peter Cary, "The Asbestos Panic Attack," *U.S. News & World Report*, 20 February 1995, pp. 61–64; Children's Defense Fund, "State of America's Children."

40. See Marina Warner, "Peroxide Mug-shot," *London Review of Books*, 1 January 1998, pp. 10–11.

41. Nathan and Snedeker, *Satan's Silence* (quote from p. 240). See also David Bromley, "Satanism: The New Cult Scare," in *The Satanism Scare*, ed. James Richardson et al. (Hawthorne, N.Y.: Aldine de Gruyter, 1991), pp. 49–71.

42. Of girls ages fifteen to seventeen who gave birth, fewer than one in ten were unmarried and had been made pregnant by men at least five years older. See Steven Holmes, "It's Awful, It's Terrible, It's . . . Never Mind," *New York Times*, 6 July 1997, p. E3.

43. CNN, "Crossfire," 27 August 1995 (contains Huffington quote); Ruth Conniff, "Warning: Feminism Is Hazardous to Your Health," *Progressive*, April 1997, pp. 33–36 (contains Sommers quote). See also Susan Faludi, *Backlash* (New York: Crown, 1991); Deborah Rhode, "Media Images, Feminist Issues," *Signs* 20 (1995): 685–710; Paula Span, "Did Feminists Forget the Most Crucial Issues?" *Los Angeles Times*, 28 November 1996, p. E8.

44. See Katha Pollitt, "Subject to Debate," *Nation*, 26 December 1994, p. 788, and idem, 20 November 1995, p. 600.

45. Henry Nelson Coleridge, ed., *Specimens of the Table Talk of the Late Samuel Taylor Coleridge* (London: J. Murray, 1935), entry for 5 October 1830. Nixon quote cited in William Safire, *Before the Fall* (New York: Doubleday, 1975), prologue.

11

RISKY BUSINESS
VIVIDNESS, AVAILABILITY, AND THE MEDIA PARADOX

JOHN RUSCIO

D o you believe that more people die in the United States each year from falling airplane parts or from shark attacks? From tornadoes or from lightning? From stomach cancer or from car accidents? From diabetes or from homicide? When we evaluate the relative degree of danger associated with different hazards, we can easily overlook two subtle biases in the sample of information that comes to mind. First, the popular media report to us, in vivid detail, a carefully selected assortment of unusual events. Second, vivid and unusual events exert a disproportionate influence on our subsequent judgments through their increased memorial availability. These two biases operate hand-in-hand to create what I call the "media paradox": The more we rely on the popular media to inform us, the more apt we are to misplace our fears.

In one widely cited study, college students ranked nuclear power as the most dangerous of thirty different activities and technologies. Experts in risk assessment, on the other hand, ranked nuclear power twentieth on the same list, less hazardous than riding a bicycle (Slovic, Fischhoff, and Lichtenstein 1979). Ross (1995) reviews several serious misperceptions of risk and poses the critical question, "Are we then turning our backs on a raging inferno while we douse the flame of a match?" (53).

From *Skeptical Inquirer* (March/April 2000): 22–26.

VIVIDNESS

Many of us rely on the popular media (television, radio, newspapers, magazines, the Internet, and so forth) for daily information to help navigate the hazards in the world around us. These sources, however, do not provide us with a representative sampling of events. For a variety of reasons—including fierce competition for our patronage within and across the various popular media outlets—potential news items are rigorously screened for their ability to captivate an audience. Stories featuring mundane, commonplace events don't stand a chance of making it onto the six o'clock news. The stories that do make it through this painstaking selection process are then crafted into accounts emphasizing their concrete, personal, and emotional content. Each of these aspects of a story promotes its vividness, which increases the likelihood that we will attend to and remember the information (Nisbett and Ross 1980; Plous 1993).

Both anecdotal and empirical evidence demonstrates the impact of vividness. Imagine that you are in the market for a new car, and you turn to *Consumer Reports* for advice.[1] Several hundred consumers' experiences, plus the opinions and road tests of automotive experts, are neatly summarized, and it appears that the cost and reliability of a Honda Civic will best meet your transportation needs. Before making a purchase, however, you happen to mention your decision to a colleague, who is shocked. "A Honda! You must be joking! A friend of mine bought one and had nothing but trouble. First the fuel injection system broke, then the brakes, and finally the transmission. He had to sell it for scrap within three years!" The vividness of this warning makes it quite compelling. How many of us can honestly say that we would treat it in a rationally appropriate manner, fairly weighing the favorable evidence from several hundred consumers plus a consensus of automotive experts against the unfavorable evidence from one second-hand account?

Of course, I would not expect to convince you of the significance of vividness with a single vivid example. Experimental investigations more definitively illustrate the impact of vivid information. For example, Borgida and Nisbett (1977) asked introductory psychology students to rate their interest in taking each of ten upper-level psychology courses. To help make these ratings, all students were randomly assigned to one of three informational conditions. Those in a "base rate" condition read a statistical summary of course evaluations from "practically all the students who had enrolled in the course the previous semester." A small panel of advanced students shared their views on the ten courses with participants in a "face-to-face" condition. The panelists prefaced their remarks by reporting the same average numerical evaluations that were provided in the statistical summary to "base rate" participants. Finally, participants in a control condition were given no information about the courses.

Compared to the control group, students receiving the statistical summary expressed slightly greater interest in the recommended courses. More important, students hearing the panel discussion expressed considerably greater interest in the recommended courses. The face-to-face presentation of information had a more pronounced impact on students' preferences than did the statistical summary of a far larger number of previous students' responses.[2] Moreover, this effect was stronger among students who had recently decided to major in psychology than among students who had declared other majors. Personal relevance appears to magnify the power of vividness.

The popular media capitalize on this power in many ways. Why, in a story on the effects of welfare reform on thousands of families across a state, does nine-tenths of the report consist of an interview with one affected individual? Why is the logic of "going beyond the statistics and onto the streets" to examine an issue persuasive to viewers, listeners, or readers? Producers are aware that a scientific analysis is not as emotionally compelling as one (carefully chosen) individual's personal experiences. Why does a television news reporter stand in front of a courthouse when sharing a landmark verdict reached earlier that day? Why does a weather correspondent endure frigid temperatures, sleet, and harsh wind on camera to inform us that a severe storm is in progress? Even superficial background elements appear to add a sense of realism and concreteness to a story.

AVAILABILITY

Having been exposed to a biased sample of vivid information through popular media outlets, what impact does this have on our subsequent decisions? Psychologists have discovered that our judgments of frequency and probability are heavily influenced by the ease with which we can imagine or recall instances of an event. Consider these two problems from the research literature. First, from among a group of ten people, are there more distinct ways to form a two-member or a five-member committee? Second, supposing that you have randomly sampled an English word from a text, is it more likely that it begins with the letter "k" or that "k" is its third letter?

Tversky and Kahneman (1973) found that participants in their studies systematically and predictably erred on both of these problems. In the first problem, it is perhaps easier to imagine forming smaller committees, which readily differ from one another, than larger ones, which overlap substantially. In fact, there are only forty-five ways to form two-member committees but 252 ways to form five-member committees. In the second problem, it is surely easier to bring to mind words that begin with "k" than words with "k" as the third letter, but extensive word-counts indicate that the latter outnumber the former by a ratio of roughly two to one. In fact, you might not have noticed that there have already been eleven words with "k" as the third letter in this article, but only one occurrence with "k" as the first letter and even that occurrence could be disqualified on the grounds that it was a proper name at the beginning of this paragraph, "Kahneman."

What these exercises reveal is that our judgments are indeed biased by the ease of imagining or recalling information. In everyday life, what makes one event more available in memory than another? One crucial determinant is vividness. When we search through our memory to reach a judgment of frequency or probability, the most easily retrieved instances are often those that are concrete, personal, and emotional. Students in the course selection experiment, for example, are more likely to remember the views expressed by panelists than the comparatively pallid statistical summaries. Likewise, a news report will leave a more lasting impression by documenting one individual's personal suffering than by providing a scientific argument based on "mere statistics."

Because our judgment is affected by the ease with which instances of an event can be recalled, rather than a careful evaluation of all the logically possible events weighted by their actual frequency of occurrence, the simple presence of one memory and absence of another can short-circuit a fully rational evaluation. We seldom take notice of *non-occurrences*, such as the *absence* of crime or accidents (Nisbett and Ross 1980). Still more rare are popular media reports on the absence of events—unless of course this absence itself represents a dramatic change from the status quo, as when a large city witnesses a significant drop in homicide rates. Richard Bach (1973) once wrote of a young couple's fear when they embarked on their first trip on an airplane:

> In all that wind and engine blast and earth tilting and going small below us, I watched my Wisconsin lad and his girl, to see them change. Despite their laughter, they had been afraid of the airplane. Their only knowledge of flight came from newspaper headlines, a knowledge of collisions and crashes and fatalities. They had never read a single report of a little airplane taking off, flying through the air and landing again safely. They could only believe that this must be possible, in spite of all the newspapers, and on that belief they staked their three dollars and their lives. (37)

THE MEDIA PARADOX

Bach's passage on a couples fear of flying highlights the joint operation of vividness and availability on our judgment, which ultimately results in the media paradox. We have likely all heard or read that, per mile traveled, flying is much safer than driving. Given this fact, media coverage of air travel catastrophes may actually steer us in the wrong direction: onto the more hazardous roadways. Indeed, a classic series of studies on the judged frequency of lethal events underscores the powerful impact that media coverage has on our perceptions of risk. College students and members of the League of Women Voters were asked to estimate the frequency with which forty-one causes of death occurred each year in the United States (Lichtenstein, Slovic, Fischhoff, Layman, and Combs 1978). Two systematic biases were uncovered in analyses of these judgments. First, frequencies of the least common causes of death were overestimated, whereas frequencies of the most common causes of death were underestimated.

In many cases, the judgments were off by more than an order of magnitude. Second, relative to the best-fitting curve that characterized the relationship between judged and actual frequencies across all forty-one causes of death, those that were overestimated tended to be the ones that received more extensive media coverage. For example, motor vehicle accidents and homicide were overestimated relative to the best-fitting curve, whereas smallpox vaccination and diabetes were underestimated.

Following up on this evidence that suggests a connection to the media, Combs and Slovic (1979) closely scrutinized the actual reporting of deaths in their regional newspapers (the Eugene, Oregon, *Register Guard* and the New Bedford, Massachusetts, *Standard Times*). During alternate months for one year, they counted the number of articles about, the number of occurrences of, and the number of reported deaths resulting from each of the forty-one causes of death. The two newspapers were almost perfectly consistent in their coverage of deaths (correlations across the causes of death were .98, .94, and .97 for the three indices listed above). This is interesting in that newspapers with vastly different readerships nonetheless still find certain types of deaths to be more "newsworthy" than others.[3] More important, there was an impressive correspondence between judged and reported frequencies of death, with a correlation of about .70. This substantial correlation was not due to a common link between both judged and reported frequencies with actual frequencies of death. In fact, when actual frequency was statistically held constant, the correlations were much higher, .89 and .85 for the two newspapers.

Tempting as it may be, however, we must be careful not to conclude on the basis of this correlational evidence alone that the media are necessarily responsible for distorting our perceptions of risk. It may be just the opposite: perhaps media professionals are simply responsive to our fears and interests, reporting what they perceive to be newsworthy to us. It may be that a "third variable"— such as the relative degree of controllability or the catastrophic nature inherent in different causes of death—causes both our fears and media coverage. A case can be made for each of these explanations for the observed link between media coverage and beliefs, as well as others, and the broad array of factors that are involved appear to be complexly intertwined.

Fortunately, however, we are in a position to evaluate this relationship armed with more than correlational evidence. Evidence from controlled experimentation shows a causal influence of vivid information on our judgments, and the additional causal influence of memorial availability on our judgments represents a likely mediator of the vividness effect. This knowledge makes it very difficult to deny that the media exerts some measure of causal influence on our fears. Debating the strength of this effect or whether it operates in a reciprocal fashion is certainly worthwhile, but it does not allow us to escape from the conclusion that any systematic departure from reality in the media is likely to be mirrored in our beliefs.

FALLING AIRPLANE PARTS REVISITED

Aside from a close miss by what was reported to be a falling airplane part early in *The Truman Show*, I cannot personally recall ever having heard of such an incident, fictitious or real. Students over the years have told me that they recall stories of people having *found* fallen airplane parts, but not of an actual fatality resulting from such falling parts. Shark attacks, on the other hand, are easily imagined and widely reported. Moreover, in the first movie that comes to my mind, the shark in *Jaws* actually did cause several fatalities. It may come as some surprise, then, to learn that in an average year in the United States thirty times more people are killed by falling airplane parts than by shark attacks ("Death Odds" 1990).

By this point, it has probably become evident how Plous (1993) constructed all four of the questions that I borrowed at the beginning of this article. Within each pair of causes of death, one tends to be reported more frequently than the other in the popular media. The correct answers (as given by Plous 1993) are: falling airplane parts, lightning, stomach cancer,* and diabetes.

Simply put, then, the media paradox operates this way: Events must be somewhat unusual in order to be considered newsworthy, but the very fact of their appearance in the news leads us to overestimate their frequency of occurrence. We may therefore come to believe that relatively rare events are common, taking precautionary measures against unlikely dangers at the neglect of more significant hazards. At any given time, we are bombarded with warnings about particular hazards that often turn out to be far less significant threats to our well-being than initially advertised. Gilovich (1991) discussed widespread media reports on the chances of contracting HIV through heterosexual sex. He quotes Oprah Winfrey as having said that "Research studies now project that one in five heterosexuals could be dead from AIDS at the end of the next three years. That's by 1990. One in five. It is no longer just a gay disease. Believe me." This has obviously turned out to be a gross exaggeration, and although the transmission of HIV through heterosexual sex is a serious public health issue, it is nonetheless important to keep the degree of danger in perspective.

A healthy dose of skepticism is one obvious way to protect ourselves from misplacing our fears. We can routinely ask ourselves simple questions, such as, "Why did the producers choose to air this story?" or "How common is the problem being described?" Gilovich (1991) outlines several other strategies for protecting ourselves from misplaced fears, such as considering the source of information, distrusting projections, and being wary of testimonials.

---

*As acknowledged by the author in July/August 2000 Letters to the Editor section of *Skeptical Inquirer*, this claim is incorrect. Car accident mortality exceeds stomach cancer mortality on average by a ratio of more than 3 to 1.—Ed.

A RADICAL CONJECTURE

To respond to Ross's (1995) question, it appears that we may sometimes dowse a match and ignore a raging inferno. I suggest something more radical still. I propose that a mindful review of cautionary advisories may paradoxically alert us to pockets of relative safety. That is, some media reports intended to shield us from danger may, upon careful reflection, actually signal precisely the opposite. Let me illustrate this notion through a pair of examples.

Once when I used to live in a suburb of Boston, a local fast food franchise was temporarily closed for violations of the health code. To put it gently, the illnesses of several patrons had been traced back to unfortunate encounters with food at the salad bar. The local media quite naturally ran stories about this. When the time came for the restaurant to reopen, at least one local newspaper printed a follow-up story to remind local residents of the danger. I would suggest that, of all the places one could grab a quick bite to eat, this particular restaurant was among the *safest*, at least in the short run. The management surely must have realized that a second problem, so soon after the last, would have spelled disaster. The knowledge that everyone—patrons and health inspectors alike—would be keeping a close watch on food quality would surely have heightened attentiveness to the issue.

If the choice of a fast-food restaurant strikes you as trivial, consider a decision with more profound, long-range consequences. On March 28, 1979, an accident occurred at the Three Mile Island (TMI) nuclear power plant in Middletown, Pennsylvania. As the twentieth anniversary of this tragic event approached, there was considerable publicity here in southcentral Pennsylvania, publicity which no doubt awakened memories and rekindled old fears. Around this time, a candidate for a faculty position at the college where I work declined a job offer because the candidate's spouse refused to live so close to TMI. Now, not only do experts in risk assessment consider nuclear power to be quite safe, but I would contend that of all the nuclear power plants in the world, TMI is likely to be among the very safest. Nobody would tolerate another accident, and the operators of TMI have been forced to take extraordinary precautions for the past two decades. They will surely continue to do so, compelled as they are by their own widelypublicized track record.

Media professionals have a penchant for dramatizing case studies of mishap, be they accidental or malicious. When an incident is brought to the public's attention, it is possible to overlook the fact that the alleged perpetrators are themselves sensitized to the issue, and thus likely to be exercising renewed vigilance. Therefore, not only should we be extremely careful about accepting media warnings at face value, but an even more robust skepticism may point to a sensible course of action 180 degrees at odds with the directions mapped out in a vivid story.

I encourage readers to consider the broader implications of the media paradox. With practice, we may learn to protect ourselves from the subtle biases that pervade popular media reports, but does this go far enough? One's own critical thinking habits will provide insufficient protection against illadvised *policy* decisions based upon prevailing misconceptions that have spread through the mass media. As spelled out in the experimental work of Shanto Iyengar (Iyengar 1991; Iyengar and Kinder 1987), media effects on ordinary citizens' political judgments raise grave concerns about the stability of a democratic system that rests upon a well-informed public.

NOTES

1. This example is adapted from Nisbett, Borgida, Crandall, and Reed (1976).

2. In order to control for the possibility that the face-to-face condition achieved a large effect by providing critical information not contained in the statistical summary, a replication of this experiment included a condition in which the base rate group received—in addition to the statistical summary—a complete written transcript of the panelists' comments. This new condition was also less influential in affecting students' preferences than was the face-to-face condition (Borgida and Nisbett 1977).

3. This is not simply a result of each newspaper reporting deaths in accordance with the actual frequencies of occurrence. For example, homicides were reported three times as often as deaths by diseases despite the fact that diseases killed about 100 times as many people.

REFERENCES

Bach, Richard. 1973. "Nothing by chance." *The American Way* 6: 32-38.

Borgida, Eugene, and Richard E. Nisbett. 1977. "The differential impact of abstract vs. concrete information on decisions." *Journal of Applied Social Psychology* 7: 258–71.

Combs, Barbara, and Paul Slovic. 1979. "Causes of death: Biased newspaper coverage and biased judgments." *Journalism Quarterly* 56: 837–43.

"Death Odds." 1990. *Newsweek*, 24 September.

Gilovich, Thomas. 1991. *How We Know What Isn't So: The Fallibility of Human Reason in Everyday Life*. New York: Free Press.

Iyengar, Shanto. 1991. *Is Anyone Responsible? How Television Frames Political Issues*. Chicago: University of Chicago Press.

Iyengar, Shanto, and Donald R. Kinder. 1987. *News That Matters*. Chicago: University of Chicago Press.

Lichtenstein, Sarah, Paul Slovic, Baruch Fischhoff, Mark Layman, and Barbara Combs. 1978. "Judged frequency of lethal events." *Journal of Experimental Psychology Human Learning and Memory* 4: 551–78.

Nisbett, Richard E., Eugene Borgida, Rick Crandall, and Harvey Reed. 1976. "Popular induction: Information is not necessarily informative." In J. S. Carroll and J. W Payne (Eds.), *Cognition and Social Behavior*. Hillsdale, N.J.: Erlbaum.

Nisbett, Richard E., and Lee Ross. 1980. *Human Inference: Strategies and Shortcomings of Social Judgment*. Englewood Cliffs, N.J.: Prentice-Hall.

Pious, Scott. 1993. *The Psychology of Judgment and Decision Making*. Philadelphia: Temple University Press.

Ross, John F. 1995. "Risk: Where do real dangers lie?" *Smithsonian* 26: 42–53.

Slovic, Paul, Baruch Fischhoff, and Sara Lichtenstein. 1979. "Rating the risks." *Environment* (April 14–20): 36–39.

Tversky, Amos, and Daniel Kahneman. 1973. "Availability: A heuristic for judging frequency and probability." *Cognitive Psychology* 4: 207–32.

PART THREE

GUN AVAILABILITY
AND VIOLENCE

Alone among the Western nations, the United States permits the unrestricted availability of handguns and alone it suffers an astronomical crime rate. The only sensible solution, in the interest of civil liberties as well as public safety (is to) attack violence at its source by banning the private possession of handguns.
Robert F. Drinan, *The Good Outweighs the Evil*

The gun control debate as an instrument of Americas political, social, and moral culture wars is infused with bias (Part One). The gun control/gun violence debate as carried on in the popular media is too often infused with bias from both cognitive and motivational sources (Part Two).

Bias is not necessarily the outcome of deliberate attempts to deceptively manipulate information. Assuming that the misinformation and distortion that characterize the debate is *necessarily* caused by the intention to deceive is to commit the fallacy of representiveness (like goes with like, Part Two). An alternative explanation is that bias, in many cases, arises out of the formation of one-sided beliefs concerning gun violence issues. These one-sided beliefs unwittingly lead us to erroneous conclusions, to detecting nonexistent patterns and next to devising causal theories to "explain" what are in fact creations of our own reasoning errors (Part Two).

A one-sided belief is defined as one whose lack of temporal focus biases the possessor's attention toward confirmations and to disregard or depreciate evidence that would decisively prove it false. Such beliefs are formed on the basis of noteworthy attention grabbing events; noteworthy because they are exceptional, at variance with the normal data of our experience. They are one-sided in the sense that their noteworthiness distracts attention from what *didn't* happen and how often it *doesn't* happen. Therefore, one-sided events are fed by every confirmation and unchecked by disconfirmations. If for example, we firmly believe that "bad things happen to people when guns are around" or that "no law will prevent a criminal who wants a gun, from getting a gun," we will search for noteworthy confirmations and therefore, not be seriously motivated to look for disconfirmations. To the extent we cannot avoid potentially disconfirming evidence we subject it to more critical inspection than confirming data and smugly declare ourselves "objective."

Is there a way around a self-confirming one-sided approach to gun violence issues? A two-sided approach as advocated in Part Two would reduce bias by forcing claims concerning guns and violence to be focused on specified predictions that would strengthen, weaken, or falsify outright theses claims.*

Allow me to state key questions in the gun debate in ways that render them two-sided.

Part Three explores a core question in the gun violence–gun control debate: Do higher levels of gun ownership in the United States cause higher rates of violent crime?

Compared to other industrialized, democratic nations, the United States has higher rates of violent crime. The United States with some exceptions has higher levels of gun ownership (up to 240 million). The United States also has higher rates of homicides committed with guns (60–70 percent) especially handguns (80 percent of gun homicides). In any given year there are between 600,000 and 700,000 nonfatal gun crimes, the majority of which involve handguns.

From these facts it is inferred that higher levels of gun ownership cause Americans higher rates of violent crime: more guns, more violence. Hence, if the availability, the levels of gun ownership, especially handgun ownership were substantially reduced or precluded violent crime rates would fall (less guns, less violence).

The argument, more guns, more violence hence less guns, less violence is certainly plausible. However, as stated it is also one-sided. It is possible that the variables—higher levels of gun ownership and higher rates of violence are coincidental, independent of one another. Or it is possible that the direction of causality is reversed—higher levels of gun ownership in the United States are the consequent, not the cause of higher crime rates. Or, it is possible that lower rates of violence in other countries are entirely independent of lower rates of gun ownership or stricter gun control laws. After all, the British or Japanese are not merely Americans without guns. Also we cannot assume that if guns were not available that gun homicides would not have occurred through the use of other

---

*Given the emotional attachment to such claims bias would not be eliminated but failure to play by the rules of inquiry in the long run might well prove embarrassing both personally and for an agenda. We humans, without and sometimes with training are not superb logicians. However, we are superb cheater detectors. Once bitten, we become excellent at detecting misdirection as both presidents and lesser mortals have discovered.

weapons. In other words as *noteworthy* as the contrasting levels of gun owner-ship and violence between nations are, they remain at the level of numerical asso-ciations, not causes (causes are antecedent events that produce or contribute to the occurrence of subsequent events). The issues of causality, its direction and inferences concerning reducing violence through reducing gun availability simply are not established by reciting these untested numerical relationships. To prove causality these numerical associations have to be rendered "two-sided" by stating them as hypotheses (proposed solutions) in which the following specified *predictions* would be tested on independent sets of data:

> *If* higher levels of gun availability are associated with higher rates of violence or lethal violence then (*predicted fact*) rates of violence will be positively associated with varying levels of gun availability.

> *If* higher levels of gun availability *cause* higher rates of violence then (*predicted fact*) geographic areas with higher gun ownership will have *as a result*, higher rates of violence.

> *If* people have access to guns (*predicted fact*) they will have *as a result* higher rates of homicides and suicides than similar people who do not have access to guns.

> *If* there is a *causal* link between gun availability and higher rates of violence, then (*predicted fact*) violent incidents with guns will *result* in higher rates of attack, injuries and death than similar incidents involving other weapons (instrumentally effect).

Therefore, if none of these predicted facts are consistently supported by evidence generated by a number of technically sound studies *then* causal links between levels of gun availability and violence rates are nonexistent or unsupported and no policy discussions are warranted. However, if all of these predicted facts are sup-ported by *consistent* evidence from a number of technically sound studies including those capable of documenting causation with no divergent or contra-dictory data produced then causal links have been established. On the basis of this evidence, a discussion of what proposed policies would best reduce gun avail-ability in the area(s) where causality has been established must include: specified predicted benefits *and* costs (economic, social, political, judicial, and constitu-tional) to whom and by when. These specifications would allow an assessment of both the probable consequences of such policies as well as criteria and time-tables to evaluate the effectiveness of such policies, if implemented. These conditions and their fulfillment would render discussions of the hypothesis that gun avail-ability contributes significantly to higher violence rates in the United States, two-sided. Also, these conditions would render discussions of policy two-sided.

One further clarification is necessary on the issue of causation as it applies to the gun availability—violence problem. All of the scholarly parties agree on one point: the availability of guns *alone* does not explain why America has a higher vio-lent crime rate than other industrialized democratic countries.[1] If guns were involved in 60 to 70 percent of homicides in the 1990s then up to 40 percent of homicides *were not* committed with guns. Without *any* gun violence America would still have higher violence rates than Japan, Britain, or Canada. And, no one believes that all of the homicides committed with guns simply wouldn't have occurred if guns were not available. Guns then are not *necessary* conditions of violence (violence occurs without guns). Nor are guns *sufficient* to cause violence (they don't make violence happen). Fifty percent of all American households contain guns and 25 percent contain handguns; however, only a small fraction of such households are involved in gun violence. What, then, is the gun availability debate about? The debate concerns the *degree* to which, if any, gun availability increases levels and rates of violence in a society which already contains more violent prone individuals than comparable advanced industrial societies. Therefore, the testable, predicted facts above are designed to resolve the question concerning *to what degree* and in what direction(s) a single technology influences (or doesn't influence) rates of violence among already violent prone individuals and subgroups.

Therefore, the following selections provide the opportunity to determine whether the *predicted facts* that support the *hypothesis* that gun availability *contributes* to higher violence rates are corroberated or in doubt. Also the information in the selections allows the reader to evaluate to what extent gun control policies are supported by what strength of evidence.

The following selections all address the issue of causality. Do higher levels of gun ownership in the U.S. cause/produce higher rates of violence?

Remember: To show that this causal relationship exists the following predicted facts must be corroberated:

1. More guns available in general are always associated with increased rates of violent acts in general.
2. More guns in a geographical area produce higher rates of violent acts.
3. Higher rates of violent acts among gun owners exist than non gun owners *who are otherwise similar.*
4. Higher rates of attack, injury and mortality occur in violent incidents where guns are used compared to similar incidents where other weapons are used.

At this point we find:

1. Has been shown to be false. The statistics that introduced this volume show that high levels of gun ownership in the 1990s are in fact associated with sharply *falling* rates of murder and violent crime.
2. The claim that more guns in a geographical are a *causing* or *producing* higher violence rates is hotly contested in Part Three (unproven [see National Research Council] "highly correlated" [Cook] positive correlations are in fact the outcome of citizens buying guns in *response* to high crime rates [Kleck]).
3. Specifically addressed in Part Four.

4. The claim that the greater destructive capacity of handguns compared to other weapons causes or produces higher and more lethal violence rates (instrumentality effect) is a primary issue in the gun debate and the primary issue addressed in the selections in Part Three. Here all researchers agree that causality has been established, but they disagree on the degree of causality that can be attributed to handguns alone. Specifically what is at issue is the degree to which violent subsets of the population, concentrated heavily in racial and ethnic minorities are rendered more lethal, more injurious and more likely to attack if they have access to guns, especially handguns.

All the parties who debate this issue accept the following facts:

African Americans are 41 percent and Hispanics 32 percent more likely than whites to be victimized by violent crime.

African Americans constitute 13 percent of the U.S. population and 45 percent of its homicide victims.

African American males constitute 7 percent of the population but individuals within this group commit over 50 percent of the murders in the United States.

Hispanics and Native Americans are also disproportionally the victims and victimizers in violent crimes.

The claim that gun availability *causes* higher rates of lethal violence then is based first on violent crimes committed by violent individuals concentrated in these groups. Gun availability produces different consequences for different groups not only in terms the numbers of people willing to use guns violently but also because guns are up to four times more lethal than the next most commonly employed weapon—knives. Therefore, the instrumentality effect of guns—their capacity to inflict more severe damage is the foundation for the causal claim that gun availability produces higher rates of serious lethal injury than when other weapons are employed.

"Mortality rates from firearm violence are high in the U.S. compared with other countries and rising especially among young black males (1991). . . . Available research does not demonstrate that greater gun availability is linked to greater numbers of violent events or injuries. However, what is clear is that gun inflicted injuries have more lethal consequences than injuries inflicted by other weapons."[2]

Therefore, the instrumentality effect theory purports to explain why, in part, higher rates as well as numbers of lethal and injuries violence events plague the more violent subsets of the population. The instrumentality effect would also explain why levels of gun availability or ownership in the general population does not correlate with violent crime rates: this population contains proportionately fewer people willing to unleash the instrumentality effect of guns.

The instrumentality effect is the foundation concept of gun control agendas.

Gun availability does not make people violent, it makes more violently inclined people, more lethal, more injurious and may enable them to commit crimes they ordinary couldn't. Whatever the causes of violent behavior, guns make that behavior more dangerous. The instrumentality effect hypothesis, if reliable, provides a factual basis for focusing on the role of the technology of guns in massacres: guns, the instrument, make massacres not only more lethal but the technology makes massacres more probable in the first place. Reduce gun availability and, you will reduce homicides, injuries, successful suicides and the lethality or occurrence of massacres. Therefore, the stronger the instrumentality effect is thought to be, the more the emphasis on control of the technology of violence. The instrumentality effect underlies the litigation of city and county governments and the threat of a federal lawsuit in behalf of public housing units to pressure gun manufacturers to make safer guns (e.g. built in trigger locks, electronic devices to insure only the owner can fire the gun) as well as altering market practices to keep guns out of criminal hands. The instrumentality effect of firearms underlies calls for the outright ban of handguns.

The gun control debate as a two-sided empirical dispute concerning causation revolves around the strength and policy implications of the instrumentality effect. The selections authored by Franklin Zimring, Gordon Hawkins, and Phillip Cook attempt to document the existence of a strong 'instrumentality effect' and its implications for gun control policies. Zimring and Hawkins argue, as they have for three decades, for a federal ban on handgun ownership as the only sure way to keep handguns out of the hands of the violent prone.

Two selections are included from *Understanding and Preventing Violence* (1993). These selections survey key violent crime, firearms violence and gun control issues, including the linkage of gun availability and the instrumentality effect to violence rates. The volume (1993) was authored by a panel of twenty social scientists sponsored by the National Research Council of the National Academy of Sciences. The panel's task was to assess the state of our understanding of the causes of violence, suggest preventative strategies and identify areas for further research. Despite four of the panel members advocacy of a strong instrumentality effect (Cook, Zimring, Kellerman, Lofton—all appearing in Parts Three and Four of this volume) the summary of the report indicated further research is needed on this subject. Also, the report endorsed enforcement of existing laws and strategies rather than new gun control initiatives.

The research of criminologists James Wright, Peter Rossi, Don Kates, and Gary Kleck in the 1980s (see *The Gun Control Debate: You Decide*, 1990) raised important questions concerning the strength of "instrumentality effect." Also, these researchers, especially Kleck, raised considerable doubts concerning the claim that correlations between high levels of gun ownership in the *general public* and high violent crime rates proved that general gun availability caused higher violent crime rates. Kleck's work purported to show just the opposite, that gun ownership by the general public was a *response* to rising crime rates in the 1970s–1980s, not a *cause* of rising violent crime rates. Also, he claimed, using research done on surveys, that defensive gun uses by the general public, out numbered criminal misuses of firearms. Therefore, prohibitionist gun control would disarm law abiding citizens more than criminals and prove a net disadvantage (*The Gun Control Debate: You Decide,* 1990). Kleck summarized these research findings, their policy implications, as well as reviewed the purported methodological failings of instrumentality effect theorists in *Point Blank: Guns and Violence in America* (1991) and updated this work in *Targeting Guns* (1997).

The selections included here from Kleck's research challenge the purported two-sidedness of research documenting a strong instrumentality effect (Zimring, Hawkins, Cook, Kellermann). Kleck's work building on the research of James Wright and Peter Rossi investigating the gun habits of felons (*Armed and Considered Dangerous,* 1986) claims that research purportedly documenting the instrumentality effect (guns are four times more lethal than knives) had confused intentionality with weapon lethality. Serious criminals he argues choose more serious weapons and hence studies not controlling for *intent* had overestimated the lethality of the weapon hence invalidating *comparisons* of lethal violence rates using different weapons.

Further, Kleck argues weapons have complex effects on violent outcomes sometimes decreasing numbers and seriousness of violent episodes, sometimes increasing numbers of and seriousness of violent episodes (e.g., guns deter attackers, victims submit without injury, guns enable attackers to attack defended targets, enable weaker people [women] to attack stronger people [men]). Also he raises the issue of substitution: given the more serious intent of gun offenders would limiting handgun availability lead to the substitution of more lethal guns (e.g., sawed-off shotguns)?

If Kleck's challenges to the two-sidedness of instrumentality effects research is sustained he and other skeptical researchers (Wright, Rossi, Kates, and Patterson) have raised serious doubts concerning a foundation concept supporting prohibitionist gun control proposals emphasizing the dangers of the technology itself. Instead, they argue that a diminished instrumentality effect, together with the fact that gun ownership among the general public is not correlated with violence rates, that citizen guns have a crime deterrant effect (Part Four) combined with the ubiquity of firearms in America support gun controls aimed only at high risk individuals (e.g., felons, violent criminals, alcoholics, the criminally insane—see Kleck, "Guns and Violence," in Part Three of this volume). Therefore, the reader must decide, preferrably using a two-sided evaluation of the strength of causal claims, which approach to gun control would provide the most benefits and the least costs and to whom.

NOTES

1. See Franklin E. Zimring and Gordon Hawkings, "Lethal Violence in America," p. 215 in this volume.

2. Albert J. Reiss and Jeffrey A. Roth, eds., *Understanding and Preventing Violence* (Washington, D.C.: National Academy Press, 1993), p. 18.

12

UNDERSTANDING AND PREVENTING VIOLENCE

ALBERT J. REISS & JEFFREY A. ROTH

SUMMARY*

In cities, suburban areas, and even small towns, Americans are fearful and concerned that violence has permeated the fabric and degraded the quality of their lives. The diminished quality of life ranges from an inability to sit on the front porch in neighborhoods where gang warfare has made gunfire a common event to the installation of elaborate security systems in suburban homes where back doors once were left open. Children in urban schools experience violence on the way to school and in the school building itself. Surveys show that large percentages of the population fear even walking in their neighborhoods at night. The nation's anxiety on the subject of violence is not unfounded. In 1990, more than 23,000 people were homicide victims. Violent deaths and incidents that result in lesser injuries are sources of chronic fear and a high level of concern with the seeming inability of public authorities to prevent them.

In 1988 the National Academy of Sciences was asked by a consortium of federal agencies—the National Institute of Justice, the National Science Foundation, and the Centers for Disease Control—to assess the understanding of violence, the implications of that understanding for preventive interventions, and the most important research and evaluation needed to improve understanding

---

*From Albert J. Reiss and Jeffrey A. Roth, eds., *Understanding and Preventing Violence* (Washington, D.C.: National Academy Press, 1993), pp. 1–27. Copyright © 1993 by the National Academy of Sciences. Courtesy of the National Academy Press, Washington, D.C.

182

and control of violence. In response, the Academy created the Panel on the Understanding and Control of Violent Behavior. . . .

The panel adopted as its definition of "violence": *behaviors by individuals that intentionally threaten, attempt, or inflict physical harm on others.* Death is the basis for defining the most serious violent crime—murder. However, with murder as with lesser acts of violence, the definition masks enormous diversity in underlying behaviors that cause death: shootings by robbers, intrafamily murders, minor disputes that turn violent, sexual attacks, and gang killings. This diversity is also masked in statistical classifications of nonfatal violent crimes such as assault, robbery, and forcible rape. Even greater diversity is seen in violent behaviors that may not be counted as crimes, such as school fights, violence among prison inmates, and violence in the home.

Other violent events involve large collectives: wars, state violence, riots, and some activities of organized crime. The panel did not attempt to analyze such collective violence in this report.

MEASURING VIOLENCE

Violent behaviors that society identifies as crimes are counted more completely and classified more accurately than those that are not. Three national measurement systems are of primary importance in counting crimes and their victims. The National Crime Survey (NCS) asks all persons age twelve and over in a national sample of households to recall and describe recent nonfatal victimizations. The Uniform Crime Reporting (UCR) system records basic information about crimes detected by or reported to police, supplementary information about homicides, and descriptions of arrestees. Homicide data are also tabulated annually from death certificates by the National Center for Health Statistics (NCHS) vital statistics program.

While murders are counted rather accurately, counts of nonfatal violent crimes are incomplete. Gaps and discrepancies occur because victimizations may not be recognized as crimes, because embarrassment or psychological stigma inhibits reporting, because victims are sometimes reluctant to involve authorities, because their consequences may not be thought worth reporting as crimes, and because of discretion in classifying and counting violent events.

Moreover, definitions of violent events as criminal or not change over time and differ among segments of society. Data are even less adequate for violent acts that authorities and the public are coining to recognize as serious crimes. Recent attention to bias crimes, for example, highlights the inadequacy of crime information on violence motivated by differences in ethnic status, religion, and sexual preference. A 1990 law requires modification of the UCR to improve statistics on bias crimes. Similarly, physical and sexual assaults against women and children by intimates and acquaintances are now increasingly recognized and reported as crimes. If all such events were included in official counts of assaults and rapes, those counts would increase substantially.

PATTERNS AND TRENDS

Nearly one-third of the nineteen million crime victimizations reported to the NCS in 1990 involved violence. The prototype violent crime is an assault. Aggravated assaults—those with weapons or causing serious nonfatal injury—accounted for nearly 300 of every 1,000 violent victimizations. Less serious simple assaults accounted for more than 500. Robbery accounted for most of the rest. Forcible rapes accounted for about 20 in every 1,000; fewer than 4 in every 1,000 violent victimizations resulted in death for the victim.

These basic patterns raise several questions:

Is the United States more violent than other societies?

In general, the answer is yes. Homicide rates in the United States far exceed those in any other industrialized nation. For other violent crimes, rates in the United States are among the world's highest and substantially exceed rates in Canada, our nearest neighbor in terms of geography, culture, and crime reporting. Among sixteen industrialized countries surveyed in 1988, the United States had the highest prevalence rates for serious sexual assaults and for all other assaults including threats of physical harm.

Is the United States more violent today than ever before?

No. The national homicide rate has peaked twice in this century; each peak was followed by a decline. The first peak was in the early 1930s and the rate then fell for the next thirty years. More recently, the national homicide rate began to increase in 1973 and peaked between 1979 and 1981, declining until 1984 and 1985. The homicide rate has since increased and is now at about its 1980 level. Historical data suggests that certain cities may have experienced still higher homicide rates during the nineteenth century. What is true is that, as a result of population growth, today's homicide rates per 100,000 residents produce total numbers of homicides that are high by historic standards. Levels of nonfatal violent crimes also rose during the late 1980s, although there is less consistency in trends across cities. Only for aggravated assault do 1990 rates exceed 1980 rates in cities of all sizes.

Who is at greatest risk of violent victimization and death?

Demographic minorities. In 1990, blacks were 41 percent and Hispanics 32 percent more likely than whites to be victims of violent crime. Ethnic differences combine with age and gender patterns so that recently young black males have been about 20 times more likely than older white females to be victimized. Homicide rates are also highest for minorities: the black rate is 5 times the white rate, and rates for Native Americans about double the rate of the entire population.

Death rates from natural causes are generally low for young persons. Correspondingly, accidents and homicides become leading causes of death at younger ages. However, because minority homicide risks are high at all ages, only about one-fourth of the lifetime homicide risk for black and white males and females is experienced before the twenty-fifth birthday. American Indian males also have higher homicide victimization rates than white males, but they are more concentrated at later ages.

What are the consequences of violent crimes?

Although the public naturally focuses on death or injury as the outcome of violent crime, injury occurs in only about one-third of violent crimes. Most injuries are minor with only about half requiring any medical treatment and 4 percent requiring an overnight hospital stay. The victim is killed in fewer than 4 of every 1,000 violent crimes. However, the fact that 23,000 people died as a result of homicide in 1990, and that these deaths occurred in only a small percentage of violent encounters, should emphasize the magnitude of the total violence problem.

Even when death or injury is avoided, losses to victims and society are sizable: an estimated average cost of $54,000 per attempted or completed rape, $19,200 per robbery, and $16,000 per assault. About 15 percent of these costs are financial—victims' monetary losses, society's costs for lost productivity, emergency response, and administration of compensation. Roughly 85 percent reflects values imputed for nonmonetary losses, such as pain, suffering, the risk of death, psychological damage, and reduced quality of life. Responses to violence by law enforcement, criminal justice, and private security agencies add additional costs. Additional losses, which have not been estimated but are very visible, include the destruction of families and neighborhoods; the fortification of schools, homes, and businesses; and the deterioration and abandonment of community resources such as parks and playgrounds.

Who commits violent crimes?

We know less about the perpetrators of violent crimes than about their victims. However, we do know that offenders and their victims share similar demographic profiles. That is, they are overwhelmingly male (89 percent of all those arrested) and are disproportionately drawn from racial and ethnic minorities. Arrestees for violent crimes are somewhat older than victims. Men in the 25–29 age range were more likely to commit violent crimes in 1988 than any other age group. Perpetrators were acquaintances of their victims in a majority of simple assaults, forcible rapes and homicides, but in only 38 percent of aggravated assaults and 26 percent of completed robberies.

One quarter of nonfatal violent victimizations are committed by multiple offenders; almost half of robberies involve co-offenders, whereas forcible rapes and simple assaults are generally solitary crimes (only 8 percent of rapes and 19 percent of simple assaults involve more than one assailant). About 8 percent of robberies involve groups of four or more.

Are violent crimes the work of "violent career criminals"?

No. While a few individuals commit violent crimes frequently, they account for a small share of total violence in the United States. Despite occasional media reports to the contrary, "serial murderers" are responsible for only about 1 or 2 percent of homicides in any year. Most recorded violent crimes occur in the course of long, active criminal careers dominated by property offenses, so that arrests for violent crimes account for no more than 1 in 8 of all arrests in European and American cohorts whose records have been analyzed. The general pattern is that while few offenders begin their criminal careers with a violent crime, most long arrest records include at least one. It is inaccurate, however, to portray this as an "escalation" from property to violent crimes.

More generally, predictions of future violent behavior from past arrests are highly inaccurate.

What effect has increasing the prision population had on levels of violent crime?

Apparently, very little. However, the question cannot be answered unambiguously. While average prison time served per violent crime roughly tripled between 1975 and 1989, reported levels of serious violent crime varied around the level of about 2.9 million per year. Estimates of the crime control effects of incarceration—by isolating violent offenders from potential victims in the community and by deterring others from committing violent crimes—are necessarily imprecise. However, if tripling the average length of incarceration per crime had a strong preventive effect, then violent crime rates should have declined in the absence of other relevant changes. While rates declined during the early 1980s, they generally rose after 1985, suggesting that changes in other factors . . . may have been causing an increase in potential crimes.

Why did average prison time served per violent crime increase so substantially between 1975 and 1989? Experience varied somewhat by crime type and state, but the data point to general increases in both the average time served if incarcerated and the chance of imprisonment if arrested.

There is currently active discussion by public officials of further increases in prison sentences as a means of crime control. Analyses suggest that a further increase in the average time served per violent crime would have an even smaller proportional incapacitation effect than the increase that occurred between 1975 and 1989. According to the best estimates available to us, a 50 percent increase in the probability of incarceration would prevent twice as much violent crime as a 50 percent increase in the average term of incarceration. Achieving such an increase in certainty would, however, require substantial improvement in crime reporting and investments in police investigation and prosecution.

This analysis suggests that preventive strategies may be as important as criminal justice responses to violence. The success of preventive strategies depends, however, on understanding how individual potentials for violent behavior develop, of what circumstances are conducive to violent events, and of what social processes foster violence. While the complex interactions among these processes are still poorly understood, careful evaluations of promising interventions are contributing knowledge that increases the ability to prevent violence. . . .

SOCIAL PROCESSES AND VIOLENT CRIME

Interaction effects are important in understanding how social processes affect violent crime. For example, ethnicity and socioeconomic status (SES) appear to interact: at low SES levels, blacks are more likely to be homicide victims than whites; but at higher SES levels the differential attenuates or disappears. What social factors account for the variation? For at least fifty years, sociologists have pointed to three structural factors—low economic status, ethnic heterogeneity, and residential mobility. Subsequent research has supported these findings and refined them. This work points to:

- *concentrations* of poor families in geographic areas and greater income differences between poor and nonpoor (income inequality);
- measures associated with *differential social organization* such as population turnover, community transition, family disruption, and housing/population density—all of which affect a community's capacity to supervise young males; and
- indicators of *opportunities* associated with violence (e.g., illegal markets in drugs and firearms).

In addition, some individual-level risk factors for violent crimes point to possible community-level causes. Ineffective parenting, drug use, school failure, and a poor employment history are all more likely to occur in communities in which illegal markets are nearer at hand than are prenatal and pediatric care, good schools protected from violence, and legitimate employment opportunities. Communities that present different distributions of occasions for learning violent behaviors can be expected to produce quite different distributions of developmental sequences.

There is a critical need to understand how these risk factors interact. For example, there are poor communities with low levels of violence. However, interactions between ethnicity and community characteristics are particularly hard to disentangle empirically because poor minorities are so much more likely than poor whites to be concentrated in communities in which a very high percentage of residents live below the poverty line.

Community Characteristics

Quantitative indicators of community disorganization include high housing density, high residential mobility, high percentages of single-parent families and the occurrence of neighborhood transitions—both economic decline and gentrification. These appear to account for more of the geographic variation in violent victimization rates than do measures of poverty and income inequality.

These indicators appear to reflect a breakdown of social capital—the capacity to transmit positive values to younger generations. This breakdown appears in such intangibles as parents' inability to distinguish neighborhood youth from outsiders, to band together with other parents to solve common problems, to question each others' children, to participate in voluntary organizations and friendship networks, and to watch neighborhood common areas. Single parents who work have less time for such activities and constant family turnover in large multidwelling housing units makes them more difficult to carry out. Many "old heads"community elders who took responsibility for local youth have left urban communities, and the status of those who remain is diminished by contrast with the rise of successful young entrepreneurs in illegal markets.

Social and Economic Structure and Organization

The economic, organizational, and social niches in which poor people tend to live are disadvantaged in ways that defy easy measurement. These include isolation from legitimate economic opportunities and from personal contacts with those who control resources in the larger society. Legitimate routes to social status, income, and power are often severely limited in these communities.

Structural economic changes of the last decade have reduced employment opportunities for low-income urban minorities and increased the numbers of such families living near or below the poverty level. There has been an exodus of economically stable and secure families, which contributes to the decline of institutions of socialization and informal control. Measuring the causal influence of these trends is difficult for many reasons-including the fact that high levels of violence themselves may encourage the most stable families to leave the central cities.

Community Culture

Ethnographic studies of urban communities, primarily black and Hispanic, provide important hypotheses about how local cultures that support violence develop as a by-product of individuals' and groups' efforts to maintain and increase their social status. . . .

THE CIRCUMSTANCES OF VIOLENCE

A promising approach to the understanding, prevention, and control of violence—a perspective with roots in both criminology and public health—is to focus on the places where violence occurs. The incidence of violent events varies widely in space—by city, neighborhood, and specific address. The greatest variation is found across locations within cities; for example, although 97.8 percent of all Minneapolis addresses generated zero robbery calls to police in 1986, eight generated more than twenty calls each.

The violence potential of a situation depends on risk factors in both encounters and places. Examples of hazardous encounters in the community include disputes, illegal drug transactions, and robberies. Among the characteristics of encounters that affect the probability of a violent event are the nature of preexisting relationships among the participants, the degree to which communications are impaired by alcohol or other psychoactive drugs, and the proximity of an individual who could intervene. The presence of firearms potentially modifies both the probability and the severity of a violent event.

Some violent events arise out of behavioral interactions or exchanges: threats and counterthreats, the exercise of coercive authority, insults and retorts, weapons displays. Violent exchanges and responses to the exercise of authority can accompany encounters between police and citizens, and inmates and custodians in prisons and jails. The dynamics of these exchanges in high-risk encounters are only partially documented, but they can be expected to differ across ethnic and socioeconomic cultures and to depend on the visibility of encounters to public view. Improved understanding of these dynamics could lead to preventive interventions to modify high-risk encounters. . . .

Firearms and Violent Events

Mortality rates from firearm violence are high in the United States compared with other countries and rising, especially among young black males. The nature of the causal relationship between the availability of firearms and mortality rates from firearm violence, especially involving handguns and so-called assault weapons, is a matter of intense public interest and often emotional debate.

Available research does not demonstrate that greater gun availability is linked to greater numbers of violent events or injuries. However, what is clear is that gun-inflicted injuries have more lethal consequences than injuries inflicted by other weapons. This suggests that making guns less available in high-risk situations (e.g., in the hands of unsupervised juveniles and others barred from legal gun markets, in homes with histories of family violence, in "fighting bars") might reduce the number of homicides.

Educational, technological, and regulatory strategies can be devised with the objectives of changing how handguns are used and stored, changing their allocation from higher-risk to lower-risk segments of the population, reducing their lethality, or reducing their numbers. For any of these policies to reduce homicides, two conditions must be met: the policy must reduce violent uses of at least some types of guns and they must not be replaced with more lethal weapons.

Over 80 percent of the firearms used in crimes are reportedly obtained by theft or through illegal or unregulated transactions. Therefore, while public debates continue over the wisdom of new regulations for firearms, we believe that priority should be placed on evaluating the effects of three strategies for enforcing existing laws governing the purchase, ownership, and use of firearms:

- disrupting illegal gun markets using both the centralized and street-level tactics currently in use for disrupting illegal drug markets;
- enforcing existing bans on juvenile possession of handguns; and
- community-oriented or neighborhood-oriented police work involving close coordination with community residents and community-based organizations to set enforcement priorities and to assist in enforcement and thereby to reduce perceived need for individual gun ownership. . . .

FIREARMS AND VIOLENCE*

An analysis of violence in the United States would be incomplete without a discussion of firearms, which are involved in about 60 percent of all homicides. The most widely debated methods of preventing gun violence involve legal restrictions on firearm owners or licensed dealers. While evaluations have found several regulations that have reduced gun homicides when they are enforced, regulations arouse controversy among law-abiding dealers and owners—some of whom acquired guns precisely because they feared gun violence. Our review of available evidence revealed several promising preventive strategies, none requiring new laws, which are ripe for rigorous evaluation. We also concluded that like "drug-related violence," "gun violence" may be best understood in terms of illegal markets and reduced through tactics that police already apply in illegal drug markets.

We begin by discussing overall patterns and trends in firearms ownership and use in violent crimes. Then, proceeding from best understood to least understood, we examine how firearms alter a series of conditional probabilities in violent events: the chance that an injury causes death, the chance that an encounter (e.g., robbery, assault) produces an injury, and the relationship of firearms availability to the frequencies of such encounters. We then discuss what little is known about the channels through which firearms reach violent crime scenes and conclude by examining the empirical basis for alternative strategies for reducing the incidence and consequences of violent firearm use.

PATTERNS AND TRENDS IN FIREARM OWNERSHIP AND VIOLENT USE

Firearms are widely owned and widely available in the United States. No precise count is available since no enumeration system exists, but the best estimates are that the national gun population was in the range of 60–100 million in 1968 (Newton and Zimring, 1969), 100–140 million in 1978 (Wright et al., 1983), 130–170 million in 1988 (Cook, 1991), and 200 million in 1990 (Bureau of Alcohol, Tobacco, and Firearms, 1991). For at least three decades, the fraction of all households owning any type of gun has remained stable at about 50 percent; however, the fraction own a handgun rose from 13 percent in 1959 to 24 percent in 1978, where it has remained, more or less, since then (Bureau of Justice Statistics, 1989, cited in Cook, 1991). Surveys generally conclude that the fraction of households owning firearms is greatest in rural areas and small towns, higher for whites than for blacks, highest in the South, lowest in the Northeast,

---

*From Albert J. Reiss and Jeffrey A. Roth, eds., *Understanding and Preventing Violence* (Washington, D.C.: National Academy Press, 1993), pp. 255–87. Copyright © 1993 by the National Academy of Sciences. Courtesy of the National Academy Press, Washington, D.C.

and higher for high-income households than for low-income households (Cook, 1991; Wright et al., 1983).

Violent uses of guns impose both human and monetary costs. In 1989 gun attacks resulted in about 12,000 homicides—about 60 percent of all homicides (Federal Bureau of Investigation, 1989). In addition, Cook (1991) estimates that 5.7 nonfatal gunshot injuries occur for every homicide—a projection on the order of 70,000 for 1989. For 1985, Rice and associates (1989) estimate the total cost of intentional and unintentional gun injuries at over $14 billion, including both the direct costs of hospital and other medical care and the indirect costs of long-term disability and premature death.

The risk of death from homicide by a gun is not uniformly distributed throughout the population; rather, it is highly elevated for adolescents, particularly black males. In 1988 the gun homicide rate per 100,000 people was 8 for teenagers ages 15 to 19, but less than 6 for the population as a whole. Among teenagers ages 15 to 19, the 1989 rate was 83.4 for black males compared with 7.5 for white males (unpublished data from the National Vital Statistics system, 1992)—a ratio of more than 11:1.

The elevated risk for teenagers reflects both a concentration of homicides in ages 15 to 34 and a peak in gun use by killers of young people. Figure 1, which displays 1989 age distributions for homicide victims in five-year intervals, shows that the largest fraction of nonfirearm homicide victims was in the 25 to 29 age range; the largest fraction of firearm homicide victims was slightly younger, in the 20 to 24 age range. The fraction of homicides committed with guns peaks even earlier, at 81 percent for victims ages 15 to 19, then declines gradually but monotonically for victims age 20 and older (figure 2).

Although the 1989 risk of gun homicide for black teenage males ages 15 to 19 was 11 times the risk for their white counterparts, black victims outnumbered white victims in that age range by only 1,163 to 547, because whites are so much more numerous in the population (unpublished data from the National Vital Statistics system, 1992). Despite the small numbers involved, the firearm homicide risk for young black males warrants special attention. Not only is the recent increase in this risk a significant social inequity, but also such a huge increase is unique to this particular intersection of sex, race, age, weapon type, intent, and time period.

Trends between 1979 and 1988 in teenage deaths were reported by Fingerhut et al. (1991). During that period, no increases of similar proportions occurred in firearm homicides of black females or white males of the same age, or among older black males ages 25 to 29 (figure 3).[1] And between 1987 and 1988 nonfirearm homicides actually declined for black male teenagers, from 10.8 per 100,000 to 9.5, essentially the 1984 level. The rate for unintentional firearm death, a measure more closely related to firearm availability, rose only about 50 percent (from 2.3 to 3.4 per 100,000) among black male teenagers between 1984 and 1988. And every rate displayed in the figure declined during the immediately preceding period, 1979–1984. The most comparable trend

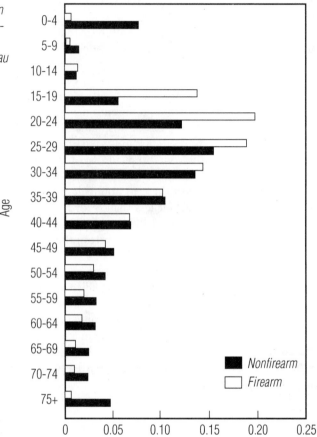

Figure 1. *Age distribution for homicide victims at five-year intervals. Source: Adapted from Federal Bureau of Investigation (1989:11).*

during the period 1984–1988 is in the other form of intentional injury: a 100 percent increase (from 3.4 to 6.8 per 100,000) in the firearm suicide rate for black male teenagers—a higher relative increase than for other race and sex categories in this age group or for older black males.

In short, the increase during the period 1984–1988 in firearm homicides cannot be explained solely in terms of either demographics or firearm availability; rather, one must look at these factors in conjunction with other events that affected young black males during those specific years.

The risks of violent gun use are not evenly distributed across type of gun. Of all guns in the United States, approximately one-third are handguns and two-thirds are long guns—a heterogeneous category that includes, for example, both small-caliber and large-caliber rifles, shotguns, and semiautomatic and automatic rifles. Handguns are disproportionately likely to be used in homicides, by a factor of more than 3 to 1. In gun homicides for which the type of weapon was known, handguns accounted for nearly 80 percent in 1989, compared with 8 percent for

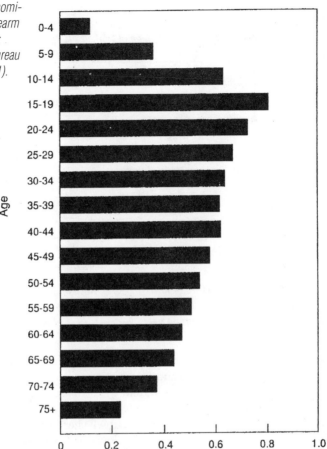

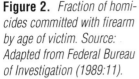

Figure 2. *Fraction of homicides committed with firearm by age of victim. Source: Adapted from Federal Bureau of Investigation (1989:11).*

rifles and 12 percent for shotguns (Federal Bureau of investigation, 1989). Despite substantial recent public attention to what are called assault weapons, we were unable to find national statistics on the availability, use, or lethality of this rather ill-defined category of firearm (Zimring, 1989; Kleck, 1991).

Even for handguns, the weapon of choice in violent crimes in the United States, the risk of violent use is not evenly distributed. Based on estimates by Cook (1981), it appears that, of each cohort of new handguns sold, about one-third are involved in crime (i.e., displayed or fired) at least once during their usable lifetimes.[2] New handguns, those acquired most recently, are especially likely to be involved in violent crimes (Zimring and Hawkins, 1987). But there is little information available about the kinds of places, encounters, handgun attributes, ownership patterns, and distribution channels that heighten the risk that a given handgun will be used in a violent manner. Research on this question is complicated by the lack of data systems to track unique identifiers of firearms and by

Figure 3. *Death rates for selected demographic groups and manners of death: United States, 1979–1988. F/H = firearm homicide; N/H = nonfirearm homicide; F/S = firearm suicide; F/U = unintentional firearm death. Source: Fingerhut et al. (1991:Table 1).*

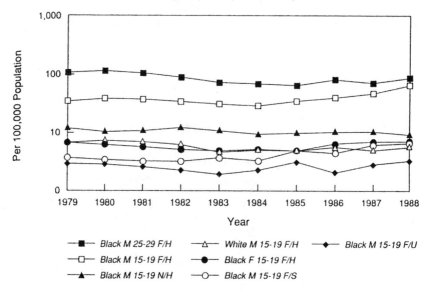

their frequent movement, through burglary, unregulated sales, and simple carrying, from one situation to another. (On request from a law enforcement agency, the Bureau of Alcohol, Tobacco, and Firearms attempts to trace the ownership paths of guns used in crime, but these do not provide a basis for comparing their ownership histories to those of other guns.) There are no accurate profiles for distinguishing "dangerous" handguns or locations from "safe" ones.

THE LETHALITY OF FIREARM INJURIES

A focus on violent injuries produces one clear correlation. The case fatality rate—the fraction of injuries that lead to death—is much greater for guns than for knives, the next most lethal weapon. Zimring (1968) reports fatality rates of 12.2 percent for gun attacks and 2.4 percent for knife attacks, a lethality ratio of about 5 to 1. Others report somewhat smaller lethality ratios, but no estimate is less than 2 to 1 (Curtis, 1974, reported in Wright et al., 1983; Vinson, 1974).

From scientific and policy perspectives, the difficulty lies in determining how much of the difference in lethality among weapons is due to instrumental effects (i.e., properties of the weapon or ammunition) and how much to the perpetrator's intent. For more than thirty years, people have argued that the perpetrators most intent on killing not only select firearms more frequently but also aim more carefully, fire more bullets, and take other steps that further increase the lethal effects (Wolfgang, 1958). In this view, intent contributes most of the lethality and, if guns became unavailable, such intent killers would succeed in killing with knives, blunt instruments, fists, or feet.

This argument is plausible for some shootings, but there is no basis for estimating how often it applies. Firearms are rarely used by serial killers, for example, who are considered among the most intent of all killers. Often guns are used to achieve some objective other than killing, such as to threaten. The use of guns to threaten that has been the best measured is robbery, in which the purpose is to get persons, usually strangers, to hand over property. Guns are also used to threaten or to inflict harm against family members or casual acquaintances in many different situations—disputes, revenge for some perceived slight or chronic harassment, and the like. Another use of threat is self-defense, in which, for example, a surprised homeowner may brandish or fire a gun primarily to frighten a burglar away.

The choice of a firearm to communicate threats has two potentially offsetting effects on lethality. if use of a gun instead enables the initiator to achieve his or her goals without firing, physical harm is prevented (Kleck, 1991). But having a gun may encourage some people to initiate robberies or altercations against others who would otherwise appear too invulnerable to challenge; occasionally the gun will be discharged in those encounters, causing physical harm.

Guns may also be fired in circumstances that involve no strategy. Such incidents include gratuitous murders at the successful conclusion of a robbery—perhaps as a manifestation of hate or of what has been termed recreational violence. Also, guns may be fired in conflicts between intimates or more casual acquaintances involving intense anger, fear, or both. Between 1976 and 1987, more than twice as many women were shot and killed by their husband or intimate partner as were killed by strangers using any means. In violent domestic disputes, the choice of a weapon may well be the nearest available object that can project force, and it seems likely that instrumentality rather than intent contributes most of the firearm's lethal effect.

Police and court records make clear that neither these scenarios nor countless others should be ignored in debates over firearms policy. The difficulty, as any trial judge knows, is that establishing the motive for an instance of gun use is a formidable, time-consuming, judgmental task, often with an uncertain outcome.

Available information is therefore indirect and imprecise. In an analysis of gun assaults in Chicago (Zimring, 1968), the victim received a single wound in over 80 percent of both fatal and nonfatal gun assaults. Since most guns have the capability to inflict multiple wounds, this suggests that at least some assaulters with guns lacked sufficient intent to exhaust all options for killing the persons they attacked.[3] An analysis of survey data for victims of 12,000 robberies (Cook, 1980) is consistent with Kleck's conclusion that guns are sometimes used to threaten victims who would otherwise be relatively invulnerable: 55 percent of commercial robberies but only 13 percent of other robberies involve guns; the few gun robberies of persons tend to target relatively invulnerable groups and young adult males; and nongun street robberies are most likely to target women, children, and elderly victims. Similarly, Sampson and Lauritsen (Volume 3) report that, between 1973 and 1982, approximately 41 percent of male victims of violent crimes other than homicide, but only 29 percent of female victims, were attacked by persons with weapons—a pattern consistent with the use of weapons to overcome victim invulnerability rather than necessarily to kill.

A survey of 1,874 incarcerated convicted felons interviewed during 1982 provides a more precise but perhaps unrepresentative distribution of the motivations of criminal gun users (Wright and Rossi, 1985). Of the 184 who fired a gun while committing the offense for which they were incarcerated, only 36 percent reported doing so "to kill the victim." More commonly reported motivations were "to protect myself" (48 percent) and "to scare the victim" (45 percent). Incarcerated offenders are not representative of all offenders and may be reluctant to report an intent to kill. Nevertheless, the data suggest strongly that many criminals who fire guns do so for reasons other than a single-minded attempt to kill. In fact, as the authors conclude, "*most of the men [76%] who actually fired guns in criminal situations claimed to have had no prior intention of so doing*" (Wright and Rossi, 1985:15; emphasis in original).

These findings indicate that, even in violent felonies, firearms are sometimes fired without a premeditated intent to kill. Consequently, a problem for future research is to measure what fraction of the difference in lethality between firearms and other weapons is due to instrumentality rather than intent. Since this fraction of lethality would be reduced if guns became less available, the research findings should be integral to debates over firearms policy.

FIREARMS, ENCOUNTERS, AND INJURY RATES

To this point, our discussion has treated the gun victim as a passive target. Usually, of course, violent gun use occurs during an encounter between two or more people and depends on the nature of their interaction. As we indicate . . . , far too little is known about these interactions generally, in part because records of representative samples of assaults are difficult to construct, compile, and analyze. However, the choice of weapon for attacks and for self-defense is important in determining the probability and severity of injury when a gun is involved.

Weapon Choice by Perpetrators

Most of the evidence about perpetrators' weapon choice and lethality comes from studies of robberies and assaults. Studies of robbery reviewed by Cook (1991) indicate that, compared with other robbers, those who carry a gun are more likely to complete their robberies without experiencing victim resistance and without injuring the victims. However, because gun injuries are so much more likely to be lethal, the fatality rate for gun robberies, 4 per 1,000, is about triple the rate in knife robberies and 10 times the rate in robberies with other weapons (Cook, 1980). Zimring and Zuehl (1986) report a similar differential for nonresidential robberies known to the police. But because nonlethal residential robberies are more likely to be reported if a gun was used, including residential robberies in the analysis attenuates the lethality differential.

Kleck and McElrath (1989) report a somewhat different pattern for assaults. The presence of a lethal weapon decreases the chance of actual physical attack. If an attack occurs, injury is less likely with a gun than with a knife. When an injury occurs, the fatality rate is higher in gun incidents than in knife incidents. The latter effect approximately offsets the first two, so that fatalities are about equally likely in gun assaults and knife assaults.

The Bureau of Justice Statistics (1986:table 12) reported, by weapon type, the distribution of injury outcomes for violent victimizations of all types, based on National Crime Survey data for the period 1973 to 1982. Escalation from threat to attack, and especially to an attack causing injury, was far less probable when the offender was armed with a gun (probability = .14) than when he or she was unarmed (.30), armed with a knife (.25), or armed with any other weapon (.45). Given that they were injured, just over half of both gun victims and knife victims required medical attention, but gun victims were somewhat more likely to be hospitalized (.83) than were knife victims (.74) if they required medical help. Nevertheless, because of the low probabilities of attack and injury when the offender displayed a gun, the overall probability of being hospitalized following victimization by a gun-wielding offender was only .06—the same as when the offender was unarmed, and less than when the offender was armed with a knife (.10) or with another weapon (.16).[4]

The data do not of course explain the low probabilities of attack and injury in events in which guns are involved. The attacker's display of the gun may intimidate the victims into submission rather than resistance; the attacker may fire the gun but miss (an event that has no analog in statistics on attacks by unarmed offenders); or the intended victims of gun wielders may themselves be more likely to be carrying guns, which they display or use in self-defense.

Firearm Use in Self-Defense

The use of guns for self-defense is one of the most controversial topics in firearms policy, and it promises to become more so if residents of high-crime areas grow more skeptical that police can or will effectively protect them and their property. In a 1979 survey, 20 percent of all gun owners and 40 percent of all handgun owners cited self-defense at home as the most important reason for their gun ownership; for handgun owners, self-defense was the most commonly cited reason (DecisionMaking Information, Inc., 1979, cited in Wright et al., 1983:96). But self-described "self-defense" is ambiguous; it may refer, for example, to homeowners with a generalized fear of burglary, to single women who have received specific threats of rape, to belligerent regular patrons of "fighting bars" who anticipate confrontations, to gang members preparing for neighborhood intrusions by violent rival gangs, to criminals fearing retaliation for their previous crimes, and even to criminals in the course of their crimes— recall that in Wright and Rossi's sample of incarcerated felons, 48 percent of those who fired guns cited self-defense as a motive. Police report anecdotally hearing "It was him or me" as an increasingly common excuse offered by alleged youthful killers with guns.

Counts of Gun Use for Self-Defense

Because self-defense is such an ambiguous term, it is not surprising that there is great dispute over how often firearms are actually used for self-defense. Using National Crime Survey data, Cook (1991) estimates incidents of self-defense firearm use at 78,000 per year, just below the number of people killed and wounded by firearms. Drawing on a number of surveys that ask about self-defense uses of guns without tying them to specific incidents, Kleck puts the annual number of self-defense uses about 10 times higher—between 700,000 (G. Kleck, personal communication to Jeffrey A. Roth, National Research Council, 1990; Kleck, 1991) and one million (Kleck, 1988) per year, about equal to the number of violent crimes involving guns.

Part of the discrepancy is no doubt accounted for by methodology. The National Crime Survey excludes commercial robberies, and it undercounts attempted and completed rapes and sexual assaults, particularly by family members; self-defense gun uses in those incidents would be missed as well. The surveys reviewed by Kleck (1988, 1991) have smaller sample sizes and longer reference periods, and they leave definitions of *self-defense* and use to respondents. Besides the ambiguity in defining self-defense, the counts may be inflated by respondents' inadvertent telescoping of incidents of self-defense into the reference period from previous periods. Also, some reported instances of self-protection are not comparable to specific criminal victimizations: respondents in some surveys could well have been concerned about animal rather than human attackers; others may have simply brought the gun nearby in anticipation of an encounter that never occurred.[5] To correct for these and various other methodological artifacts, Kleck uses a number of adjustment factors, some of which rely on untested assumptions. He presents no sensitivity analyses of alternative adjustment procedures, and some of them are incompletely documented. our calculations indicate that making alternative plausible assumptions would substantially decrease Kleck's estimates of annual selfdefense uses.[6]

Because of the likely undercounts in the National Crime Survey and the uncertainties surrounding Kleck's sources and adjustments, the discrepancy about how and how often guns are used for self-defense remains approximately 80,000 to 700,000. Some of it can be accounted for by Kleck's adjustment factors. But an additional cause is almost certainly that some of what respondents designate as their own self-defense would be construed as aggression by others.

As recommended by Cook (1991), there is a need for estimates that are free of the threshold and reporting problems associated with the National Crime Survey and the FBI's Supplementary Homicide Reports but that differentiate among self-defense uses and that rest on surveys of sufficiently high quality to eliminate the need for dubious adjustment procedures.

The Probability of Gun Use for Self-Defense

In making the decision whether to purchase a gun for protection, it is less relevant to know how often guns are used for self-defense than to know either the probability of using the gun if victimized or the consequences of using it. According to National Crime Survey tabulations, victims rarely defend themselves with firearms—1.2 percent of robberies, 1.4 percent of assaults, 3.1 percent of all residential burglaries, and 4.6 percent of residential burglaries by strangers.[7] Self-defense gun use, however, is associated with a reduced risk of physical attack and injury. Of intended robbery victims who defended themselves with guns, only 17 percent reported being injured, compared with 33 percent overall and 25 percent of those who made no self-protection effort. For assaults, the injury rates were 12 percent for targets who used guns, compared with 30 percent overall and 27 percent who took no self-protective action (Kleck, 1988:table 4).

Statistical associations such as these have been interpreted as demonstrations of the self-defense value of guns. However, since such self-defense uses are so rare in victimizations, they may well represent anomalies—scenarios in which, for example, the initiator failed to surprise the intended victim. In losing the advantage of surprise, the initiator may simultaneously become more vulnerable to any form of self-defense and give a gun-owning intended victim time to arm himself. Without detailed comparisons of situational dynamics in events in which gun-owning victims did and did not use their guns in self-defense, claims that average victims can successfully defend themselves with guns against robbery, burglary, and assault remain unproven.

Firearm ownership can carry substantial risks. In confrontations with assailants, even experienced owners of firearms can find their weapons turned against them. Between 1984 and 1988, 93 percent of all law enforcement officers killed in the line of duty died of gunshot wounds. Sixty-four of these officers (19 percent) lost their lives when their service weapons were turned against them (unpublished data, Federal Bureau of Investigation).

Guns in the home may also increase a family's risk of serious injury or death through mishandling, family violence, or suicide. Kellermann and Reay (1988) studied all gunshot deaths occurring in King County, Washington, between 1978 and 1983 and found that 52 percent occurred in the home where the firearm involved was kept. For every time a gun in the home was involved in a self-protection homicide, they noted 1.3 unintentional deaths, 4.5 criminal homicides, and 37 firearm suicides. Wintemute et al. (1987) studied 88 incidents in which young California children fatally shot a playmate or themselves and noted that 75 percent occurred while children were playing with a gun or demonstrating its use. In at least 48 percent of fatal residential shootings, children gained access to unlocked firearms that were stored loaded. Below the age of 8, few children can reliably distinguish a toy gun from a real one.

Firearm Availability and Violence

How is the availability of guns related to overall levels of violence? The discussion above has established that greater gun availability is associated with more robberies, home burglaries, assaults, and homicides using guns—but this is only one of several countervailing relationships to be considered. By reducing robbery and home burglary completion rates, self-defense gun use theoretically decreases the rewards for these crimes and increases the perceived risks to offenders. Yet guns in the homes of lawabiding citizens are themselves tempting targets for burglars. Moreover, by analogy from theoretical models of international arms races (Downs, 1991), the fear that potential victims or adversaries may be armed may simply encourage someone planning an attack to acquire superior firepower and carry out the attack regardless. Because of these conflicting potential incentives, it is not clear a priori whether greater firearms availability should be expected to increase or decrease aggregate violence levels.

Indirect empirical evidence on this question is available from four kinds of studies: multivariate statistical analyses of nonfatal violent crime levels, using the prevalence of gun use in homicides and suicides as a proxy measure for gun availability (Cook, 1979, 1985); crossnational comparisons of gun availability measures and gun crimes (van Dijk et al., 1990); time-series analyses of gun availability measures and homicide rates (Phillips et al., 1976; Kleck, 1984; McDowall, 1991); and comparisons between jurisdictions in which substantial availability differences are generally acknowledged without being precisely measured (Sloane et al., 1988).

Studies of all these types are discussed by Cook (1991). They find no relationship between gun availability and the number of nonfatal violent crimes. For crimes that end in death, they generally find that greater gun availability is associated with somewhat greater use of firearms and somewhat greater rates of felony murder, but do not account for a large fraction of the variation.[8] Cook (1979) finds no discernible effect of gun ownership prevalence on robbery rates. Comparing experience in Seattle and Vancouver, two neighboring jurisdictions that are demographically and socioeconomically similar but have different gun laws, Sloane et al. (1988) found no differences in event measures—burglary and simple and aggravated assault rates—but Seattle, which has more permissive gun laws, had an overall homicide rate more than 60 percent higher and a firearm homicide rate 400 percent higher.

Even where positive correlations are found between measures of gun availability and nonfatal violent crime, the direction of the causal chain is unclear. Some households may be arming themselves in response to increases in violent crime rates (G. Kleck, personal communication to Jeffrey A. Roth, National Research Council, 1990). Differences across nations, states, and communities may reflect separate local traditions about guns and about violence, rather than any direct connection between guns and violence (Cook, 1991). To the extent that alienation from public institutions exists in black communities . . . , it could account for higher levels of gun ownership and of violent crime; mistrust of the police and courts could trigger a "vigilante" mentality in which citizens arm themselves in order to be prepared to settle disputes without recourse to the civil or criminal justice system.

The strongest empirical evidence on how variations in firearms availability affect levels of violent crime and felony homicides can be obtained from carefully controlled evaluations of changes in laws and especially in enforcement efforts, that reduce firearms availability. As background for a such a discussion, we summarize what little is known about the sources of firearms used in violent events.

Sources of Firearms

According to recent estimates, only about one firearm of every six used in crimes was legally obtained. The high rate of handgun murders in cities such as New York and Washington, which have highly restricted legal access to handguns, is further evidence that guns are often obtained illegally, as is the recent increase in firearm homicides among black males ages 15 to 19, since minors are legally prohibited nearly everywhere from owning handguns,

Most published research on illegal and unregulated sources of firearms is several years old and is, as one might expect, sketchy and unrepresentative. But at least during the 1970s and early 1980s, the path from manufacturer to gun felon involved theft and unregulated private transfers far more often than licensed dealers. The small volume of illegal sales by dealers is usually a small-scale, decentralized, off-the-books activity involving used guns rather than a trade in new guns dominated by large organizations.

Theft—from licensed dealers, from residences, and from other criminals—is an important source of firearms used in felonies. Moore (1981) reports the results of manufacturer-to-user traces by the Bureau of Alcohol, Tobacco, and Firearms of 113 handguns used in Boston felonies during 1975–1976. Of the guns whose histories could be traced, 40 percent were stolen at some point: 12 percent of those used in assaults, and 56 percent of those used in other crimes, which presumably were more likely to involve advance planning. Another 29 percent were purchased directly from licensed retailers (27 percent by legally eligible purchasers, and 2 percent by proscribed persons), and 20 percent involved a chain of private transfers, which are not federally regulated.

In a survey of 1,874 incarcerated felons, 32 percent of those who used guns in the instant offense reported stealing them, 16 percent purchasing them from dealers, and 52 percent buying or borrowing them from private sources (Wright and Rossi, 1985). Of special interest are the 52 percent of respondents who rated "need gun to do crime" as a "somewhat" or "very" important motive for obtaining their guns. Of these, 45 percent reported stealing them and 30 percent reported buying them on black markets—compared with only 24 percent and 22 percent, respectively, among respondents for whom use in crime was rated "not important" as a motive for obtaining their guns (calculated from Wright and Rossi, 1985:table 21).

To explore the nature of the illegal market in firearms, Moore (1981) tabulated the investigative files for 131 cases of "dealing without a license" that were closed by the Bureau of Alcohol, Tobacco, and Firearms during 1974 and 1976; these were virtually all the cases closed in seven regional offices. According to these files, the trade is of small scale: the majority of traders had no inventories at the time of arrest, only 10 percent had more than 20 guns on hand, and the majority sold fewer than 5 guns per month. Despite the small scale of operations, the sources of illegally sold guns were diverse: thefts from residences and other dealers, legal purchases from other dealers, and unregulated purchases from private owners were all represented in substantial numbers.

While this information must be considered dated and imprecise, it establishes four points about the acquisition of guns used in crimes during the 1970s and early 1980s. First, all distribution channels: legal and illegal purchases from licensed dealers, unregulated private transactions, and theft-are potentially important sources of guns used in violent crime. Second, illegal sources were most important for those acquiring guns in explicit preparation for later crimes. Third, illegal sellers of firearms tend to be small-scale independent operators rather than members of large organizations. Fourth, most people who buy guns from licensed dealers that they later use in crimes were legally entitled to make their purchases.

If these findings still hold today, they suggest that illegal firearms transactions more closely resemble today's decentralized crack trade than the earlier highly organized distribution of heroin and powdered cocaine. In turn, this suggests that local-level interdiction efforts in illegal firearms traffic may reduce firearm violence more effectively than expanded federal regulation of licensed dealers and interstate commerce. This inference was drawn by Moore more than a decade ago, and it is echoed (for different reasons) in the call by participants in the December 1990 Forum on Youth Violence in Minority Communities for greater community involvement in the formulation of local firearm policy (Centers for Disease Control, 1991). However, there is as yet no strong evidence bearing on which centralized or decentralized approaches, if any, are most effective in enforcing existing firearms regulations, and on the importance of community involvement in increasing the effectiveness of enforcement.

INTERVENTIONS TO REDUCE FIREARM VIOLENCE

The strongest evidence on how firearms availability affects levels of violent crime and felony homicides can be obtained from carefully controlled evaluations of interventions that reduce firearms availability. This principle is true not only of interventions to modify the availability of firearms, but also of interventions to modify their uses, their allocation across owner categories, and their lethality. (This classification of interventions appears in Moore, no date; other useful classifications appear in Zimring, 1991; and Kellermann et al., 1991.) The need for evaluations encompasses legal interventions; technological interventions that modify firearms, ammunition, and shields; and interventions involving public education about uses and misuses of firearms. Although substantial experience has been gained with several of these intervention strategies, there is a dearth of evaluations sound enough to permit us to learn from that experience.

Table 1 lists legal, technological, and public education interventions classified by their objective: to alter the uses, allocation, lethality, or availability of firearms. These objectives are not mutually exclusive, and some interventions are intended to achieve several of them simultaneously. For example, the Federal Gun Control Act of 1968 contained provisions to reduce gun availability (by restricting imports) and allocation (by prohibiting sales to convicted felons, minors, and certain others). Statutory waiting periods for purchases from licensed gun dealers, which are intended primarily to affect firearms allocation (by improving enforcement of the 1968 act), may affect uses (e.g., if a prospective purchaser's passionate anger subsides during the waiting period).

Theoretically, some of these intervention strategies may reinforce each other if introduced as a package. For example, mandatory waiting periods may be more effective if accompanied by interventions to disrupt illegal gun distribution channels. Or public education on safe use and storage of guns may be a useful requirement as part of an owner licensing program; however, experience with driver's education in reducing automobile deaths is not encouraging (Robertson, 1983). Registration of guns to particular owners, like automobile registration, might facilitate other interventions intended to achieve one of the listed objectives (Moore, no date).

Unfortunately, there is little evidence that bears on these speculations about control strategies. The technological strategies—many of which arise from the public health approach to injury control—are relatively untested. And there are few evaluations of the effects of legal strategies embodied in existing federal, state, and local laws (Wright et al., 1983:244). The opportunities to learn from enactment and enforcement of restrictions are sometimes overlooked by both their advocates and their opponents in public debates.

The Legal Environment

As background, a brief overview follows of laws that attempt to implement the strategies in table 1. The reader is referred to Wright et al. (1983) for a comprehensive overview as of a decade ago, and to Bureau of Alcohol, Tobacco and Firearms (1988, 1989) for more detailed compilations of federal, state, and local laws.

Briefly, the Federal Gun Control Act of 1968 attempts to restrict imports of military weapons and to interdict interstate retail trade in all firearms by limiting

Table 1. Evaluation Status of Strategies and Interventions for Reducing Gun Violence

Strategy and intervention	Evaluated?	Effective?
Strategy 1: Alter gun uses or storage		
Place and manner laws		
Restrict carrying		
Bartley-Fox Amendment	Yes	Yes
Enhance sentences for felony gun use		
Michigan	Yes	Partial[a]
Pennsylvania	Yes	Partial[a]
Increase probability of sentences for felony gun use		
Operation Triggerlock	No	?
Civil/administrative laws		
Owner liability for damage by gun	No	?
Technological		
Enhance/maintain firearm detectability	No	?
Metal detectors in dangerous places	No	?
Enhance visibility of dangerous illegal uses	No	?
Shields for vulnerable employees	No	?
Public education		
Safe use and storage	No	?
Role in self-defense	Yes	?
Strategy 2: Change gun allocation		
Civil/administrative laws		
Permissive licensing of owners (e.g., all but felons, drug users, minors, etc.)	No	?
Waiting periods for gun purchases	No	?
Restrict sales to high-risk purchasers Gun Control Act of 1968	Yes	No
Law enforcement		
Disrupt illegal gun markets	No	?
Mandatory minimum sentences for gun theft	No	?
Technological		
Combination locks on guns	No	?
Strategy 3: Reduce lethality of guns		
Protective clothing in dangerous encounter	No	?
Reduce barrel length and bore	No	?
Reduce magazine size	No	?
Ban dangerous ammunition	No	?
Strategy 4: Reduce number of guns		
Restrictive licensing systems D.C. Firearms Control Act of 1968	Yes	Yes
Restrict imports	No	?
Prohibit ownership	No	?

[a]Reduced gun homicides, no consistent effect on robberies, assaults, or nongun homicides.

legal firearms shipments to federally licensed dealers. Licensed dealers are prohibited from selling guns through the mail or across state lines except to other licensed dealers. The law also prohibits gun sales to certain categories of persons: minors, illegal aliens, felons convicted or under indictment, drug users, and former involuntarily committed mental patients. The 1968 act is enforced by the Bureau of Alcohol, Tobacco and Firearms. Bureau staffing decreased by about 24 percent between 1981 and 1983 and did not return to 1981 levels until 1989, despite its assumption of new responsibilities in arson and drug law enforcement (General Accounting Office, 1991:1315). There have been no rigorous evaluations of the effects of these changes in enforcement resource levels. However, the General Accounting Office (1991:39) noted a recent doubling of the police waiting time for routine traces of firearms used in crimes. Also, newspaper accounts provide anecdotal reports of convicted felons and active drug dealers obtaining licenses as federal firearms dealers; the licenses enable them to obtain large numbers of firearms for personal use for off-the-books sales to others (Isikoff, 1991).

Federally licensed dealers are also required to comply with state and local requirements, most of which are intended to keep guns away from designated high-risk categories of persons. The most common such restriction is a requirement that gun purchasers obtain a permit or license before taking possession. In most of the twenty-one states with license requirements as of 1989, eligibility for a license was "permissive" (i.e., open to most categories of persons), but a few jurisdictions have adopted "restrictive" licensing requirements, with eligibility limited to a few select groups. Among the nation's most restrictive laws is the District of Columbia's 1977 Firearms Control Act, which prohibits handgun possession by virtually anyone except police officers, security guards, and those who owned their handguns before the law went into effect. Nevertheless, Isikoff (1991) reported that there were forty-one federally licensed dealers in Washington, D.C.

A fundamental political and ethical issue in firearms regulation is the trade-off between the effects on deaths and injuries and the costs imposed on members of law-abiding society who use guns for recreation or other legal purposes—a policy evaluation criterion noted by Zimring (1991), Wright et al. (1983), and others. Consequently, some firearm regulations apply a strategy to a limited domain: only "high-risk" firearms, firearm users, or firearm uses. Examples include bans on Saturday night specials or assault weapons (considered high-risk weapons, respectively, because of concealability and rapid-fire capability), computer systems to verify that prospective gun buyers are not members of a prohibited category, and "place and manner" laws that prohibit designated high-risk firearm uses such as carrying concealed weapons or firing them in densely populated areas.

In short, there is a variety of legal, public education, and technological strategies for interventions with licensed firearm dealers, firearm owners, and the firearms themselves. For several reasons, it is impossible to predict a priori their effects on frequencies of violent events and violent deaths. The effects of strategies to alter firearm uses depend on individuals' behavioral responses to public education and to the disincentives of legal penalties; these cannot be known in advance. Interventions intended to reduce the lethality of firearms, or to reduce the availability of firearms in certain categories, may be thwarted by the substitution of other, more lethal categories; one cannot know the extent of substitution in advance. And interventions to alter the allocation or availability of firearms may be circumvented by illegal markets, to an extent that cannot be known in advance. Therefore, carefully controlled evaluations represent the only way of ascertaining intervention effects.

Findings from Previous Evaluations

As previously mentioned, there have been few evaluations of the legal, technological, and public education intervention strategies displayed in table 1. We summarize findings from those that are available.

Strategy 1: Alter Gun Uses or Storage

Of the tactics listed in the table to alter gun uses or storage, three have been more or less rigorously evaluated: restrictions on carrying firearms, sentence enhancements for using guns to commit felonies, and public education concerning gun use for self-defense. Evaluations provide strong evidence that carrying restrictions and sentence enhancements reduced the harm from gun violence in the urban jurisdictions in which they were evaluated. The evaluations of gun use promotion for self-defense were of poorer quality, and so their violence control effectiveness remains to be demonstrated. Although we could find no evaluations of actual experience with technological protections against dangerous uses of firearms or with owner liability laws for gun injuries or damage, their logic seems sufficiently persuasive to warrant systematic evaluation programs.

The most thoroughly evaluated restriction on gun uses is the 1974 Bartley-Fox Amendment, which expanded Massachusetts licensing procedures and mandated a one-year sentence for unlicensed carrying of firearms in public. Process evaluations suggest that the law was vigorously enforced immediately following passage, but that over the following two years police confusion about the law and growing judicial discretion in its application partially undercut its intent (Beha, 1977; Rossman et al., 1979). Early evaluations of the law's effects in Boston produced conflicting findings, but a more extensive evaluation that compared statewide trends with trends in neighboring states demonstrated rather clearly that the law decreased gun use in assaults and robberies and also decreased gun homicides during the two-year evaluation period (Pierce and Bowers, 1979).

Another approach to restricting high-risk gun use is a mandatory sentence increase for felonies in which a gun is used. This approach has been evaluated in six jurisdictions, and a meta-analysis of the findings concludes that the sentence enhancements decreased gun homicides, left nongun homicide levels unchanged, and produced no consistent effect on gun robberies or assaults (McDowall et al., 1992a, b). The homicide effects are consistent with a strong instrumental effect for guns and very little substitution of other weapons in homicides. The mixed results for robberies and assaults are puzzling because the one-year sentence enhancement is a smaller relative increment to the average homicide sentence than to the average assault or robbery sentence. It may well be that a clearer picture would have emerged if the available data had permitted a separate evaluation for commercial robberies (in which guns are most likely to be used) and provided more systematic recording and classification of assaults.

Currently, under Operation Triggerlock, special investigation and prosecution efforts are being employed to increase the *probability* of punishment for felony firearm use. Evaluation results are not available at this writing.

There have been at least two evaluations of interventions to promote the use of firearms for self-defense. Both involved simple comparisons of violent crime levels before and after the interventions, with no measures taken of gunshot injuries, fatal homicides, or firearm accidents. A highly publicized antirape police initiative that trained some 2,500 women residents of Orlando, Florida, in the safe use of firearms was followed by an 88 percent decrease in the recorded rape rate the following year (Kleck and Bordua, 1983). But the recorded rape rate in one year not long before the intervention had actually dropped to zero, suggesting problems with recording accuracy. Green (1987, cited in Cook, 1991) questioned the reliability of the police department's records in evaluating its own antirape program, and McDowall et al. (1991) found the decrease well within the bounds of normal year-to-year variation at that time. Similarly, a local ordinance requiring each household to own a firearm was passed in Kenesaw, Georgia, in 1982 and was followed by a drop in burglary rates (Kleck, 1988). However, a subsequent analysis of long-term trends by McDowall et al. (1991) demonstrated that the drop was well within the bounds of year-to-year variation in Kenesaw's burglary rates. Further evaluations, preferably involving randomized experiments and multiple outcome measures, are needed to yield a strong conclusion on the effectiveness of this approach.

Strategy 2: Change the Allocation of Firearms

Of the tactics for changing the allocation of firearms, we could find a rigorous evaluation of only one: the provision of the Federal Gun Control Act of 1968 that prohibits gun dealers from selling to certain categories of persons designated "dangerous." This provision seems to have had no significant effect on firearms injuries or deaths.

Because this law focused on interstate transactions, its effects on handgun use in assaults and homicides should have been evident in New York and Boston, where the incentives for out-of-state purchases were high because of unusually restrictive local license requirements. In fact, Zimring (1975) found that, before and after the law was enacted, trends in those jurisdictions were not significantly different from trends in other large cities.

The lack of effect may have been due to a lack of enforcement effort. A 1970 crackdown to enforce the federal gun law in the District of Columbia, involving a seven- to tenfold increase in enforcement agents on the street, did accompany a six-month decrease in gun homicides, while other homicides remained constant. But evaluation results for the 1968 act may also reflect the fact that purchases by ineligible persons from licensed dealers make only a small contribution to gun use in violent crimes. We consider interventions in gun markets involving unlicensed dealers in the conclusion to this chapter.

Strategy 3: Reduce the Lethality of Available Firearms

The third strategy is to designate certain firearms dangerous because of their concealability, firepower, or other characteristic, then either to restrict access to them by law or to make them less dangerous through technological means.

Recently, the most conspicuous proposals to implement this strategy have focused on assault weapons. The term has no generally accepted precise definition but seems to apply to rifles and pistols capable of automatic or semiautomatic fire and having a military appearance (Kleck, 1991). Except for military cosmetics (e.g., plastic rather than wood stocks, nonreflective rather than reflective surfaces) and a shift from American to foreign brands, the semiautomatic rifles that have recently become more visibly associated with urban homicides differ little from semiautomatic weapons that have been available for decades. This fact, which receives little attention from either advocates or opponents of special restrictions on these weapons, has complicated the problem of drafting legislation.

There is controversy over how much more lethal assault weapons are than other rifles and pistols (Kleck, 1991). But this controversy has been carried out entirely in terms of laboratory observations of the firepower of particular weapons. Resolution of that controversy in laboratory settings would provide little useful information about actual use of such weapons in violent crimes.

Given the imprecision of the term assault weapon, it should not be surprising that there are no generally accepted estimates of the number of such weapons in the United States, of ownership patterns, of their lethality compared with other weapons, or of their uses in crimes (Zimring, 1991). Therefore, legislative efforts to restrict their availability are proceeding with very little basis in knowledge.

Even if workable restrictions on assault weapons can be specified and implemented, past experience suggests that continuing enforcement efforts would be required to avoid circumvention through illegal markets. Therefore, the needs for evaluation cited in connection with Strategy 2 apply here as well.

Strategy 4: Reduce the Availability of Firearms

Perhaps the most ambitious effort to reduce the number of firearms in a community was the 1977 District of Columbia Firearms Control Act, which prohibited handgun ownership by virtually everyone except police officers, security guards, and previous gun owners. Three evaluations of this intervention are available: U.S. Conference of Mayors (1980), Jones (1981), and Loftin et al.

(1991). As discussed by Cook (1991), the first two evaluations indicate that, during periods of vigorous enforcement, the District of Columbia law did reduce the rates of gun robbery, assault, and homicide during the three years following implementation. The effect was especially strong for homicides arising from disputes among family members and acquaintances. The Loftin et al. (1991) evaluation found decreases of about one-fourth in D.C. gun homicides and suicides immediately after passage of the law. The effect persisted until 1988, when gun homicides associated with crack markets increased, and it was not mirrored by trends in D.C. nongun homicides or suicides, or in gun homicides or suicides in nearby suburban areas that were not subject to the law. While none of these findings should be considered conclusive or universally applicable, their convergence—despite different approaches—suggests that local restrictive licensing laws, when enforced, may reduce firearm homicides and warrant evaluations in other communities.

RESEARCH AND EVALUATION NEEDS

Violence involving firearms exacts a large toll in terms of deaths, injuries, and monetary costs. The risk of firearm violence is high and rising, especially among young black males.

Research is needed to determine answers to a number of questions about the multiple complex relationships between firearms and violence. Ignorance is especially profound concerning socalled assault weapons, a poorly defined category.

One or more surveys are needed to develop accurate estimates of ownership by gun type, of motives and sources for obtaining guns, and especially of gun acquisition patterns among juveniles and criminals. Case control, ethnographic survey, and other studies are needed of robberies and assaults involving guns to discover the risk factors associated with actual shootings and the role of guns in self-defense.

Existing data are inadequate for measuring the annual incidence of self-defense gun use. The National Crime Survey is subject to event threshold and recall problems, and other estimates are subject to definitional ambiguities and other methodological problems that cannot be solved without resorting to dubious adjustment factors. For informing individuals' choices about gun ownership, however, the more important questions are how often and under what circumstances intended victims deploy their guns in self-defense and how the deployment affects the outcome of the event. These questions bear further analysis not only through victimization surveys but also through analyses of event records.

Analyses of natural variation have established that increased firearm availability is associated with increased firearm use in violent crime. But the methods used to date have been insufficient to answer a more basic question: Do changes in gun availability cause changes in violence levels overall? To answer this question, evaluations are needed of the effects of gun supply reduction initiatives on violence levels in particular geographic areas.

Educational, technological, and legal strategies can be devised with the objectives of changing how handguns are used and stored, changing their allocation from higher-risk to lower-risk segments of the population, reducing their lethality, or reducing their numbers. For any of these policies to reduce homicides, they must reduce violent uses of at least some types of guns to an extent that is not offset by substitution of other more lethal weapons.

It is not clear in advance whether this condition would be met for any policy focused on handguns. While intentional firearm injuries are two to five times as lethal as injuries from knives, the next most lethal weapon, it is not known how much of this difference in lethality is due to weapon characteristics and how much to more lethal intentions by those who attack with guns. We also do not know the extent to which long guns or assault weapons would be substituted if handguns became less available, or indeed whether those weapons are more lethal than handguns when used in violent crimes.

Without a priori knowledge, an assessment must depend on evaluations of experience, which are conditionally encouraging. Examples exist of reductions in violent gun uses caused by legal restrictions on carrying guns, by enhanced sentences for felony gun use, and by restrictive licensing of firearms in particular jurisdictions. However, the success of legal strategies depends critically on the nature and intensity of enforcement efforts, since illegal or unregulated gun transfers supply most of the guns used in crimes.

Enforcement efforts directed against illegal gun markets combine elements of the first three strategies shown in table 1. Also, unlike interventions involving licensed dealers and gun owners, most of whom are law abiding, disruption of illegal markets focuses on persons who are violating laws. Interventions against illegal drug markets should be more effective if they are informed by more specific research on the nature of those markets—their size, their distribution channels, and their retail-level marketing techniques. As a starting point, however, efforts to disrupt local illegal gun markets might reasonably borrow tactics that are currently being used against illegal drug markets. These could include buy-bust operations,[9] high-priority investigation and prosecution of alleged unregulated gun dealers, the development of minors arrested in possession of guns as informants against gun sources, phony fencing operations for stolen guns, high-priority investigations and prosecutions of burglaries and robberies in which guns are stolen, and high mandatory minimum sentences for those who steal or illegally sell guns.

. . . Community support was . . . cited as a necessary ingredient of firearm policy development at the December 1990 Forum on Youth Violence in Minority Communities (Centers for Disease Control, 1991). This suggests that community-oriented or neighborhood-oriented police work involving close coordination with community-based organizations may be useful in reducing residents' motivations to acquire guns for self-defense, in encouraging community members to notify police anonymously about illegal gun transactions and persons illegally carrying guns, and in supporting market disruption tactics when necessary.

In view of the lack of available evidence, a high priority should be placed on evaluations of the violence-reduction effects—on gun and nongun violence and on illegal and unregulated gun transfers—of interventions to reduce illegal sales of firearms.

Specifically, high priority should be placed on evaluating the effects of three intervention strategies:

- disrupting illegal gun markets using the centralized and street-level tactics currently in use for disrupting illegal drug markets;
- enforcing existing bans on juvenile possession of handguns; and
- a community-oriented or neighborhood-oriented police work involving close coordination with residents and community-based organizations.

At this writing, the Department of justice is expanding its pilot testing of "Operation Weed and Seed"—a program under which these and other initiatives involving police—community cooperation could be systematically evaluated.

Rigorous evaluations should also be made of the effects of strategies other than law enforcement interventions: public education interventions to change how guns are stored and used and technological interventions to reduce the lethality of firearms. To the extent that consideration is given to reducing the availability of assault weapons through new statutes, there is a need to reach consensus on a definition of that term, and then to ascertain their level of violent use their lethality in actual use, and the effects of alternative enforcement strategies in reducing the violence associated with them.

NOTES

1. For legibility, trends in the 1984–1988 firearm homicide rate for black males are not displayed in figure 3 for all available age groups. The rate for ages 15–19 increased from 30 to 68 per 100,000, a 126 percent increase. The corresponding increases were from 2.1 to 4.5 (114 percent) for ages 10–14; from 63 to 104 (65 percent) for ages 20–24; from 70 to 90 (29 percent) for ages 25–29; and from 62 to 69 (11 percent) for ages 30–34 (Fingerhut et al., 1991).

2. Cook has estimated that for each new cohort of 100 guns, 33 uses in crime are reported. But because the frequency of repeat uses is unknown, the fraction that is ever used in this way is unknown.

3. Wright et al. (1983) point out that in some of the 80 percent, the shooter may have shot a second time but missed, and in others the killer may have failed to shoot a second time because the victim appeared to be dead already. It seems likely that both explanations apply to some incidents but that even together they are insufficient to account for all oneshot incidents.

4. Because National Crime Survey data include only nonfatal victimizations, the publication does not report conditional probabilities of being hospitalized or killed. Because deaths are so rare, however, those probabilities would not be substantially altered.

5. Respondents to one of the surveys of the uses of self-defense (Decision-Making Information, Inc., 1979) stated that only 31 percent of the incidents involving gun use for self-defense were "important enough to report to the police."

6. As one example, in a survey by Decision-Making Information (1979, cited in Wright et al., 1983:96), 15 percent of respondents reported "ever" using a gun for self-protection. To convert this

lifetime prevalence to an annual prevalence, Kleck multiplies it by the ratio 1.4/8.6, the ratio of annual to lifetime prevalence rates for self-defense uses obtained in another survey and obtains an estimate of 897,000 annual self-defense uses. Yet elsewhere in the same publication, he reports that the mean duration of gun ownership in a representative sample of gun owners is 23.4 years. if one accepted the 1.4 percent rate as accurate but assumed that selfdefense uses were distributed uniformly over the life of each gun, the implied adjustment ratio would be 1.4/23.4, which would reduce Kleck's annualized estimate to 329,000.

As another example, Kleck (1988:5 and table 2) adjusts justifiable civilian homicides with guns for assumed underreporting in the Uniform Crime Reports Supplementary Homicide Report. The adjustment involves 57 "other civilian legal defensive homicides" (OCLDHs) in Detroit and leads to a national estimate of 2,819 total firearm OCLDHs for 1980. Yet the estimation method for the Detroit OCLDHs is not explained, their cited source does not appear in the reference list, and no more than one OCLDH was estimated for any of the other five large jurisdictions included in Kleck's Table 2. Omitting the Detroit OCLDHs from the adjustment would reduce the national estimate from 2,819 to 1,711.

7. Because some incidents of self-defense with a firearm in events outside the home entail illegal firearms carrying, the rates for assaults and robberies may be underreported to interviewers. However, given the difficulty of gun deployment during a surprise robbery or assault, it seems unlikely that the rates for assaults and robberies are as high as those for residential burglaries, in which self-defense with a gun is generally legal.

8. Based on a multivariate analysis, Cook (1979) finds that a 10 percent reduction in the prevalence of gun ownership in a city is associated with about a 5 percent reduction in the gun robbery rate and a 4 percent reduction in the robbery murder rate. Killias (1990, cited in Cook, 1991) reports a correlation of .72 between the gun fraction in homicide and the prevalence of gun ownership for 11 countries.

9. In a buy-bust operation, a dealer is arrested following one or more illegal sales to undercover officers, which are usually recorded on videotape for use as evidence.

REFERENCES

Beha, J. A., III. 1977. " 'And nobody can get you out': The impact of a mandatory prison sentence for the illegal carrying of a firearm on the use of firearms and the administration of criminal justice in Boston." *Boston University Law Review* 57:96–146, 289–33.

Bureau of Alcohol, Tobacco, and Firearms. 1988. (Your Guide to) Federal Firearms Regulation, 1988–89. Bureau of Alcohol, Tobacco, and Firearms publication No. 5300.4. Washington, D.C.: U.S. Government Printing Office.

———. 1989. State Laws and Published Ordinances—Firearms. Washington, D.C.: U.S. Government Printing Office.

———. 1991. "How many guns?" ATF News (Press release). May 22.

Bureau of Justice Statistics. 1986. *The Use of Weapons in Committing Crimes.* Washington, D.C.: U.S. Government Printing Office.

———. 1989. *Criminal Victimization in the United States, 1987.* Washington, D.C.: U.S. Bureau of Justice Statistics.

———. 1992. *Criminal Victimization in the United States, 1990.* Washington, D.C.: U.S. Government Printing Office.

Centers for Disease Control. 1991. "Forum on Youth Violence in Minority Communities: Setting the Agenda for Prevention, December 10–12, 1990." Summary of the proceedings. *Public Health Reports* 106(3):225–77.

Cook, P. J. 1979. "The effect of gun availability on robbery and robbery murder: A cross section study of fifty cities." *Policy Studies Review Annual* 3.

———. 1980. "Reducing injury and death rates in robbery." *Policy Analysis* 6(1):21–45.

———. 1981. "Guns and crime: The perils of long division." *Journal of Policy Analysis and Management* 1:120–25.

———. 1985. *Report on a City-Specific Gun Prevalence Index.* Mimeographed. Durham, N.C.: Duke University, Institute of Policy Sciences.

———. 1991. "The technology of personal violence." In *Crime and Justice: A Review of Research.* Vol. 14. Edited by M. Tonry. Chicago: University of Chicago Press, pp. 1–72.

Curtis, L. A. 1974. *Criminal Violence: National Patterns and Behavior.* Lexington, Mass.: D.C. Heath.

Decision-Making Information, Inc. 1979. *Attitudes of the American Electorate Toward Gun Control.* Santa Ana, Calif.: Decision-Making Information, Inc.

Downs, G. W. 1991. "Arms race and war." In *Behavior, Society and Nuclear War.* Edited by P. E. Tetlock, J. L. Husbands, R. Jervis, P. C. Stern, and C. Tilly. New York: Oxford University Press, pp. 73–109.

Federal Bureau of Investigation. 1989. *Crime in the United States, 1988: Uniform Crime Reports.* Washington, D.C.: U.S. Government Printing Office.

———. 1991. *Uniform Crime Reports for the United States: 1990.* Washington, D.C.: U.S. Government Printing Office.

Fingerhut, L. A., J. C. Kleinman, E. Godfrey, and H. Rosenberg. 1991. "Firearm mortality among children, youth, and young adults 34 years of age, trends and current status: United States, 1979–88." *Monthly Vital Statistics Report* 39 (11, Supplement). Hyattsville, Md.: National Center for Health Statistics.

General Accounting Office. 1991. *BATF: Management Improvements Needed to Handle Increasing Responsibilities.* Report to the Chairman, Subcommittee on Oversight, Committee on Ways and Means, House of Representatives. GAO publication No. GGD91-67. Washington, D.C.: U.S. General Accounting Office.

Green, G. S. 1987. "Citizen gun ownership and criminal deterrence: Theory, research, and policy." *Criminology* 25:63–82.

Isikoff, Michael. 1991. "Gun dealers' 'great scam': U.S. licenses grow popular with criminals." *Washington Post*, 8 May, pp. A1, A8.

Jones, E. D., III. 1981. "The District of Columbia's Firearms Control Regulations Act of 1975: The toughest handgun control law in the United States or is it?" *Annals of the American Academy of Political and Social Science* 455:138–49.

Kellermann, A. L., and D. T. Reay. 1988. "Protection or peril? An analysis of firearm related deaths in the home." *New England Journal of Medicine* 319:1256–62.

Kellermann, A. L., R. K. Lee, J. A. Mercy, and J. Banton. 1991. "The epidemiologic basis for the prevention of firearm injuries." *Annual Review of Public Health* 12:17–40.

Killias, Martin. 1990. "Gun ownership and violent crime: The Swiss experience in international perspective." *Security Journal* 1(3):169–74.

Kleck, G. 1984. "The relationship between gun ownership levels and rates of violence in the United States." In *Firearms and Violence: Issues of Public Policy.* Edited by D.B. Kates Jr. Cambridge, Mass.: Ballinger.

———. 1988. "Crime control through the private use of armed force." *Social Problems* 35:1–22.

———. 1991. *Point Blank: Guns and Violence in America.* New York: Aldine de Gruyter.

Kleck, G., and D. J. Bordua. 1983. "The factual foundation for certain key assumptions of gun control." *Law and Policy Quarterly* 5:271–98.

Kleck, G., and K. McElrath. 1989. *The Effects of Weaponry on Human Violence.* Mimeographed. Tallahassee, Fla.: Florida State University, School of Criminology.

Loftin, C., D. McDowall, B. Wiersema, and T. J. Cottey. 1991. "Effects of restrictive licensing of handguns on homicide and suicide in the District of Columbia." *New England Journal of Medicine* 325 (December 5):1615–20.

McDowall, D. 1991. "Firearm availability and homicide rates in Detroit, 1951–1986." *Social Forces* 69(4):1085–1101.

McDowall, D., A. J. Lizotte, and B. Wiersema. 1991. "General deterrence through civilian gun ownership: An evaluation of the quasi-experimental evidence." *Criminology* 29(4):541–59.

McDowall, David, Colin Loftin, and Brian Wierserna. 1992a. "A comparative study of the preventive effects of mandatory sentencing laws for gun crimes." *Journal of Criminal Law and Criminology*, forthcoming.

——. 1992b. "Preventive effects of mandatory sentencing laws for gun crimes." In *Proceedings of the Social Statistics Section*, pp. 87–94. Annual meeting of the American Statistical Association, Atlanta, Ga., August 18–22, 1991. Alexandria, Va.: American Statistical Association.

Moore, M. H. 1981. "Keeping handguns from criminal offenders." *The Annals of the American Academy of Political and Social Science* 455:92–109.

No Alternative Policy Approaches to the Control of Handgun Abuse. Unpublished manuscript available from the Kennedy School of Government, Harvard University.

Newton, G. D., Jr., and F. E. Zimring. 1969. *Firearms and Violence in American Life*. Washington, D.C.: U.S. Government Printing Office.

Phillips, L., H. L. Votey Jr., and J. Howell. 1976. "Handguns and homicide: Minimizing losses and the costs of control." *Journal of Legal Studies* 5:463–78.

Pierce, G. L., and W. J. Bowers. 1979. "The Impact of the Bartley-Fox Gun Law on Crime in Massachusetts." Unpublished manuscript. Boston: Northeastern University, Center for Applied Social Research.

Rice, Dorothy P., Ellen J. MacKenzie, and Associates. 1989. *Cost of Injury in the United States: A Report to Congress*. San Francisco, Calif.: Institute for Health and Aging, University of California and Injury Prevention Center, Johns Hopkins University.

Robertson, L. S. 1983. *Injuries: Causes, Control Strategies, and Public Policy*. Lexington, Mass.: Lexington Books.

Rossman, D., P. Froyd, G.L. Pierce, J. McDevitt, and W. Bowers. 1979. *The Impact of the Mandatory Gun Law in Massachusetts*. Boston University School of Law: Center for Criminal Justice.

Sloane, J. H., A. L. Kellermann, D. T. Rey, J. A. Ferris, T. Koepsell, F. P. Rivara, C. Rice, L. Gray, and J. LoGerfo. 1988. "Handgun regulations, crimes, assaults, and homicide: A tale of two cities." *New England Journal of Medicine* 319:1256–62.

U.S. Conference of Mayors. 1980. *The Analysis of the Firearms Control Act of 1975: Handgun Control in the District of Columbia*. Mimeographed. Washington, D.C.

van Dijk, Jan J.M., Pat Mayhew, and Martin Killias. 1990. *Experiences of Crime Across the World: Key Findings From the 1989 International Crime Survey*. Deventer, Netherlands: Kluwer Law and Taxation Publishers.

Vinson, T. 1974. "Gun and knife attacks." *Australian Journal of Forensic Science* 7(2):76–83.

Wintemute, G. J., S. P. Teret, J. F. Kraus, and M. A. Wright. 1987. "When children shoot children. 88 unintentional deaths in California." *Journal of the American Medical Association* 257:3107–3109.

Wolfgang, M. 1958. *Patterns in Criminal Homicide*. New York: Wiley.

Wright, J. D., and P. H. Rossi. 1985. *The Armed Criminal in America: A Survey of Incarcerated Felons*. National Institute of Justice Research Report (July).

Wright, J. D., P. H. Rossi, and K. Daly. 1983. *Under the Gun: Weapons, Crime, and Violence in America*. Hawthorne, N.Y.: Aldine Publishing Company.

Zimring, F. E. 1968. "Is gun control likely to reduce violent killings?" *University of Chicago Law Review* 35:721–37.

——. 1975. "Firearms and federal law: The gun control act of 1968." *Journal of Legal Studies* 4:133–98.

——. 1989. "The problem of assault firearms." *Crime & Delinquency* 35(4):538–45.

——. 1991. "Firearms, violence, and public policy." *Scientific American* (November):48–54.

Zimring, F. E., and G. Hawkins. 1987. *The Citizen's Guide to Gun Control*. New York: Macmillan Publishing Company.

Zimring, F.E., and J. Zuehl. 1986. "Victim injury and death in urban robbery: A Chicago study." *Journal of Legal Studies* 15(1):1–40.

13

LETHAL VIOLENCE IN AMERICA

FRANKLIN E. ZIMRING & GORDON HAWKINS

FIREARMS AND LETHAL VIOLENCE*

W hen discussing American lethal violence with any foreign criminologist, guns are always the first factor to be mentioned as an explanation of the distinctively high rates of death in the United States. What sets the foreign criminologists' comments apart from our American colleagues is not the unanimity with which they focus on guns, however, because this topic is inevitably mentioned by American criminologists as well. But our foreign colleagues are frequently unwilling to discuss any other feature of American society or government *except* gun ownership and use. In Europe or Japan, any mention of social, demographic, or economic factors as a cause of homicide is commonly regarded as an evasion of the most obvious reason why American violence is specially dangerous. This singular preoccupation with guns and gun use overstates the degree to which U.S. lethal violence can be explained by a single cause, but not by much. Firearms use is so prominently associated with the high death rate from violence that starting with any other topic would rightly be characterized as an intentional evasion.

This [section] discusses the role of firearms use in explaining the high rate of lethal interpersonal violence in the United States. This is but one element of a complex set of issues that concerns that relationship between guns and violence

*From Franklin E. Zimring and Gordon Hawkins, *Crime Is Not the Problem: Lethal Violence in America* (New York: Oxford University Press, 1997), pp. 106–23. Copyright © 1997 by Oxford University Press, Inc. Used by permission of Oxford University Press, Inc.

in the United States. Self-inflicted and accidental gunshot cases are excluded from this analysis. We will not discuss general patterns of gun ownership and use . . . or survey the many different types of control strategy that might reduce gun violence. The central concern here is whether and to what extent our distinctive patterns of gun use explain the high death rates from American violence. . . .

Why Guns?

There are two features of the approach . . . that put special emphasis on gun use: the emphasis on lethal violence and the frequent use of crossnational comparisons. Figure 1 shows the special connection between gun use and deadly violence in the United States by comparing the proportion of police-reported gun use in total index felonies, violent felonies in the crime index, and killings resulting from intentional injury.

The estimates presented in the figure probably understate gun use in index and violent felonies recorded because gun use is not reported for forcible rape and cannot be assessed for noncontact property crime. . . . The 4 percent estimate for the proportion of total index offenses involving guns confirms what the National Rifle Association has been insisting upon for some time: only a very small proportion of all criminal offenses in the United States are known to involve guns. If all crimes are of equally serious concern to citizens and policy makers, the low prevalence of firearms in serious crime would be a significant reason to look for other instrumentalities and approaches when attempting to reduce crime.

What the middle bar shows is that when the crimes analyzed are restricted to those that threaten or inflict bodily injury—homicide, rape, robbery, and aggravated assault—the proportion of gun involvement increases fivefold, from 4 to 20 percent. When the subject of the inquiry shifts again to criminal injuries that take life, the prevalence of guns jumps again, this time rising to 70 percent. A shorthand way of communicating the importance of the shift to lethal violence as the focus of inquiry is this: If crime is nominated as the problem, guns are involved in one of every twenty-five cases; if lethal violence is nominated as the problem, then guns are implicated in seven of every ten cases.

The contrast between the one-in-five share of violent felonies committed with guns and the 70 percent gun share for American homicide makes guns appear very much more important when the focus shifts from all violence to lethal violence; this contrast also provides a preliminary basis for concluding that attacks with guns are more dangerous than attacks with other weapons. The 20 percent share of violent crime committed with guns in the United States is significant, but very far from cornering the market. The majority of robberies, rapes, and criminal assaults are committed with personal force, knives, or blunt objects. Even the elimination of all firearms incidents would leave a very high volume of violent offenses. But the 70 percent of all lethal attacks committed with firearms represents a statistical dominance that is difficult to ignore or to minimize. Guns alone account for more than twice as much homicide in the United States as all other means combined.

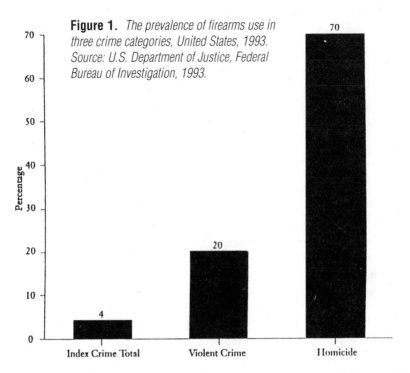

Figure 1. *The prevalence of firearms use in three crime categories, United States, 1993. Source: U.S. Department of Justice, Federal Bureau of Investigation, 1993.*

And the contrasting percentage of gun use for lethal and nonlethal violence also provides circumstantial evidence that guns are far more dangerous than any other instruments when used in violent assaults. If 25 percent of all aggravated assaults produce 70 percent of the lethal outcomes, then that 25 percent of gun attacks are seven times more likely to produce death on the average than the 80 percent of all serious assault that does not involve guns and that cumulatively accounts for only 30 percent of all killings. These are only preliminary indications, because gun attacks may be the product of different motives and situations from attacks employing other means. But the dominance of gun cases in the whole of the lethal violence category makes firearms use a necessary first step in the explanation of American lethal violence.

While solely domestic statistics implicate firearms as a dominant cause of American lethal violence, the sort of international statistical comparison that we have used as a primary tool in earlier analysis also calls attention to firearms. No large industrial democracy other than the United States reports firearms as the cause of a majority of its homicides. Thus, scholars engaging in international comparison are confronted with two extraordinary distinctions between homicide in the United States and in the rest of the developed Western world: very much higher rates of homicide in the United States, and a uniquely high percentage of gun use in U.S. violence. Concluding that the elevated gun use is a cause of the distinctively high homicide experience seems natural.

Table 1. Gun and Nongun Homicides, England and Wales and the United States, 1980–1984

Type of murder	Homicides		Average annual rate per one million population[a]		England and Wales to United States ratio
	England and Wales	United States	England and Wales	United States	
All gun[b]	213	63,218	.86	54.52	1 to 63.4
Handgun[b]	57	46,553	.23	40.15	1 to 174.6
Nongun[b]	2,416	41,354	9.75	35.67	1 to 3.7
Total[c]	2,629	104,572	10.61	90.19	1 to 8 5

[a]Annual average population for 1980–1984: United States, 231.9 million; England and Wales, 49.55 million.
[b]Figures for the United States involved some extrapolation from homicides for which weapon was known.
[c]Figures for England and Wales relate to offenses currently recorded as homicide.
Source: Clarke and Mayhew 1988, table 2, p. 107.

One example of this reasoning from a statistical comparison may be found in an essay by Ronald V. Clarke and Pat Mayhew, "The British Gas Suicide Story and Its Criminological Implications." Clarke and Mayhew compare homicide rates per one million population for England and Wales and the United States for firearms, handguns (also counted in the firearms category), and all means other than firearms. Their results are set out in a table, which is reproduced here as table 1.

All forms of homicide are more frequent in the United States than in England and Wales. Killings by all means other than guns occur in the United States at a rate per million population that is 3.7 times the nongun homicide rate reported in England and Wales. But homicides by handguns occur in the United States at a rate per million population that is 175 times as great. This comparison leads the authors to conclude that "there is little doubt that limiting the availability of firearms in the United States would have a substantial effect on homicide and probably also on other violent crime" (Clarke and Mayhew 1988:106).

Even though this conclusion cannot be established solely from populati on statistics of the sort presented in table 1, the tendency to reach it is inevitable when both the magnitude of gun use and the aggregate death toll differences are that high. The fact that homicide rates with handguns in the United States are 175 times as high as in Great Britain may be only coincidental to the large difference in total homicide rates between the two countries. But few who have studied these international differences are willing to accept the coincidence hypothesis. Instead, those who analyze American violence by first making international comparisons tend to be adamant in their belief that gun use is a major explanation of the elevated death toll from violence. As we have said, it is hard to get them to consider anything else.

And the obvious conclusion about the relationship between firearms and lethal violence in the United States is also the correct one. High levels of gun use in assault and robbery are a very important contributory cause to elevated

U.S. death rates from violence. While the magnitude of the difference that can be attributed solely to gun use cannot be determined with precision, as much as half of the difference between American and European homicide rates may be explained by differential resort in the United States to the most lethal of the commonly used instruments of violence.

On Global Comparisons

The type of data featured in figure 1 and in table 1 are global statistical comparisons that show the extent of the overlap between firearms and violence in the United States. We use the phrase "global comparison" to denote efforts to estimate the impact of gun use on the death rate from violence by obtaining a correlation between variations in gun use and variations in homicide rates. Such comparisons do not directly address issues of causation. A further limitation of most global comparative analyses is that they do not directly distinguish what features of firearms use might contribute to elevating death rates from those associated with other types of violent attack. So the global comparative approach should never be the endpoint of any analysis of firearms and violence. Nevertheless, the cautious use of basic comparison can tell us a great deal about the extent to which gun use increases death rates from violence.

One early test of global relationship was reported by Stephen Seitz in 1972 (Seitz 1972). Seitz observed a 0.98 correlation between the firearms homicide rate in a U.S. state in 1967 and the total rate of homicide experienced in that state, so that a higher-than-average death rate from firearms injury would almost predict a higher-than-average death rate from injury by all means. The interpretation of this relationship was: "It is almost impossible to conclude that the relation between firearms and criminal homicide is merely coincidental" (Seitz 1972:597).

The problem with inferring a causal connection between gun homicide and total homicide from this sort of correlation is that this type of relationship studied by Seitz has been categorized as a "part-whole correlation." Gun homicides constitute the majority of all homicides in the United States. Thus, if a state has a higher-than-average gun homicide rate, the total homicide rate would automatically tend to vary in the same direction as the gun homicide statistics.

The problem can be illustrated by imagining a study of the effect of weight loss strategies that found that those men and women who lost the largest amount of weight from their thighs, legs, and feet during a diet period also tended to lose the largest total amount of body weight. Does this tell us that a priority strategy of a diet regime should be weight reduction in the thighs, legs, and feet? The alternative to concluding that thighs are of special significance in weight reduction is understanding that the bottom half of the body is an important part of the body's weight and for that reason alone persons who lost considerable weight from their legs would have lost more total weight on a diet than those who lost a smaller percentage of their southern extremity poundage. Losing a substantial amount of weight in the legs, far from being an independent variable causing success in a dietary regime, is one of the major effects of having been on a diet.

Is there a way of eliminating the impact that death rates from firearms would have on total homicide rates only because they are such a substantial part of the homicide total? One promising approach would be to measure the influence, not of the number of people killed by guns in any given state, but of the proportionate use of guns rather than other methods of inflicting death. Suppose we compare, for each state, the proportion of fatal attacks using firearms with the total homicide rate for the particular state instead of comparing the rate of gun deaths with the total rate of all deaths, the notorious part-whole correlation. We are now predicting that a high proportionate use of guns will yield a higher-than-average homicide rate while states with lower relative gun use in deadly attacks will also have smaller-than-average total homicide rates. The correlation when we use a percentage homicide variable rather than the gun homicide rate for the fifty states in 1967 is 0.55, suggesting that gun use explains about 30 percent of cross-state variations in homicide in the year that the Seitz analysis was run.

There are a variety of different global comparisons of gun use and death rates that point to gun use as a positive influence on homicide rates. One strategy is to study the relationship between gun use and homicide rates over time in the United States. The correlation between total gun share of homicide and total homicide rates in the United States for the years 1964–1990 is 0.77, indicating that years in which the proportion of all killings committed by guns is high are associated with high total homicide rates by all means, and vice versa.

To the same effect, a recent research note by one of us finds the correlation over time between percentage gun use and total homicide rate for offenders under eighteen was 0.9 over the years 1977–1992, and that changes in gun use were also efficient predictors of which age groups would exhibit the largest increase in homicide (Zimring 1996).

Even this variety of correlational study results cannot establish a definitive causal sequence. Perhaps both the rate of gun use and the death rate from attacks increase because more people who intend to kill their victims select guns to achieve that goal. Because the proportion of all assaults committed with guns may signal changes in the nature of violent attackers as well as in violent attacks, it is not possible to isolate firearms as a cause of increases in death rate through the use of this kind of comparison.

In the second place, even if we believe that global comparisons make it probable that gun use causes an increased death rate, this kind of global statistical analysis cannot reveal what characteristics of guns or their use in attacks is the operative cause of increased lethality. What is there about guns that produces more homicides than other weapons when they are used in assaults? Simply knowing that those periods of maximum gun use in the recent history of the United States are associated with much higher death rates from intentional injury cannot produce any insight into why gun assaults acquire their extra measure of dangerousness. In this sense, then, global statistical comparison is important as an estimate of the strength of the general relationship between gun use and death from homicide and as a precursor to more specific investigation of the mechanism of guns and the effect of these on violent assault.

The basic problem that limits the policy significance of the global comparison is that changes in gun use may signal changed intentions by attackers as well as increasing the chances that an attack will result in death because the gun is a more lethal instrument. When Clarke and Mayhew assert that reducing gun availability will reduce deaths, they either assume that more deadly intentions are not the cause of a high rate of death from gun assault or believe that the absence of available guns will modify or frustrate an attacker's lethal intentions.

The prudent conclusion from global comparison is that when gun use increases, both the larger capacity of firearms to cause death and the greater manifest desire of the attacker to risk a victim's death will increase the death rate. The global comparison can estimate the joint impact of altered instruments and intentions, but cannot apportion any effects on death rate between these two elements.

As to the magnitude of the relationship between gun use and homicide rates, studies over time in the United States are associated with substantial estimates of gun use effects. More than half of the variations of homicide rates in the United States are linked systematically to variations in the proportion of shooting fatalities in the 0.77 correlated reported previously. And parallel statistics for selected cities and subgroups produce even larger correlations (see Zimring 1996).

No matter how large the noted association between guns and homicide, however, the global comparison is a self-limiting methodology. The more likely it is that such comparisons implicate gun use as a cause of homicide, the more important it becomes to supplement such statistics with different empirical strategies that promise to provide information about why guns are particularly lethal.

The Causes of Differential Lethality

Guns may cause increases in the death rate from assault in a variety of different ways. The use of guns as opposed to other weapons in assault may be associated with both mechanical and social changes in violent assault that can increase death rates. Among the mechanical or instrumentality aspects of gun use that can increase death rates are: the greater injurious impact of bullets, the longer range of firearms, and the greater capacity of firearms for executing multiple attacks. Among the features in social setting related to gun use are: the need to use more lethal instruments of assault in situations where an attacker fears that his adversary may have a gun, the need to sustain or intensify a deadly assault because an opponent possesses or is using firearms, and the increased willingness to use guns and other lethal weapons in personal conflict because such weapons are used generally. All of these aspects may increase the lethality of assaults committed with guns, but by no means to the same degree. There are also two social impacts of gun possession and use that can lower death rates: the deterrence of assaults because of fear of gun-owning victims and the prevention of attempted assaults by an armed victim.

Instrumentality Effects

Of all the possible ways that gun use increases the deadliness of attacks, the theory that gunshot wounds inflict more damage than other methods of personal attacks is considered the most important and has been the subject of the most research.

The early debate about the influence of guns on deaths from assault involved different theories of the types of intention that produced assaults that lead to death. Marvin Wolfgang in his landmark study of homicide doubted that the weapon used in an attack made much difference in the chance that a death would result since so many different weapons could produce death if an attacker tried hard enough (Wolfgang 1958). Zimring responded to this assertion with a study of knife and gun assaults and killings in Chicago (Zimring 1968).

Zimring's data suggested that many homicides were the result of attacks apparently conducted with less than a single-minded intent to kill. Unlike the Wolfgang study where only fatal attacks were examined, the first Zimring study compared fatal and nonfatal gun and knife assaults in Chicago over four police periods. The study found that 70 percent of all gun killings in Chicago were the result of attacks that resulted in only one wound to the victim, and most attacks with guns or knives that killed a victim looked quite similar to the knife and gun attacks that did not kill (Zimring 1968). From this data, Zimring argued that most homicides were the result of ambiguously motivated assaults, so that the offender would risk his victim's death, but usually did not press on until death was assured.

Under such circumstances, the capacity of a weapon to inflict life-threatening injury would have an important influence on the death rate from assault. The 1968 Chicago study found that gun attacks were about five times as likely to kill as knife attacks, and this ratio held when the comparison was controlled for the number of wounds inflicted and the specific location of the most serious wounds (Zimring 1968). Since knives were the next most deadly frequently used method of inflicting injury in attacks, the large difference in death rate suggested that substituting knives or other less dangerous instruments for guns would reduce the death rate from assault.

This weapon dangerousness comparison was first reported for Chicago in 1968 and has been replicated in other sites (Vinson 1974; Sarvesvaran and Jayewardene 1985). Follow-up studies have shown that a difference in a weapon as subtle as firearm caliber can double the death rate from gun assaults (Zimring 1972). The summary conclusion from this line of research can be simply stated: the objective dangerousness of a weapon used in violent assaults appears to be a major influence on the number of victims who will die from attacks. This "instrumentality effect" is the major documented influence of guns on death rate (see Cook 1991).

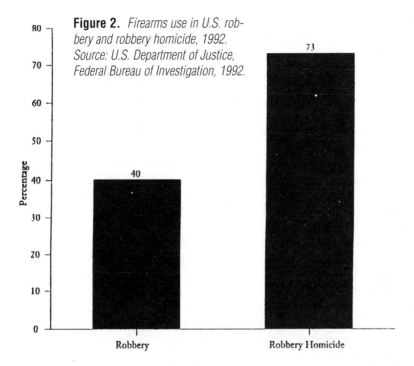

Figure 2. *Firearms use in U.S. robbery and robbery homicide, 1992. Source: U.S. Department of Justice, Federal Bureau of Investigation, 1992.*

The use of guns in robbery is different from their use in wounding since the weapon is not necessarily used to inflict harm. Because robberies with guns frighten their victims into complying with the robbers' demands more than other robberies, a smaller number of gun robberies result in woundings than personal force robberies and robberies with knives. Still, the greater dangerousness of guns when fired more than compensates for the lower number of wounds. For street robberies and those that take place in commercial establishments, the death rate for every 1,000 gun robberies is about three times that generated by robberies at knife point and about ten times the death rate from robberies involving personal force (see Zimring and Zuehl 1986; Cook 1991:17).

Another way of estimating the impact of gun use on the dangerousness of robbery is to focus on the prevalence of gun use in fatal and nonfatal robbery incidents. Figure 2 contrasts the firearms share of robberies and robbery killings in the United States for 1992.

The contrast in figure 2 is about half that noted between violent crime and homicide in figure 1. Firearms are responsible for 40 percent of robberies and 73 percent of all robbery killings in the United States, so that the apparent death rate from gun robbery nationwide is four times that of nongun robberies in the aggregate. The data presented in New York City robbery estimate a 10-to-1 difference in death rate.

The death rate comparison in figure 2 is subject to at least two qualifications. In the first place, the difference in death rate noted in the figure already takes into account whatever savings of life results from the lower rate of resistance to gun-using robbers. So the difference in death rate from gun robbery as a result of the greater injury potential of bullet wounds may be larger than the 4-to-1 ratio derived from the data in figure 2.

The second qualification cuts in the opposite direction. Many of the robberies committed with guns involve commercial entities and other relatively well-defended robbery targets. These robberies might involve a greater risk of injury or death that is to some degree independent of the weapon used by the robber. The switch to knives or blunt instruments in such cases might lead to a higher rate of victim injury or death than is generated by other types of knife and blunt instrument robbery. Of course, some of these difficult target robberies might not be committed if firearms were not available. So the calculus of comparison between gun robberies and other types of robbery is both multidimensional and complex.

There is one sense in which what we call global gun-versus-nongun comparisons in robbery are less problematic than global comparisons involving assault. Because persons committing assault intend to injure, the weapons they select may be probative of their intention to risk a lethal outcome. Since robbery involves only the threat of force, the choice of weapon may not directly reflect an intention to do harm and the choice of more dangerous weapons may not as closely reflect a more serious intention to injure. The robber may not intend any harm at the point of choosing weapons, and differences in total death rate may thus reflect only instrumentality effects.

Range

One obvious way in which firearms differ from other frequently used instruments of personal attack is the long distance across which bullets remain potent messengers of lethal force. Sticks, stones, knives, and blunt objects can be used to deadly effect, but not at great range. Killing with a knife or a blunt instrument is both hard work and close work. The only practical limit to the range of a firearm as an instrument of deadly attack is the marksmanship of the shooter. Hunting rifles are designed to inflict life-threatening force at great distances. The bullets fired from handguns can travel considerable distances before losing their capacity for injury, although most handguns are more difficult to employ with accuracy at long range.

How important the greater range of firearms might be in elevating the death rate from assault depends on the types of situation and the distance between victim and assailant that occur in life-threatening assaults. The majority of life-threatening assaults in the United States are carried out at close range even when a firearm is the instrument of attack. For this reason, the long range of guns should not be a major influence on the death rate from attacks in most cases. Indeed, handguns are nine times as likely to be involved in a homicidal assault in the United States as long guns even though the longer barreled weapons are much more efficient in respect of aim and accuracy over great distances. Lethal violence in the United States is for the most part hand-to-hand combat where the handgun's maneuverability is more important than the long gun's superior long-range accuracy.

In those circumstances where attacks are initiated or completed at long range, a firearm is a necessary weapon. Included in such attacks are sniper incidents, many assassination attempts, other assaults from a distance at a defined and frequently guarded target, as well as more common "drive-by" shootings where a target may or may not have been preselected, but where the defining characteristic of the attack is shooting at long range. The official records on such killings are not complete. The Federal Bureau of Investigation reported a total of ninety-seven sniper killing cases between 1990 and 1992, but did not have a code for drive-by shootings. The Los Angeles police estimated about thirty drive-by fatalities in 1991 out of about 1,000 cases (no national-level estimates are available).

Capacity for Multiple Attack

Most firearms have the capacity to shoot many separate bullets in a relatively short period of time and with a minimum of physical effort on the part of the shooter. A revolver typically has a six-shot capacity and is easy to reload. Pistols typically carry six to nine rounds and can carry many more. Rifles vary from single-shot weapons to some with very large capacity clips and magazines.

There are two ways in which the capacity for multiple-wound infliction can produce a higher death rate from assault than would occur if more time and effort were required to repeat or intensify an attack. In the first place, several shots can be fired at the same victim producing wounds where the first attempt missed or resulting in multiple wounds that involve a much higher probability of death. In the second place, the multiple-shot capacity of many firearms can mean that more than one victim can be wounded—and put at risk of death—during the same assault.

Very little research has addressed explicitly the impact of a firearm's capacity for multiple attack on the outcome of gun assault. There are a number of different questions to be studied. First, single-victim attacks could be studied to assess whether attacks with guns result in a greater number of woundings than attacks with knives. Second, firearms assaults could be studied to determine whether attacks made with weapons that carry a single load of many bullets produce a higher number of multiple wounds and a higher rate of fatality.

The assault studies conducted in the late 1960s and early 1970s did not show a high proportion of multiple-wound attacks. Indeed, the failure of most shooters to exhaust the capacity of their firearms is cited as strong evidence against the proposition that most gun fatalities were not the result of kill-at-any-cost intentions (Zimring 1972). The more specific study of whether firearms with multiple capacity are more often used to produce multiple wounds has not yet been attempted.

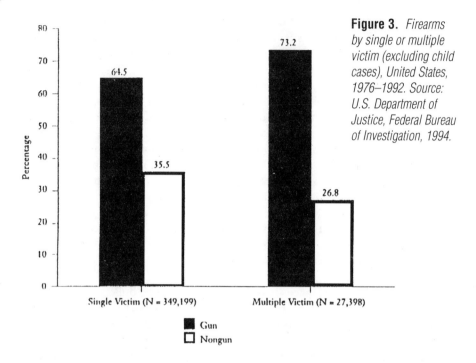

Figure 3. *Firearms by single or multiple victim (excluding child cases), United States, 1976–1992. Source: U.S. Department of Justice, Federal Bureau of Investigation, 1994.*

Crude empirical soundings regarding whether guns are more often used in multiple-victim killings are not difficult to conduct in the age of the computer, but an all-fatality sample may be biased. Using data from the Federal Bureau of Investigation's Supplementary Homicide Reports for the years 1976–1992, we tested the hypothesis that guns would more often be the instrument of attack in assaults that resulted in more than one fatality than in assaults in which only one victim died. We found a modest but consistent confirmation of the hypothesis. In all seventeen years covered by the data set, the proportion of gun use in multiple-victim killings was higher than in single-victim killings. When cases involving young children are deleted from the analysis, weapons other than guns are used, in about one out of every four multiple-victim incidents, as compared with one out of three single-victim killings, as shown by figure 3.

The larger proportion of multiple killings committed with guns probably represents an increase in death rate on top of the differential deadliness effects discussed earlier, but these two effects overlap in a study that considers only multiple killings. A larger proportion of attacks on multiple victims with knives or clubs may result in only one death because other victims survive a knife attack but are killed in a gun attack. The research question is whether gun attacks on multiple victims produces even higher differential deadliness over knife attacks than is found in single-victim assaults. A study of nonfatal as well as fatal attacks might decide this issue, but has not yet been undertaken.

Social Factors

The mechanical factors just discussed are characteristics of guns that may influence the death rate from attacks committed with firearms. What we call social factors are the many ways in which a social environment where many people possess and use firearms in interpersonal assault may have an influence on the extent to which assaults lead to fatal conclusions. There are at least three different theories as to how a social environment of high gun use can increase killings and at least two theories about how a social environment of extensive gun ownership and use might reduce violent deaths. But precise and specific empirical evaluation of theories about social and environmental effects is not easy.

One way in which a social environment of frequent gun assaults can increase the death rate from assault is by making those engaged in physical combat resort to more lethal instruments of assault and also to continue and intensify an assault because an opponent is armed. A social environment of frequent gun use multiplies the number of cases where both sides in a conflict possess lethal weapons. This should increase the death rate from both gun and knife attacks by motivating more sustained application of lethal force because of the counterforces risked if the attacker desists too soon.

One common feature of a two-way gun fight is that each combatant is unwilling to stop shooting until it seems clear that his opponent is incapable of shooting back. For this reason, it seems likely that the death rate from bilateral gun fights will be much higher than in situations where one party is armed with a gun and the other party has no deadly weapon. An attack where only one participant uses lethal force should be less likely to produce death because the combatant who controls the lethal force can stop pressing his attack without risking being shot or stabbed.

A second environmental influence closely related to the problem of bilateral lethal force is the way in which fear that others may have guns may motivate people to arm themselves with deadlier weapons than they might otherwise feel would be necessary for either self-defense or attack. When approaching a conflict in which guns are believed to be present, a potential combatant is more likely to feel it necessary to arm himself with a knife or a gun. The irony here is that one element that may increase the use of firearms in combat is a fear of guns in the hands of others. In this way increases in gun use can, in many social settings, become self-fulfilling prophecies.

A third effect of an environment where gun use is frequent that might increase mortality rates from assault is that a high frequency of gun use might lead citizens to expect that firearms are used in interpersonal conflict. On this theory, an increase in gun use would occur, not only out of fear, but out of social habit as the widespread practice of carrying and using guns generates a belief that gun use is a normal part of interpersonal conflicts. The use of a gun in many serious conflicts may no longer be regarded as deviant behavior. This could increase gun use over time substantially. We know of no way to directly measure the extent of this type of legitimation of the use of deadly force, but it is an influence that could be of considerable significance.

There are two current theories about how a social environment of frequent gun use might reduce the death toll from criminal violence: self-defense and deterrence. The self-defense theory argues that a larger number of firearms produces a larger proportion of gun ownership and self-defense gun use. Potential crime victims will use guns to prevent or thwart attack and thus reduce the death toll—at least among nonoffenders—from assault. The extent of this direct self-defense dividend from high gun ownership is the subject of a lively debate (cf. Meck 1991 with McDowall and Wiersema 1994).

One major methodological problem with measuring self-defense is that asking persons in a survey whether they have used a gun to prevent a criminal act produces self-serving statements that cannot be verified. Each party to an argument that turned violent is likely to regard the other party as a criminal aggressor, and to think that his own use of force was permissible self-defense. When talking to only one of two combatants, the story one is likely to hear is that a crime was prevented by a gun even though the respondent's opponent would swear that in fact a crime was committed by the person representing himself as the victim. Official police statistics on assault involve an umpire's decision made by police about the culpability of the parties. But survey research cannot generate a valid test of the allegations of a self-serving respondent.

A final theory of social influence argues that widespread gun ownership and use deters criminal assault because would-be offenders recognize the high probability that a criminal attack will be met with lethal force. The probability of substantial across-the-board crime reduction from this kind of armed citizen deterrence is emphasized frequently by opponents of gun control legislation in the United States. And it has been associated with legislative proposals to loosen restrictions on carrying concealed guns. Indeed one small city in Georgia passed an ordinance requiring citizen possession of firearms for which the stated rationale was deterrence (see Benson 1984).

The measurement of the types of social impact that have been outlined is difficult and some of the most important social influences are the most difficult to assess empirically. The degree to which widespread ownership and use of guns leads to the expectation that they will be used in personal assaults could have a substantial impact on the amount of lethal violence experienced in a society incrementally over a long period of time. But the rigorous empirical assessment of this would be practically impossible to execute because it would be a process taking place gradually over decades without any specific landmarks to be the focus of evaluation. Yet the potential importance of this factor in determining a society's rate of lethal interpersonal violence is not smaller merely because it is not susceptible to rigorous measurement.

Some of the theories of social influence outlined above can be tested in relatively straightforward ways. The quantity and quality of self-defense uses of firearms can be assessed using police statistics and, to a lesser extent, surveys. Police statistics can provide a minimum estimate of incidents of citizen self-defense where a neutral factfinder affirms that the person using the force was not to blame for the event. Survey reports of self-defense can be useful in defining issues even if the factual accounts in the survey cannot be verified. When surveys show that 70 percent of all claimed incidents of crime prevention concern the offense of aggravated assault, the criminologist can pay specific attention to assault and homicide statistics in studying the influence of gun ownership and use on crime.

Another opportunity for straightforward evaluation is the comparison of multiple-wounding and case-fatality rates in one- and two-way gun battles. That sort of specific assessment would be a logical next step in the epidemiological research into intentional injury that is in progress in the United States (see Kellerman and Reay 1986; Winternute 1995).

There are a number of hypotheses that cannot be isolated and separately measured. If high gun ownership environments are associated with higher-than-average proportionate use of guns in assault, is this because would-be attackers are afraid their opponents may be armed or is it another manifestation of a general social expectation that it is permissible to use guns in certain types of social conflict? If the widespread availability of handguns prevents some lethal attacks but also increases the death rate from attacks, how can these two countervailing tendencies be isolated and measured?

To some extent, the difficulties of isolating each element of gun influence for individual assessment are intractable, but the precise measure of individual influences on death rates may also be relatively unimportant. From a social policy standpoint, the sort of global assessment that was discussed earlier may tell us all that we have to know because it provides an estimate of the magnitude of the net effect of variations in gun use over time and crossnationally.

The major problem with many such global estimates by themselves, however, is the issue of causal ordering. But once the mechanical ways in which gun use increases the death rate from assault have been identified and measured, it may be possible to approach the sort of global estimates discussed earlier with more confidence that variations in gun use are, for the most part, independent variables in the equation and that variations in homicide rates are, again for the most part, the dependent variables. If so, a large positive correlation between percentage firearms use in homicide and rates of homicide over time tells us that mechanical and social elements that accompany increases in gun use have a much greater elevating influence on death rates than any restraining influence that may be concurrent. If lethal violence is the focus of social concern, such an aggregate conclusion may be more important than the precise assessment of the impact of specific aspects of firearms use.

Firearms Use as Contributing Cause

The use of firearms in assault and robbery is the single environmental feature of American society that is most clearly linked to the extraordinary death rate from interpersonal violence in the United States. But the strength of this relationship does not mean that firearms ownership and use has a simple, invariable, or independent influence on homicide rates. In this section, we consider the question of the causal connection between gun use and lethality. We do this not only because it is an important issue in relation to firearms and lethal violence, but also because reflecting on the questions of causation that arise in connection with firearms teaches us an important lesson about the role of many other environmental influences on the incidence of lethal violence.

The American debate about guns has produced one of the few causal critiques ever to appear on a bumper sticker: the famous "Guns don't kill people, people kill people." Behind the strong sentiment that inspired this and a multitude of related appeals lies an important logical point. Firearms ownership and use is neither a necessary nor a sufficient cause of violent death in the United States. Firearms are not a necessary cause of killings because of the wide array of alternative methods of killing that are available ranging from the strangler's hands to car bombs. Even in the United States in 1996, nearly 30 percent of all killings did not involve guns. Moreover, the widespread availability of firearms is not a sufficient condition for intentional homicide by a wide margin. One-half of all American households own guns and it is estimated that one-quarter of all households own a handgun—the weapon used in three-quarters of all gun homicides. Yet only a small fraction of all gun owners become gun attackers. The logical point here is that guns do not become dangerous instruments of attack if they are not used in an attack.

If gun use is neither a necessary nor a sufficient cause of violent death, what is the proper descriptive label for the role gun use plays in deaths due to intentional injury? The most accurate label for the role of firearms in those cases of death and injury from intentional attacks in which they are used is contributing cause. Even where the availability of a gun plays no important role in the decision to commit an assault, the use of a gun can be an important contributing cause in the death and injury that results for gun attacks. When guns are used in a high proportion of such attacks, the death rate from violent attack will be high. Current evidence suggests that a combination of the ready availability of guns and the willingness to use maximum force in interpersonal conflict is the most important single contribution to the high U.S. death rate from violence. Our rate of assault is not exceptional—our death rate from assault is exceptional.

The role of gun use as a contributing cause means that the net effect of firearms on violence will depend on the interaction of gun availability with other factors that influence the rate of violent assaults in a society and the willingness of people to use guns in such assaults. So the precise contribution of firearms to the death toll from violence is contingent on many other factors that may influence the number and character of violent attacks.

Some implications of this contingency deserve emphasis. Introducing 10,000 loaded handguns into a social environment where violent assault is a rare occurrence will not produce a large number of additional homicide deaths unless it also increases the rate of assault. The percentage increase in homicide might be considerable if guns become substitutes for less lethal weapons. But the additional number of killings would be small because of the low rate of attack. Introducing 10,000 handguns into an environment where rates of attack and willingness to use handguns in attack are both high is a change that would produce many more additional deaths. The net effect of guns depends on how they are likely to be used.

One corollary of viewing guns as an interactive and contributing cause to intentional homicide is that societies with low rates of violent assault will pay a lower price if they allow guns to be widely available than will societies with higher rates of violence. The sanguine sound bite encountered in American debates about guns is: "An armed society is a polite society" (Handgun Control Inc. 1995). This does not seem particularly plausible to us, but it seems likely that only a very polite society can be heavily armed without paying a high price.

The United States of the 1990s is far from that polite society. Our considerable propensity for violent conflict would be a serious societal problem even if gun availability and use were low. But the very fact that the United States is a high-violence environment makes the contribution of gun use to the death toll from violence very much greater. When viewed in the light of the concept of contributing causation, the United States has both a violence problem and a gun problem, and each makes the other more deadly.

ON PRIORITY CONCERNS FOR AMERICAN VIOLENCE CONTROL*

The inductive logic of public health analysis allows the major elements of a general problem to emerge from careful analysis of its distinguishing characteristics. The search is for the characteristics that seem most prominently associated with the problem under study. When fatal car crashes are examined, the analyst discovers abnormal concentrations of driver blood alcohol, a large proportion of crashes where the deceased hit the windshield, and a disproportionate number of high-speed collisions. The identification of particular risk conditions is an important step toward finding remedies to the most pressing problems. If speed makes crashes more likely to kill, speed limits may save lives. If passengers who are thrown out of vehicles are at particular risk, then systems to restrain passengers are likely to reduce fatality risks. By providing a more specific reading of the problems that most need to be addressed, these risk comparisons help to direct the search for specific remedies.

What would a comprehensive survey of incidents of lethal violence tell us about the priority concerns for violence control? There are three conditions prominently associated with lethal violence in the United States that must be addressed by any agenda for the control of life-threatening violence. These are

---

*From Franklin E. Zimring and Gordon Hawkins, *Crime Is Not the Problem: Lethal Violence in America* (New York: Oxford University Press, 1997), pp. 199–214. Copyright © 1997 by Oxford University Press, Inc. Used by permission of Oxford University Press, Inc.

handgun availability and use, high rates of lethal violence among African Americans, and the high incidence of homicides where victim and offender were previously unacquainted.

Guns as Sine Qua Non

The characteristic that most dominates the landscape of American lethal violence is the use of firearms in attacks, particularly the use of handguns. Firearms use predominates in American homicide, accounting for seventy percent of all cases known to the police. Even though handguns are about one-third of all the guns in circulation in the United States, they are used in three-quarters of deaths caused by firearms.

While rates of firearms use are high in many kinds of robbery and assault, the co-occurrence is particularly striking between firearms as a means of attack and death as an outcome of attack. Police in the United States report rates of serious assault with knives and other cutting instruments that are as high as rates of firearms assault, but the deaths from firearms assault are five times as numerous. International comparisons also identify as distinctive the overlap between high rates of assault fatality in the United States and extraordinary concentrations of gun use in assault. The circumstantial indications that implicate gun use as a contributing cause to American lethal violence are overwhelming.

. . . The literal translation of the phrase "sine qua non" is "without which not." The phrase is used [here] to emphasize an important implication of shifting the focus of concern from crime, generally, and from violence, generally, to the special problem of lethal violence. No program for the prevention of lethal violence can possess even superficial credibility without paying sustained attention to guns. Without strategies for the reduction of firearm use in assaults, no policy can be accurately characterized as directed at the reduction of American lethal violence.

The design of appropriate strategies of firearms control involves a mixture of relatively easy choices and very difficult ones. A specific focus on handguns is an easy choice in the sense that it emerges from a profile of the firearms at risk for every major category of lethal violence. With regard to homicide generally, the per unit involvement of handguns is nine times as great as for long guns, and the concentration in particular subsets of lethal violence, such as robbery, is even greater. Handguns are differentially at risk also for suicide and fatal accidents. So effective measures of reducing the handgun share of interpersonal assault seem likely to generate benefits in the prevention of self-destructive violence.

There are also substantial indications in the statistical profile of firearms and violence that reductions in handgun violence do not result in compensatory increases in the use of rifles and shotguns in assault and robbery. There is, first, the disproportionate use of handguns in the United States, which indicates that the portable and concealable handgun is not regarded as interchangeable with long guns by its users.

A second indication of limited substitution is that where handguns are subject to special regulations and restrictions, a major problem in gun use remains illicit handguns rather than more easily available rifles and shotguns. This is overwhelmingly the case in the United States, where illegal handguns are still easily available, and is even evident in foreign countries where special restrictions on handguns succeed in reducing the supply of handguns.

Thus, special regulation of handguns is a rational framework for the United States; but what kind of regulation? The basic choice is between trying to deny handguns to only high-risk groups and attempting to curtail the availability and use of handguns generally. The current system in most of the United States is to deny handguns to the immature, to persons with records of felony conviction, and to other persons regarded as special risks. This system fails in two respects. It does not even attempt to restrict the access to guns of many who will misuse them; and its aim to keep guns out of the reach of the young and the previously criminal is frustrated by the large number of handguns in general circulation.

One pattern of reform advocated for gun control in the United States is to strengthen the mechanisms designed to keep guns from the limited classes currently not eligible to own them. Systems that check the criminal records of prospective handgun purchasers are designed to make it more difficult for the ineligible to obtain guns. Systems that make legal owners accountable for each gun that is owned are a second method of reducing the flow of guns from qualified owners to the unqualified.

The alternative basic approach to handgun regulation is to restrict the availability of such weapons generally. The goal of such a scheme is not to keep handguns from particular groups of citizens who are regarded as dangerous, but to keep guns out of general circulation because they are regarded as dangerous. In the permissive system where all but unqualified owners are permitted access to guns, the target of regulation is dangerous gun users. In restrictive licensing schemes where only limited access to handguns is allowed, the target of the regulations is a class of guns that is regarded as too dangerous for general ownership.

The current system of handgun regulation in most of the United States is permissive and the number of handguns in circulation is quite large, in the range of 50 to 70 million. While some guns have been generally restricted in the United States (machine guns, sawed-off shotguns), no weapon in mass circulation has ever been so curtailed. While other industrial democracies have instituted and maintained restrictive handgun regulations, no such system has ever been instituted after generations of mass availability.

If the basic choice for American handgun control is between a permissive or restrictive strategy, each approach seems subject to a decisive disadvantage. The problem with handgun controls that attempt to restrict the availability of weapons is that they depend on radical changes in citizen behavior. Critics of such restrictions make pointed reference to the lessons of alcohol prohibition in the United States (Kaplan 1985; Jacobs 1986). Using the criminal law to change folkways is always a high-risk venture, and handgun restrictions are certainly no exception to this principle.

The decisive objection to permissive handgun controls is that the level of lethal violence that would persist under even the most effective of these modest controls would be substantial. Unless the lethal assault rate in the United States drops by more that half its 1992 level, homicide rates in the United States will remain at more than double the next highest industrial democracy's level. Anything short of drastic change in gun policy is either an acceptance of very high death rates or a gamble on very sharp reductions in violent assault.

So the choice in handgun control is between two unpalatable alternatives. Gun control in the twenty-first century will either be an expensive, unpopular, and untested attempt at bringing the U.S. handgun policy to the standard of the rest of the developed world, or it will consist of minor adjustments to current regulations that will all but guarantee persisting high rates of death. It is likely that this hard choice will amount to the definitive referendum on lethal violence in the United States.

The African American Imperative

Even cursory exposure to the data justifies special attention to loss-reduction programs for African Americans. The distribution of American lethal violence is highly skewed, much more than is crime, much more than are other forms of violence. African Americans constitute 13 percent of the U.S. population, but more than 45 percent of all homicide victims, and more than half of all killers.

The impact of this concentration on health statistics is not small. In the early 1990s, homicide was the leading cause of death for young African American males. The threat of violent death inhibits processes of community organization by undermining trust and a sense of physical security. The prospect of lethal violence is one defining element of coming of age for many young African American men.

Death rates from violence are substantial, but why an African American "imperative"? The point we wish to underscore is a statistical rather than a moral obligation. The concentration of lethal violence among African Americans is so great that it would not be possible for loss-reduction programs to succeed generally without producing substantial results in this key segment of victims and offenders. The urban neighborhoods where high proportions of African Americans reside are the laboratories of necessity for efforts to reduce death and injury from violence in the United States.

This emphasis on one population group is not to suggest that the forces that generate lethal violence are any different in African American neighborhoods than in other neighborhoods, or to imply that different tactics of loss reduction might be appropriate for minority populations. The rationale for emphasis on African American violence concerns not the content of a treatment program, but only its target population. There is no reason to suppose that the effects of mechanisms for reducing lethal violence vary with the skin color of the population at risk, any more than do the effects of seat belts, speed limits, and air bags.

There is, however, one benefit associated with the high rates of lethal violence among the African American population, a variation of the point made earlier about economies of scale in violence loss prevention. The higher the base rate of lethal violence, the more likely it is that any program that reduces levels of violence will generate benefits greater than the costs of the intervention. The higher the costs currently suffered, the larger the benefits a successful intervention can produce. In this sense, the measurement of programmatic effects in high violent death-rate communities provides a sensitive barometer of the potential value of countermeasures in lower-rate environments. . . .

How Large a Problem?

. . . How large a problem is lethal violence in the United States of the late 1990s?

The earlier analysis . . . would deny that objective data about death and injury can provide a reliable measure of the social cost of intentional injury because the anxiety associated with lethal violence creates fear of public social life for many citizens. The ripple effects of such fear are considerable. Many of the victims of violence in American society have received no physical injuries; instead the boundaries of their public opportunities are narrowed, and fear of public environments diminishes the quality of personal life. Under these circumstances, the lives lost and injuries sustained from violence may provide some rough measure of the magnitude of the problem at one time as compared with another, or when different places are being compared. But the costs imposed by lethal violence are far higher than any body count would indicate.

There can be no doubt that subjective evaluations by the public are an important element in defining the magnitude of lethal violence as a social problem. This does not mean, however, that government policy must slavishly follow public fears in allocating resources for safety. Even if large segments of the public imagine that visitors from outer space are a clear and present urban danger, this should not generate a governmental responsibility to invest resources in the detection of space invaders. If the public fear is sincere, there is a responsibility generated for a government response, but the appropriate government response may be public education when particular fears do not reflect reality. The public Roads and Traffic Authority informs visitors to Sydney, Australia, that pedestrian road accidents caused 500 times as many deaths in Australia as shark attacks over the eleven years between 1983 and 1993 (Roads and Traffic Authority 1995). This is a perfectly appropriate effort to bring public appreciation of risks into a more accurate relation to objective facts. However, the effect of presenting such statistics is likely to be more fear of pedestrian risks rather than greater public comfort about the prospect of shark attacks. With only one death a year in a country of 18 million, public authorities in Australia would still be well advised to maintain the shark nets surrounding their public beaches.

The point of the shark example is not to assert that lethal violence is a one in 18 million problem in the United States. Instead, the shark story suggests a model of governmental response to public fear in which the public importance of a problem generates the obligation either to alter public priorities through an educational process or to respect those priorities in the allocation of prevention resources.

Even widespread fear does not require exhausting the public treasury in shark nets while preventable pedestrian fatalities pile up on Sydney streets. Still, spending more money per life saved on shark precautions may make good sense if a feeling of safety from sharks on beaches is an indivisible public good of special value, in the same sense that additional expenditures for commercial airline safety can be justified as an important benefit to airline passengers and the public at large. The same notion may justify spending larger resources on reducing the risk of lethal violence if the public cost of current feelings of insecurity is sufficiently substantial.

On these grounds alone, the degree of public fear of lethal violence in the United States becomes an important element in determining the appropriate governmental response. What do we know about the magnitude of lethal violence as a societal problem in the United States of the 1990s? What can this tell us about the appropriate priority of loss prevention from lethal violence in the competition for scarce resources?

By most measurements of public opinion, lethal violence is a major problem in the United States of the mid-1990s, a problem that seems more important in current circumstances than was evident in 1980 when the death toll from violence was somewhat higher. There are two reasons why subjective measurements of violence as a problem might have increased while the objective manifestations of violence have not. In the first place, the number of serious problems pressing for public attention in the United States was somewhat larger in 1980 than in 1997. In 1980, epic inflation in the United States and acute Cold War tensions abroad may have diverted attention from annual homicide rates, then at their highest point in the twentieth century. This comparative perspective on societal problems suggests that the same general level of lethal violence may generate more public anxiety in good times than in bad times when the population has so many other things to worry about. The current heightened concern about life-threatening violence in the streets may thus be a byproduct of peace and prosperity.

The peace and prosperity analysis above would predict a cyclical pattern to concern about lethal violence, a pattern where the relative standing of violence as a societal problem can be expected to decline in the next economic recession. But there is a second possibility, that social tolerance of lethal violence is declining over time in the United States so that the same number of killings can be expected to produce a larger problem response steadily over time. On this interpretation, die increased worry about violence in the United States will not abate in the next recession. Instead, a volume of violence equal to current rates can be expected to provoke more public reaction with the passing of time.

Has the tolerance for lethal violence in American society changed in recent years? Should one describe the social tolerance for lethal violence as high or low in the United States? A sophisticated student of American social history might argue that Americans have historically displayed high levels of tolerance for some forms of lethal violence and low levels of toleration for other types of lethal violence; that little notice was taken of assault-generated homicide involving minority male victims and offenders in urban ghetto locations, while killing of higher social status persons, particularly violent attacks that crossed social and geographic boundaries into America's nicer neighborhoods, have always generated high levels of fear and low social toleration.

This two-track pattern of social toleration of violence continues in the United States, and huge differences continue in rates of victimization by race, class, and location. But the two tracks of social concern may be moving closer together because the perceived distance between the usual scenes of killing and woundings in the United States and the physical and social locations where most citizens live has declined. Part of this may be due to mass media, as television has brought citizens in more proximate contact with local violence. Part of this diminishing distance reflects increasing social integration of the American workplace and some schools. Many more Americans know and care about people who are at high risk of lethal violence than in the past.

The lesson here again is that increasing public fear and anxiety about lethal violence can frequently be a product of social progress. Social changes that lower tolerance for lethal violence produce higher levels of public discomfort with the same amount of violence. But if increasing discomfort is the consequence of rising social expectations, it can stand as a positive sign of public health. Indeed, a society that was untroubled by current American rates of lethal violence would represent a significant retrogression in social development.

REFERENCES

Amir, Menachem. 1971. *Patterns in Forcible Rape.* Chicago: University of Chicago Press.

Andenaes, Johannes. 1974. *Punishment and Deterrence.* Ann Arbor: University of Michigan Press.

Archer, Dane, and Rosemary Gartner. 1984. *Violence and Clime in Cross-National Perspective.* New Haven, Conn.: Yale University Press.

Baron, James N., and Peter C. Reiss. 1985. "Same Time, Next Year: Aggregate Analyses of the Mass Media and Violent Behavior." *American Sociological Review* 50:347–63.

Benson, Bruce L. 1984. "Guns for Protection and Other Private Sector Responses to the Fear of Rising Crime." In *Firearms and Violence: Issues of Public Policy,* ed. Don B. Kates Jr. Cambridge, Mass.: Ballinger.

Bentham, Jeremy. 1841a. "Introduction to the Principles of Morals and Legislation [1789]." In *The Works of Jeremy Bentham,* ed. J. Bowring, Vol. 1, pp. 1–54. London: Simpkin, Marshall.

———. 1841b. "Principles of Penal Law [1802]." In *The Works of Jeremy Bentham,* ed. J. Bowring, Vol. 1, pp. 365–580. London: Simpkin, Marshall.

Block, Richard. 1977. *Violent Crime: Environment, Interaction, and Death.* Lexington, Mass.: Lexington Books.

Block, Richard, and Franklin E. Zimring. 1973. "Homicide in Chicago, 1965–1970." *Journal of Research in Crime and Delinquency* 10:1–12.

Blumstein, Alfred, Jacqueline Cohen, Jeffrey A. Roth, and Christy A. Visher, eds. 1986. *Criminal Careers and "Career Criminals."* Washington, D.C.: National Academy Press.

Bollen, Kenneth A., and David P. Phillips. 1981. "Suicidal Motor Vehicle Fatalities in Detroit: A Replication." *American Journal of Sociology* 87:404–12.

———. 1982. "Imitative Suicides: A National Study of the Effects of Television News Stories." *American Sociological Review* 47:802–809.

Bonger, WA. 1943. *Race and Crime.* Trans. Margaret M. Hordk, New York: Columbia University Press.

Broder, John M. 1995. "Dole Castigates Hollywood for Debasing U.S. Culture." *Los Angeles Times,* June 1, p. Al.

Butterfield, Fox. 1997. "Number of Slain Police Officers Is Lowest Since 1960." *New York Times,* January 1, Section 1, p. 12

Centerwall, Brandon S. 1989a. "Exposure to Television as a Risk Factor for Violence." *Public Communication and Behavior* 2:1–58.

———. 1989b. "Exposure to Television as a Cause of Violence." *American Journal of Epidemiology* 129:643–52.

———. 1992. "Television and Violence: The Scale and the Problem and Where to Go from Here." *Journal of the American Medical Association* 267:3059–63.

Chappell, Duncan, Gilbert Geis, Stephen Schafer, and Larry Siegel. 1977. "A Comparative Study of Forcible Rape Offenses Known to the Police in Boston and Los Angeles." In *Forcible Rape: The Crime, the Victim, and the Offender,* ed. Duncan Chappell, Robley Geis, and Gilbert Geis, pp. 227–44. New York: Columbia University Press.

Clarke, Ronald V. 1995. "Situational Crime Prevention." In *Crime and Justice: A Review of Research,* ed. Michael Tonry and David P. Farrington, Vol. 19, p. 91. Chicago: University of Chicago Press.

Clarke, Ronald V., and Pat Mayhew. 1988. "The British Gas Suicide Story and Its Criminological Implications." In *Crime and Justice. A Review of Research,* ed. Michael Tonry and Norval Morris, Vol. 10, p. 107. Chicago: University of Chicago Press.

Cohen, Albert K. 1983. "Sociological Theories." In *Encyclopedia of Clime and Justice,* ed. Stanford H. Kadish, Vol. 1, pp. 342–53. New York: Free Press.

Cohen, Jacqueline, and José Canela-Cacho. 1994. "Incapacitation and Violent Crime." In *Understanding and Preventing Violence,* ed. Albert J. Reiss Jr. and Jeffrey A. Roth, Vol. 4, pp. 296–388. Washington, D.C.: National Academy of Sciences.

Comer, Joseph P. 1985. "Black Violence and Public Policy." In *American Violence and Public Policy,* ed. Lynn A. Curtis, pp. 63–86. New Haven, Conn.: Yale University Press.

Cook, Philip J. 1991. "The Technology of Personal Violence." In *Crime and Justice: A Review of Research,* ed. Michael Tonry. Chicago: University of Chicago Press.

Corman, Hope, Theodore Joyce, and Naci Mocan. 1991. "Homicide and Crack in New York City." In *Searching for Alternatives: Drug Control Policy in the United States,* ed. Melvyn B. Krauss and Edward P. Lazear, pp. 112–37. Stanford, Calif.: Hoover Institution Press.

De Fleur, Melvin L., and Sandra Ball-Rokeach. 1975. *Theories of Mass Communication,* 3d edition. New York: David McKay Company.

Dilulio, John. 1994. "The Question of Black Crime." *The Public Interest,* Fall, p. 3.

Eliany, Marc, ed. 1989. *Licit and Illicit Drugs in Canada.* Canada: Ministry of Supply and Services.

Eron, L. D. 1972. "Parent-Child Interaction, Television Violence, and Aggression in Children." *American Psychologist* 37:197–211.

Fagan, Jeffrey. 1990. "Intoxication and Aggression." In *Crime and Justice,* ed. Michael Tonry and James Q. Wilson, Vol. 13, pp. 241–320. Chicago: University of Chicago Press.

Federal Highway Administration (1990). *Highway Statistics.* Washington, D.C.: U.S. Government Printing Office.

Feshbach, Seymour, and Robert D. Singer. 1971. *Television and Aggression.* San Francisco: Josey-Bass.

Freedman, Jonathan L. 1984. "Effect of Television Violence on Aggressiveness." *Psychological Bulletin* 96:227–46.

Friedman, David, and William Sjostrom. 1993. "Hanged for a Sheep. The Economics of Marginal Deterrence." *Journal of Legal Studies* 22:345–66.

Friedman, Milton. 1991. "The War We Are Losing." In *Searching for Alternatives: Drug Control Policy in the United States*, ed. Melvyn B. Krauss and Edward P. Lazear, pp. 53–67. Stanford, Calif.: Hoover Institution Press.

Gastil, Raymond D. 197 1. "Homicide and a Regional Culture of Violence." *American Sociological Review* 36:412–27.

Goldstein, Michael J., and Harold S. Kent. 1974. *Pornography and Sexual Deviation*. Berkeley: University of California Press.

Goldstein, Paul J. 1985. "The Drugs/Violence Nexus: A Tripartite Conceptual Framework." *Journal of Drug Issues* 15:493–506.

Goldstein, Paul J., Henry H. Brownstein, Patrick J. Ryan, and Patricia A. Bellucci. 1990. "Crack and Homicide in New York City, 1988: A Conceptually Based Event Analysis." *Contemporary Drug Problems* 16:651–87.

Gottfredson, Don H., and Michael R. Gottfredson, 1980. "Data for Criminal Justice Evaluation: Some Resources and Pitfalls." In *Handbook of Criminal Justice Evaluation*, ed. Malcolm W. Klein and Katherine S. Teilmann. Beverly Hills/London: Sage Publications.

Greenwood, Peter W., with Allan Abrahamse. 1982. *Selective Incapacitation*, Report R-2 815 -NIJ. Santa Monica, Calif.: Rand Corporation.

Hackney, Sheldon. 1969. "Southern Violence." *American Historical Review* 74:906–25.

Haddon, William, Edward A. Suchman, and David Klein. 1964. *Accident Research: Methods and Approaches*. New York: Harper and Row.

Handgun Control Inc. 1995. *Carrying Concealed Weapons. Questions and Answers*. Washington, D.C.: Handgun Control Inc.

Hartnoll, Richard. 1994. *Multi-City Study: Drug Misuse Trends in Thirteen European Cities*. Strasbourg, France: Council of Europe Press.

Hindelang, Michael J., and Bruce L. Davis. 1977. "Forcible Rape in the United States: A Statistical Profile." In *Forcible Rape: The Crime, the Victim, and the Offender*, ed. Duncan Chappell, Robley Geis, and Gilbert Geis, pp. 87–114. New York: Columbia University Press.

Home Office (1961, 1991–1993). *Criminal Statistics in England and Wales*. London: Her Majesty's Stationery Office.

———. 1984. *Statistics of the Misuse of Drugs, United Kingdom, 1983*. Home Office Statistical Bulletin 18/84. London: Her Majesty's Stationery Office.

———. 1987. *Statistics of the Misuse of Drugs, United Kingdom, 1986*. Home Office Statistical Bulletin 28/87. London: Her Majesty's Stationery Office.

———. 1988. *Statistics of the Misuse of Drugs, United Kingdom, 1987*. Home Office Statistical Bulletin 2 5/88. London; Her Majesty's Stationery Office.

———. 1995. Personal correspondence from P.H. White, Research and Statistics Department, to Franklin E. Zimring, July 24, 1995.

Hoover, J. Edgar. 1938. *Persons in Hiding*. Boston: Little, Brown.

Information Please Almanac, Atlas, and Yearbook. 1995. Boston: Houghton Mifflin.

Istituto Nazionale di Statistica. 1961, 1991. *Annuario Statistico Italiano 1991*. Rome: Istituto Nazionale di Statistica.

Jacobs, James. 1986. "Exceptions to a General Prohibition on Handgun Possession: Do They Swallow Up the Rule?" *Law and Contemporary Problems* 49:5.

Johnson, Bruce. D., Paul J. Goldstein, Edward Preble, James Schmeidler, Douglas S. Lipton, Barry Spunt, and Thomas Miller. 1985. *Taking Care of Business: The Economics of Crime by Heroin Abusers*. Lexington, Mass.: Lexington Books.

Kaplan, John. 1985. "The Wisdom of Gun Prohibition." *Annals* 455:11.

Katz, Jack. 1988. *The Seductions of Crime*. New York: Basic Books.

Kellermann, Arthur L., and Donald T. Reay 1986. "An Analysis of Firearms Related Deaths in the Home." *New England Journal of Medicine* 314:1557.

Kleck, Gary. 1991. *Point Blank: Guns and Violence in America*. New York: Aldine.

Kristof, Nicholas. 1996. "In Japan, Nothing to Fear but Fear Itself." *New York Times*, May 19, Section 4, p. 4.

Kropotkin, Peter. 1887. *In Russian and French Prisons*. Reprint. 1971. New York: Schocken Books.

Laurence, Michael, John Snortum, and Franklin E. Zimring, eds. 1988. *Social Control of the Drinking Driver*. Chicago: University of Chicago Press.

Law Enforcement Assistance Administration (1972). *San Jose Methods Test of Known Crime Victims*, Statistics Technical Report No. 1. Washington, D.C.: U.S. Government Printing Office.

Leuw, Ed. 1991. "Drugs and Drug Policy in the Netherlands." In *Crime and Justice: A Review of Research*, ed. Michael Tonry, Vol. 14, pp. 229–76. Chicago: University of Chicago Press.

Loftin, Colin, and Robert H. Hill. 1974. "Regional Subculture and Homicide." *American Sociological Review* 39:714–24.

London Research Centre, Demographic and Statistical Studies Department. 1993. *Annual Abstract of Greater London Statistics*. London: London Research Centre.

McClintock, F. Y., and Evelyn Gibson. 1961. *Robbery in London*. London: Macmillan.

McDowall, David, and Brian Wiersema. 1994. "The Incidence of Defensive Firearm Use by U.S. Crime Victims, 1987–1990." *American Journal of Public Health* 84:1982.

McLuhan, Marshall. 1964. *Understanding Media: The Extensions of Man*. New York: McGraw-Hill.

Milavsky, J. R., H. H. Stipp, R. C. Kessler, and W. S. Rubens. 1982. *Television and Aggression: A Panel Study*. New York: Academic Press.

Ministere de L'Economie et Des Finances. 1961, 1991. *Annuaire Statistique de la France 1991*. Paris: Imprimerie Nationale.

Monahan, John. 1988. "Risk Assessment of Violence Among the Mentally Disordered: Generating Useful Knowledge." *International Journal of Law and Psychiatry* 11:249–57.

Morris, Norval. 1974. *The Future of Imprisonment*. Chicago: University of Chicago Press.

———. 1984. "On 'Dangerousness' in the Judicial Process." *Rec. A.B. City N.Y.* 39:102–28.

Morris, Norval, and Gordon Hawkins. 1971. *Letter to the President on Crime Control*. Chicago: University of Chicago Press.

Morris, Norval, and Michael H. Tonry. 1984. "Black Crime, Black Victims." In *The Pursuit of Criminal Justice*. ed. Gordon Hawkins and Franklin E. Zimring. Chicago: University of Chicago Press.

Mukherjee, Satyanshu. 1981. *Crime Trends in Twentieth-Century Australia*. Sydney: Australian Institute of Criminology.

Nixon, Richard M. 1973. Radio Address on Law Enforcement and Drug Abuse Prevention. *Weekly Compendium of Presidential Documents* 9:246. Washington, D.C.: U.S. Government Printing Office.

Office of Criminal Justice Plans and Analysis. 1991. *Homicide in the District of Columbia*. Washington, D.C.: U.S. Government Printing Office.

Office of National Drug Control Policy. 1989. *National Drug Control Strategy*. Washington, D.C.: U.S. Government Printing Office.

Pearson, Geoffrey. 1991. "Drug Control Policies in Britain." In *Crime and Justice: A Review of Research*, ed. Michael Tonry, Vol. 14, pp. 167–227. Chicago: University of Chicago Press.

Phillips, David P. 1978. "Airplane Accident Fatalities Increase Just After Stories About Murder and Suicide." *Science* 201:148–50.

———. 1979. "Suicide, Motor Vehicle Fatalities, and Mass Media: Evidence Toward a Theory of Suggestion." *American Journal of Sociology* 84:1150–74.

———. 1980. "Airplane Accidents, Murder, and the Mass Media: Towards a Theory of Imitation and Suggestion." *Social Forces* 58:1001–24.

———. 1983. "The Impact of Mass Media Violence on U.S. Homicides." *American Sociological Review* 48:560–68.

Phillips, David P., and Kenneth A. Bollen. 1985. "Same Time, Last Year: Selective Data Dredging for Negative Findings." *American Sociological Review* 50:364–71.

Rand Corporation. 1995. "'Three Strikes': Serious Flaws and a Huge Price Tag." *Rand Research Review* 19:1–2.

Reiss, Albert J., Jr., and Jeffery A. Roth, eds. 1993. *Understanding and Preventing Violence.* Washington, D.C.: National Academy Press.

Roads and Traffic Authority. 1995. *Sydney's Best Map.* Sydney: Roads and Traffic Authority.

Ruggiero, Vincenzo, and Anthony A. Vass. 1992. "Heroin Use and the Formal Economy: Illicit Drugs and Licit Economies in Italy." *British Journal of Criminology* 92:273–91.

Russell, Diana E. H. 1982. *Rape in Marriage.* New York: Macmillan.

Sarvesvaran, R., and C. H. S. Jayewardene. 1985. "The Role of the Weapon in the Homicide Drama." *Medicine and Law* 4:315.

Seitz, Steven Thomas. 1972. "Firearms Homicide and Gun Control Effectiveness." *Law and Society Development Magazine,* p. 595.

Silberman, Charles E. 1978. *Criminal Violence, Criminal Justice.* New York: Random House.

Statistics Bureau, Management and Coordination Agency. 1961, 1991. *Japan Statistical Yearbook.* Tokyo: Japan Statistical Association.

Statistics Canada, Communications Division. 1961, 1991. *Canada Year Book.* Manitoba: D.W. Friesen & Sons.

Statistisches Bundesamt. 1962, 1991. *Statistisches Jahrbuch für die Bundesrepublik Deutschland.* Wiesbaden: Metzler Poeschel.

Tarde, Gabriel. 1890. *Penal Philosophy.* Trans. R. Howell. Reprint. 1912. Boston: Little, Brown and Company.

Tennenbaum, Abraham N. 1994. "The Influence of the Garner Decision on Police Use of Deadly Force." *Journal of Criminal Law and Criminology* 85:241.

United Nations. 1955–1989. *Statistical Yearbook.* New York: United Nations.

———. 1991. *Demographic Yearbook.* New York: United Nations.

U.S. Department of Commerce, Bureau of the Census. 1976. *Historical Statistics of the United States: Colonial Times to 1970.* Washington, D.C.: U.S. Government Printing Office.

———. 1990. *Current Population Reports.* Washington, D.C.: U.S. Government Printing Office.

———. 1990. *Statistical Abstract of the United States,* 112th edition. Washington, D.C.: U.S. Government Printing Office.

U.S. Department of Health and Human Services. 1991. *Vital Statistics of the United States, Volume II—Mortality.* Hyattsville, Md.: U.S. Department of Heath and Human Services.

U.S. Department of Justice, Bureau of Justice Statistics. 1992. *A National Report: Drugs, Crime, and the Justice System.* Washington, D.C.: U.S. Government Printing Office.

———. 1993. *Criminal Victimization in the United States.* Washington, D.C.: U.S. Government Printing Office.

U.S. Department of Justice, Federal Bureau of Investigation. 1947–1958, 1961–1980, 1990–1993, 1994a. *Crime in the United States.* Washington, D.C.: U.S. Government Printing Office.

———. 1994b. *Uniform Crime Reports. Supplementary Homicide Reports, 1976–1992.* 1st ICPSR version.

U.S. Department of Justice, National Institute of Justice. 1990. *Research in Action, March 1990.* Washington, D.C.: U.S. Government Printing Office.

U.S. National Commission on the Causes and Prevention of Violence. 1969a. Mass Media and Violence, Staff Report, Vol. XI. Washington, D.C.: U.S. Government Printing Office.

———. 1969b. *To Establish Justice, to Insure Domestic Tranquility. Final Report.* Washington, D.C.: U.S. Government Printing Office.

van den Haag, Ernest. 1975. *Punishing Criminals.* New York: Basic Books.

van Dijk, Jan, and Pat Mayhew. 1992. *Criminal Victimization in the Industrial World.* The Hague: Ministry of Justice.

———. 1993. "Criminal Victimization in the Industrialized World: Key Findings of the 1989 and 1992 International Crime Surveys." In *Understanding Crime: Experiences of Crime and Crime Control,* ed. Anna Alvazzi del Frate, Ugljesa Zvekic, and Jan van Dijk. Rome: United Nations Interregional Crime and Justice Research Institute.

Vinson, Tony. 1974. "Gun and Knife Attacks." *Australian Journal of Forensic Science* 7:76.

Wilinsky, Adam. 1995. The Crisis of Public Order. *The Atlantic Monthly* (July): 39.

Webster, Daniel. 1993. "The Unconvincing Case for School-Based Conflict Resolution Programs for Adolescents." *Health Affairs* 12:126.

Wintemute, Garen J. 1995. *Trauma in Transition: Trends in Deaths from Firearm and Motor Vehicle Injuries.* Sacramento, Calif.: Violence Prevention Research Program.

Wilson, James Q. 1975. *Thinking About Crime.* New York: Vintage Books.

Wilson, James Q., and Richard J. Herrnstein. 1985. *Crime and Human Nature.* New York: Simon and Schuster.

Wilson, James Q., and George L. Kelling. 1982. "Broken Windows." *Atlantic Monthly*, March, pp. 29–38.

Wolfgang, Marvin. 1958. *Patterns in Criminal Homicide.* Philadelphia: University of Pennsylvania Press.

Wolfgang, Marvin E., and Bernard Cohen. 1970. *Crime and Race: Conceptions and Misconceptions.* New York: Institute of Human Relations Press, American Jewish Committee.

Wolfgang, Marvin, Robert Figlio, and Thorsten Sellin. 1972. *Delinquency in the Binh Cohort.* Chicago: University of Chicago Press.

World Health Organization. 1955–1993. *World Health Statistics Annual.* Geneva: World Health Organization.

Zimring, Franklin E. 1968. "Is Gun Control Likely to Reduce Violent Killings?" *University of Chicago Law Review* 35:721–37.

———. 1972. "The Medium Is the Message: Firearms Caliber as a Determinant of Death from Assault." *Journal of Legal Studies* 1:97–123.

———. 1981. "Kids, Groups, and Crime: Some Implications of a Well-Known Secret." *Journal of Criminal Law and Criminology* 72:867–85.

———. 1988. "Law, Society, and the Drinking Driver: Some Concluding Reflections." In *Social Control of the Drinking Driver*, ed. Michael Laurence, John Snortum, and Franklin Zimring. Chicago: University of Chicago Press.

———. 1994. " 'Three Strikes' Law Is Political Fool's Gold." *Christian Science Monitor*, April 11, p. 23.

1996. "Kids, Guns, and Homicide: Policy Notes on an Age-Specific Epidemic." *Law and Contemporary Problems* 59:25–37.

Zimring, Franklin E., and Gordon Hawkins. 1970. "The Legal Threat as an Instrument of Social Change." *Journal of Social Issues* 27:33–48.

———. 1973. *Deterrence: The Legal Threat in Crime Control.* Chicago: University of Chicago Press.

———. 1991. *The Scale of Imprisonment.* Chicago: University of Chicago Press.

———. 1992. *Prison Population and Criminal Justice Policy in California.* Berkeley, Calif: Institute of Governmental Studies.

———. 1992b. *The Search fir Rational Drug Control.* New York: Cambridge University Press.

———. 1995. *Incapacitation: Penal Confinement and the Restraint of Crime.* New York: Oxford University Press.

Zimring, Franklin E., Gordon Hawkins, and Hank Ibser. 1995. "Estimating the Effects of Increased Incarceration on Crime in California." *California Policy Seminar Brief*, Vol. 7, July, pp. 1–12. Berkeley: California Policy Seminar.

Zimring, Franklin E., and James Zuehl. 1986. "Victim Injury and Death in Urban Robbery: A Chicago Study." *Journal of Legal Studies* 15:1–40.

14

THE TECHNOLOGY OF PERSONAL VIOLENCE

PHILIP J. COOK

The core issues for researchers concerned with the technology of personal violence were identified two decades ago in *Firearms and Violence in American Life* (Newton and Zimring 1969), a report of the National Commission on the Causes and Prevention of Violence. The first issue is to establish the causal importance of weapon type in influencing the volume, patterns, and lethality of personal violence. The second is to measure the effects of gun availability on the propensity to use guns in crime and suicide, where "availability" refers both to the prevalence of gun ownership and to the legal regulations governing transfer and use. The third core issue is to analyze how the threat of criminal victimization influences the use of guns in self-defense, and to what effect. These were the central concerns of Newton and Zimring's seminal report, and they remain central today.

Obviously, these concerns are motivated by the ongoing debate over the proper regulation of guns. This policy context not only sets the agenda; it also tends to politicize scholarly interpretation and criticism of the results. In this context, it is too easy to lose sight of the fact that, at least in principle, research can be evaluated on the basis of its scientific merits independent of whether it seems more supportive of the "pro" or "anti" position on gun control. Furthermore, some of these issues are relevant to a basic scientific understanding of violence. This review aspires to apply the norms of science in evaluating research methods and results while taking note of the policy context.

From *Crime and Justice*, vol. 14, ed. Michael Tonry (Chicago: University of Chicago Press, 1991), pp. 1–71. Reprinted with permission.

There has been a shift in the emphasis of weapons research in the two decades since publication of *Firearms and Violence in American Life*. During the 1970s, the primary focus was on the criminal misuse of guns (Cook 1982; Wright, Rossi, and Daly 1983). But during the 1980s, the focus has broadened to include much greater attention to suicide and gun accidents. This shift is the result of the involvement of the public health research community as one aspect of its emerging concern with traumatic injury as a public health problem. Milestones in this new effort are the publication of *Injury in America: A Continuing Public Health Problem by the Committee on Trauma Research of the National Research Council* (1985) and the subsequent creation of a research program on intentional injury by the Centers for Disease Control (Mercy and Houk 1988).

The involvement of the public health community has a number of virtues besides generating increased scholarly attention to suicides and accidents. It also brings a new capacity to improve data collection on gunshot wounds and consideration of a variety of policy instruments for responding to this problem: improving emergency medical response to gunshot cases, encouraging physicians to advise their patients on how to prevent gun injuries in the home, and developing regulations on the design of guns to reduce accidental shootings. But even with the broader objectives dictated by the public health framework, the most important capacities for reducing gun violence continue to reside in the criminal justice system and government apparatus for regulating gun transfer, possession, and use.

My objective here is not to review the literature as much as to review and supplement current knowledge concerning weapons and violence.[1] While there are a few international comparisons offered, the bulk of the essay is limited to research using data from the United States . . . interesting trends in the use of guns in personal violence during this period and a remarkable surge in homicide among black youths since 1984. [The section "Instrumentality"] assesses the evidence on "instrumentality," concluding that the deadliness of the weapon used in a robbery or assault has an important effect on whether the victim lives or dies. The type of weapon also influences the likelihood that a robbery or assault will be "successful." ["Patterns of Gun Use in Personal Violence"] explores one logical implication of these findings, namely, that criminals who are equipped with a gun will be empowered to commit robberies or assaults on people who could defend themselves against attacks with less potent weapons; a gun is indeed the "great equalizer." The likelihood that a gun will be used is closely related to its relative value given the vulnerability of the victim. ["Availability"] then considers how the general availability of guns influences their use in personal violence. There is considerable geographic variation in the prevalence of gun ownership, and the prevalence of gun ownership is highly correlated with the fractions of homicides, robberies, and suicides committed with a gun. Evidence is sketchy on whether regulations governing the possession, transfer, and use of guns have any additional effect. . . . ["Directions for Future Research"] outlines a research agenda that identifies projects that appear feasible (given sufficient funding) and important from a policy perspective.

Virtually every issue discussed in this essay has been debated by partisans in the "great American gun war," and almost any conclusions concerning the scientific evidence would be controversial. Nonetheless, a number of policy-relevant conclusions are offered in this essay, albeit with what I hope is an appropriate degree of scholarly caution. These conclusions are briefly summarized in the next few paragraphs.

One familiar bumper sticker asserts, "Guns don't kill people: people kill people," meaning, perhaps, that it is the intent of the assailant rather than the type of weapon he uses that determines whether the victim lives or dies. But there is persuasive evidence that both intent and weapon matter. A policy that was successful in inducing a substitution of knives for guns in acts of interpersonal violence would save lives. It may be true that a resourceful person can always find a way to kill someone if he is determined to do so. But many homicides are not the result of a sustained, deliberate intent to kill but rather are etiologically indistinguishable from a larger set of assaults and robberies in which the victim does not die. The lethality of the weapon is a major independent determinant of the lethality of the attack. The importance of the weapon in this respect is perhaps the best-establihed shed finding relevant to the gun control debate.

Another familiar bumper sticker reads, "When guns are outlawed, only outlaws will have guns." If this is not a tautology, then it expresses the belief that the violent criminals will always find a way to obtain guns, regardless of legal efforts to restrict availability. Undoubtedly, laws restricting gun possession, transfer, and carrying are difficult to enforce in the American context in which there are about 150 million firearms in private hands. However, it is notable that the tendency to use guns in crime differs widely among cities and is highly correlated with the local prevalence of gun ownership. A similar pattern holds in international comparisons. It is interesting that the prevalence of gun ownership does not appear to have much effect on the overall robbery rate; guns are simply substituted for other weapons when they are readily available. The consequence is not more robberies, but rather a higher death rate in those robberies that do occur. There is some evidence that assault is similar to robbery with respect to the effect of these weapons.

Are guns useful in self-defense? The answer is surely yes. Based on the best available evidence, the National Crime Survey (NCS), it appears that there are about 80,000 instances each year in which people attempt to defend themselves with guns against assault, robbery, rape, or burglary, and in most such cases they are successful. Unfortunately, guns are used far more often to perpetrate violent crimes—over 800,000 per year—than to defend against them. And guns acquired for self defense often end up being used to shoot family members, either accidentally or intentionally. One survey found that as many handgun owners reported being involved in a gun accident as reported using the gun in self-defense. In considering the social costs and benefits of the widespread ownership of firearms, the assertion that it produces a gent effect on predatory crime is worth considering. But the general deterrent evidence on this issue is inconclusive.

The rules of engagement over gun control policy have been rewritten during the 1980s with the involvement of the public health community. The focus and perspective of public health officials on mortality and morbidity has the effect of reordering the implicit priorities in gun violence; in particular, suicide, which accounts for a majority of gunshot deaths each year, becomes much more important in a public health framework than in a criminal justice framework. And there is some evidence for "instrumentality" in suicide. The availability of deadly weapons that are acceptable in some sense to the suicidal person arguably plays an independent causal role in whether the person dies of selfinflicted injury. If suicide becomes a central focus of the debate over gun control, then much is changed. Those at greatest risk for suicide are the demographic mirror image of homicide victims (except with respect to sex), so that the "gun problem" becomes an affliction of the middle class and middle aged in this perspective. And there exist policies that arguably would make it more difficult for a suicidal person to obtain a gun but would be irrelevant to curtailing criminal violence: one such policy is counseling family members about keeping guns away from suicidal people.

The overarching conclusion from this essay is that the widespread involvement of firearms in personal violence is not just an incidental detail but, rather, has an important influence on the patterns and lethality of this violence. . . .

Instrumentality

Only a fraction of those who are shot, stabbed, cut, or bludgeoned in criminal assaults die of their wounds. That fraction is much higher for gunshot wounds than for wounds inflicted with other common weapons. One interpretation of this weapon-specific difference in case fatality rates comes from Zimring (1968, 1972), Who suggested that the death or survival of the victim of personal violence is largely a matter of chance, and that that chance depends in part on the lethality of the weapon used to inflict injury. This "weapon instrumentality effect," which ascribes causal importance to the type of weapon, is a fundamental tenet of gun control advocates, and is, hence, one of the key points of debate in both the politics and the social science of this issue.

There is no question that case fatality rates for assaults, robberies, and other violent encounters are much higher when the assailant uses a gun than a knife, club, or bare hands; the controversy has focused on the interpretation of this finding. Marvin Wolfgang (1958, 83) states in his seminal study of homicide in Philadelphia that "it is the contention of this observer that few homicides due to shooting could be avoided merely if a firearm were not immediately present, and that the offender would select some other weapon to achieve the same destructive goal." Wolfgang believed that the choice of weapon by an assailant was an indication of his lethal intent, and that the relatively high case fatality rates for gun assaults simply reflected the relative prevalence of would-be killers among the gun users. Zimring's quite different conclusion was supported by his analysis of gun and knife assaults in Chicago; he found that gun assaults in his sample were five times as likely to result in death as knife assaults, despite the apparent similarity between gun and knife assaults in other observable respects. "These figures support the inference that if knives were substituted for guns, the homicide rate would drop significantly" (Zimring 1968, p. 728).

The debate over the weapon instrumentality effect can be clarified by a thought experiment. Imagine that it was possible to intervene just before the first blow was struck in a violent encounter, replacing the assailant's weapon with another that is less lethal, and then observe the outcome. In particular, Zimring's question was whether the death rate would be reduced in cases where a loaded gun was replaced with a knife. His affirmative answer is supported by his argument that many gun homicides are committed by people who have no clear intention to kill. If the assailant's intent were ambiguous or unsustained, then the fatality rate would fall because killing with a knife ordinarily requires greater strength and more sustained effort than killing with a gun. Indeed, despite his conclusion quoted above, Wolfgang suggested one mechanism for this possibility: "The offender's physical repugnance to engaging in direct physical assault by cutting or stabbing his adversary, may mean that in the absence of a firearm no homicide occurs" (Wolfgang 1958, p. 79). In other cases the assailant may cease the attack after inflicting a wound or two, simply because the violent urge that prompted the attack is satisfied. Rarely does the assailant administer the coup de grace that would ensure the victim's death. In Zimring's gun sample, only 16 percent of nonfatal cases and 19 percent of fatal cases involved more than one gunshot wound (1968, p. 737).

Wright, Rossi, and Daly (1983) provide the most prominent critique of Zimring's work on instrumentality. They focus on Zimring's conclusion that a large fraction of killers attack their victims with no clear intention of killing them and, in that respect, are similar to other assailants whose victims survive. Wright, Rossi, and Daly agree that some killers lack clear homicidal intent but do not accept Zimring's evidence as establishing that ambiguous intent characterizes a large percentage of homicidal attacks (Wright, Rossi, and Daly 1983, p. 192) and is hence so prevalent as to account for the large observed differences in weapon-specific case fatality rates.

The evidence in question is of three sorts. First, Zimring (1968) notes that homicides in Chicago in 1967 typically involved relatives or acquaintances caught up in altercations in which the assailant or victim had been drinkingcircumstances that he asserts tend to be associated with ambiguous intent (p. 722). Second, he demonstrates that homicide cases are similar to serious assault cases with respect to the demographic characteristics of killers and victims, with greatly disproportionate involvement of males and blacks (p. 724). In that respect, then, fatal and nonfatal cases are similar, suggesting (says Zimring) that they may also be similar with respect to the assailants' state of mind. Third, he reports the results of a detailed study of the wounds inflicted in gun and knife attacks, concluding that despite the lower death rate in knife attacks, a greater percentage of knife than gun attacks appear to be "in earnest," based on the location and number of wounds inflicted (pp. 730–35). Zimring (1968) analyzed Chicago Police Department assault records for the period November 9–December 6, 1967. During this period there were 366 serious knife attacks, of which eight were fatal, and 247 serious gun attacks, of which thirty-four were fatal. He analyzed the number and location of wounds resulting from each of these attacks as a basis for judging the seriousness and intent of the assailant.

Wright, Rossi, and Daly's response to this evidence is that it is insufficient to offer persuasive support for Zimring's conclusion regarding ambiguous intent. However, Wright, Rossi, and Daly are impressed by Zimring's data on the seriousness of many nonfatal knife attacks, concluding that this evidence "does at least suggest that a substantial portion of knife attacks are indeed 'in earnest,' and this constitutes the strongest evidence yet encountered that the motives of gun and knife attackers may be similar" (Wright, Rossi, and Daly 1983, p. 200). The implication is that if these "earnest" knife attackers had used guns, a higher percentage of victims would have died; that is, Wright, Rossi, and Daly appear to accept the validity and importance of the weapon instrumentality effect while remaining unconvinced that Zimring's explanation for this effect (ambiguous intent) is correct.

Zimring buttressed the conclusions from his first study, which compared knife and gun attacks, with a later (1972) study comparing attacks with large- and small-caliber guns. The basic data for the caliber comparison came from an analysis of fatal and nonfatal firearm attacks reported to the Chicago police between March 5 and July 22, 1970. In all, 1,115 gun attacks resulting in 156 fatalities were reported. For the purpose of comparing death rates by caliber, Zimring excluded from this sample all robberies and also all attacks with shotguns and large-caliber rifles and also excluded a number of cases (most of which were not fatal) in which the caliber of the gun was not known to police. The actual number of cases available for detailed study is not clear from Zimring's report.

He found that the fatality rate increased with caliber, as predicted by the weapon instrumentality effect. The alternative explanation takes the same form as in the case of guns versus knives: that assailants who use larger-caliber weapons tend to have more deadly intent, and that the fatality rate differential between large- and small-caliber guns reflects this difference in intent rather than the lethality of the weapon. This alternative explanation receives some support from the fact that shooters using a .38 or higher-caliber weapon were more likely to inflict multiple wounds than those using a .22-caliber weapon (26 percent vs. 11 percent) (Zimring 1972, p. 104). But the caliber-related differences in the death rate are large even when the number and location of wounds are controlled for. In any event, Wright, Rossi, and Daly (1983), despite their generally critical review of Zimring's work, are convinced by it that weapon lethality does have an independent causal effect on the probability of death: "One apparently certain implication of Zimring's result is that the substitution of higher-caliber for lowercaliber handguns would almost certainly cause the rate of handgun deaths to increase" (Wright, Rossi, and Daly 1983, p. 203).

While Zimring's work focused on weapon-specific case fatality rates for assaults, it is also of interest to observe how the weapon instrumentality effect fares in the context of other violent felonies. Homicides committed during the commission of a felony such as robbery, rape, or burglary account for about 20 percent of all criminal homicides, of which half are robberies (Cook 1985b). My studies of robbery violence offer support for the instrumentality effect in that context (Cook 1979, 1980a, 1987). Robbery is generally defined as theft or attempted theft by force or the threat of violence, including muggings and holdups. The overall robbery fatality rate is about 1 in 750 (Cook 1987), much lower than for serious assaults (where the rate is roughly one in 100).[2] But as in the case of assault, robbery fatality rates differ widely, depending on the type of weapon used. The fatality rate is four per thousand for gun robberies, which is about three times higher than for knife robberies and ten times higher than for robberies involving other weapons. Demonstrating that all or part of this difference in weapon-specific fatality rates is due to the weapon itself requires a statistical method for controlling for other factors that influence the probability that a robbery will result in the death of a victim.

One approach that I developed for testing weapon instrumentality in robbery was quite different from Zimring's. I reasoned that if the type of weapon had an independent causal effect on the probability of death, then a city's robbery murder rate should be more sensitive to variations in its gun robbery rate than to its nongun robbery rate. This prediction was confirmed in my study of changes in robbery and robbery murder in forty-three cities for the period 1976-83 (Cook 1987, p. 373). On the average, an additional 1,000 gun robberies produced an additional 4.8 murders, whereas an additional 1,000 nongun robberies added only 1.4 additional murders. . . .

In sum, the weapons-specific differences in fatality rates in assault as well as for robbery have been clearly established; more lethal weapons are associated with higher fatality rates. Further, there is persuasive evidence that these differences in fatality rates are, in large part, the direct consequence of the differential lethality of the weapons, rather than simply a statistical artifact of some other causal process (such as differences in intent that influence both weapon choice and outcome). However, the various mechanisms that are responsible for the instrumentality effect have not been completely analyzed or documented.

The mechanism suggested by Zimring is that in a large percentage of violent attacks the assailant's intent is ambiguous. His data and those of others make clear that for every killing there are several other nonfatal attacks for which there was a real chance that the assailant's actions would cause death; for example, for everyone in his (1972) sample who (died from a single gunshot wound in the chest, there were 1.8 others who suffered a single gunshot wound in the chest and survived. Surely the element of chance is important here, and in an unsustained attack, the lethality of the first blow will be a major determinant of the chance of death. But there are other mechanisms that may also be important in instrumentality.

In the mechanism suggested by Zimring, the key attribute of a gun is that it can kill without sustained effort; relatively small amounts of energy and time are sufficient. But another quality of firearms may also be relevant; it empowers someone to attack a stronger victim and kill him or her, which may be physically impossible with a less powerful weapon. Surely the power of a gun to overcome or forestall resistance helps explain why all successful presidential assassinations and over 90 percent of murders of police officers have been committed with a gun (Federal Bureau of Investigation 1979). . . .

Whatever the mix of mechanisms that account for it, the instrumentality effect is not a complete explanation for observed weapons-specific differences in fatality rates. The death rate for assault may vary for reasons unrelated to weapon choice. For example, Swersey (1980) documented a large increase in the homicide rate in Harlem between 1968 and 1973 which was accompanied by a more than doubling of the fraction of gun attacks resulting in death; Swersey concluded that much of the change was due to an increase in intentional killings resulting from disputes involving narcotics activities. But the type of weapon, while not the sole determinant of the probability that a violent encounter will result in death, is one of the important determinants of this probability.

Other Instrumentality Effects

The effect of weapon type on the likelihood of death in a violent encounter is of paramount concern, but it is by no means the only weapon instrumentality effect. The type of weapon also influences the likelihood and severity of injury and the likelihood that the assailant will succeed in whatever purpose motivated the attack. As noted by Kleck and McElrath (1989), "The ultimate goal behind an act of violence is not necessarily the victim's death or injury, but rather may be money, sexual gratification, respect, attention, or the humiliation and domination of the victim." Their analysis of National Crime Survey data on assaults by strangers found that half of these cases were mere threats without any attack; in only about half of those cases where the assailant did attack was the victim injured. The type of weapon affects the likelihood of physical attack and injury in an assault, as well as the likelihood of "success."

Most of the previous research on this issue has focused on robbery. The principal role of a weapon in robbery is to aid the robber in coercing the victim (by force or threat) to part with his valuables. If the threat is sufficiently convincing, physical force is not necessary. For this reason, it is hardly surprising that the use of force is closely related to the weapon type in robbery, being very common in unarmed robbery and relatively rare in gun robbery. Using National Crime Panel data for twenty-six cities, I found that the likelihood of physical attack in a noncommercial robbery committed by one or more adult males differed with the type of weapon used as follows: gun, 22.1 percent; knife, 39.4 percent; other weapon, 60.4 percent; and strong-arm, 73.5 percent (Cook 1980a). As an immediate consequence, the likelihood of injury is less in a gun robbery than for robberies with other weapons (Conklin 1972; Cook 1976; Skogan 1978); indeed, the pattern of injury across the four weapon categories is exactly the reverse of the pattern of fatality rates. But if we confine our attention to injuries serious enough to require hospitalization, then this pattern largely disappears; when other factors are held constant (via a multivariate statistical analysis) gun and knife robberies are about equally likely to result in serious injury.[3] Thus, more lethal weapons are less likely to be used to inflict injury but when they are, the injury tends to be more serious. That is why the likelihood of death is much higher in gun robberies than in knife robberies, as noted above.

Kleck and McElrath (1989) report a similar analysis for assaults by strangers reported to the National Crime Survey during the years 1979–85. They found that the presence of a gun or knife reduces the likelihood that there will be any sort of physical attack during the assault; if there are lethal weapons present, it is more likely that the assault will terminate with a threat. Given that there is an attack during the assault by a stranger, it is less likely that the victim will sustain injury if the attack is perpetrated with a gun than with a knife, presumably because attack with a gun includes the possibility of shooting at but missing the victim, a possibility that has no analog for other types of weapons. If there is an injury, the probability that it will result in the death of the victim is much higher in the case of gunshot wounds than knife wounds.[4]

The inverse relation between weapon lethality and use of force is compatible with the notion that violence plays a tactical role in robbery—that it is employed when the robber believes it is needed to overcome or forestall victim resistance, and that this need is less likely to arise when the robber uses a gun. (See Cook [1980a] for a complete discussion of this issue. Not all violence in robbery is tactical.) Thus, the type of weapon is an important determinant of the nature of the interaction between robber and victim.

The type of weapon is also important in determining whether a robbery is completed successfully. The powerful threat produced by the display of a gun generally ensures compliance. According to National Crime Survey data for 1987, success rates in noncommercial robbery ranged from 70 percent for gun cases down to 55 percent for knife robberies and 49 percent for robberies with clubs and other weapons (Bureau of Justice Statistics 1989a, p. 64). Furthermore, the value of items taken in completed robberies is over twice as high in gun robberies as for other armed robberies (Cook 1976).

Handgun versus Long Gun

Comparisons of fatality and injury rates across different categories of weapons conceal the potentially important diversity within each category. The "knife" category includes everything from scissors and pen knives to large hunting knives, while "gun" incorporates homemade "zip" guns, assault rifles, and everything in between. Laws regulating the transfer and use of firearms incorporate certain distinctions among different types of firearm. For example, current federal law bans the transfer of automatic rifles and sawed-off shotguns and bans the importation of small cheap handguns commonly known as Saturday night specials. State laws tend to regulate handguns more stringently than long guns (Cook and Blose 1981). If these legal distinctions affect the mix of guns used in assault and robbery, then they may thereby influence the fatality rate in these crimes.

Zimring's (1972) most persuasive demonstration of the instrumentality effect in assault used the finding that wounds made by larger-caliber bullets are more likely to result in death than were otherwise comparable wounds made by smaller-caliber bullets. Other characteristics of a bullet are also important in determining the lethality of a wound, including its shape and velocity. In particular, while tissue damage inflicted by a low-velocity bullet is primarily limited to the track of the bullet through the body, high-velocity bullets injure tissue distant from the bullet track, because of the large temporary cavity formed by the shock wave (Fackler 1988; Hollerman 1988).

Rifles are more deadly than handguns in part because of the difference in the velocity of the bullet. For example, a .22-caliber bullet fired from a rifle will travel at a muzzle velocity of about 1,700 feet per second, compared with a velocity of 950 feet per second for a bullet from the same cartridge fired from a handgun (Hollerman 1988, p. 238). The difference in velocity is the direct result of the difference in barrel length; a longer barrel provides a longer time for the force of the gunpowder explosion to accelerate the bullet. A corollary is that bullets fired from snub-nosed handguns have lower muzzle velocity than bullets fired from handguns with standard barrels.

Shotguns add a new dimension to the analysis of the intrinsic lethality of firearms since a single shotshell contains a number of projectiles. According to one expert, shotgun wounds are most commonly caused by a one-ounce load of no. 6 birdshot containing 225 pellets, fired from a twelve-gauge shotgun (Hollerman 1988, p. 241). The spread of the shot pattern and the trauma inflicted by multiple wounds enhance the case fatality rate for shotgun wounds.

Given a choice, one would prefer being shot at by someone using a handgun than a rifle or shotgun. This conclusion follows both from the wound ballistics information summarized above and because long guns are more accurate and easier to aim than handguns. A number of authors have considered the possible implications for the regulation of guns (Benenson and Kates 1979; Wright, Rossi, and Daly 1983; Kleck 1984a), concluding that a policy that regulates handguns more stringently than long guns may have the perverse effect of increasing the death rate from gun assaults. For example, if the only effect of a handgun prohibition were that shooters would use sawed-off shotguns instead, then there is no question that the result of the prohibition would be to increase the homicide rate. However, if the principal effect of the prohibition were to reduce the rate of gun assault, with only a relatively few cases in which another type of firearm was substituted for the handgun, then the homicide rate would fall. Note that "substitution" in this case is not a simple phenomenon; the elimination of handguns would presumably have some effect on all of the following: the rate of robberies and other potentially violent confrontations, the weapons deployed in these confrontations, the likelihood that if a gun were deployed it would be fired, the likelihood that if fired it would hit the intended victim, and finally, the likelihood that the wound would be fatal. There is no precise information on any of the links of this chain, and the net effect on the homicide rate is in doubt.

Those who favor more stringent regulation of handguns are impressed by the greatly disproportionate involvement of such guns in violent crime. There are more than twice as many long guns in private hands as handguns. Yet handguns were used in over 80 percent of the gun homicides in 1988 (Federal Bureau of Investigation 1989, p. 12) and over 90 percent of the noncommercial gun robberies in 1987 (Bureau of Justice Statistics 1989a, p. 64); among handgun crimes, most involve weapons with barrels that are shorter than the average of those in circulation (Cook 1981a). One consequence of the disproportionate use of handguns in crime is a rather high probability that a privately owned handgun has been or will be used in crime; by one estimate, a representative group of 100 handguns sold new in 1977 were, over the course of their lifetimes, involved in crime at the rate of .33 (one crime per three guns) (Cook 1981b).[5] This number is still higher for snubnosed handguns. This relatively high rate of crime involvement, an order of magnitude higher for handguns than for long guns, suggests that handguns are especially well suited to criminal use and that the criminal use of guns would decline if handguns were somehow eliminated.

Kleck (1984a) has laid out a useful road map for estimating the effects of a handgun prohibition. If we knew the relative death rates for handgun wounds and long gun wounds resulting from criminal assault under current conditions of gun availability, then it would be possible to make at least a rough estimate of the effect of substitution on the homicide rate. Unfortunately, this information is not available. The overall death rate from gunshot wounds in assault is about one in seven (Cook 1985a), which can be viewed as an average of the long gun and handgun ratios. But data on gunshot wounds do not usually distinguish between long guns and handguns, so separate fatality rates cannot be calculated. Indirect methods employed by Kleck (1984a) suggest that the death rate for gunshot wounds inflicted by long guns may be three or four times as high as for wounds inflicted by handguns; the validity of these methods is not known due to the lack of direct evidence on this matter. The best evidence that is available is provided by Kleck himself, in a subsequent study (Kleck and McElrath 1989). He and his coauthor created a unique data set by combining the NCS reports of injuries resulting from stranger assaults with supplementary homicide reports of homicides by strangers for the year 1982. Based on these combined data, they estimated the effects of different weapon types on the likelihood of death, controlling for some other variables. Their estimates imply that the likelihood of death in handgun assaults is virtually identical to the likelihood of death in assaults with other guns.[6] They do not comment on this result, but the apparent implication is that other guns are no more lethal in practice than handguns.

One interesting aspect of the controversy concerning the possible effects of regulating some guns more stringently than others is that all parties to the debate seem to have accepted the validity of the weapon instrumentality effect. Thus there is a consensus among the researchers in this area that the type of weapon matters, not just as a signal of the intent or personality of the assailant, but as a distinct causal factor. Whether a shooting victim lives or dies depends in part on the length of the gun barrel and the size of the bullet.

Suicide

As with homicide, about 60 percent of suicides are committed with guns. And, as in the case of criminal attacks, there is evidence that the instrument chosen by suicide attempters affects whether the attempt proves fatal or not (Clarke and Lester 1989). Case fatality rates are much higher for gun attempts than for those involving other means that are frequently employed, such as drugs and razors; for example, Dallas Police Department data indicate a fatality rate of 76 percent for gun suicide attempts, compared with just 4 percent for all other means combined (SOURCE: Special unpublished tabulation, Dallas Police Department [1983]). In another study (Card 1974), it was found that 92 percent of suicide attempts by firearms were successful, compared with 78 percent for carbon monoxide, 9 percent for other gases, 78 percent for hanging, 67 percent for drowning, 23 percent for poisoning, and 4 percent for cutting. This impressive difference does not, of course, prove the instrumentality claim. It can be argued that the choice of weapon in a suicide attempt reflects the seriousness of purpose of the attempter and makes no independent contribution to the outcome. The debate over instrumentality in suicide proceeds parallel to the debate over instrumentality in homicide.

The case for suicide instrumentality is weaker than for homicide. First, while Zimring's claim is plausible that a large fraction of the shooters in homicide cases have no clear intent to kill, a similar assertion for gun suicides is far less plausible. Surely someone who purposefully points a gun at a vital area and pulls the trigger expects to die. Further, if a gun is not available for some reason, then there are always alternatives that are nearly as lethal, including hanging and jumping from a high place (Card 1974). And while homicides are usually the result of transitory altercations or confrontations, we know that many suicides result from a chronic condition such as pathological depression or a terminal painful disease. In such cases, there is time to contemplate alternative means and select one that will succeed. It is noteworthy in this regard that Japan and some European countries have far higher suicide rates than the United States despite the fact that private ownership of guns is relatively rare in those countries and gun suicides make up only a small fraction of the total. Kates (1990, p. 42) tabulated suicide rates for various years in the mid-1980s. The U.S. rate was 12.2 per 100,000, compared with Japan (20.3), West Germany (20.4), France (21.8), Austria (26.9), Denmark (28.7), and Rumania (66.2).

Nevertheless, there is some evidence that the instrumentality effect is important in suicide. That some other countries have higher suicide rates despite the relatively rare use of guns does not undercut this conclusion. The argument here is not that the availability of lethal means is the sole determinant of suicide rates but, rather, that the availability of lethal means influences the extent to which suicidal impulses are translated into complete suicides. Depriving a suicidal person of a lethal and attractive means of self-destruction may well save his life. . . .

. . . But while there is some evidence that, if deprived of their favored means of death, some suicidal people may choose to live (e.g., Clarke and Mayhew 1988), this evidence is far from conclusive.

A recent study of risk factors in adolescent suicide is directly relevant to the issue of gun instrumentality and confirms (albeit for a small local sample) that suicidal youths are more likely to kill themselves if there is a gun in their home than otherwise (Brent et al. 1988). The authors conclude that "clinicians who work with suicidal adolescents should strongly advocate the removal of firearms from the home environment" (p. 587). This conclusion seems very reasonable, even in the absence of a definitive experiment. Sloan et al. (1990)* used an entirely different method to reach a similar conclusion about youthful suicide: in their comparison of suicide rates in King County (Seattle) and Vancouver for the years 1985–87, they found that King County, with a much higher prevalence of gun ownership, had a 37 percent higher rate of suicide for youths age fifteen to twenty-four; King County had a much higher gun suicide rate for this group and a slightly lower nongun rate. However, the apparent importance of gun availability in influencing the overall suicide rate is limited to youths; for older people, the suicide rate was actually somewhat higher in Vancouver than in King County. It should be noted, in any event, that this comparison between two jurisdictions is not a reliable basis for making generalizations.

From what little is known of the suicide process, it appears plausible that there is an instrumentality effect, and in particular in the United States, where guns are the favored means, that depriving suicidal people of guns would save some lives. But the evidence available at this point is not strong and includes findings that contradict the instrumentality hypothesis. Nevertheless, if I had a deeply depressed teenage son or daughter, I would take care that there were no loaded guns in the house.

Conclusion

The discussion on instrumentality begins with the undeniable observation that death rates in assault, robbery, and parasuicide differ widely depending on the "instrument" used. The more lethal the weapon, the higher the fraction of injuries that prove fatal. The difficult question is how to interpret this empirical pattern. If the type of weapon in a violent encounter were chosen at random,

---

*See John Henry Sloan, "Handgun Regulations, Crime, Assaults, and Homicide," in Part Four of this volume.—Ed.

then the significance of the observed pattern would be clear: the type of weapon has a direct influence on the outcome. But in practice, the choice of weapon in an assault or suicide attempt is not strictly random; to some extent it is a signal of intent, and other things equal, those with more deadly intent are more likely to kill. The debate over instrumentality, over whether the weapon "matters," is a debate over whether systematic differences in intent are sufficient to account for the large observed differences in weapon-specific death rates. While the evidence is mixed for suicide, it is more clear cut in assaultive crimes that the weapon does indeed matter.

This conclusion follows from close scrutiny of samples of assaults and from analysis of patterns in aggregate data. And it comports with common sense. The type of weapon matters in personal violence just as it does in warfare. If violent people did not have access to guns, there would still be as much violence in the United States as there is now, or more, but it would be much less deadly.

Patterns of Gun Use in Personal Violence

Firearms were used in 61 percent of the homicides, 33 percent of the robberies, and 21 percent of the aggravated assaults reported to the police in 1988 (Federal Bureau of Investigation 1989). These percentages have varied over time and differ across jurisdictions. . . . [Here we] focus on the patterns of gun use across the different circumstances in which these crimes occur. What characteristics of the assailant, the victim, and the immediate environment of the criminal act influence the likelihood that a gun is employed, rather than another type of weapon?

A gun has a number of characteristics that make it superior to other readily available weapons for use in violent crime: even in the hands of a weak and unskilled assailant, a gun can be used to kill. The killing can be accomplished from a distance without much risk of effective counterattack by the victim, and the killing can be completed quickly, without sustained effort, and in a relatively impersonal fashion. Furthermore, because everyone knows that a gun has these attributes, the mere display of a gun communicates a highly effective threat. In most circumstances, a gun maximizes the probability of success for a would-be robber or murderer.

Evidence that criminals who use guns are influenced by tactical considerations such as these comes from a survey of prisoners by James Wright and Peter Rossi (1986). They persuaded 1,874 convicted male felons in ten states to fill out questionnaires concerning their criminal histories and their use of weapons. This sample, it should be noted, is a sample of convenience, rather than a representative sample of all male prisoners, and no clear inferences can be drawn from the quantitative results. In the absence of other data, however, the Wright-Rossi survey is useful in providing a general qualitative impression. Respondents who had used guns in some of their crimes (almost all of whom admitted to committing robberies, among other crimes) cited a number of motives for this choice of weaponry. A majority indicated that each of the following reasons, related to their ability to forestall or overcome victim resistance and get away unscathed, was "very important" or "somewhat important": "chance victim would be armed," "prepared for anything," "ready to defend myself," "easier to do crime," "might need gun to escape," "need gun to do crime," "people don't mess with you." The most cited reason for using a gun was "don't have to hurt victim."

Given all these advantages, the obvious question is why only a minority of violent crimes are committed with a gun. Wright and Rossi asked felons in their sample who used weapons other than guns "why not carry a gun?" The most frequent reasons were "just asking for trouble," "get a stiffer sentence," "never needed a gun for my crimes." Lack of familiarity was important for a large minority of respondents, who checked "never owned a gun" or "don't like guns." One-third of respondents checked "against the law for me to own a gun" as an important reason. Twenty-one percent of this group checked "too much trouble to get one." Thus, the respondents who used weapons other than guns were generally concerned about the legal consequences and other trouble resulting from carrying a gun to use in crime. Tastes, familiarity, and legal restrictions on ownership also played a role in their decisions. Availability is cited as an important consideration by only a few of the respondents, but that by no means "proves" that availability is generally unimportant. The respondents may have had a tendency to exaggerate their competence in obtaining whatever weapon they wanted. Further, the Wright-Rossi sample gives a highly distorted representation of the population of violent criminals; all respondents were prisoners, and prisoners tend to be older and perhaps more sophisticated about crime than the population of active criminals on the outside.

A variety of evidence gives clear indication that the decision about whether to go armed with a gun is closely linked to decisions about what crimes to commit and the likely success or failure of these crimes. The tool determines the task, and the task determines the tool. These links are clearly illustrated by the patterns of gun use in robbery, murder, and assault. . . .

Assault

For a large percentage of violent crimes, it is in the assailant's interest to take care to avoid killing the victim. Robbery murder, for example, is a capital crime in many jurisdictions—even if the killing is an "accident" or a spontaneous reaction to victim resistance. Conklin (1972, p. 111) interviewed several robbery convicts who used an unloaded-gun (for fear that otherwise they might end up shooting their victims, and the same concern was reflected in some of the responses from Wright and Rossi's (1986) sample of prisoners. In other violent confrontations, such as fights between family members, this same concern may deter the combatants from reaching for a gun—even when there is one readily available. A loaded gun is not an appropriate weapon when the assailant's intent is to hurt, but not kill, the victim.

Some unknown fraction of assault cases is similar to robbery in that the assailant's objective is to coerce the victim's compliance—the assailant wants the victim to stop attacking him (physically or verbally) or stop dancing with his girl-friend or get off his favorite bar stool or turn down the stereo. Moreover, as in the case of robbery, the probability of a physical attack in such cases may be less if the assailant has a gun than otherwise, because the victim will be less inclined to ignore or resist a threat enforced by the display of a gun. (It may also be true that the assailant would be more hesitant to use a gun than another weapon to make good his threat.) In general support of these ideas, evidence from the National Crime Survey indicates that assaults with a gun are less likely to involve attack or injury than are assaults with other weapons (Kleck and McElrath 1989).

Conclusion

Consideration of the tactical concerns of criminals helps make sense of a number of patterns in weapon use in violent crime. A robber equipped with a gun can stage a successful robbery against a target that might effectively resist an assailant using a less powerful weapon. A woman who decides to kill a man who is larger and stronger than she will have a hard time of it with a knife, but a gun would do the job. Guns are most likely to be used where they have greatest value compared to other, less lethal weapons. This conclusion inspires an obvious question: if guns became more scarce, would there be relatively less violent crime of the sort for which guns are most valuable? In the case of robbery, for example, would there be a reduction in the victimization rate for commercial places? If so, would crim-inals substitute other targets or other types of crime for commercial robbery? These questions cannot be answered from the available literature but are relevant in assessing the policy-relevant effects from a change in gun availability. . . .

Availability

About one-half of the households in the United States possess at least one firearm, and the total number of firearms in private hands is on the order of 150 million. Nevertheless, guns are a scarce commodity, costly to obtain and to use. For a criminal, the costs may include not only the purchase price but also the various legal risks of obtaining, possessing, and using the gun in crime. These costs help explain why guns are not used in a higher proportion of violent crimes. . . . For example, gun robberies tend to be considerably more lucrative than others, yet less than one-third of all robberies are committed with a gun.

Advocates of gun control measures seek to make guns more scarce, espe-cially to criminals and criminal use. "Gun control" generally encompasses three basic strategies (Zimring 1990): deprive dangerous people (convicted felons, mental patients) of guns; restrict high-risk uses (carrying concealed); and forbid commerce in certain kinds of firearms (machine guns, Saturday night specials). Evidence on the effectiveness of such measures in reducing the misuse of guns is sketchy. There have been only a few evaluations of specific ordinances, and these are reviewed below; more work has been done on how gun availability, defined generically, affects the prevalence of gun misuse.

The most obvious indicator of "availability" is the prevalence of ownership. . . .

Recent Trends and Patterns in Gun Ownership

The number of firearms in private hands has been estimated both from survey data and from data on manufactures and imports. The most thorough study of this matter is by Wright, Rossi, and Daly (1983), who estimate that there were 100–140 million firearms in 1978, of which 30–40 million were handguns. Since then there have been 52 million firearms manufactured or imported into the United States for sale to households, businesses, and law-enforcement agencies (Bureau of Alcohol, Tobacco and Firearms 1989). Of the 52 million new guns, there were 6.6 million recorded exports (Bureau of Alcohol, Tobacco and Firearms 1989) and possibly millions more of illegal export. Further, some portion of the stock of guns existing in 1978 has been discarded, rendered useless by breakage and rust, or confiscated by authorities, so some of the new guns are "replacements" for older guns. If the stock in existence in 1978 depreciated by just 1 percent per year, then the total stock as of 1988 was 150 million give or take 20 million. (This estimate accepts the 100–140 million range for 1978 as correct and ignores illegal imports and exports since then.) While the trend probably continues upward, it is notable that fewer new guns were sold in the United States during the decade ending in 1988 than during the preceding decade.

The 1989 Gallup poll estimated 47 percent of households possessed a gun, a result that affirms one of the remarkable constants in American life: the fraction of American households owning a gun has remained at about one-half for at least the last three decades (Bureau of Justice Statistics 1989b, p. 232). There has, however, been a substantial increase in the fraction of households that own a handgun, from 13 percent in 1959 to about 24 percent in 1978 and thereafter; thus in recent years, about half of the gun-owning households own a handgun. Most gun-owning households have several guns, with an average of three as of 1978 (based on a poll of voters conducted by Decision Making Information, Inc. that year; see Wright 1981). Only one in six gun-owning households is limited to handguns; three-quarters of those who own a handgun also own a rifle or shotgun. These statistics are relevant to the question of how many guns are in private hands; between 1978 and 1988, the number of households increased by 12 million, while the fraction of households owning a gun remained roughly constant. These data support the conclusion that the total stock of guns in private hands has increased, but whether it has increased in proportion to the number of households depends on whether there has been any change in the average number of guns per gun-owning household during this period.[7]

The incidence of firearms ownership is not uniform across society. The General Social Surveys conducted by the National Opinion Research Center have included an item about gun ownership since 1973; they consistently find that the fraction of households owning a gun increases with income, decreases with city size, is substantially higher for whites than blacks, and is highest in the South and lowest in the Northeast (Wright and Marston 1975; Bureau of Justice Statistics 1989b). An analysis of regional patterns of ownership for residents of large cities, using National Opinion Research Center polls taken in the mid-1970s, found a range for gun ownership from 10 percent for residents of large cities in New England and the Mid-Atlantic up to 50 percent for the East South Central region (Louisville, Kentucky; Memphis and Nashville, Tennessee; Birmingham, Alabama). The South Atlantic, Mountain, and West South Central regions all had ownership rates of 40 percent or higher (Cook 1979).

The Costs of Obtaining a Gun

The density of gun ownership is one dimension of gun availability since gun owners obviously have more ready access to guns than do other people. The term "gun availability" also refers to the cost and difficulty of acquiring a gun. The purchase price of a new gun will differ widely depending on its characteristics. The trend in the average prices of new guns has followed the overall trend in consumer prices since 1960 (Cook 1982). Since about half of all gun transfers involve used guns (Blose and Cook 1980), it would also be relevant to assess price trends in that market. In the absence of any useful data on this subject, it seems safe to assume that prices in the secondhand market exhibit the same trend as prices in the market for new guns, as is true for autos and other consumer durables.

In addition to the purchase price, the cost of obtaining a gun may be increased by federal and state laws that regulate firearms commerce. What is required in this respect differs from state to state and sometimes also differs among jurisdictions within a state.

Regulations Governing Transfers and Possession

The Gun Control Act of 1968 established the framework for the current system of controls on gun transfers. All shipments of firearms are limited to federally licensed dealers who are required to obey all applicable state and local ordinances. This act also stipulates several categories of people who are denied the right to receive or possess a gun, including illegal aliens, convicted felons and those under indictment, and people who have at some time been involuntarily committed to a mental institution. People with a history of "substance abuse" are also proscribed from possessing a gun. Dealers are not allowed to sell handguns to people younger than twenty-one, or to sell long guns to those younger than eighteen, although there is no federal prohibition of gun possession by youths. Under the Gun Control Act, the various prohibitions are implemented by a requirement that the buyer sign a form stating that he does not fall into any of the proscribed categories.

The Gun Control Act imposed a national ban on mail-order purchases of firearms except by licensed dealers. There are also some restrictions on sales to people from out of state. The intended effect of these regulations was to insulate the states from each other so that the stringent regulations on firearms commerce adopted in some states would not be undercut by the greater availability of guns in other states.[8]

A number of states have adopted significant restrictions on commerce in firearms, especially handguns. Twenty-one states, including about two-thirds of the population, currently require that handgun buyers obtain a permit or license (or at least send an application to the police) before taking possession of the gun (Bureau of Justice Statistics 1989b, p. 169). Local jurisdictions in several other states have regulations of this sort in place. All but a few state transfer-control systems are "permissive," in the sense that most people are legally entitled to obtain a gun. In a few jurisdictions, however, it is very difficult to (obtain a handgun legally. For example, Washington, D.C., stipulates that only law-enforcement officers and security guards are entitled to obtain a handgun (Jones 1981).

The effect of a permissive transfer-control system is to increase the effective cost of a legally purchased handgun by imposing a permit fee and a waiting period and by requiring applicants to do some paperwork and submit to a criminal record check. These requirements may discourage some people from purchasing handguns and motivate others to evade the transfer regulations by purchasing from friends or other sources that lack a dealer's license. Of course, purchase from a nondealer may be costly and inconvenient in other ways.

Evading Regulations on Gun Transfers

Interstate differences in the stringency of transfer regulations produce a vigorous illegal commerce in guns moving across state lines (Bureau of Alcohol, Tobacco, and Firearms 1976; Moore 1981). Even in jurisdictions that lack stringent regulations, there is an active market in stolen guns and off-the-book transfers. From their survey of prisoners, Wright and Rossi (1986, p. 185) report that few respondents acquired their guns by purchasing them from a licensed dealer. Of those who had owned a handgun, one-third reported having stolen their most recent one. For others, "family and friends" were the most common source of guns purchased, traded for, or borrowed. Many of the guns obtained from these sources had been stolen by someone else. These findings are suggestive although, as noted above, the Wright-Rossi study is based on a sample of convenience that is not representative of the population of active criminals.

It seems reasonable to conclude that gun availability to criminals has much to do with the ease of stealing a gun or obtaining one on the black market or from an acquaintance. Given these sources, the difficulty of obtaining a gun is presumably closely related to the density of gun ownership. For example, the fraction of burglaries that result in the theft of guns increases with the fraction of households that own guns (Moore 1981), so the black market for stolen guns will be more active in cities where gun ownership is prevalent. Further, criminals will find it easier (and perhaps cheaper) to buy or borrow a gun from an acquaintance in cities with high rates of gun ownership. Thus, the costs of obtaining a gun for those who are not inclined to buy from a dealer will depend on the general prevalence of gun ownership.

Carrying Guns in Public

Since most violent crimes occur away from the assailant's home, mere possession of a gun is not enough to guarantee that it is available for use when the occasion arises. Hence, the propensity to go armed in public is an important aspect of gun availability. Presumably, the prevalence of going armed is highly correlated with the prevalence of ownership across cities, but it may also be influenced by the vigor with which anticarrying laws are enforced and by other factors.

State and local legislation tends to make a sharp distinction between keeping a gun in one's home or business and carrying a gun in public. All but a few states either ban concealed weapons entirely or require a special license for carrying concealed weapons. One national survey found that 7 percent of respondents carried a handgun outside of their homes for protection (Wright 1981).

Measuring Gun Availability

The preceding discussion developed the notion of gun availability in terms of the prevalence of ownership, the costs of obtaining a gun, and the propensity to go armed in public. These three dimensions of availability are closely related, but it would be useful to distinguish among them in measuring the effects of gun availability on violent crime and suicide. Unfortunately, none of these dimensions can be measured directly from existing data. Instead, researchers make use of indicators that have some logical relation to availability, and are arguably correlated with one or more of the relevant dimensions of availability. But the interpretation of empirical studies of this sort is inevitably somewhat uncertain.

1. *Gun Use in Homicide as an Availability Measure.* Perhaps the most commonly used measure of gun availability is the fraction of criminal homicides committed with a gun. A number of authors have related this gun fraction to the homicide rate across jurisdictions or over time in a single jurisdiction. A positive correlation is interpreted as evidence that increased gun availability causes increases in the murder rate. . . .

The gun fraction in homicide is not the only available proxy for gun availability. Measurement theory suggests that we can obtain a more reliable indicator for this underlying trait by combining two or more proxy variables. One possibility in this regard is to average the gun fraction in homicide with the gun fraction in suicide (Cook 1979, 1985c). The latter also reflects the choices of a sample of people (suicides), and those choices reflect the ease of obtaining a gun, among other things (Clarke and Lester 1989). And the "sample" reflected in suicide statistics is quite different from the sample reflected in homicide statistics. In particular, the demographics of suicide and homicide are quite different, and in some ways are virtually mirror images. For example, the homicide death rate peaks in the third decade and drops sharply thereafter, while the suicide death rate tends to increase throughout the normal age span. The homicide rate for blacks is over six times as high as for whites, while the white suicide rate is almost double that of blacks. Most suicides occur at home, while most homicides occur away from home. Despite these differences and others, the use of guns in homicide and suicide exhibits a similar geographic pattern. For 1973 and 1974 data combined, the gun fractions for suicide and assaultive homicide were highly correlated across fifty large cities (r = .82), suggesting an environmental determinant of gun use. . . .

This index was then used as a measure of gun availability in a regression analysis of robbery rates. Controlling for other variables important in explaining intercity differences in robbery,[9] the principal results were as follows: a 10 percent reduction in the prevalence of gun ownership in a city is associated with about a 5 percent reduction in the gun robbery rate and a 4 percent reduction in the robbery murder rate but has no discernible effect on the overall robbery rate. These results suggest that gun density influences the choice of weapon in robbery and its lethality but not the overall volume of robbery.

These estimates do not allow for the possibility that the prevalence of gun ownership is influenced in some way by the robbery rate. While it is true that a small fraction of guns are acquired for self-defense purposes (Kleck 1988; Smith and Uchida 1988), most of these are purchased by households that have acquired other guns for sporting purposes; three-quarters of those who own a handgun also own a rifle or shotgun (Wright 1981). The overall geographic pattern of gun ownership appears to have much more to do with regional culture than with the objective threat of crime.

While the geographic patterns of gun use in homicide and suicide are very similar, the same is not true for temporal patterns in gun use. As noted earlier, there has been a mild downward trend in gun use in homicide since 1975, while the trend in suicide has been toward somewhat greater use of guns (see also Cook 1985c).

2. *Survey Data.* Since there have been a number of national surveys that include items on gun ownership, an obvious question arises as to why the results cannot be used to measure geographic patterns of availability. The problem is that the national samples are too small to produce reliable estimates of ownership rates for cities or states. Markush and Bartolucci (1984) employed NORC survey data to estimate gun prevalence for each of nine regions; they increased the sample size and hence reliability of the estimates by combining data from four surveys. Their study was limited to suicide; across the nine regions, the suicide and gun ownership rates were highly correlated (r = .81). Unfortunately, with such a small sample, they are unable to take account of other factors besides gun availability that may also influence suicide rates, so the proper interpretation of their result is not clear (see also Lester 1988).

The 1989 International Crime Survey (van Dijk, Mayhew, and Killias 1990) surveyed households in fourteen countries, and for the first time makes possible a valid international comparison of gun ownership and violent crime patterns. Killias (1990) looked at a subsample of eleven countries for which there were data on homicide by weapon type: for what it is worth, the correlation between the gun fraction in homicide and the prevalence of gun ownership is r = .72.[10]

3. *Manufacturing, Import, and Sales Data.* Newton and Zimring (1969) assembled a historical series on gun manufacture and import as a basis for estimating the current private stocks of handguns and long guns. These data are flawed by the facts (acknowledged by Newton and Zimring) that imports are not measured accurately, and data are lacking on exports, breakage, confiscation, and other removals from the stock. Nonetheless, this series has been used as a measure of gun availability by several researchers.

Four studies have analyzed the effect of the stock of guns, as estimated by the Newton-Zimring method, on temporal movements in the national homicide rate (Phillips, Votey, and Howell 1976; Kleck 1979, 1984b; Magaddino and Medoff 1984). All use multivariate statistical methods to control for some of the other variables that influence homicide rates, and all but Kleck (1984b) conclude from their analysis that the stock of guns has a positive effect on the homicide rate. The difficulty with this type of analysis, in addition to the flaws in the measure of gun availability, is the uncertainty concerning the proper specification of the statistical model; the social process that generates year-to-year changes in the homicide rate is poorly understood, and the estimates of how the gun stock affects homicide are sensitive to what assumptions are made about other factors. (It should be noted that specification uncertainty is also a problem in crosssectional studies such as reported in Cook 1979.)

Comparisons without Explicit Measures of Availability

There is a tradition in debates over gun control to compare homicide rates across countries that are known to differ widely with respect to the private ownership of guns (Bruce-Briggs 1976). It is not necessary to have a precise measure of availability to be sure that guns are much scarcer in Japan than in the United States. The problem with such comparisons is that countries that differ widely with respect to availability also differ with respect to various other factors that influence rates of personal violence. Japan, where few individuals own a gun, has a very low homicide rate and a high suicide rate by American standards. Kates (1990, p. 42) indicates that Japan's suicide rate was 20.3 per 100,000, compared to a U.S. rate of 12.2 in 1982; Japan's homicide rate was 0.9 per 100,000, compared with a rate of 7.6 in the United States. All we can safely conclude from this comparison is that guns are not the only thing that matters in personal violence.

A recent study by Sloan et al. (1988) claims to have solved the problem of finding two jurisdictions that are quite different with respect to gun availability but alike in other respects relevant to personal violence. Seattle and Vancouver share a common geography, climate, and history and are remarkably similar in terms of demographic and socioeconomic characteristics. But guns are more widely owned and more easily obtained in Seattle than in Vancouver, as indicated by differences in laws governing ownership, the number of gun permits issued, and the fractions of homicides and suicides committed with a gun. The two cities have similar rates of aggravated assault, but more of Seattle's assaults were committed with a gun. The homicide rate in Seattle averaged 11.3 per 100,000 (1980–86), compared with 6.9 for Vancouver; all the difference was in the rate of gun homicide. These results are intriguing, but there must remain some doubt about their proper interpretation.

In one view, the Seattle-Vancouver comparison should be considered a sort of natural controlled experiment, in which the people living in the two cities are two samples that have been "drawn" at random from the same population and assigned to either the Seattle "treatment" (more guns) or the Vancouver "treatment" (fewer guns). The probability statements in the article by Sloan and his associates only make sense in the context of a model such as this. There is certainly reason to doubt this model; the two "samples" are obviously not the result of random assignment (e.g., they differ substantially with respect to the ethnic composition of the nonwhite populations), and the two "treatments" differ in more ways than gun availability.

A quite different view of the Seattle-Vancouver comparison is that the relevant unit of observation is the city, rather than the individuals who make up the city populations. And in that perspective, the sample size here is just two. The fundamental finding is that the city with more guns also has a higher homicide rate, and that finding is compatible with the generalization that gun availability has a direct causal effect on the homicide rate. But with a sample of two, this conclusion is not persuasive. Quantifying the uncertainty in this case is difficult, and requires some careful thought about the appropriate model in which to view the two-city comparison.

Conclusions Concerning Gun Availability Studies

Assessing the effects of gun availability on personal violence is made difficult by problems in defining and measuring availability as well as by the usual problems in interpreting results generated from nonexperimental data (Cook 1980b). It is clear from this work that the geographic differences in gun ownership are highly correlated with the fractions of homicides, suicides, assaults, and robberies involving guns. One explanation for this relation is that the weapon choices of violent and suicidal people are influenced by the ease of obtaining a gun.

Given the weapon instrumentality effect, greater use of guns in assaults and robberies is likely to increase the death rates from these types of violence. If an increase in gun availability produces an increase in the fraction of violent acts committed with a gun, then the end result will be more deaths. This conclusion is plausible and supported by a number of the studies reviewed above but difficult to document persuasively in the absence of a natural experiment. The case-control approach represented in the comparison of Vancouver and Seattle seems promising, though it is difficult, in practice, to identify suitable pairs of jurisdictions, and one pair is not enough. An alternative approach to assessing the effect of gun availability on personal violence is to evaluate the effects of legal interventions designed to reduce availability. Such evaluations are of particular interest because they are directly relevant to policy.

Directions for Future Research

Research on weapons and violence has provided some answers or partial answers to questions relevant to evaluating alternative gun control strategies. At the same time, this research has demonstrated that the "technology" of personal violence is an important piece of the etiological puzzle. Further research in a number of areas would enhance our scientific understanding of personal violence and inform the policy debate on how best to combat this pressing problem. Below is a menu of promising and feasible projects.

Data Collection

There remains considerable uncertainty concerning the number of firearms in private households. This uncertainty could be greatly reduced by a carefully designed national survey that included items on whether there were any guns in the house, and if so, how many and of what sort. Other items of interest include information on how these guns are stored and used, who within the household has access to them, and how the guns were obtained.

There is a lack of information on the use of guns in self-defense. The National Crime Survey currently includes items that provide information on self-defense in violent confrontations and against burglars, but no information on other uses such as scaring trespassers away from private property. There is also need for better data on justifiable homicides than are currently available from the Federal Bureau of Investigation's supplementary homicide reports (Kleck 1988).

We need reliable estimates of the number of gunshot woundings in accidents, assaults, and suicide attempts, including detailed information on the type of gun. Without such data, it is not possible to develop a clear picture of the relative costs of gun misuse in different circumstances. The data that are currently routinely available, which are limited to fatal shootings, may tend to understate the importance of accidents (fatal or otherwise) relative to criminal or self-inflicted shootings. If this is true, then policy interventions directed specifically at reducing the accident rate are undervalued.

Finally, it is worth considering an expanded program of data collection on homicide and suicide, perhaps using the Fatal Accident Reporting System (FARS) as a model.[11] FARS is maintained by the National Highway Traffic Safety Administration, which collects detailed crash information from police records. Suicide and homicide data could be collected separately, or FARS could be expanded into a traumatic death reporting system; in either case, data elements would include information on the weapons that caused death, together with demographic characteristics, immediate circumstances, blood alcohol content of the participants, and so forth.

Measuring Gun Availability

Gun "availability" has been viewed by some researchers as virtually synonymous with the prevalence of gun ownership. It would be of great interest to evaluate this assumption by analyzing how violent people obtain their guns in a sample of jurisdictions that differ with respect to prevalence of ownership. Potential sources of information on this issue include traces of confiscated crime guns, police investigations of fences, drug dealers, and other black market operators, and interviews of the sort conducted by Wright and Rossi (1986), but with a broader and more representative sample.

In addition to this effort to develop better qualitative understanding of gun availability, it would be useful to conduct evaluations of various indicators of gun availability as a basis for studying the effect of availability on crime patterns. The most commonly used indicator, the percentage of homicides that are committed with a gun, is flawed by its sensitivity to differences in the composition of homicide over time and across jurisdictions.

The promising new effort to collect internationally comparable data on crime and the prevalence of gun ownership should be encouraged and broadened to include suicide. Casual international comparisons have long been a part of the rhetoric for and against gun-control measures, and it would be of value to be able to make these comparisons more systematically.

Methodology

The research on guns and crime that has received the attention in recent memory is the comparison of homicide rates in Seattle and Vancouver, conducted by Sloan, Kellermann, and others (1988). There is an interesting methodological question about this type of comparison, relating to the degree of uncertainty that attaches to the results. Should this be viewed as a controlled laboratory experiment in which the two cities are identical in every relevant respect except gun availability? Or should this single comparison be viewed as an interesting anecdote that must be confirmed by results from many other pairs of cities before the result is well established in a statistical sense? I favor the second view but would welcome a careful analysis of the methodological issues here.

Evaluations of Policy Changes

Evaluations of the effects of changes in policies affecting gun availability and use offer the most direct evidence on the question of what generally can be accomplished through such measures. Of course, the consequences of any particular intervention will be influenced by the immediate context and the effort devoted to implementation, so there will always be a question about what generalizations can safely be drawn. But that simply argues for doing as many evaluations as possible and not resting strong conclusions on single cases.

Systematic evaluation of a policy change in one jurisdiction is relevant to predicting the consequences of a similar change proposed for another jurisdiction. In some cases it may also serve as a test of general propositions concerning guns and violence. A case in point is the Bartley-Fox Amendment in Massachusetts. Several studies found that its threat of severe punishment for carrying a gun illegally reduced illegal carrying and some types of violent crime, including homicide, although the nongun assault rate appears to have increased. In addition to providing information about the effects of this particular ordinance, this pattern of results is powerful evidence in support of the instrumentality effect.

These recommendations for research directions are not intended to exhaust the list of interesting possibilities but, rather, to suggest that there is much useful work that remains to be done. Indeed, even after two decades of systematic research on weapons and personal violence and results indicating the powerful and pervasive influence of weapon type on the patterns and outcomes of violent encounters, this area of research has yet to realize its great potential. Criminologists who set out to understand personal violence rarely devote much attention to weapons questions; they are apparently perceived as a distinct topic, which has not yet been "mainstreamed" into etiological research. Public health researchers appear to be moving more quickly in this respect, and guns have been established in the public health literature as a widely acknowledged environmental risk factor.

The type of weapon is more than an incidental detail of a violent encounter, and the general availability of guns in a community cannot be ignored when seeking to understand patterns of interpersonal violence and suicide. That is the bottom line and the basis for encouraging more research in this area.

NOTES

1. This essay is an update and extension of Cook (I 1983a). The earlier review includes a discussion of the market for guns, a topic that is not included here, but this essay includes several new topics, most important, suicide and self-defense.

2. The estimated number of aggravated assaults in 1987, based on the National Crime Survey, is 1.5 million (Bureau of Justice Statistics 1989a). There were about 20,000 criminal homicides in that year, of which about 20 percent were in felony circumstances (Federal Bureau of Investigation 1988). The remaining homicides would have been classified as aggravated assaults if the victims had survived.

3. "Serious injury" is defined here as "hospitalized overnight" (Cook 1987, p. 361). Robberies committed with clubs and other weapons (besides guns and knives) have the highest probability of serious injury.

4. The authors were able to estimate "likelihood of death" equations by merging NCS data on nonfatal assaults with supplementary homicide report data. Kleck and McElrath (1989) do not replicate for assaults the analysis of robbery data reported in Cook (1986); that is, they do not estimate the effect of weapon type on the probability that the victim will sustain a serious injury given that there was an assault.

5. This estimate is the ratio of crimes committed with handguns in 1977 (estimated from National Crime Survey data) to the number of new handguns sold in that year. This method of estimating the lifetime crime involvement of the 1977 cohort of new handguns is valid under the assumption that handgun sales and handgun crime rates are constant over time. It underestimates handgun crime involvement if crime increases after 1977 or if the 1977 cohort of new handguns turns out to be small relative to subsequent cohorts.

6. In fact, in their probit estimate, the coefficient estimate for "handgun" is slightly higher than for "other gun," but the difference is small. It should be noted that Kleck and McElrath (1989), in constructing their data set, are forced, due to insufficient information, to omit over half of the homicides by strangers.

7. Gary Kleck (1990), in a personal communication, notes that data from a December 1989 poll imply that the average respondent who said there was at least one gun in the household had an average of 4.4 guns, considerably higher than the three-per-household estimate from a 1978 poll mentioned above.

8. The McClure-Volkmer Amendments of 1986 eased the restriction on out-of-state purchases of long guns. Such purchases are now legal so long as they comply with the regulations of both the buyer's state of residence and the state in which the sale occurs.

9. The control variables include the following characteristics of the cities: percent of the population that are youthful black males; population per square mile; fraction of the standard metropolitan statistical area in the city; fraction of the population in relative poverty; number of Uniform Crime Report crimes per policeman; number of retail stores per capita; and an indicator for those cities in states with relatively stringent gun-control regulations.

10. For these eleven countries, the percent of households possessing a firearm is as follows: Australia, 20. 1; Belgium, 16.8; Canada, 30.8; England and Wales, 4.7; Federal Republic of Germany, 9.2; Finland, 25.5; France, 24.7; Netherlands, 2.0; Norway, 31.2; Switzerland, 32.6; and United States, 48.9. France is excluded from the correlation due to lack of homicide data.

11. Arthur Kellermarm (1990) suggested this approach in a personal communication.

REFERENCES

Beha, James A., III. 1977. "'And Nobody Can Get You Out': The Impact of a Mandatory Prison Sentence for the Illegal Carrying of a Firearm on the Use of Firearms and the Administration of Criminal justice in Boston." *Boston University Law Review* 57:96–146, 289–33.

Benenson, Mark, and Don B. Kates Jr. 1979. "Handgun Prohibition and Homicide: A Plausible Theory Meets the Intractible Facts." In *Restricting Handguns: The Liberal Skeptics Speak Out.* Edited by Don B. Kates Jr. Crotonon-Hudson, N.Y.: North River.

Berger, Lawrence R. 1988. "Suicides and Pesticides in Sri Lanka." *American Journal of Public Health* 78:826–28.

Blose, James, and Philip J. Cook. 1980. "Regulating Handgun Transfers: Current State and Federal Procedures, and an Assessment of the Feasibility and Costs of the Proposed Procedures in the Handgun Crime Control Act of 1979." Working paper. Durham, N.C.: Duke University, Institute of Policy Sciences.

Boor, M. 1981. "Methods of Suicide and Implications for Suicide Prevention." *Journal of Clinical Psychology* 37:70–75.

Brearly, Harrington C. 1932. *Homicide in the U.S.* Chapel Hill: University of North Carolina Press.

Brent, David A., Joshua A. Perper, Charles E. Goldstein, David J. Kolko, Marjorie J. Allan, Christopher J. Allman, and Janice P. Zelenak. 1988. "Risk Factors for Adolescent Suicide." *Archives of General Psychiatry* 45:581–88.

Bruce-Briggs, B. 1976. "The Great American Gun War." *Public Interest* 45: 1–26.

Bureau of Alcohol, Tobacco, and Firearms. 1976. *Project Identification: A Study of Handguns Used in Crime.* Washington, D.C.: U.S. Department of the Treasury.

———. 1989. "Ready Reference Statistics." Mimeographed. Washington, D.C.: U.S. Department of the Treasury.

Bureau of Justice Statistics. 1984. *Family Violence.* Bureau of Justice Statistics Special Report. Washington, D.C.: U.S. Bureau of Justice Statistics.

———. 1989a. *Criminal Victimization in the United States, 1987.* Washington, D.C.: U.S. Bureau of Justice Statistics.

———. 1989b. *Sourcebook of Criminal Justice Statistics—1988.* Washington, D.C.: U.S. Bureau of Justice Statistics.

Card, J. J. 1974. "Lethality of Suicidal Methods and Suicide Risk: Two Distinct Concepts." *Omega* 5:37–45.

Clarke, Ronald V., and David Lester. 1989. *Suicide: Closing the Exits.* New York: Springer-Verlag.

Clarke, Ronald V., and Pat Mayhew. 1988. "The British Gas Suicide Story and Its Criminological Implications." In *Crime and Justice: A Review of Research.* Vol. 10. Edited by Michael Tonry and Norval Morris. Chicago: University of Chicago Press.

Committee on Trauma Research, National Research Council. 1985. *Injury in America: A Continuing Public Health Problem.* Washington, D.C.: National Academy Press.

Conklin, John E. 1972. *Robbery and the Criminal Justice System.* Philadelphia: Lippincott.

Cook, Philip J. 1976. "A Strategic Choice Analysis of Robbery." In *Sample Surveys of the Victims of Crimes.* Edited by Wesley Skogan. Cambridge, Mass.: Ballinger.

———. 1979. "The Effect of Gun Availability on Robbery and Robbery Murder: A Cross Section Study of Fifty Cities." In *Policy Studies Review Annual.* Vol. 3. Edited by Robert H. Haveman and B. Bruce Zellner. Beverly Hills, Calif.: Sage.

———. 1980a. "Reducing Injury and Death Rates in Robbery." *Policy Analysis* 6(1):21–45.

———. 1980b. "Research in Criminal Deterrence: Laying the Groundwork for the Second Decade." In *Crime and Justice: An Annual Review of Research.* Vol. 2. Edited by Norval Morris and Michael Tonry. Chicago: University of Chicago Press.

———. 1981a. "The 'Saturday Night Special': An Assessment of Alternative Definitions from a Policy Perspective." *Journal of Criminal Law and Criminology* 72:1735–45.

———. 1981b. "Guns and Crime: The Perils of Long Division." *Journal of Policy Analysis and Management* 1: 120–25.

———. 1982. "The Role of Firearms in Violent Crime: An Interpretive Review of the Literature, with Some New Findings and Suggestions for Future Research." In *Criminal Violence.* Edited by Marvin Wolfgang and Neil Weiner. Beverly Hills, Calif.: Sage.

———. 1983a. "The Influence of Gun Availability on Violent Crime Patterns." In *Crime and Justice: An Annual Review of Research.* Vol. 4. Edited by Michael Tonry and Norval Morris. Chicago: University of Chicago Press.

———. 1983b. "Does Gun Ownership Deter Burglary?" Mimeographed. Durham, N.C.: Duke University, Institute of Policy Sciences.

———. 1985a. "The Case of the Missing Victims: Gunshot Woundings in the National Crime Survey." Journal of Quantitative Criminology 1:91-102.

———. 1985b. "Is Robbery Becoming More Violent? An Analysis of Robbery Murder Trends since 1968." *Journal of Criminal Law and Criminology* 76:480–89.

———. 1985c. "Report on a City-specific Gun Prevalence Index." Mimeographed. Durham, N.C.: Duke University, Institute of Policy Sciences.

———. 1986. "The Relationship between Victim Resistance and Injury in Noncommercial Robbery." *Journal of Legal Studies* 15:405–16.

———. 1987. "Robbery Violence." *Journal of Criminal Law and Criminology* 78:357–76.

Cook, Philip J., and James Blose. 1981. "State Programs for Screening Handgun Buyers." *Annals of the American Academy of Political and Social Science* 455:80–91.

Cook, Philip J., and Daniel Nagin. 1979. *Does the Weapon Matter?* Washington, D.C.: Institute for Law and Social Research.

Curtis, Lynn A. 1974. *Criminal Violence*. Lexington, Mass.: Lexington.

Dallas Police Department. 1983. Personal communication with author.

Deutsch, Stuart Jay. 1979. "Lies, Damn Lies, and Statistics: A Rejoinder to the Comment by Hay and McCleary." *Evaluation Quarterly* 3:315–28.

Deutsch, Stuart Jay, and Francis B. Alt. 1977. "The Effect of Massachusetts' Gun Control Law on Gun-related Crimes in the City of Boston." *Evaluation Quarterly* 1:543–68.

District of Columbia. 1989. *Homicide in the District of Columbia*. Washington, D.C.: Office of Criminal Justice Plans and Analysis.

Etzioni, Amitai, and Richard Remp. 1973. *Technological Shortcuts to Social Change*. New York: Russell Sage.

Fackler, Martin L. 1988. "Wound Ballistics: A Review of Common Misconceptions." *Journal of the American Medical Association* 259(18):2730–36.

Federal Bureau of Investigation. 1979. *Crime in the United States, 1978*. Washington, D.C.: U.S. Government Printing Office.

———. 1988. *Crime in the United States, 1987*. Washington, D.C.: U.S. Government Printing Office.

———. 1989. *Crime in the United States, 1988*. Washington, D.C.: U.S. Government Printing Office.

Fisher, Joseph. 1976. "Homicide in Detroit: The Role of Firearms." *Criminology* 13:387–400.

Geisel, Martin S., Richard Ross, and R. Stanton Wettick Jr. 1969. "The Effectiveness of State and Local Regulation of Handguns: A Statistical Analysis." *Duke Law Journal* 4:647–76.

Green, Gary S. 1987. "Citizen Gun Ownership and Criminal Deterrence: Theory, Research, and Policy." *Criminology* 25:63–82.

Hollerman, Jeremy J. 1988. "Gunshot Wounds." *American Family Physician* 37(5):231–46.

Jones, Edward D., III. 1981. "The District of Columbia's 'Firearms Control Regulations Act of 1975': The Toughest Handgun Control Law in the United States—or Is It?" *Annals of the American Academy of Political and Social Science* 455:138–49.

Kakalik, James S., and Sorrell Wildhorn. 1972. *The Private Security Industry: Its Nature and Extent*. Santa Monica, Calif.: RAND.

Kates, Don B., Jr. 1983. "Handgun Prohibition and the Original Meaning of the Second Amendment." *Michigan Law Review* 82:204–73.

———. 1989. "Firearms and Violence: Old Premises and Current Evidence." In *Violence in America: The History of Crime*. Edited by Ted Robert Gurr. Newbury Park, Calif.: Sage.

———. 1990. *Guns, Murders, and the Constitution: A Realistic Assessment of Gun Control*. San Francisco: Pacific Research Institute.

Kellermann, Arthur L. 1990. Personal communication with author.

Kellermann, Arthur L., and James A. Mercy. 1990. "Sex, Lies, and Safety: Should Women Buy Handguns for Self Defense?" Unpublished manuscript. Memphis: University of Tennessee, Department of Medicine.

Kellermann, Arthur L., and Donald T. Reay. 1986. "Protection or Peril? An Analysis of Firearm-related Deaths in the Home." *New England Journal of Medicine* 314:1557–60.

Killias, Martin. 1990. "Gun Ownership and Violent Crime: The Swiss Experience in International Perspective." *Security Journal* 1(3):169–74.

Kleck, Gary. 1979. "Capital Punishment, Gun Ownership, and Homicide." *American Journal of Sociology* 84:882–910.

———. 1984a. "Handgun-only Control: A Policy Disaster in the Making." In *Firearms and Violence: Issues of Public Policy*. Edited by Don B. Kates Jr. Cambridge, Mass.: Ballinger.

———. 1984b. "The Relationship between Gun Ownership Levels and Rates of Violence in the

United States." In *Firearms and Violence: Issues of Public Policy.* Edited by Don B. Kates Jr. Cambridge, Mass.: Ballinger.

———. 1988. "Crime Control through the Private Use of Armed Force." *Social Problems* 35:1–22.

———. 1990. Personal communication with author.

Kleck, Gary, and David J. Bordua. 1983. "The Factual Foundation for Certain Key Assumptions of Gun Control." *Law and Policy Quarterly* 5:271–98.

Kleck, Gary, and Karen McElrath. 1989. "The Effects of Weaponry on Human Violence." Mimeographed. Tallahassee: Florida State University, School of Criminology.

Kreitman, Norman, 1976. "The Coal Gas Story: United Kingdom Suicide Rates, 1960–71." *British Journal of Preventive Social Medicine* 30:86–93.

Lester, David. 1988. "Research Note: Gun Control, Gun Ownership, and Suicide Prevention." *Suicide and Life-Threatening Behavior* 18(2):176–80.

Lester, David, and Mary E. Murrell. 1982. "The Prevention Effect of Strict Gun Control Laws on Suicide and Homicide." *Suicide and Life-Threatening Behavior* 12(3):131–40.

McDowall, David, Brian Wiersema, and Colin Loftin. 1989. "Did Mandatory Firearm Ownership in Kennesaw Prevent Burglaries?" Working paper. College Park: University of Maryland, Institute of Criminal Justice and Criminology.

Magaddino, Joseph P., and Marshall H. Medoff. 1984. "An Empirical Analysis of Federal and State Firearm Control Laws." In *Firearms and Violence: Issues of Public Policy.* Edited by Don B. Kates Jr. Cambridge, Mass.: Ballinger.

Markush, R. E., and A. A. Bartolucci. 1984. "Firearms and Suicide in the United States." *American Journal of Public Health* 74:123–27.

Medoff, Marshall H., and Joseph P. Magaddino. 1983. "Suicides and Firearm Control Laws." *Evaluation Review* 7(3):357–72.

Mercy, J. A., and V. N. Houk. 1988. "Firearm Injuries: A Call for Science." *New England Journal of Medicine* 319:1283–85.

Moore, Mark. 1981. "Keeping Handguns from Criminal Offenders." *Annals of the American Academy of Political and Social Science* 455:92–109.

Murray, Douglas It. 1975. "Handguns, Gun Control Laws, and Firearms Violence." *Social Problems* 23:81–93.

National Center for Health Statistics. 1970–86. *Vital Statistics of the United States*, vol. IIA: Mortality. Washington, D.C.: U.S. Government Printing Office.

———. 1976. *Persons Injured and Disability Days by Detailed Type and Class of Accident, United States, 1971–1972.* Vital and Health Statistics Series no. 10/ 105. Washington, D.C.: U.S. Government Printing Office.

———. 1987. Personal communication with author.

Newton, George D., Jr., and Franklin E. Zimring. 1969. *Firearms and Violence in American Life.* Washington, D.C.: U.S. Government Printing Office.

Penick, Bettye K., and Maurice E. B. Owens III. 1976. *Surveying Crime.* Washington, D.C.: National Academy of Sciences.

Phillips, Llad, Harold L. Votey Jr., and John Howell. 1976. "Handguns and Homicide: Minimizing Losses and the Costs of Control." *Journal of Legal Studies* 5:463–78.

Pierce, Glenn L., and William J. Bowers. 1979. "The Impact of the Bartley-Fox Gun Law on Crime in Massachusetts." Unpublished manuscript. Boston: Northeastern University, Center for Applied Social Research.

———. 1981. "The Bartley-Fox Gun Law's Short-Term Impact on Crime in Boston." *Annals of the American Academy of Political and Social Science* 455:120–37.

Rushforth, N. B., A. B. Ford, C. S. Hirsh, N. M. Rushforth, and L. Adelson. 1977. "Violent Death in a Metropolitan County: Changing Patterns in Homicide (1958–74)." *New England Journal of Medicine* 297:531–38.

Seiden, Richard. 1977. "Suicide Prevention: A Public Health/Public Policy Approach." *Omega* 8:267–76.

Silver, Carol Ruth, and Don B. Kates Jr. 1979. "Self-Defense, Handgun Ownership, and the Independence of Women in a Violent, Sexist Society." In *Restricting Handguns: The Liberals Skeptics Speak Out*. Edited by Don B. Kates Jr. Croton-on-Hudson, N.Y.: North River.

Skogan, Wesley G. 1978. "Weapon Use in Robbery: Patterns and Policy Implications." Unpublished manuscript. Evanston, Ill.: Northwestern University, Center for Urban Affairs. Washington, D.C.: U.S. 1981. Issues in the Measurement of Victimization. Department of Justice, Bureau of Justice Statistics.

———. 1990. "The National Crime Survey Redesign." *Public Opinion Quarterly* 54:256–72.

Sloan, J. H., A. L. Kellermann, D. T. Reay, J. A. Ferris, T. Koepsell, F. P. Rivara, C. Rice, L. Gray, and J. LoGerfo. 1988. "Handgun Regulations, Crimes, Assaults, and Homicide. A Tale of Two Cities." *New England Journal of Medicine* 319:1256–62.

Sloan, J. H., F. P. Rivara, D. T. Reay, J. A. Ferris, and A. L. Kellermann. 1990. "Firearm Regulations and Community Suicide Rates: A Comparison of Two Metropolitan Areas." *New England Journal of Medicine* (forthcoming).

Smith, Douglas A., and Craig D. Uchida. 1988. "The Social Organization of Self-Help: A Study of Defensive Weapon Ownership." *American Sociological Review* 53(1):94–102.

Swersey, Arthur J. 1980. "A Greater Intent to Kill: The Changing Pattern of Homicide in Harlem and New York City." Unpublished manuscript. New Haven, Conn.: Yale School of Organization and Management.

U.S. Conference of Mayors. 1980. "The Analysis of the Firearms Control Act of 1975: Handgun Control in the District of Columbia." Mimeographed. Washington, D.C.: U.S. Conference of Mayors.

van Dijk, Jan J. M., Pat Mayhew, and Martin-Killias. 1990. *Experiences of Crime across the World: Key Findings from the 1989 International Crime Survey*. Boston: Dordrecht.

Wolfgang, Marvin E. 1958. *Patterns in Criminal Homicide*. Philadelphia: University of Pennsylvania Press.

Wright, James D. 1981. "Public Opinion and Gun Control: A Comparison of Results from Two Recent National Surveys." *Annals of the American Academy of Political and Social Science* 45 5:24–39.

———. 1984. "The Ownership of Firearms for Reasons of Self-Defense." In *Firearms and Violence: Issues of Public Policy*. Edited by Don B. Kates Jr. Cambridge, Mass.: Ballinger.

Wright, James D., and Linda L. Marston. 1975. "The Ownership of the Means of Destruction: Weapons in the United States." *Social Problems* 23:81–107.

Wright, James D., and Peter H. Rossi. 1986. *The Armed Criminal in America: A Survey of Incarcerated Felons*. Hawthorne, N.Y.: Aldine.

Wright, James D., Peter H. Rossi, and Kathleen Daly. 1983. *Under the Gun: Weapons, Crime, and Violence in America*. Hawthorne, N.Y.: Aldine.

Yeager, Matthew G. 1976. *How Well Does the Handgun Protect You and Your Family?* Washington, D.C.: U.S. Conference of Mayors.

Zimring, Franklin E. 1968. "Is Gun Control Likely to Reduce Violent Killings?" *University of Chicago Law Review* 35:721–37.

———. 1972. "The Medium Is the Message: Firearm Calibre as a Determinant of Death from Assault." *Journal of Legal Studies* 1:97–124.

———. 1975. "Firearms and Federal Law: The Gun Control Act of 1968." *Journal of Legal Studies* 4:133–98.

———. 1990. "Firearms, Violence, and Public Policy." *Scientific American* (forthcoming).

15

GUNS AND VIOLENCE
AN INTERPRETIVE REVIEW OF THE FIELD
GARY KLECK

INTRODUCTION

T his [essay] summarizes the research literature on guns, violence, and gun control. The full empirical basis for most of the conclusions can be found in my book *Point Blank: Guns and Violence in America* (Kleck 1991), and the approximately 570 references which are cited therein. Interested readers may consult that book for a more extensive body of supporting citations, empirical evidence, and detailed argumentation.

WHY THE ISSUE MATTERS

In 1991, about 38,000 persons were killed with guns (National Safety Council 1994). and at least another 130,000 people suffered nonfatal gunshot wounds (Kleck 1991:62). Nearly half of the deaths, 48 percent, were suicides, 46 percent were homicides, 4 percent were fatal gun accidents, and 1 percent each were due to legal intervention (police officers killing suspects in the line of duty) and to death where it was undetermined whether injury was intentionally or accidentally inflicted. Among all deaths due to "external cause," i.e., accident, suicide or homicide, guns were involved in 26 percent of them, handguns in about 17 percent of them. Guns were involved in 1.7 percent of all deaths, from all causes, 61

From *Social Pathology* vol. 1, no. 1 (January 1995): 12–47.

percent of suicides, 66 percent of homicides, and 1.5 percent of accidental deaths in 1990 (National Safety Council 1994). The majority of all gun deaths involve handguns, mainly because 86 percent of the gun homicide deaths involved handguns (U.S. Federal Bureau of Investigation 1993:18). There were also at least 690,000 nonfatal (i.e., excluding homicides) violent crime incidents involving offenders armed with guns in 1991, over 540,000 of them (78 percent) involving handguns. Offenders were armed with guns in about 12 percent of all violent crime incidents, and handguns in about 9 percent. The majority of these gun crimes were assaults, mostly threats without any injury or any element of theft or rape (U.S. Bureau of Justice Statistics 1992: 82–83).

GUN OWNERSHIP

The prospects for reducing violence by restricting guns depends to a great extent oil how many guns there are, how people get them, why they own them, and how strongly they would resist or evade gun controls in order to hold onto them. Also, one's interpretation of a positive relationship between violence rates and gun ownership rates depends on the degree to which one believes that violence can drive up gun ownership, by motivating people to get guns for protection, as distinct from gun ownership driving up violence.

There were probably over 225 million guns in private hands in the United States by the end of 1994, about a third of them handguns (extrapolation from data through 1987 in Kleck 1991:50, assuming average additions to the gun stock for 1983–1987 continued to prevail through 1994). One straightforward policy implication is that policies which seek to reduce gun violence by reducing the overall supply of guns, as distinct from reducing possession just within high-risk subsets of the population, face an enormous obstacle in this huge existing stock. Even if further additions to the stock could somehow be totally and immediately stopped, the size of the stock and durability of guns imply that, in the absence of mass confiscations or unlikely voluntary surrenders of guns, it might be decades before any impact of a strategy based on overall supply-reduction would start to become apparent. Probably fewer than 2 percent of handguns and well under 1 percent of all guns will ever be involved in a violent crime (Kleck 1986). Thus, the problem of criminal gun violence is concentrated within a very small subset of guns and of gun owners, indicating that gun control aimed at the general population faces a daunting needle-in-the-haystack problem.

The size of the private gun stock increased rapidly from the 1960s through the 1980s, especially for handguns. Some of the increase was due to the formation of new households and to growing affluence enabling gun owners to acquire still more guns; however, a substantial share of the increase was also a response to rising crime rates among people who previously did not own guns. Most handguns are owned for defensive reasons, and many people get guns in response to high or rising crime rates. Therefore, at least some (and possibly all) of the positive association sometimes observed between gun ownership levels and crime rates is due to the effect of crime on guns, rather than the reverse (Kleck 1984a; Kleck and Patterson 1993). Nevertheless, most guns, especially long-guns, are owned primarily for recreational reasons unconnected with crime (DMI 1979:71; Crocker 1982:256; Kleck 1984a:105).

From the mid-1960s to the mid-1980s, scattered evidence suggests that, while gun ownership increased in general, it did so even more among criminals and violence-prone people than it did among the nonviolent majority of the population (Kleck 1984a). Because these "high-risk" groups are largely unrepresented in national surveys, this would partially account for the fact that household gun prevalence, as measured in national surveys, remained fairly constant during this period, despite huge numbers of guns being manufactured and imported for the private market (Kleck 1991:49–52, 451–60).

Gun owners are not, as a group, psychologically abnormal, nor are they more racist, sexist, or proviolent than nonowners (Diener and Kerber 1979; Lizotte et al. 1981:503; Kleck 1991:35–38). Most gun ownership is culturally patterned and linked with a rural hunting subculture. The culture is transmitted across generations, with recreation-related gun owners being socialized by their parents into gun ownership and use from childhood. Defensive handgun owners, on the other hand, are more likely to be disconnected from any gun subcultural roots, and their gun ownership is usually not accompanied by association with other gun owners or by training in the safe handling of guns. Defensive ownership is more likely to be an individualistic response to life circumstances perceived as dangerous. Defensive ownership is also a response to the perception that the police cannot provide adequate protection (Lizotte and Bordua 1980; Lizolle et al. 1981; Stinchconibe et al. 1980). This response to dangers, however, is not necessarily mediated by the emotion of fear, but rather may be part of a less emotional preparation for the possibility of future victimization.

The strongest and most consistent predictors of gun ownership are hunting, being male, being older, higher income, residence in rural areas or small towns, having been reared in such small places, having been reared in the South, and being Protestant (Wright and Marston 1975; Williams and McGrath 1976; DeFronzo 1979; Lizotte and Bordua 1980; Lizotte et al. 1981; Stinchcombe et al. 1980; McClain 1983; Kleck 1991:40–41; Kleck 1994). The social origins of Rs consistently predict having firearms, supporting the view that early socialization into gun owning subcultures is important in explaining gun ownership. However, traits like racial prejudice and punitiveness towards criminals are not important.

Most gun ownership in the general public is related to outdoor recreation like hunting and its correlates, rather than crime. Indeed, one of the most striking patterns evident in survey data is that so many of those segments of the population which have the lowest rates of violent behavior also have the highest rates of gun ownership—whites, older people, those with higher incomes, white-collar workers, and married people (Wright and Marston 1975; Williams and McGrath 1976; DeFronzo 1979; Lizotte and Bordua 1980; Lizotte et al. 1981;

Stinchcombe et al. 1980; McClain 1983; Kleck 1991:40–41, 56–57). On the other hand, ownership of handguns may well be linked with fear of crime and prior burglary victimization, though findings are necessarily ambiguous due to questions of causal order—fear could motivate gun acquisition, but having a gun could also reduce the owner's fear.

The pattern of results as a whole is compatible with the thesis that gun ownership is a product of socialization into a rural hunting culture. The findings support a simple explanation of the high level of gun ownership in the United States, an explanation which rejects the notion that weak gun laws are somehow responsible. Unlike European nations with a feudal past, the United States has had both widespread ownership of farmland and millions of acres of public lands available for hunting. Rather than hunting being limited to a small land-owning aristocracy, it has always been accessible to the majority of ordinary Americans. Having the income and leisure to take advantage of these resources, millions of Americans have hunted for recreation, long after it was no longer essential to survival for any but an impoverished few. Hunting in turn encouraged other recreational uses of guns, including target and other sport shooting, and collecting, of both handguns and long guns. Rather than high gun ownership being the result of a lack of strict gun control laws, it is more likely that causation ran in the other direction, i.e., that high gun ownership discouraged the enactment of restrictive gun laws, and that the prevalence of guns was mostly a product of the prevalence of recreational hunting. Only since the mid-1960s has a large share of gun ownership been attributable to concerns about crime (Kleck 1991:41).

Criminal gun users most commonly get their guns by buying them from friends and other nonretail sources, or by theft (Wright and Rossi 1986:183–87; U.S. Bureau of Justice Statistics 1993c:19). Therefore, gun regulation would be more likely to succeed in controlling gun violence if it could effectively restrict nondealer acquisitions and possession of guns by this small high-risk subset of gun owners.

FOCUSSING ON SPECIAL GUN TYPES

Since about half of U.S. households have a gun, broadly directed restrictions on the acquisition, possession, and use of guns impinge on the lives of millions of Americans, not just a small, politically powerless subset of them. This is the essential political obstacle which faces advocates of strict gun control—legislators who vote for strong gun laws must face the prospect of offending large numbers of gun-owning voters. Many advocates of more restrictive controls have therefore directed their focus away from measures which regulate all types of guns and toward those which regulate special subtypes of firearms, i.e., types of guns which are owned by smaller numbers of voters and which are consequently more politically vulnerable to regulation.

Procontrol groups have increasingly stressed the need to control various special weapon categories such as machineguns, "assault weapons," "assault rifles," plastic guns, Saturday night special handguns, and "cop-killer" bullets, or sometimes all handguns. For each weapon or ammunition type, it is argued that (he object is especially dangerous or particularly useful for criminal purposes, while having little or no counterbalancing utility for lawful purposes. A common slogan is "The [type of gun] is good for only one purpose—killing people."

The specific weapon type so described shifts from one year to the next, in response to shifts in the political winds rather than actual criminologically significant shifts in criminal use of guns. For example, when the so-called cop killer bullets were restricted in 1986, they had never, as far as investigating Congressional committees could tell, killed a cop (*Los Angeles Times* 12-18-85:16). Therefore, there obviously could not have been an increase, around 1986, in the number of police officers killed by the bullets. Likewise, the all-plastic guns restricted in 1988, which would have been undetectable by airport security equipment, were never actually manufactured (*New York Times* 5-5-86), and thus had never been involved in even a single act of violence.

"Assault rifles" and "assault weapons" became important objects of gun control efforts in the late 1980s and early 1990s. Contrary to widespread claims, these semiautomatic "military-style" weapons are rarely used by criminals in general or by drug dealers or juvenile gang members in particular. While both legitimate ownership and involvement of semiautomatic pistols in violence has been common in the United States since the 1920s, probably fewer than 2 percent of gun crimes involve those models of military-style semiautomatic weapons which are commonly labelled "assault weapons" (Kleck 1991, chap. 5; Suter 1994). Ironically, legislative activity concerning these weapons increased after 1989, at a time when their always-slight involvement in crime was apparently declining to even lower levels (U.S. Congressional Research Service 1992:10, 11, 16, 19, 20).

"Assault weapons" are almost never used to kill police officers, are generally less lethal than ordinary hunting rifles, and are not easily converted to fully automatic fire. They do offer a rate of fire somewhat higher than some other gun types such as revolvers, but no higher than their civilian-style counterparts among semiautomatic firearms. In any case, revolvers can be fired at a rate which is more than fast enough to carry out any known gun crimes, including even the extreme cases of mass shootings. "Assault weapons" can be used with magazines holding large numbers of cartridges, but there is at present no reason to believe that magazine capacity has ever affected the outcome of any significant number of gun crimes, since so few involve large numbers of rounds being fired in circumstances where neither reloading nor use of multiple guns was possible (Kleck 1991:70–82).

Saturday night specials (SNSs) are small, cheap handguns. They have been the target of special control efforts in the past because it was claimed that they were the preferred weapon of criminals, and were especially useful for criminal purposes, based on the twin notions that they are especially concealable because of their small size, and that their low price makes them especially affordable for predominantly low-income criminals. The best available information indicates the following about SNSs. Only about 10 to 27 percent of crime handguns (in the 1970s) fit the U.S. Bureau of Alcohol, Tobacco and Firearms (BATF) definition of SNSs (barrel length under three inches, .32 caliber or less, and price under $50 in mid-1970s dollars) (Kleck 1986). Thus, most crime handguns were not SNSs, nor did they claim a share even approaching a majority. Because only about 14 percent of violent crimes involve a handgun, SNSs were therefore involved in only about 2 to 4 percent of all violent crimes.

Further, the SNS share of crime guns appears to be no larger than the SNS share of the general civilian handgun stock, since at least 20 percent of all handguns introduced into the general civilian stock were SNSs. Thus, there is no strong reason to believe that criminals are any more likely to use SNSs than are noncriminal members of the general public. More specifically, criminals are no more likely to use cheap or small caliber handguns than noncriminal gun owners. Therefore, there is no meaningful sense in which criminals can be said to "prefer" SNSs. On the other hand, there is some mixed support for the idea that some criminals prefer short-barrelled handguns over longer-barrelled ones, though the weapons tend to be middle or large caliber and of good quality. At most, perhaps 7 percent, and more realistically 1–2 percent, of SNSs will ever be involved in even one violent crime (Kleck 1986). In sum, most handgun criminals do not use SNSs, and few SNSs are owned or used for criminal purposes. Instead, most are probably owned by poor people for protection.

One policy implication of the last conclusion is that gun control efforts directed specifically at SNSs would have their greatest impact in reducing the availability of defensive handguns among low-income people. Effective SNS-specific measures would disproportionately affect the law-abiding poor, since it is they who are most likely to own SNSs and obey the laws, but are least likely to have the money to buy better quality guns.

A SNS-specific control policy could be worse than merely ineffectual. If it actually did deprive any criminals of SNSs, some would adapt by substituting larger and/or marginally more expensive guns, which would imply the substitution of larger caliber, longer barrelled handguns. Wounds inflicted with larger caliber handguns are more like to result in a death (Zimring 1972); longer barrelled guns fire bullets with greater accuracy and a higher muzzle velocity, thereby increasing their deadliness. Consequently, among those persons who previously would have used SNSs but who, as a result of the control policy, substituted larger handguns, the attack fatality rate would almost certainly increase (Kleck 1986; 1991:85–91).

Most U.S. gun laws are aimed largely or solely at handguns. This focus has the same flaw as the focus only on SNSs, but on a larger scale. While some potentially violent people denied handguns would do without guns of any kind, others would substitute shotguns and rifles, which are generally more lethal than handguns. Under any but the most optimistic circumstances, this would result in a net increase in the number of homicide deaths (Kleck 1984b). One of the political temptations of handgun-only control is that it appears to be a satisfactory compromise between doing nothing about gun violence, which would alienate procontrol voters, and restricting all gun types, which would alienate many long gun owners. It is tempting to assume that the results of this apparent compromise policy would correspondingly lie somewhere between the results of a policy of doing nothing and the results of one restricting all guns. This assumption is false—the "middle" course of restricting only handguns is worse than either of the other two alternatives (Kleck 1991:91–94).

A clear policy recommendation follows from what should be a basic principle of weapons regulations: Never place controls on a subcategory of weapons without also placing controls at least as stringent on more deadly, easily substituted alternative weapons.

Focusing on specialized weapon categories will be an unproductive, but unfortunately increasingly popular gun control strategy in the foreseeable future. The very features that make the piecemeal approach ineffective also make it politically attractive. Thus, policies focusing on "assault weapons," machine guns, plastic guns, and armor-piercing bullets are inoffensive to most voters and have little cost, but they also address weapons and ammunition that are only very rarely used by criminals.

So far, this is merely a special case of a political universal applying to any policy area—weak approaches carry less risk to policy makers, while also having less impact on the target problem. However, many special-weapon gun control measures are worse than this, since they have serious potential for making the violence problem worse. Policies targeting only less lethal weaponry, such as handguns generally or Saturday night specials specifically, can increase the gun death total by inadvertently encouraging the substitution of more lethal types of guns.

DEFENSIVE USE OF GUNS BY CRIME VICTIMS

Policy analysts seeking to assess the relative costs and benefits of gun control sometimes simplify their task by implicitly assuming that gun ownership has no significant benefits, beyond the relatively minor ones of recreational enjoyment of shooting sports like hunting. Under this assumption, it is unnecessary to show that a given law produces a large reduction in violence, since even one life saved would outweigh the supposedly negligible benefits of gun ownership. This simplification, however, is unrealistic, because it erroneously assumes that gun ownership and use has no defensive or deterrent value, and thus no potential for preventing deaths or injuries.

Each year there are at least 2.5 million defensive uses of guns by crime victims, about four to five times the number of crimes committed with guns (Kleck and Gertz 1994). (National Crime Victimization Survey estimates of defensive gun use frequency are demonstrably erroneous, covering no more than 3 percent of the actual number of uses—[Kleck and Gertz 1994*].) These huge figures are less surprising in light of the following facts. About a third of U.S. households

*See Gary Kleck and Marc Gertz, "Armed Resistance to Crime: The Prevalence and Nature of Self-Defense with a Gun," in Part Four of this volume.—Ed.

keep a gun at least partially for defensive reasons (DMI 1979); at any one time nearly a third of gun owners have a firearm in their home (usually a handgun) which is loaded Quinley 1990); about a quarter of retail businesses have a gun on the premises (U.S. Small Business Administration 1969); and perhaps 5 percent of U.S. adults regularly carry a gun for self-defense (DIALOG 1990).

Keeping a gun for home defense makes most defensive gun owners feel safer, and most also believe they are safer because they have a gun (Quinley 1990; Mauser 1990; tabulations from a 1981 *Los Angeles Times* survey reported in Kleck 1991:120). The belief is not unrealistic. Previous research has consistently indicated that victims who resist with a gun or other weapon are less likely than other victims to lose their property in robberies (Hindelang 1976; Ziegenhagen and Brosnan 1985; Kleck 1988; Kleck and DeLone 1993:68) or in burglaries (Cook 1991:57). Previous research has also consistently indicated that victims who use guns or other weapons to resist attack are less likely to be injured compared either to victims who do not resist or to those who resist without weapons. This is true whether the research relied on victim surveys or on police records, and whether the data analysis consisted of simple cross-tabulations or more complex multivariate analyses. These findings have been obtained both with respect to robberies (Ziegenhagen and Brosnan 1985; Kleck 1988; Kleck and DeLone 1993) and assaults (Kleck 1988).

Cook* (1991:58) offers the unsupported personal opinion concerning robbery victims that resisting with a gun is only prudent if the robber does not have a gun. The primary data source on which Cook himself relies, however, flatly contradicts this opinion. National Crime Victimization Survey (NCVS) data indicate that even in the very disadvantageous situation where the robber has a gun, victims who resist with guns are still substantially less likely to be injured than those who resist in other ways, and even slightly less likely to be hurt than those who do not resist at all (Kleck and DeLone 1993:75).

With regard to studies of rape, while samples typically include too few cases of self-defense with a gun for separate analysis, McDermott (1979), Quinsey and Upfold (1985), Lizotte (1986), and Kleck and Sayles (1990) all found that victims who resisted with some kind of weapon were less likely to have the rape attempt completed against them. Findings concerning the impact of armed resistance on whether rape victims suffer additional injuries beyond the rape itself are less clear, due to a lack of information on whether acts of resistance preceded or followed the rapist's attack (Kleck and Sayles 1990:154, 157). The only two rape studies with the necessary sequence information found that forceful resistance by rape victims usually follows, rather than precedes, rapist attacks inflicting additional injury, undercutting the proposition that victim resistance increases the likelihood that the victim will be hurt (Quinsey and Upfold 1985:46–47, Ullman and Knight 1992:39). This is consistent with findings on robbery and assault (Kleck 1988:9). Criminals take the gun away from the victim in less than

---

*See Philip J. Cook, "The Technology of Personal Violence," in Part Three of this volume.—Ed.

1 percent of these incidents. Thus, the evidence does not support the idea that nonresistance is safer than resisting with a gun or other weapon (see reviews in Kleck 1988; Kleck and Sayles 1990; Kleck and DeLone 1993).

Widespread civilian gun ownership might also deter some criminals from attempting crimes in the first place. There probably will never be definitive evidence on this deterrence question, since it revolves around the issue of how many crimes do not occur because of victim gun ownership. However, scattered evidence is consistent with a deterrence hypothesis. Gun use by private citizens against violent criminals and burglars is common and more frequent than legal actions like arrests, is a more prompt negative consequence of crime than legal punishment, and is more severe, at its most serious, than legal system punishments (Kleck 1988). In prison surveys criminals report that they have refrained from committing crimes because they thought a victim might have a gun (Wright and Rossi 1986). "Natural experiments" indicate that rates of "gun deterrable" crimes have declined after various highly publicized incidents related to victim gun use, including gun training programs, incidents of defensive gun use, and passage of a law which required household gun ownership. Widespread gun ownership may also deter burglars from entering occupied homes, reducing confrontations with residents, and thereby reducing deaths and injuries. U.S. burglars are far less likely to enter occupied premises than burglars in nations with lower gun ownership (Kleck 1988; Kleck 1991:134–13p).

The most parsimonious way of linking these previously unconnected and unknown or obscure facts is to tentatively conclude that civilian ownership and defensive use of guns deters violent crime and reduces burglar-linked injuries. Rates of robbery, assault, rape, and injury linked with residential burglary might be still higher than their already high levels were it not for the dangerousness of the prospective victim population. Gun ownership among prospective victims may well have as large a crime-inhibiting effect as any crime-generating effects of gun possession among prospective criminals. This would account for the failure of so many researchers to find a significant net relationship between measures of general gun ownership and rates of crime like homicide and robbery. . . . The two effects may roughly cancel each other out.

Guns are potentially lethal weapons whether wielded by criminals or victims. They are frightening and intimidating to those they are pointed at, whether the subjects are predators or the preyed upon. Guns thereby empower both those who would use them to victimize and those who would use them to prevent their victimization. Consequently, they are a source of both social order and disorder, depending on who uses them, just as is true of the use of force in general.

THE RISKS OF PROHIBITIONIST MEASURES

The failure to fully acknowledge this reality can lead to grave errors in devising public policy to minimize violence through gun control. While some gun laws are intended to reduce gun possession only among relatively limited "high-risk" groups such as convicted felons, through such measures as laws licensing gun owners or requiring permits to purchase guns, other laws are aimed at reducing gun possession in all segments of the civilian population, both criminal and non-criminal. Examples would be the Morton Grove, Illinois, handgun possession ban, near approximations of such bans in New York City, Chicago, and Washington, D.C., laws prohibiting the carrying of concealed weapons, and general bans on the sale or possession of handguns, Saturday night specials, or assault weapons.

By definition, laws are most likely to be obeyed by the law-abiding, and gun laws are no exception. Therefore, measures aimed at reducing gun availability among both criminals and noncriminals are almost certain to reduce gun possession more among the latter than the former. Because very little serious violent crime is committed by persons without previous records of serious violence (Kleck and Bordua 1983:291–94; Kates 1990:45–49), there are at best only modest direct crime control benefits to be gained by reductions in gun possession among noncriminals. Consequently, one has to take seriously the possibility that prohibitionist gun control measures could decrease the crime-control effects of noncriminal gun ownership more than they would decrease the crime-causing effects of criminal gun ownership. For this reason, more narrowly targeted gun control measures like gun owner licensing and permit-to-purchase systems are preferable to prohibitionist measures.

People skeptical about the value of gun control sometimes argue that while a world in which there were no guns would be desirable, it is also unachievable. The evidence summarized here raises a more radical possibility—that a world in which no one had guns might actually be less safe than one in which nonaggressors had guns and aggressors did not. As a practical matter, the latter world may be no more achievable than the former, but the point is worth raising as a way of clarifying what the goals of rational gun control policy should be. If gun possession among prospective victims tends to reduce violence, then reducing such gun possession is not, in and of itself, a social good. Instead, the best policy goal to pursue may be to shift the distribution of gun possession as far as practical in the direction of likely aggressors being disarmed and noncriminal prospective victims being armed. To disarm noncriminals in the hope this might indirectly help reduce access to guns among criminals is a dangerous gamble with potentially lethal consequences.

EFFECTS OF GUNS ON ASSAULTIVE VIOLENCE

The power which weaponry confers has conventionally been treated as exclusively violence-enhancing—it has commonly been assumed that weapon possession and use (at least among aggressors) serves only to increase the likelihood of the victim's injury and death (e.g., Newton and Zimring 1969). This is an unduly restrictive conceptualization of the significance of weaponry. A broader perspective starts with a recognition of weaponry as a source of power, frequently used instrumentally to achieve goals by inducing compliance with the user's demands. The ultimate goal behind an act of violence is often not the victim's death or injury, but rather the acquisition of money, sexual gratification, respect, attention, or the terrorizing, humiliation, or domination of the victim. Power can be, and usually is, wielded so as to obtain these things without actually inflicting physical injury. Threats, implied or overt, usually suffice and are often preferred to physical attack (Goode 1971).

The effects of guns in the hands of aggressors can be better understood if we view violent events as being composed of an ordered series of stages, with the occurrence and outcome of each stage being contingent on the outcomes of previous stages. . . .

1. **Confrontation**. In order for a violent exchange to occur, the prospective aggressor and victim must first come in contact with one another, entering into a potentially conflictual encounter. Possession of a gun can embolden both victims and aggressors to go where they like, including dangerous places where they might adventitiously encounter a stranger who, in the course of the interaction, becomes an adversary, or it may encourage them to stop avoiding, or even deliberately seek out, contact with persons with whom they already had a hostile relationship. Thus, gun ownership could increase the rate of assaultive violence by giving people freedom of movement without regard to the risks of entering into dangerous circumstances, thereby increasing the rate of hostile encounters. There is, however, no systematic evidence on these possible effects.

2. **Threat**. Once aggressor and victim find themselves confronting one another in a hostile encounter, a gun in the possession of the aggressor could encourage him to threaten the victim, with words or a gesture, possibly alluding to the gun. On the other hand, the prospective victim's possession of a gun could, if it was known to the would be aggressor, discourage the aggressor from expressing a threat. Again, there is no systematic evidence bearing directly on these possible effects.

3. **Attack**. Some hostile encounters go beyond verbal or gestural threats, escalating to an attempt to physically injure the victim, i.e., proceeding to an attack. An aggressor's possession of a gun can either increase or decrease the probability that he will attack his victim. At least four kinds of effects on attack can be conceptualized: facilitation, triggering, inhibition, and redundancy.

Facilitation. A gun could make it possible or easier to commit an attack which would otherwise be physically or emotionally impossible, dangerous, or difficult to carry out. It has often been remarked that a gun serves as an "equalizer," that it is a way of making power relations more equal than they otherwise would be. Just as a prospective victim's possession of a gun can give him power greater than or equal to his adversary and discourage an attack, the aggressor's possession of a gun could encourage it. The gun might assure the aggressor that his attack will so effectively hurt his victim that counterattack will be impossible, or at least that his victim will be afraid to strike back, even if physically capable of doing so. Guns can thereby encourage weaker adversaries to attack stronger ones. Thus, guns are more commonly used when women attack men than when women attack other women, are more common when an individual attacks a group than when the situation is reversed, and so forth (Cook 1982; Kleck 1991:156–58, 204).

Guns also facilitate attack from a distance. Further, a gun may psychologically facilitate an attack by a person who is unwilling to attack in a way which involves physical contact with his victim, or by a person too squeamish to use a messier weapon like a knife or club.

Triggering. This is the effect which experimental psychologists label the "weapons effect." Since it is but one of many effects of weaponry, this term is unsuitable. I have relabelled it the "triggering effect." Psychologists have argued that a person who is already angered may attack when they see a weapon, due to the learned association between weapons and aggressive behavior. The experimental research literature on this hypothesis is almost exactly divided between nine studies supporting it (Berkowitz and LePage 1967; Boyanowsky and Griffiths 1982; Caprara et al. 1984; Frodi 1973; Leyens and Parke 1975; Mendoza 1972; Page and O'Neal 1975; Simons and Turner 1975; Turner and Goldsmith 1976), nine studies failing to support it (Buss et al. 1972; Cahoon and Edwards 1984; 1985; Ellis et al. 1971; Fisher et al. 1969; Halderman and Jackson 1979; Page and Scheidt 1971; Tannenbaum 1971; Turner and Simons 1974), and two obtaining mixed findings (Fraczek and Macauley 1971; Turner et al. 1975). Generally, the more realistic the study's conditions and the more relevant to real-world aggression, the less supportive the results were (Kleck 1991:158–61, 205–206). There may be triggering effects, but they appear to be very contingent effects, which depend on settings and conditions not yet very well-specified.

Inhibition. Some of the "weapons effect" studies found evidence that weapons could inhibit aggression as well as trigger it (Fisher et al. 1969; Fraczek and Macauley 1971; Turner et al. 1975). While the reasons for these findings in experimental settings are not clear, in real world contexts one reason for such an effect might be that a gun provides an aggressor with a more lethal weapon than he wants. Most aggressors do not want to kill, but this could easily happen if they attacked with a gun. Therefore, an aggressor may refrain from attacking altogether, for fear that he might end up inflicting more harm than he intended.

Redundancy. This inelegant term alludes to the possibility that possession of a gun could make a physical attack unnecessary, by making it possible for an aggressor to get what he wants without attacking. Weapons are an important source of power frequently wielded to achieve some emotional or material goal—to obtain sexual gratification in a rape or money in a robbery, or, more frequently, to frighten and dominate victims in some other kind of assault. All of these things can be gained with threats rather than an actual attack. Possession of a gun can therefore serve as a substitute for attack, rather than its vehicle. In robberies, offenders without guns often feel they must attack their victims in order to insure that the victims will not resist, while robbers with guns are confident they can gain the victim's compliance merely by pointing their gun at them. In assaults, a gun can enable aggressors to terrify their victims or emotionally hurt them, making a physical attack unnecessary.

It is not yet possible to separately assess the relative importance of each of these possible causal effects. However, the total effect of all of them considered together is fairly clear. The net effect of aggressor gun possession on whether the aggressor attacks is negative. The results of at least sixteen prior studies have indicated, without exception, that aggressors with guns were less likely than other aggressors to attack and/or injure their victims (Normandeau 1968:199–202; Conklin 1972:116–20; McDonald 1975:139; Hindelang 1976:213; Block 1977:80; Skogan 1978:65, Cook and Nagin 1979:35; Skogan and Block 1983:224; Ziegenhagen and Brosnan 1985:691–92; Zimring and Zuehl 1986:23; Rand, DeBerry, Klaus, and Taylor 1986:4; Cook 1987:361; King 1987:13–14, 17; Weiner 1987, Table 3; Kleck and McElrath 1990:683, 685; Kleck and DeLone 1993:69).

4. **Injury**. Once an aggressor makes an attack, it may or may not result in injury. That is, only some attempts to injure are successful. The rate at which attacks result in physical injury to the victim is lower when the attacker fires a gun than when he throws a punch, attempts to cut or stab his victim, or tries to strike the victim with a blunt instrumemt of some kind (Rand et al. 1986:4; Kleck 1991:209). This presumably is because it is difficult to shoot a gun (usually a handgun) accurately, especially under the emotionally stressful conditions which prevail in most violent encounters. Only about 18 percent of incidents where an aggressor shot at a victim result in the victim suffering a gunshot wound (Rand 1994), while the comparable attack completion rate is about 45 percent for knife attacks (Rand et al. 1986:5). Since guns encourage aggressors to attempt attacks at greater distances and attacks against more difficult targets, they may thereby also reduce the attack completion rate (Kleck and McElrath 1991).

5. **Death**. Finally, if the aggressor does inflict a physical injury on the victim, it may or may not result in death. Less than 1 percent of all criminal assaults, and less than 2 percent of violent crimes committed by offenders armed with guns, result in death (compare national homicide estimates in U.S. Federal Bureau of Investigation 1993:58 with nonfatal assault estimates in U.S. Bureau of Justice Statistics 1993a:82–83). The measured fatality rate is under 15 percent even if we limit attention just to crimes involving an actual gunshot wounding (Cook 1985). Further, because nonfatal attacks are substantially undercounted, while fatal attacks are fairly completely counted, the true fatality rate in gunshot woundings is almost certainly still lower.

Nevertheless, the measured wounding fatality rate for guns, in all crimes considered together, is about four times higher than that of woundings with knives, the next most lethal weapon, among those which could be used in the same circumstances as guns (Kleck 1991:207). This might seem to indicate that if guns became scarce and attackers use knives rather than guns, only one fourth as many victims would die. This reasoning, however, is invalid because it implicitly attributes all of the difference in fatality rates to the weapon itself, and assumes that all else, including the intentions and motives of the aggressors, is equal in gun and knife attacks.

This assumption is unrealistic. Evidence indicates that aggressors who use guns choose them over other available weapons—a gun is not used just because "it was there"; weapon choice is not random. Rather, more serious aggressors use more serious weaponry. For example, aggressors with longer records of violence in their past are more likely to use guns (Kleck 1991:208). Thus, some of the 4-to-1 difference in fatality rates between guns and knives is due to differences in the people who used the weapons, rather than just the technical differences between the weapons themselves (Hardy and Stompoly 1974; Wright et al. 1983:191–97; Kleck 1991:163–69).

Since weapon scarcity would presumably not alter the intentions and aggressive drives of aggressors, this implies that the fatality rate would drop by a factor of less than four if knives were substituted for guns. It is impossible to say how much less, since no one has directly measured and controlled for the intentions and intensity of an aggressor's anger and willingness to hurt his victim at the moment of the attack. Some studies that have imperfectly controlled for aggressor traits thought to be correlated with these factors indicate that guns still appear to be more lethal than knives (Cook 1987; Kleck and McElrath 1991). On the other hand, when relatively homogenous samples of violent crimes are analyzed (e.g., samples of just robberies), differences in fatality rates between gun and knife woundings are small (reviewed in next section, on robbery). Likewise, a medical study of a homogenous sample of assault wounds (all were "penetrating wounds of the abdomen") found the wound fatality rates to he 13.3 percent for butcher knife wounds, 14.3 percent for ice pick wounds, and an only slightly larger 16.8 percent for pistol wounds (Wilson and Sherman 1961:643).

To summarize, an aggressor's possession and use of a gun apparently reduces the probability that he will attack, reduces the probability that the attack will result in an injury, and increases the probability that the injury will be fatal. Therefore, it is not at all obvious that threatening situations with a gun-armed aggressor are more likely to result in the victim's death, since it is not obvious what the relative balance of these three countervailing effects is. The only empirical study of real-life violent incidents which assessed all of these effects indicated that the net effect is very close to zero (Kleck and McElrath 1991:687). That is, the overall probability of a threatening situation ending in the victim's death is about the same when the aggressor is armed with a gun as it is when the aggressor is unarmed. This pattern has been obscured in earlier studies of weapons effects because researchers limited their attention to cases in which a wound had been inflicted, thereby focussing attention solely on the last stage of the violence process, the only stage where the effects of guns are known to be predominantly violence-increasing. Guns have many strong effects on violent encounters, but the effects operate in both violence-increasing and violence-decreasing directions, and the limited information we have at present indicates that these effects apparently more or less cancel each other out with respect to the likelihood that the victim will die.

Note that this conclusion takes no account of gun effects on confrontations and threats. It is still possible that gun availability in a population could affect the rates of assault and murder, despite the foregoing conclusions, if it significantly encouraged people to more frequently enter into dangerous confrontations and to issue threats or otherwise initiate hostile interactions. On the other hand, an analysis focussing solely on individual violent incidents also cannot take account of possible deterrent effects of victims having guns, which would tend to discourage aggressors from seeking contact with victims or threatening them. Consequently, the net impact of widespread gun ownership must be assessed using data on aggregates like cities or states, where the combined impact of all of these separate effects can be estimated. These kinds of studies will be summarized later.

EFFECTS OF GUNS IN ROBBERIES

A robber's goal is to get his victim's property. Injury to the victim appears to usually be more of an unintended by-product of the crime than an important goal, in contrast to homicides and assaults. Consequently, guns have some additional effects peculiar to robberies, beyond the effects observable in assaultive crimes. They may have a facilitative effect similar to that connected with assaultive crimes, since they may encourage some people to rob who would not be willing to do so without a gun. They also appear to encourage robbers to tackle more difficult, better guarded (and more lucrative) targets, such as stores or groups of people on the street, rather than lone individuals. While this might seem to imply that gun availability should increase the robbery rate, the best available evidence indicates that the former has no apparent net effect on the latter (Cook 1979; McDowall 1986; Kleck and Patterson 1993). This may be due partly to deterrent effects of victim gun ownership, especially the impact of defensive gun ownership and use by store owners on commercial robberies. However, gun possession by robbers also may have its own negative effect. Because the average "take" in gun robberies is higher than in nongun robberies, a robber with a gun can acquire a given amount of money (e.g., that needed to support a drug habit) with fewer robberies than his unarmed counterparts (Hindelang 1976, Cook 1976).

Concerning the attacks, injuries, and deaths linked with robberies, the effects of robber gun use parallel those observed in assaults, with some additional elements also apparent. Robber gun use appears to inhibit victim resistance, thereby reducing the robber's need to attack and injure the victim (Cook and Nagin 1979). And indeed, studies have invariably indicated that gun robbers are less likely to attack or injure their victims than are unarmed robbers (summarized in Kleck and DeLone 1993:62). On the other hand, if the victim is injured, he is more likely to die if shot with a gun than if injured in some other way (Cook 1987). As with assaultive crimes, it is unclear how much of this greater fatality rate is attributable to the weapons and how much to robber differences.

When these countervailing, opposite-sign effects of robber gun possession are considered together, what is the net overall effect on the likelihood that a robbery will result in the victim's death? According to national police-based data, the rate of robbery killings per 1,000 robberies in 1992 was 6.2 in gun robberies and 4.7 in knife robberies (computed from U.S. Federal Bureau of Investigation 1993:20, 29, 58), a ratio of just 1.33, far short of the 3-1 or 4-1 ratios commonly discussed. Presumably if one could control for the greater "lethality" of robbers who use guns, this ratio would be reduced even further.

Cook (1987:371) reported data from just large (250,000 population or larger) cities in 1977, which indicated a 3-to-1 difference between gun and knife robbery fatality rates. These extremely different results suggest that either big city robberies are radically different from robberies elsewhere, and/or patterns prevailing in 1977 no longer described robbery as it was by 1992. Zimring and Zuehl's (1986) single-city data imply identical death rates (6.75 robbery deaths per 1,000 robberies) in gun robberies and knife robberies (computed from data on pp. 2, 23, weighted up to population totals). In this study, the net effect of the robber's gun possession on whether the victim died appears to be about the same as it was in Kleck and McElrath's analysis of a general sample of violent crimes of all types: close to zero.

IMPACT OF GUN OWNERSHIP LEVELS ON VIOLENT CRIME RATES

The findings of aggregate studies are . . . almost evenly split between thirteen studies supporting the idea that higher gun levels are associated with higher crime rates and eleven studies that do not. All but a handful of the studies are technically very weak. They rely on small samples, sometimes including as few as nine, or even four cases; only Bordua (1986) and Kleck and Patterson (1993) had more than fifty cases. In combination with the multicollinearity that often characterizes aggregate data, this implies very unstable estimates. Most studies used measures of gun ownership which are either known to be invalid or whose validity is unknown. Eight of the studies did not control for any other factors that might be associated with gun ownership and that could affect crime rates, making it impossible to judge whether any observed associations between gun and violence levels were spurious, while eleven other studies controlled for no more than two other variables.

The most critical flaw in the aggregate-level studies is the failure to model the twoway relationship between crime rates and gun levels. Higher crime rates cause more people to acquire guns for self-defense (Kleck 1979; 1984a; Lizotte et al. 1981:501; Smith and Uchida 1988:100–101; Kleck 1994; Kleck and Patterson

1993). Consequently, any significant positive associations generated in studies failing to model the possible two-way relationship will at least partially reflect the effect of crime rates on gun rates, rather than the reverse (Cook's 1979 study is a good example of this problem). Whether there is also any effect of guns on violence is impossible to detect from the findings of studies flawed in this way. Of twenty-four aggregate studies, the problem was adequately addressed in only four of them. Three of these four studies found no impact of gun ownership levels on violent crime rates, the 1979 Kleck study being the sole exception.

EFFECTS OF GUNS ON SUICIDE

In a suicide, victim and offender are the same person, so there is no victim resistance to overcome. This radically changes the nature of the technology needed to carry the act out. The gun's capacity to facilitate attacks against strong victims or attacks at a distance is irrelevant. On the other hand, its lethality, and the quickness with which it can be used, may be significant for suicides.

Gun availability might increase suicide rates by giving suicide attempters a more lethal method. It could be argued that, in the absence of a gun, while some attempters would still persist after a nonfatal suicide attempt, others would not make any subsequent attempts and lives would therefore be saved. This argument differs, however, from, the parallel argument made for gun effects in assaultive crimes. Unlike in the assault case, there are many common methods of committing suicide which are nearly as lethal, and in other ways even more satisfactory, than guns. The fatality rate in gun suicide attempts is about 85 percent, but it is about 80 percent in hanging attempts, 77 percent with carbon monoxide, and 75 percent with drowning (Kleck 1991:258). These are only slight differences, and some or all of them could be due to greater seriousness of intent among gun users. There is evidence that suicide attempters who use putatively more lethal methods are more intent on killing themselves, rather than merely making an attempt as a "cry for help" to those around them, and also that attempts with putatively more lethal methods are less impulsive (Tuckman and Youngman 1963; 1968; Eisenthal et at. 1966, Fox and Weissman 1975).

Other ways of committing suicide are in many ways as satisfactory or even superior to using a gun. For example, compared to suicide with a gun, using carbon monoxide in the form of exhaust fumes does not disfigure the victim as much, is not as messy, is less painful, is nearly as lethal, and is quieter and therefore less likely to summon people who might intervene to save the attempter's life (Kleck 1991:257 and accompanying text). Consequently, there is more reason with suicide than with homicide to expect that nongun methods could be substituted for guns with equally frequent fatal results.

Consistent with this assessment, previous research has indicated that while gun ownership levels are consistently related to the rate of gun suicides, they are usually unrelated to the total suicide rate. That is, where guns are common, people will more frequently use them to kill themselves, but this does not seem to affect the total number of people who die. Apparently, gun availability affects only method choice, not the frequency of fatal outcomes.

GUN ACCIDENTS

While gun accidents contribute only about 4 percent of the deaths linked with guns, they play an important rhetorical role in the gun control debate. They are used in attempts to persuade people that keeping guns in their homes for protection is foolish because the risks of a gun accident exceed any defensive benefits. Gun accidents play a different rhetorical role in the debate from homicides or suicides because most people can tell themselves that there is no one in their household likely to assault another person or attempt suicide, while it is harder to confidently state that no one will be involved in an accident. Since anybody can have an accident, the argument goes, every household with a gun is at risk of suffering a gun accident.

There are several problems with this argument. First, gun accidents are quite rare relative to the numbers of people exposed to them. The rate of accidental death per 100,000 guns or per 100,000 gun-owning households is less than 4–6 percent of the corresponding rates for automobiles, i.e., far less than the risks routinely taken on by millions of Americans. The gun accident rate has also been sharply declining for over 25 years, despite rapid increases in the size of the gun stock (Kleck 1991:306–307; National Safety Council 1994). The approximately 1,400 annual fatal gun accidents (National Safety Council 1994) are also extremely rare compared to the 2.5 million annual defensive uses of guns (Kleck and Gertz 1994).

Second, the risk of a gun accident is not randomly distributed across the gun-owning population and thus is not a significant risk for more than a small fraction of owners. Gun accidents are apparently largely confined to an unusually reckless subset of the population, with gun accidents disproportionately occurring to people with long records of motor vehicle accidents, traffic tickets, drunk driving arrests, and arrests for violent offenses (Waller and Whorton 1973). Accidents in general are most common among alcoholics and people with personality traits related to recklessness, impulsiveness, impatience, and emotional immaturity (e.g., Tillman and Hobbs 1949; Conger et al. 1959., Shaw 1965; Schuman et al. 1967). The circumstances of gun accidents commonly involve acts of unusual recklessness, such as "playing" with loaded guns, pulling the trigger to see if a gun is loaded, and playing Russian roulette with a revolver (Metropolitan Life Insurance Company 1948; 1953, 1956; 1959; 1968; Heins et al. 1974; Copeland 1984; Morrow and Hudson 1986; Wintemute et al. 1987). Gun accidents are largely confined to defensive gun owners, and less than one sixth of accidental deaths are connected with hunting (Kleck 1991:289–91, 316). Consequently, gun accidents are quite rare for ordinary gun owners, especially when compared with the frequency of defensive uses.

Contrary to impressions generated by the news media, gun accidents almost never involve preadolescent children. There were 142 fatal gun accidents, with about 50–60 of them involving handguns, involving children under age 13 in the entire nation in 1991 (see National Safety Council 1994:22 re. total child gun accident deaths, and Kleck 1991:309 re. the share of those deaths which involve handguns). Instead, gun accidents are largely concentrated in the same age groups where intentional assaultive violence is concentrated: adolescent and young adult males (Kleck 1991:276–80, 309).

Most gun safety training is aimed at hunters, rather than the defensive gun owners who make up the bulk of people involved in gun accidents. Because of this narrow coverage, it probably has little impact outside of the hunting community. Further, because the training does not treat alcoholism or modify the shooter's personality, it seems useful primarily for reducing the minority of accidents which are attributable to shooter ignorance rather than chronic recklessness. There is some weak evidence that the training is effective for hunters, implying that extending its coverage to other gun owners might be moderately useful (Kleck 1991:296–300, 318). On the other hand, trying to reduce gun accidents through gun laws looks less promising in light of evidence that existing gun laws have no apparent impact on gun accident rates (Kleck and Patterson 1993:274).

TYPES OF GUN CONTROLS

"Gun control" encompasses many different forms of laws intended to regulate human behavior in some way related to firearms (Kleck 1991, chap. 8). Some controls regulate gun acquisition, restricting the purchasing, trading, or receiving of guns. Gun owner license laws require that people have a license in order to lawfully possess a gun, even in the home, and in order to acquire the gun in the first place. This license is not issued until the applicant has passed through a check of official records to see if the person has a prior criminal conviction, and possibly to see if they have some other disqualifying traits, such as alcoholism or mental illness. Purchase permit laws require a person to get a permit before buying a gun, and applicants must first pass through a records check. "Application-to-purchase" systems are similar to purchase permit systems, except that the records check is typically optional, and the system usually requires a minimum waiting period between initial purchase attempt and final delivery of the gun (Blose and Cook 1980). Registration requirements mandate recording the acquisition or possession of a gun, linking each gun with a particular owner, but do not mandate screening for unqualified gun buyers.

Other laws regulate gun transactions from the other end, regulating the selling, manufacture, or importation of guns. Still others regulate various kinds of gun use. Some laws completely forbid the carrying of guns in public places, while others require licenses to do so. Restrictions are generally stronger regarding concealed carrying than open carrying, and stronger with respect to carrying on the person than carrying in a motor vehicle (Jones and Reay 1980; Blackman 1985). Some attach mandatory penalties to unlawful carrying. Other laws attempt to discourage gun use in crimes by attaching additional (some discretionary, others mandatory) or minimum penalties to various dangerous felonies when they are committed with a gun.

Almost all states prohibit possession of guns by high-risk subgroups of the population, most commonly convicted criminals, mentally ill people, drug addicts, alcoholics, and minors (Ronhovde and Sugars 1982:204–205). These laws do not specifically restrict the original acquisition of guns, but instead are intended to make it more legally risky to be in possession of guns at any one time.

The strongest gun laws of all impose bans on the possession, sale, and/or manufacture of various categories of guns. While no U.S. jurisdiction forbids ownership of all types of guns, New York City, Chicago, and Washington, D.C. have de facto bans on the private possession of handguns, and some small towns have formal handgun bans. A number of states have banned the sale and manufacture of Saturday night specials, usually defined in practice as guns made of cheap metal with a low melting point (Kleck 1991, chap. 8).

PUBLIC OPINION AND SUPPORT FOR GUN LAWS

Levels of support for gun control have shown no clear long-term trends in the past decades. There is short-term volatility in reported levels of support for some measures, consistent with evidence that opinion is easily changed and that gun control is not a salient issue for many Americans, despite the emotional intensity of debates among activist minorities (Bordua 1983; U.S. Congress 1975; Crocker 1982:263–64; Kleck 1991:363–66). The intensity of support for gun control appears to he weaker than the intensity of opposition, in the sense that opponents report that they are much more likely to actually do something based on their beliefs, such as writing a letter to a public official or contributing money to an organization connected with the issue (Schuman and Presser 1981).

Much of the support for gun control is not utilitarian or instrumentalist in character. That is, many people support gun control even though they do not believe it is an effective tool for reducing violence (Wright 1981; Crocker 1982). For example, in a national survey, nearly half of those stating that they supported stricter gun controls also stated that they believed that stricter controls would not reduce (or might even increase) crime (Mauser 1990, discussed in Kleck 1991:371). Instead, positions on gun control seem symptomatic of culture conflict, with gun law used as a way of declaring gun ownership and gun owners to be morally inferior (Kaplan 1979, Kates 1979: 1990:6–16; Kleck 1991:375–77), parallel to the way alcohol prohibition was used as a way for rural and small-town Anglo-Saxon Protestants to condemn the culture of supposedly free-drinking urban Catholics from Irish or Southern and Eastern European backgrounds (Gusfield 1963).

. . . There are a large number of weak or moderate controls which a majority of Americans will endorse if asked, though few will volunteer "gun control" as an answer if asked an open-ended question soliciting their opinion about how crime might be reduced (U.S. Congress 1975, Dialog 1990, discussed in Kleck 1991:364). Prohibition of gun ownership by the general public does not have majority support, but many moderate regulatory measures do. Controls on handguns enjoy more support than controls on the more widely owned rifles and shotguns. There is more support for "getting tough on criminals" than for controls likely to restrict or impose costs on ordinary gun owners. In short, Americans support controls unlikely to have any direct impact on themselves, while opposing those which might impose some costs on them or interfere with their own gun ownership.

THE IMPACT OF GUN CONTROL LAWS ON VIOLENCE RATES

. . . Given the previously noted lack of support for the notion that guns have a net violence-increasing impact on either violence rates or the outcomes of individual violent incidents, it is not surprising that research has failed to indicate consistent support for the view that gun laws reduce violence. Most studies do not support this idea, and the few that do are extremely weak methodologically. . . .

Kleck and Patterson (1993) sought to avoid all of these technical problems. Their analysis covered all forms of violence which involves guns, encompassed every large (over 100,000 population) city in the nation, and assessed all major forms of existing gun control in the U.S. Their findings . . . indicate that gun ownership levels have no net positive effect on any violent crime rate, and that, with few exceptions, existing gun control laws have no significant net negative effect on violence rates.

The likely exceptions to the latter generalization were owner licensing, which seems to reduce homicides, discretionary add-on penalties for committing crimes with a gun, which appear to reduce homicide and rape, mandatory penalties for unlawful gun carrying, which also seem to reduce robbery, and state or local licensing of gun dealers, which rather surprisingly appears to reduce robberies.

POLICY CONCLUSIONS

Despite enormous variation in gun ownership levels across U.S. cities, the best available evidence indicates that general gun ownership levels have no measurable net impact on violent crime levels, although they do affect the frequency with which guns are used in some kinds of violence. On the other hand, the frequency with which guns are carried may have an impact on robbery which gun ownership levels do not, and gun ownership within special high-risk subsets of the population may have an impact on violence rates which general gun ownership levels do not.

The significance of the few gun control measures found to be effective should not be overlooked. There is some empirical support for a few moderate gun controls. I favor a national "instant records check," which would screen for high-risk gun buyers similar to owner license and purchase permit systems, but without the delays and arbitrary administration which sometimes characterizes those controls. The system should cover nondealer transactions as well as dealer sales, and apply to rifles and shotguns, as well as handguns. Also, tighter licensing of gun dealers and increased enforcement of carry laws may be useful.

Gun control is a very minor, though not entirely irrelevant, part of the solution to the violence problem, just as guns are of only very minor significance as a cause of the problem. The United States has more violence than other nations for reasons largely unrelated to its extraordinarily high gun ownership. Fixating on guns seems to be, for many people, a fetish which allows them to ignore the more intransigent causes of American violence, including its dying cities, inequality, deteriorating family structure, and the all-pervasive economic and social consequences of a history of slavery and racism. And just as gun control serves this purpose for liberals, equally useless "get tough" proposals, like longer prison terms, mandatory sentencing (e.g., "three strikes and you're out" proposals), and more use of the death penalty serve the purpose for conservatives. All parties to the crime control debate would do well to give more concentrated attention to more difficult, but far more relevant, issues like how to generate stable good-paying jobs for the underclass, an issue which is at the heart of the violence problem.

REFERENCES

Beha, James. 1977. "And Nobody Can Get You Out." *Boston University Law Review* 57:96–146, 289–333.

Berkowitz, Leonard, and Anthony LePage. 1967. "Weapons as Aggression-Eliciting Stimuli." *Journal of Personality and Social Psychology* 7:202–207.

Blackman, Paul H. 1985. "Carrying Handguns for Personal Protection." Paper presented at the Annual Meeting of the American Society of Criminology, San Diego, California.

Block, Richard. 1977. *Violent Crime*. Lexington, Mass.: Lexington Books.

Block, Richard. 1981. "Victim-Offender Dynamics in Violent Crime." *Journal of Criminal Law & Criminology* 72:743–61.

Blose, James, and Philip J. Cook. 1980. *Regulating Handgun Transfers*. Durham, N.C.: Institute of Policy Sciences and Public Affairs, Duke University.

Boor, Myron, and Jeffrey H. Bair. 1990. "Suicide Rates, Handgun Control Laws, and Sociodemographic Variables." *Psychological Reports* 66:923–30.

Bordua, David J. 1983. "Adversary polling and the construction of social meaning." *Law & Policy Quarterly* 5:345–66.

———. 1986. "Firearms Ownership and Violent Crime: A Comparison of Illinois Counties." In *The Social Ecology of Crime*. Edited by James M. Byrne and Robert J. Sampson. New York: Springer-Verlag, pp. 156–88.

Boyanowsky, Ehor O., and Curt T. Griffiths. 1982. "Weapons and Eye contact as Instigators or Inhibitors of Aggressive Arousal in Police-Citizen Interaction." *Journal of Applied Social Psychology* 12:398–407.

Brearley, H. C. 1932. *Homicide in the United States.* Chapel Hill: University of North Carolina Press.

Brill, Steven. 1977. *Firearm Abuse: A Research and Policy Report.* Washington, D.C.: Police Foundation.

Buss, Arnold, Ann Booker, and Edith Buss. 1972. "Firing a Weapon and Aggression." *Journal of Personality and Social Psychology* 22:296–302.

Cahoon, Delwin D., and Ed M. Edmonds. 1984. "Guns/No Guns and the Expression of Social Hostility." *Bulletin of the Psychonomic Society* 22:305–308.

———. 1985. "The Weapons Effect: Fact or Artifact." *Bulletin of the Psychonomic Society* 23:57–60.

Caprara, G. V., P. Renzi, P. Amolini, G. D'Imperio, and G. Travaglia. 1984. "The Eliciting Cue Value of Aggressive Slides Reconsidered in a Personological Perspective: The Weapons Effect and Irritability." *European Journal of Social Psychology* 14:313–22.

Clarke, Ronald V., and Peter R. Jones. 1989. "Suicide and Increased Availability of Handguns in the United States." *Social Science and Medicine* 28:805–809.

Conger, J. J., H. S. Gaskill, D. D. Glad, L. Hassel, R. V. Rainey, and W. L. Sawrey. 1959. "Psychological and Psycho-physiological Factors in Motor Vehicle Accidents." *Journal of the American Medical Association* 169:1581–87.

Conklin, John E. 1972. *Robbery and the Criminal Justice System.* Philadelphia: Lippincott.

Cook, Philip J. 1976. "A Strategic Choice Analysis of Robbery." In *Sample Surveys of the Victims of Crime.* Edited by Wesley Skogan. Cambridge: Ballinger, pp. 173–87.

———. 1979. "The Effect of Gun Availability on Robbery and Robbery Murder." In *Policy Studies Review Annual.* Edited by Robert Havernan and B. Bruce Zellner. Beverly Hills: Sage, pp. 743–81.

———. 1985. "The Case of the Missing Victims: Gunshot Woundings in the National Crime Survey." *Journal of Quantitative Criminology* 1:91–102.

———. 1987. "Robbery Violence." *Journal of Criminal Law and Criminology* 78:357–76.

Cook, Philip J., and Daniel Nagin. 1979. *Does the Weapon Matter?* Washington, D.C.: INSLAW.

Copeland, Arthur R. 1984. "Accidental Death by Gunshot Wound—Fact or Fiction." Forensic *Science International* 26:25–32.

Crocker, Royce. 1982. "Attitudes Toward Gun Control: A Survey." In *Federal Regulation of Firearms.* Edited by Harry L. Hogan. Washington, D.C.: U.S. Government Printing Office, pp. 229–67.

DeFronzo, James. 1979. "Fear of Crime and Handgun Ownership." *Criminology* 17:331–39.

Deutsch, Stephen Jay, and Francis B. Alt. 1977. "The Effect of Massachusetts' Gun Control Law on Gun-Related Crimes in the City of Boston." *Evaluation Quarterly* 1:543–68.

DeZee, Matthew R. 1983. "Gun Control Legislation: Impact and Ideology." *Law and Policy Quarterly* 5:367–79.

DIALOG. 1990. Computer search of DIALOG database, POLL file of public opinion survey results. Palo Alto, Calif.: DIALOG Information Services, Inc.

Diener, Edward, and Kenneth W. Kerber. 1979. "Personality Characteristics of American Gun Owners." *Journal of Applied Psychology* 107:227–38.

DMI (Decision-Making-information). 1979. *Attitudes of the American Electorate Toward Gun Control.* Santa Ana, Calif.: DMI.

Eisenthal, Sherman, Norman L. Farberow, and Edwin S. Shneidman. 1966. "Followup of Neuropsychiatric Patients in Suicide Observation Status." *Public Health Reports* 81:977–90.

Ellis, Desmond P., Paul Weinir, and Louie Miller III. 1971. "Does the Trigger Pull the Finger? An Experimental Test of Weapons as Aggression-Eliciting Stimuli." *Sociometry* 34:453–65.

Fischer, Donald G., Harold Kelm, and Ann Rose. 1969. "Knives as Aggression-Eliciting Stimuli." *Psychological Reports* 24:755–60.

Fisher, Joseph C. 1976. "Homicide in Detroit: The Role of Firearms." *Criminology* 14:387–400.

Turner, Charles W., and Lynn Stanley Simons. 1974. "Effects of Subject Sophistication and Evaluation Apprehension on Aggressive Responses to Weapons." *Journal of Personality and Social Psychology* 30:341–48.

Ullman, Sarah E., and Raymond A. Knight. 1992. "Fighting Back: Women's Resistance to Rape." *Journal of Interpersonal Violence* 7:31–43.

U.S. Bureau of Justice Statistics. 1993a. *Criminal Victimization in the United States, 1992.* Washington, D.C.: U.S. Government Printing Office.

———. 1993b. *Sourcebook of Criminal Justice Statistics, 1992.* Washington, D.C.: U.S. Government Printing Office.

———. 1993c. *Survey of State Prison Inmates, 1991.* Washington, D.C.: U.S. Government Printing Office.

U.S. Congress. 1975. "Gun Control." *Congressional Record* 121 (December 19): 1–10.

U.S. Congressional Research Service. 1992. "'Assault Weapons': Semiautomatic Military-Style Firearms Facts and Issues." (Revised as of June 4, 1992) Washington, D.C.: The Library of Congress. U.S. Federal Bureau of Investigation (FBI).

U.S. Federal Bureau of Investigation 1993. *Crime in the United States (1992)—Uniform Crime Reports.* Washington. D.C.: U.S. Government Printing Office.

U.S. Small Business Administration. 1969. *Crime Against Small Business.* Senate Document No. 91-14. Washington, D.C.: U.S. Government Printing Office.

Weiner, Neil A. 1987. "Situational Dynamics and Juvenile Interpersonal Violence." Paper presented at the annual meetings of the American Society of Criminology, Montreal, Canada.

Williams, J. Sherwood, and John H. McGrath. 1976. "Why People Own Guns." *Journal of Communication* 26:22–30.

Wilson, H., and R. Sherman. 1961. "Civilian Penetrating Wounds of the Abdomen." *Annals of Surgery* 153:639–49.

Wintemute, Garen J., Stephen P. Teret. Jesse F. Kraus, Mona A. Wright, and Gretchen Bradfield. 1987. "When Children Shoot Children: 88 Unintended Deaths in California." *Journal of the American Medical Association* 257:3107–3109.

Wisconsin. 1960. *The Regulation of the Firearms by the States.* Research Bulletin 130. Madison, Wisc.: Wisconsin Legislative Reference Library.

Wright, James D. 1981. "Public Opinion and Gun Control." *The Annals* 455:24–39.

———. 1984. "The Ownership of Firearms for Reasons of Self-Defense." In *Firearms and Violence*, edited by Don B. Kates Jr. Cambridge, Mass.: Ballinger, pp. 301–27.

Wright, James D., and Linda Marston. 1975. "The Ownership of the Means of Destruction Weapons in the United States." *Social Problems* 23:93–107.

Wright, James D., and Peter H. Rossi. 1986. *Armed and Considered Dangerous: A Survey of Felons and Their Firearms.* New York: Aldine.

Wright, James D., Peter H. Rossi, and Kathleen Daly. 1983. *Under the Gun: Weapons, Crime, and Violence in America.* New York: Aldine.

Ziegenhagen, Eduard A., and Dolores Brosnan. 1985. "Victim Responses to Robbery and Crime Control Policy." *Criminology* 23:675–95.

Zimring, Franklin E. 1972. "The Medium is the Message: Firearm Caliber as a Determinant of Death from Assault." *Journal of Legal Studies* 1:97–123.

———. 1975. "Firearms and Federal Law: The Gun Control Act of 1969." *Journal of Legal Studies* 4:133–98.

Zimring, Franklin E., and James Zuehl. 1986. "Victim Injury Death in Urban Robbery: A Chicago Study." *Journal of Legal Studies* 15:140.

PART FOUR

THE ARMED CITIZEN
MORE VIOLENCE OR LESS?

Despite the widely held belief that guns are effective for protection, our results suggest they pose a substantial threat to members of the household (therefore) people should be strongly discouraged from keeping guns in their homes.
Arthur Kellermann et al., 1993

Allowing citizens to carry concealed handguns reduces violent crimes . . . mass shootings in public places are reduced when law abiding citizens are allowed to carry concealed handguns.
John Lott, 1998

This volume has emphasized that, from a two-sided perspective, the core issues of the gun debate concern causality. This perspective would link degrees and kinds of restrictions on firearms to evidence that conclusively establishes causal links between levels of gun ownership and elevated violence rates. To the extent there is such a causal linkage then restrictions of gun ownership would presumably reduce violence rates.

As was argued in Part Three, if a causal linkage between gun availability and violence rates is to be sustained (more guns produce more violence) then four predicted facts must be co-oroberated by consistent evidence provided by studies capable of documenting causality:

1. Higher levels of gun ownership will always be associated with increased rates of lethal violence.

2. Higher levels of gun ownership in a geographic area *will produce* higher violence rates
3. Higher rates of attack, injury, and mortality occur in violent incidents where guns are involved compared to similar incidents where other weapons are employed.
4. Higher rates of violent acts will occur among gun owners than nongun owners who are similar.

In Part Three we saw that predicted fact 1 was contradicted by statistical data. Higher levels of gun availability are not consistently associated with higher rates of violent acts or rates of lethal violence (witness the 1990s). Predicted fact 2, that higher levels of gun ownership in a geographic area produces higher rates of violent acts was as yet unproven and needed further research (National Research Council selections) or "highly correlated" (Cook) or a confusion of the direction of causation—more citizens acquiring guns as a response to higher violence rates (Kleck).

Predicted fact 3 was intensively debated in Part Three: that higher rates of attack, injury, and mortality will occur in violent incidents where guns are involved than similar incidents where other weapons are employed. Although all researchers acknowledged that guns were more lethal than other weapons (instrumentality effect) there was serious disagreement concerning the degree of lethality that guns *alone* contributed to violence generated by violence prone subsets of the population. These violent subsets were concentrated in racial and ethnic minorities.

However, criticisms aside of the extent that the added lethality of guns alone contribute to violence rates among the violent prone, the instrumentality effect hypothesis suffers a serious *political* weakness when used to support policy recommendations for prohibitions on public handgun ownership (Zimring, Hawkins).

If defensive gun ownership among the nonviolent is based upon fear of crime and/or prudently acquiring an instrument to defend oneself if circumstances arise, then why would noncriminals support legislated disarmerment as a way to make criminals less lethally violent? As noted, gun violence is identified as a problem that primarily effects racial and ethnic minorities (see Zimring and Hawkins, "Lethal Violence in America" in Part Three of this volume). So far, the attempt to persuade the nonminority community to support gun prohibition to solve the gun violence problems in minority communities has not met with success (see Zimring and Hawkins, "Lethal Violence in America" in Part Three of this volume). Therefore, more *politically* powerful has been the argument that since law-abiding citizens are more likely to obey the law than the violently criminal population gun prohibitions would therefore yield criminals a net gain (see Kleck, "Guns and Violence," in Part Three of this volume). People who own guns for personal protection do so to reduce vulnerability and to deter attack. This population fears that gun prohibitions would restrict their ability to defend themselves especially against criminals carrying guns. Therefore, gun prohibition in the defensive gun owners view renders them more vulnerable relative to the criminal and therefore is politically unacceptable as a policy remedy.

In light of the above, those who favor restricting citizen access to handguns for home and self-defense must prove for political and policy reasons the truth of predicted fact 4:

> Higher rates of violent acts will occur among gun owners than nongun owners who are similar.

That is, publically restrictive gun policies will be politically persuasive especially among the wider nongun owning public if it can empirically demonstrated that:

1. Guns in the homes of ordinary, noncriminal, nondrug plagued, non-mentally unstable citizens cause significantly elevated violence rates (homicides, fatal accidents, suicides) when compared to similar people who don't own guns.
2. Guns are a seldom employed and neglible deterrent to criminal attacks in and outside of home.
3. Citizens *legally* carrying guns for self-protection ("packing heat") produce elevated violence rates in that group.

In short, it must be proved that the costs of gun ownership for self-defense outweigh any purported benefits. Hence, policies discouraging gun ownership, especially handgun ownership, for defensive ownership by the *noncriminal public* would be empirically justified.

The necessary proof that guns owned for self-defense cause or produce more harm than benefit depends on the strength of statistical evidence produced by studies. Studies employing techniques of statistical analysis aim to establish the degree, if any, to which variables (subjects you are interested in) are related or correlated. Correlations are numerical measures of how closely the growth of one variable (e.g., lethal violence rates) are related to the growth of the other variables (e.g., levels of gun ownership). However, the fact that as one variable increases, so does the other, does not prove that one variable is affecting or influencing the other.

For example, critics of studies that find positive correlations between levels of gun availability (however measured) and elevated rates of lethal violence emphasize that these relationships don't establish causality. To establish that a variable contributes to whatever degree to the likelihood of the occurrence of another variable, the alleged cause must be shown to have preceded its effect. Cross-sectional (gallup-poll type studies) that establish positive associations between gun availability and violence rates do not establish temporal antecedence. They survey a cross section of the population at a fixed time. If, for example, using such a study, you found an association between poverty and heavy drinking, you couldn't tell from your data to what extent heavy drinking caused poverty or whether it was poverty causing heavy drinking. Likewise in cross-sectional studies the direction of causality between guns and violence rates remains undetermined (e.g., Do higher violence rates cause more people to buy guns?). These studies therefore can help establish hypotheses (more guns cause more or less violence) but in themselves they don't prove causation (see Lott, "More Guns, Less Crime," in Part Four of this volume).

To prove causality, we could do an experiment. We would place firearms in a randomly selected number of households and compare violence rates in that group to a randomly selected group of households in which we have not placed firearms (see Lott, "More Guns, Less Crime," Part Four of this volume). Ethically, we cannot do this for it might put people's lives at risk without their consent.

The next best device that would model this experimental situation is a cohort or longitudinal study. This type of study is *prospective*. It does not rely on existing data that may be incomplete or inaccurate. Instead it follows groups of people over many years who are initially free of the condition you are investigating (e.g., lethal behavior). The researchers then monitor the group over time to see which members develop the condition (e.g., lethally violent behavior) and compare them to those who don't develop the behavior (controls). The occurrence or nonoccurrence of the behavior is related to the characteristics of the subjects (e.g., gun ownership) to identify causes (e.g., what's different). This sort of study since it takes place over time establishes the sequence of events and allows for a careful matching of characteristics shared by those who develop the behavior under investigation and those who don't.

Unfortunately, cohort studies are time consuming, expensive, and subject to losing track of the original individuals involved in the study (e.g., they move). In short, such studies require a willingness to define the problem as important enough to assign significant money, time, and research staff to the project.

Lacking money and people we can try to establish causality using cheaper, less time intensive but unfortunately less reliable *retrospective* methods to model our experimental situation—the case-control study. Case-control studies compare the people who develop the condition under investigation (cases) to people who are similar in important respects but don't develop the condition (controls). The careful matching of cases with controls is the key to creating the *possibility* of establishing causality; remembering however, that since the study is retrospective the reliability of evidence depends on the accuracy of existing records as well as the memory and the truthfulness of interviewees.

These types of studies (and others) are the tools of epidemiology, which relates characteristics of people to health or disease. Studies that attempt to model experimental situations where clinical trials are not possible, are the mainstays of the public health approach to disease control. Such studies are also the mainstays of the public health approach to gun control.

Researchers attempt to relate guns to violence in ways that would establish the direction and degrees of causality of these associated variables. In fact, the public health literature has become the major support for restrictive or prohibitionist approaches to gun control. This approach purports to establish conclusive causal links to gun ownership and violence by comparing different violence rates between gun owners and nongun owners who in all other important respects are similar. Therefore, samples of this research are included in this section as well as skeptic's attempts to rebut their findings by focusing on their alleged methodological failings.

One of the most influential and widely quoted examples of this research is included in this section. An analysis of some of the methodological issues will alert us to key points of contention. These points of contention must be understood in order for us to evaluate the degree of "two-sided" support for the last predicted fact in the gun-ownership–violence hypothesis—that gun ownership by ordinary people similar in other respects cause them to be more violent.

Arthur Kellermann et al. (1993) published a case-control study in the *New England Journal of Medicine* in which the researchers concluded: "Despite the widely held belief that guns are effective for protection, our results suggest they pose a substantial threat to members of the household . . . [therefore] people should be strongly discouraged from keeping guns in their homes."

The study was accompanied by a strongly worded editorial urging strict gun control (see Kassirer, "Guns in the Household," in Part Four of this volume) citing support from Kellerman's research among other evidence. The editorial called for registration of firearms, liscencing of gun owners, mandatory gun locks, mandatory loaded gun indicators, bans on the sale of automatic and semi-automatic weapons as well as denunciations of the National Rifle Association for successfully resisting necessary gun control legislation. How did Kellerman et al. arrive at the conclusion that "people should be strongly discouraged from keeping guns in their homes"? They used a case-control study.

In this research homicide victims killed in their homes (cases) were matched by sex, age, and race with nonvictims (controls) in a three-county area who lived in the same neighborhoods. Interviews with the victims survivors alleged to establish that handgun ownership was much more common in homes of homicide victims (36 percent) than among nonvictimized controls (23 percent). It was acknowledged that the victim group (cases) had higher rates of physical violence, arrests, and drug usage than the controls. Statistical methods were used to adjust for these behaviors. Therefore, increased risks of homicide victimization in the home were statistically linked to gun ownership for the entire U.S. population based upon this sample and this study. The methodological issues here are twofold. Was this sample representative of the general population? Was a causal relationship established between gun ownership and increased rates of homicide by comparing the populations in the study? In short, does this study model the experimental situation described earlier—randomly placing guns and not placing guns in randomly selected households and seeing if violence rates differ? The answers to these questions have significance for the entire public health literature which claims to document causal relationships between gun ownership and increased risks for homicide, accidents, and suicides in the home (instrumentality effect) by comparing people(s) similar in all respects but one—gun ownership.

Readers of Part Three will suspect that skeptics will attack these purported causal linkages and generalizations by again raising the issues of comparability and intentionality. To what extent did this study control for intent? If it did not, then it is claimed that comparisons and generalizations found in the study are invalidated. Skeptics argue that people are motivated to own firearms for different reasons. Therefore, case-control studies that find positive associations between gun-availability and elevated violence rates have not proved causation unless they have controlled for different motivations for firearm ownership. People who are nonviolent, noncriminal, nonreckless, etc. may have different motivations for defensive ownership of guns than their high-risk contraries. If you are a drug dealer, gang member or their cohort, your reasons for defensive gun ownership may well be different than a noncriminal afraid of violent crime or wanting an insurance weapon against possible attack by people very different than he or she. Therefore, generalizing from a population of high risk gun owners (drug users, people with histories of physical violence and arrest records) to the general population is to use a unrepresentative sample (see Kates et al., "The Myth that Murderers Are Ordinary Gun Owners," in Part Four of this volume). More subtly however, skeptics (see Kleck, "Case-Control Research on Homicidal Behavior" and Lott, "More Guns, Less Crime" in Part Four of this volume) raise questions concerning the comparability of cases and controls *within* this higher risk subset. Do higher rates of gun ownership among gun homicide victims (cases) indicate a more dangerous life style than lived by nongun owning, nonhomicide victims (the controls)? In short, do the reasons *why* a person chooses to own a gun or not to own a gun among people in this higher risk subset, make them different? These are exactly the same kind of questions involving intentionality and comparability that were at the center of the controversy over how much lethality guns added to violent encounters over other weapons (instrumentality effect). Skeptics maintain that the public health approach consistently fails to control for intentionality and hence routinely makes unrepresentative comparisons between violent subsets of the population and the general population as well as between nations (see Kates et al., "The Myth that Murderers Are Ordinary Gun Owners"; Kleck, "The Medical/Public Health Literature on Guns and Violence"; Kopel, "Children and Guns"; and Lott, "More Guns, Less Crime," in Part Four of this volume).

A second issue involving public health literature concerns its objectivity. Skeptics (see Kates et al., "The Myth that Murderers Are Ordinary Gun Owners"; Kleck, "The Medical/Public Health Literature on Guns and Violence"; and Kopel, "Children and Guns," in Part Four of this volume) raise questions concerning intentionality and comparability, unrepresentative samples, one-sidedness and outright distortion of statistics in medical literature concerning claims of gun availability and high risks of homicide, suicides, and accidents, especially among children (instrumentality effect). To what extent are gun homicides, suicides, and accidents illegitimately mixed together (intentionality and comparability) to produce "big numbers"? To what extent are people who have gun accidents representative of the general population? To what extent have trends in gun accident numbers and rates, especially among American children been accurately represented in the medical literature? To what extent can comparisons between nations with different histories, customs, and populations establish causality concerning gun availability levels and violence? To what extent does the public health approach seek only confirmations and disregard or discount divergent information concerning these issues? The reader is provided with examples of both government and privately authored studies as well as critical pieces to decide on the purported "one-sidedness" of treatment.

The last and perhaps the most controversial issue addressed in this section is the degree, if any, to which citizens' guns provide a widely employed, effective deterrent against criminals (deterrence effect). As shown earlier, advocates of restrictivist or prohibitionist gun control policies must not only prove causal linkages between guns for self-defense and higher violence rates for gun owners when compared to similar nongun owners but also that guns are not widely employed or effective deterrents to crime. Even if, for example, the public health literature was able to demonstrate that the violence rates of ordinary, noncriminal gun owners exceeded those of ordinary, noncriminal, nongun owners (instrumentality effect) it also could be true that citizen gun ownership suppresses violent crime to a degree that outweighed its costs (deterrence effect). And, if the methodological criticisms and claims of outright one-sidedness of that literature are sustained, proof of the widespread employment and deterrence effectiveness of citizen guns would strongly support the case that handgun prohibitions would benefit criminals more than noncriminals (see Kleck, "Guns and Violence," in Part Three of this volume; Kleck, "Gun Decontrol," Lott, "More Guns, Less Violence" in Part Four of This volume). And, even if Lott's research (see "More Guns, Less Crime"), which claims legally carried weapons reduce crime is not conclusive; if it only proves that guns don't increase lethal violence rates (see Kleck, "Gun Decontrol," in Part Four of this volume), then the claims that guns *alone* contribute to higher lethal violent rates (instrumentality effect—see Zimring, and Hawkins, "Lethal Violence in America," and Cook, "The Technology of Personal Violence," in Part Three of this volume) would be weakened.

Hence in this last part of the debate concerning the causal capacity of owning, employing, or carrying weapons to deter crime (deterrence effect) the roles of the participants are reversed. Gun control skeptics such as Gary Kleck, Marc Gertz, and John Lott will now attempt to prove that citizen guns are a crime deterrent; that is, to document the extent to which American men and women arm themselves for self-defense (50 percent of handgun owners, 27 percent of all gun owners—see Kleck, "Guns and Violence," in Part Three of this volume), the extent to which guns are employed annually for self-defense (up to 2.5 million times—see Kleck and Gertz, "Armed Resistance to Crime," in Part Four of this volume), and the extent to which citizens legally carrying guns cause violent crime to diminish (a 1 percent increase in gun ownership reduces violent crime by 4.1 percent—see Lott, "More Guns, Less Crime," in Part Four of this volume).

Instrumentality effect advocates (see Cook, "Self-Defense," in Part Four of this volume) and those who produce evidence to prove that citizens legally carrying weapons cause gun murder rates to rise (see McDowell et al., "Easing Concealed Firearm Laws," in Part Four of this volume) and those who question the number of defensive gun uses per year claimed by Kleck and Gertz (see also Cook, "Self-Defense," in Part Four of this volume) now become the skeptics and seek to provide evidence to discredit the claims that guns in citizen hands are widely used and effective crime deterrents.

The methodological and substantiative issues involved in the deterrence debate discussed here in Part Four focus on:

Standards to measure the deterrence effects of guns (the number of criminals killed—Kellerman et al., "Gun Ownership as a Risk Factor for Homicide in the Home") or the number of times citizens report employing guns for defensive purposes against criminals (Kleck and Gertz, "Armed Resistance to Crime") or the number of times explicit threats with guns were made unnecessary because criminals feared citizens were armed (Lott, "More Guns, Less Crime") or the drop in violent crime rates after concealed-carry permits were issued to all non-criminals who applied for them in thirty-one states (Lott).

The representiveness of samples (issues of intentionality and comparability) that establish either higher rates of defensive gun usage (Kleck and Gertz, "Armed Resistance to Crime") or lower rates (National Research Council—Part III, Cook, "Self-Defense")

The specification of what constitutes representative, sufficient sized samples and sufficient controls to determine if concealed carry permits raised or lowered rates of gun violence (McDowell, et. al., "Easing Concealed Firearm Laws"; Kleck, "Gun Decontrol"; Lott, "More Guns, Less Crime")

These methodological and substantive issues as well as assumptions that are central to the contemporary deterrence effect debate grew out of earlier research. In the 1980s James Wright and Peter Rossi challenged the view that the deterrence effect of guns was accurately measured by the numbers of criminals killed (see also B. Bruce-Briggs, "The Great American Gun War," in Part One of this volume). For example, the deterrence effect of arming police would not be measured by how many criminals they annually shot and killed. Rather, their effectiveness is measured in terms of crimes not committed (falling crime rates) as well as feelings of security of the citizenry. With these standards in mind Wright and Rossi surveyed 1,874 incarcerated felons and published their findings (*Armed and Considered Dangerous*, 1986). In the surveys, felons reported that they feared being shot by citizens more than they feared being caught and punished by the criminal justice system (34 percent reported being scared off, shot at, or wounded by citizens). They also reported making rational choices in selecting victims. They made as sure as possible that the potential victim was not armed. Burglars tried to estimate if a house owner was away before entering so as to avoid being shot. That is, general gun ownership conferred an advantage on even those who weren't armed or didn't have a gun in the home because citizen guns influenced criminal's estimations of risks.

Criminologist Gary Kleck added further fuel to the deterrence debate with research published in 1988 ("Crime Control Through the Use of Armed Force"—see selected bibliography). Kleck, using a 1988 national survey done by pollster Peter Hart which asked questions concerning defensive handgun use, estimated such guns were used about 645,000 times annually to defend against criminal intrusions. He concluded that "gun ownership among potential crime victims may exert as much effect on violent crime and burglary as to criminal justice activities."

The above research had explosive political consequences for the gun debate. The National Rifle Association eagerly embraced the work of Wright, Rossi, and Kleck. Gun control advocates attacked it. They had always emphasized the negative consequences of gun ownership (homicides, suicides, accidents—see Kellerman et al., "Gun Ownership as a Risk Factor for Homicide in the Home," in Part Four of this volume), and claimed that since few criminals are ever killed by citizens that guns had limited defensive utility against crime (costs outweigh benefits). Gun control advocates eagerly embraced the work of Philip Cook ("Self-Defense," in Part Four of this volume) citing the National Crime Victimization Survey (NCVS) done by the Department of Justice, which showed only 64,000 to 80,000 annual defensive gun users (*see also*, National Research Council, 1993—Part Three). Cook argued that the NCVS, a federally administered large-scale survey, was much more accurate than the Hart survey that Kleck had used.

Also, critics leveled methodological criticisms at all the surveys which measured defensive gun uses (DGUs). For example, to what extent are people reporting DGUs criminals? Criminals frequently victimize other criminals; hence, to what extent are surveys merely recording gun battles between criminal aggressors and criminal victims? Further, since surveys are retrospective, rely on memory, to what extent are people misremembering, lying, exaggerating or misunderstanding questions (e.g., confusing gun ownership with gun defense, defenses against animals with defenses against humans)?

The Kleck-Gertz research ("Armed Resistance to Crime," 1995) included in Part Four addresses all of these issues and comes up with a new estimation of defensive gun users—up to 2.5 million per year, a majority with handguns. Have Kleck and Gertz proved their case? The selection by gun control academic Marvin Wolfgang is suggestive ("A Tribute to a View I Have Opposed," in Part Four of this volume). His concession to the methodological rigor of the Kleck-Gertz research keeps the deterrence-effect hypothesis at the center of the two-sided gun debate. Also, the policy implications of such purported widespread use of citizen guns puts such work at the center of an empirically oriented policy debate. If the Kleck-Gertz estimates are correct, prohibitionary handgun restrictions would eliminate a widely employed crime deterrent. But just how costly as well as effective is that deterrent?

In 1987 Florida changed the way concealed-carry handgun permits were issued. Until 1987 each county issued permits at its discretion to citizens of "good moral character." In countries with large urban populations and high crime rates permits were rarely issued. In October 1987, the system was changed to make concealed carry permit issuance both uniform and mandatory. Unless one was a minor, felon, drug addict, alcoholic, previously committed to a mental institution or mentally incompetent, for $125 and passing a gun safety program, you received a concealed carry permit. By 1996, the number of permits issued had reached 194,356—about 1.3 percent of Floridas' population (see Kleck, "Gun Decontrol," in Part Four of this volume).

These changes created the opportunity for a natural experiment to test both the instrumentality effect hypothesis (more guns, more violence) and the deterrence-effect hypothesis (more guns, less crime). A natural experiment is one where fortuitous circumstances provides data that allows for controlled testing of a hypothesis.

The instrumentality effect hypothesis would predict that in the Florida situation higher rates of violence would occur in the permit holder group *after* they received those permits. That is, although they had been certified as law abiding, noncriminals the fact that they had applied for permits (only 1 percent of the eligible population applied), assumes they perceived themselves at high risk. Comparing their post-permit rate of violence to their pre-permit rate of violence (0 percent) would therefore control for intent. If the instrumentality effect hypothesis is correct, we would expect then that the carrying of guns, alone, would produce escalated violence rates in this group; e.g., road rage events, alcohol-fueled aggressive altercations, etc. (since their offending rate was initially 0 percent the possibility that they carried guns illegally before the law change would not effect the experiment). But, if the expected escalation of violence rates does not occur, then the instrumentality effect hypothesis, the assertion that guns alone increase violence rates or rates of lethal violence, would be falsified when applied to defense-minded law-abiding citizens. The selections in Part Four from McDowell et al. (Easing Concealed Firearm Laws"), Kleck ("Gun Decontrol"), and Lott ("More Guns, Less Crime") all deal with this natural experiment.

And conversely by building on such data, we could test the deterrence effect. If gun carrying deters crime, we would predict that as more people acquired such permits over time (controlling for other variables), that violent crime rates would be reduced the greatest in the areas that had the greatest number of concealed carry permit holders. Conversely, we would predict that criminals would move into contiguous areas with fewer concealed carry permit holders. And, testing the deterrence effect hypothesis is what John Lott and David Mustard have done..

In 1997 (*Journal of Legal Studies*) they published a complex statistical analysis of 3,054 U.S. counties in 28 states comparing violence rates and gun ownership patterns from 1977 to 1992. The aim of the study was to determine the benefits and costs of gun ownership and gun laws in terms of lives saved and lost. The conclusions which supported the deterrence effect of citizens carrying concealed weapons, touched off both political and media controversy and detailed and complex debates concerning a multitude of statistical issues. In 1998, John Lott published *More Guns, Less Crime* which explained his research assumptions, the specific problems to be resolved, the methodologies employed to resolve them, and the conclusions reached.

Specifically, Lott, an economist, based his research on the assumption that criminals, like other groups, respond to incentives and disincentives, in a self-interested manner: "When crime becomes more difficult, less crime is committed. Higher arrest and conviction rates dramatically reduce crime." Criminals move out of areas where tough crime control measures are instituted and move into areas where enforcement is weaker. Also, citizens can take actions that deter crime. Allowing citizens to carry concealed handguns reduces violent crimes and "the reductions coincide very closely with the numbers of concealed handgun permits issued. Mass shootings in public places are reduced when law abiding citizens are allowed to carry concealed handguns" (Lott, "More Guns, Less Crime").

Specifically, Lott claims a 1 percent increase in gun ownership lowers violent crime by 4.1 percent. A more direct challenge to the instrumentality effect and the policies it supports would be impossible.

Outside of Gary Kleck's critical comments ("Gun Decontrol"—in Part Four of this volume) concerning whether the Lott-Mustard study established causality no further critical pieces are included. The reasons are threefold:

First, published criticisms focus on statistical issues involving regression analysis, too technical for nonexperts to understand.

Second, Lott provides a very unusual and valuable feature in his book *More Guns, Less Crime*. He devotes an entire chapter ("The Political and Academic Debate") in which he provides, in the critics words, all the main objections to his research. He then responds in detail to each of the critics.

Third, and most importantly, it appears, from a two-sided perspective it may be too early to decide whether Lott has proven causation. However, his rigorous methodology, combined with the fact that more data is becoming available (thirty-one states are now issuing, mandatory concealed carry permits with more probably to follow) means attempted and enhanced replications of his work are inevitable. Key questions concerning causality will be settled: As more and higher percentages of concealed carry permits are issued will violent crime rates continue to fall faster in those areas of higher issuance? As more and higher percentages of citizens acquire concealed carry permits will the now nonexistent instrumentality effect emerge in those groups?

In short, further inquiry over time and extended databases will determine if Lott's deterrent effect hypothesis has established causality or whether his samples (1 percent of the eligible concealed-carry permit population) were too small to be representative and capable of reducing crime to the degree Lott claims.

This section concerning the costs and benefits of citizen guns as a crime deterrent (as well as the rest of the volume) provides the reader with a few helpful instruments to view the central issues of the gun debate in a more "two-sided" manner. Framing the debate as one in which causal claims must be established through the methods and standards of experimental logic (specified predicted facts either confirmed or disconfirmed through consistent evidence produced by technically sound procedures) makes it a different debate than what occurs in the media and political treatment of gun control issues. That is, despite the obvious polarization of the social science debate over guns, the rules of inquiry make a 'one-sided' treatment of gun control issues more difficult to conceal. Hence, the degrees of certainty of conclusions have to be matched to the methodological soundness of the means to those conclusions.

However, the degree to which even practitioners of these methodologies accuse each other of cognitive and motivational bias in the gun debate should alert us to how difficult such biases are to overcome especially when issues become part of larger political, social and, cultural struggles. But, the alternative is a disturbing one: the ongoing utilization of the propaganda campaigns of media, politicians, and advocacy groups or judicial fiat as a means of reaching public policy decisions on important issues.

16

HANDGUN REGULATIONS, CRIME, ASSAULTS, AND HOMICIDE

JOHN HENRY SLOAN ET AL.*

Approximately 20,000 persons are murdered in the United States each year, making homicide the eleventh leading cause of death and the sixth leading cause of the loss of potential years of life before age sixty-five.[1-3] In the United States between 1960 and 1980, the death rate from homicide by means other than firearms increased by 85 percent. In contrast, the death rate from homicide by firearms during this same period increased by 160 percent.[3]

Approximately 60 percent of homicides each year involve firearms. Handguns alone account for three-fourths of all gun-related homicides.[4] Most homicides occur as a result of assaults during arguments or altercations; a minority occur during the commission of a robbery or other felony.[2,4] Baker has noted that in cases of assault, people tend to reach for weapons that are readily available.[5] Since attacks with guns more often end in death than attacks with knives, and since handguns are disproportionately involved in intentional shootings, some have argued that restricting access to handguns could substantially reduce our annual rate of homicide.[5-7]

To support this view, advocates of handgun control frequently cite data from countries like Great Britain and Japan, where the rates of both handgun ownership and homicide are substantially lower than those in the United States.[8]

From the *New England Journal of Medicine* 319, no. 19 (November 10, 1988): 1256–62. Copyright © 1998 Massachusetts Medical Society. All rights reserved. Reprinted by permission of the publisher.

*Arthur L. Kellermann, Donald T. Reay, James A. Ferris, Thomas Koepsell, Frederick P. Rivara, Charles Rice, Laurel Gray, and James LoGerfo.

Rates of injury due to assault in Denmark are comparable to those in north-eastern Ohio, but the Danish rate of homicide is only one fifth as high as Ohio's.[5,6] In Denmark, the private ownership of guns is permitted only for hunting, and access to handguns is tightly restricted.[6]

Opponents of gun control counter with statistics from Israel and Switzer-land, where the rates of gun ownership are high but homicides are relatively uncommon.[9] However, the value of comparing data from different countries to support or refute the effectiveness of gun control is severely compromised by the large number of potentially confounding social, behavioral, and economic fac-tors that characterize large national groups. To date, no study has been able to separate the effects of handgun control from differences among populations in terms of socioeconomic status, aggressive behavior, violent crime, and other fac-tors.[7] To clarify the relation between firearm regulations and community rates of homicide, we studied two large cities in the Pacific Northwest: Seattle, Wash-ington, and Vancouver, British Columbia. Although similar in many ways, these two cities have taken decidedly different approaches to handgun control.

METHODS

Firearm Regulations

Although similar in many ways, Seattle and Vancouver differ markedly in their approaches to the regulation of firearms. In Seattle, handguns may be purchased legally for self-defense in the street or at home. After a thirty-day waiting period, a permit can be obtained to carry a handgun as a concealed weapon. The recre-ational use of handguns is minimally restricted.[15]

In Vancouver, self-defense is not considered a valid or legal reason to purchase a handgun. Concealed weapons are not permitted. Recreational uses of handguns (such as target shooting and collecting) are regulated by the province, and the pur-chase of a handgun requires a restricted-weapons permit. A permit to carry a weapon must also be obtained in order to transport a handgun, and these weapons can be discharged only at a licensed shooting club. Handguns can be transported by car, but only if they are stored in the trunk in a locked box.[16,17]

Although they differ in their approach to firearm regulations, both cities aggressively enforce existing gun laws and regulations, and convictions for gun-related offenses carry similar penalties. For example, the commission of a class A felony (such as murder or robbery) with a firearm in Washington State adds a minimum of two years of confinement to the sentence for the felony.[18] In the Province of British Columbia, the same offense generally results in 1 to 14 years of imprisonment in addition to the felony sentence.[16] Similar percentages of homicides in both communities eventually lead to arrest and police charges. In Washington, under the Sentencing Reform Act of 1981, murder in the first degree carries a minimum sentence of 20 years of confinement.[19] In British

Columbia, first-degree murder carries a minimum sentence of 25 years, with a possible judicial parole review after 15 years.[20] Capital punishment was abolished in Canada during the 1970s.[21] In Washington State, the death penalty may be invoked in cases of aggravated first-degree murder, but no one has been executed since 1963.

Rates of Gun Ownership

Because direct surveys of firearm ownership in Seattle and Vancouver have never been conducted, we assessed the rates of gun ownership indirectly by two independent methods. First, we obtained from the Firearm Permit Office of the Vancouver police department a count of the restricted-weapons permits issued in Vancouver between March 1984 and March 1988 and compared this figure with the total number of concealed-weapons permits issued in Seattle during the same period, obtained from the Office of Business and Profession Administration, Department of Licensing, State of Washington. Second, we used Cook's gun prevalence index, a previously validated measure of intercity differences in the prevalence of gun ownership.[14] This index is based on data from forty-nine cities in the United States and correlates each city's rates of suicide and assaultive homicide involving firearms with survey-based estimates of gun ownership in each city. Both methods indicate that firearms are far more commonly owned in Seattle than in Vancouver.

Identification and Definition of Cases

From police records, we identified all the cases of robbery, burglary, and assault (both simple and aggravated) and all the homicides that occurred in Seattle or Vancouver between January 1, 1980, and December 31, 1986. In defining cases, we followed the guidelines of the U.S. Federal Bureau of Investigation's uniform crime reports (UCR).[22] The UCR guidelines define aggravated assault as an unlawful attack by one person on another for the purpose of inflicting severe or aggravated bodily harm. Usually this type of assault involves the actual or threatened use of a deadly weapon. Simple assault is any case of assault that does not involve the threat or use of a deadly weapon or result in serious or aggravated injuries.

A homicide was defined as the willful killing of one human being by another. This category included cases of premeditated murder, intentional killing, and aggravated assault resulting in death. "Justifiable homicide," as defined by the UCR guidelines, was limited to cases of the killing of a felon by a law-enforcement officer in the line of duty or the killing of a felon by a private citizen during the commission of a felony.[22] Homicides that the police, the prosecuting attorney, or both thought were committed in self-defense were also identified and noted separately.

Statistical Analysis

From both Seattle and Vancouver, we obtained annual and cumulative data on the rates of aggravated assault, simple assault, robbery, and burglary. Cases of aggravated assault were categorized according to the weapon used. Data on homicides were obtained from the files of the medical examiner or coroner in each community and were supplemented by police case files. Each homicide was further categorized according to the age, sex, and race or ethnic group of the victim, as well as the weapon used.

Population-based rates of simple assault, aggravated assault, robbery, burglary, and homicide were then calculated and compared. These rates are expressed as the number per 100,000 persons per year and, when possible, are further adjusted for any differences in the age and sex of the victims. Unadjusted estimates of relative risk and 95 percent confidence intervals were calculated with use of the maximum-likelihood method and are based on Seattle's rate relative to Vancouver's.[23] Age adjusted relative risks were estimated with use of the Mantel-Haenszel summary odds ratio.[24]

RESULTS

During the seven-year study period, the annual rate of robbery in Seattle was found to be only slightly higher than that in Vancouver (relative risk, 1.09; 95 percent confidence interval, 1.08 to 1.12). Burglaries, on the other hand, occurred at nearly identical rates in the two communities (relative risk, 0.99; 95 percent confidence interval, 0.98 to 1.0). During the study period, 18,925 cases of aggravated assault were reported in Seattle, as compared with 12,034 cases in Vancouver. When the annual rates of assault in the two cities were compared for each year of the study, we found that the two communities had similar rates of assault during the first four years of the study. In 1984, however, reported rates of simple and aggravated assault began to climb sharply in Seattle, whereas the rates of simple and aggravated assault remained relatively constant in Vancouver. This change coincided with the enactment that year of the Domestic Violence Protection Act by the Washington State legislature. Among other provisions, this law required changes in reporting and arrests in cases of domestic violence.[25] It is widely believed that this law and the considerable media attention that followed its passage resulted in dramatic increases in the number of incidents reported and in related enforcement costs in Seattle.[26] Because in Vancouver there was no similar legislative initiative requiring police to change their reporting methods, we restricted our comparison of the data on assaults to the first four years of our study (1980 through 1983).

During this four-year period, the risk of being a victim of simple assault in Seattle was found to be only slightly higher than that in Vancouver (relative risk, 1.18; 95 percent confidence interval, 1.15 to 1.20) The risk of aggravated

Table 1. Annual Crude Rates and Relative Risks of Aggravated Assault, Simple Assault, Robbery, Burglary, and Homicide in Seattle and Vancouver, 1980 through 1986.*

Crime	Period	Seattle	Vancouver	Relative Risk	95% CI
		n./ 100,000			
Robbery	1980–1986	492.2	450.9	1.09	1.08–1.12
Burglary	1980–1986	2952.7	2985.7	0.99	0.98–1.00
Simple assault	1980–1983	902	767.7	1.18	1.15–1.20
Aggravated assault	1980–1983	486.5	420.5	1.16	1.12–1.19
Firearms		87.9	11.4	7.70	6.70–8.70
Knives		78.1	78.9	0.99	0.92–1.07
Other		320.6	330.2	0.97	0.94–1.01
Homicides	1980–1986	11.3	6.9	1.63	1.38–1.93
Firearms		4.8	1.0	5.08	3.54–7.27
Knives		3.1	3.5	0.90	0.69–1.18
Other		3.4	2.5	1.33	0.99–1.78

*CI denotes confidence interval. The "crude rate" for these crimes is the number of events occurring in a given population over a given time period. The relative risks shown are for Seattle in relation to Vancouver.

assault in Seattle was also only slightly higher than in Vancouver (relative risk, 1.16; 95 percent confidence interval, 1.12 to 1.19). However, when aggravated assaults were subdivided by the type of weapon used and the mechanism of assault, a striking pattern emerged. Although both cities reported almost identical rates of aggravated assault involving knives, other dangerous weapons, or hands, fists, and feet, firearms were far more likely to have been used in cases of assault in Seattle than in Vancouver (table 1). In fact, all the difference in the relative risk of aggravated assault between these two communities was due to Seattle's 7.7-fold higher rate of assaults involving firearms.

Over the whole seven-year study period, 388 homicides occurred in Seattle (11.3 per 100,000 person-years). In Vancouver, 204 homicides occurred during the same period (6.9 per 100,000 person-years). After adjustment for differences in age and sex between the populations, the relative risk of being a victim of homicide in Seattle, as compared with Vancouver, was found to be 1.63 (95 percent confidence interval, 1.28 to 2.08). This difference is highly unlikely to have occurred by chance.

When homicides were subdivided by the mechanism of death, the rate of homicide by knives and other weapons (excluding firearms) in Seattle was found to be almost identical to that in Vancouver (relative risk, 1.08; 95 percent confidence interval, 0.89 to 1.32). Virtually all of the increased risk of death from homicide in Seattle was due to a more than fivefold higher rate of homicide by firearms (table 1). Handguns, which accounted for roughly 85 percent of the homicides involving firearms in both communities, were 4.8 times more likely to be used in homicides in Seattle than in Vancouver.

To test the hypothesis that the higher rates of homicide in Seattle might be

Table 2. Annual Age-Adjusted Homicide Rates and Relative Risks of Death by Homicide in Seattle and Vancouver, 1980 through 1986, According to the Race or Ethnic Group of the Victim.*

Race or Ethnic Group	Seattle	Vancouver	Relative Risk	95% CI
	n./ 100,000			
White (non-Hispanic)	6.2	6.4	1	0.8– 1.2
Asian	15.0	4.1	3.5	2.1– 5.7
Excluding Wah Mee murders	9.5	—	2.3	1.4– 4.0
Black	36.6	9.5	2.8	0.4–20.4
Hispanic	26.9	7.9	5	0.7–34.3
Native American	64.9	71.3	0.9	0.5– 1.5

*CI denotes confidence interval. The relative risks shown are for Seattle in relation to Vancouver.

due to more frequent use of firearms for self-protection, we examined all the homicides in both cities that were ruled "legally justifiable" or were determined to have been committed in self-defense. Thirty-two such homicides occurred during the study period, 11 of which involved police intervention. After the exclusion of justifiable homicide by police, 21 cases of homicide by civilians acting in self-defense or in other legally justifiable ways remained, 17 of which occurred in Seattle and 4 of which occurred in Vancouver (relative risk, 3.64; 95 percent confidence interval, 1.32 to 10.06). Thirteen of these cases (all of which occurred in Seattle) involved firearms. The exclusion of all 21 cases (which accounted for less than 4 percent of the homicides during the study interval) had little overall effect on the relative risk of homicide in the two communities (age- and sex-adjusted relative risk, 1.57; 95 percent confidence interval, 1.22 to 2.01).

When homicides were stratified by the race or ethnic group of the victim, a complex picture emerged (table 2). The homicide rates in table 2 were adjusted for age to match the 1980 U.S. population. This technique permits fairer comparisons among racial and ethnic groups with differing age compositions in each city. The relative risk for each racial or ethnic group, however, was estimated with use of the Mantel-Haenszel summary odds ratio.[24] This method, in effect, uses a different set of weights for the various age strata, depending on the distribution of persons among the age strata for that racial or ethnic group only. Hence, these estimates of relative risk differ slightly from a simple quotient of the age-adjusted rates.

Whereas similar rates of death by homicide were noted for whites in both cities, Asians in Seattle had higher rates of death by homicide than their counterparts in Vancouver. This difference persisted even after the exclusion of the 13 persons who died in the Wah Mee gambling club massacre in Seattle in 1983. Blacks and Hispanics in Seattle had higher relative risks of death by homicide than blacks and Hispanics in Vancouver, but the confidence intervals were very wide, given the relatively small size of both minorities in Vancouver. Only one black and one Hispanic were killed in Vancouver during the study period. Native Americans had the highest rates of death by homicide in both cities.

DISCUSSION

Previous studies of the effectiveness of gun control have generally compared rates of homicide in nations with different approaches to the regulation of firearms. Unfortunately, the validity of these studies has been compromised by the large number of confounding factors that characterize national groups. We sought to circumvent this limitation by focusing our analysis on two demographically comparable and physically proximate cities with markedly different approaches to handgun control. In many ways, these two cities have more in common with each other than they do with other major cities in their respective countries. For example, Seattle's homicide rate is consistently half to two-thirds that reported in cities such as Chicago, Los Angeles, New York, and Houston,[4] whereas Vancouver experiences annual rates of homicide two to three times higher than those reported in Ottawa, Toronto, and Calgary (Canadian Centre for Justice Statistics, Homicide Program, Ottawa: unpublished data).

In order to exclude the possibility that Seattle's higher homicide rate may be explained by higher levels of criminal activity or aggressiveness in its population, we compared the rates of burglary, robbery, simple assault, and aggravated assault in the two communities. Although we observed a slightly higher rate of simple and aggravated assault in Seattle, these differences were relatively small—the rates in Seattle were 16 to 18 percent higher than those reported in Vancouver during a period of comparable case reporting. Virtually all of the excess risk of aggravated assault in Seattle was explained by a sevenfold higher rate of assaults involving firearms. Despite similar rates of robbery and burglary and only small differences in the rates of simple and aggravated assault, we found that Seattle had substantially higher rates of homicide than Vancouver. Most of the excess mortality was due to an almost fivefold higher rate of murders with handguns in Seattle.

Critics of handgun control have long claimed that limiting access to guns will have little effect on the rates of homicide, because persons who are intent on killing others will only work harder to acquire a gun or will kill by other means.[7,21] If the rate of homicide in a community were influenced more by the strength of intent than by the availability of weapons, we might have expected the rate of homicides with weapons other than guns to have been higher in Vancouver than in Seattle, in direct proportion to any decrease in Vancouver's rate of firearm homicides. This was not the case. During the study interval, Vancouver's rate of homicides with weapons other than guns was not significantly higher than that in Seattle, suggesting that few would-be assailants switched to homicide by other methods.

Ready access to handguns has been advocated by some as an important way to provide law-abiding citizens with an effective means to defend themselves.[27–29] Were this true, we might have expected that much of Seattle's excess rate of homicides, as compared with Vancouver's, would have been explained by a higher rate of justifiable homicides and killings in self-defense by civilians. Although such homicides did occur at a significantly higher rate in Seattle than in Vancouver, these cases accounted for less than 4 percent of the homicides in both cities during the study period. When we excluded cases of justifiable homicide or killings in self-defense by civilians from our calculation of relative risk, our results were almost the same.

It also appears unlikely that differences in law-enforcement activity accounted for the lower homicide rate in Vancouver. Suspected offenders are arrested and cases are cleared at similar rates in both cities. After arrest and conviction, similar crimes carry similar penalties in the courts in Seattle and Vancouver.

We found substantial differences in the risk of death by homicide according to race and ethnic group in both cities. In the United States, blacks and Hispanics are murdered at substantially higher rates than whites.[2] Although the great majority of homicides in the United States involve assailants of the same race or ethnic group, current evidence suggests that socioeconomic status plays a much greater role in explaining racial and ethnic differences in the rate of homicide than any intrinsic tendency toward violence.[2,30,31] For example, Centerwall has shown that when household crowding is taken into account, the rate of domestic homicide among blacks in Atlanta, Georgia, is no higher than that of whites living in similar conditions.[32] Likewise, a recent study of childhood homicide in Ohio found that once cases were stratified by socioeconomic status, there was little difference in race-specific rates of homicide involving children five to fourteen years of age.[33]

Since low-income populations have higher rates of homicide, socioeconomic status is probably an important confounding factor in our comparison of the rates of homicide for racial and ethnic groups. Although the median income and the overall distribution of household incomes in Seattle and Vancouver are similar, the distribution of household incomes by racial and ethnic group may not be the same in Vancouver as in Seattle. For example, blacks in Vancouver had a slightly higher mean income in 1981 than the rest of Vancouver's population (statistics Canada, 1981 Census Custom Tabulation: unpublished data). In contrast, blacks in Seattle have a substantially lower median income than the rest of Seattle's population.[34] Thus, much of the excess risk of homicide among blacks in Seattle, as compared with blacks in Vancouver, may be explained by their lower socioeconomic status. If, on the other hand, more whites in Vancouver have low incomes than whites in Seattle, the higher risk of homicide expected in this low-income subset may push the rate of homicide among whites in Vancouver higher than that for whites in Seattle. Unfortunately, neither hypothesis can be tested in a quantitative fashion, since detailed information about household incomes according to race is not available for Vancouver.

Three limitations of our study warrant comment. First, our measures of the prevalence of firearm ownership may not precisely reflect the availability of guns in the two communities. Although the two measures we used were derived independently and are consistent with the expected effects of gun control, their validity as indicators of community rates of gun ownership has not been conclusively established. Cook's gun prevalence index has been shown to correlate with data derived from national surveys, but it has not been tested for accuracy in cities outside the United States. Comparisons of concealed weapons permits in Seattle with restricted-weapons permits in Vancouver are probably of limited validity, since these counts do not include handguns obtained illegally. In fact, the comparison of permit data of this sort probably substantially underestimates the differences between the communities in the rate of handgun ownership, since only a fraction of the handguns in Seattle are purchased for use as concealed weapons, whereas all legal handgun purchases in Vancouver require a restricted-weapons permit. Still, these indirect estimates of gun ownership are consistent with one another, and both agree with prior reports that estimate the rate of handgun ownership in Canada to be about one-fourth that in the United States.[35]

Second, although similar in many ways, Seattle and Vancouver may well differ in other aspects that could affect their rates of homicide. For example, differences in the degree of illegal drug-related activity, differences in the rate of illicit gun sales, or other, less readily apparent differences may confound the relation between firearm regulations and the rate of homicide. Although such differences may exist, striking socioeconomic similarities between the cities and the fact that they had similar rates of burglary, robbery, and both simple and aggravated assault during comparable reporting periods make such confounding less likely. Unfortunately, changes in the rules for reporting assault cases in Seattle, mandated by the state of Washington in 1984, precluded a valid comparison of the rates of simple and aggravated assault over the entire seven-year period.

Third, conclusions based on a comparison of two cities in the Pacific Northwest may not be generalizable to other urban areas in North America. Given the complex interaction of individual behavior, environment, and community factors in the pathogenesis of violent death, we cannot predict the precise impact that Canadian-style gun control might have in the United States. Even if such a major change in public policy were to take place, the current high rates of handgun ownership might blunt any effects of tougher handgun regulations for years to come.

Our analysis of the rates of homicide in these two largely similar cities suggests that the modest restriction of citizens' access to firearms (especially handguns) is associated with lower rates of homicide. This association does not appear to be explained by differences between the communities in aggressiveness, criminal behavior, or response to crime. Although our findings should be corroborated in other settings, our results suggest that a more restrictive approach to handgun control may decrease national homicide rates.

REFERENCES

1. *Homicide Surveillance: 1970–78* (Atlanta: Centers for Disease Control, September, 1983).

2. *Homicide Surveillance: High Risk Racial and Ethnic Groups—Blacks and Hispanics, 1970 to 1983* (Atlanta: Centers for Disease Control, November, 1986).

3. S. P Baker, B. O'Neill, and R. S. Karpf, *The Injury Fact Book* (Lexington, Mass.: Lexington Books, 1984).

4. Department of Justice, Federal Bureau of Investigation, *Crime in the United States* (Uniform Crime Reports) (Washington, D.C.: U.S. Government Printing Office, 1986).

5. S. P. Baker, "Without Guns, Do People Kill People?" *American Journal of Public Health* 75 (1985): 587–88.

6. J. Hedeboe, A. V. Charles, J. Nielsen, et al. "Interpersonal Violence: Patterns in a Danish Community," *American Journal of Public Health* 75 (1985): 651–53.

7. J. Wright, P. Rossi, K. Daly, and E. Weber-Burdin. *Weapons, Crime, and Violence in America: A Literature Review and Research Agenda* (Washington, D.C.: Department of Justice, National Institute of Justice, 1981).

8. J. M. A. Weiss,"Gun Control: A Question of Public/Mental Health?" *Journal of Operational Psychiatry* 12 (1981): 86–88.

9. B. Bruce-Briggs, "The Great American Gun War," *Public Interest* 45 (1976): 37–62.

10. Bureau of Census, *1980 Census of population, Washington* (Washington, D.C.: U.S. Government Printing Office, 1981).

11. Statistics Canada: 1981 census of Canada, Vancouver, British Columbia (Ottawa, Ont.: Minister of Supply and Services, 1983).

12. Seattle local market TV ratings, 1985–86. (Based on Arbitron television ratings.) Provided by KING TV, Seattle, Washington.

13. Vancouver local market TV ratings, 1985–86. Provided by Bureau of Broadcast Measurement, Toronto.

14. P. J. Cook, "The Role of Firearms in Violent Crime," in *Criminal Violence,* ed. M. Wolfgang (Beverly Hills, Calif.: Sage, 1982), pp. 236–90.

15. Revised Code of State of Washington. RCW chapter 9.41.090,9.41.095,9.41.070, 1986.

16. Criminal Code of Canada, Firearms and Other Offensive Weapons, Martin's Criminal Code of Canada, 1982. Part 11.1 (Sections 81-016.9, 1982).

17.Criminal Code of Canada, Restricted Weapons and Firearm Control Regulations Sec. 106.2 (11); Amendment Act, July 18, 1977, 1982.

18. Revised Code of State of Washington, Sentence Reform act Chapter 9 94A. 125.1980.

19. Revised Code of State of Washington, Murder 1, 9A.32.040.1984.

20. Criminal Code of Canada, Application for Judicial Review Sentence of Life Imprisonment, 1988 Part XX 669-67,1(1).

21.Criminal Code of Canada, Act to Amend Criminal Code B. II C94, 1976.

22. Department of Justice, Federal Bureau of Investigation, *Uniform Crime Reporting Handbook* (Washington, D.C.: U.S. Government Printing Office, 1984).

23. K. J. Rothman and J. D. Boice Jr., *Epidemiologic Analysis with a Programmable Calculator* (Boston: Epidemiology Resources, 1982).

24. P. Armitage and G. Berry, *Statistical Methods in Medical Research,* 2d ed. (Oxford: Blackwell, 1987).

25. Revised Code of State of Washington. RCW Chapter 10.99.010-.100,1984.

27. Seattle Police Department. Inspectional Service Division Report, Domestic Violence Arrest Costs: 1994–87, Seattle, 1986.

28. R. B. Drooz, "Handguns and Hokum: A Methodological Problem." *JAMA* 238 (1977): 43–45.

29. A. R. Copeland, "The Right to Keep and Bear Arms—A Study of Civilian Homicides Committed against Those Involved in Criminal Acts in Metropolitan Dade County from 1957 to 1982," *Journal of Forensic Science* 29 (1984): 584–90.

30. G. Kleck, "Crime Control through the Private Use of Armed Force," *Social Problems* 35 (1988): 1–21.

31. C. Loftin, and R. H. Hill. "Regional Subculture and Homicide: An Examination of the Gastil-Hackney Thesis," *American Sociology Review* 39 (1974): 714–24.

32. K. R. Williams, "Economic Sources of Homicide: Reestimating the Effects of Poverty and Inequality," *American Sociological Review* 49 (1984): 283–89.

33. B. S. Centerwall, "Race, Socioeconomic Status, and Domestic Homicide, Atlanta, 1971–72," *American Journal of Public Health* 74 (1994): 813–15.

34. J. E. Muscat, "Characteristics of Childhood Homicide in Ohio, 1974–84." American Journal of Public Health 78 (1988): 822–24.

35. Seattle City Government, *General Social and Economic Characteristics, City of Seattle: 1970–1980*. Planning Research Bulletin no. 45. (Seattle: Department of Community Development, 1983).

36. G. Newton and F. Zimring, *Firearms and Violence in American Life: A Staff Report to the National Commission on the Causes and Prevention of Violence* (Washington, D.C.: Government Printing Office, 1969).

17

RATES OF HOMICIDE, SUICIDE, AND FIREARM-RELATED DEATH AMONG CHILDREN— 26 INDUSTRIALIZED COUNTRIES

MORBIDITY AND MORTALITY WEEKLY REPORT

During 1950–1993, the overall annual death rate for U.S. children aged [less than] 15 years declined substantially,[1] primarily reflecting decreases in deaths associated with unintentional injuries, pneumonia, influenza, cancer, and congenital anomalies. However, during the same period, childhood homicide rates tripled, and suicide rates quadrupled.[2] In 1994, among children aged 1–4 years, homicide was the fourth leading cause of death; among children aged 5–14 years, homicide was the third leading cause of death, and suicide was the sixth.[3] To compare patterns and the impact of violent deaths among children in the United States and other industrialized countries, CDC [the Centers for Disease Control] analyzed data on childhood homicide, suicide, and firearm-related death in the United States and twenty-five other industrialized countries for the most recent year for which data were available in each country.[4] This report presents the findings of this analysis, which indicate that the United States has the highest rates of childhood homicide, suicide, and firearm-related death among industrialized countries.

In the 1994 World Development Report,[5] 208 nations were classified by gross national product; from that list, the United States and all twenty-six of the other countries in the high-income group and with populations of [greater than or equal to] 1 million were selected because of their economic comparability and the likelihood that those countries maintained vital records most accurately. In January and February 1996, the ministry of health or the national statistics institute in each of the twenty-six countries were asked to provide denominator data and counts by

From *Morbidity and Mortality Weekly Report* 46, no. 5 (February 7, 1997): 101.

sex and by five-year age groups for the most recent year data were available for the number of suicides (International Classification of Diseases, Ninth Revision [ICD-9], codes E950.0-E959), homicides (E960.0-E969), suicides by firearm (E955.0-E955.4), homicides by firearm (E965.0-E965.4), unintentional deaths caused by firearm (E922.0-E922.9), and firearm-related deaths for which intention was undetermined (E985.0-E985.4); twenty-six (96 percent) countries, including the United States, provided complete data.* Twenty (77 percent) countries provided data for 1993 or 1994; the remaining countries provided data for 1990, 1991, 1992, or 1995. Cause-specific rates per 100,000 population were calculated for three groups (children aged 0–4 years, 5–14 years, and 0–14 years). The rates for homicide and suicide by means other than firearms were calculated by subtracting the firearm-related homicide and firearm-related suicide rates from the overall homicide and suicide rates. Rates for the United States were compared with rates based on pooled data for the other twenty-five countries. Of the 161 million children aged [less than] 15 years during the first year for which data were provided, 57 million (35 percent) were in the United States and 104 million (65 percent) were in the other twenty-five countries.

Overall, the data provided by the twenty-six countries included a total of 2,872 deaths among children aged [less than] 15 years for a period of one year. Homicides accounted for 1,995 deaths, including 1,177 (59 percent) in boys and 818 (41 percent) in girls. Of the homicides, 1,464 (73 percent) occurred among U.S. children. The homicide rate for children in the United States was five times higher than that for children in the other twenty-five countries combined (2.57 per 100,000 compared with 0.51) (table 1).

Suicide accounted for the deaths of 599 children, including 431 (72 percent) in boys and 168 (28 percent) in girls. Of the suicides, 321 (54 percent) occurred among U.S. children. The suicide rate for children in the United States was two times higher than that in the other twenty-five countries combined (0.55 compared with 0.27) (table 1). No suicides were reported among children aged [less than] 5 years.

A firearm was reported to have been involved in the deaths of 1,107 children; 957 (86 percent) of those occurred in the United States. Of all firearm-related deaths, 55 percent were reported as homicides; 20 percent, as suicides; 22 percent, as unintentional; and 3 percent, as intention undetermined. The overall firearm-related death rate among U.S. children aged [less than] 15 years was nearly twelve times higher than among children in the other twenty-five countries combined (1.66 compared with 0. 14) (table 1). The firearm-related homicide rate in the United States was nearly sixteen times higher than that in all of the other countries combined (0.94 compared with 0.06); the firearm-related suicide rate was nearly

---

*Complete data were provided by Australia, Austria, Belgium, Canada, Denmark, England and Wales, Finland, France, Germany, Hong Kong, Ireland, Israel, Italy, Japan, Kuwait, Netherlands, New Zealand, Northern Ireland, Norway, Scotland, Singapore, Sweden, Spain, Switzerland, Taiwan, and the United States. In this analysis, Hong Kong, Northern Ireland, and Taiwan are considered as countries.

Table 1. Rates* of homicide, suicide, and firearm-related death† among children aged [less than] 15 years—United States and twenty-five other industrialized countries.§

Age group (yrs)	Total homicide	Total suicide	Firearms-related deaths				
			Homicide	Suicide	Unintentional	Intention undetermined	Total
0-4							
U.S.	4.10	0	0.43	0	0.15	0.01	0.59
Non-U.S.	0.95	0	0.05	0	0.01	0.01	0.07
Ratio U.S.:Non-U.S.	4.3:1		8.6:1		15.0:1	1.0:1	8.4:1
5-14							
U.S.	1.75	0.84	1.22	0.49	0.46	0.06	2.23
Non-U.S.	0.30	0.40	0.07	0.05	0.05	0.01	0.18
Ratio U.S.:Non-U.S.	5.:1	2.1:1	17.4:1	9.8:1	9.2:1	6.0:1	12.4:1
0-14							
U.S.	2.57	0.55	0.94	0.32	0.36	0.04	1.66
Non-U.S.	0.51	0.27	0.06	0.03	0.04	0.01	0.14
Ratio U.S.:Non-US.	5.0:1	2.0:1	15.7:1	10.7:1	9.0:1	4.0:1	11.9:1

*Per 100,000 children in each age group and for 1 year during 1990–1995.

†Homicides (International Classification of Diseases, Ninth Revision, codes E960.0-E969), suicides (E950.0E959), homicides by firearrn (E965.0-E965.4), suicides by firearm (E955.0-E955.4), unintentional deaths caused by firearm (E922.0-E922.9), and firearm-related deaths for which intention was undetermined (E985.0-E985.4).

§All countries classified in the high-income group with populations [is greater than or equal to] I million (5) that provided complete data (Australia, Austria, Belgium, Canada, Denmark, England and Wales, Finland, France, Germany, Hong Kong, Ireland, Israel, Italy Japan, Kuwait, Netherlands, New Zealand, Northern Ireland, Norway, Scotland, Singapore, Sweden Spain, Switzerland and Taiwan). In this analysis, Hong Kong, Northern Ireland, and Taiwan are considered as countries.

elevent times higher (0.32 compared with 0.03); and the unintentional firearm-related death rate was nine times higher (0.36 compared with 0.04). For all countries, males accounted for most of the firearm-related homicides (67 percent), firearm-related suicides (77 percent), and unintentional firearm-related deaths (89 percent). The nonfirearm-related homicide rate in the United States was nearly four times the rate in all of the other countries (1.63 compared with 0.45), and nonfirearm-related suicide rates were similar in the United States and in all of the other countries combined (0.23 compared with 0.24).

The rate for firearm-related deaths among children in the United States (1.66) was 2.7-fold greater than that in the country with the next highest rate (Finland, 0.62) (figure 1). Except for rates for firearm-related suicide in Northern Ireland and firearm-related fatalities of unknown intent in Austria, Belgium, and Israel, rates for all types of firearm-related deaths were higher in the United States than in the other countries. However, among all other countries, the impact of firearm-related deaths varied substantially. For example, five countries, including three of the four countries in Asia, reported no firearm-

FIGURE 1. Rates* of firearm-related death† among children aged <15 years — 26 indus-trialized countries§

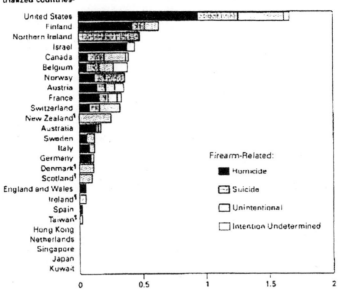

*Per 100,000 children in each aged <15 years and for 1 year during 1990–1995.

†Homicides by firearm (*International Classification of Diseases, Ninth Revision*, codes E965.0-E954), suicides by firearm (E955.0-E955.4), unintentional deaths caused by firearm (E922.0-E922.9), and firearm-related deaths for which intention was undetermined (E985.0-E985.4).

§All countries classified in the high-income group with populations 21 million (5) that provided complete data. In this analysis, Hong Kong, Northern Ireland, and Taiwan are considered as countries.

¶Reported only unintentional firearm-related deaths.

related deaths among children. In comparison, firearms were the primary cause of homicide in Finland, Israel, Australia, Italy, Germany, and England and Wales. Five countries (Denmark, Ireland, New Zealand, Scotland, and Taiwan) reported only unintentional firearm-related deaths.

Reported by: Div of Violence Prevention, National Center for Injury Prevention and Control, CDC.

Editorial Note: The findings in this report document a high rate of death among U.S. children associated with violence and unintentional firearm-related injuries, particularly in comparison with other industrialized countries. Even though rates in all other countries were lower than those in the United States, rates among other countries varied substantially and were particularly low in some countries. Although specific reasons for the differences in rates among countries are unknown, previous studies have reported on the associations between rates of violent childhood death and low funding for social programs,[6] economic stress related to participation of women in the labor force,[7,8] divorce, ethnic-linguistic heterogeneity, and social acceptability of violence.[9]

The findings of the analysis in this report are subject to at least three limitations. First, although the data were obtained from official sources and were based on ICD-9 codes, the sensitivity and specificity of the vital records and reporting systems may have varied by country. Second, because 21 countries (81 percent) each reported [less than] 10 firearm-related deaths among children aged 0–14 years, the firearm-related death rates for those countries, when not pooled, are unstable and may vary substantially for different years. Finally, only one half of the countries (including the United States) reported all four digits of the ICD-9 codes for firearm-related deaths; the fourth digit distinguishes whether deaths were caused by injuries from firearms or by other explosives. For countries in which this distinction could not be made, the firearm-related death rates may be overestimated slightly.

In May 1996, the 49th World Health Assembly adopted a resolution that declared violence a leading worldwide public health problem and urged all member states to assess the problem of violence and to communicate their findings to the World Health Organization.[10] Crosscultural comparisons may identify key factors (e.g., attitudinal, behavioral, educational, socioeconomic, or regulatory) not evident from intranational studies that could assist in the development of new country-specific strategies for preventing such deaths.

NOTES

1. G. K. Singh, S. M. Yu, "US childhood mortality, 1950 through 1993: trends and socioeconomic differentials," *American Journal of Public Health* 86 (1996): 505–12.

2. National Center for Health Statistics, *Health, United States, 1994* (Hyattsville, Md.: U.S. Department of Health and Human Services, Public Health Service, CDC, 1995).

3. G. K. Singh, K. D. Kochanek, and M. E. MacDorman, *Advance report of final mortality statistics, 1994* (Hyattsville, Md.: U.S. Department of Health and Human Services, Public Health Service, CDC, National Center for Health Statistics, 1996). (Monthly vital statistics report; vol 45, no. 3, suppl).

4. K. G. Krug, L. L. Dahlberg and K. E. Powell "Childhood homicide, suicide, and firearm deaths: an international comparison." *World Health Statistics Quarterly* 49, no. 4 (1996).

5. World Bank, *World development report* (New York: Oxford University Press, 1994) pp. 251–52.

6. R. Garnter "Family structure, welfare spending, and child homicide in developed democracies, *Journal of Marriage and Family* 53 (1991): 231–40.

7. R. Fiala, G. LaFree "Cross-national determinants of child homicide," *American Sociological Review* 53 (1988): 432–45.

8. R. Gartner "The victims of homicide: a temporal and cross-national comparison," *American Sociological Review* 55 (1990): 92–106.

9. C. M. Briggs, and P. Cutright "Structural and cultural determinants of child homicide: a cross-national analysis," *Violence Vict* 9 (1994): 3–16.

10. World Health Assembly,. *Prevention of violence: public health priority* (Geneva, Switzerland: World Health Organization, 1996). (Resolution no. WHA49.25).

18

INTERNATIONAL COMPARISONS AND THE KILLIAS RESEARCH

GARY KLECK

One of the least productive lines of inquiry in the gun control debate has been to make pairwise comparisons of the United States with other nations. It is unproductive because the game has been played in such a way that either side can win regardless of whether there is any merit to their claims. Gun control supporters like to selectively contrast the high-gun ownership/high-violence United States with nations having both low-gun ownership and low-violence rates (homicide data are usually cited), such as Great Britain or Japan, concluding that low gun ownership must have contributed to the low violence rates. On the other hand, opponents like to selectively cite high-gun/low-violence nations such as Switzerland or low-gun/high-violence nations such as Mexico, and conclude that gun ownership either has no impact on violence, or actually reduces it. Obviously, pairwise comparison of two selected cases is useless for establishing causal connections, or the lack thereof (see Sloan et al. [1988] for a particularly egregious example). Assuming there is not a perfect association between gun and violence levels, out of any large number of possible pairings, it is safe to say that at least a few pairs can be found to appear to support either side, just as one can find, in a large sample, some smokers without lung cancer and some nonsmokers with lung cancer.

In some cases the comparisons of nations are patently ridiculous. To do no

Reprinted with permission from Gary Kleck, *Targeting Guns: Firearms and Their Control* (Hawthorne, N.Y.: Aldine de Gruyter, 1997), pp. 251–55. Copyright © 1997 by Walter de Gruyter, Inc., New York.

more than compare homicide rates in Japan and the United States and claim to know whether any of the huge difference in homicide rates is attributable to differences in gun ownership levels is ludicrous. The two nations differ enormously on almost all hypothesized determinants of homicide rates, including degree of social solidarity, cultural and ethnic homogeneity, history of racial conflict, hierarchical rigidity, obedience to authority, and subjective sense of unjust deprivation. Further, most of these differences are not currently measured, making it impossible to empirically disentangle effects of these variables from effects of gun levels on homicide.

One way one might crudely and partially control for United States-Japan cultural differences is to compare homicide rates among Japanese-Americans, who live where guns are plentiful, with the homicide rates of their presumably culturally more similar counterparts in Japan, where private gun ownership is nearly nonexistent. Certainly this pair of populations is more comparable than the population of Japan compared with the entire U.S. population. Up through 1979, the FBI reported homicide arrests sorted by racial breakdowns that included "Japanese." For the period 1976–1978, only 21 of 48,695 arrests for murder and nonnegligent manslaughter were of Japanese-Americans, or 0.04 percent (U.S. FBI [Uniform Crime Reports] 1977–1979). Applying this fraction to the total of 57,460 homicides yields an estimate of 24.78 killings by Japanese-Americans for 1976–1978, or about 8.26 per year. With 791,000 persons of Japanese ancestry in the United States in 1980 (U.S. Bureau of the Census 1984), this translates into an annual rate of 1.04 homicides per 100,000 population. For the same 1976–1978 period, the annual homicide rate in Japan averaged 2.45 (United Nations 1982:192, 718). Thus, crudely controlling for Japanese culture in this way indicates that in Japan, where civilian gun ownership is virtually nonexistent and gun control laws are extremely strict, the homicide rate is 2.3 times as high as it is among Japanese-Americans living where guns are easily available and gun laws are far less restrictive.

A critic could object that there are still many uncontrolled differences between these two populations, and such a critic would be quite correct. These sorts of primitive crossnational comparisons tell us little about the guns-violence link. One would hope, however, that this criticism would be even-handedly applied to all such comparisons, whether used to spuriously buttress either progun or antigun arguments. The preceding exercise merely served to demonstrate that one simple "control" can make a large crossnational violence rate difference disappear altogether, and even reverse its direction.

The reasoning used in crossnational comparisons is also very selective. Great Britain is often compared with the United States and it is noted that the former has a much lower total homicide rate, and also a lower gun homicide rate. This fact is supposed to nail down the claim that it is gun ownership that causes the homicide rate differences. However, the absurdity of the logic becomes evident once it is applied to nongun homicides. Britain's rates of killings with hands and feet are also far lower than the corresponding rates in the United States, but no one is foolish enough to infer from these facts that the lower violence rates were due to the British having fewer hands and feet than Americans (Greenwood 1972:37).

In earlier research, a major obstacle to judging whether gun ownership accounts for any of the homicide rate differences between nations was the absence of any actual data on gun ownership levels in the foreign nations compared to the United States. Recently, international data based on a more direct measure of gun ownership have become available for a small sample of nations, allowing research to go beyond crude comparison of just two nations. Telephone surveys asking about gun ownership were conducted in 1989 and 1992 in eighteen countries, including the United States. The percentage of households with guns in these countries was reported by Killias (1993b), along with their homicide rates. There were significant correlations between gun prevalence and both the gun homicide and total homicide rates, so Killias concluded that higher gun ownership levels cause higher homicide rates. Killias, however, did not inform his readers that the positive "international" guns-homicide association is entirely attributable to the inclusion of a single extreme observation, the United States. Contrary to his claim that "the overall correlation is not contingent upon a few countries with extreme scores on the dependent and independent variable" (ibid.:294), reanalysis of the data reveals that if one excludes only the United States from the sample there is no significant association between gun ownership and the total homicide rate. Killias reported a marginally significant correlation of .441 (p = .044) with two of his eighteen nations excluded, but the correlation based on a sample with *only* the United States excluded is only .120 (p = .324). Thus, the homicide-guns association reported by Killias was not international at all, but merely reflected the unique status of the United States as a high-gun ownership/high-violence nation. Killias also did nothing to distinguish the effects of gun levels on homicide rates from the effects of homicide rates on gun ownership rates. Since the positive association Killias observed was entirely dependent on the U.S. case, where self-defense is a common reason for gun ownership, this supports the conclusion that the association was attributable to the impact of the homicide rates on gun levels. Note that none of this prevented McDowall and Loftin from referring to Killias's crude bivariate analysis as "excellent work" (1994:1158).

Data on a larger and more diverse sample of nations have recently become available. Krug and colleagues at CDC (1996) obtained homicide and suicide mortality data for thirty-six nations (including the United States) for the period 1990–1995. Because the data distinguished gun deaths from nongun deaths, they allow the computation of the percentage of suicides committed with guns, which has an almost perfect correlation with the percentage of households reporting gun ownership in surveys (r = .86 in Kleck 1991:194–95, across 170 U.S. cities; r = .91 in Killias 1993b:295, across sixteen nations). My computations indicate that across these thirty-six nations, the correlation between gun ownership levels and the total homicide rate was .2735 (p = .053), or .2004 (p = .124) if the United States is excluded. Thus, with or without the United States, there is no significant (at the 5 percent level) association between gun ownership levels and the total homicide rate in the largest sample of nations available to study this topic. (Associations with the total suicide rate were even weaker.)

Crossnational research holds little promise for assessing the impact of gun levels on violence levels, for several reasons. First, gun availability data are still available for only a handful of nations, making results extremely vulnerable to slight changes in the composition of the samples analyzed. Second, outside the United States, there is far less variation in gun prevalence across those nations for which data are available than there is across cities, states, or counties within the United States. For example, in the Killias sample, excluding the United States, the percentage of households with guns was confined to the range from 2 to 32 percent, while in the United States it ranges from as low as 1 or 2 percent in urban areas in the Northeast (Kleck and Patterson 1993) to as high as 80 percent or higher in rural areas of the West or South. For example, a 1990 survey of Montana adults found that 78 percent of Montana households report at least one gun (Floyd and Wilson 1990:17). Third, there are virtually no internationally comparable data on national cultures and other determinants of violence rates likely to be correlated with gun levels, making it impossible to separate the effects of gun levels from the effects of other possible determinants of violence rates. Finally, there are no internationally comparable data on the "instrument" variables that would allow an analyst to properly model the possible two-way relationship between gun and violence levels. In sum, crossnational comparisons do not provide a sound basis for assessing the impact of gun levels on crime or violence rates.

REFERENCES

Floyd, Joe, and Graig Wilson. 1990. "The Eastern Montana College poll of national, state, and local issues, February, 1990." Billings: Easter Montana College.

Greenwood, Colin. 1972. *Firearms Control: A Study of Armed Crime and Firearms Control in England and Wales.* London: Routledge.

Killas, Martin. 1993b. "Gun ownership, suicide, and homicide: An international perspective." In *Understanding Crime: Experiences of Crime and Crime Control.* Edited by Anna del Frate, Uglijesa Zvekic, and Jan J. M. van Diijk. Rome: UNICRI, pp. 289–303.

Kleck, Gary. 1991. Point Blank: Guns and Violence in America. Hawthorne, N.Y.: Aldine de Gruyter.

Kleck, Gary, and E. Britt Patterson. 1993. "The impact of gun control and gun ownership levels on violence rates." *Journal of Quantitative Criminology* 9: 249–88.

McDowall, David, and Colin Loftin. 1994. Letter to the Editor. *New England Journal of Medicine* 330:1158–59.

U.S. Bureau of the Census. 1971; 1976; 1979; 1981; 1982; 1983; 1984; 1986; 1987; 1988. Statistical Abstract of the United States 1976 (1981); 1982–83; 1984; 1987; 1988; 1989). Washington, DC: U.S. Government Printing Office.

U.S. Federal Bureau of Investigation. 162–1996. Crime in the United States (year)—Uniform Crime Reports (for years 1961–1995) Washington, D.C.: U.S. Government Printing Office.

Sloan, John Henry, Arthur L. Kellermann, Donald T. Reay, James A. Ferris, Thomas Koepsell, Frederick P. Rivara, Charles Rice, Laurel Gray, and James LoGerfo. 1990. "Handgun regulations, crime, assaults and homicide." *New England Journal of Medicine* 319:1256–62.

19

GUNS IN THE HOUSEHOLD

J. P. KASSIRER

Last October several bizarre coincidences led to the death of a sixteen-year-old Japanese exchange student in a suburb of Baton Rouge, Louisiana. The student and an American friend, looking for a Halloween party, missed the correct house by a few doors and rang the doorbell. The exchange student, in the spirit of holiday, was moving around in mimicry of John Travolta in the movie *Saturday Night Fever*, and the frightened woman who answered the door called to her husband to get his gun. The husband mistook a camera in the student's hand for a weapon, and when the student failed to respond to the command "Freeze!" he shot the boy in the chest with a .44 Magnum.[1-3]

We could be resigned about this unusual sequence of events: perhaps it is inevitable that unlikely coincidence time to time create just the right circumstances for such a tragedy. But we should not forget that the Japanese student would almost certainly be alive today if not for the presence in that house of a loaded handgun. Given the circumstances and the penchant for having such guns available for protection the jury's decision to acquit the husband was not surprising, and perhaps it was even appropriate. In the United States accidental and intentional deaths due to guns in and around the home are commonplace in most major cities, and a substantial proportion of an entire generation of young people are armed and prepared to shoot with little or no provocation.[4] People in Japan, however, lacked a framework for understanding either the

From the *New England Journal of Medicine* 329, no. 15 (October 7, 1993): 1117–19. Copyright © 1993 Massachusetts Medical Society. All rights reserved.

shooting or the verdict; with few exceptions, private ownership of guns is not permitted in their country.[3]

The study reported in this issue of the *Journal* by Kellermann and his colleagues[5] is the second of two population-based case-control studies that have focused on the home as a site of gun-related deaths. The current study focuses on homicides; the same authors reported on suicides about a year ago.[6] In the current study, carried out in three counties in Tennessee, Ohio, and Washington, interviews with proxies of homicide victims and matched controls disclosed that homes where homicides occurred were significantly more likely to contain firearms than neighboring homes that were not the scenes of homicides. After matching for four potentially confounding variables (age range, sex, race, and neighborhood) and controlling for five other variables, the investigators found that keeping a firearm in the home was associated with a risk of homicide nearly three times as high. Almost all of this increase was due to a greater risk of homicide by a family member or close acquaintance. Not unexpectedly, illicit drug use and domestic violence were important independent risk factors for homicide. In the earlier study, of suicide, there was a nearly fivefold increase in the risk of suicide in homes where guns were kept.[6] These are not the first studies to document the risk associated with having guns in the home, but they are among the most persuasive and, I believe, justify routine warnings about this risk by physicians and other health workers.

If we know that keeping handguns around the house is so dangerous, why do millions of people continue to do so? Paradoxically, the primary reason is for protection. Surveys of gun owners indicate that they believe guns protect them from intruders,[7,8] and the enormous increase in gun sales in the Los Angeles area following the riots in the spring of 1992 is further evidence of that conviction. Yet, we actually know little about the collective efficacy of guns in the home in warding off attacks. Estimates of the number of times per year that guns protect citizens (not necessarily only in the home) vary widely, from 80,000 to a million,[7-9] but neither statistics kept by law-enforcement agencies nor any existing polls of citizens have provided accurate data. And the anecdotal reports of crime rates that fall after part or all of the populace of small towns is armed are badly flawed.[7,10] We do know that when guns are readily available, children accidentally kill their siblings and friends, depressed people impulsively kill themselves (they are more successful when the weapon is a gun), teenagers settle minor arguments with guns rather than with words or fists, drive-by shootings are reported nearly every week, and psychologically scarred people kill fellow workers and others seemingly at random. The study by Kellermann and his colleagues found no protective benefit of gun ownership in the home even in the homicide cases that followed forced entry.[5]

Meanwhile, congress is idle on gun control. The Brady bill, which mandates a five-day waiting period and background checks before a gun may be purchased, failed to be enacted last year, but it will be introduced again this fall.* I

---

*The Brady Act was implemented in 1994.—Ed.

doubt that the Brady bill is strong enough to make a difference in handgun-associated deaths, and I favor more stringent regulations and restrictions on handguns and assault weapons. Although assault rifles account for less than 3 percent of the privately owned firearms in this country, they are used in a proportionately larger fraction of crimes. Despite the limitations of the Brady bill, it is a reasonable beginning. Might passage of this bill be the beginning of a series of more restrictive statutes? Yes, it could be and should be.

How can we get meaningful gun control legislation passed given the putative power of the gun lobby, which uses its funds to support national and local political candidates who oppose gun control, harasses gun control advocates with thousands of letters and telephone calls, and carries out public relations campaigns to persuade citizens to support its views?[13] There are promising signs. The National Rifle Association (NRA) is not the monolith its popular image projects; instead, it is chronically beset by internal squabbling over power.[13] Even more encouraging, the popular movement to control the availability of guns is gaining acceptance. Many citizens have now concluded that we have exceeded the "killing threshold,"[14] and a great many have decided that something must be done about private ownership of handguns and assault weapons.[15] Polls for the past 15 years have consistently shown that about two-thirds of citizens support stricter gun control laws,[16] and in a nationwide poll of adults reported only a few months ago, 52 percent favored a federal ban on handgun ownership, 63 percent supported a federal ban on the sale of automatic and semiautomatic weapons, and 82 percent favored handgun registration by federal authorities. Nearly 90 percent of those sampled (and 68 percent of NRA members) declared their support for the Brady bill.[15]

Many parts of society have begun to act. In recent years police departments across the country have led a campaign against possession of certain types of weapons and ammunition, and at least five states (California, Connecticut, Hawaii, New Jersey, and New York) have banned assault rifles.[17,18] In some states (Arkansas, Missouri, and Texas) legislation has been defeated that would have allowed citizens to carry concealed weapons,[19] and other states have defeated attempts to turn back gun control legislation already on the books. Some cities have mounted gun buy-back programs. In 1993 alone, gun control advocates have scored victories in 11 states (Arkansas, California, Connecticut, Indiana, Minnesota, Missouri, New Jersey, New York, Ohio, Texas, and Virginia). Even the Federal Bureau of Investigation has broken its tradition of neutrality on gun control and proposed national restrictions, including a five-day waiting period before a gun could be purchased, regulation of gun dealers, and restrictions on the possession of assault rifles and certain kinds of ammunition.[20] And finally, Attorney General Janet Reno recently urged the American people to rise up against the gun lobby's unswerving opposition to gun control.[21]

High-quality epidemiologic research is the latest challenge to the gun lobby. Although a cadre of gun advocates (some of them physicians) try hard to discredit all research of this kind, solid data are accumulating on the populations at risk for injury from firearms, the kinds of weapons involved, and the trade-off between the risks and benefits of private gun ownership.[22–24] Fortunately, the facts speak for themselves, as the two studies by Kellermann and his colleagues[5,6] illustrate. Considerably more federal support for research of this kind is warranted.

Although the gun lobby has deep pockets, its resources are not infinite. Over the past two years the NRA has posted multimillion-dollar losses, and it anticipates a continued large loss this year.[25] In two local political battles alone (New Jersey and Virginia), the NRA spent close to a million dollars[26] (and Katz L: personal communication). Some of its members have expressed serious concern about its deficit spending.[25] As an index of its financial status, the NRA has had to shift funds out of its education and sport-shooting divisions over the past decade into its political arm.[13] Resourceful advocates of gun control might consider enlisting the help of more courageous politicians, such as governors Florio and Wilder, Congressman Andrews, and Senator DeConcini and mounting campaigns to introduce gun control legislation around the country. Countering such efforts could be quite expensive for the NRA.

Gun control advocates should not be unrealistic, however. Rather than set their sights next on a total ban on gun possession, they might try first to craft proposals that would receive wide public support. They could espouse new design standards for firearms, for example, mandating devices that indicate whether a gun is loaded and requiring locks on guns that can be unlocked only by those knowing the code. They could support the registration of firearms and licensing of all gun owners to make it easier for police to trace stolen weapons. They could introduce federal legislation that would proscribe bringing a gun into a school. And they could support a federal ban on the sale of automatic and semiautomatic weapons. If such laws were implemented we could assess their efficacy; if we still found them wanting we would be justified in supporting even more stringent restrictions.

No matter how reasonable some of these less restrictive proposals seem, the gun lobby in recent years has regularly taken an absolutist position, attempting to thwart all gun control legislation and trying not only to maintain the status quo but also to roll back existing legislation. The efforts of this lobby should not be underestimated. One of their spokesmen, promising to use funds to unseat legislators in New Jersey who "betrayed" him, declared; "We're in this forever because we're fighting for freedom. You don't quit on freedom."[26] Even more compelling is a letter I received from a surgeon on the West Coast after publication of my 1991 editorial[14] (Hunt TK: personal communication). He said, "Guns are single simple answers for situations they (members of the NRA) fear they will face. If anyone asks you, send them to me. I once had to go from the operating room to tell a young couple that their little boy was dead—shot while playing with his father's handgun. The mother collapsed into tears. The father, who told me he was an NRA member, did not cry, but became visibly angry, saying, 'I taught the dumb kid how to use it right.' That kind of passion dies hard."

NOTES

1. "Defense depicts Japanese boy as 'scary,'" *New York Times*, May 1991, p. A10.

2. "Acquittal in doorstep killing of Japanese student," *New York Times*, 14 May 1993, p. Al.

3. T. R. Reid, "Japanese media disparage acquittal in 'freeze case': commentators see America as a sick nation," *Washington Post*, 25 May 1993, p. A14.

4. "A survey of experiences, perceptions, and apprehensions about guns among young people in America New York." LH Research, July 1993.

5. Al Kellermann, F. P. Rivara, N. B. Rushforth et al., "Gun ownership as a risk factor for homicide in the home," *New England Journal of Medicine* 329 (1993): 1084–91.

6. Al Kellermann, F. P. Rivara, G. Somes et al. "Suicide in the home in relation to gun ownership," *New England Journal of Medicine* 327 (1992): 467–72.

7. P. J. Cook, "The technology of personal violence," in *Crime and Justice: A Review of Research*, vol. 14, ed. M. Tonry (Chicago: University of Chicago Press, 1991), pp. 1–71.

8. G. Kleck *Point Bank: Guns and Violence in America* (New York: Aldine de Gruyter, 1991).

9. L. Pratt "Little guns, big equalizers," *Wall Street Journal*, 3 April 1992A.

10. D. McDowall, A. J. Uzone, and B. Wiersema, "General deterrence through civilian gun ownership: an evaluation of the quasi-experimental evidence," *Criminology* 29 (1991): 541–59.

11. W. Edel, "Assault weapons are designed for murder," *New York Times*, 23 September 1992, p. A26.

12. R. O'Harrow Jr. and B. Miller, "Power, price, and availability make assault weapon popular," *Washington Post*, 28 January 1993, p. B4.

13. O. G. Davidson, "Under fire: the NRA and the battle for gun control," New York: Henry Holt, 1993.

14. J. P. Kassirer, "Firearms and the killing threshold." *New England Journal of Medicine* 325 (1991): 1647–50.

15. *A survey of the American people on guns as a children's health issue* (New York: LH Research, June 1993).

16. W. Schneider, "Why such trouble now for gun lobby?" *Boston Herald*, 11 March 1993, p. 17.

17. K. Sack, "Gun-control battles reveal gradual shifts," *New York Times*, 13 June 1993, pp. 37–41,

18. "Handguns, politics, and people," *Washington Post*, 16 June 1993, p. A20.

19. "Gunfighting: state by state," *Newsweek*, 21 June 1993, p. 8.

20. D. Johnston, "F.B.I., in shift, proposes backing gun control," *New York Times*, 8 July 1993, p. A13.

21. I. F. Engardio, "Reno calls on NRA lobby to get lost," *Boston Globe*, 13 August 1993, pp. 1, 10.

22. M. F. Goldsmith, "Epidemiologists aim at new target: health risk of handgun proliferation," *JAMA* 161 (1989): 675–76.

23. P. Cotton, "Gun-associated violence increasingly viewed as public health challenge," *JAMA* 267 (1992): 11714.

24. G. Taubes, "Violence epidemiologists test the hazards of gun ownership," *Science* 258 (1992): 213–15.

25. P. H. Stone, "Is the NRA bleeding internally?" *National Journal*, 13 March 1993, p. 626.

26. M. Gladwell, "New Jersey gun ban survives repeal vote," *Washington Post*, 16 March 1993, p. A3.

20

GUN OWNERSHIP AS A RISK FACTOR FOR HOMICIDE IN THE HOME

ARTHUR L. KELLERMANN, M.D., M.P.H., ET AL.*

*A*bstract *Background*. It is unknown whether keeping a firearm in the home confers protection against crime or, instead, increases the risk of violent crime in the home. To study risk factors for homicide in the home, we identified homicides occurring in the homes of victims in three metropolitan counties.

Methods. After each homicide, we obtained data from the police or medical examiner and interviewed a proxy for the victim. The proxies' answers were compared with those of control subjects who were matched to the victims according to neighborhood, sex, race, and age range. Crude and adjusted odds ratios were calculated with matched-pairs methods.

Results. During the study period, 1860 homicides occurred in the three counties, 444 of them (23.9 percent) in the home of the victim. After excluding 24 cases for various reasons, we interviewed proxy respondents for 93 percent of the victims. Controls were identified for 99 percent of these, yielding 388 matched pairs. As compared with the controls, the victims more often lived alone or rented their residence. Also, case households more commonly contained an illicit-drug user, a person with prior arrests, or someone who had been hit or hug in a fight in the home. After controlling for these characteristics, we found that keeping a gun in the home was strongly and independently associ-

From the *New England Journal of Medicine* 329, no. 15 (October 7, 1993): 1084–91. Copyright © 1993 Massachusetts Medical Society. All rights reserved.

*Frederick P. Rivara M.D., M.P.H., Norman B. Rushforth, Ph.D., Joyce G. Banton, M.S., Donald T. Reay, M.D., Jerry T. Francisco, M.D., Ana B. Locci, Ph.D., Janice Prodzinski, B.A., Bela B. Hackman, M.D., and Grant Somes, Ph.D.

ated with an increased risk of homicide (adjusted odds ratio, 2.7; 95 percent confidence interval, 1.6 to 4.4). Virtually all of this risk involved homicide by a family member or intimate acquaintance.

Conclusions. The use of illicit drugs and a history of physical fights in the home are important risk factors for homicide in the home. Rather than confer protection, guns kept in the home are associated with an increase in the risk of homicide by a family member or intimate acquaintance (*New England Journal of Medicine* 329 [1993]: 1084–91).

Homicide claims the lives of approximately 24,000 Americans each year, making it the eleventh leading cause of death among all age groups, the second leading cause of death among all people 15 to 24 years old, and the leading cause of death among male African Americans 15 to 34 years old.[1] Homicide rates declined in the United States during the early 1980s but rebounded thereafter.[2] One category of homicide that is particularly threatening to our sense of safety is homicide in the home.

Unfortunately, the influence of individual and household characteristics on the risk of homicide in the home is poorly understood. Illicit-drug use, alcoholism, and domestic violence are widely believed to increase the risk of homicide, but the relative importance of these factors is unknown. Frequently cited options to improve home security include the installation of electronic security systems, burglar bars, and reinforced security doors. The effectiveness of these protective measures is unclear, however.

Many people also keep firearms (particularly handguns) in the home for personal protection. One recent survey determined that handgun owners are twice as likely as owners of long guns to report "protection from crime" as their single most important reason for keeping a gun in the home.[3] It is possible, however. that the risks of keeping a firearm in the home may outweigh the potential benefits.[4]

To clarify these issues, we conducted a population-based case-control study to determine the strength of the association between a variety of potential risk factors and the incidence of homicide in the home.

METHODS

Identification of Cases

Shelby County, Tennessee; King County, Washington; and Cuyahoga County, Ohio, are the most populous counties in their respective states. The population of King County is predominantly white and enjoys a relatively high standard of living. In contrast, 44 percent of the population of Shelby County and 25 percent of the population of Cuyahoga Country are African American. Fifteen percent of the households in Shelby County and 11 percent in Cuyahoga County live below the povery level, as compared with 5 percent in King County.[5–7]

All homicides involving residents of King County or Shelby County that occurred between August 23, 1987, and August 23, 1992, and all homicides involving residents of Cuyahoga County that occurred between January 1, 1990, and August 23, 1992, were reviewed to identify those that took place in the home of the victim. Any death ruled a homicide was included, regardless of the method used. Assault-related injuries that were not immediately fatal were included if death followed within three months. Cases of homicide involving children twelve years of age or younger were excluded at the request of the medical examiners.

Selection of Case Subjects and Recruitment of Case Proxies

A home was defined as any house, apartment, or dwelling occupied by a victim (i.e., a case subject) as that person's principal residence. Homicides occurring in adjacent structures (e.g., a garage) or the surrounding yard were also included. Murder-suicides and multiple homicides were considered a single event. In the case of a murder-suicide, the homicide victim was included if he or she was older than the suicide victim; in multiple homicides, the oldest victim was included.

Reports made at the scene were collected to ensure that study criteria were met. In King County, the medical examiner's staff conducted all investigations of the homicide scene. In Shelby County and Cuyahoga County, police detectives conducted these investigations. In addition to recording the details of the incident for law enforcement purposes, investigators obtained the names of persons close to the victim who might provide us with an interview at a later date, thereby serving as proxies for the victim. These lists were supplemented with names obtained from newspaper accounts, obituaries, and calls to funeral homes.

Approximately three weeks after a victim's death, each proxy was sent a signed letter outlining the nature of the project. A $10 incentive was offered, and a follow-up telephone call was made a few days later to arrange a time and place for an interview. At the time of this meeting, informed consent was obtained.

Selection and Recruitment of Controls

After each interview with a case proxy, we sought a control subject matched to the case subject according to sex, race, age range (15 to 24 years, 25 to 40 years, 41 to 60 years, and 61 or older), and neighborhood of residence. To minimize selection bias, the controls were identified by a previously validated procedure for the random selection of a matching household in the neighborhood.[8-10] After marking off a one-block avoidance zone around the home of the case subject, the interviewer started a neighborhood census at a randomly assigned point along a predetermined route radiating out from the case subject's residence. Households where no one was home were approached twice more, at different times of day and on different days of the week. If contact could not be established after three tries, no further efforts were made. After each neighborhood census was completed, an adult (a person 18 years old or older) in the first household with a member who met the matching criteria was offered a $10 incentive and asked to provide an interview. Whenever possible, attempts were made to interview a proxy for the actual matching control subject. When no interview was granted, the next matching household on the route was approached. If a closer match on the route was found on the second or third visit to the neighborhood, an adult respondent in the closer household was interviewed and any earlier, more distant interviews were discarded. Overall, census data were obtained from 70 percent of the households approached to identify each match. Eighty-four percent of the interviews were obtained from the closest matching household, 13 percent from the second, 3 percent from the third, and less than 1 percent from the fourth.

Interviews

Case and control interviews were identical in format, order, and content. Each was brief, highly structured, and arranged so that more sensitive questions were not broached until later in the interview. Items drawn from the Short Michigan Alcoholism Screening Test,[11] the Hollingshead-Wilson two-factor index of social position,[12] and a 1978 poll of gun ownership by Decision Making Information[13] were included. Particularly sensitive questions were preceded by "permissive" statements, such as the following: "Many people have quarrels or fights. Has anyone in this household ever been hit or hurt in a fight in the home?"

Statistical Analysis

Data from reports prepared by medical examiners and police were used to describe the study population. Interview data were used for risk assessment, because these were collected in an analogous manner from the case proxies and matching control households. Since members of a household might acquire firearms or remove them from the home in response to a homicide in the neighborhood, answers were adjusted to reflect the state of affairs on the date of the homicide. Mantel-Haenszel chi-square analysis for matched pairs was used to calculate the crude odds ratio associated with each variable. Multivariate analyses used conditional logistic regression, the appropriate technique for a matched-pairs design.[14]

Potentially confounding variables were identified and controlled for by a two-step process. First, models containing closely related variables (such as those describing the use of alcohol in the home) were constructed to identify the variable or variables in each set that were most predictive of whether the household in question was a case or a control household. Next, a model that incorporated the variables selected in this initial step was constructed to select those that remained significant after we controlled for the effects of the remaining variables in the model. An additional model was constructed to look for interaction effects among the significant variables. Since no interaction terms significantly altered the adjusted odds ratios. the final model included six variables and was based on complete data from 316 matched pairs. After this analysis, an alternative modeling procedure was used to retain potentially confounding variables if they were even marginally significant (P<0.20). Although this approach added two variables, it did not significantly alter the adjusted odds ratios of the six included in our final model.

After completing this initial series of calculations, we examined the relation between homicide in the home and gun ownership, using various strata of the full study sample. To limit bias resulting from potentially faulty reporting, one analysis was limited to pairs with a case interview obtained from a proxy who lived in the home of the victim. To determine whether gun ownership was associated with an increased risk of homicide by firearms as compared with homicide by other means. cases were stratified according to method. To discern whether guns in the home decrease the risk of an intruder-related homicide or increase the risk of being killed by a family member, additional analyses stratified according to circumstance and the relationship between the victim and the offender were also conducted. After these were completed, a comparable series of stratified analyses was performed to assess more clearly the relation between homicide and previous violence in the home.

RESULTS

Study Population

There were 1,860 homicides in the three counties during the study period. Four hundred forty-four (23.9 percent) took place in the home of the victim. After we excluded the younger victim in 19 double deaths, 2 homicides that were not reported to project staff, and 3 late changes to a death certificate, 420 cases (94.6 percent) were available for study.

Reports on the Scene

Most of the homicides occurred inside the victim's home (table 1). Eleven percent occurred outside the home but within the immediate property lines. Two hundred sixty-five victims (63.1 percent) were men; 36.9 percent were women. A majority of the homicides (50.9 percent) occurred in the context of a quarrel or a romantic triangle. An additional 4.5 percent of the victims were killed by a family member or an intimate acquaintance as part of a murder-suicide. Thirty-two homicides (7.6 percent) were related to drug dealing, and 92 homicides (21.9 percent) occurred during the commission of another felony, such as a robbery, rape, or burglary. No motive other than homicide could be established in 56 cases (13.3 percent).

The great majority of the victims (76.7 percent) were killed by a relative or

Table 1. Characteristics of 420 Homicides Committed in the Homes of the Victims.*

Characteristic	No. (%) of victims	Characteristic	No. (%) of victims
Scene		Relationship of offender to victim	
Inside residence	373 (88.8)	Spouse	70 (6.7)
Within immediate property line	47 (11.2)	Intimate acquaintance	58 (13–8)
Sex of victim		First-degree relative	40 (9.5)
Female	155 (36.9)	Other relative	12 (2.9)
male	265 (63.1)	Roommate	12 (2.9)
Race or ethnic group of victim		Friend or acquaintance	130 (31.0)
White	140 (33.3)	Police officer	4 (1.0)
Black	260 (61.9)	stranger	15 (3.6)
Native American, Eskimo, Aleut	4 (1.0)	Unknown (unidentified suspect)	73 (17.4)
Asian or Pacific Islander	7 (1.7)	Other	6 1.4
Other	9 (2.1)	Method of homicide	
Age group of victim (yr)		Handgun	180 (42.9)
15–24	58 (13.8)	Rifle	10 (2,4)
25–40	171 (40.7)	Shotgun	15 (3.6)
41–60	106 (25.2)	Unknown firearm	4 (1.0)
≥61	85 (20.2)	Knife or sharp instrument	111 (26.4)
Circumstances		Blunt instrumentt	49 (11.7)
Altercation or quarrel	185 (44.0)	Strangulation or suffocation	27 (6.4)
Romantic triangle	29 (6.9)	Burns, smoke, scalding	0 (2.4)
Murder-suicide	19 (4.5)	Other	14 (3.3)
Felony-related	92 (21,9)	Victim resisted assailant	
Drug dealing	32 (7.6)	Yes	184 (43.8)
Homicide only	56 (13.3)	No	140 (33.3)
Other	7 (1.7)	Not noted	96 (22.9)
		Evidence of forced entry	
		Yes	59 (14.0)
		No	354 (84.3)
		Not noted	7 (1.7)

*Because of rounding, so all percentages total 100.

someone known to them. Homicides by a stranger accounted for only 15 cases (3.6 percent). The identity of the offender could not be established in 73 cases (17.4 percent). The remaining cases involved other offenders or police acting in the line of duty.

Two hundred nine victims (49.8 percent) died from gunshot wounds. A knife or some other sharp instrument was used to kill 111 victims (26.4 percent). The remaining victims were either bludgeoned (11.7 percent), strangled (6.4 percent), or killed by other means (5.7 percent).

Evidence of forced entry was noted in 59 cases (14.0 percent). Eighteen of these involved an unidentified intruder; six involved strangers. Two involved the police. The rest involved a spouse, family member, or some other person known to the victim.

Table 2. Demographic Characteristics of 388 Pairs of Case Subjects and Controls.*

Characteristic	Case Subjects	Controls
Sex (%)		
Male	63.1	63.1
Female	36.9	36.9
Race or ethnic group		
White	32.9	34.5
Black	62.1	61.6
Native American, Eskimo, Aleut	1.0	0.5
Asian or Pacific Islander	2.8	2.8
Other	1.0	0.5
Age group—yr (%)		
15–24	13.1	13.1
25–40	40.2	40.5
41–60	26.0	26.0
≥61	20.6	20.4
Median years of education of household head	12	12
Median socioeconomic status of household head †	4	4
Type of dwelling (%)		
House	54.6	60.3
Other	45.4	39.7
Rented	70.4	47.3
Owned	29.6	52.7
Median no. of residents/room	0.5	0.6
Lived alone (%)	26.8	11.9
Telephone interview (%)	40.1	12.6
Proxy respondents interviewed	100	48.2

*Because of rounding, not all percentages total 100

†Socioeconomic status was measured according to the Hollingshead Score on a scale of 1 to 5, with 1 as the highest score.[12]

Attempted resistance was reported in 184 cases (43.8 percent). In 21 of these (5.0 percent) the victim unsuccessfully attempted to use a gun in self-defense. In 56.2 percent of the cases no specific signs of resistance were noted. Fifteen victims (3.6 percent) were killed under legally excusable circumstances. Four were shot by police acting in the line of duty. The rest were killed by another member of the household or a private citizen acting in self-defense.

Comparability of Case Subjects and Controls

Potential proxy respondents were identified for 405 of the 420 case subjects (96.4 percent). Interviews were obtained from 93 percent of those approached in Shelby County, 99 percent in Cuyahoga County, and 98 percent in King County. The households of those who agreed to be interviewed did not differ from the households of those who refused with respect to the age, sex, or race of the victim or the method of homicide (firearm versis other).

Interviews with a matching control were obtained for 99.7 percent of the case interviews, yielding 388 matched pairs. Three hundred fifty-seven pairs were matched for all three variables, 27 for two variables, and 4 for a single variable (sex). The demographic characteristics of the victims and controls were similar, except that the case subjects were more likely to have rented their homes (70.4 percent versus 47.3 percent) and to have lived alone (26.8 percent versus 11.9 percent) (table 2). Although efforts were made to conduct every interview in person, proxy respondents for the case subjects were much more 11 likely than the controls to request a telephone interview (40.2 percent versus 12.6 percent). Despite efforts to interview a proxy respondent for each control, only 48.2 percent of the control interviews were obtained in this manner.

Univariate Analysis

Alcohol was more commonly consumed by one or more members of the households of case subjects than by members of the households of controls (table 3). Alcohol was also more commonly consumed by the case subjects themselves than by their matched controls. Case subjects were reported to have manifested behavioral correlates of alcoholism (such as trouble at work due to drinking) much more often than matched controls. Illicit-drug use (by the case subject or another household member) was also reported more commonly by case households than control households.

Previous episodes of violence were reported more frequently by members of case households. When asked if anyone in the household had ever been hit or hurt in a fight in the home, 31.8 percent of the proxies for the case subjects answered affirmatively, as compared with only 5.7 percent of controls. Physical fights in the home while household members were drinking and fighting severe enough to cause injuries were reported much more commonly by case proxies than controls. One or more members of the case households were also more likely to have been arrested or to have been involved in a physical fight outside the home than members of control households.

Similar percentages of case and control households reported using deadbolt locks, window bars, or metal security doors. The case subjects were slightly less likely than the controls to have lived in a home with a burglar alarm, but they were slightly more likely to have controlled security access. Almost identical percentages of case and control households reported owning a dog.

One or more guns were reportedly kept in 45.4 percent of the homes of the case subjects, as compared with 35.8 percent of the homes of the control subjects (crude odds ratio, 1.6; 95 percent confidence interval, 1.2 to 2.2). Shotguns and rifles were kept by similar percentages of households, but the case households were significantly more likely to have a handgun (35.7 percent versus 23.3 percent; crude odds ratio, 1.9; 95 percent confidence interval, 1.4

Table 3. Univariate Analysis of Hypothesized Risk on Protection Factors Derived from Data on 388 Matched Pairs of Case Subjects and Controls

Variable	Case Subjects	Controls	Crude Odds Ratio (95% CI)*
	no. (%)†		
Behavioral factors			
Any household member drank alcoholic beverages	277 (73.3)	217 (55.9)	2.4 (1.7–3.3)
Case subject or control drank alcoholic beverages	238 (62.8)	162 (41.9)	2.6 (1.9–3.5)
Drinking caused problems in the household	92 (24.8)	22 (5.7)	7.0 (4.2–11.8)
Any household member had trouble at work because of drinking	32 (9.0)	3 (0.8)	10.7 (4.1–27.5)
Case subject or control had trouble at work because of drinking	20 (5.5)	1 (0.3)	20.0 (4.9–82.4)
Any household member hospitalized because of drinking	41 (11.4)	9 (2.3)	9.8 (4–2–22.5)
Case subject or control hospitalized because of drinking	28 (7.6)	2 (0.5)	14.0 (4.7–41.6)
Any household member used illicit drugs	111 (31.3)	23 (6.0)	9.0 (5.4–15.0)
Case subject or control used illicit drugs	74 (20.3)	16 (4.2)	6.8 (3.8–12.0)
Any physical fights in the home during drinking	92 (25.3)	13 (3.4)	8.9 (5.2–15.3)
Any household member hit or hurt in a fight in the home	117 (31.8)	22 (5.7)	7.9 (5.0–117)
Any family member required medical attention because of a fight in the home	62 (17.3)	8 (2.1)	10.2 (5.2–20.0)
Any adult household member involved in a physical fight outside the home	103 (29.9)	70 (18.8)	2.1 (1.4–3.0)
Any household member arrested	193 (52.7)	90 (23.4)	4.2 (3.0–6.0)
Case subject or control arrested	132 (36.0)	60 (15.7)	3.5 (2.4–5.2)
Environmental factors			
Home rented	271 (70.4)	183 (47–6)	5.9 (3.8–9.2)
Public housing	41 (11.1)	38 (9.8)	1.5 (0.7–3.3)
Case subject or control lived alone	103 (26.8)	46 (11.9)	3.4 (2.2–5.1)
Deadbolt locks	243 (68.8)	292 (75.3)	0.8 (0.5–1.0)
Window bars	71 (19.2)	81 (20–9)	0.8 (0.5–13)
Metal security door	95 (25.4)	104 (26.8)	0.9 (0.6–1.3)
Burglar alarm	26 (7.1)	43 (11.1)	0.6 (0.4– 1.0)§
Controlled security access to residence	52 (13.9)	38 (9.8)	2.3 (1.2–4.4)
Dog or dogs in home	94 (24.2)	87 (22.4)	1.1 (0.8–1.6)
Gun or guns in home	174 (45.4)	139 (35.8)	1.6 (1.2–2.2)
Handgun	135 (35.7)	90 (23.3)	1.9 (1.4–2.7)
Shotgun	50 (13.6)	65 (16.8)	0.7 (0.5–1.1)
Rifle	45 (12.2)	54 (13.9)	0–8 (0.5–1.3)
Any gun kept unlocked	105 (29.6)	69 (17.8)	2.1 (1.4–3.0)
Any gun kept loaded	93 (26.7)	48 (12.5)	2.7 (1.8–4.0)
Gun kept primarily for self–defense	125 (32.6)	86 (22.2)	1.7 (1.2–2.4)

*Results were calculated with the Mantel–Haenszel chi-square analysis for matched pairs, CI denotes confidence interval.

†Percentages reflect the proportion of subjects who responded yes among all subjects who gave a response.

§The value is statistically significant: the upper bound of the 95 percent confidence interval is 1.0 because of bounding.

to 2.7). Case households were also more likely than control households to contain a gun that was kept loaded or unlocked (table 3).

Multivariate Analysis

Six variables were retained in our final conditional logistic–regression model: home rented, case subject or control lived alone, any household member ever hit or hurt in a fight in the home, any household member ever arrested, any household member used illicit drugs, and one or more guns kept in the home (table 4). Each of these variables was strongly and independently associated with an increased risk of homicide in the home. No home-security measures retained significance in the final model. After matching for four characteristics and controlling for the effects of five more, we found that the presence of one or more firearms in the home was strongly associated with an increased risk of homicide in the home (adjusted odds ratio, 2.7; 95 percent confidence interval, 1.6 to 4.4).

Stratified analyses with our final regression model revealed that the link between guns and homicide in the home was present among women as well as men, blacks as well as whites, and younger as well as older people (table 5). Restricting the analysis to pairs with data from case proxies who lived in the home of the victim demonstrated an even stronger association than that noted for the group overall. Gun ownership was most strongly associated with homicide at the hands of a family member or intimate acquaintance (adjusted odds ratio, 7.8; 95 percent confidence interval, 2.6 to 23.2). Guns were not significantly linked to an increased risk of homicide by acquaintances, unidentified intruders, or strangers. We found no evidence of a protective benefit from gun ownership in any subgroup, including one restricted to cases of homicide that followed forced entry into the home and another restricted to cases in which resistance was attempted. Not surprisingly, the link between gun ownership and homicide was due entirely to a strong association between gun ownership and homicide by firearms. Homicide by other means was not significantly linked to the presence or absence of a gun in the home.

Living in a household where someone had previously been hit or hurt in a fight in the home was also strongly and independently associated with homicide, even after we controlled for the effects of gun ownership and the other four variables in our final model (adjusted odds ratio, 4.4; 95 percent confidence interval, 2.2 to 8.8) (table 4). Previous family violence was linked to an increased risk of homicide among men as well as women, blacks as well as whites, and younger as well as older people. Virtually all of this increased risk was due to a marked association between prior domestic violence and homicide at the hands of a family member or intimate acquaintance (adjusted odds ratio, 20.4; 95 percent confidence interval, 3.9 to 104.6).

DISCUSSION

Although firearms are often kept in homes for personal protection, this study shows that the practice is counterproductive. Our data indicate that keeping a gun in the home is independently associated with an increase In the risk of homicide in the home. The use of illicit drugs and a history of physical fights in the home are also important risk factors. Efforts to increase home security have largely focused on preventing unwanted entry, but the greatest threat to the lives of household members appears to come from within.

We restricted our study to homicides that occurred in the home of the victim, because these events can be most plausibly linked to specific individual and household characteristics. If, for example, the ready availability of a gun increases the risk of homicide, this effect should be most noticeable in the immediate environment where the gun is kept. Although our case definition excluded the rare instances in which a nonresident intruder was killed by a homeowner, our methodology was capable of demonstrating significant protective effects of gun ownership as readily as any evidence of increased risk.

Previous studies of risk factors for homicide have employed correlational analysis[15] or retrospective-cohort[16] or time-series[17] designs to link rates of homicide to specific risk factors. However, hazards suggested by ecologic analysis may not hold at the level of individual households or people.[18] In contrast to these approaches, the case-control method studies individual risk factors in relation to a specific outcome of interest. Case-control research is particularly useful when the list of candidate risk factors is large and the rate of adverse outcomes is relatively low. Under these circumstances, it is usually the analytic method of choice.[19]

Although case-control studies offer many advantages over ecologic studies, they are prone to several sources of bias. To minimize selection bias, we included all cases of homicide in the home and rigorously followed an explicit procedure for randomly selecting neighborhood control subjects. High response rates among case proxies (92.6 percent) and matching controls (80.6 percent) minimized nonresponse bias. Case respondents did not differ significantly from nonrespondents with regard to the age, sex, and race of the victim, and the type of weapon involved. Although double homicides and murder-suicides were considered single events to avoid overrepresenting their effects, the number of cases excluded for this reason was small.

Other threats to the validity of the study were less easy to control. A respondent's recollection of events can be powerfully affected by a tragedy as extreme as a homicide in the home. To diminish the effect of recall bias, we delayed our contact with the case proxies to allow for an initial period of grief. We also used a simple, forced-cholice questionnaire to ascertain information in a comparable manner from case proxies and controls. We tried to obtain data on victims and controls as similarly as possible by interviewing proxy respondents for the controls whenever possible. Although we were able to do so only 48 percent of the

Table 4. Variables Included in the Final Conditional Logistic-Regression Model Derived from Data on 316 Matched Pairs of Case Subjects and Controls.*

Variable	Adjusted Odds Ratio (95% CI)
Home rented	4.4 (2.3–8.2)
Case subject or control lived alone	3.7 (2.1–6.0)
Any household member hit or hurt in a fight in the home	4.4 (2.2–8.8)
Any household member arrested	2.5 (1.6–4.1)
Any household member used illicit drugs	5.7 (2. 6–12.6)
Gun or guns kept in the home	2.7 (1.6–4.4)

*Conditional logistic-regression analysis requires that data on all the variables of interest be available for both case subjects and their matched controls. Therefore, 72 pairs with missing data on any of the six variables of interest were excluded from this analysis. CI denotes confidence interval.

time, the responses we obtained from this subgroup were consistent with those obtained from the study population overall.

Potential misreporting of sensitive information was a serious concern since we had no way to verify each respondent's statements independently. If case proxies or controls selectively withheld sensitive information about illicit-drug use, alcoholism, or violence in the home, inaccurate estimates of risk could results. We attempted to minimize this problem by reassuring our respondents of the confidentiality of their responses. We also placed "permissive" statements before each potentially, intrusive question to encourage honest replies. Very few respondents refused to answer our questions, although all were assured that they were free to do so.

The rate of domestic violence reported by our control respondents was somewhat less than that noted in a large telephone survey.[20] This may be due to regional or temporal differences in rates of battering, variations in the way we phrased our questions (e.g., screening as compared with an exploratory line of inquiry), or the increased anonymity afforded by telephone interviews as compared with our face-to-face encounters.

Underreporting of gun ownership by control respondents could bias our estimate of risk upward. We do not believe, however, that misreporting of gun ownership was a problem. In two of our three study communities, a pilot study of homes listed as the addresses of owners of registered handguns confirmed that respondents' answers to questions about gun ownership were generally valid.[21] Furthermore, the rate of gun ownership reported by control respondents in each study community was comparable to estimates derived from previous social surveys[22] and Cook's gun-prevalence index.[15]

Four limitations warrant comment. First, our study was restricted to homicides occurring in the home of the victim. The dynamics of homicides occurring in other locations (such as bars, retail establishments, or the street) may be quite different. Second, our research was conducted in three urban counties that lack a substantial percentage of Hispanic citizens. Our results may therefore not be generalizable to more rural communities or to Hispanic households. Third, it is possible that reverse causation accounted for some of the association we observed between gun ownership and homicide—i.e., in a limited number of cases, people may have acquired a gun in response to a specific threat. If the source of that threat subsequently caused the homicide, the link between guns in the home and homicide may be due at least in part to the failure of these weapons to provide adequate protection from the assailants. Finally, we cannot exclude the possibility that the association we observed is due to a third unidentified factor. If, for example, people who keep guns in their homes are more psychologically prone to violence than people who do not, this could explain the link between gun ownership and homicide in the home. Although we examined several behavioral markers of violence and aggression and included two in our final logistic-regression model, "psychological confounding" of this sort is difficult to control for. "Psychological autopsies" have been used to control for psychological differences between adolescent victims of suicide and inpatient controls with psychiatric disorders,[23,24] but we did not believe this approach was practical for a study of homicide victims and neighborhood controls. At any rate, a link between gun ownership and a psychological tendency toward violence or victimization would have to be extremely strong to account for an adjusted odds ratio of 2.7.

Given the univariate association we observed between alcohol and violence, it may seem odd that no alcohol-related variables were included in our final multivariate model. Although consumption of alcoholic beverages and the behavioral correlates of alcoholism were strongly associated with homicide, they were also related to other variables included in our final model. Forcing the variable "case subject or control drinks" into our model did not substantially alter the adjusted odds ratios for the other variables. Furthermore, the adjusted odds ratio for this variable was not significantly greater than 1.

Large amounts of money are spent each year on home-security systems, locks, and other measures intended to improve home security. Unfortunately, our results suggest that these efforts have little effect on the risk of homicide in the home. This finding should come as no surprise, since most homicides in the home involve disputes between family members, intimate acquaintances, friends, or others who ready have access to the home. It is important to realize, however, that these data offer no insight into the effectiveness of home-security measures against other household crimes such as burglary, robbery, or sexual assault. In a 1983 poll, Seattle homeowners feared "having someone break into your home while you are gone" most and "having someone break into your home while you are at home" was fourth on a list of sixteen crimes.[15] Although homicide is the most serious of crimes, it occurs far less frequently than other types of household crime. Measures that make a home more difficult to enter are probably more effective against these crimes.

Despite the widely held belief that guns are effective for protection, our results suggest that they actually pose a substantial threat to members of the household. People who keep guns in their homes appear to be at greater risk of homicide in the home than people who do not. Most of this risk is due to a substantially greater risk of homicide at the hands of a family member or intimate acquaintance. We did not find evidence of a protective effect of keeping a gun in the home, even in the small subgroup of cases that involved forced entry.

Saltzman and colleagues recently found that assaults by family members or other intimate acquaintances with a gun are far more likely to end in death than those that involve knives or other weapons.[26] A gun kept in the home is far more likely to be involved in the death of a member of the household than it is to be used to kill in self-defense.[4] Cohort and interrupted time-series studies have demonstrated a strong link between the availability of guns and community rates of homicide.[2,15–17] Our study confirms this association at the level of individual households.

Previous case-control research has demonstrated a strong association between the ownership of firearms and suicide in the home.[10,23,24] Also, unintentional shooting deaths can occur when children play with loaded guns they have found at home.[27] In the light of these observations and our present findings people should be strongly discouraged from keeping guns in their homes.

The observed association between battering and homicide is also important. In contrast to the money spent on firearms and home security, little has been done to improve society's capacity to respond to the problem of domestic violence.[28,29] In the absence of effective intervention, battering tends to increase in frequency and severity over time.[28–30] Our data strongly suggest that the risk of homicide is markedly increased in homes where a person has previously been hit or hurt in a family fight. At the very least, this observation should prompt physicians, social workers, law-enforcement officers, and the courts to work harder to identify and protect victims of battering and other forms of family violence. Early identification and effective intervention may prevent a later homicide.[31,32]

NOTES

1. M. Hammett, K. E. Powell, P. W. O'Carroll, and S. T. Clanton, "Homicide surveillance United States, 1979–1988." MMWR CDC Surveill Summ 41 (1992): 1–33

2. A. J. Reiss Jr. and J. A. Roth, eds., *Understanding and Preventing Violence: Panel on the Understanding and Control of Violent Behavior* (Washington, D.C.: National Academy Press, 1993), pp. 42–97.

3. D. S. Weil and D. Hemenway, "Loaded guns in the home: analysis of a national random survey of gun owners," *JAMA* 267 (1992): 3033–37.

4. Al Kellermann and D. T. Reay, "Protection or peril? An analysis of firearm related deaths in the home," *New England Journal of Medicine* 314 (1986): 1557–60.

5. Bureau of the Census, *1990 census of population: Tennessee* (WashingtonD.C.: U.S. Government Printing Office, 1992). (Publication nos. CPH-5-44 and CP1-44.)

6. Bureau of the Census, *1990 census of population: Washington* (Washington, D.C.: U.S. Government Printing Office, 1992). (Publication nos. CPH-5-49 and CP-1-49.)

7. Bureau of the Census, *1990 census of population: Ohio* (Washington, D.C.: U.S. Government Printing Office, 1992). (Publication nos. CPH-5-37 and CP-1-37.)

8. M. C. Yu, T. Mack, R. Hanisch, R. L. Peters, B. F. Henderson, and M. C. Pike, "Hepatitis

alcohol consumption, cigarette smoking, and hepatocellular carcinoma in Los Angeles." *Cancer Research* 43 (1983): 6077–79.

9. T. M. Mack, M. C. Yu, R. Hanisch, and B. E. Henderson, "Pancreas cancer and smoking, beverage consumption, and past medical history," *National Cancer Institute* 76 (1986): 49–60.

10. Al Kellerman, F. P. Rivara, and G. Somes et al., "Suicide in the home in relation to gun ownership," *New England Journal of Medicine* 327 (1992): 467–72.

11. M. L. Selzer, A. Vinokur, and L. van Rooijen, "A self-administered Short Michigan Alcoholism Screening Test (SMAST)," *Journal of Studies on Alcohol* 36 (1975): 117–26.

12. "The index of social position: appendix two," in A. B. Hollingshead, *Redlich Social class and mental illness: a community study* (New York: John, 1958), pp. 381–97.

13. *Attitudes of the American electorate toward gun control* (Santa Ana, Calif.: Decision Making Information, 1978).

14. D. W. Hosmer and S. Lemeshow, *Applied Logistic Regression* (New York: John Wiley, 1989).

15. P. J. Cook, "The effect of gun availability on robbery and robber murder: a cross section study of fifty cities," *Policy Studies Review Annual* 3 (1979): 743

16. J. H. Sloan, Al Kellermann, and D. T. Reay, et al., "Handgun regulations, crime, assaults. and homicide: a tale of two cities," *New England Journal of Medicine* 319 (1899): 1256.

17. C. Loftin, D. McDowall, B. Wiersema, and T. DJ. Cottey "Effects of restrictive licensing of handguns on homicide and suicide in the District of Columbia, *New England Journal of Medicine* 325 (1991): 1615–20.

18. H. Morgenstern, "Uses of ecologic analysis in epidemiologic research," *American Journal of Public Health* 72 (1982): 1336–44.

19. J. J. Schlesselman, ed., *Case Control Studies: Design, Conduct, Analysis* (New York: Oxford University Press, 1982).

20. M. A. Strauss, R. J. Gelles, and S. K. Steinmetz, *Behind Closed Doors: Violence in the American Family* (Garden City, N.Y.: Anchor Press, 1980).

21. Al Kellermann, F. P. Rivara, J. Banton, D. Reay, and C. L. I'lligneir "Validating survey responses to questions about gun ownership among owners of registered handguns," *American Journal of Epidemiology* 131 (1990): 1080–84.

22. J. D. Wright, P. Rossi, K. Daly, and E. Weber-Burdin, *Weapons, Crime, and Violence in America: A Literature Review and Research Agenda* (Washington, D.C.: U.S. Government Printing Office, 1983), pp. 212–60, 361–411.

23. D. A. Brent, J. A. Perper, C. F. Goldstein, et al., "Risk factors for adolescent suicide: a comparison of adolescent suicide victims with suicidal inpatients," *Archives of General Psychiatry* 45 (1998): 581–88.

24. D. A. Brent, J. A. Perper, D. J. Allman, G. M. Moritz, M. E. Wartella, and J. P. Zelenak "The presence and accessibility of firearms in the homes of adolescent suicides: a case-control study," *JAMA* 266 (1991): 2989–95.

25. M. Warr and M. Stafford, "Fear of victimization: a look at the proximate causes," *Social Forces* 61 (1983): 1033–43.

26. L. E. Saltzman, J. A. Mercy, P. W. O'Carroll, M. L. Rosenberg, and P. H. Rhodes, "Weapon involvement and injury outcomes in family and intimate assaults," *JAMA* 267 (1992): 3043–3047.

27. G. J. Winternute, S. P. Teret, J. F. Kraus, M. A. Wright, and G. Bradfield, "When children shoot children: 88 unintended deaths in California," *JAMA* 257 (1987): 3107–3109.

28. American Medical Association, "Violence against women: relevance for medical practitioners," *JAMA* 267 (1992): 3184–89.

29. National Committee for Injury Prevention and Control. "Domestic violence," *American Journal of Preventitive Medicine* 5, supplement (1989): 223–32.

30. E. Stark and A. H. Flitcraft, "Spouse abuse," in *Violence in America: A Public Health Approach,* ed. M. L. Rosenberg, and M. A. Fenley (New York: Oxford University Press, 1991), pp. 123–57.

31. J. A. Mercy and L. E. Saltzman, "Fatal violence among spouses in the United States, 1976–1985," *American Journal of Public Health* 79 (1989): 595–99.

32. Al Kellermann and J. A. Mercy, "Men, women, and murder: gender-specific differences in rates of fatal violence and victimization," *Journal of Trauma* 33 (1992): 1–5.

21

CASE-CONTROL RESEARCH ON HOMICIDAL BEHAVIOR

GARY KLECK

A case-control study is a retrospective comparison of individuals possessing a given trait (the "cases"), often a relatively rare one (e.g., delinquency, violent behavior, lung cancer) with individuals lacking the trait (the "controls"), and it commonly involves the rare individuals somehow being oversampled (Schlesselman 1982). The case-control design helps solve the problem of how to study the causes of rare phenomena and ensure that the investigator has enough of the rare cases to compare with the more numerous persons who lack the rare attribute.

Arthur Kellermann and his colleagues applied this design to homicide victimization in an attempt to link it with household gun ownership. They obtained lists of persons killed in their homes in three urban counties and then located persons of the same sex, race, and approximate age living in the same neighborhood. After interviewing survivors of the homicide victims and the matched controls (or their proxies), they found that gun ownership was more common in the households of the homicide victims and concluded, in very strongly worded terms, that guns kept in the home "pose a substantial threat to members of the household" and that therefore "people should be strongly discouraged from keeping guns in their homes" (1993:1009). The conclusions were phrased in unambiguously causal terms and were not in any way qualified with respect to the subsets of the population to which they might apply.

Reprinted with permission from Gary Kleck, *Targeting Guns: Firearms and Their Control* (Hawthorne, N.Y.: Aldine de Gruytner, 1997), pp. 243–47. Copyright © 1997 by Walter de Gruyter, Inc., New York.

Kellermann and his colleagues did not establish a causal link between gun ownership and homicide victimization. (The following discussion is based on the detailed critique of this study in Kleck and Hogan 1996.) Although the authors described the association they discovered (an odds ratio of 2.7) as a "strong" one, in fact it was not even large enough to qualify as the minimum taken seriously by epidemiologists who study risk factors and disease (an odds ratio of 3; Lilienfeld and Stolley 1994; Taubes 1995:165). More importantly, this was almost certainly a largely or entirely spurious association, that is, a noncausal association due to antecedent confounding factors that the researchers failed to control. Virtually all known factors that increase the risk of homicide victimization could also increase the likelihood that persons exposed to those factors would acquire a gun for self-protection. Thus, one would expect a positive association between gun ownership and violent victimization, even if the former had no causal effect whatsoever on the latter. Indeed, much of the research on gun ownership [is] premised on the idea that various predictors of future victimization risk (such as past victimization or living in a high-crime place) would influence some people to acquire guns, especially handguns. For example, Kellermann et al. failed to control for whether subjects were drug dealers or members of street gangs, persons who are both much more likely to own guns and far more likely to become victims of homicide. Callahan and Rivara (1992:3042) found that street gang members were 8.8 times more likely to own handguns than other youths, and that those who sold illicit drugs were 3.7 times more likely to own a handgun. In turn, gang members are 19 times more likely, and drug dealers at least six times more likely, to be homicide victims (Kleck and Hogan 1996, based on data in Hutson et al. 1995; Harrison and Gfroerer 1992). These risk factors would easily be large enough to create a spurious odds ratio of 2.8. More generally, Kellermann et al. failed to control for any risks existing outside the home, despite the fact that their own data indicated that most of the known offenders, even in killings occurring in the victim's home, did not live with the victim.

While claiming that keeping a gun in one's home raises the risks that one will be killed, the authors did not document a single case in which the victim was killed with a gun kept in the victim's home. Indeed, based on their data on victim-offender relationships, most of the victims killed in their homes were killed by persons who lived elsewhere, and who presumably used their own guns, kept in their own homes. Based on the share of home gun homicides that involved offenders likely to live in the victim's home, a gun kept in the victim's home was probably used in no more than 4 percent of the total homicides committed in the three counties studied. Also, because of the way the sample was chosen, the results cannot be generalized beyond the predominantly black, low-income residents of high-crime urban areas included in the study (Kleck and Hogan 1996).

The observed gun-homicide association is so weak that it could easily be due entirely to a higher rate of concealing gun ownership among controls than among cases. The authors' own test of the validity of survey reports of gun ownership indicated that 11.4 percent of gun owners may deny gun ownership (Kellermann et al. 1990). . . .

Unfortunately, it has not been possible to definitively explore all of the defects in this study because Dr. Kellermann has repeatedly refused scholars' requests (including a request by the present author) for a copy of his data for reanalysis (see also Kates et al. 1995:590–91;* Polsby 1995a:211). In the final analysis, about the only effective deterrent to distorted or honestly mistaken analysis of research data is the possibility of the analyst's distortions being discovered by other analysts. Consequently, it is customary among scientists that their data be provided to others for purposes of reanalysis. Unfortunately, the government agency on which Kellermann and many other medical researchers have primarily relied for support, the federal Centers for Disease Control and Prevention, does not require its grant recipients to make their data available to other scholars. Consequently, even though a body of data like the one gathered by Kellermarm was paid for with public funds, CDC-funded researchers are allowed to treat the data as their own private property, to distribute or not as they see fit.

There was an enormous gap between the authors' strong conclusions and their very weak evidence, using the ordinary norms of conventional science. Under the most generous interpretation, one might conclude that victims keeping guns in their households might have played a role of some unknown magnitude in their deaths in less than 4 percent of the homicides committed in the study area, but only if one ignored the effects of failures to control important confounding factors and of errors in measuring household gun ownership, and if one stressed that this is a conclusion that cannot be generalized beyond the predominantly high-crime neighborhoods studied in three nonrandomly chosen urban counties. Less generously, one might conclude that the authors spent a great deal of time and money to rediscover a criminological commonplace: the same factors that increase the risk of violent victimization also increase the likelihood a person will acquire a gun for self-defense.

This has not, however, been the way this study's findings have been interpreted by the authors' medical colleagues, based on citations to this study in the medical literature. Instead, these weak findings have been unambiguously interpreted as clear proof that keeping a gun in one's home raises the residents' risk of becoming a homicide victim (see citations listed in footnote 313 of Kates et al. 1995).

A NATIONAL CASE-CONTROL STUDY OF HOMICIDE OFFENDING

Some of the difficulties of Kellermarm and his coauthors can be traced to their decision to indirectly address the guns-homicide link by conceptualizing their

---

*See Don B. Kates et al., "The Myth That Murders Are Ordinary Gun Owners," in Part Three of this volume.—Ed.

project as a study of homicide victimization, contrasting victims and nonvictims, rather than a study of homicide *offending*, contrasting killers and nonkillers. If guns in a potential homicide victim's household are a source of risk to the victim, it is only because an attacker, typically another household member, can use the gun to kill. That is, the risk to the victim exists only if gun availability somehow affects aggressive behavior and its possibly lethal consequences, indicating that the problem is more directly conceptualized as the effect of gun ownership on homicide offending.

Kleck and Hogan (1996) improved on the Kellermann et al. study in at least four ways: (1) they directly studied homicide offending, rather than studying it indirectly by focusing on homicide victimization, (2) they used nationally representative samples of the incarcerated homicide offender population and the general adult (nonkiller) population, allowing generalizations to the U.S. adult population, (3) they used a far larger sample, providing more stable estimates and greater statistical power to estimate a guns-homicide association, and (4) they controlled directly for attributes of individual offenders and controls, rather than attributes of their fellow household members.

Their sample was a combination of two separate samples: (1) inmates in state prisons in 1991 who had committed a homicide between 1980 and 1991 and who were interviewed in the U.S. Census Bureau's Survey of State Prison Inmates (the "cases"), and (2) a general sample of noninstitutionalized U.S. adults (age eighteen or older) interviewed in the General Social Surveys (GSS) between 1980 and 1991 (the "controls"). In the inmate sample, only those who had committed an intentional homicide when age eighteen or older were included, to match the age range covered by the GSS. Thus, the Survey of State Prison Inmates sample is a nationally representative sample of persons sent to state prisons for committing intentional homicides while adults, and the GSS sample is a nationally representative sample of noninstitutionalized U.S. adults, of whom we can be confident that 99 percent had *not* committed homicides. Combining the samples together produced a representative sample of U.S. adults, of whom a disproportionately large share were known killers.

Are gun owners more likely to kill than nonowners? The results indicated that persons with a gun in their household are about 1.36 times more likely to commit a homicide than persons without a gun. Because of the large sample size, this is a statistically significant association, but it is a far smaller association than Kellermann et al. found with respect to homicide victimization, and by the conventional standards of epidemiology is probably not large enough to rely on as demonstrating a causal effect. There are, moreover, the same doubts surrounding the meaning of this weak association that characterized the Kellermarm association. It was not possible to control for all confounding factors, so it is likely that some or all of this association was spurious, due to the effects of risk factors (e.g., drug dealing, gang membership) that elevate both homicide offending and acquisition of guns for self-protection.

REFERENCES

Callahan, Charles M., and Frederick P. Rivara. 1992. "Urban high school youth and handguns." *Journal of the American Medical Association* 267:3038–42.

Kates, Don B., Henry E. Schaffer, John K. Lattimer, George B. Murray, and Edwin H. Cassem. 1995. "Guns and public health: Epidemic of violence or pandemic of propaganda?" *Tennessee Law Review* 62:513–96.

Kellermann, Arthur L., Frederick P. Rivara, Joyce Banton, Donald Reay, and Corinte L. Fligner. 1990. "Validating survey responses to questions about gun ownership among owners of registered handguns." *American Journal of Epidemiology* 131:1080–84.

Kellermann, Arthur L., Frederick P. Rivara, Norman B. Rushforth, Joyce G. Banton, Donald T. Reay, Jerry T. Francisco, Ana B. Locci, Janice Prodzinski, Bela B. Hackman, and Grant Somes. 1993. "Gun ownership as a risk factor for homicide in the home." *New England Journal of Medicine* 329:1084–91.

Kleck, Gary, and Michael Hogan. 1996. "A National case control study of homicide offending and gun ownership." Revised version of a paper presented at the annual meetings of the American Society of Criminology, Chicago, November 21.

Lilienfeld, D. E., and P. D. Stolley. 1994. *Foundations of Epidemiology*, 3rd rev. ed. New York: Oxford University Press.

Polsby, Daniel D. 1995a. "Firearms costs, firearms benefits, and the limits of knowledge." *Journal of Criminal Law and Criminology* 86:207–20.

_____. 1995b. "Daniel D. Polsby replies." *Journal of Criminal Law and Criminology* 86:227–30.

22

THE MYTH THAT MURDERERS
ARE ORDINARY GUN OWNERS

DON B. KATES ET AL.*

The case for reducing firearm availability to ordinary people rests on two inter-related myths endorsed explicitly and implicitly in the health advocacy literature on firearms. First is the myth that "most [murderers] would be considered law-abiding citizens prior to their pulling the trigger."[1] Second is the myth that "most shootings are not committed by felons or mentally ill people, but are acts of passion that are committed using a handgun that is owned for home protection."[2] From these myths other falsehoods follow: that firearm availability to ordinary citizens is the "primary cause" of murder,[3] that murder would radically decrease if ordinary citizens were deprived of those guns, and that it is unnecessary to worry much about the enforceability of gun bans because, even if criminals will not disarm, the law-abiding will—and they are the ones committing most murders.

The problem is that it simply is not true that previously law-abiding citizens commit most murders or many murders or virtually any murders. Thus, disarming them would not, and could not, eliminate most, many, or virtually any murders. Homicide studies show that murderers tend not to be ordinary law-abiding citizens, but rather extreme aberrants.[4] The great majority of murderers have life histories of violence, felony records, and substance abuse.[5] These facts are so firmly established that they even appear in medico-health discussions of violence,[6] yet they are never discussed in connection with the health advocate

The full text of this article appears in *Tennessee Law Review* 62 (1995): 513. This portion appears by permission of the Tennessee Law Review Association, Inc.

*Don B. Kates, Henry E. Shaffer, John K. Lattimer, George B. Murray, and Edwin H. Cassem.

sages' mythology about ordinary citizens murdering relatives and acquaintances with guns.

Looking only to official criminal records, data over the past thirty years consistently show that the mythology of murderers as ordinary citizens does not hold true. Studies have found that approximately 75 percent of murderers have adult criminal records,"[7] and that murderers average a prior adult criminal career of six years, including four major adult felony arrests.[8] These studies also found that when the murder occurred "about 11 percent of murder arrestees [were] actually on pre-trial release"—that is, they were awaiting trial for another offense.[9]

The fact that only 75 percent of murderers have adult crime records should not be misunderstood as implying that the remaining 25 percent of murderers are noncriminals. The reason over half of those 25 percent of murderers don't have adult records is that they are juveniles.[10] Thus, by definition they cannot have an adult criminal record. Juvenile criminal records might well show these murderers to have extensive serious criminal records. "The research literature on characteristics of those who murder yields a profile of offenders that indicates that many have histories of committing personal violence in childhood, against other children, siblings, and small animals."[11] Though juvenile criminal records are not generally available, they occasionally become known in connection with some high-profile cases. In one recent case which generated nationwide publicity, a five-year-old boy was thrown from a fourteenth story window by two other boys because he had refused to steal candy for them.[12] Police revealed that both killers, ages ten and eleven, had prior arrests for theft, aggravated battery, and unlawful use of a weapon.[13] At the time of the murder, one of the perpetrators was supposed to be confined to his home on a weapons conviction.[14]

The antigun health advocacy literature avoids the fact that murderers tend to be extreme aberrants by just falsifying the facts. A truly startling example, because it contradicts his own writings, is the CDC's point man for prohibition, Dr. Mark Rosenberg.[15] Dr. Rosenberg, director of the CDC's National Center for Injury Prevention and Control, recently extolled the CDC's hope to create a public perception of firearms as "dirty, deadly, and banned."[16] To mislead readers into blaming firearms for crime rather than criminals, Dr. Rosenberg actually goes so far as to claim that "most of the perpetrators of violence are not criminals by trade or profession. Indeed, in the area of domestic violence, most of the *perpetrators* are never accused of any crime. The victims and perpetrators are *ourselves—ordinary citizens*, students, professionals, and *even public health workers*."[17] A comparison of this statement to Dr. Rosenberg's other statements reveals its falsity. In the same work, Dr. Rosenberg stated: "Violence is foreign to the lives of most public health professionals."[18] In another article, Dr. Rosenberg recognized that "most family homicides involve spouses and occur after a series of prior assaultive incidents."[19]

We do not suggest that all statements promoting this mythology in the health advocacy literature constitute conscious misrepresentations. Some reflect only a combination of ignorance and intellectual confusion. For instance, Jeremiah Barondess comments in *JAMA*:

In relation to the contention that homicide by firearms is carried out by estab-lished felons, the Federal Bureau of Investigation has reported that of the 15,377 reported firearm-related murders in 1992, a total of 7,505 fell under the category of "other than felony type," such as "romantic triangle, arguments over money or property, other arguments"; *thus*, many who kill for the first time are not felons until they commit the act.[20]

But for the tragic seriousness of the subject matter, this comment would be truly hilarious as an example of class-based myopia. It is evident that the image the term "argument" conveys to Barondess et al. is a heated disagreement between doctors. It seems entirely to have escaped Barondess and his coauthors that "argument" may mean something very different when it occurs among young men in areas where the willingness and capacity to employ extreme vio-lence is respected, where young men raised in violent families live in an envi-ronment whose most attractive employment opportunities are in the violent drug trade.[21] These are young men who "believe that to survive, one must be tough, be willing to fight, carry a gun, and be willing to shoot it."[22] They are young men who "engage in high-risk activities partly because they believe their chances of living beyond age thirty are slim anyway"[23] and who participate in "often deadly battles over respect"[24] which is of heightened concern to them because they are "deprived of [any] legitimate opportunities to acquire symbols of status."[25] The same intellectual confusion characterizes Jeffrey B. Kahn's claim that "most firearm-related violence is being committed" not by criminals, but "by relatives and friends of victims and in the course of arguments."[26]

Their myopia leads Barondess and Kahn to the unexamined and absurd assump-tion that felons don't have friends, relatives, or acquaintances, and don't engage in "romantic triangle[s] arguments over money or property, [or in] other argu-ments."[27] Only by indulging in that absurd assumption could they falsely conclude that the murderers in the study were ordinary citizens "who kill[ed] for the first time [and were] not felons until they commit[ted] the act."[28] Kahn and Barondess fall into this absurdity only by ignoring the studies which describe terms like "acquain-tance homicide" and murder in the course of . . . romantic triangle[s], arguments over money or property, other arguments."[29] These are not previously law-abiding people killing each other, but abusive men killing women they have savaged on many prior occasions, or gang members and drug dealers killing each other.[30] But for their gun-averse dyslexia, Kahn and Barondess could have discovered these well-estab-lished facts about homicide by just reviewing studies in their own discipline.[31]

As for child abusers and wife batterers, Dr. Rosenberg correctly observes that many are never arrested. That is yet another reason why 25 percent of mur-derers don't have a record, though most domestic murderers do have prior records.[32] Although Dr. Rosenberg is correct that most child abusers and wife batterers; are never arrested, he is as wrong factually as he is morally to minimize child abuse and wife beating as essentially normal behavior engaged in by "ordi-nary citizens, students, professionals, and even public medico-health workers."[33]

Those abusers who eventually murder resemble other murderers in that they are highly aberrant individuals with life histories of substance abuse and brutalizing family members, often in irrational outbursts of violence.

> There are significant differences between men who commit [domestic] partner homicide and men in the general noncriminal population. For instance, men who kill their [domestic] partners are more often drug abusers, are more prone to abuse alcohol and are intoxicated more often, and are more frequently given to [prior verbal] . . . threats and [physical violence] than are other men.[34]

In 90 percent of domestic homicide cases, the police had been called to the same address at least once within the preceding two years; the median number of prior police calls to the same address was five during that period.[35] A leading analyst of domestic homicide has noted that "the day-to-day reality is that most family murders are preceded by a long history of assaults.[36]

It is difficult to avoid the conclusion that antigun health advocates suppress and misrepresent these facts because the facts are embarrassing to the antigun argument for two reasons. First, laws are already in place to prevent gun ownership by felons, drug abusers, and juveniles. Sensible though these laws are, in practice they have proven only marginally effective. To reiterate the obvious, murderous aberrants see little reason to obey laws which prohibit gun ownership. The failure of these laws suggests that it is senseless, and indeed counterproductive, to strain police resources further by committing them to enforcing a gun ban against the general populace, which does not misuse guns anyway. Second, since owning guns does not cause ordinary people to murder—and certainly doesn't cause them to rob, rape, or burgle—it is difficult to identify and justify the basis for confiscating their property and depriving them of the freedom to choose to own arms for the defense of self, home, and family.[37]

"GUN OWNERNSHIP AS A RISK FACTOR FOR HOMICIDE IN THE HOME"

This is the title of a 1993 article whose authors include several of Sloan's coauthors on the Vancouver-Seattle comparison.[38] The 1993 article having, like its predecessor, appeared in the *New England Journal of Medicine*. we refer to it as *NEJM-1993*. This article is particularly appropriate for a detailed critique of the antigun position because it has received widespread publicity[39] and voluminous citation in the health advocacy literature.[40]*

Moreover, *NEJM-1993* continues a long series of widely publicized health advocacy studies and would be more appropriately cited in a statistics text as a cautionary example of multiple statistical errors.

---

*See Arthur L. Kellermann et al., "Gun Ownership as a Risk Factor for Homicide in the Home," in Part Four of this volume.—Ed.

Statistical analyses are used to reach conclusions in the face of certain types of uncertainty. Uncertainty results from such factors as inherent variation in the subjects being studied, the effects of many other influences, both known and unknown, and limited resources which restrict the amount of data that can be collected and studied. Statistical analyses may result 'in erroneous conclusions for a variety of reasons, some acceptable, others not. In this discussion, we shall ignore errors in recording data and of calculation, because though unacceptable, these errors have become less common with the use of computers and statistical analysis programs. However, many other types of errors can occur and are of grave concern when the conclusions will be used to make important policy decisions. In any case, use of flawed statistical studies may lead to fatal consequences.

When What You See Is Not Necessarily What You Get

We assume here that the statistical analysis program on the computer performs the calculations of the statistical analysis correctly, although this is not always true. Moreover, data entry errors are sufficiently common to require careful checking by the analyst to catch them. However, neither calculation errors nor data entry errors will be biased in favor of any particular agenda the analyst may have.

More serious methodological concerns involve errors by the analyst which relate to a conscious or unconscious agenda. The analyst is responsible for choosing the correct type of analysis, for ensuring that the assumptions in the statistical analysis are met, and for confirming that the results are described correctly. When errors occur in any of these areas, the conclusions reached can be partially or completely wrong even in the absence of any other errors. While the presence of these errors in a study does not guarantee that the conclusions are invalid, the conclusions are then unsubstantiated, and the scientific impartiality of the analyst may be called into question. Errors are of particular concern when they occur in such a manner as to facilitate conclusions which confirm the previous positions of the analyst.

It is seldom possible to conduct a scientific study in which only the effects to be tested are operating to compel a particular conclusion. The statistical field of "Experimental Design" is concerned with methods which detect the effects to be studied even when other effects are operating.[41] Failure to separate the effects to be studied from extraneous effects leads to the unintentional "confounding"[42] of extraneous effects with the effects to be studied. The resulting conclusions, then, are not based on tests of the effects being studied. Rather, they reflect some unknown combination of those effects and extraneous effects confounded with them. Thus, the hypotheses supposedly being studied are not in fact being studied. Hence, what you see is not what you get.

Purpose and Design of NEJM-1993

The hypothesis allegedly under study by *NEJM-1993* was "Whether keeping a firearm in the home confers protection against crime or, instead, increases the risk of violent crime in the home."[43] Simplistically described, the study compares a sample of households in which homicide occurred to a supposedly similar sample in which they did not.[44] It finds that the households where homicide occurred were more likely to have contained guns.[45] From this finding, it concludes that guns are more of a danger than a protection.[46]

The study utilized data, from three urban counties where homicide occurred in the home during chosen time periods.[47] As a comparison with these homicide cases, a control was selected for each homicide victim.[48] These control subjects were matched to the homicide victim with respect to sex, race, age, and neighborhood of residence.[49] The authors then obtained additional kinds of information by reading police or other official reports relating to the homicide cases, by interviewing another occupant of the household where the homicide occurred (a case-proxy), and by interviewing either the control subject or another occupant of the control subject's household (a control-proxy).[50]

Study Design Exaggerates Risks of Defensive Gun Ownership

The data presented in *NEJM-1993* does not show that even one homicide victim was killed with a gun ordinarily kept in that household. Indeed, the indirect evidence indicates that most of the homicide victims in the study were killed using guns not kept in the victim's home: 70.9 percent of the homicide victims were killed by people whose relationship to the victim[51] indicates that the killer did not live in the victim's household, and thus presumably used a gun not kept in the victim's household.

Incidentally, we do not mean to deny that it may be relevant that the murder household had a gun even though that gun had no direct involvement in the murder, but the nature of that relevance compromises *NEJM-1993*'s conclusions about the supposed risk of home gun ownership. What if it turns out that people who are at higher risk of being murdered are more likely to own guns than those at lesser risk? This is not only intuitively plausible, but it is also supported by the finding In some high density urban areas that victims of homicide and other severe violence tend to be engaged in criminal activity, including drug activity, or have criminal records.[52] If these higher risk people own guns more often, *NEJM-1993*'s conclusion that murder victims owned guns at a higher rate than the control group of nonvictims does not at all prove that owning a gun is risky. On the contrary, far from showing that the murder victims were at higher risk because they were more likely to own guns, the comparison may only demonstrate that they owned guns because they were at highter risk than the members of the supposedly comparable control group. We take up this point in the next section.

The study's authors make a tacit assumption by consistently using the word "victim," and by asserting that "violent crime in the home" is being considered.[53] The authors assume that the victim of the crime and the victim of the homicide are the same person. However, the deceased may actually have been the attacker, and thus the homicide should have been considered a benefit rather than a risk. The cases in which the "offender" is listed as "Police officer" seem likely to fall under this misleading classification, as does even the categorization of "Police" as "offender."[54]

Inadequate Consideration of High Risk Career Criminality

The authors of *NEJM-1993* were aware of the problem that the homicide cases in their study might contain a disproportionate number of high risk people. In an attempt to avoid the problem, they tried to compare the homicide cases to the controls to see if there were differences in a variety of risk factors, including drinking and drug problems, histories of domestic violence, whether the home was owned or rented, and particularly emphasizing gun ownership.[55] *NEJM-1993* then reports differences in the presence of these risk factors as being associated with an increase in the risk of homicide.[56]

In this connection, note that gun ownership, the supposed risk factor *NEJM-1993* emphasizes, was far from the most strongly associated with being murdered. Drinking and drug problems, a history of family violence, living alone, and living in a rented home were all greater individual risk factors associated with being murdered than gun ownership, based on the study's results.[57] Even so, it is clear that other risk factors, such as the number of criminal associates or frequency of high risk or criminal activity, were not taken into account. These factors, and others which are ignored in this study, have had their effects combined with the effects of the risk factors supposedly being studied, thus resulting in inadvertent statistical "confounding." An "association" due to these ignored confounding factors would be more accurately described as a "spurious association." Proper statistical design requires an effort to identify all risk factors and to take the relevant ones into account by properly collecting the data and choosing the appropriate statistical analysis. To the contrary, *NEJM-1993* simply did not do this adequately. Thus, the study's strongly worded conclusions about the included factors are not warranted. For instance, although the authors accounted for whether any member of either the homicide victim household or the control group had been arrested, the authors failed to account for the seriousness of the crime for which the arrest was made, for conviction of the crime, for whether the specific murder victim had been arrested or convicted of a crime, or for other high risk activity or gang affiliations of any member of the household.

These issues are particularly important because criminological studies indicate that the overall population may be divided into three categories: (1) the overwhelming majority, who are law-abiding citizens; (2) a minority of people who commit infrequent or trivial crimes; and (3) "career criminals" who commit the majority of crimes, especially the more serious ones.[58] It may plausibly be postulated that a group containing more career criminals will have both a higher rate of gun ownership and a greater likelihood of being murdered than a supposedly similar control group of people who commit relatively less frequent and less serious crimes. If so, that is a confounding factor which would produce a spurious association between owning a gun and being murdered.

This leads us to a more fundamental problem with the entire *NEJM-1993* study design. Let us suppose that the data problems arising from the comparison of the murdered group to the control group had all been solved. Still, the cases involve high-risk households unrepresentative of the general population. The controls, having been drawn from atypically high violence geographical areas, are unrepresentative of the general population. Therefore, there is no formal research basis for applying any conclusions from this study regarding the effects of gun ownership to the general population.[59] Nonetheless, *NEJM-1993* reaches unqualified conclusions and presents them as applying to the general population.[60]

False Minimization of Sampling Bias

Whenever only a portion of a phenomenon is studied, the conclusions reached may be in error if the portion selected for study is not representative of all of the cases. One way to avoid this error, called a "bias," is to scrupulously include all of the cases in the study. The authors of *NEJM-1993* are aware of this, and claim: "To minimize selection bias, we included all cases of homicide in the home. . . . High response rates among case proxies (94.6 percent) and matching controls (80.6 percent) minimized nonresponse bias."[61]

Unforturtately, a rather different picture emerges from close examination of the numbers. During the time period selected, 444 cases of homicide in the home were reported in the counties studied.[62] Nineteen of the 444 cases were dropped from consideration because the authors deemed them murder-suicides and multiple homicides as a single event and included only one homicide per event.[63] Five additional homicides were dropped for reasons relating to reporting or death certificate change.[64] The remaining cases account for the 94.6 percent of the total cases that the authors state were left in the study.[65] An additional 7 percent were dropped because of failure to interview the proxy, and 1 percent more due to failure to find a control.[66]

This left 388 matched pairs, or only 87.4 percent of the cases. This lower percentage is not mentioned by the authors, though they do give the individual drop percentages, thereby downplaying the cumulative effect and the possible biases which could result. The authors were unable to obtain complete data on all of the matched pairs, but the multivariate statistical analysis used requires complete data. Therefore, 72 of the 388 matched pairs had to be excluded in the final multivariate analysis.[67]

The end result is that only 316 matched pairs were used in the final analyses, representing only 71.2 percent of the 444 homicide cases.[68] It is very difficult, therefore, to accept *NEJM-1993*'s claim of having examined "all cases" in an analysis that was actually based on 71.2 percent of the cases. We hasten to add that this does not prove that there was any selection or response bias in this study. It shows only that there was ample room for such biases to act. It also shows that the authors avoided coming to grips with this issue and presented the data in a manner which would mislead the readers into thinking that little or no such bias existed.

Further analysis of the 28.8 percent of the cases which were dropped might shed some light on whether, and to what extent, *NEJM-1993* is compromised by the existence of such biases. Nevertheless, the senior author refuses to make these data available to others for reanalysis.[69]

Control Group Selection Did Not Assure Comparability

The validity of *NEJM-1993*'s conclusions depends on the precise matching of the control group with the homicide cases, except, of course, for the occurrence of a homicide. The importance of proper control selection cannot be overemphasized where medical or policy implications are at stake. Use of an inappropriate control can lead to erroneous conclusions, and perhaps to harmful practices: "It is thus, for want of an adequately controlled test, that various forms of treatment have in the past, become unjustifiably, even sometimes harmfully, established in everyday medical practice. . . ."[70] The need for the control groups to differ only with respect to the factor being studied is called an "obviosity" because it is so glaringly obvious.[71] In *NEJM-1993*, however, the control group falls to match the cases in important ways. The incomplete matching produced a control group which was not representative of the counties studied, and therefore further decreased the inferences which can be legitimately drawn from the data of this study.

While the study did match the control group to the case group using several categorizations such as sex, race, age, and neighborhood of residence, this matching method selected controls which were not necessarily matched with the case group on other important factors. The control selection involved random selection of households that were at least a "one-block avoidance zone" away from the case homicide.[72] The matching criteria did not 'include any lifestyle or related indicators. A number of lifestyle indicators, referred to as "behavioral factors," were studied,[73] but the large differences between the cases and the control group for these factors invariably shows more substance abuse and other problems in the cases than in the controls. This indicates that matching was not done for these lifestyle indicators. Other lifestyle indicators, such as single parent versus two parent homes, were not included in the study or are not shown in the article.

If the selected population is composed of subpopulations which differ in homicide rates, the matching control must come from the same subpopulation as the case which it is supposed to match. This could happen with the matching method *NEJM-1993* used only if the subpopulations were settled in distinct and different large geographic areas. These areas would have to be larger than one block in size because of the avoidance method used. How much larger is hard to tell, since the study does not reveal how far outside the zone it was necessary to travel to find a matching control who would agree to cooperate.

In any event risk subpopulations are not distributed in such a coarse-grain manner. Criminal residences and crime areas which define the homicide risk subgroup factors, such as drug use and drug dealing, violent criminal events, and violently abusive family relationships, are often fine-grained in their distribution.

Differences exist in areas within a city, but there is population heterogeneity within these areas.[74] Choosing a control group living one or more blocks away will not assure matching with respect to the subpopulation.

Of particular interest here is the small, violent high-risk subpopulation that may be disproportionately represented in the homicide cases. The chances are good that the controls with which they will be matched will come from the much larger nonviolent, or less violent, subpopulations, producing a "spurious association."[75]

The control group may or may not differ from the homicide cases in another central characteristic. The conclusion that gun ownership is a risk factor for homicide derives from the finding that 45.4 percent of the homicide case households owned a gun, but only 35.8 percent of the control households owned one.[76] Whether that finding is accurate, however, depends on the truthfulness of control group 350 interviewees in admitting the presence of a gun or guns in the home.[77] The question, therefore, becomes whether much confidence can be reposed in the truth of persons asked about gun ownership by a surveyor.

The authors of *NEJM-1993* admit that "underreporting of gun ownership by control respondents could bias our estimate of risk upward."[78] They realize that this is a critical point, but they conclude that there is no underreporting.[79] Predictably, they do not mention the fact that false denial of gun ownership by survey respondents has long been deemed a major problem with calculating the true size of American gun ownership. Nor do they cite Professor Kleck's exhaustive discussion of this issue.[80]

The authors of *NEJM-1993* justify their dismissal of the problem of underreporting by noting that "a pilot study [conducted by four of the *NEJM-1993* authors plus one other person] of homes listed as the addresses of owners of registered handguns confirmed that respondents' answers to questions about gun ownership were generally valid."[81] It is reasonable to ask what "generally" means. In the pilot study, 97.1 percent of the families listed as the location of a registered handgun admitted to having guns in the home, either at the time or recently.[82] Superficially this appears to be an impressive record of openness. It becomes less impressive, however, when the numbers are placed in full perspective. Seventy-five homes were chosen from new handgun registration records.[83] Due to false addresses and other difficulties, only fifty-five could be found, and of these, only thirty-five consented to the interview.[84] These families are unrepresentative in an even more significant respect. These are people who have chosen to let the government know that they own guns, and who have undergone a governmental approval process. To learn that this sample is willing to admit the same facts to survey interviewers can tell us nothing about gun owners in general, let alone about the lower income gun owners in *NEJM-1993*.

In comparison with this sample of registered gun owners, it is likely that owners of unregistered guns would be even more reluctant to admit to ownership. Among other things, it may involve admission of a criminal offense.[85] Moreover, the control group could be further biased if criminals and owners of illicit guns are more likely to refuse to be interviewed for a study such as this, let alone to admit to gun ownership. With these possible discrepancies between measures of gun ownership in the homicide case and control homes, it appears that the authors quote their own previous work in a way which overstates its strength.

To reiterate, *NEJM-1993*'s conclusions depend entirely on an accurate estimation of the control group's gun ownership. In this case, it would take only 35 of the 388 controls falsely denying gun possession to make the control ownership percentage exactly equal that of the homicide case households. If indeed the controls actually had gun ownership equal to that of the homicide case households, then a false denial rate of only 20.1 percent among the gun owning controls would produce 35 false denials, thereby equaling ownership. Such a false denial rate is smaller than either the "Refused consent for interview" category of the pilot study, or the "inaccurate registration data" category.[86] Therefore, the results of the pilot study air consistent with a false denial rate sufficiently high to bring the control group gun ownership rate up to a level equal to, or even higher than, the homicide case household rate, although the authors cite the pilot study to the reverse effect.[87] Neglect of the false denial rate can produce a bias large enough, by itself, to account for the entire association between gun ownership and homicide claimed in this study.

INAPPROPRIATE METHOD OF STATISTICAL ANALYSIS

NEJM-1993's authors chose to use the Case Control Method (CCM).[88] This method is accepted in medical research as an investigatory tool with a strength in its ability to generate hypotheses, rather than as a final test of hypotheses.[89] A relevant weakness of the CCM is that it has a susceptibility to bias.[90] In the social sciences it is seldom possible to do the properly blinded, randomized, controlled studies which would be used to confirm a hypothesis. Thus, it becomes even more important to be sensitive to the possible existence of biases, and to attempt to minimize them. *NEJM-1993* makes conclusory claims about the association found between gun ownership and homicide, rather than asserting a tentative hypothesis.[91] According to the author's conclusion in the abstract,[92] "guns kept in the home are associated with an increase in the risk of homicide," and "our study confirms this association."[93] The authors' occasional qualification of their results[94] indicates that they understand the tentative nature of the results of Case Control Method studies, yet this does not appear to have tempered the presentation of their conclusions.

CONCLUSION

We believe we have documented an emotional antigun agenda in the treatment of firearms issues in the medical and public health literature. While the antigun editorials and articles discussed had the superficial form of academic discourse, the basic tenets of science and scholarship have too often been lacking. We call them "antigun health advocacy literature" because they are so biased and contain so many errors of fact, logic, and procedure that we cannot regard them as having a legitimate claim to be treated as scholarly or scientific literature.

Criminological and sociological analysis provides important, even crucial, information as to the role of firearms in violence and the utility and viability of potential gun control strategies. Virtually all of this information is ignored or affirmatively suppressed in the health advocacy literature. That literature also shows consistent patterns of making misleading international comparisons, mistaking the differences between handguns and long guns, and exaggerating the number of children injured or killed, thereby building up the emotional content. Other distortions include presenting gun ownership in such a manner as to ignore or minimize the benefits, and measuring defensive benefits purely in terms of attackers killed, rather than considering attacks deterred or attackers repelled. To the contrary, the criminological and sociological research literature demonstrates the existence of high-risk groups for firearms misuse, and of the "career" criminals who commit many of the serious crimes in our society. Yet the antigun health advocacy literature consistently overlooks these data and attributes equal propensity to commit violent crime to all people.

The health advocacy literature exists in a vacuum of lock-step orthodoxy almost hermetically sealed from the existence of contrary data or scholarship. Such data and scholarship routinely goes unmentioned and the adverse emotional reaction of the gatekeepers of the health journals assures the elimination of contrary views from their pages. In the rare instances in which works with contrary views are cited at all, they tend to be dismissed with ad hominem comments, but without the presentation of evidence or analysis refuting them. The antigun health advocacy literature can be described with the derogatory term "sagecraft," implying that academics have gone beyond the pale. Superficialities of scientific methodology and presentation are used to counterfeit scholarship supporting an antigun agenda while the basics of sound research are ignored. This shameful performance implies the willing collaboration of the researchers, the journals, and the CDC as a federal governmental funding agency. While many medical and public health journals have participated in this sagecraft, the *New England Journal of Medicine* has been one of the most noticeable. It has an editorial policy which is strongly and explicitly antigun, has published poorly written antigun articles, and has excluded articles which disagree with its editorial policy. These actions forfeit its claim to be a research journal rather than just a political advocacy publication.

This indictment of the antigun health advocacy literature is extremely troubling in an era in which research and data are often sought as a basis for debate over guns and formulation of public policy. When emotionally based antigun, pseudoscientific advocacy is presented in the guise of research, ill-founded policy decisions may ensue, wasting public resources and harming many people. The medical and public health journals need to eschew their emotionally based advocacy role in favor of presenting scientific research results.

Finally, some remark must be made on the idea of violence as an epidemic and a public health emergency. For that purpose, we are delighted to adopt recent comments by a preeminent neutral scholar in criminology, Professor James D. Wright:

> And there is a sense in which violence is a public health problem. So let me illustrate the limitations of this line of reasoning with a public-health analogy.
>
> After research disclosed that mosquitos were the vector for transmission of yellow fever, the disease was not controlled by sending men in white coats to the swamps to remove the mouth parts from all the insects they could find. The only sensible, efficient way to stop the biting was to attack the environment where the mosquitos bred.
>
> Guns are the mouth parts of the violence epidemic. The contemporary urban environment breeds violence no less than swamps breed mosquitos. Attempting to control the problem of violence by trying to disarm the perpetrators is as hopeless as trying to contain yellow fever through mandible control.[95]

NOTES

1. Webster et al., supra note 4, p. 73; see also Calhoun, supra note 4, p. 15 (most murderers "are neither felons nor crazy," but rather "people involved in family fights and fights over jobs and money, and people who are sad or depressed").

2. Christoffel, supra note 10, p. 300.

3. Goldsmith, supra note 4, p. 675 (quoting the president of the American College of Epidemiology); cf. "Brady Bill Has Medicine's Support," *American Medical News* (May 20, 1991): 25 ("Uncontrolled ownership and use of firearms" is "one of the main causes of intentional and unintentional injury and death."); Calhoun, supra note 4, p. 17 ("Guns are not just an inanimate object, but in fact are a social ill."); Somerville, supra note 4, p. 9 ("Guns are a virus that must be eradicated.").

4. See notes 5–11.

5. See, e.g., Bureau of Justice Statistics, U.S. Department of Justice, *Murder in Families* (1994): 5, table 7 [hereinafter *Murder in Families*]; Bureau of Justice Statistics, U.S. Department of Justice, Murder In Large Urban Counties (1993): 1988.

6. See Injury Prevention, supra note 4, p. 265 (asserting that prior criminal and assaultive behavior of murderers supports the utility of background checks for firearms purchasers); Eugene D. Wheeler and S. Anthony Baron, *Violence in Our Schools, Hospitals, and Public Places: A Prevention and Management Guide* (Ventura, Calif.: Pathfinder Pub., 1993), p. 166 ("A history of violence is the best predictor of [whether persons are likely to murder or commit other] violence."); "Centers for Disease Control and Prevention, Homicides Among 15–19 Year Old Males—United States 1963–1991," *Morbidity and Mortality Weekly Report* (1994): 725, 726–27. (noting drastically rising homicide among inner city youth and suggesting that "the immediate and specific causes" may include "the recruitment of juveniles into drug markets"); Andrew L. Dannenberg et al., "Intentional and Unintentional Injuries in Women: An Overview," *Annals Epidemiology* 4 (1994): 133, 137 ("Risk factors for [wifebattering] may include prior episodes of physical abuse"); Dowd et al., supra note 10, p. 871 (showing one study's finding that "75 percent of the 26 perpetrators for whom criminal status was known had a history of one or more arrests by the Kansas City police department"): Sheilagh Hidgins, "Mental Disorder, Intellectual Deficiency, and Crime: Evidence From a Birth Cohort," *Archives General Psychiatry* 49 (1992): 476 (citing numerous studies from

the United States, Canada, and Europe which indicate that persons suffering from major mental disorders, persons with subpar intelligence and substance abusers were each several times more likely to engage in violent crime than ordinary citizens).

7. An FBI data run of murder arrestees nationally over a four year period in the 1960s found 74.7 percent to have had prior arrests for violent felony or burglary. In one study, the Bureau of Criminal Statistics found that 76.7 percent of murder arrestees bad criminal histories as did 78 percent of defendants in murder prosecutions nationally. In another FBI data run of murder arrestees over a one year period, 77.9 percent had prior criminal records. Federal Bureau of Investigation *Uniform Crime Report* 38 (1971).

The annual Chicago Police Department bulletin *Murder Analysis* shows the following figures for the percentage of murderers who had prior crime records:

1991: 77.15%
1990: 74.63%
1989: 74.22%
1988: 73.59%
1987: 73.81%

Five-year average for 1987–1991: 74.68%

8. Federal Bureau of Investigation, *Uniform Crime Report* 43 (1975).

9. John Dilulio, "The Question of Black Crime," *Public Interest* 117 (1994): 3, 16.

10. See Kathleen M. Heide, "Weapons Used by Juveniles and Adults to Kill Parents," *Behavioral Science and Law* 11 (1993): 397, 398.

11. Ronald M. Holmes and Stephen T. Holmes, *Murder in America* (Thousand Oaks, Calif.: Sage Publications, 1994), pp. 8–9.

12. "Boy, 5, Is Killed for Refusing to Steal Candy," *New York Times*, 15 October 1994, p. 9 [hereinafter "Refusing to Steal"]; Dowd seems to have had special access to city-level police data including juvenile records because the age of shooting perpetrators averaged 19.5 and 75 percent had previously been arrested at least once by the local police. Dowd et al., supra note 10, p. 871.

13. "Refusing to Steal," p. 9.

14. Ibid.

15. Raspberry, supra note 5, p. A23.

16. Ibid.

17. Mark L. Rosenberg et al., "Violence as a Public Health Problem: A New Role for CDC and a New Alliance with Educators," *Educational Horizons* (1984): 124, 1226–27 (emphasis added).

18. Ibid., p. 124.

19. Mark L. Rosenberg et al., "Interpersonal Violence: Homicide and Spouse Abuse," in *Public Health and Preventive Medicine*, ed. John M. Lasted, 12th ed (Norwalk, Conn.: Appleton-Century-Crofts, 1986), pp. 1399–1426; see also Mark L. Rosenberg et al., "Violence: Homicide, Assault, and Suicide," in *Closing the Gap: The Burden of Unnecessary Illness*, ed. Robert W. Amler and H. Bruce Dull (New York: Oxford University Press, 1987), pp. 164–78.

20. Jeremiah A. Barondess, "Correspondence," *JAMA* 272 (1994): 1409 (emphasis added).

21. Daniel W. Webster, "The Unconvincing Case for School-Based Conflict Resolution Programs for Adolescents," *Health* AFF. 12 (1994): 126, 132.

22. Ibid.

23. Ibid., p. 133.

24. Ibid., p. 138.

25. Ibid., p. 137.

26. Kahn, supra note 10, p. 567.

27. Barondess, supra note 291, p. 1409.

28. Ibid. See notes 5 to 11 and accompanying text.

29. Barondess, supra note 291, p. 1409.

30. See Paul J. Goldstein, "Homicide Related to Drug Traffic," *Bulletin New York Academy of Medicine* 62 (1986): 509. Tardiff et al., supra note 10, p. 46; Franklin E. Zimring and James

Zuehl, "Victim Injury and Death in Urban Robbery: A Chicago Study," *Journal of Legal Studies* 15 (1986): 1, 9–12.

31. See, e.g., Michael D. McGonigal et al., "Urban Firearm Deaths: A Five-Year Perspective," *Journal of Trauma* 35 (1993): 532, 536–37. "Eighty-four percent of victims in 1990 had ante-mortem drug use or criminal history." Ibid., p. 532. H. Range Hutson et al., "Adolescents and Children Injured or Killed in Drive-By Shootings in Los Angeles," *New England Journal of Medicine* 330 (1994): 324, 325 (stating that 71 percent of children and adolescents injured in drive-by shootings "were documented members of violent street gangs").

Medical studies suggest that a minimum of 2,000 murders annually are drug-related, including one-third to one-half or more of the murders in some major cities. *Injury Prevention*, supra note 4, p. 206; Daniel W. Webster et al., "Epidemiologic Changes in Gunshot Wounds in Washington, D.C., 1983–1990," *Archives Surgery* 127 (1992): 694–98. Studies in three major trauma care centers reported finding urban knife and bullet wounds to be "a chronic recurrent disease peculiar to unemployed, uninsured law breakers." R. Stephen Smith et al., "Recidivism in an Urban Trauma Center," *Archives Surgery* 127 (1992): 694–98 (describing the conclusions in Deborah W. Sims et al., "Urban Trauma: A Chronic, Recurrent Disease," *Journal of Trauma* 29 [1989]: 940); Thomas B. Morrissey et al., "The Incidence of Recurrent Penetrating Wound Trauma in an Urban Trauma Center," *Journal of Trauma* 31 (1991): 1536.

32. *Murder in Families.*

33. Rosenberg et al., "Violence, Homicide, Assault, and Suicide," pp. 126–27.

34. Holmes and Holmes, *Murder in America*, p. 28.

35. Murray A. Straus, "Domestic Violence and Homicide Antecedents," 62 *Bulletin, New York Academy of Medicine* 446, 457 (1986).

36. Ibid., p. 454.

37. See Kleck & Bordua, supra note 1] 8.

38. Arthur L. Kellermann et al., "Gun Ownership as a Risk Factor for Homicide in the Home," *New England Journal of Medicine* 327 (1993): 1084 [hereinafter *NEJM-1993*].

39. Daniel D. Polsby, "The False Promise of Gun Control," *Atlantic Monthly*, March 1994, pp. 59, 60 (stating that "within two months [of its publication, *NEJM-1993*] received almost 100 mentions in publications and broadcast transcripts indexed in the Nexis data base," including "prominent coverage" in the *New York Times, Los Angeles Times, Washington Post, Boston Globe*, and *Chicago Tribune*).

40. Since its appearance it has been cited in at least the following articles: Adler et al., supra note 4, p. 1283; Dannenberg et al., supra note 277, p. 137; Mercy et al., supra note 12, p. 28; Jeffrey J. Sacks et al., "Correspondence," *JAMA* 272 (1994): 847, 848; Yvonne D. Senturia et al., "Reply," *Pediatrics* 97 (1994): 777, 778; Susan B. Sorenson and Audrey F. Saftlas, "Violence and Women's Health: The Role of Epidemiology," *Annnals Epidemiology* 4 (1994): 140, 145; Webster and Wilson, supra note 5, p. 622.

41. See generally William G. Cochran and Gertrude M. Cox, *Experimental Designs*, 2d ed. (New York: Wiley, 1992) (providing background information on the field).

42. Klaus Hinkelmann and Oscar Kempthorne, *Design and Analysis of Experiments: Introduction to Experimental Design* (New York: Wiley, 1994), p. 361 (discussing intentional confounding).

43. *NEJM-1993*, p. 1084.

44. Ibid., pp. 1084–85.

45. Ibid., pp. 1087–90.

46. Ibid., p. 1090.

47. Ibid., p. 1084. The three counties included Shelby County, Tennessee, containing Memphis; King County, Washington, containing Seattle; and Cuyahoga County, Ohio. containing Cleveland.

48. Ibid., p. 1085.

49. Ibid.

50. Ibid.

51. Ibid., p. 1086, table 1. Other data in table 1, taken in conjunction with the data in table 3, and other data discussed in the text, shows that in a substantial number of the homicides by gun,

the gun was brought in from outside, presumably by the perpetrator. *NEJM-1993*'s authors refuse to disclose their study data to scholars who want to evaluate their findings. Without access to the data, it is not possible to determine the actual fraction of guns which were brought into the household and used in homicide.

52. See, eg., Cook, supra note 87, p. n.4 ("The Metropolitan [District of Columbia] Police Department classified most homicides by motive: the fraction classified as drug-related increased from 21 percent to 80 percent between 1985 and 1988."); Ann D. Helms, "In Charlotte, Risk of Being Shot Seems Tied to Lifestyle, Study Says," *Charlotte Observer*, 25 November 1994, p. 1A (discussing all gunshot wounds reported to the Charlotte, N.C., Police Department from 1992 to 1993). Of the 632 known gunshot victims, 71 percent of the 545 adult victims had known criminal records. Ibid., p. 14A. The juvenile victims could not be analyzed for criminal records because of the unavailability of juvenile criminal records.

53. *NEJM-1993*, pp. 1084–85.

54. Ibid., p. 1086.

55. Ibid., pp. 1086–88.

56. Ibid., p. 1088.

57. Ibid., pp. 1086–88.

58. See generally Jan M. Chaiken and Marcia R. Chaiken, *Varieties of Criminal Behavior* (Santa Monica, Calif.: Rand Corp., 1982). Based on a survey of 2,190 felons in California, Michigan, and Texas prisons of the crimes they had committed in the two years prior to their incarceration. Chaiken and Chaiken determined that a small minority were responsible for most crimes, and particularly the serious ones. The average "violent predator" (their term for these career criminals) reported committing eight assaults, 63 robberies, 172 burglaries, 1,252 drug deals and 214 miscellaneous other thefts in a one year period. Ibid.; Jan M. Chaiken and Marcia R. Chaiken, "Offender Types and Public Policy," *Delinquency* 30 (1984): 195; cf. Paul E. Tracy et al., *Delinquency Careers in Two Birth Cohorts* (New York: Plenum, 1990) (showing that between their tenth and eighteenth years, of 13,160 Philadelphia boys born in 1958, 67.2 percent were never arrested, 25.3 percent were arrested four or fewer times, 7.5 percent were arrested five or more times accounting for 60.6 percent of the arrests in the total birth cohort); Marvin E. Wolfgang, *Delinquency in a Birth Cohort* (Chicago: University of Chicago Press, 1972) (showing that between their tenth and eighteenth years, of 9,945 Philadelphia boys born in 1945, 65.1 percent had no offenses, 16.2 percent had one offense, 12.4 percent had a few offenses, and 6.3 percent committed 51.9 percent of the offenses in the cohort).

59. By way of analogy, suppose a study of people who had had one heart attack, and then later died of another, showed that more of them had taken up strenuous exercise after their first heart attack than had a control group of heart attack victims who had not taken up strenuous exercise after the first attack. That result would suggest that strenuous exercise was a risk factor for people who are at high risk of having a heart attack. But it would not prove anything about the level of risk that strenuous exercise imposes on low, or ordinary, risk people who have never had a heart attack.

60. *NEJM-1993*, pp. 1084–87.

61. Ibid., p. 1088 (emphasis added). The effect of excluding cases of homicide of children under thirteen years of age is not clear, but the authors note that this was done "at the request of the medical examiners." Ibid., p. 1084.

62. Ibid., p. 1085.

63. Ibid.

64. Ibid.

65. Ibid.

66. Ibid., p. 1086.

67. Ibid., p. 1089.

68. Ibid., pp. 1085, 1087.

69. Letter from Arthur L. Kellermann to Henry Schaffer (October 12, 1994). This research was supported by grants from the Centers for Disease Control and Prevention of the National Institutes of Health. The CDC does not require that data resulting from their grants be made available

to the public. This is in contrast to the policy of the National Institute of Justice, which requires that comparable datasets be made publicly available.

70. A. Bradford Hill, *Statistical Methods in Clinical and Preventitive Medicine* (New York: Oxford University Press, 1962), quoted in J. B. Chassan, *Research Design in Clinical Psychology and Psychiatry*, 2d ed. (New York: Wiley, 1979), p. 100.

71. Hinklemann and Kempthorne, p. 22.

72. *NEJM-1993*, p. 1085.

73. Ibid., p. 1088. Table 3 includes excessive alcohol use, illicit drug use, and presence or absence of an arrest record.

74. See generally Christopher S. Dunn, "Crime Area Research," in *Crime: A Spatial Perspective*, ed. Daniel E. Georges-Abeyie and Keith D. Harries (New York: Columbia University Press, 1980), p. 5.

75. See note 57 and above accompanying text.

76. *NEJM-1993*, pp. 1087–88.

77. While the problem of unwillingness to admit gun ownership is not entirely absent as to the homicide case households, it is much less acute. *NEJM-1993*'s authors had police reports as to these households. Ibid., p. 1084. In cases where the murder weapon was left near the body the police report would presumably so indicate. In cases where it was not, the report would presumably indicate whether the home was searched for guns, whether other occupants, if any, were asked about gun ownership, and whether registration records were consulted to see if a gun was registered to a person living in the household. The family of the deceased in the case-subject home also had time between the homicide and the interview to go through the effects of the deceased and to discover a gun, if one was owned. None of this, however, eliminates the possibility that a gun was kept in the homicide household. That possibility is far better minimized as to the homicide case households than as to the control households. There. the accuracy of *NEJM-1993*'s gun ownership finding is entirely dependent on the truthfulness of the interviewees

78. Ibid., p. 1089.

79. Ibid.

80. Kleck, *Point Blank*, supra note 2, p. 455. We must remark that the quantitative difference between the paragraph they devote to this issue, and the appendix that Kleck devotes to it, is emblematic of the qualitative difference in scholarship between Kleck and the entire health advocacy literature.

81. *NEJM-1993*, p. 1089 (emphasis added) (citing Kellermann et al., "Validating Survey Responses to Questions About Gun Ownership Among Owners of Registered Handguns," *American Journal of Epidemiology* 131 [1990]: 1080–84 [hereinafter Kellermann et al., "Validating Survey"]).

82. Kellerman et al., "Validating Survey," p. 1080.

83. Ibid.

84. Ibid. The correct degree of openness should be based not just on these final 35, but on the larger original sample. Only 31 of the 55 homes contacted (61.84 percent) admitted to gun ownership and only 31 of the total of 75 homes (45.3 percent) selected were contacted and then willing to admit gun ownership. The failure to find or contact 22 of the 75 registered owners (29.3 percent) may relate to their unwillingness to be connected with ownership. The owners who could not be reached (24 percent) might also have the same root cause. With only 45.3 percent of the registered handgun owners finally admitting to gun ownership, little substantiation is provided for the assumption that all guns owned by the control group would be admitted. Ibid.

85. Ibid., p. 1083. For example, the state of Tennessee and the city of Cleveland have various handgun registration or transfer regulations. Owners who violate these regulations have committed an offense which varies in seriousness depending on place of residence. The state of Washington also has a permit system for dealer transfer. Additionally, some handgun owners may have heard of the extremely severe limitations on handgun possession in many large cities. such as Washington, D.C., New York, and Chicago. All of these regulations would tend to make the owner reluctant to admit to the presence of an unregistered handgun. *NEJM-1993* does not mention how many of the guns in either the homicide or the control groups were owned legally.

86. Ibid.

87. *NEJM-1993*, p. 1089.

88. Ibid., p. 1084.

89. Thomas B. Newman et al., "Designing a New Study: II. Cross-sectional and Case-control Studies," in *Designing Clinical Research*, ed. Stephen B. Hulley and Steven R. Cummings (Baltimore: Williams and Wikins, 1988), pp. 78–86.

90. Ibid., p. 80. "Case control studies are a cheap and practical way to investigate risk factors for rare diseases, or to generate hypotheses about new diseases or unusual outbreaks. These are great strengths, but they are achieved at a considerable cost. . . . The biggest weakness of case-control studies is their increased susceptibility to bias." Ibid.

91. *NEJM-1993*, supra note 311, p. 1084.

92. Ibid.

93. Ibid., p. 1090.

94. Ibid., p. 1089 "People who keep guns in their homes appear to be at greater risk homicide in the home than people who do not." Ibid (emphasis added).

95. James D. Wright, "Bad Guys, Bad Guns," *National Review* (March 6, 1995): p. 51

23

NONFATAL AND FATAL FIREARM-RELATED INJURIES

JOURNAL OF THE AMERICAN MEDICAL ASSOCIATION

Abstract: The rate of death and injury from firearms dropped substantially between 1993 and 1997. According to statistics from the National Electronic Injury Surveillance System (NEISS) of the U.S. Consumer Product Safety Commission, the death rate from firearm injuries dropped 21 percent during this time period. The number of nonfatal injuries decreased 41 percent. This is consistent with a 21 percent drop in violent crime during the same time period. Surveys of high school students also show a 25 percent decline in the number of students who carry a gun on school property.

In 1997, 32,436 deaths resulted from firearm-related injuries, making such injuries the second leading cause of injury mortality in the United States after motor-vehicle-related incidents.[1] Also in 1997, an estimated 64,207 persons sustained nonfatal firearm-related injuries and were treated in U.S. hospital emergency departments (EDs); approximately 40 percent required inpatient hospital care. National firearm-related injury and death rates peaked in 1993, then began to decline.[2] This report presents national data from 1993 through 1997, which showed that the decline in nonfatal and fatal firearm-related injury rates was substantial and consistent by sex, race/ethnicity, age, and intent of injury. . . .

Overall, annual nonfatal and fatal firearm-related injury rates declined consistently from 1993 through 1997. The annual nonfatal rate decreased 40.8 percent, from 40.5 per 100,000 (95 percent CI = 22.6–58.4) in 1993 to 24.0 per

From the *Journal of the American Medical Association* 283 (January 5, 2000): 47–48.

100,000 (95 percent CI = 13.8–34.1) in 1997. This decline was accompanied by a decrease of 21.1 percent in the annual death rate from 15.4 per 100,000 (95 percent CI = 15.2–15.5) in 1993 to 12.1 per 100,000 (95 percent CI = 12.0–12.3) in 1997.

The declines in nonfatal and fatal firearm-related injury rates generally were consistent across all population subgroups. The declines in nonfatal and fatal injury rates were similar for males (40.7 percent for nonfatal, 20.9 percent for fatal) and for females (42.1 percent for nonfatal, 23.2 percent for fatal). Declines in death rates for blacks and Hispanics were similar, and were both greater than the decline observed for non-Hispanic whites. For nonfatal injury rates, no consistent pattern was found in the estimated decline across age groups, but for fatal injury rates, age and percentage change were inversely related. With respect to intent, the declines in nonfatal injury rates were seen in assault related, intentionally self-inflicted, and unintentional firearm-related injuries. However, the declines in homicide and unintentional injury death rates were approximately three times greater than that of the suicide rate.

Overall, quarterly fatal and nonfatal firearm-related injury rates showed statistically significant downward trends over the 5-year period adjusting for seasonal changes (overall predicted percentage declines were 36.6 percent and 17.3 percent for nonfatal and fatal injury rates, respectively, from first quarter 1993 through fourth quarter 1997; p [less than] 0.01 for both). For males aged 15–24 years, quarterly assaultive firearm-related injury rates also declined significantly from 1993 through 1997 (overall predicted percentage declines were 37.5 percent and 16.0 percent for nonfatal and fatal injury rates, respectively, from first quarter 1993 through fourth quarter 1997; p [less than] 0.01 for both). For males aged 15–24 years, the cyclical seasonal pattern was consistent for both fatal and nonfatal assaultive firearm-related injury rates, with the highest rates occurring during July, August, and September. These summer rates were significantly higher than rates during the other three quarters for fatal injuries (p [less than] 0.01) but not for nonfatal injuries (p = 0. 17).

Reported by: Office of Statistics and Programming and Division of Violence Prevention, National Center for Injury Prevention and Control, CDC.

CDC Editorial Note: The overall percentage decline in nonfatal and fatal firearm-related injury rates in the U.S. population from 1993 through 1997 is consistent with a 21 percent decrease in violent crime during the same time.[4] Since 1950, unintentional fatal firearm-related injury rates have declined. NEISS data also suggest a decline since 1993 in the rate of nonfatal unintentional firearm-related injuries treated in hospital EDs. Most of these nonfatal injuries occurred among males aged 15–44 years, were self-inflicted, and were associated with hunting, target shooting, and routine gun handling (i.e., cleaning, loading, and unloading a gun).[5] Additional investigation should focus on factors that may have contributed to the decrease, such as gun safety courses and information campaigns, the proportion of the population that uses guns for recreational purposes, and legislation.

Numerous factors may have contributed to the decrease in both nonfatal and fatal assaultive firearm-related injury rates. Possible contributors include improvements in economic conditions; the aging of the population; the decline of the crack cocaine market; changes in legislation, sentencing guidelines, and law-enforcement practices; and improvements associated with violence prevention programs.[6] However, the importance and relative contribution of each of these factors have not been determined, and the reasons are not known for the declines in firearm-related suicide and suicide attempt rates.

This analysis also indicates that using NEISS is an effective means for tracking national estimates of nonfatal firearm-related injuries. Quarterly nonfatal firearm-related injury rates based on NEISS data track closely with firearm-related death rates based on death-certificate data. For males aged 15–24 years, a known high-risk group for assaultive injury,[2,3] both fatal and nonfatal quarterly assaultive firearm-related rates show cyclical seasonal trends over the five-year study period, with the highest rates occurring during the summer months.

A limitation of NEISS is that it is not designed to provide data to examine trends at the state and local level. State and local data are needed for jurisdictions to design and evaluate firearm-related injury-prevention programs. CDC has collaborated with states and communities to design and implement successful firearm-related injury surveillance and data systems,[7] which can serve as models for future efforts.

Although firearm-related injuries have declined substantially across all intent categories and population subgroups, recent school-related shootings, multiple shootings, and homicide-suicide incidents are reminders that firearm-related injuries remain a serious public health concern. Even with the significant declines in nonfatal and fatal firearm-related injury rates, approximately 96,000 persons in the United States sustained gunshot wounds in 1997. However, results from the Youth Risk Behavior Survey also indicate a decline in violence-related behavior among high school students, including a 25 percent decline in carrying guns on school property and a 9 percent decline in engaging in a physical fight on school grounds during this five-year period.[8] Prevention efforts should continue to design, implement, and evaluate public health, criminal justice, and education programs to further reduce firearm-related injuries in the United States.

NOTES

1. D. L. Hoyert, K. D. Kochanek, and S. L. Murphy, "Deaths: final data for 1997," *Monthly Vital Statistics Report* 47 (1999): 9.

2. D. Cherry, J. L. Annest, J. A. Mercy, M. Kresnow, and D. A. Pollock, "Trends in nonfatal and fatal firearm-related injury rates in the United States, 1985-1995." Ann Emerg Med 32 (1998): 51–59.

3. J. L. Annest, J. A. Mercy, D. R. Gibson, and G. W. Ryan, "National estimates of nonfatal firearm-related injuries: beyond the tip of the iceberg." *JAMA* 273 (1995): 1749–54.

4. M. Rand, *Criminal Victimization 1997: Changes 1996–1997 with Trends 1993–1997* (Washington, D.C.: U.S .Department of Justice, Bureau of Justice Statistics, December 1998).

5. N. Sinauer, J. L. Annest, and J. A. Mercy, "Unintentional, nonfatal firearm-related injuries: a preventable public health burden," *JAMA* 275 (1996): 1740–43.

6. M. H. Moore and M. Tonry, "Youth violence in America," in *Crime and Justice: A Review of the Research*, vol 24, ed. M. Tonry and M. H. Moore (Chicago, Illinois: The University of Chicago Press, 1998), pp.1–26.

7. R. M. Ikeda, J. A. Mercy, and S. P. Teret, eds., "Firearm-related injury surveillance," *American Journal of Preventive Medicine* 15 (1998): (3S).

24

THE MEDICAL/PUBLIC HEALTH LITERATURE ON GUNS AND VIOLENCE

GARY KLECK

The normal historical pattern in science is for the technical quality of research to improve over time, since each researcher seeking to add to the sum of human knowledge is obliged to read the reports of previous researchers and to improve on their work in some way. The pattern in the guns-violence field over the period since the early 1980s has been just the opposite, with a pronounced deterioration in the average technical quality of published research. The main cause of this unfortunate pattern has been the flood of unprofessional work published in medical and public health journals.

For a researcher to be a "professional" implies, at minimum, two things: (1) a mastery of the existing body of knowledge, and (2) advanced formal training in the research methods of the field, sufficient to enable the person to make useful new contributions that improve on prior research. Merely publishing articles in professional journals is no guarantee that the author is a professional. Judging from what is allowed into print in medical journals, the referees evaluating paper submissions to the journals seem to be amateurs, whose only claim to expert status may be a record of previous publications in medical journals, publications likewise refereed by amateurs.

While it is possible for amateurs to make useful contributions with respect to topics requiring more modest skills, such as simple descriptions of phenomena,

Reprinted with permission from Gary Kleck, *Targeting Guns: Firearms and Their Conterol* (Hawthorne, N.Y.: Aldine de Gruyter, 1997), pp. 56–62. Copyright © 1997 by Walter de Gruyter, Inc., New York.

they are far more likely to make serious mistakes in tackling more complex topics, such as the causal linkages between phenomena. Based solely on the quality of published work, it is clear that the researchers who publish their work on guns and violence primarily in medical journals are almost all amateurs, in the sense that they have neither an adequate mastery of the body of relevant substantive knowledge nor professional-level skills in applying the appropriate research methods. Although there is nothing about a medical degree that disqualifies someone from doing research on the links between guns and violence, there is also nothing in medical school training that adequately prepares one to do such work.

As a result of these limitations, combined with a willingness to combine scholarship with personal advocacy of a political agenda (Kates et al. 1995; see Teret et al. 1990 for an overt defense of advocacy research), research on guns published in medical outlets is commonly of abysmal quality. The major exception is research providing simple descriptions of gun homicides, suicides, accidents, and nonfatal woundings, usually based on examination of hospital and medical examiner records, a type of research that requires only modest skills, along with the access to records more readily released to medical researchers.

Unfortunately, the central research issues in the guns-violence field are ones of causal linkages. Does greater gun availability cause more violence? Do higher violence rates cause higher gun ownership rates? Does the use of a gun by an aggressor cause higher risks of attack, injury, or death for the victim? Does the use of a gun by a victim cause lower risks of attack, injury, or death for the victim? It is fair to describe the work of medical researchers on these issues as almost uniformly incompetent and consistently biased.

This sort of sweeping assessment should be backed up by specifics as to the ways in which this research is substandard. The following is a brief and undoubtedly incomplete list of some of the more common and serious shortcomings of medical studies drawing conclusions about guns-violence causal links:

1. An ignorance of prior research, and an almost complete ignorance of the technically sound research, with reviews limited to the generally primitive research published in medical journals (consult any review published in a medical journal and compare it to studies cited herein).

2. As a result of the preceding problem, an ignorance of the basic issues, i.e., what questions need to be addressed. For example, the important policy issue is not the association of gun levels with rates of *gun* violence (e.g., the gun homicide rate or the gun suicide rate) but rather the association of gun levels with rates of *total* violence (e.g., the total homicide rate or the total suicide rate) (e.g., Violence Prevention Task Force of the Eastern Association for the Surgery of Trauma 1995:165).

3. Related to the preceding problem, confusing the effects of the weapon on violence with effects of the intentions of the user of the weapon (or a failure to recognize and acknowledge that this is even an issue). That is, fatality rates in gun attacks may be higher than in knife attacks because those who choose guns

are more lethal in their intentions, and this, rather than the weapon itself, may at least partly account for the fatality rate difference.

4. The failure to address (or even be aware of) the possible two-way relationship between gun availability and violence, leading to a confusion of cause and effect. Thus, in cases where higher violence levels caused more people to acquire guns, researchers misinterpreted the positive association to mean that higher gun levels had caused higher violence rates (e.g., Sloan, Kellermann, et al. 1988; Killias 1993a).

5. The use of small, unrepresentative, nonprobability local convenience samples that preclude generalization to large populations and increase the likelihood of sample bias (e.g., Brent et al. 1988, based on twenty-seven adolescent suicide victims in the Pittsburgh area and matching controls; Kellermann et al. 1993,* who drew conclusions about the entire gun-owning population based on a nonprobability sample of households in the high-homicide areas of just three nonrandomly selected urban counties; Bergstein, Hemenway, Kennedy, Quaday, and Ander 1996, who drew conclusions about "urban youth" based on convenience samples of seventh and tenth graders in two cities).

6. The use of primitive bivariate data analytical methods that fail to control for confounding factors (e.g., Sloan, Kellermann, et al. 1988; Killias 1993a; Lester 1989b). The Sloan, Kellermann, et al.† comparison of Seattle and Vancouver, published in America's most prestigious medical journal, the *New England Journal of Medicine*, was arguably the most technically primitive study of guns-violence links ever published in a professional journal, in a field where poor research abounds. It used dubious measures of gun ownership that turned out to be inaccurate, bivariate data analysis, and a sample consisting of a grand total of *two* nonrandomly selected cities. It was described by Professor James Wright as "little more than polemics masquerading as serious research" (1989:46).

The reaction in the community of medical researchers, on the other hand, was very different. The study was lavishly praised by Dr. Garen Wintemute as "an elegant evaluation of firearm mortality" (1989–1990:21) and commended by CDC employees James Mercy and Vernon Houk for its application of "scientific methods" (1988:1284).

7. Ignorance about valid measures of gun availability or about the limits of those measures (e.g., Sloan, Kellermann, et al. 1988), or the willingness to assert an association between gun availability and violence when the authors did not even measure gun availability (e.g., Farmer and Rohde 1980; Boyd 1983; Boyd and Mowscicki 1986; Wintemute 1987; Marzuk, Tardiff, Smyth, Stajic, and Leon 1992; Tardiff et al. 1994).

The consequences of ignorance about gun measurement flaws are especially apparent in the comparison of Seattle with Vancouver by Sloan, Kellermann, and

---

*See Arthur L. Kellermann et al., "Gun Ownership as a Risk Factor for Homicide in the Home," in Part Four of this volume.—Ed.

†See John Henry Sloan, "Handgun Regulations, Crime, Assaults, and Homicide," in Part Four of this volume.—Ed.

their colleagues (1988). They compared noncomparable rates of issuance of very different kinds of gun permits (Wright 1989:46) and inappropriately applied an indirect measure of "gun prevalence." When direct survey measures later became available, however, those data indicated that the household prevalence levels of gun ownership in the two cities were essentially identical: 23 percent in greater Vancouver (Mauser 1989) and 24 percent in Seattle (Callahan, Rivara, and Koepsell 1994:475).

8. Selective reporting of findings favorable to procontrol or antigun conclusions and nondisclosure of unsupportive findings (e.g., Lester 1991a and Killias 1993b; see also examples cited in Kates et al. 1995).

9. Lumping together disparate gun-related forms of violence such as intentionally and unintentionally inflicted injuries, and self-inflicted and other-inflicted injuries, and drawing conclusions about all gun violence as a single entity, in a way that obscures the radically different influences guns have on each different form of violence (e.g., Sadowski et al. 1989).

10. Lumping together children and adolescents, in a way that conceals how little gun violence involves the former and how much involves the latter. For example, Teret and Wintemute claimed that "almost 1,000 children die each year from unintentional gunshot wounds" (1983:341), a statistic that turned out to actually refer to all persons aged 0–24; almost all of the gun accident deaths in this age range involved adolescents and young adults, not children (PB:277,309). In 1992, only 18 percent of accidental gun deaths in this age range involved children age 0–12, among whom the death rate is virtually zero (National Safety Council 1995:32; PB:277). This practice serves propagandistic purposes by playing on people's strong feelings about children and on their greater willingness to view children, in contrast to adolescents, as innocent victims of violence. It also directs disproportionate attention to potential solutions that are relevant only to the rare childinvolved case (e.g., "child-proofing" guns to prevent gun accidents involving shooters young enough to be affected by the measures; see Nelson, Grant-Worley, Powell, Mercy, and Holtzman 1996:1746 for an example).

11. Unprofessional bias in interpretation of results, such that all results lead to procontrol/antigun conclusions, regardless of the character of the evidence. That is, the procontrol/antigun propositions are treated as nonfalsifiable hypotheses. For example, Callahan and his colleagues' (1994) evidence indicated, by their own admission, that a gun "buy-back' program was ineffective, prompting the authors to call for more and better turn-in programs. Thus, it was clear that these authors were prepared to support buy-back programs no matter how negative their research results were (for a critique, see Kleck 1996b:31–32).

Likewise, Bergstein, Hemenway, and their colleagues (1996) tested the hypothesis that "easy access" to guns increases unsupervised gun handling and gun carrying among urban youth. With two measures of "access" ("could get a gun if they wanted one" and "gun in the home") and two gunrelated behaviors, they had four chances for their hypothesis to be supported. All four multivariate results were negative: neither measure of "easy access" to guns was related to either unsupervised gun handling or gun carrying (ibid.:797). The authors' conclusions nevertheless were that gun carrying is indeed "related to" easy access (ibid.:794), and their recommended strategy for reducing gun handling and carrying was "reducing access to guns" (ibid.:797). Leaving aside whether this conclusion is actually reasonable, it clearly did not follow from the authors' research findings. Given that the authors were willing to conclude that access to guns should be reduced, in the face of totally unsupportive results, it is hard to see what findings could have induced the authors to reject their procontrol hypothesis.

12. A lack of simple common sense, as when medical researchers attempted to establish how rarely gun owners conceal their gun ownership when interviewed in surveys, by studying a sample of registered gun owners (Kellermann, Rivara, Banton, Reay, and Fligner 1990). Given that all registered gun owners have, by definition, already shown themselves to be willing to let strangers know that they own guns, the fact that most of this small and unrepresentative sample of gun owners told interviewers that they own guns obviously can tell us nothing about how large a share of the general gun owner population is not willing to tell strangers that they own guns. Or consider Kellermann's assumption that if few victims of "home invasions" tell police about their defensive uses of guns, it means that they rarely occur (Kellermann, Westphal, Fischer, and Harvard 1995).

FALSE CITATION OF PRIOR RESEARCH

One final problem in the medical/public health literature on gun-sviolence links is so widespread, serious, and misleading that it deserves extended attention: the false citation of previous research as supporting antigun/procontrol conclusions, buttressing the author's current findings, when the studies actually did no such thing.

In a typical example, a researcher might assert that gun levels increase homicide rates and cite five supposedly supportive studies. Of the five, one might provide weak and debatable support, one might be merely a previous expression of similar personal opinion on the issue (often in an editorial or propaganda publication), another might not even address the topic, still another might have drawn non sequitur conclusions based on irrelevant information, and the last might even have generated evidence indicating the exact opposite conclusion.

Consider, for example, a widely cited article by Arthur Kellermann* and his colleagues, wherein they claim that "cohort and interrupted time-series studies have demonstrated a strong link between the availability of guns and community rates of homicide" (1993:1090), citing four previous studies in support (their citations 2, 15–17). Naive readers might assume that Kellermann et al. were citing four "cohort and interrupted time-series studies" that had empirically documented a guns-homicide association. In fact, the first of the cited publications was not an empirical study at all, but rather a review of the literature (their citation 2) that did not support this assertion. The part of this report cited by

---

*See Arthur L. Kellermann et al., "Gun Ownership as a Risk Factor for Homicide in the Home," in Part Four of this volume.—Ed.

the Kellermann et al. (ibid.:42–97) did not even address the issue in question, while the part that did address it did not conclude that there was a strong guns-homicide link. Instead, the review authors cited an earlier review as having indicated that studies "*generally* find that greater gun availability is associated with . . . *somewhat* greater rates of felony murder, but *do not account for a large fraction of the variation*" (Reiss and Roth 1993:268, emphasis added) and drew an unmistakably "no decision" conclusion, noting problems of causal order that Kellermann and his medical colleagues have consistently ignored. Perhaps Kellermann simply did not know enough of the rudiments of statistics to understand that to state that one variable does not account for a large fraction of the variation in the other variable means that the association is not strong, i.e., exactly the opposite of the conclusions Kellermann et al. were citing the Reiss and Roth review to support.*

Among the remaining three supposedly supportive studies, one did not even measure "the availability of guns," nor did its authors claim to have done so, and thus it could not possibly have established any guns-homicide association, never mind a strong one (their citation 17, to Loftin, McDowall, Wiersema, and Cottey 1991). The third cited study only weakly supported the authors' claim (citation 15, Cook 1979). This study addressed only robbery homicides, which accounted for only 10 percent of U.S. homicides the year Kellermann et al. wrote (U.S. FBI 1994:21), and apparently confused an effect of robbery murders on rates of gun ownership with an effect of gun levels on robbery murder rates. Finally, the authors also cited a crude two-city study of their own (Sloan, Kellermann, Reay, et al. 1988) that simply ignored the causal order issue, used indirect measures of gun ownership that turned out to be inaccurate, and drew conclusions that ignored differences between the cities that were responsible for some or all of the observed differences in homicide.

In sharp contrast, the authors completely omitted any mention of the most sophisticated research that did address the causal order issue, measured gun ownership levels, and used multivariate controls. Perhaps it is just coincidence that these more sophisticated but uncited analyses generally found no causal effect of gun levels on homicide rates (Kleck 1984a; Magaddino and Medoff 1984 [only some of whose results were based on models taking two-way relationships into account; see pp. 251, column 1, p. 253, column 1 and p. 258, for the relevant results]; Kleck 1991:191–201, 219–22; but see Kleck 1979, whose results were superseded by Kleck 1984a). Perhaps Kellermarm and his colleagues felt that studies that did not even measure gun availability provided a sounder basis for drawing conclusions about the guns-homicide link than studies that did.

There are unfortunately dozens of similar miscitations in the medical literature on guns and violence. They include authors

---

*See Albert J. Reiss and Jeffrey A. Roth, "Understanding and Preventing Violence," in Part Three of this volume.—Ed.

1. citing studies for support when the studies in fact contained no relevant information (Teret and Wintemute 1983:347; Schetky 1985:229; Webster, Gainer, and Champion 1993:1604; Tardiff et al. 1994:45; U.S. Centers for Disease Control 1992b:452);

2. citing studies as if they contained supporting empirical evidence, without informing readers that the citations merely referred to other authors who had expressed similar personal opinions in editorials, etc. (Rivara and Stapleton lf82:37; Saltzman, Mercy, O'Carroll, Rosenberg, and Rhodes 1992:3045; Bergstein, Hemenway et al. 1996:797);

3. citing nonexistent statistics (Schetky 1985:229; Kellermann and Reay 1986:1559; Callahan and Rivara 1992:5041; Hemenway, Solnick, and Azrael 1995a:48; Sinauer, Annest, and Mercy 1996); and even

4. citing as supportive of the author's views studies that actually reached contrary conclusions (Rushforth, Hirsch, Ford, and Adelson 1975:503; Sloan, Kellermann, et al. 1988:1256; Runyan and Gerken 1989:2275; U.S. Centers for Disease Control 1991; Kellermarm et al. 1992:467; 1993:1090; Callahan et al. 1994).

For details on what studies were miscited and how the citations were in error, as well as additional examples, see Kleck 1997b.

It bears stressing that the authors were not the only people complicit in these miscitations. In each case, inaccurate citations that would have been conspicuous to genuinely expert reviewers went uncorrected because both journal editors and the supposedly expert referees who reviewed the papers failed to recognize the mistakes and ensure that they were fixed, indicating that these parties either were not familiar enough with the research in this field to recognize the inaccuracies or were not concerned enough about miscitations in a procontrol direction to make sure that they were corrected. Kates and his colleagues identified the costs of incompetent and biased peer review: "An atmosphere in which criticism in general, and peer review in particular, comes from only one perspective not only allows error, but promotes it" (1995:530).*

CONCLUSIONS

Would it be any wonder if readers of medical journals and federal government reports were convinced that research overwhelmingly supports the guns-cause-violence thesis? Surrounded by selective, biased, and systematically misstated summaries of what prior research found, almost all radically biased to favor pro-control conclusions regardless of the evidence, even open-minded readers would have a hard time acquiring even an approximately accurate and representative picture of the full body of evidence. The body of medical/public health litera-

---

*See Don B. Kates et al., "The Myth That Murderers Are Ordinary Gun Owners," in Part Fourt of this volume.—Ed.

ture on guns violence links in particular is so thoroughly tainted by either dishonesty, ignorance, or gross incompetence that readers who take on faith the conclusions expressed therein do so at their peril.

REFERENCES

Bergstein, Jack M., David Hemenway, Bruce Kennedy, Shere Quaday, and Roseanna Ander. 1996. "Guns in young hands." *Journal of Trauma* 41:794–98.

Callahan, Charles M., Frederick P. Rivara, and Thomas D. Koepsell, 1994. "Money for guns: evaluation of the Seattle gun buy-back program." *Public Health Reports* 104:472–77.

Hemenway, David, Sara J. Solnick, and Deborah R. Azrael. 1995a. "Firearm training and storage." *Journal of the American Medical Association* 273:48–50.

———. 1995b. "Firearms and community feelings of safety." *Journal of Criminal Law and Criminology* 86: 121–32.

Kates, Don B., Henry E. Schaffer, John K. Lattimer, George B. Murray, and Edwin H. Cassem. 1995. "Guns and public health: Epidemic of violence or pandemic of propaganda?" *Tennessee Law Review* 62:5113–96.

Kellermann, Arthur L. 1993. "Obstacles to firearm and violence research." *Health Affairs* 12:142–53.

Kellermann, Arthur L., and Donald T. Reay. 1986. "Protection or peril? An analysis of firearm-related deaths in the home." *New England Journal of Medicine* 314:1557–60.

Kellermann, Arthur L., Frederick P. Rivara, Joyce Banton, Donald Reay, and Corinte L. Fligner. 1990. "Validating survey responses to questions about gun ownership among owners of registered handguns." *American Journal of Epidemiology* 131:1080–84.

Kellermann, Arthur L., Frederick P. Rivara, Roberta K. Lee, Joyce G. Banton, Peter Cummings, Bela B. Hackman, and Grant Somes. 1996. "Injuries due to firearms in three cities." *New England Journal of Medicine* 335:1438–44.

Kellermann, Arthur L., Frederick P. Rivara, Norman B. Rushforth, Joyce G. Banton, Donald T. Reay, Jerry T. Francisco, Ana B. Locci, Janice Prodzinski, Bela B. Hackman, and Grant Somes. 1993. "Gun ownership as a risk factor for homicide in the home." *New England Journal of Medicine* 329:1084–91.

Kellermann, Arthur L. Frederick P. Rivara, Grant Somes, Donald T. Reay, Jerry Francisco, Joyce Gillentine Banton, Janice Prodzinski, Corinne Fligner, and Bela B. Hackman. 1992. "Suicide in the home in relation to gun ownership." *New England Journal of Medicine* 327:467–72.

Kellermann, Arthur L., Lori Westphal, Laurie Fischer, and Beverly Harvard. 1995. "Weapon involvement in home invasion crimes." *Journal of American Medical Association* 273:1759–62.

Kleck, Gary. 1979. "Capital punishment, gun ownership, and homicide." *American Journal of Sociology* 84:882–910.

———. 1984a. "The relationship between gun ownership levels and rates of violence in the United States." In *Firearms and Violence: Issues of Public Policy*. Edited by Don B. Kates Jr. Cambridge, Mass.: Ballinger, pp. 99–135.

———. 1984b. "Handgun-only gun control." In *Firearms and Violence: Issues of Public Policy*. Edited by Don. B. Kates Jr. Cambridge: Ballinger, pp. 167–99.

———. 1985. "Life support for ailing hypotheses." *Law and Human Behavior* 9:271–85.

———. 1986a. "Policy lessons from recent gun control research." *Law and Contemporary Problems* 49:35–62.

———. 1986b. "Evidence that 'Saturday Night Specials' not very important for crime." *Sociology and Social Research* 70:303–7.

———. 1988. "Crime control through the private use of armed force." *Social Problems* 35:1–21.

———. 1991. *Point Blank: Guns and Violence in America*. Hawthorne, N.Y.: Aldine de Gruyter.

———. 1992. "Suicide in the home in relation to gun ownership." *New England Journal of Medicine* 327:1878.

———. 1993. "The incidence of gun violence among young people." *Public Perspective* 4:3–6.

———. 1994. "Bad data and the 'Evil Empire': Interpreting poll data on gun control." *Violence and victims* 8:367–76.

———. 1995a. "Guns and violence: An interpretive review of the field." *Social Pathology* 1:12–47.

———. 1995b "Using speculation to meet evidence: Reply to Alba and Messner." *Journal of Quantitative Criminology* 11(4):411–24.

———. 1996a. "Crime, culture conflict and sources of support for gun control: A multi-level application of the General Social Surveys." *American Behavioral Scientist* 39(4):387–404.

Killias, Martin. 1993b. "Gun ownership, suicide, and homicide: An international perspective." In *Understanding Crime: Experiences of Crime and Crime Control.* Edited by Anna del Frate, Uglijesa Zvekic, and Jan J. M. van Diik. Rome: UNICRI, pp. 289–303.

Loftin, Colin, David McDowall, Brian Wiersema, and Talbert J. Cottey. 1991. "Effects of restrictive licensing of handguns on homicide and suicide in the District of Columbia." *New England Journal of Medicine* 325:1615–20.

Mauser, Gary A. 1989. "Firearms ownership in British Columbia." Unpublished paper, Faculty of Business Administration, Simon Fraser University, Burnaby, BC.

———. 1990. Unpublished tabulations from a 1990 national survey, produced at the author's request.

Mauser, Gary A. and Michael Margolis. 1990. "The politics of gun control." Paper presented at the annual meetings of the American Political Science Association, San Francisco.

National Safety Council. 1981. *Accident Facts,* 1981 edition. Chicago: Author.

———. 1988. *Accident Facts,* 1988 edition: Chicago: Author.

———. 1995. *Accident Facts,* 1995 edition: Itasca, Illinois: Author.

———. 1996. *Accident Facts,* 1996 edition: Itasca, Illinois: Author.

Sadowski, Laura S., Robert B. Edwin, H. Cairs, and Jo Anne Earp. 1989. "Firearm ownership among nonurban adolescents." *American Journal of Diseases of Children* 143:1410–30.

Sloan, J. H., A. L. Kellermann, D. T. Reay, J. A. Ferris, T. Koepsell, F. P. Rivara, C. Rice, L. Gray, and J. LoGerfo. 1988. "Handgun Regulations, Crimes, Assaults, and Homicide. A Tale of Two Cities." *New England Journal of Medicine* 319:1256–62.

Tardiff, Kenneth, Peter M. Marzuk, Andrew C. Leon, Charles S. Hirsch, Marina Stajic, Laura Portera, and Nacy Hartwell. 1994. "Homicide in New York City: Cocaine use and firearms." *Journal of the American Medical Association* 272:43–46.

Taubes, Gary. 1995. "Epidemiology faces its limits." *Science* 269:164–69.

Teret, Stephen P., Greg R. Alexander, and Linda A. Bailey. 1990. "The passage of Maryland's gun law: Data and advocacy for injury prevention." *Journal of Public Health Policy* (spring):26–38.

Violence Prevention Task Force of the Eastern Association for the Surgery of Trauma. 1995. "Violence in America: A public health crisis—the role of firearms." *Journal of Trauma* 38:163–68.

Wintemute, Garen J. 1987. "Firearms as a cause of death in the United States, 1920–1982." *Journal of Trauma* 27:532–36.

———. 1989–1990. "Closing the gap between research and policy: Firearms." *Injury Prevention Network* 7:20–21.

Wright, James D. 1981. "Public opinion and gun control." *Annals* 455:24–39.

———. 1984. "The ownership of firearms for reasons of self-defense." In *Firearms and Violence.* Edited by Don B. Kates Jr. Cambridge, Mass.: Ballinger, pp. 301–37.

———. 1989. "Guns and sputter." *Reason* (July): 46–47.

———. 1990. "In the heat of the moment." *Reason* (August/September):44–45.

25

CHILDREN AND GUNS

DAVID B. KOPEL

INTRODUCTION

The evidence of a national crisis involving children and guns seems overwhelming:

- "One child under fourteen is accidentally shot to death every day in the U.S.A." (Center to Prevent Handgun Violence).[1]
- "In the past decade, more than 138,000 Americans were shot just by children under the age of six" (*Hartford Courant*).[2]
- One hundred thirty-five thousand children carry guns to school each day. (Senators Biden and Chafee).[3]
- "Firearms are responsible for the deaths of 45,000 infants, children, and adolescents per year" (American Academy of Pediatrics).[4]
- Eleven percent of children in grades six through twelve have been shot at with a gun; 9 percent have shot a gun at somebody (Lou Harris, Governor Roy Romer).[5]

These statistics are horrifying, and few people who read them can avoid concluding that some kind of gun control—any kind, in fact—is an urgent necessity. Fortunately, every one of the above statistics is false. The correct statistics are presented in the relevant sections of this chapter.

From David B. Kopel, ed., *Guns: Who Should Have Them?* (Amherst, N.Y.: Prometheus Books, 1995), pp. 309–22.

Gun control strategists recognize that children are their most effective issue, even for controls that would apply to adults. Senator John Chafee (R-Rhode Island), who supported the Brady Bill as a minimal first step, has proposed the confiscation of all American handguns. The most important reason Senator Chafee offered for his drastic proposal was that handguns are "infecting" America's schools. The confiscation legislation won immediate support from America's "prochild" lobbies such as the Children's Defense Fund and the American Academy of Pediatrics.

America's rising tide of teenage homicide has prompted demands from elected officials and the media for severe gun control, although the connection between the crime and the purported solution is sometimes unclear. When a pair of teenage runaways with a stolen revolver murdered a Colorado state trooper in 1992, then State Senator Regis Groff moved quickly to introduce legislation for a handgun waiting period and an "assault weapon" ban. The *Atlantic* plastered an M-11 handgun on its cover and printed a story about a child in Virginia Beach, Virginia, who used the ugly but low-caliber handgun to murder a teacher; the story intoned that adults should be allowed to own handguns only after receiving official permission and passing government tests.[6]

Gun control advocates are hammering at the issue of children and guns as never before, in the not unrealistic hope that creating an atmosphere of panic about children will allow the enactment of severe gun controls aimed at adults. As Senator Chafee puts it, America must "do something" about the current "handgun slaughter," in which "our children are being killed and are killing," for "sooner rather than later every family in the United States will be touched by handgun violence."

The ploy of insisting that we curtail the rights of adults in order to protect children has at various times in American history brought success to campaigns to outlaw alcohol, marijuana, sexually explicit literature, homosexual behavior, lawn darts, and just about everything else that prohibitionists have wanted to eradicate.

America *does* face a crisis with children and guns. But the true facts of the crisis have very little to do with the politicized fearmongering of some gun prohibition advocates. If Americans are to respond effectively to the problems associated with children and guns—particularly the extremely high murder rate of inner-city black teenage males—it will be necessary to understand the true scope and history of the problems, and to analyze carefully which solutions will make things better, and which will make things even worse.

ACCIDENTS

How many children die in gun accidents? One of America's leading gun-control advocates, Dr. Stephen Teret, puts the figure at "almost 1,000 children" per year.[7] A lobbyist for Handgun Control, Inc., when asked, "Is it true that many accidents in this country involve children playing with a parent's gun and

Table 1. Yearly Fatal Gun Accidents for Children 0–14

1970	530	1982	279
1972	470	1983	243
1974	532	1984	287
1975	495	1985	278
1976	428	1986	230
1977	392	1987	250
1978	349	1988	277
1979	364	1989	273
1980	316	1990	236
1981	298	1991	227

Source: National Safety Council, Accident Facts (Itacsa, Ill., various years)

shooting some one accidentally?" responded, "That is right. Fourteen hundred children die in such tragic accidents each year. . . ."[8]

In 1991, the most recent year for which precise numbers are available, there were twenty-four fatal gun accidents involving children under age five, and 203 involving children aged five to fourteen (for a total of 227 for all children under fifteen).[9] Preliminary estimates put the 1993 figures at forty for children under five, and 180 for children under fifteen.[10]

In recent decades, the American firearms supply has risen, and now stands at over two hundred million guns, a third of them handguns. But as the number of guns has risen, the number of childhood gun accidents has fallen sharply, declining by nearly 50 percent in the last two decades. Table 1 illustrates the happy trend.

From 1968 to 1993, the rate of fatal gun accidents for all ages fell from 1.2 per 100,000 population per year to 0.6—a decline of 50 percent. In the same period, the motor vehicle fatal accident rate fell from 27.5 to 16.3—a 41 percent decline.[11] Work deaths declined 58 percent.[12]

While there are enormous bureaucracies devoted to reducing work accidents (the Occupational Safety and Health Administration) and automobile accidents (the Department of Transportation), there is no government body charged with reducing firearms accidents. Yet thanks to voluntary, private educational efforts, including programs sponsored by the National Rifle Association (NRA), the Boy Scouts, 4-H, and other groups, the number of firearm accidents has declined at about the same rate as that of other activities over which federal bureaucracies have charge.

The true number of childhood gun accidents might be even lower than the official figures suggest. Some fatalities, involving older teenagers, may in fact be homicides, in which the perpetrator claims that pointing the gun at the victim's head or torso and then pulling the trigger was "an accident." In addition, a number of so-called accidents may be child-abuse homicides perpetrated by adults.[13]

Few causes of childhood death have fallen as steeply as have gun accidents, and the fall has taken place without any government programs. The situation might be considered evidence that private safety programs can be more effective than government regulation, and that there is no persuasive case for restrictive gun controls designed to fight childhood gun accidents.

Many gun control advocates are not persuaded, however. In the push for restrictive laws to deal with accidents, they attempt, often successfully, to create the impression that gun accidents involving children are extremely common. While the actual numbers are readily available from the National Safety Council (NSC) and while the NSC reports have never been challenged for underestimating true accident numbers, gun control advocates sometimes claim far higher numbers of childhood accidents, without giving any source for their data.[14]

Another approach of gun control advocates is to discuss accidents in a way that avoids mentioning the actual number of fatalities, and the sharp downward trend in the number. For example, it may be pointed out, accurately, that firearms are the fourth-leading cause of accidental deaths for children aged five to fourteen (behind auto accidents, drowning, and fires and burns); and the third-leading cause for fifteen- to twenty-four-year-olds.[15] What is omitted by the emphasis on ranking is how small a role firearms actually play in accidental deaths, since the leading causes of accidental deaths (principally motor vehicles) so hugely outnumber the lesser causes. Guns account for only 3 percent of accidental deaths of children fourteen and under.[16] A child fourteen or under is five times more likely to drown than to die in a gun accident, five times more likely to die in a fire, and fourteen times more likely to die in an auto accident.[17]

It is to be expected that accidents and other "man-made" factors would be leading causes of death for young persons. In an era of advanced medical care, young people (other than infants) rarely die of natural causes. Accordingly, any cause of death in the under-fourteen or under-twenty-four age groups—even if it occurs infrequently—may have a relatively high rank.

In any case, showing the particular ranking of a cause of injury is hardly the same as proving that the factor related to that injury should be outlawed or drastically restricted. Among children aged five to nine, the rate of reported dog bites is higher than the combined rate of reportable childhood diseases (such as measles).[18] The fact does not by itself prove that dogs should be outlawed, or that the law should require that dogs always be locked up if children might come nearby.

Some medical researchers have suggested that a firearm in the home of a normal, healthy family poses a grave risk to that family's health. For example, the *Journal of the American Medical Association* (JAMA) published a report which concluded that a "firearm in the home" is a risk factor for home firearm accidents.[19] The conclusion was certainly correct, since it was nearly a tautology. Having a swimming pool in the home is a risk factor for swimming pool accidents, having a motorcycle in the home is a risk factor for motorcycle accidents, and having an appendix is a risk factor for appendicitis. The report did not prove that the presence of a gun in the home causes a significant increase in the risk of accidental death; given the very low rate of deaths from childhood gun accidents, it would be impossible to prove such a conclusion.

Although the number of childhood gun accidents is low and getting lower, some gun prohibitionists contend that outlawing or drastically restricting firearms would be appropriate, "if it saves one life."

If any object associated with about 227 accidental childhood deaths a year should be outlawed, then it would be logical to call for the prohibition of bicycles (over 300 child deaths a year).[20] An even larger number of children are killed by motor vehicles (3,087).[21] Four hundred and thirty-two children die annually in fires caused by adults who fall asleep while smoking;[22] these 432 deaths would, by the handgun-banning logic, make a persuasive case for outlawing tobacco.

If the focus is on children under age five, then outlawing swimming pools, bathtubs, and five-gallon buckets (450 home drowning deaths) or cigarette lighters (90 deaths) would save many more children under five from accidental deaths than would a gun ban (24 deaths).[23]

Thus, the "if it saves one life" antiaccident logic applies with much greater force to bicycles, automobiles, bathtubs, swimming pools, tobacco, and cigarette lighters than to guns. Gun-prohibition advocates might reply that swimming pools or cars have legitimate purposes, while guns do not. Whereas banning swimming pools or cars in order to "save one life" would deprive people of necessary or useful items, a ban on guns would cause no such deprivation. But guns, like swimming pools, are commonly used for sport and recreation. And although bicycles, bathtubs, and cigarette lighters make life more convenient, these objects do not save lives or prevent injury.

Guns, however, do save lives and prevent crime every day. [Elsewhere I have] presented various studies which found that guns are used for protection against criminal attack at least several hundred thousand times per year, and perhaps over two million times a year. These data are consistent with the polling of felony convicts in state prison systems conducted for the National Institute of Justice (NIJ). Felons apparently have a high level of fear of armed victims, and try to avoid armed targets.[24]

Even if the criminologists' figures for self-defense are ten times too high, the true number of protective gun uses is still far higher than the number of times—namely none—that bicycles, bathtubs, and cigarette lighters are used for self-defense each year. Few persons who want to save "just one life" by banning handguns to eliminate child handgun accidents would propose saving many more children's lives by banning bicycles, bathtubs, and cigarette lighters. Is it possible that the motivation for banning handguns is something other than saving lives?

PROPOSED SOLUTIONS FOR ACCIDENTS

While safety education has already saved many lives, it is opposed by many gun control organizations. Instead, these organizations favor a variety of restrictive laws that would impair the rights of all gun owners.

"Loaded" Indicators

Former Senator Howard Metzenbaurn (D-Ohio), a leading gun control advocate, proposed giving the Consumer Product Safety Commission (CPSC) authority over firearms.[25] If the CPSC had jurisdiction for firearms, it would have power to order manufacturers to initiate recalls of any or all privately owned firearms and ammunition that did not meet the commission's criteria for safety. Likewise, the commission could, by unilateral administrative action, ban the future production of any and all firearms and ammunition. Currently the CPSC is forbidden to regulate firearms precisely because Congress is afraid that regulation could become a subterfuge for gun prohibition.

One proposed federal safety criterion that tens of millions of guns would fail (and hence be subject to recall) is for the gun to have a "loaded" indicator. The "loaded" indicator, as the name implies, signals whether a gun is loaded. The General Accounting Office (GAO) reports that 23 percent of accidental firearms deaths could be prevented by having a "loaded" indicator.[26]

Although a "loaded" indicator would prevent some accidents, it might cause others. First of all, unless the requirement for a "loaded" indicator were made retroactive, so that the entire United States gun stock was recalled for retrofitting, some guns would have "loaded" indicators and many would not. Accordingly, persons who had learned to rely on "loaded" indicators might treat a loaded gun without the "loaded" signal as if the gun were unloaded.

In addition, it is foolish to expect that the half of American households that own guns would turn over their firearms for retrofitting. When Sturm, Ruger & Co. did a recall of some old revolvers, offering a free retrofit to prevent accidental discharges, only about 10 percent of the guns that had been sold were returned for the free modification, even though Ruger wrote to all known owners and advertised the free retrofit for many years.[27] A government-ordered retrofit would probably be less successful than Ruger's 10 percent, since government involvement might raise fears about gun confiscation or registration.[28]

Even assuming that most guns could be retrofitted, reliance on a "loaded" indicator is contrary to safe firearms-handling rules. Using a "loaded" indicator legitimizes treating a gun as unloaded, and thus engaging in all sorts of inappropriate behavior, such as pointing the "safe" gun at someone. The more cautious approach, fostered by safety training, is to treat every gun as if it were loaded. Even if a person is certain that a gun is unloaded, that gun should never be pointed at anyone except in self-defense.

Finally, the "loaded" indicator is meaningless except to persons who have taken firearms safety classes and have been taught the indicator's meaning, or who have read an owner's manual for the gun. Anyone who has taken a safety class will have been drilled never to point a gun at a person and to treat every gun as loaded. Anyone who reads the safety manual will have read similar safety instructions. Accordingly, the "loaded" indicator is a superfluity for the only segment of the population that would learn of it. And, of course, those who read safety manuals and take safety classes are the type of people least likely to cause accidents in the first place.

Childproof Devices

Another gun redesign program suggested by GAO is that all firearms include a device, such as a pressure-sensitive grip, which could prevent them from being fired by young children. GAO estimates that 8 percent of gun accidents could be prevented by some kind of childproof device.[29] (The GAO estimate was probably twice as high as it should have been, since the GAO study included twice as high a percentage of young children as the population data mandated.[30])

A childproof device of any type could only reliably be expected to protect children under six (or thereabouts), who would have neither the strength nor the ingenuity to defeat a safety device.[31] Even then, the device might not work if the child pulled the trigger with a thumb rather than a finger (as a child could do if pointing the gun at himself). Design standard modifications would be of little benefit in reducing the more common type of childhood gun accident, that involving preteen and older boys.[32]

During the 1880s, Daniel Baird Wesson, head of the Smith & Wesson gun company, ordered his engineers to produce a childproof gun after he read a newspaper account of a child killed in a gun accident. The new gun, with a safety lever in the grip, and a very hard trigger pull, was marketed as the New Departure Model Safety Hammerless. It is said that one evening Mr. Wesson was entertainmg guests in his mansion and, to demonstrate his safety innovation, handed a boy a loaded Safety Hammerless and told him, "Go ahead and pull the trigger." The boy did, and a bullet instantly tore through an expensive Persian carpet, lodging itself in the floor near Mr. Wesson's feet.[33]

Although the GAO report implicitly builds the case for a recall of all handguns, child-resistant devices are readily available as aftermarket items, and can be attached to a gun by a consumer who wants one.

Interestingly a large number of modern handguns already incorporate child-resistant design, but these are the very guns some antigun groups wish to see banned. Most semiautomatic handguns have a safety lever or switch to prevent the gun from being accidentally fired. Only if the safety is turned off can the trigger mechanism be operated. In addition, to load a round into a semiautomatic pistol, a person must pull back on the top part of the gun (the slide) to chamber the round. Pulling the slide requires substantial physical force, more than many young children can muster. And of course many children will be unaware of how to engage the slide at all, and thus be unable to load the gun.[34]

Partly because semiautomatic handguns are so accident-resistant, a loaded, accessible handgun is statistically less likely to be involved in a fatal accident than a loaded, accessible long gun.[35]

Locks and Similar Devices

Many gun owners store their gun with a trigger lock, a device that prevents the trigger from being squeezed until the lock is removed with a key. Other gun owners store their guns in safes or in "quick-lock" safety boxes which pop open when a combination of buttons is pressed. Some gun owners store their gun separately from their ammunition, or with an essential component (such as the bolt) removed. Any of these steps may be a sensible way to deal with the presence of guns and children in the same house. NRA safety training strongly urges that any gun kept only for sporting purposes be stored in a condition so that it cannot be readily fired.

Does it makes sense legally to mandate such storage conditions? No. The United States Constitution and most state constitutions guarantee the right to own a gun for defense, and mandatory trigger locks nullify that right. A gun that must be locked up may not be readily available in an emergency. A blanket policy of making guns not easily accessible to people who are under attack will harm, not enhance, public safety.

Moreover, the circumstances of protection in each individual home are too varied to mandate any one policy. The mother of a three-month-old baby, who lives in a dangerous neighborhood, could safely keep a loaded gun in a bedside drawer. When the child grew older, she might store the gun's magazine (the device containing the ammunition) on a high closet shelf, with the hope that she could retrieve and insert the magazine if she heard someone breaking into her home. If an ex-boyfriend started harassing her by phone, and threatened to come over that night and kill her, it would be sensible for her to keep the loaded gun top of her bedside table while she slept, and even to carry the gun in a holster when she was awake. No single safety rule, written in the crime-free confines a legislative chamber, can determine what the best practices for gun storage will be in all situations. In addition, safe storage laws are often vague and gun owners have difficulty discerning what kind of storage, short of a safe, will satisfy the requirements.

Interestingly, the advocates of requiring all firearms to be locked up do not propose that parents be forced to lock up, or otherwise render inaccessible to children, substances such as liquor, household cleansers, or automobile keys. Every year children die from the poisonous effects of rapid ingestion of hard liquor and household cleansers, or from attempting to "drive" their parents' car. Certainly no adult has a self-defense "need" for rapid access to unlocked liquor cabinets, cleansers, or car keys.

Owner Liability Laws

Another approach to dealing with childhood gun accidents is to enact laws making the owner of the gun involved in the accident guilty of a crime. For example, California makes the offense a three-year felony. Florida, New Jersey, Illinois, and Connecticut are among those states with similar laws.[36] These laws are generally superfluous gestures. Existing laws against reckless endangerment provide ample authority for prosecution in cases where it is warranted.

Does significant good come from handcuffing the grieving parent of a dead child, and adding even more pain and sorrow to what the grief-stricken family must already bear? Sending the adult involved to prison may satisfy a social desire for revenge, and may generate newspaper stories warning against careless behavior. At the same time, it may be asked whether the brothers and sisters of the deceased child should also lose their parent to a prison term.

While most criminal laws are considered to do good by incapacitating criminals, the beneficial impact of criminal storage laws may come from the publicity that attends them. Florida State Representative Harry Jennings, sponsor of Florida's criminal liability law, suggests that the most important effect of his law is not the number of prosecutions (there are only a few every year) but the change in the accident rate. From 1987 to 1989 (before the law), there were an average of sixteen fatal gun accidents in Florida involving children under fourteen. From 1990 to 1992 (after the new law), the number fell to six per year. "We scared the 'hell out of people around the state," he observed.[37]

Publicity about the new law was not the only educational program in Florida at the time; besides intense media attention paid to the gun accidents themselves (which often cluster around the end of school, in May and June, so that one accident story follows on the heels of the previous one), the Eddie Eagle gun accident prevention program (discussed below), was also going into effect all over Florida. Although determining the precise safety benefit of any particular educational item is impossible, it is intuitively plausible that each item of public education (including publicity about the law) helped. Still, criminal laws should imprison only people who should be imprisoned, and it is questionable whether criminal storage laws do so.

Harassment Lawsuits

Lawsuits against gun owners, gun stores, and gun manufacturers have become a potent tool of antigun organizations. Such suits have met with limited success to date, since they are based on the theory that the manufacturer knew that the gun would be a crime weapon when, in fact, a very small percentage of handguns of any type are ever used in crime.[38]

Taking a different tack, a Texas plaintiff's attorney sued the Boy Scouts of America, claiming that the Boy Scouts magazine *Boys' Life* had enticed a twelve-year-old boy into fatal play with a .22 rifle because the magazine had run a sixteen-page advertising supplement involving firearms.[39]

Yet while the antigun lawsuits are rarely found to have merit, they succeed on another level. Even in cases where the defendant prevails, he must spend huge sums on defense costs, with no hope of recovering the costs after the lawsuit has been thrown out. Although courts legally have the power to sanction attorneys who bring frivolous cases, sanctions are rarely imposed.

Safety Education

When a teenage girl in Colorado found a loaded gun at a friend's house, picked it up, began playing with it, pointed it at her brother, squeezed the trigger, and saw her brother die, the children's parent explained, "We talked to our kids about AIDS, about alcohol, about drugs—but not guns. In our wildest dreams, we never thought they'd pick up a gun at a party." [40] Just as parents who do not drink and keep no alcohol in the house have a responsibility to teach their children about alcohol, all parents have a responsibility to teach their children about the dangers of guns. Similarly, even parents who do not own swimming pools should still drownproof their children.

A third to a half of fatal gun accidents occur outside the child's own home. Thus, parents' removing guns from a home, or never acquiring guns, is not enough to protect a child from gun accidents. Since there are over two hundred million firearms in the United States, it is possible that a child may at some point encounter an unattended gun. "Childproofing" guns is not a safe approach, since any safety device can be defeated. What is more important is to "gunproof" every child. All children, including those from gunless homes, ought to be taught the fundamentals of gun safety.

Only a minority of accidental deaths could be prevented by modifying gun design. In contrast, safety education addresses the vast majority of gun accidents, for about 84 percent of accidental shootings involve the violation of basic safe rules.[41] The owners of guns involved in accidental deaths of children are unlikely to have received safety training.[42]

Groups such as the Boy Scouts of America, 4-H, the American Camping Association, and the NRA have long instructed children in the safe use of sporting arms. Junior target shooting programs and the like have helped millions of children and teenagers learn that guns must always be handled with extreme care, according to a strict set of safety rules from which no deviation is ever permitted.

Sadly, some of the groups that complain the most about childhood gun accidents also complain about programs to prevent such accidents. The Educational Fund to End Handgun Violence bemoans the fact that "nearly 23 percent of the accredited camps in the country offer some kind of shooting program. The affiliation of these programs with the National Rifle Association can run from the camp purchasing badges and certificates from the organization to a much more involved relationship."[43]

Programs that teach the safe sporting use of guns are beneficial, but they can reach only a fraction of the childhood population. Children of parents with no interest in the sporting use of firearms will never hear these safety lessons, and it is these children-ignorant of the actual mechanics of guns and bereft of instruction in gun safety-who may be at risk of causing a gun accident. Accordingly, it is necessary that gun safety programs be expanded to reach the broadest group of children possible.

One successful effort to promote safety training for all children is the NRA's

"Eddie Eagle" Elementary Gun Safety Education Program. The Eddie Eagle Program offers curricula for children in grades K–1, 2–3, and 4–6, and uses teacher-tested materials including an animated video, cartoon workbooks, and fun safety activities. The hero, Eddie Eagle, teaches a simple safety lesson: "If you see a gun: Stop! Don't touch. Leave the area. Tell an adult." The Eddie Eagle program is a more elaborate version of the approach taken by the Pennsylvania Division of the American Trauma Society, which offers a free coloring book warning children about various potential dangers; for firearms, the children are warned, "If you find a gun, don't touch it. Tell your parents. Remember—no gun is a toy!"[44]

Eddie Eagle includes no political content, no statements about the Second Amendment, and nothing promoting the sporting use of guns. The program and its creator, Marion Hammer, won the 1993 Outstanding Community Service Award from the National Safety Council.[45] It has been adopted in most Florida counties and endorsed by the Police Athletic League. The Georgia legislature and the Oklahoma City city council (as well as some smaller bodies) have enacted resolutions urging schools under their supervision to adopt the Eddie Eagle program.[46] As of early 1995, Eddie Eagle had reached more than six million children.

Unfortunately, some persons in positions of authority over school safety programs have refused to allow Eddie Eagle to be used in their schools, because they disagree with the NRA's position on policy questions.[47]

While safety education in general would seem to be noncontroversial, some actively oppose it. Some antigun advocates warn that safety education may promote interest in firearms.[48] (The argument parallels some of the opposition to teaching sex education in the schools.) While no one has ever studied whether educating children about guns promotes interest in guns, research of adult-oriented safety education has not found evidence that education promotes gun use.[49]

The American Academy of Pediatrics (AAP) dismisses safety education, asserting, "No published research confirms effectiveness of gun-safety training for adolescents. Most preventive gun safety education is directed at hunters and marksmen, but hunting and target-shooting are a small part of the adolescent firearms problem."[50] Thus, claims the AAP, only a complete ban on handguns can deal with the problem of childhood gun accidents.

The AAP's point about published research, while technically true, is meaningless. No formal research has been done on whether gun-safety programs for children or teenagers reduce gun accidents. Research involving adult training has shown that it promotes safer firearms practices for adults.[51] Most parents sensibly believe that education reduces accidents, which is why schools teach young children about staying out of traffic, and instruct teenagers on how to drive safely.

Notably, hunter-safety programs have been proven to reduce hunting accidents. In the last several decades, states have required new hunters (but not those who were already hunters) to pass a safety certification class before being granted a hunting license. Today, the majority of hunters have completed safety training, and this group is involved in disproportionately fewer accidents than hunters without training.[52] Hunting accident fatalities have fallen by 75 percent since the late 1960s.[53] There is no reason to assume that safety education suddenly becomes worthless when removed from the hunting context. The AAP's antieducation reasoning is equivalent to advocating a ban on swimming pools because some people may not pay attention to water safety instruction.

The antieducation attitudes of American gun prohibitionists starkly contrast with strategies elsewhere. In New Zealand, the Mountain Safety Council (the leading outdoor sports organization) has worked with the police to produce a pamphlet which promotes responsible gun use by children. The booklet observes that "airgun ownership can contribute in a positive way to growing up."[54] The council also publishes, again in conjunction with the police, a gun safety comic series called "Billy Hook" which teaches children gun safety rules.[55] The official police instruction book for gun owners, the *Arms Code*, advises parents: "While children should not handle a firearm except under the supervision of a firearms license holder, it can ease their curiosity to show them your firearm and explain that it must never be touched except when you are there."[56] Over the last half-century, there has been a significant decline in firearms deaths and injuries in New Zealand, even as the number of guns has soared.[57]

While schools and other social institutions have an important role to play in gun safety, the primary responsibility rests with parents. A child who can, under parental supervision, invite a classmate to shoot a .22 rifle at a target range may be considerably less awed by the possibility of surreptitiously playing with a friend's father's old pistol.

Given the benefits of gun-safety education, should it be made mandatory, either in schools or for gun owners? Either form of mandatory education would probably reduce accidents, but other factors should be considered. America's public schools already labor under a huge weight of legislative mandates. Many education reformers suggest that we should be removing, rather than increasing, the mandate burden on local schools. Accordingly, decisions about gun-safety classes might best be left to principals and school boards, rather than legislatures. In addition, mandatory education regarding any controversial subject (including guns or sex) must be carefully constructed so as not to offend the personal and family values of students. The Eddie Eagle program, which carefully avoids stating that guns are *per se* good or bad, or that any particular gun laws are good or bad, meets the standard of neutrality. Other gun-safety programs may not; for example, the Milwaukee police use a "safety" program which encourages children to call the police if they find out that their parents own a gun.[58]

Requiring prospective handgun owners to pass a safety class before buying a handgun is currently the law in California. Such a law might reduce the gun accident rate, but would impose other, unacceptable social costs. First, the safety training acts as a de facto waiting period. A person may not be able to obtain a gun for months while waiting to take the class. In some cities with safety training laws, the only approved class is one taught by the police, and the class is taught only a few times a year. Waiting periods may be a net loss to public safety: persons who need a gun for immediate protection cannot obtain one, whereas those who are capable of murder on one day generally remain capable of murder a few weeks later. The experience of jurisdictions that impose mandatory safety training suggests that some police administrators will attempt to use safety training not to ensure that gun owners are well trained, but to set up administrative roadblocks to gun ownership.[59] For people who, as a matter of principle, want the government to limit gun ownership, mandatory safety training "for the sake of our children" offers a handy wedge.[60]

From a Constitutional viewpoint, mandatory safety training is dubious. No other Constitutional right is limited by a requirement that persons seeking to exercise that right prove their competence to do so. (Driving is not a right, and no driver's license is needed on private roads or other private property.) Many other nations license journalists, and the number of people harmed by libel and other a mistakes would probably decline if journalists were required to take a government-mandated "safe journalism" class covering the fundamentals of libel law fact verification. If such a law were proposed, most journalists would not bother to argue that the number of truly reckless journalists is small, or that the number of people killed because of media mistakes is negligible.[61] Instead, journalists would argue, correctly, that because the First Amendment guarantees a right rather than privilege, the government may not impose tests on people who seek to exercise their rights. The same principle is true regarding the Second Amendment, and every other amendment.

Finally, many accidents involving adults (the only people who are old enough to be gun buyers, and hence be required to take mandatory safety classes) are the result of recklessness more than ignorance. Adults and older teenagers who cause firearms accidents are unlike the rest of the population. They are "disproportionately involved in other accidents, violent crime and heavy drinking."[62] Without guns, they would likely find some other way to kill themselves "accidentally," such as by reckless driving. Indeed, they tend to have a record of reckless driving and automobile accidents. Safety education can accomplish little for this group.

While children can be helped by affirmative programs that teach gun responsibility, they can also be harmed by media images that glamorize recklessness.[63] Consider a child whose exposure to firearms consists of television imagery. Studies have shown that even very young children learn skills by watching television demonstrations.[64] Television "teaches" (by example) that the first thing you do when you get a gun is put your finger on the trigger, and then point the gun at someone. These television demonstrations violate two key gun-safety rules: keep your finger off the trigger unless you are ready to shoot; and never point a gun at another person (except in self-defense).

While the media can at least claim to be ignorant of actual gun-safety rules, the antigun organizations have less excuse. No matter how important a lobbying group believes its political goals to be, those goals should not be furthered through advertising which directly endangers children. One of the most famous posters of the antigun movement, dramatizing the supposedly high rate of childhood gun accidents, shows a baby looking down the barrel of a gun.65 Even presuming that the gun was unloaded (or was an imitation gun), the baby/victim in the poster has been unintentionally taught that looking down the barrel of a gun is permissible and interesting. And so have all the preliterate children who see that poster.

The poster is also extremely misleading in its attempt to create an image of a widespread and frequent problem. About one child under the age of one dies in a gun accident in an average year.66

As a nation, the United States has no shortage of social pathologies, including pathologies worsened by heavy-handed government. Despite the claims of, some gun control advocates, the problem of childhood gun accidents is relatively small, and is continuing to decline. Prudence suggests that the safest course is to continue the voluntary educational strategies which appear to be working.

NOTES

1. John Darling, former member of the Board of Directors of the Center to Prevent Handgun Violence, "You Must Educate Your Children," *USA Today*, 19 June 1989.

2. Marc B. Goldstein, "Guns Don't Kill But They Sure Make it Easier," *Hartford Courant*, 5 July 1992, p. 14.

3. Sen. Joseph Biden, "Statement of Senator Joseph R. Biden, Jr., Chairman, Senate Judiciary Committee, 'Children and Guns: Why the Recent RiseT " Senate Committee on the Judiciary, October 1, 1992, p. 2 ("135,000 children are carrying guns to school everyday [*sic*]"); Senator John Chafee, "Testimony of Senator John H. Chafee before the Senate Judiciary Committee during Hearings on 'Kids and Guns,' " 1 October 1992, p. 1 ("An estimated 135,000 boys carry guns to school every day"); Dr. Katherine Christoffel, American Academy of Pediatrics, testimony on "Children and Guns," House Select Committee on Children, Youth and Families, June 15, 1989 ("An estimated 135,000 boys carried handguns to school daily in 1987 . . . "), Also, "When Guns Go to School," *USA Today*, 28 February 1992; *Crime Control Digest*, 5 August 1991, p. 9.

Senator Christopher Dodd pegs the number even higher. "Statement of Senator Christopher J. Dodd," Hearing on "Children of War: Violence and America's Youth," Senate Subcommittee on Children, Family, Drugs, and Alcoholism, July 23, 1992, p. 1. ("Each day, 186,000 students bring a gun to school, many out of fear.")

4. American Academy of Pediatrics, reported in "Doctors Worry about Gun Deaths," *Aurora Beacon News*, 23 October 1989 (Associated Press). The 45,000 figure is much larger than the total number of gun deaths for all ages combined.

5. The Lou Harris poll, released in July 1993, surveyed 2,508 students in grades six through twelve, at ninety-six schools. Louis Harris Research, Inc., "A Survey of Experiences, Perceptions, Apprehensions about Guns among Young People in America," conducted for the Harvard School of Public Health under a grant from the Joyce Foundation, July 1993 (poll conducted April 19–May 21, 1993). The poll is discussed in Gary Kleck, "The Incidence of Gun Violence among Young People," *The Public Perspective*, September/October 1993, pp. 3–6.

No politician has done more to raise the issue of "children and guns" to a level of national hysteria than Colorado Governor Roy Romer. At a special "emergency" session of the Colorado legislature in September 1993, which the governor called to deal with juvenile violence, he quoted the Lou Harris data in his address to the General Assembly.

Other parts of Governor Romer's understanding of the children and guns issue were also disconnected from reality. For example, in his September 1993 speech, at town meetings during the preceding summer, and in a *New York Times* op-ed, Romer said, "If the NRA in Washington is so out of touch with Colorado that it cannot even support the simple proposition that a 14-year-old has no business carrying a loaded gun to school, then the NRA is part of the problem." Roy Romer, "Under 18? Hand Over That Gun," *New York Times*, 21 October 1993, p. 23. Actually, since 1989, Colorado has had a law forbidding anyone (not just fourteen-year-olds) to bring guns to school. Colorado Revised Statutes, § 18–12–105(1)(d)(enacted by House Bill 89-1245). In 1993, legislation was proposed to strengthen the law; the NRA endorsed the bill, and without the NRA's lobbying, the bill probably would not have passed the Colorado House of Representatives. Governor Romer signed the strengthened law in June 1993; a few weeks later, he was touring the state, fulminating that the NRA was opposing the governor's reasonable, new proposal that 14-year-olds should not carry guns to school.

After the special 1993 legislative session ended, Governor Romer informed politicians and media all over the country how he "beat" the NRA. In fact, the bill that the governor promoted during the weeks preceding the special session—a licensing system for juvenile handgun possession-received so little support that no licensing bill was even introduced. After the special session ended, the governor told the *New York Times* (and anyone else who would listen) that the legislature had enacted a complete ban on juvenile handgun possession, and "The only exceptions to the ban are for licensed hunting, target practice, or shooting competition." "Under 18? . . ." Actually, the stringent ban the governor described was contained in the governor's (modified) flagship bill, introduced on the first day of the special session. The bill was killed that very day by the first committee to hear the bill, on a seven-to-two vote. The juvenile handgun bill that the legislature enacted was neither drafted with nor initially endorsed by Governor Romer. It was written by Republican Jeannie Adkins. After negotiations (and after the Romer bill was killed), Governor Romer and the NRA both endorsed the Adkins bill, which was less restrictive than the governor's initial proposals, but more restrictive than the NRA's initial proposals.

6. Erik Larson, "The Story of a Gun," The *Atlantic*, January 1993, p. 48 (excerpt from Erik Larson, *Lethal Passages: The Journey of a Gun* [New York: Crown, 1994]).

7. Teret and Wintemute, "Handgun Injuries: The Epidemiologic Evidence for Assessing Legal Responsibility," *Hamline Law Review* 6 (1983): 341, 346.

8. "Gun Violence in America: An Interview with Robert J. Walker of Handgun Control, Inc.," *Highlights* (American Association of Retired Persons), January/February 1995, p. 7.

9. National Safety Council, *Accident Facts*—1994 (Itacsa, Ill.: National Safety Council, 1994), p. 12.

For children under fifteen, accidental deaths are about 43 percent of total firearms deaths. For persons over fifteen, however, accidents constitute only 5 percent of firearms deaths. For children under fifteen, males are three times as likely to suffer a fatal accident as females, and whites ate more likely to suffer an accident than blacks. Patti J. Patterson and Alfonso H. Holguin, study of Texas incidents published in *Texas Medicine*, and discussed in "Survey Says 43 percent of Childhood Firearms Deaths Unintentional," *Crime Victims Digest*, July 1990, p. 9.

There are as many as 105 nonfatal accidental injuries for every accidental fatality. Data from ten cities, reported in United States General Accounting Office, *Accidental Shootings: Many Deaths and Injuries Caused by Firearms Could Be Prevented*, March 1991 (hereinafter "GAO Report"), p. 2.

Including nonfatal accidents, gun accidents cause one billion dollars in lifetime medical costs per year for all age groups. GAO Report, p. 3. Total American medical expenditures in a given year are about four hundred billion dollars.

10. *Accident Facts—1994*, p. 5.

11. Ibid., p. 33.

12. Ibid., p. 37.

13. Gary Kleck, *Point Blank* (Hawthorne, N.Y: Aldine, 1991), p. 276.

14. For example, an American Academy of Pediatrics advisor claims "five hundred annually." Dr. Robert Tanz, Northwestern University Medical School, quoted in loan DeClaire, "Kids & Guns," *View* (September/October 1992): 30, 33.

15. GAO Report, p. 2.

16. *Accident Facts—1994*, p. 12 (227 of 7,286 accidental deaths in that age group).

17. Ibid., p. 12 (3,087 motor vehicle; 1,142 drowning; 1,104 fires, burns).

18. Jane Matter Vachon, "Should You Trust a Tail-Wagging Dog?" *Reader's Digest*, November 1992, p. 134.

19. R. K. Lee and J. J. Sacks, "Latchkey Children and Guns at Home," *JAMA* 264 (1990): 3120. The study also asserted, but offered no evidence to prove, that latchkey children were a risk factor for gun accidents.

20. *Accident Facts—1994*, p. 69.

21. Ibid., p. 22.

22. Centers for Disease Control, *Morbidity and Mortality Weekly Report*, 11 March 1988, pp. 144–45.

23. *Accident Facts—1994*, p. 101 (drowning; figure is an estimate for 1993; number of estimated accidental deaths of children under five for 1993 is twenty); John H. Cushman, "Tales from the 104th: Watch Out, or the Regulators Will Get You!" *New York Times*, February 28, 1995, p. A10 (thirty-six child deaths from five-gallon buckets in 1994; 500 in last ten years); *Consumer's Research*, May 1988, p. 34 (cigarette lighters).

The chances that a child between the ages of one and nine will die from a firearms-related injury are about one in 10,000. (Based on Maryland data for 1980–86 contained in the article "Firearms Fatalities: A Leading Cause of Death in Maryland," and prepared by the Johns Hopkins School of Hygiene and Public Health.)

24. James Wright and Peter Rossi, *Armed and Considered Dangerous: A Survey of Felons and Their Firearms* (New York: Aldine, 1986).

25. See GAO Report, p. 4. The senator introduced the bill as S. 892 in the 102d Congress. The laws restricting the CPSC are found at 15 U.S.C. § 2052(a)(1)(E) & § 2080(d)&(e).

26. GAO Report, p. 24 (345 of 1,501 accidental deaths studied). It should be noted that GAO prepared the study at Senator Metzenbaum's request, and it is not impossible that the agency tried to arrive at policy conclusions that would please the powerful senator.

27. Paul Blackman, *Children and Firearms: Lies the CDC Loves*, paper presented at the annual meeting of the American Society of Criminology, New Orleans, November 4–7, 1992, p. 17 n.23.

28. Also, the Ruger refit benefitted any owner who thought that he might accidentally drop the gun one day. The government retrofit would benefit only those owners who expected the gun to one day be handled by a person reckless enough to point a gun at someone else for fun.

29. GAO Report, p. 3.

30. About 3.5 percent of accidents included children under five, but the GAO study made children under five 8 percent of the sample. Conversely, 40 percent of firearms accidents involve persons over thirty, but the GAO sample included only 16 percent from this age group. Office of Policy, Assistant Comptroller General, Letter to Dr. Paul Blackman, National Rifle Association, May 31, 1991. Accordingly, GAO's estimate that a childproof grip would save $170 million per year in medical costs was likely at least twice as high as it should have been. GAO Report, p. 4.

GAO also likely overestimated the number of handguns involved in gun accidents, since the GAO sample overrepresented urban areas, where the handgun to long-gun ratio is apt to be higher.

The GAO's estimate of the medical costs which arguably could be saved through increased gun regulations may be compared to the two billion dollars annually spent on medical care for persons injured while sliding into base during softball games. There are about 1.7 million sliding injuries per year, which cost an average of $1,223 to treat.

31. GAO Report, p. 3.

32. "Modifications in gun design are unlikely to reduce injury, since those at greatest risk are preteen and teenage boys, both of whom possess adult abilities to circumvent gun safety features." American Academy of Pediatrics, Committee on Adolescence, "Policy Statement: Firearms and Adolescents," *AAP News*, January 1992 (approved by AAP Executive Board in 1991, released in January 1992), p. 21.

33. Massad Ayoob, Gun Proof Your Children (Concord, N.H.: Police Bookshelf, 1986), p. 8.

34. In regards to rifles, many so-called assault weapons can use plastic, translucent magazines (ammunition-feeding devices), which make it easier for the user to tell if the gun is loaded.

35. Kleck, *Point Blank*, pp. 280–81.

36. Fla. Stat. §§ 784.05, 791,175.

37. "More Children Using Weapons Frequently in Schools," Associated Press, 23 May 1993.

38. For example, *Farley* v. *Guns Unlimited and S.W. Daniel, Inc.*, Virginia Beach, Virginia Circuit Court, no. 89-2047; *Bengston* v. *Intratec U.S.A.*, Superior Court of Middlesex, Conn., No CV-87-00487025 (case dismissed).

39. The trial court threw out the suit against the Boy Scouts, but allowed the suit against the advertisers to proceed. *Way* v. *Boy Scouts of America*, no. 90-12265-1, discussed in "Boy Scout Gun Suit Rejected," *ABA Journal* (January 1992): 21.

40. Kevin Simpson, "While Children Die, Colorado Balks at Firearms Reforms," *Denver Post*, 26 September 1991, p. B1.

41. GAO Report.

42. M. Heins, R. Kahn, and J. Bjordnal, "Gunshot Wounds in Children," *American Journal of Public Health* 64 (1974): 326–30.

43. William W. Treanor and Marjolijn Bijlefeld, *Kids & Guns: A Child Safety Scandal*, 2d ed. (Educational Fund to End Gun Violence), p. 17.

44. American Trauma Society, Pennsylvania Division, *"Ouch!" Anybody Can Get Hurt*. One shortcoming of the Pennsylvania brochure is that it teaches by negative example. Rather than showing a child refusing to touch the gun, the comic shows the child accidentally shooting a friend. In contrast, the fire safety example shows a child leaving a burning house, rather than a child being burned to death after he fails to evacuate.

45. Laurie Cassady, "Shorstein, NRA Aim to Save Kids," *Florida Times-Union*, 2 November 1994, p. B-2.

46. Even the *Washington Post* calls Eddie Eagle a "must for any parent who keeps a gun in the home." *Washington Post*, 7 January 1992, p. B5.

47. Cheryl Jackson, "Gun Safety Backers Shun NRA Material," (Cleveland) *Plain Dealer*, 27 March 1992. Similar opposition has kept Eddie Eagle out of the Denver public schools.

48. National Committee for Injury Prevention and Control, *Injury Prevention: Meeting the Challenge* (New York: Oxford, 1989), p. 266. Similarly, a government researcher in Western Australia concluded that firearms safety classes in high schools might reduce injuries.

Nevertheless, the researcher opposed the idea because classes might encourage an interest in firearms and because instructors might suggest it was legitimate to own firearms. O. F. Dixon, *Review of Firearms Legislation: Report to the Ministerfor Police and Traffic* (Perth, Australia: Government Printer, 1981).

49. Ronald E. Vogel and Charles Dean, "The Effectiveness of a Handgun Safety Education Program," *Journal of Police Science and Administration* 14 (1986): 242–49. The program failed to change the reckless habits of the small percent of handgun owners who do not ensure that their gun is unloaded before cleaning it.

50. American Academy of Pediatrics, Committee on Adolescence, *News Release*, p. 21.

Authors writing in the AAP's journal express dismay at the "unrealistic expectations" of the half of all gun-owning parents who believe that "active strategies" such as education and supervision are the best method to prevent gun accidents in children over twelve. D. W. Webster et al., "Parents' Beliefs about Preventing Gun Injuries to Children," *Pediatrics* 89, no. 5 (1992): 908–14.

51. In a test program in Charlotte, North Carolina, the city's Police Department made April 1985 "Handgun Safety Month," and blitzed the city with public service announcements, brochures, and speeches. Followup polling showed that the program significantly increased the percentage of handgun owners who kept their gun locked; but it did not increase the number of owners who took additional safety classes or who taught their children about handguns. Vogel and Dean, "The Effectiveness of a Handgun Safety Education Program."

A rather implausible criticism of Eddie Eagle was offered by Diane Sawyer of ABC's *Primetime Live*. In a program that described the problems of accidental shootings by children, and also detailed the Eddie Eagle gun safety education program, Ms. Sawyer stated, "in the last year we could find figures available, there was a 25 percent increase in the number of 16-year-old kids committing homicides with guns, so coloring books are not working." "Real Young Guns," ABC News *Prime-time Live*, 22 February 1990, show #129, transcript p. 2. Ms. Sawyer's conclusion failed to consider that (1) Eddie Eagle is intended to prevent accidents involving preteen children, rather than intentional murders by teenagers, and (2) no person aged sixteen at the time Ms. Sawyer's statistics were compiled could have taken the Eddie Eagle safety class.

52. Kleck, *Point Blank*, pp. 299–300; Hunter Education Association, *Hunting Accident Report with Graphics of 1986–1990 Data* (Seattle: Outdoor Empire Pub., 1991).

53. National Safety Council, *Accident Facts*, 1968 ed. and *Accident Facts, 1994*, p. 92 (139 fatal and 1,132 nonfatal hunting accidents in 1992).

54. New Zealand Police and New Zealand Mountain Safety Council, *Beginning with Airguns* (Wellington, Government Printer, 1986), p. 2.

55. In *Billy Hook Goes to Manuka Lodge*, young Billy learns essential gun safety rules. Home from the lodge, he goes target shooting with his father. See also New Zealand Police and New Zealand Mountain Safety Council, *Gun Safety with Billy Hook* (n.d.).

56. New Zealand Police, *Arms Code: Firearms Safety Manual Issued by the New Zealand Police* (Upper Hutt, New Zealand: Wright and Carman, n.d.), p. 33.

57. Charles I. H. Forsyth, *Firearms in New Zealand* (Thorndon, Wellington: New Zealand Mountain Safety Council, 1985), pp. 2, 121.

58. The Milwaukee police, in conjunction with McDonalds restaurants, produced a cartoon "safety" book featuring talking, animated guns with names like "Sammy Saturday Night Special." The use of talking guns (in contrast to Eddie Eagle's realistic, inanimate guns) obviously detracts from the realism and the effectiveness of the gun-safety message.

Moreover, the comic book tells children to call the police if they find a gun in their parents' home. In the Milwaukee/McDonalds comic, the gun that triggers the phone call happens to be a stolen one, which the father bought without knowing it was hot. But the children didn't know that, nor did the police in the comic, until they had seized the gun and taken it in for tracing.

59. David B. Kopel, *The Samurai, the Mountie, and the Cowboy: Should America Adopt the Gun Controls of Other Democracies?* (Amherst, N.Y.: Prometheus Books, 1992), pp. 22, 442 (Japan, Detroit).

60. One study found that gun owners who have received training are more likely to store their guns loaded and unlocked, perhaps because they are more confident of their ability to handle the firearm properly without causing an accident. David Hemenway, Sara J. Solnick, and Deborah R. Azrael, "Firearm Training and Storage," *JAMA* 273, no. 1 (January 4, 1995): 46–50. Gun owners who are more interested in personal protection may also be more likely to seek training. Although Hemenway et al. accept the received wisdom of the public health literature that loaded guns in the home are per se pernicious, they do not study whether the trained owners' loaded guns were stored where irresponsible children could get hold of them.

61. The number of deaths resulting from misleading, sloppy journalism is not zero. To cite but one example, almost every commercial airplane crash anywhere in the world is covered by media, but car crashes are rarely reported, even in the state where they occur. The media almost never report the data showing that, per passenger mile, commercial air travel is far safer than driving. As a result of the media's unbalanced coverage of air safety, some people choose to drive rather than fly to a distant destination, in the mistaken belief that driving is safer. Statistically speaking, it is a certainty that by indirectly encouraging some people to drive rather than fly, the media cause an increase in transportation fatalities. See generally, Richard B. McKenzie and Dwight R. Lee, *Ending Free Airplane Rides for Infants: A Myopic Method of Saving Lives*, Briefing Paper no. 11 (Washington, D.C.: Cato Institute, August 30, 1990).

62. Philip Cook, "The Role of Firearms in Violent Crime: An Interpretative Review of the Literature," in M. Wolfgang and N. Weiler, eds., *Criminal Violence* (Beverly Hills, Calif.: Sage, 1982), pp. 236, 269. Also, Roger Lane, "On the Social Meaning of Homicide Trends in America," in Ted R. Gurr, ed., *Violence in America* 1 (1989): 59 ("the psychological profile of the accident-prone suggests the same kind of aggressiveness shown by most murderers"); Kleck, *Point Blank*, pp. 282–87.

63. In a highly publicized shooting of a ten-year-old boy by a playmate, the playmate was reportedly watching a movie called *Gotcha*. The playmate asked his friends if they wanted to see a real gun, and went to his father's closet to get a .357 Magnum, which he then loaded and accidentally fired. "Real Young Guns," ABC News, *Primetime Live*, 22 February 1990, Program #129, transcript, p. 1.

64. A. N. Meltzoff, "Imitation of Televised Models by Infants," *Child Development* 59 (1988): 1221. In the Meltzoff study, children aged fourteen and twenty-four months watched an adult manipulate a novel toy in a particular way. Twenty-four hours later, the children were shown the real toy, and they used the toy in imitation of the way the man on television had used it.

65. William W. Treanor and Marjolijn Bijlefeld (Educational Fund to End Gun Molencr), *Kids & Guns: A Child Safety Scandal*, 2d ed. The photo is also used by Handgun Control, Inc.'s, tax-exempt affiliate, Center to Prevent Handgun Violence, "Handgun Violence: An American Epidemic" (no date) (fund raising flyer).

66. *Accident Facts*, 1992, 1994 editions.

26

SELF-DEFENSE

PHILIP J. COOK

T hat one-half of American households own guns is primarily a reflection of the widespread involvement in hunting and target shooting. But for one-fifth of those who own a gun and two-fifths of handgun owners, the most important reason is self-defense at home (Wright, Rossi, and Daly 1983, p. 96). The concern reflected in this defensive demand for guns is quite reasonable, given the burglary statistics. During the period 1979–87, there was an annual average of one million residential burglaries in which a household member was present, yielding a household victimization rate of over 1 percent.[1] Thirty-four percent of these burglaries of occupied dwellings resulted in an assault, robbery, or rape. Thus, the need to take precautions against intruders is real, and a gun seems to offer an inexpensive means of self-defense against intruders who are neither discouraged by locks nor deterred by the presence of someone in the home.

A number of studies have questioned whether a gun, in fact, offers much protection against burglars since most people who are burglarized while at home do not attempt to defend themselves with a gun even when there is one available. The larger issue is whether the presence of a gun in the home poses a risk to household members that outweighs whatever protection it may confer; a handgun obtained for self-protection may end up causing accidental injury or suicide (Kellermann and Reay 1986). There may, however, be a public benefit to the widespread ownership of guns, particularly in deterring burglary of occu-

From Philip J. Cook, "The Technology of Personal Violence," in *Crime and Justice*, vol. 14, ed. Michael Tonry (Chicago: University of Chicago Press, 1991), pp. 52–63. Reprinted with permission.

pied dwellings. And the use of guns for self-protection away from home raises the same issues; people who go armed in public may have a better chance to defend themselves against robbery and assault while at the same time increasing the rates of accidental shootings and other forms of misuse. Indeed, it is entirely reasonable that private gun ownership has mixed effects on personal violence and crime. This paper documents these effects and reviews the evidence on their importance.

THE DEMAND FOR GUNS FOR SELF-PROTECTION

The qualities of a gun that make it effective in fending off assailants and intruders are the same as those that make it an effective tool in personal crimes of violence. A gun greatly enhances most people's capacity to intimidate or incapacitate an assailant. The defensive demand for guns extends even to those who routinely engage in violent crime; a majority of the gun-using felons who responded to Wright and Rossi's survey cited self-defense as an important reason for their practice of carrying a gun (Wright and Rossi 1986, p. 128).

As a means of defense against crime, guns supplement alarms, guard dogs, and "target-hardening" measures (door locks, window grilles, safes), both in residences and retail shops. A 1968 survey of small businesses found that the demand for guns and other protection devices increased with the threat of victimization. Businesses in the ghetto were more likely to have a gun than were those located in other areas of the central city, which, in turn, were more likely to have a gun than were businesses located in the suburbs (Kakalik and Wildhorn 1972). This pattern of gun ownership is not found among households since most people buy guns to hunt rather than for defending their homes; thus, urban households are less likely to own a gun than rural households. However, there is evidence that the propensity to obtain a gun specifically for self-protection is influenced by the threat of criminal victimization. Smith and Uchida (1988) demonstrate this result with data from a survey of three urban areas conducted in 1977. For the overall sample of 9,021 respondents, 14.3 percent reported that they or another member of their household had purchased a "gun or other weapon" for protection of home and family. The authors' multivariate analysis of these responses demonstrated that defensive weapon acquisition was more likely if a household member had been victimized in the last year, or if the respondent perceived an increase in his neighborhood's crime rate in the last year. They also found a strong negative association between weapon acquisition and the respondent's rating of police services. The authors conclude that obtaining a weapon for protection is a response to perceived vulnerability to crime. This result is surely credible though not definitive; the data do not allow them to distinguish between guns and other weapons and do not include any objective indicator of neighborhood crime rates.

USE OF GUNS FOR SELF-PROTECTION

If guns are obtained in part for self-protection, how often are they actually used for that purpose? Attempts to answer this question have relied primarily on survey data since there are no official records that are directly relevant.

Gary Kleck (1988) reviewed a number of surveys and other sources in an attempt to demonstrate the value of guns in defending against crime. He noted in particular the results of the 1981 Hart poll of registered voters; 4 percent of respondents said they or members of their household had used a handgun in the previous five years for self-protection or for protection of property at home, work, or elsewhere. (Respondents were instructed to limit their report to uses against people, as opposed to animals, and to exclude military and police-work uses.) On the assumption that respondents define "household" the same way as the Census Bureau, Kleck concludes that there were 3.2 million households (4 percent of 80 million) in which someone used a handgun to threaten or shoot at another person in an effort to defend life or property. Unfortunately, there are no details provided in the Hart poll concerning the distribution of circumstances for these events, nor any data on defensive uses of long guns. Kleck overcomes the latter problem by multiplying the incidence of handgun uses by a factor of 1.57. His justification is based on a poll conducted in 1978, which inquired whether guns in the home were owned primarily for self-defense. He concludes from the responses that there are 21 million handguns and 12 million long guns kept for self-defense, or .57 long guns for every handgun. He then assumes that long guns are used for self-defense in this same ratio (Kleck 1988, p. 4). He concludes that guns are used in self-defense about one million times each year.

The National Crime Survey (NCS) provides much more specific data on the use of guns in self-defense against personal violence. National Crime Survey data for 1979–85 yield an estimate of 386,000 instances in which victims of assault and robbery defended themselves with a gun (Kleck 1988). This implies an annual average of 55,000 defensive uses of firearms in crimes of violence, which is less than 6 percent of Kleck's estimate of the overall frequency of self-defense uses. The logical implication, if one believes Kleck's estimate, is that there are about 950,000 other "defensive" uses of guns that do not involve violent crimes. But Kleck comes to a different conclusion. He uses California survey data as a basis for arguing that most of the defensive uses of guns do involve crimes of personal violence, occurring primarily at home. His explanation for the seemingly gross inconsistency among his various statistics is that the NCS respondents underreport assaults occurring at home. The undercount would have to be vast indeed for this to be an adequate explanation, but perhaps it is: conceivably, respondents are so reticent about reporting domestic violence incidents to NCS interviewers that the NCS estimate misses all but 1 or 2 percent of them.[2]

Alternatively, or in addition, the Hart poll may be in error. The Hart poll on which Kleck's estimate is based requires respondents to recall events from years earlier and, in particular, to distinguish between those that occurred within five years and those that occurred earlier. Experiments conducted in the course of designing the National Crime Survey demonstrated that respondents made systematic errors in placing their personal victimization experiences in time; if asked to report victimizations occurring within the previous twelve months, they would tend to "telescope" in important experiences that had occurred outside of that time frame, while forgetting to mention other victimizations that occurred within the time frame (Penick and Owens 1976; Skogan 1981). The Hart poll asked respondents to deal with a time frame of five years, rather than one, and the question concerned experiences for any member of the "household," rather than just personal experience. Given these difficulties, it is likely that some of the respondents who gave a positive response were remembering events that, in fact, had occurred more than five years earlier or events that occurred to family members who were not members of the "household" as that term would be defined by the Bureau of the Census. In short, there are severe methodological problems with the Hart poll as a basis for estimating the prevalence of gun use in self-defense.

The National Crime Survey is a much larger and more sophisticated effort, based on questionnaires that have been devised and refined through a program of extensive testing to produce a reliable basis for estimating the volume of crime. Still, Kleck is correct in pointing out that the NCS data miss a large fraction of domestic assaults and the defensive uses of guns that may occur in that context. My conclusion is to accept the NCS-based estimate of 50,000 defensive uses per year against rape, robbery, and assault with the proviso that this figure excludes almost all defensive uses against members of the same household. The NCS data probably also miss most of the instances in which guns are used by criminals and others who are unlikely to cooperate with the National Crime Survey interviewers (Cook 1985a). Of course, there is no reason to believe that the Hart poll would do any better in this respect.

The National Crime Survey also offers some information on the frequency of gun use in protecting property. In particular, newly available results on burglaries provide the first direct measure of self-defense measures taken against burglars of occupied dwellings. Data from the National Crime Survey for the nine-year period 1979–87 were pooled to provide reliable estimates. Special tabulations were provided in personal correspondence to me from Michael Rand of the Bureau of Justice Statistics. During this period, there was an average of 6.8 million residential burglaries a year, of which in 1.0 million cases (14.7 percent), there was someone at home at the time. In about one-half of these burglaries (52.6 percent), some self-defense action was taken. Of greatest interest here is the use of weapons in self-defense: only 3.1 percent of occupants used a gun to defend against the intruder, while 2.0 percent used a knife or other weapon. Thus, there are about 32,000 instances each year in which someone uses a gun to scare off or defend against an intruder. In other words, a gun is used once in every 220 burglaries, or once in every thirty burglaries of an occupied residence.[3]

Given these results, it is possible to estimate the total number of defensive gun uses against burglary and violent crime. Of the 32,000 annual uses against burglary, about 9,000 involved violent crimes as well. Avoiding double counting, the total National Crime Survey-based estimate of gun uses against predatory crime is about 80,000 per year.

SUCCESS AND FAILURE
IN SELF-DEFENSE EFFORTS

The statistical record suggests that people who use a weapon to defend against robberies, assaults, and burglaries are generally successful in foiling the crime and avoiding injury. In the case of burglary, the National Crime Survey sample for 1979-87 of burglaries of occupied residences indicate that gun defense is associated with a relatively low rate of successful theft (14 percent of gun-defense cases versus 33 percent overall). If we restrict the sample to those cases in which theft was actually attempted (41 percent of the total), there remains a large difference in success rates: 80 percent of all such attempts were successful in burglaries of occupied residences, but when the victim used a gun in self-defense, only 48 percent of attempts were successful. (The estimated theft success rate is only 46 percent when the victim defended himself or herself with a knife or other weapon.)

Robbery statistics also suggest the effectiveness of using a gun or other weapon in self-defense. Kleck's (1988) analysis of National Crime Survey data for the period 1979–85 found that the likelihood that a robbery would be completed successfully when the victim resisted with a gun was only 31 percent, the same as the rate for robberies where knives or other weapons were used to resist. (The overall rate of successful completion was 65 percent.) However, it was relatively rare for guns to be used to defend against robbery. Defense with guns occurred in only 1.2 percent of incidents, and knives or other weapons were used in another 2.3 percent of incidents. Proportionately, few victims have a gun handy when they are robbed, and most of those who do are surely not in a position to use it effectively. A skilled robber takes control of the victim quickly through violence or threats (Conklin 1972). Thus, the sample of robberies in which the victim uses a gun in self-defense is surely unrepresentative of the universe of robberies in a number of dimensions, including the competence of the robbers and the types of weapon they use. For that reason, the National Crime Survey tabulations are not a reliable guide to the costs and benefits of using a gun in self-defense in any specific robbery circumstances (Cook 1986).[4]

INJURY TO VICTIMS

There is always a danger that victim resistance will provoke an assailant to greater violence and result in more serious injury to the victim than if no resistance had been made. It is interesting that National Crime Survey data (Kleck 1988) suggest that physical attack and injury are much less likely to occur in robberies and assaults in which the victim is able to deploy a gun than in other circumstances. But that difference, in the absence of information on the sequence of events in the violent encounter, is subject to several interpretations (Cook 1986). It could be that resistance with a gun forestalls attack, or, alternatively, that an attack prevents the victim from deploying his gun. While both explanations may be valid, the latter is surely more important. In the usual sequence of events, the robber's attack on the victim initiates the encounter, as in a mugging or yoking. Thus instead of concluding that "gun resisters are unlikely to be attacked," it is more accurate to conclude that "victims who are attacked are unlikely to have the opportunity to deploy their gun."

The sparse National Crime Survey data on this subject say nothing at all about the likelihood that the victim will be killed since homicide is not a logical possibility in victim survey data. Police files on robbery murder do offer some information on the importance of resistance, however. I collected data from police files in Dade County, Florida, and Atlanta, Georgia, for several years in the mid-1970s (Cook 1980a). Out of thirty robbery murders in Dade County, there were just three in which the victim offered forceful resistance. In twenty-six robbery murders in Atlanta, there was evidence of forceful resistance in two cases, including one that involved a gun: a police officer was shot when he interrupted a robbery and attempted to draw his weapon (Cook and Nagin 1979, p. 33). It appears, then, that robbery murder is rarely the result of escalation of violence stemming from the victim's use of force.

In sum, while using a gun to resist a robber may sometimes result in serious injury or death to the victim, that result is not common. Only about 1 percent of victims of noncommercial robbery resist with a gun, and in those instances the resistance effort is usually successful. Of course, resisting with a gun is only possible if the robber fails to take immediate control of the situation and only prudent if the robber lacks a gun himself.

DETERRENCE AND OTHER GENERAL EFFECTS

While relatively few victims of burglary and personal violence attempt to defend themselves with guns, the possibility of encountering an armed victim poses a definite risk to predatory criminals. That risk may influence a number of crime-related decisions, including the kinds of crimes to commit, the selection of targets, the modus operandi, and even the decision of when to retire. The widespread availability of guns surely does have some influence on such decisions and, hence, on the overall volume and pattern of predatory crime. The pertinent question is whether these effects are large or small.

Wright and Rossi's (1986) survey of prisoners found a large minority with relevant personal experience. Overall, two-fifths said there had been one or more times in their life when they "decided not to do a crime because [they] knew or believed that the victim was carrying a gun" (p. 155). One-third had been "scared off, shot at, wounded, or captured by an armed victim." Wright and Rossi point out that there is an ambiguity in these results concerning the nature of the armed victim; no doubt some were law-abiding citizens, but others would be criminal associates of the respondent whom they fought or attempted to rob (p. 159). On the broader issue of deterrence, Wright and Rossi asked their respondents what felons worry about when contemplating criminal activity: "might get shot at by victim" was a frequent worry for 34 percent of the respondents, the same fraction as those whose concern was "might get shot at by police" (Wright and Rossi, p. 148). (By comparison, half of the respondents indicated that they worried about being caught.) These results, while based on a sample that is not representative of violent criminals, are at least suggestive that the threat of effective victim resistance is relevant in understanding criminal behavior.

The objective threat that armed victims pose to predatory criminals is difficult to measure. Wright and Rossi's (1986) data do not allow an estimate of the fraction who had been shot during the course of a crime. National Crime Survey data on self-defense do not include an item on whether the assailant was injured. Police departments file supplementary homicide reports with the Federal Bureau of Investigation that include cases of "civilian justifiable homicide"—instances in which a civilian killed a criminal in the act of committing a felony—but it is not always possible to determine the circumstances in which these homicides occur. One attempt to use these data focused on robbery (Cook 1979). I tabulated all such killings that occurred during robberies, 1973–74, in nineteen cities. The death rate per 100,000 exposures ranged from about four, for cities in the Northeast and Pacific regions, to a high of forty-eight for Atlanta. Assuming that the death rate from justifiable shootings in robberies is about 10 percent,[5] then an order-of-magnitude estimate for the risk a robber faces in a city with high gun ownership is 0.2 percent. This relative frequency is an average of commercial and noncommercial robberies; the former may be the more risky, given the presence of security guards in some cases. In any event, a probability on the order of 0.2 percent seems so low as to be readily ignored in a robber's calculations, yet for a robbery "career" of 100 robberies, the implication is an 18 percent probability of being shot at least once.

Do high rates of gun ownership have a deterrent effect on robbery? A multivariate analysis of city robbery rates, reported above, found that there was no statistically discernible effect of gun prevalence on the robbery rate (Cook 1979). Of course, "no effect" may be the net result of a negative deterrent effect and a positive effect stemming from the greater ease of robbers obtaining guns for use in crime.

There is a smattering of evidence on the likelihood that a residential burglar will be shot. The most often cited is Newton and Zimring's (1969, p. 63) order-of-magnitude estimate of 0.2 percent, based on a single city during a period when there were just seven justifiable homicides in burglaries. In any event, there is no evidence that higher gun ownership rates deter burglary. Indeed, I found that burglary rates tend to increase with gun ownership across large cities, other things equal (Cook 1983b). Presumably, this is the result of the greater average payoff to burglary in cities where guns are likely to be part of the loot.[6]

A number of authors have suggested that the threat of being shot by an occupant has the effect of deterring burglary of occupied dwellings (Kates 1983; Wright and Rossi 1986). In support of this proposition, Kleck (1988) observes that the occupancy rate for burglaries in the United States is far lower than in three countries for which the relevant burglary data exist (Canada, Great Britain, and the Netherlands) and where gun ownership is less prevalent.

There are two well-known instances in which a jurisdiction has implemented a policy of encouraging citizens to use guns in self-defense against crime. In both cases, short-term changes in crime statistics have been interpreted as evidence that the intervention had a large deterrent effect. Yet this interpretation of the data is open to serious doubt.

The first such intervention was in Orlando, Florida, where the police trained 6,000 women in the safe use of firearms between October 1966 and March 1967. The program was highly publicized as an antirape intervention. According to Kleck and Bordua (1983), the rape rate in Orlando dropped 88 percent from 1966 to 1967 and did not return to its former level until 1972. During that same period, the rape rate in the rest of Florida nearly doubled. But Green (1987) questioned the reliability of the Orlando Police Department's crime records as a basis for evaluating the effects of the gun training program. He pointed out that the recorded rape rate in Orlando fluctuated widely throughout the 1960s and actually dropped to zero in 1963. The pattern that is interpreted as a deterrent effect by Bordua and Kleck may be an artifact of poor data.

The second intervention was in Kennesaw, Georgia; in March 1982, the town council passed an ordinance requiring every household in the city to keep a firearm in their home. The law was enacted to make a public statement rather than to change behavior; there was no penalty for violation, and it exempted those who objected to firearms. Nevertheless, the burglary rate dropped sharply immediately following adoption of this ordinance, and it has continued to be touted as evidence of the crime-deterrent value of a well-armed citizenry (Kleck 1988; Kates 1989).

An analysis of the Kennesaw burglary data over the period from 1976 to 1986 suggests a different conclusion (McDowall, Wiersema, and Loftin 1989). They demonstrate that the burglary rate fluctuated widely from year to year (as one would expect in such a small city) but that there is no evidence that the gun ordinance produced a downward shift in the trend. They make a persuasive case that the ordinance had no effect on burglary rates in Kennesaw.

CONCLUSION

Despite the fact that there is a gun in half of American households, it is relatively rare for victims of burglary and crimes of violence to use them in self-defense.

The National Crime Survey data suggest about 55,000 uses in robbery and assault each year, with an additional 25,000 uses against burglary. The National Crime Survey underestimates the volume of domestic violence, hence, underestimates the frequency with which guns are used to defend against family members. For other circumstances, however, the National Crime Survey estimates are a reasonable approximation of reality.

When guns are used in self-defense, the result is usually favorable; the victim is able to foil the robbery or assault attempt. There is little evidence that the use of a gun in self-defense tends to escalate violence, although it surely happens in some cases. Of course, an assailant who has obtained the upper hand quickly enough can forestall effective resistance, and the data reflect that fact.

The threat of a burglar or robber being shot by a civilian during the commission of a crime is small, on the average, though higher in more heavily armed jurisdictions than elsewhere. While predatory criminals are aware of this danger and surely adopt precautions in some cases, it is not true that jurisdictions with high gun ownership have lower robbery or burglary rates than others. The two famous quasi-experiments in Kennesaw and Orlando may have produced some deterrent effects, but the data are such as to vitiate confidence in this conclusion.

Finally, it is important to comment on the several studies (including Newton and Zimring 1969; Yeager 1976; Rushforth et al. 1977; Kellermann and Reay 1986) that demonstrate that guns kept in the home are far more likely to kill a family member or friend than an intruder. This is a strange comparison, in a way, since the defensive purpose of keeping a gun is not to kill intruders but to scare them off (Silver and Kates 1979). Wright (1984) has suggested that a more relevant comparison is between the likelihood of a gun accident and the likelihood of having occasion to use a gun in self-defense; based on one national survey, these appear to be approximately equal, on the average. But that comparison ignores the fact that a gun in the house may increase the risk that a household member will commit suicide. Thus, the objective benefit of gun ownership is measured by the likelihood of using the gun to defend successfully against burglary and assault, whether or not the perpetrator is shot in the process. The cost of gun ownership is the risk of an accidental shooting, or, more problematically, of suicide. There is an asymmetry here: no cost is incurred unless there is injury, but the beneficial use of the gun does not require that anyone be injured.

Undoubtedly, anyone who is contemplating obtaining a gun should consider the risks, whose magnitude depends on how carefully a weapon is stored and handled, whether any family members are suicidal, and other factors. These risks can be compared to a realistic assessment of the benefit, that there is some small chance of being able to use the gun in self-defense if there were an intruder who could not otherwise be scared off. The upshot of this calculation will depend on the circumstances. Finally, the public benefit of having a heavily armed citizenry remains to be demonstrated.

NOTES

1. An unpublished tabulation provided the author by the U.S. Bureau of Justice Statistics estimated that, during the period 1979–87, there were 9.042 million burglaries in which a household member was present.

2. The National Crime Survey (NCS) has encountered severe problems in counting repetitive crimes (known as "series incidents") and excludes them from its published estimates (Skogan 1990). This problem combined with the underreporting engendered by special sensitivities with domestic violence produces a considerable bias in estimates of household assaults (Bureau of Justice Statistics 1984). Presumably the Hart poll would suffer from the same problems.

3. About half (54 percent) of burglaries against an occupied dwelling are perpetrated by a relative or acquaintance of the victim. But only one-third of the instances of defensive gun use against intruders involve relatives or acquaintances. When a stranger burglarizes an occupied dwelling, the likelihood the victim will use a gun in self-defense is about 4.6 percent.

4. Victims are much less likely to resist gun robbers than those with other weapons.

5. The "deterrence" explanation is speculative and should not be taken seriously until it is possible to rule out other explanations. As reported above, in the United States, it appears that burglary of occupied dwellings is a much different phenomenon than burglary of unoccupied dwellings. Half the former cases involve relatives or acquaintances, and, in most cases, their objective is something other than theft by stealth. Given this characterization, it is easy to believe that international differences in the relative frequency of burglary of occupied dwellings reflect societal differences.

6. Alternatively, it could reflect the reverse causal process, in the sense that the demand for guns may be enhanced by a high burglary rate. However, as noted above, gunownership patterns are largely determined by the demand for use in hunting and other sports, rather than for use in self defense.

REFERENCES

Conklin, John E. 1972. *Robbery and the Criminal Justice System*. Philadelphia: Lippincott.

Cook, Philip J. 1979. "The effect of Gun Availability on Robbery and Robbery Murder: A Cross Section Study of Fifty Cities." In *Policy Studies Review Annual*. Vol. 3. Edited by Robert H. Haveman and B. Bruce Zellner. Beverly Hills, Calif.: Sage.

Cook, Philip J. 1980a. "Reducing Injury and Death Rates in Robbery." *Policy Analysis* 6(1):21–45.

Cook, Philip J. 1986. "The Relationship between Victim Resistance and Injury in Noncommercial Robbery." *Journal of Legal Studies* 15:405–16.

Cook, Philip J., and Daniel Nagin. 1979. *Does the Weapon Matter?* Washington, D.C.: Institute for Law and Social Research.

Federal Bureau of Investigation. 1979. *Crime in the United States, 1978*. Washington, D.C.: U.S. Government Printing Office.

———. 1988. *Crime in the United States, 1987*. Washington, D.C.: U.S. Government Printing Office.

———. 1989. *Crime in the United States, 1988*. Washington, D.C.: U.S. Government Printing Office.

Green, Gary S. 1987. "Citizen Gun Ownership and Criminal Deterrence: Theory, Research, and Policy." *Criminology* 25:63–82.

Kakalik, James S., and Sorrell Wildhorn. 1972. *The Private Security Industry—Its Nature and Extent*. Santa Monica, Calif.: RAND.

Kates, Don B., Jr. 1983. "Handgun Prohibition and the Original Meaning of the Second Amendment." *Michigan Law Review* 82:204–73.

Kellermann, Arthur L., and Donald T. Reay. 1986. "Protection or Peril? An Analysis of Firearm-related Deaths in the Home." *New England Journal of Medicine* 314:1557–60.

Kleck, Gary. 1988. "Crime Control through the Private Use of Armed Force." *Social Problems* 35:1–22.

Kleck, Gary, and David J. Bordua. 1983. "The Factual Foundation for Certain Key Assumptions of Gun Control." *Law and Policy Quarterly* 5:271–98.

Newton, George D., Jr., and Franklin E. Zimring. 1969. *Firearms and Violence in American Life.* Washington, D.C.: U.S. Goverment Printing Office.

Penick, Bettye R., and Maurice E. B. Owens III. 1976. *Surveying Crime.* Washington, D.C.: National Academy of Sciences.

Rushforth, N. B., A. B. Ford, C. S. Hirsh, N. M. Rushforth, and L. Adelson. 1977. "Violent Death in a Metropolitan County: Changing Patterns in Homicide (1958–74)." *New England Journal of Medicine* 297:531–38.

Seiden, Richard. 1977. "Suicide Prevention: A Public Health/Public Policy Approach." *Omega* 8:267–76.

Silver, Carol Ruth, and Don B. Kates Jr. 1979. "Self-Defense, Handgun Ownership, and the Independence of Women in a Violent, Sexist Society." In *Restricting Hnadguns: The Liberals Skeptics Speak Out.* Editied by Don B. Kates Jr. Croton-on-Hudson. N.Y.: North River.

Skogan, Wesley G. 1978. "Weapon Use in Robbery: Patterns and Policy Implications." Unpublished manuscript. Evanston, Ill.: Northwestern University, Center for Urban Affairs.

Smith, Douglas A., and Craig D. Uchida. 1988. "The Social Organization of Self-Help: A Study of Defensive Weapon Ownership." *American Sociological Review* 53(1):94–102.

27

ARMED RESISTANCE TO CRIME

THE PREVALENCE AND NATURE OF SELF-DEFENSE WITH A GUN

GARY KLECK & MARC GERTZ

INTRODUCTION

Crime victims used to be ignored by criminologists. Then, beginning slowly in the 1940s and more rapidly in the 1970s, interest in the victim's role in crime grew. Yet a tendency to treat the victim as either a passive target of another person's wrongdoing or as a virtual accomplice of the criminal limited this interest. The concept of the victim precipitated homicide highlighted the possibility that victims were not always blameless and passive targets, but that they sometimes initiated or contributed to the escalation of a violent interaction through their own actions, which they often claimed were defensive.

Perhaps due to an unduly narrow focus on lower-class male-on-male violence, scholars have shown little openness to the possibility that a good deal of "defensive" violence by persons claiming the moral status of a victim may be just that. Thus, many scholars routinely assumed that a large share of violent interactions are "mutual combat" involving two blameworthy parties who each may be regarded as both offender and victim. The notion that much violence is one-sided and that many victims of violence are largely blameless is dismissed as naive.

A few criminologists have rejected the simplistic mutual combat model of violence, though they sometimes limit its rejection to a few special subtypes of violence, especially family violence, rape, and, more generally, violence of men

From the *Journal of Criminal Law and Criminology* 86, no. 1 (1995): 150–87. Copyright © 1995 by Northwestern University, School of Law. Reprinted with permission.

against women and of adults against children.[2] However, the more one looks, the more exceptions become evident, such as felony killings linked with robberies, burglaries, or sexual assaults, contract killings, mass killings, serial murders, and homicides where the violence is one-sided. Indeed, it may be more accurate to see the mutual combat common among lower-class males to be the exception rather than the rule. If this is so, then forceful actions taken by victims are easier to see as genuinely and largely defensive.

Once one turns to defensive actions taken by the victims of property crimes, it is even easier to take this view. There are few robberies, burglaries, larcenies, or auto thefts where it is hard to distinguish offender from victim or to identify one of the parties as the clear initiator of a criminal action and another party as a relatively legitimate responder to those initiatives. The traditional conceptualization of victims as either passive targets or active collaborators overlooks another possible victim role, that of the active resister who does not initiate or accelerate any illegitimate activity, but uses various means of resistance for legitimate purposes, such as avoiding injury or property loss.

Victim resistance can be passive or verbal, but much of it is active and forceful. Potentially, the most consequential form of forceful resistance is armed resistance, especially resistance with a gun. This form of resistance is worthy of special attention for many reasons, both policy-related and scientific. The policy-related reasons are obvious: if self-protection with a gun is commonplace, it means that any form of gun control that disarms large numbers of prospective victims, either altogether, or only in certain times and places where victimization might occur, will carry significant social costs in terms of lost opportunities for self-protection.

On the other hand, the scientific reasons are likely to be familiar only to the relatively small community of scholars who study the consequences of victim self-protection: the defensive actions of crime victims have significant effects on the outcomes of crimes, and the effects of armed resistance differ from those of unarmed resistance. Previous research has consistently indicated that victims who resist with a gun or other weapon are less likely than other victims to lose their property in robberies[3] and in burglaries.[4] Consistently, research also has indicated that victims who resist by using guns or other weapons are less likely to be injured compared to victims who do not resist or to those who resist without weapons. This is true whether the research relied on victim surveys or on police records, and whether the data analysis consisted of simple cross-tabulations or more complex multivariate analyses. These findings have been obtained with respect to robberies[5] and to assaults.[6] Cook[7] offers his unsupported personal opinion concerning robbery victims that resisting with a gun is only prudent if the robber does not have a gun. The primary data source on which Cook relies flatly contradicts this opinion. National Crime Victimization Survey (NCVS) data indicate that even in the very disadvantageous situation where the robber has a gun, victims who resist with guns are still substantially less likely to be injured than those who resist in other ways, and even slightly less likely to be hurt than those who do not resist at all.[8]

With regard to studies of rape, although samples typically include too few cases of self-defense with a gun for separate analysis, McDermott,[9] Quinsey and Upfold,[10] Lizotte,[11] and Kleck and Sayles[12] all found that victims who resisted with some kind of weapon were less likely to have the rape attempt completed against them. Findings concerning the impact of armed resistance on whether rape victims suffer additional injuries beyond the rape itself are less clear, due to a lack of information on whether acts of resistance preceded or followed the rapist's attack. The only two rape studies with the necessary sequence information found that forceful resistance by rape victims usually follows, rather than precedes, rapist attacks inflicting additional injury, undercutting the proposition that victim resistance increases the likelihood that the victim will be hurt.[13] This is consistent with findings on robbery and assault.[14]

THE PREVALENCE OF DEFENSIVE GUN USE (DGU) IN PREVIOUS SURVEYS

The National Crime Victimization Survey (NCVS)

However consistent the evidence may be concerning the effectiveness of armed victim resistance, there are some who minimize its significance by insisting that it is rare.[15] This assertion is invariably based entirely on a single source of information, the National Crime Victimization Survey (NCVS).

Data from the NCVS imply that each year there are only about 68,000 defensive uses of guns in connection with assaults and robberies,[16] or about 80,000 to 82,000 if one adds in uses linked with household burglaries.[17] These figures are less than one ninth of the estimates implied by the results of at least thirteen other surveys, most of which have been previously reported.[18] The NCVS estimates imply that about 0.09 of 1 percent of U.S. households experience a defensive gun use (DGU) in any one year, compared to the Mauser survey's estimate of 3.79 percent of households over a five year period, or about 0.76 percent in any one year, assuming an even distribution over the five year period, and no repeat uses.[19]

The strongest evidence that a measurement is inaccurate is that it is inconsistent with many other independent measurements or observations of the same phenomenon; indeed, some would argue that this is ultimately the only way of knowing that a measurement is wrong. Therefore, one might suppose that the gross inconsistency of the NCVS-based estimates with all other known estimates, each derived from sources with no known flaws even remotely substantial enough to account for nine-to-one, or more, discrepancies, would be sufficient to persuade any serious scholar that the NCVS estimates are unreliable.

Apparently it is not, since the Bureau of Justice Statistics continues to disseminate their DGU estimates as if they were valid,[20] and scholars continue to cite the NCVS estimates as being at least as reasonable as those from the gun surveys.[21] Similarly, the editors of a report on violence conducted for the prestigious National Academy of Sciences have uncritically accepted the validity of the NCVS estimate as being at least equal to that of all of the alternative estimates.[22] In effect, even the National Academy of Sciences gives no more weight to estimates from numerous independent sources than to an estimate derived from a single source which is, as explained below, singularly ill-suited to the task of estimating DGU frequency.

This sort of bland and spurious even-handedness is misleading. For example, Reiss and Roth withheld from their readers that there were at least nine other estimates contradicting the NCVS-based estimate; instead they vaguely alluded only to "a number of surveys,"[23] as did Cook,[24] and they downplayed the estimates from the other surveys on the basis of flaws which they only speculated those surveys *might* have. Even as speculations, these scholars' conjectures were conspicuously onesided, focusing solely on possible flaws whose correction would bring the estimate down, while ignoring obvious flaws, such as respondents (Rs) forgetting or intentionally concealing DGUs, whose correction would push the estimate up. Further, the speculations, even if true, would be wholly inadequate to account for more than a small share of the enormous nine-to-one or more discrepancy between the NCVS-based estimates and all other estimates. For example, the effects of telescoping can be completely cancelled out by the effects of memory loss and other recall failure, and even if they are not, they cannot account for more than a tiny share of a discrepancy of nine-to-one or more.

Equally important, those who take the NCVS-based estimates seriously have consistently ignored the most pronounced limitations of the NCVS for estimating DGU frequency. The NCVS is a nonanonymous national survey conducted by a branch of the federal government, the U.S. Bureau of the Census. Interviewers identify themselves to Rs as federal government employees, even displaying, in face-to-face contacts, an identification card with a badge. Rs are told that the interviews are being conducted on behalf of the U.S. Department of Justice, the law enforcement branch of the federal government. As a preliminary to asking questions about crime-victimization experiences, interviewers establish the address, telephone number, and full names of all occupants, age twelve and over, in each household they contact. In short, it is made very clear to Rs that they are, in effect, speaking to a law enforcement arm of the federal government, whose employees know exactly who the Rs and their family members are, where they live, and how they can be recontacted.

Even under the best of circumstances, reporting the use of a gun for self-protection would be an extremely sensitive and legally controversial matter for either of two reasons. As with other forms of forceful resistance, the defensive act itself, regardless of the characteristics of any weapon used, might constitute an unlawful assault or at least the R might believe that others, including either legal authorities or the researchers, could regard it that way. Resistance with a gun also involves additional elements of sensitivity. Because guns are legally regulated, a victim's possession of the weapon, either in general or at the time of the DGU, might itself be unlawful, either in fact or in the mind of a crime victim who used one. More likely, lay persons with a limited knowledge of the extremely complicated law of either self-defense or firearms regulation are unlikely to know for sure whether their defensive actions or their gun possession was lawful.

It is not hard for gun-using victims interviewed in the NCVS to withhold information about their use of a gun, especially since they are *never directly asked whether they used a gun for self-protection*. They are asked only general questions about whether they did anything to protect themselves.[26] In short, Rs are merely given the opportunity to volunteer the information that they have used a gun defensively. All it takes for an R to conceal a DGU is to simply refrain from mentioning it, i.e., to leave it out of what may be an otherwise accurate and complete account of the crime incident.

Further, Rs in the NCVS are not even asked the general self-protection question unless they already independently indicated that they had been a victim of a crime. This means that any DGUs associated with crimes the Rs did not want to talk about would remain hidden. It has been estimated that the NCVS may catch less than one-twelfth of spousal assaults and one-thirty-third of rapes,[27] thereby missing nearly all DGUs associated with such crimes.

In the context of a nonanonymous survey conducted by the federal government, an R who reports a DGU may believe that he is placing himself in serious legal jeopardy. For example, consider the issue of the location of crimes. For all but a handful of gun owners with a permit to carry a weapon in public places (under 4 percent of the adult population even in states like Florida, where carry permits are relatively easy to get),[28] the mere possession of a gun in a place other than their home, place of business, or in some states, their vehicle, is a crime, often a felony. In at least ten states, it is punishable by a punitively mandatory minimum prison sentence.[29] Yet, 88 percent of the violent crimes which Rs reported to NCVS interviewers in 1992 were committed away from the victim's home,[30] i.e., in a location where it would ordinarily be a crime for the victim to even possess a gun, never mind use it defensively. Because the question about location is asked before the self-protection questions,[31] the typical violent crime victim R has already committed himself to having been victimized in a public place before being asked what he or she did for self-protection. In short, Rs usually could not mention their defensive use of a gun without, in effect, confessing to a crime to a federal government employee.

Even for crimes that occurred in the victim's home, such as a burglary, possession of a gun would still often be unlawful or of unknown legal status; because the R had not complied with or could not be sure he had complied with all legal requirements concerning registration of the gun's acquisition or possession, permits for purchase, licensing of home possession, storage requirements, and so on. In light of all these considerations, it may be unrealistic to assume that more than a fraction of Rs who have used a gun defensively would be willing to report it to NCVS interviewers.

The NCVS was not designed to estimate how often people resist crime using a gun. It was designed primarily to estimate national victimization levels; it incidentally happens to include a few self-protection questions which include response categories covering resistance with a gun. Its survey instrument has been carefully refined and evaluated over the years to do as good a job as possible in getting people to report illegal things which *other* people have done *to* them. This is the exact opposite of the task which faces anyone trying to get good DGU estimates—to get people to admit controversial and possibly illegal things which the *Rs themselves have done*. Therefore, it is neither surprising nor a reflection on the survey's designers to note that the NCVS is singularly ill-suited for estimating the prevalence or incidence of DGU. It is not credible to regard this survey as an acceptable basis for establishing, in even the roughest way, how often Americans use guns for self-protection.

The Gun Surveys

At least thirteen previous surveys have given a radically different picture of the frequency of DGUs. The surveys, can be labelled the "gun surveys" because they were all, at least to some extent, concerned with the ownership and use of guns. Some were primarily devoted to this subject, while others were general purpose opinion surveys which happened to include some questions pertaining to guns. They are an extremely heterogeneous collection, some conducted by academic researchers for scholarly purposes, others by commercial polling firms. Moreover, their sponsors differed; some were sponsored by pro–gun control organizations, others were sponsored by anticontrol organizations, while still others were paid for by news media organizations, governments, or by research grants awarded to independent academics.

None of the surveys were meant as exclusive studies of DGU. Indeed, they each contained only one or two questions on the subject. Consequently, none of them are very thorough or satisfactory for estimating DGU frequency, even though they otherwise seem to have been conducted quite professionally. Some of the surveys were flawed by asking questions that used a lifetime recall period ("Have you ever . . . "), making it impossible to estimate uses within any specified time span. Some surveys limited coverage to registered voters, while others failed to exclude defensive uses against animals, or occupational uses by police officers, military personnel, or private security guards. Some asked the key questions with reference only to the R, while others asked Rs to report on the experiences of all of the members of their households, relying on second-hand reports. Methodological research on the NCVS indicates that substantially fewer crime incidents are reported when one household member reports for all household members than when each person is interviewed separately about their own experiences.[32] The same should also be true of those crime incidents that involve victims using guns.

The least useful of the surveys did not even ask the defensive use question of all Rs, instead it asked it only of gun owners, or, even more narrowly, of just handgun owners or just those who owned handguns for protection purposes.[33] This procedure was apparently based on the dubious assumption that people who used a gun defensively no longer owned the gun by the time of the survey, or that the gun belonged to someone else, or that the R owned the gun for a reason other than protection or kept it outside the home.

Most importantly, the surveys did not ask enough questions to establish exactly what was done with the guns in reported defensive use incidents. At best, some of the surveys only established whether the gun was fired. The lack of such detail raises the possibility that the guns were not actually "used" in any meaningful way. Instead, Rs might be remembering occasions on which they merely carried a gun for protection "just in case" or investigated a suspicious noise in their backyard, only to find nothing.

Nevertheless, among these imperfect surveys, two were relatively good for present purposes. Both the Hart survey in 1981 and the Mauser survey in 1990 were national surveys which asked carefully worded questions directed at all Rs in their samples. Both surveys excluded uses against animals and occupational uses. The two also nicely complemented each other in that the Hart survey asked only about uses of handguns, while the Mauser survey asked about uses of all gun types. The Hart survey results implied a minimum of about 640,000 annual DGUs involving handguns, while the Mauser results implied about 700,000 involving any type of gun.[34] It should be stressed, contrary to the claims of Reiss and Roth,[35] that neither of these estimates entailed the use of "dubious adjustment procedures." The percent of sample households reporting a DGU was simply multiplied by the total number of U.S. households, resulting in an estimate of DGU-involved households. This figure, compiled for a five year period, was then divided by five to yield a per-year figure. . . .

The National Self-Defense Survey

Methods

The present survey is the first survey ever devoted to the subject of armed self-defense. It was carefully designed to correct all of the known correctable or avoidable flaws of previous surveys which critics have identified. We use the most anonymous possible national survey format, the anonymous random digit dialed telephone survey. We did not know the identities of those who were interviewed, and made this fact clear to the Rs. We interviewed a large nationally representative sample covering all adults, age eighteen and over, in the lower fortyeight states and living in households with telephones.[36] We asked DGU questions of all Rs in our sample, asking them separately about both their own DGU experiences and those of other members of their households. We used both a five-year recall period and a one-year recall period. We inquired about uses of both handguns and other types of guns, and excluded occupational uses of guns and uses against animals. Finally, we asked a long series of detailed questions designed to establish exactly what Rs did with their guns; for example, if they had confronted other humans, and how had each DGU connected to a specific crime or crimes.

We consulted with North America's most experienced experts on gun-related surveys, David Bordua, James Wright, and Gary Mauser, along with survey expert Seymour Sudman, in order to craft a state-of-the-art survey instrument designed specifically to establish the frequency and nature of DGUs.[37] A professional telephone polling firm, Research Network of Tallahassee, Florida, carried out the sampling and interviewing. Only the firm's most experienced interviewers, who are listed in the acknowledgments, were used on the project. Interviews were monitored at random by survey supervisors. All interviews in which an alleged DGU was reported by the R were validated by supervisors with call-backs, along with a 20 percent random sample of all other interviews. Of all eligible residential telephone numbers called where a person rather than an answering machine answered, 61 percent resulted in a completed interview. Interviewing was carried out from February through April of 1993.

The quality of sampling procedures was well above the level common in national surveys. Our sample was not only large and nationally representative, but it was also stratified by state. That is, forty-eight independent samples of residential telephone numbers were drawn, one from each of the lower forty-eight states, providing forty-eight independent, albeit often small, state samples. Given the nature of randomly generated samples of telephone numbers, there was no clustering of cases or multistage sampling as there is in the NCIVS;[38] consequently, there was no inflation of sampling error due to such procedures. To gain a larger raw number of sample DGU cases, we oversampled in the south and west regions, where previous surveys have indicated gun ownership is higher.[39] We also oversampled within contacted households for males, who are more likely to own guns and to be victims of crimes in which victims might use guns defensively.[40] Data were later weighted to adjust for oversampling.

Each interview began with a few general "throat-clearing" questions about problems facing the R's community and crime. The interviewers then asked the following question: "Within the past *five years*, have you yourself or another member of your household *used* a gun, even if it was not fired, for self-protection or for the protection of property at home, work, or elsewhere? Please do *not* include military service, police work, or work as a security guard." Rs who answered "yes" were then asked: "Was this to protect against an animal or a person?" Rs who reported a DGU against a person were asked: "How many incidents involving defensive uses of guns against persons happened to members of your household in the past five years?" and "Did this incident [any of these incidents] happen in the *past twelve months*?" At this point, Rs were asked "Was it *you* who used a gun defensively, or did someone else in your household do this?"

All Rs reporting a DGU were asked a long, detailed series of questions establishing exactly what happened in the DGU incident. Rs who reported having experienced more than one DGU in the previous five years were asked about their most recent experience. When the original R was the one who had used a gun defensively, as was usually the case, interviewers obtained his or her firsthand account of the event. When the original R indicated that some other member of the household was the one who had the experience, interviewers made every effort to speak directly to the involved person, either speaking to that person immediately or obtaining times and dates to call back. Up to three call-backs were made to contact the DGU-involved person. We anticipated that it would some-times prove impossible to make contact with these persons, so interviewers were instructed to always obtain a proxy account of the DGU from the original R, on the assumption that a proxy account would be better than none at all. It was rarely necessary to rely on these proxy accounts only six sample cases of DGUs were reported through proxies, out of a total of 222 sample cases.

While all Rs reporting a DGU were given the full interview, only a one-third random sample of Rs not reporting a DGU were interviewed. The rest were simply thanked for their help. This procedure helped keep interviewing costs down. In the end, there were 222 completed interviews with Rs reporting DGUs, another 1,610 Rs not reporting a DGU but going through the full inter-view by answering questions other than those pertaining to details of the DGUs. There were a total of 1,832 cases with the full interview. An additional 3,145 Rs answered only enough questions to establish that no one in their household had experienced a DGU against a human in the previous five years (unweighted totals). These procedures effectively undersampled for non-DGU Rs or, equiva-lently, oversampled for DGU-involved Rs. Data were also weighted to account for this oversampling.

Questions about the details of DGU incidents permitted us to establish whether a given DGU met all of the following qualifications for an incident to be treated as a genuine DGU: (1) the incident involved defensive action against a human rather than an animal, but not in connection with police, military, or secu-rity guard duties; (2) the incident involved actual contact with a person, rather than merely investigating suspicious circumstances, etc.; (3) the defender could state a specific crime which he thought was being committed at the time of the incident; (4) the gun was actually used in some way—at a minimum it had to be used as part of a threat against a person, either by verbally referring to the gun (e.g., "get away—I've got a gun") or by pointing it at an adversary. We made no effort to assess either the lawfulness or morality of the Rs' defensive actions.

An additional step was taken to minimize the possibility of DGU frequency being overstated. The senior author went through interview sheets on every one of the interviews in which a DGU was reported, looking for any indication that the incident might not be genuine. A case would be coded as questionable if even just one of four problems appeared: (1) it was not clear whether the R actu-ally confronted any adversary he saw; (2) the R was a police officer, member of the military or a security guard, and thus might have been reporting, despite instructions, an incident which occurred as part of his occupational duties; (3) the interviewer did not properly record exactly what the R had done with the gun, so it was possible that he had not used it in any meaningful way; or (4) the

R did not state or the interviewer did not record a specific crime that the R thought was being committed against him at the time of the incident. There were a total of twenty-six cases where at least one of these problematic indications was present. It should be emphasized that we do not know that these cases were not genuine DGUs; we only mean to indicate that we do not have as high a degree of confidence on the matter as with the rest of the cases designated as DGUs. Estimates using all of the DGU cases are labelled herein as "A" estimates, while the more conservative estimates based only on cases devoid of any problematic indications are labelled "B" estimates.

Results

Table 1 displays a large number of estimates of how often guns are used defensively. These estimates are not inconsistent with each other; they each measure different things in different ways. Some estimates are based only on incidents which Rs reported as occurring in the twelve months preceding the interview, while others are based on incidents reported for the preceding five years. Both telescoping and recall failure should be lower with a one year recall period, so estimates derived from this period should be superior to those based on the longer recall period. Some estimates are based only on incidents which Rs reported as involving themselves, (person-based estimates), while others were based on all incidents which Rs reported as involving anyone in their household (household-based estimates). The person-based estimates should be better because of its first-hand character. Finally, some of the figures pertain only to DGUs involving use of handguns, while others pertain to DGUs involving any type of gun. . . .

The present estimates are higher than earlier ones primarily due to three significant improvements in the present survey: (1) a shorter recall period; (2) reliance on person-based information rather than just household-based information; and (3) information on how many household DGUs had been experienced in the recall period by those Rs reporting any such experiences. Using a shorter recall period undoubtedly reduced the effects of memory loss by reducing the artificial shrinkage to which earlier estimates were subject. Although telescoping was also undoubtedly reduced, and this would, by itself, tend to reduce estimates, the impact of reducing telescoping was apparently smaller than the impact of reducing case loss due to forgetting. Evidence internal to this survey directly indicates that a one year recall period yields larger estimates than a five year recall period; compare figures in the right half of table 1 with their counterparts in the left half. This phenomenon, where less behavior is reported for a longer recall period than would be expected based on results obtained when using a shorter period, also has been observed in surveys of self-reported use of illicit drugs.[41]

Furthermore, basing estimates on Rs reports about DGUs in which they were personally involved also increases the estimates. One of the surprises of this survey was how few Rs were willing to report a DGU which involved some other member of their household. Eighty-five percent of the reports of DGUs we

Table 1. Prevalence and Incidence of Civilian Defensive Gun Use, U.S., 1988–1993[a]

Recall Period:	Past Year				Past Five Years			
Base:	Person		Household		Person		Household	
Gun Types:	All Guns	Handguns	All Guns	Handguns	All Guns	Handguns	All Guns	Handguns
Weighted Sample Cases A:c	66	49	79	55	165	132	194	148
B:c	56	40	68	46	148	115	172	129
% Used[b] A:	1.326	0.985	1.587	1.105	3.315	2.652	3.898	2.974
B:	1.125	0.804	1.366	0.924	2.974	2.311	3.456	2.592
Persons/ Households A:	2,549,862	1,893,079	1,540,405	1,072,434	6,374,655	5,099,724	3,782,767	2,885,822
B:	2,163,519	1,545,571	1,325,918	896,945	5,717,872	4,442,941	3,353,794	2,515,345
Annual Uses A:	2,549,862	1,893,079	1,540,405	1,072,434	1,884,348	1,442,941	1,158,283	515,345
B:	2,163,519	1,545,371	1,325,918	896,945	1,683,342	888,588	1,029,615	505,069

Population Bases: Estimated resident population, age eighteen and over, U.S., April, 1993: 190,538,000; estimated households (assuming the 1992–1993 percentage increase was the same as the 1991–1992 increase): 97,045,525 (U.S. Bureau of the Census 1993, at 17, 55).

Notes:

a. Defensive uses of guns against humans by civilians (i.e., excluding uses by police officers, security guards, or military personnel). All figures are based on weighted data (see text).

b. Percent of persons (households) with at least one defensive gun use during the five years (one year) preceding the interview.

c. A estimates are based on all reported defensive gun uses reported in the survey. B estimates are based on only cases with no indications that the case might not be a genuine defensive gun use.

obtained involved the original R, the person with whom the interviewer first spoke. Given that most households contain more than one adult eligible to be interviewed, it was surprising that in a DGU-involved household the person who answered the phone would consistently turn out to be the individual who had been involved in the DGU. Our strong suspicion is that many Rs feel that it is not their place to tell total strangers that some other member of their household has used a gun for self-protection. Some of them are willing to tell strangers about an incident in which they were themselves involved, but apparently few are willing to "inform" on others in their household. Still others may not have been aware of DGUs involving other household members. Evidence internal to the present survey supports this speculation, since person-based estimates are 66 to 77 percent higher than household-based estimates; a figure that suggests that there was more complete reporting of DGUs involving the original respondent than those involving other household members.[42] For this reason, previous surveys including those which yielded only household-based estimates, four of the six gun surveys which yielded usable annual estimates, and all of those which were national in scope, probably substantially underestimated DGUs. We also had information on the number of times that DGU-involved households had experienced DGUs during the five-year recall period. While it was necessary in computing previous estimates to conservatively assume that each DGU-involved person or household had experienced only one DGU, our evidence indicates that repeat experiences were not uncommon, with 29.5 percent of DGU-involved households reporting more than one DGU within the previous five years. The average number of DGUs in this time span was 1.5 per DGU-involved household. This information alone could account for a roughly 50 percent increase in DGU incidence estimates based on the five year recall period.

Finally, our survey was superior to the NCVS in two additional ways: it was free of the taint of being conducted by, and on behalf of, employees of the federal government, and it was completely anonymous. . . .

Are these estimates plausible? Could it really be true that Americans use guns for self-protection as often as 2.1 to 2.5 million times a year? The estimate may seem remarkable in comparison to expectations based on conventional wisdom, but it is not implausibly large in comparison to various gun-related phenomena. There are probably over 220 million guns in private hands in the United States,[43] implying that only about 1 percent of them are used for defensive purposes in any one year—not an impossibly high fraction. In a December 1993 Gallup survey, 49 percent of U.S. households reported owning a gun, and 31 percent of adults reported personally owning one.[44] These figures indicate that there are about 47.6 million households with a gun, with perhaps 93 million, or 49 percentof the adult U.S. population living in households with guns, and about 59.1 million adults personally owning a gun. Again, it hardly seems implausible that 3 percent (2.5 million/93 million) of the people with immediate access to a gun could have used one defensively in a given year.

Huge numbers of Americans not only have access to guns, but the overwhelming majority of gun owners, if one can believe their statements, are willing to use a gun defensively. In a December 1989 national survey, 78 percent of American gun owners stated that they would not only be willing to use a gun defensively in some way, but would be willing to *shoot* a burglar.[45] The percentage willing to use a gun defensively in *some* way, though not necessarily by shooting someone, would presumably be even higher than this.

Nevertheless, having access to a gun and being willing to use it against criminals is not the same as actually doing so. The latter requires experiencing a crime under circumstances in which the victim can get to, or already possesses, a gun. We do not know how many such opportunities for crime victims to use guns defensively occur each year. It would be useful to know how large a fraction of crimes with direct offender-victim contact result in a DGU. Unfortunately, a large share of the incidents covered by our survey are probably outside the scope of incidents that realistically are likely to be reported to either the NCVS or police. If the DGU incidents reported in the present survey are not entirely a subset within the pool of cases covered by the NCVS, one cannot meaningfully use NCVS data to estimate the share of crime incidents which result in a DGU. Nevertheless, in a ten state sample of incarcerated felons interviewed in 1982, 34 percent reported having been "scared off, shot at, wounded or captured by an armed victim."[46] From the criminals' standpoint, this experience was not rare.

How could such a serious thing happen so often without becoming common knowledge? This phenomenon, regardless of how widespread it really is, is largely an invisible one as far as governmental statistics are concerned. Neither the defender/victim nor the criminal ordinarily has much incentive to report this sort of event to the police, and either or both often have strong reasons *not* to do so. Consequently, many of these incidents never come to the attention of the police, while others may be reported but without victims mentioning their use of a gun. And even when a DGU is reported, it will not necessarily be recorded by the police, who ordinarily do not keep statistics on matters other than DGUs resulting in a death, since police record-keeping is largely confined to information helpful in apprehending perpetrators and making a legal case for convicting them. Because such statistics are not kept, we cannot even be certain that a large number of DGUs are *not* reported to the police.

The health system cannot shed much light on this phenomenon either, since very few of these incidents involve injuries.[47] In the rare case where someone is hurt, it is usually the criminal, who is unlikely to seek medical attention for any but the most life-threatening gunshot wounds, as this would ordinarily result in a police interrogation. Physicians in many states are required by law to report treatment of gunshot wounds to the police, making it necessary for medically treated criminals to explain to police how they received their wounds.

Finally, it is now clear that virtually none of the victims who use guns defensively tell interviewers about it in the NCVS. Our estimates imply that only about 3 percent of DGUs among NCVS Rs are reported to interviewers.[48] Based on other comparisons of alternative survey estimates of violent events with NCVS estimates, this high level of underreporting is eminently plausible. Loftin and Mackenzie reported that rapes might be thirty-three times as frequent as NCVS estimates indicate, while spousal violence could easily be twelve times as high.[49]

There is no inherent value to knowing the exact number of DGUs any more than there is any value to knowing the exact number of crimes which are committed each year. The estimates in table 2 are at best only rough approximations, which are probably too low. It is sufficient to conclude from these numbers that DGU is very common, far more common than has been recognized to date by criminologists or policy makers, and certainly far more common than one would think based on any official sources of information.

What does "very common" mean? One natural standard of comparison by which the magnitude of these numbers could be judged is the frequency with which guns are used for criminal purposes. The highest annual estimate of criminal gun use for the peak year of gun crime is the NCVS estimate for 1992, when there were an estimated 847,652 violent crime incidents in which, according to the victim, at least one offender possessed a gun.[50] This NCVS figure is not directly comparable with our DGU estimates because our DGU estimates are restricted only to incidents in which the gun was actually used by the defender, as opposed to incidents in which a victim merely possessed a gun. Many of the "gun crimes" in the NCVS, on the other hand, do not involve the gun actually being used by the criminal. Thus, the NCVS estimate of "gun crimes" overstates the number of crimes in which the offender actually used the gun. The only "gun crimes" reported in NCVS interviews that one can be confident involved offenders actually using guns are those in which they shot at a victim; but these were only 16.6 percent of "handgun crimes" reported in the NCVS from 1987 to 1992.[51]

Another 46.8 percent of the "handgun crimes" are labelled "weapon present" cases by the Bureau of justice (BJS)[52] and an unknown fraction of these *could* involve actual use of a gun in a threat; but NCVS data do not permit us to know just how large a fraction. For these cases, the relevant NCVS interview items are ambiguous as to whether the gun was used to threaten a victim. Response category four of question fourteen ("How were you threatened?") of the NCVS Crime Incident Report reads: "Weapon present or threatened with weapon."[53] When this category is recorded by the interviewer, it is impossible to determine whether the victim was actually threatened with a gun or merely reported that the offender possessed a gun. In the remaining 36.6 percent of the "handgun crimes,"[54] there is no indication at all that the gun allegedly possessed by the offender was actually used.

Even the presence of a weapon is debatable, since victims are not asked why they thought the offender possessed a gun or if they saw a gun. This raises the possibility that some victims assumed that the offender had a gun, or inferred it from a bulge in the offender's clothing, or accepted the word of an offender who was bluffing about having a gun.

Thus, somewhere between 16.6 percent and 63.4 percent[55] of NCVS-defined "handgun crime" victimizations involve the gun actually being used in an attack or threat. Applying these figures to the estimates of 847,652 gun crime incidents and 689,652 handgun crime incidents, we can be confident that in 1992 there were at least 140,710 nonfatal crime incidents in which offenders used guns, 114,482 with handguns or about 157,000 total gun crime incidents, and 129,000 with handguns, when one includes gun homicides.[56] Or, generously assuming that all of the ambiguous "weapon present" cases involved guns being used to threaten the victim, estimates of 554,000 total, fatal and nonfatal, gun crime incidents and 451,000 handgun crime incidents are obtained.

All of these estimates are well short of even the most conservative estimates of DGUs in table 1. The best estimates of DGUs (first two columns), even if compared to the more generous estimates of gun crimes, are 4.6 times higher than the crime counts for all guns, and 4.2 times higher for handguns, or 3.9 and 3.4, respectively, if the more conservative *B* estimates of DGU are used. In sum, DGUs are about three to five times as common as criminal uses, even using generous estimates of gun crimes.

There is good reason to believe that survey estimates of both criminal and defensive gun uses, including the DGU estimates presented here, are too low. Cook has shown that NCVS estimates of gunshot wounds are far too low.[57] Our estimates of DGUs are probably also too low, partly because, unlike the NCVS, our survey did not cover adolescents, the age group most frequently victimized in violence. Furthermore, our use of telephone surveying excludes the 5 percent of the nation's households without telephones, households which are disproportionately poor and/or rural. Low income persons are more likely to be crime victims,[58] while rural persons are more likely to own guns and to be geographically distant from the nearest police officer.[59] Both groups therefore may have more opportunities to use guns for self-protection and excluding them from the sample could contribute to an underestimation of DGU.

Both parameters also are subject to underestimation due to intentional respondent underreporting. It is also probable that typical survey Rs are more reluctant to tell interviewers about questionable acts that they themselves have committed, such as threatening another person with a gun for purportedly defensive reasons, than they are to report criminal acts that other people have committed *against* them. Assuming this is correct, it would imply that DGUs, even in the best surveys, are underreported more than gun crime victimizations, and that correcting for underreporting would only increase the degree to which DGUs outnumber gun crimes.

The only known significant source of overestimation of DGUs in this survey is "telescoping," the tendency of Rs to report incidents which actually happened earlier than the recall period, such as reporting a six-year-old incident as having happened in the past five years. It is likely that telescoping effects are more than counterbalanced by Rs who actually experienced DGUs failing to report them. Nevertheless, it is worth discussing how much effect telescoping could have on these estimates. In evaluating the ability of crime victims to recall crime events in victim surveys, the U.S. Census Bureau selected a sample of crimes that were reported to the police, and then interviewed the victims of these known crime events. Using a twelve-month recall period (the same as we used in the present survey), they surveyed victims who had been involved in crimes which had actually occurred *thirteen to fourteen* months before the interview, i.e., one or two months before the recall period. Of these ineligible crimes, 21 percent were telescoped forward—wrongly reported as having occurred in the twelve month recall period.[60]

Since the months just before the start of the recall period will show the highest rates of telescoping, the rate should be even smaller for crimes which occurred earlier. Nevertheless, even if it is assumed that the 21 percent rate applied to events that occurred as much as one year earlier, thirteen to twenty-four months before the interview, telescoping could inflate the DGU estimates for a one year recall period by only 21 percent. Adjusting the 2.5 million DGU estimate downward for telescoping effects of this magnitude would reduce it to about 2.1 million (2.5 million/1.21=2.1 million), an adjustment which would have no effect on any of our conclusions. Telescoping would inflate estimates based on the five year recall period even less, since the ratio of memory loss errors over telescoping errors increases as the recall period lengthens.[61] Nevertheless, it should be stressed that this is just a numerical demonstration. There is no reason to believe that these modest telescoping effects outweigh the effects of Rs failing to report DGUs, and therefore, no reason to believe that these estimates are even slightly too high.

THE NATURE OF DEFENSIVE GUN USE

A total of 222 sample cases of DGUs against humans were obtained. For nine of these, the R broke off discussion of the incident before any significant amount of detail could be obtained, other than that the use was against a human. This left 213 cases with fairly complete information. Although this dataset constitutes the most detailed body of information available on DGU, the sample size is nevertheless fairly modest. While estimates of DGU frequency are reliable because they are based on a very large sample of 4,977 cases, results pertaining to the details of DGU incidents are based on 213 or fewer sample cases, and readers should treat these results with appropriate caution.

Apart from the sample size, the results of this survey also are affected by sample censoring. Beyond the incidents our interviewers were told about, there were almost certainly other DGUs which occurred within the recall period but which Rs did not mention to interviewers. In debriefings by the authors, almost all of our interviewers reported that they had experienced something like the following: they asked the key DGU question, which was followed by a long silence on the other end of the line, and/or the R asking something like "Who wants to know?" or "Why do you want to know?" or some similarly suspicious remark, followed by a "no" answer. In contrast, only one interviewer spoke with a person he thought was inventing a nonexistent incident. One obvious implication is that the true frequency of DGU is probably even higher than our estimates indicate.

Another is that the incidents which were reported might differ from those that were not.

We believe that there are two rather different kinds of incidents that are especially likely to go unreported: (1) cases that Rs do not want to tell strangers on the phone, because the Rs deem them legally or morally dubious or they think the interviewer would regard them that way; and (2) relatively minor cases that Rs honestly forget about or did not think were serious enough to qualify as relevant to our inquiries. Thus, in addition to the mostly legitimate and serious cases covered in our sample, there are still other, less legitimate or serious DGU incidents that this or any other survey are likely to miss. This supposition would imply two kinds of bias in our descriptive results: (1) our DGUs would look more consistently "legitimate" than the entire set of all DGUs actually are, and (2) our DGUs would look more serious, on average, than the entire set of DGUs really are. These possibilities should be kept in mind when considering the following descriptive information.

Table 2 summarizes what our sample DGU incidents were like. The data support a number of broad generalizations. First, much like the typical gun crime, many of these cases were relatively undramatic and minor compared to fictional portrayals of gun use. Only 24 percent of the gun defenders in the present study reported firing the gun, and only 8 percent report wounding an adversary.[62] This parallels the fact that only 17 percent of the gun crimes reported in the NCVS involve the offender shooting at the victim, and only 3 percent involve the victim suffering a gunshot wound.[63]

Low as it is, even an 8 percent wounding rate is probably too high, both because of the censoring of less serious cases, which in this context would be cases without a wounding, and because the survey did not establish how Rs knew they had wounded someone. We suspect that in incidents where the offender left without being captured, some Rs "remembered with favor" their marksmanship and assumed they had hit their adversaries. If 8.3 percent really hit their adversaries, and a total of 15.6 percent fired at their adversaries, this would imply a 53 percent (8.3/15.6) "incident hit rate," a level of combat marksmanship far exceeding that typically observed even among police officers. In a review of fifteen reports, police officers inflicted at least one gunshot wound on at least one adversary in 37 percent of the incidents in which they intentionally fired at someone.[64] A 53 percent hit rate would also be triple the 18 percent hit rate of criminals shooting at crime victims.[65] Therefore, we believe that even the rather modest 8.3 percent wounding rate we found is probably too high, and that typical DGUs are less serious or dramatic in their consequences than our data suggest. In any case, the 8.3 percent figure was produced by just seventeen sample cases in which Rs reported that they wounded an offender.

About 37 percent of these incidents occurred in the defender's home, with another 36 percent near the defender's home.[66] This implies that the remaining 27 percent occurred in locations where the defender must have carried a gun through public spaces. Adding in the 36 percent which occurred near the

Table 2. The Nature of Defensive Gun Use Incidents[a]

		%
A.	**What the Defender Did with the Gun**[b]	
	Brandished or showed gun	75.7
	Verbally referred to gun	57.6
	Pointed gun at offender	49.8
	Fired gun (including warning shots)	23.9
	Fired gun at offender, trying to shoot him/her	15.6
	Wounded or killed offender	8.3
B.	**Location of Incident**	
	In defender's home	37.3
	Near defender's home	35.9
	At, in, near home of friend, relative, neighbor	4.2
	Commercial place (bar, gas station, office, factory)	7.5
	Parking lot, commercial garage	4.5
	School (in building, on school property, playground)	0.3
	Open area, on street or public transportation	7.4
	Other locations	2.3
C.	**Type of Crime Defender Thought Was Being Committed**[b]	
	Burglary	33.8
	Robbery	20.5
	Other theft	6.2
	Trespassing	14.8[c]
	Rape, sexual assault	8.2
	Other assault	30.4
	Other crime	9.5
D.	**Did Offender Get Away with Money or Property?**	
	% of property crimes with property loss	11.0
E.	**Violence Directed at Defender**	
	No threat or attack	46.8
	Threatened only	32.3
	Attacked but not injured	15.3
	Attacked and injured	5.5
	(In incidents where defender was threatened or attacked): Who was first to threaten or use force?	
	Defender	15.3
	Offender	83.3
	Someone else	1.3
F.	**Offender's Weapons**[b]	
	None (unarmed)	51.9
	Weapon	48.1
	Handgun	13.4
	Other gun	4.5
	Knife	17.8
	Other sharp object	2.0
	Blunt object	9.9
	Other weapon	5.9

G.   Shooting

Did offender shoot at defender?

% of all incidents	4.5
% of incidents with offender armed with gun	26.2

Did both parties shoot?

% of all incidents	3.1

H.   Type of Gun Used by Defender

Revolver	38.5
Semiautomatic pistol	40.1
Other, unspecified handgun	1.1
Rifle	6.4
Shotgun	13.9

I.   Relationship of Offender to Defender

Stranger	73.4
Casual acquaintance	8.3
Neighbor	1.3
Boyfriend, girlfriend	1.0
Other friend, coworker	1.0
Brother, sister	0.0
Son, daughter	0.5
Husband, wife	3.1
Other relationship	4.2
Unknown	7.3

J.   Number of Offenders

1	47.2
2	26.1
3–4	17.6
5–6	4.0
7 or more (includes 3 cases where defender could only say there was a very large number)	5.0

K.   Defender's Perceived Likelihood that Someone Would Have Died Had Gun Not Been Used for Protection

Almost certainly not	20.8
Probably not	19.3
Might Have	16.2
Probably would have	14.2
Almost certainly would have	15.7
Could not say	13.7

L.   Were Police Informed of Incident or Otherwise Find Out?   64.2

Notes:

a. Table covers only defensive uses against persons, and excludes nine cases where respondents refused to provide enough detail to confirm incidents as genuine defensive uses.

b. Percentages will sum to more than 100% because respondents could legitimately select or report more than one category.

c. Only 3.7% of incidents involved trespassing as only crime.

defender's home and which may or may not have entailed public carrying, 36 to 63 percent of the DGUs entailed gun carrying.

Guns were most commonly used for defense against burglary, assault, and robbery.[67] Cases of "mutual combat," where it would be hard to tell who is the aggressor or where both parties are aggressors, would be a subset of the 30 percent of cases where assault was the crime involved. However, only 19 percent of all DGU cases involved only assault and no other crime where victim and offender could be more easily distinguished. Further, only 11 percent of all DGU cases involved only assault and a male defender—we had no information on gender of offenders—some subset of these could have been male-on-male fights. Thus, very few of these cases fit the classic mutual combat model of a fight between two males. This is not to say that such crimes where a gun-using combatant might claim that his use was defensive are rare, but rather that few of them are in this sample. Instead, cases where it is hard to say who is victim and who is aggressor apparently constitute an additional set of questionable DGUs lying largely outside of the universe of more one-sided events that our survey methods could effectively reach.

This survey did not attempt to compare the effectiveness of armed resistance with other forms of victim self-protection, since this sort of work has already been done and reviewed earlier in this paper. Panels D and E nevertheless confirm previous research on the effectiveness of self-defense with a gun—crime victims who use this form of self-protection rarely lose property and rarely provoke the offender into hurting them. In property crime incidents where burglary, robbery, or other thefts were attempted, victims lost property in just 11 percent of the cases. Gun defenders were injured in just 5.5 percent of all DGU incidents. Further, in 84 percent of the incidents where the defender was threatened or attacked, it was the offender who first threatened or used force. In non of the eleven sample cases where gun defenders were injured was the defender the first to use or to threaten force. The victim used a gun to threaten or attack the offender only after the offender had already attacked or threatened them and usually after the offender had inflicted the injury. There is no support in this sample for the hypothesis that armed resistance provokes criminals into attacking victims; this confirms the findings of prior research.[68]

While only 14 percent of all violent crime victims face offenders armed with guns,[69] 18 percent of the gun-using victims in our sample faced adversaries with guns.[70] Although the gun defenders usually faced unarmed offenders or offenders with lesser weapons, they were more likely than other victims to face gun-armed criminals. This is consistent with the perception that more desperate circumstances call forth more desperate defensive measures. The findings undercut the view that victims are prone to use guns in "easy" circumstances which are likely to produce favorable outcomes for the victim regardless of their gun use.[71] Instead, gun defenders appear to face more difficult circumstances than other crime victims, not easier ones.

Nevertheless, one reason crime victims are willing to take the risks of forcefully resisting the offender is that most offenders faced by victims choosing such an action are unarmed, or armed only with less lethal weapons. Relatively few victims try to use a gun against adversaries who are themselves armed with guns. According to this survey, offenders were armed with some kind of weapon in 48 percent of DGU incidents but had guns in only 18 percent of them.[72]

The distribution of guns by type in DGUs is similar to that of guns used by criminals. NCVS and police-based data indicate that about 80 percent of guns used in crime are handguns,[73] and the present study indicates that 80 percent of the guns used by victims are handguns.[74]

Incidents where victims use a gun defensively are almost never gunfights where both parties shoot at one another. Only 24 percent of the incidents involved the defender firing their gun, and only 16 percent involved the defender shooting *at* their adversary.[75] In only 4.5 percent of the cases did the offender shoot at the defender.[76] Consequently, it is not surprising that only 3 percent of all the incidents involved both parties shooting at each other.

Among our sample cases, the offenders were strangers to the defender in nearly three quarters of the incidents.[77] We suspect that this again reflects the effects of sample censoring, just as the NCVS appears to detect less than a tenth of domestic violence incidents,[78] our survey is probably missing many cases of DGU against family members and other intimates.

While victims face multiple offenders in only about 24 percent of *all* violent crimes,[79] the victims in our sample who used guns faced multiple offenders in 53 percent of the incidents.[80] This mirrors the observation that criminals who use guns are also more likely than unarmed criminals to face multiple victims.[81] A gun allows either criminals or victims to handle a larger number of adversaries. Many victims facing multiple offenders probably would not resist at all if they were without a gun or some other weapon. Another possible interpretation is that some victims will resort to a defensive measure as serious as wielding a gun only if they face the most desperate circumstances. Again, this finding contradicts a view that gun defenders face easier circumstances than other crime victims.

Another way of assessing how serious these incidents appeared to the victims is to ask them how potentially fatal the encounter was. We asked Rs: "If you had *not* used a gun for protection in this incident, how likely do you think it is that you or someone else would have been *killed*? Would you say almost certainly *not*, probably not, might have, probably would have, or almost certainly would have been killed?" Panel K indicates that 15.7 percent of the Rs stated that they or someone else "almost certainly would have" been killed, with another 14.2 percent responding "probably would have" and 16.2 percent responding "might have."[82] Thus, nearly half claimed that they perceived some significant chance of someone being killed in the incident if they had not used a gun defensively.

It should be emphasized that these are just stated perceptions of participants, not objective assessments of actual probabilities. Some defenders might have been bolstering the justification for their actions by exaggerating the seriousness of the threat they faced. Our cautions about sample censoring should also be kept in mind—minor, less life-threatening events are likely to have been left out of this sample, either because Rs forgot them or because they did not think them important enough to qualify as relevant to our inquiries.

If we consider only the 15.7 percent who believed someone almost certainly would have been killed had they not used a gun, and apply this figure to estimates in the first two columns of table 1, it yields national annual estimates of 340,000 to 400,000 DGUs of any kind, and 240,000 to 300,000 uses of handguns, where defenders stated, if asked, that they believed they almost certainly had saved a life by using the gun. Just how many of these were truly life-saving gun uses is impossible to know. As a point of comparison, the largest number of deaths involving guns, including homicides, suicides, and accidental deaths in any one year in U.S. history was 38,323 in 1991.[83]

Finally, we asked if Rs had reported these incidents to the police, or if the police otherwise found out about them; 64 percent of the gun-using victims claimed that the incidents had become known to the police. This figure should be interpreted with caution, since victims presumably want to present their use of guns as legitimate and a willingness to report the incident to the police would help support an impression of legitimacy. Rs who had in fact not reported the incident to the police might have wondered whether a "no" reply might not lead to discomforting follow-up questions like "why not?" (as indeed it does in the NCVS). Further, it is likely that some Rs reported these incidents but did not mention their use of a gun.

WHO IS INVOLVED IN DEFENSIVE GUN USE?

Finally, this article will consider what sorts of people use guns defensively, and how they might differ from other people. Table 3 presents comparisons of five groups: (1) "defenders," i.e., people who reported using a gun for defense; (2) people who personally own guns but did not report a DGU; (3) people who do not personally own a gun; (4) people who did not report a DGU, regardless of whether they own guns; and (5) all people who completed the full interview.

Some of the earlier gun surveys asked the DGU question only of Rs who reported owning a gun. The cost of this limitation is evident from the first two rows of table 3. Nearly 40 percent of the people reporting a DGU did not report personally owning a gun at the time of the interview. They either used someone else's gun, got rid of the gun since the DGU incident, or inaccurately denied personally owning a gun. About a quarter of the defenders reported that they did not even have a gun in their household at the time of the interview. Another possibility is that many gun owners were falsely denying their ownership of the "incriminating evidence" of their DGU.

Many of the findings in table 3 are unsurprising. Gun defenders are more likely to carry a gun for self-protection, consistent with the large share of DGUs which occurred away from the defender's home. Obviously, they were more

Table 3. Comparison of Defenders with Other People (Weighted Percentages)

	Defenders	No-DGU Gun owners	Sample[a] Non-owners	No DGU	All Persons
Personally owns gun	59.3	100.0	0.0	23.9	25.5
Gun in household	79.0	100.0	16.3	36.3	37.9
Carries gun for protection	47.3	23.3	2.1	7.3	8.8
Burglary victim, past year	19.3	4.5	4.9	4.9	5.3
Robbery victim, past year	12.9	1.9	2.0	2.1	2.5
Assault victim as adult	46.8	29.3	18.3	21.5	22.5
Nights away from home, monthly average					
0	8.2	5.2	8.9	8.2	8.2
1–6	27.3	24.1	33.4	31.3	31.2
7–13	23.2	28.2	22.7	23.8	23.9
14+	42.0	42.3	35.0	36.8	36.6
Must depend on self rather than cops	77.0	69.7	50.0	55.0	35.8
Supports death penalty	72.4	85.2	65.8	70.5	70.6
Courts not harsh enough	75.2	78.9	71.5	74.0	74.0
Gender (% male)	53.7	75.4	37.1	46.4	46.7
Age					
18–24	25.7	10.2	14.3	13.1	13.5
25–34	36.9	21.6	22.6	22.1	22.6
35–44	20.6	26.8	25.2	25.3	25.4
45–64	14.2	30.6	25.9	27.3	26.8
65+	2.6	10.9	12.1	12.0	11.7
Race					
White	72.4	90.3	83.0	84.6	84.1
Black	16.8	5.1	9.7	8.6	8.9
Hispanic	8.0	3.2	4.9	4.6	4.8
Other	2.8	1.3	2.4	2.2	2.1
Place of Residence					
Large City (over 500,000)	32.3	14.7	24.7	22.2	22.6
Small city	29.8	32.2	27.7	29.4	29.3
Suburb of large city	25.5	28.1	32.6	31.3	31.1
Rural area	12.2	24.9	15.1	17.2	17.0
Marital Status					
Married	50.8	69.1	57.5	60.5	60.1
Widowed	0.6	2.2	6.5	6.2	6.0
Divorced/Separated	15.3	10.9	11.2	11.8	12.0
Never married	33.3	17.8	24.8	21.4	21.9
Annual Household Income					
Under $15,000	12.3	7.4	15.3	13.6	13.5
$15,000–29,999	30.1	23.2	27.9	26.9	27.2
$30,000–44,999	22.2	30.3	23.0	24.5	24.4
$45,000–59,999	18.6	17.8	20.0	19.2	19.2
$60,000–79,999	7.9	12.1	8.0	8.9	8.9
$80,000 or more	8.8	9.2	5.8	6.8	6.9
Gun-related Occupation	2.4	4.9	2.0	3.2	3.1

Notes:

a. "Defenders" are persons who reported a defensive gun use against another person in the receding five years, excluding uses in connection with military, police, or security guard duties. This sample 'includes nine cases where such a use was reported, but the respondent did not provide further details.

"No-DGU gun owners" are persons who report personally owning a gun but did not report a defensive gun use.

"Nonowners" are persons who did not report personally owning a gun and who did not report a defensive gun use. These persons may, however, live in a household where others own a gun.

"No DGU" are persons who did not report a defensive gun use, regardless of whether they reported owning a gun.

likely to have been a victim of a burglary or robbery in the past year, a finding which is a tautology for those Rs whose DGU was in connection with a robbery or burglary committed against them in the preceding year. They were also more likely to have been a victim of an assault since becoming an adult.

Defenders are more likely to believe that a person must be prepared to defend their homes against crime and violence rather than letting the police take care of it compared to either gun owners without a DGU and nonowners. Whether this is cause or consequence of defenders' defensive actions is impossible to say with these data.

Some might suspect that DGUs were actually the aggressive acts of vengeful vigilantes intent on punishing criminals. If this were true of gun defenders as a group, one might expect them to be more supportive of punitive measures like the death penalty. In fact, those who reported a DGU were no more likely to support the death penalty than those without such an experience, and were somewhat *less* likely to do so compared with gun owners as a group. Similarly, gun defenders were no more likely than other people to endorse the view that the courts do not deal harshly enough with criminals.

Perhaps the most surprising finding of the survey was the large share of reported DGUs that involved women. Because of their lower victimization rates and lower gun ownership rates, one would expect women to account for far less than half of DGUs. Nevertheless, 46 percent of our sample DGUs involved women. This finding could be due to males reporting a lower fraction of actual DGUs than women. If a larger share of men's allegedly DGUs were partly aggressive actions, a larger share would be at the "illegitimate" end of the scale and thus less likely to be reported to interviewers. Further, women may be more likely than men to report their DGUs because they are less afraid of prosecution. Consequently, although there is no reason to doubt that women use guns defensively as often as this survey indicates, it is probable that males account for a larger number and share of DGUs than these data indicate.

A disproportionate share of defenders are African American or Hispanic compared to the general population and especially compared to gun owners. Additionally, defenders are disproportionately likely to reside in big cities compared to other people, and particularly when compared to gun owners, who reside disproportionately in rural areas and small towns. Finally, defenders are disproportionately likely to be single. These patterns are all presumably due to the higher rates of crime victimization among minorities, big city dwellers, and single persons.[84] On the other hand, defenders are not likely to be poor. The effect of higher victimization among poor people may be cancelled out by the lower gun ownership levels among the poor.[85]

One might suspect that, despite instructions not to report such events, some of the Rs reporting a DGU might have been describing an event which occurred as part of their occupational activities as a police officer, a member of the military, or a security guard. This could not have been true for more than a handful of our DGU cases since only 2.4 percent (five sample cases) involved a person who had this type of occupation. Even these few cases may have occurred off-duty and thus would not necessarily be occupational DGUs. Gun defenders were in fact somewhat *less* likely to have a gunrelated occupation than other gun owners.

CONCLUSION

If one were committed to rejecting the seemingly overwhelming survey evidence on the frequency of DGU, one could speculate, albeit without any empirical foundation whatsoever, that nearly all of the people reporting such experiences are simply making them up. We feel this is implausible. An R who had actually experienced a DGU would have no difficulty responding with a "no" answer to our DGU question because a "no" response was not followed up by further questioning. On the other hand, lying with a false "yes" answer required a good deal more imagination and energy. Since we asked as many as nineteen questions on the topic, this would entail spontaneously inventing as many as nineteen plausible and internally consistent bits of false information and doing so in a way that gave no hint to experienced interviewers that they were being deceived.

Suppose someone persisted in believing in the anomalous NCVS estimates of DGU frequency and wanted to use a "dishonest respondent" hypothesis to account for estimates from the present survey that are as much as thirty times higher. In order to do this, one would have to suppose that twenty-nine out of every thirty people reporting a DGU in the present survey were lying. There is no precedent in criminological survey research for such an enormous level of intentional and sustained falsification.

The banal and undramatic nature of the reported incidents also undercuts the dishonest respondent speculation. While all the incidents involved a crime, and usually a fairly serious one, only 8 percent of the alleged gun defenders claimed to have shot their adversaries, and only 24 percent claim to have fired their gun. If large numbers of Rs were inventing their accounts, one would think they would have created more exciting scenarios.

By this time there seems little legitimate scholarly reason to doubt that defensive gun use is very common in the United States, and that it probably is substantially more common than criminal gun use. This should not come as a surprise, given that there are far more gun-owning crime victims than there are gun-owning criminals and that victimization is spread out over many different victims, while offending is more concentrated among a relatively small number of offenders.

There is little legitimate reason to continue accepting the NCVS estimates of DGU frequency as even approximately valid. The gross inconsistencies between the NCVS and all other sources of information make it reasonable to suppose that all but a handful of NCVS victims who had used a gun for protection in the reported incidents refrained from mentioning this gun use. In light of evidence on the injury-preventing effectiveness of victim gun use, in some cases where the absence of victim injury is credited to either nonresistance or some unarmed form of resistance, the absence of injury may have actually been due to resistance with a gun, which the victim failed to mention to the interviewer.

The policy implications of these results are straightforward. These findings do *not* imply anything about whether moderate regulatory measures such as background checks or purchase permits would be desirable. Regulatory measures which do not disarm large shares of the general population would not significantly reduce beneficial defensive uses of firearms by noncriminals. On the other hand, prohibitionist measures, whether aimed at all guns or just at handguns, are aimed at disarming criminals and noncriminals alike. They would therefore discourage and presumably decrease the frequency of DGU among noncriminal crime victims because even minimally effective gun bans would disarm at least some noncriminals. The same would be true of laws which ban gun carrying. In sum, measures that effectively reduce gun availability among the noncriminal majority also would reduce DGUs that otherwise would have saved lives, prevented injuries, thwarted rape attempts, driven off burglars, and helped victims retain their property.

Since as many as 400,000 people a year use guns in situations where the defenders claim that they "almost certainly" saved a life by doing so, this result cannot be dismissed as trivial. If even one-tenth of these people are accurate in their stated perceptions, the number of lives saved by victim use of guns would still exceed the total number of lives taken with guns. It is not possible to know how many lives are actually saved this way, for the simple reason that no one can be certain how crime incidents would have turned out had the participants acted differently than they actually did. But surely this is too serious a matter to simply assume that practically everyone who says he believes he saved a life by using a gun was wrong.

This is also too serious a matter to base conclusions on silly statistics comparing the number of lives taken with guns with the number of criminals *killed* by victims.[86] Killing a criminal is not a benefit to the victim, but rather a nightmare to be suffered for years afterward. *Saving* a life through DGU would be a benefit, but this almost never involves killing the criminal; probably fewer than 3,000 criminals are *lawfully* killed by gun-wielding victims each year,[87] representing only about $\frac{1}{1000}$ of the number of DGUs, and less than 1 percent of the number of purportedly life-saving DGUs. Therefore, the number of justifiable homicides cannot serve as even a rough index of life-saving gun uses. Since this comparison does not involve any measured benefit, it can shed no light on the benefits and costs of keeping guns in the home for protection.[88]

NOTES

1. Marvin E. Wolfgang, *Patterns in Criminal Homicide* (Philadelphia: University of Philadelphia Press, 1958), p. 245.

2. Richard A. Berk et al., "Mutual Combat and Other Family Violence Myths," in *The Dark Side of Families*, ed. David Finkelhor et al.(Beverly Hills: Sage Publications, 1983), p. 197.

3. See generally Michael J. Hindelang, *Criminal Victimization in Eight American Cities* (1976); Gary Kleck, "Crime Control Through the Private Use of Armed Force," *Social Problems* 35 (1988):1; Gary Kleck and Miriam Al DeLone, "Victim Resistance and Offender Weapon Effects in Robbery," *Journal of Quantitative Criminology* 9 (1993): 55; Eduard A. Ziegenhagen and Dolores Brosnan, "Victim Responses to Robbery and Crime Control Policy," *Criminology* 23 (1985): 675.

4. See generally Philip J. Cook, "The Technology of Personal Violence," *Crime and Justice*; vol. 14, ed. Michael Tonry. (Chicago: University of Chicago Press, 1991), pp. 1, 57.

5. Ziegenhagen and Brosnan, "Victim Responses"; Kleck "Crime Control Through the Private Use of Armed Force"; Kleck and DeLone, "Victim Resistance."

6. Kleck, "Crime Control Through the Private Use of Armed Force."

7. Cook, "The Technology of Personal Violence," p. 58.

8. Kleck and DeLone, "Victim Response," p. 75.

9. Joan M. McDermott, *Rape Victimization in 26 American Cities* (Washington, D.C.: U.S. Government Printing Office, 1979).

10. Quinsey and Upfold, "Rape Completion and Victim Injury as a Function of Female Resistance Strategy," *Canadian Journal of Behavioral Science* 17 (1985): 40.

11. Alan J. Lizotte, "Determinants of Completing Rape and Assault," *Journal of Quantitative Criminology* 22 (1986): 203.

12. Gary Kleck and Susan Sayles, "Rape and Resistance," *Social Problems* 37 (1990): 149.

13. Quinsey and Upfold, "Rape Completion and Victim Injury," pp. 46–47. See generally Sarah E. Ullman and Raymond A. Knight, "Fighting Back: Women's Resistance to Rape," *Journal of Interpersonal Violence* 7 (1992): 31.

14. See Kleck, p. 9.

15. Cook, "The Technology of Personal Violence"; David McDowall and Brian Wiersema, "The Incidence of Defensive Firearms Use by U.S. Crime Victims, 1987 Through 1990," *American Journal of Public Health* 84 (1994): 1982; *Understanding and Preventing Violence*, ed. Albert J. Reiss and Jeffrey A. Roth (Washington, D.C.: National Academy Press, 1993), p. 265.

16. Kleck, "Crime Control Through the Use of Private Force," p. 8.

17. Cook, "The Technology of Personal Violence," p. 56; Michael R. Rand, "Bureau of Justice Statistics, Guns and Crime" (Crime Data Brief) (1994).

18. See Kleck, "Crime Control Through the Use of Private Force," p. 3; Gary Kleck, *Point Blank: Guns and Violence in America* (New York: Aldine de Gruyter, 1991), p. 146.

19. Gary A. Mauser, "Firearms and Self-Defense: The Canadian Case, Presented at the Annual Meetings of the American Society of Criminology" (October 28, 1993).

20. Rand, "Bureau of Justice Statistics, Guns and Crime."

21. Cook, "The Technology of Personal Violence," p. 56; McDowall and Wiersema, "The Incidence of Defensive Firearms Use by U.S. Crime Victims, 1987 Through 1990."

22. *Understanding and Preventing Violence*, pp. 265–66.

23. Ibid., p. 265.

24. Cook, "The Technology of Personal Violence," p. 54.

25. *U.S. Bureau of the Census National Crime Survey Interviewer's Manual, NCS550, Part D —How To Enumerate NCS* (1986).

26. U.S. Bureau of Justice Statistics, *Criminal Victimization in the United States 1992* (1994), p. 128.

27. Colin Loftin and Ellen J. MacKenzie, "Building National Estimates of Violent Victimization," (April 1–4, 1990), pp. 21–23 (unpublished background paper prepared for the Symposium on the Understanding and Control of Violent Behavior, sponsored by the National Research Council).

28. Patrick Blackman, "Carrying Handguns for Personal Protection" (1985), p. 31 (unpublished paper presented at the annual meetings of the American Society of Criminology) (November 13–16, 1985); Kleck, *Point Blank*, p. 412.

29. Kent M. Ronhovde and Gloria P. Sugars, "Survey of Select State Firearm Control Laws," in *Federal Regulation of Firearms*, ed. H. Hogan (1982), pp. 204–205 (report prepared for the U.S. Senate Judiciary Committee by the Congressional Research Service).

30. U.S. Bureau of Justice Statistics, *Criminal Victimization in the United States 1992*, p. 75.

31. Ibid., pp. 124, 128.

32. U.S. Bureau of Justice Statistics, *Criminal Victimization in the United States 1992*, p. 144.

33. Cambridge Reports, Inc., *An Analysis of Public Attitudes Towards Handgun Control* (1978); The Ohio Statistical Analysis Center, *Ohio Citizen Attitudes Concerning Crime and Criminal Justice* (1982); H. Quinley, Memorandum reporting results from Time/CNN Poll of Gun Owners, dated Feb. 6, 1990 (1990).

34. Kleck, *Point Blank*, pp. 106–107.

35. *Understanding and Preventing Violence*, p. 266.

36. Completed interviews, n=4,977.

37. See, e.g., David J. Bordua et al., *Illinois Law Enforcement Commission, Patterns of Firearms Ownership, Regulation and Use in Illinois* (1979); Seymore Sudman and Norman Bradburn, *Response Effects in Surveys* (1974); James Wright and Peter Rossi, *Armed and Considered Dangerous* (1986); Alan J. Lizotte and David J. Bordua, "Firearms Ownership for Sport and Protection," *American Sociological Review* 46 (1980): 499; Gary Mauser, "A Comparison of Canadian and American Attitudes Towards Firearms," *Canadian Journal of Criminology* 32 (1990): 573; Gary Mauser, "'Sorry, Wrong Number': Why Media Polls on Gun Control Are Often Unreliable," POL. Comm. 9 (1992): 69; Mauser, "Firearms and Self-Defense."

38. U.S. Bureau of Justic Statistics, *Criminal Victimization in the United States* 1992, pp. 141–42.

39. Kleck, *Point Blank*, p. 57.

40. Ibid., p. 56.

41. See Jerald Bachman and Patrick O'Malley, "When Four Months Equal a Year: Inconsistencies in Student Reports of Drug Use," *Public Opinion Quarterly* 45 (1981): 536, 539, 543.

42. See table 1.

43. Kleck, *Point Blank*, p. 50 (extrapolating up to 1994, from 1987 data).

44. David W. Moore and Frank Newport, "Public Strongly Favors Stricter Gun Control Laws," *The Gallup Poll Monthly* 340 (1994): 18.

45. Quinley, Memorandum reporting results from Time/CNN Poll of Gun Owners, dated February 6, 1990.

46. Wright and Rossi, *Armed and Considered Dangerous*, p. 155.

47. See table 2, panels A, E.

48. The 85,000 DGUs estimated from the NCVS, divided by the 2.5 million estimate derived from the presented survey equals .03.

49. Loftin and MacKenzie, "Building National Estimates of Violent Victimization," pp. 22–23.

50. Computed from U.S. Bureau of Justice Statistics, *Criminal Victimization in the United States 1992*, pp. 82–83.

51. Rand, "Bureau of Justice Statistics, Guns and Crime," p. 2.

52. Ibid.

53. U.S. Bureau of Justice Statistics, *Criminal Victimization in the United States 1992*, p. 126.

54. 100%, minus the 16.6% where the victim was shot at, minus the 46.8% where the victim reported a 'weapon present or threatened with a weapon" = 36.6%.

55. 16.6% plus the 46.8% in the ambiguous 'weapon present" category.

56. Federal Bureau of Investigation, U.S. Department of Justice, *Crime in the United States 1992—Uniform Crime Reports* (1993), pp. 18, 58.

57. Philip J. Cook, "The Caw of the Missing Victims: Gunshot Woundings in the National Crime Survey," *Journal of Quantitative Criminology* 1 (1985): 91.

58. U.S. Bureau of Justice Statistics, *Criminal Victimization in the United States 1992*, p. 33.

59. Kleck, *Point Blank*, p. 57.

60. Richard W. Dodge, "The Washington, D.C. Recall Study," in *The National Crime Survey: Working Papers: Current and Historical Perspectives*, vol. 1, ed. Robert G. Lehnen and Wesley G. Skogan (Washington, D.C.: U.S. Government Printing Office, 1981), p. 14.

61. Henry S. Woltman et al., "Recall Bias and Telescoping in the National Crime Survey," in

The National Crime Survey: Working Papers: Methodological Studies, vol. 2, ed. Robert G. Lehnen and Wesley G. Skogan (Washington, D.C.: U.S. Government Printing Office, 1981), p. 14; Sucintan Sudman and Bradburn, "Effects of Time and Memory Factors on Response in Surveys."

62. See table 2, panel A.

63. Rand, "Bureau of Justice Statistics, Guns and Crime."

64. William A. Geller and Michael S. Scott, *Deadly Force: What We Know* (Washington, D.C.: Police Executive Research Forum, 1993), pp. 100–106.

65. Rand, "Bureau of Justice Statistics, Guns and Crime."

66. See table 2, panel B.

67. Ibid., panel C.

68. Kleck, "Crime Control Through the Private Use of Armed Force," pp. 7–9; Kleck and DeLone, "Victim Residence," pp. 75–77.

69. U.S. Bureau of Justice Statistics, *Criminal Victimization in the United States 1992*, p. 83.

70. See table 2, panel F.

71. For a related speculation, see *Understanding and Preventing Violence*, p. 266.

72. Ibid.

73. U.S. Bureau of Justice Statistics, *Criminal Victimization in the United States 1992* p. 83; U.S. Federal Bureau of Investigation, p. 18.

74. See table 2, panel H.

75. Ibid., panel A.

76. Ibid., panel G.

77. Ibid., panel I.

78. Loftin and MacKenzie, "Building National Estimates of Violent Victimization," pp. 22–23.

79. U.S. Bureau of Justice Statistics, *Crime in the United States 1992—Uniform Crime Reports*, p. 82.

80. See table 2, panel J.

81. Cook, "The Technology of Personal Violence."

82. See table 2, panel K.

83. National Safety Council, *Accident Facts* (1994), p. 11. This assumes that 95 percent of "legal intervention" deaths involved guns.

84. U.S. Bureau of Justice Statistics, *Crime in the United States 1992—Uniform Crime Reports*, pp. 25–26, 31, 38–39.

85. Kleck, *Point Blank*, p. 56.

86. Arthur L. Kellermann and Donald T. Reay, "Protection or Peril?" *New England Journal of Medicine* 314 (1986): 1557.

87. Kleck, *Point Blank*, p. 111–17.

88. See ibid., pp. 127–29 for a more detailed critique of these "junk science" statistics. See *Understanding and Preventing Violence*, p. 267, for an example of a prestigious source taking such numbers seriously.

28

A TRIBUTE TO A VIEW
I HAVE OPPOSED

MARVIN E. WOLFGANG

I am as strong a guncontrol advocate as can be found among the criminolo-gists in this country. If I were Mustapha Mond of *Brave New World*, I would eliminate all guns from the civilian population and maybe even from the police. I hate guns—ugly, nasty instruments designed to kill people.

What troubles me is the article by Gary Kleck and Marc Gertz. The reason I am troubled is that they have provided an almost clearcut case of method-ologically sound research in support of something I have theoretically opposed for years, namely, the use of a gun in defense against a criminal perpetrator. Maybe Franklin Zimring and Philip Cook can help me find fault with the Kleck and Gertz research, but for now, I have to admit my admiration for the care and caution expressed in this article and this research.

Can it be true that about two million instances occur each year in which a gun was used as a defensive measure against crime? It is hard to believe. Yet, it is hard to challenge the data collected. 'We do not have contrary evidence. The National Crime Victim Survey does not directly contravene this latest survey, nor do the Mauser and Hart studies. . . . The methodological soundness of the current Kleck and Gertz study is clear. I cannot further debate it.

There is no one part of the early section of their paper with which I disagree. These authors argue against the mutual offensive behavior of offender and victim in homicide cases. They then refer to robbery, burglary and lesser assault cases. They cite me relative to homicide.

From the *Journal of Criminal Law and Criminology* 86, no. 1 (1995): 188–92. Copyright © 1995 by Northwestern University, School of Law. Reprinted with permission.

Robbery and burglary are quite different offenses from homicide. Robbery and burglary commonly involve stranger relationships between offender and victim. Not so with homicide, although stranger and unknown relationships, according to the *Uniform Crime Reports*, have greatly increased over the past thirty years.

Still, many homicides have victims who are demographically like their offenders. My victim-precipitated homicide thesis is not diminished by any contemporary homicide research.

Defensive gun usage, as reported in the current study by Kleck and Gertz, includes mostly robbery and burglary, in which offenses there is little "mutual combat" compared to homicides.

My *Patterns in Criminal Homicide* stands as solidly viable with respect to the offender-victim drama, the prior record of victims, and the victim-precipitated model, as indicated in studies in Chicago by Blocks, in Alberta by Silverman, in Montreal by Normandeau and many other places.

The Kleck and Gertz study impresses me for the caution the authors exercise and the elaborate nuances they examine methodologically. I do not like their conclusions that having a gun can be useful, but I cannot fault their methodology. They have tried earnestly to meet all objections in advance and have done exceedingly well.

29

EASING CONCEALED FIREARM LAWS

EFFECTS ON HOMICIDE IN THREE STATES

DAVID MCDOWALL, COLIN LOFTIN, & BRIAN WIERSEMA

INTRODUCTION

Restrictions on carrying concealed weapons are among the most common gun control policies.[1] These statutes limit who may have a deadly weapon—usually a handgun—hidden on their person when outside the home. By reducing access to guns in public, concealed weapons laws seek to make firearms less available for violence.[2]

Details of concealed weapons laws vary greatly among localities, but most approaches fall into two categories. One of these is a discretionary system, sometimes called "may issue" licensing.[3] Under this policy, legal authorities grant licenses only to those citizens who can establish a compelling need for carrying a gun.

The other approach is a nondiscretionary, or "shall issue," system.[4] Here the authorities must provide a license to any applicant who meets specified criteria. Because legal officials are often unwilling to allow concealed weapons, adopting a shall issue policy usually increases the number of persons with permits to carry guns.[5]

In 1985, the National Rifle Association announced that it would lobby for shall issue laws.[6] Several states, including Florida, Mississippi, and Oregon, have since changed from may issue to shall issue systems. Advocates of shall issue laws argue that such laws will both prevent crime and reduce homicides.[7]

From the *Journal of Criminal Law and Criminology* 86, no. 1 (1995): 193–206. Reprinted with permission.

This article examines the frequency of homicides in the large urban areas of Florida, Mississippi, and Oregon, before and after their shall issue laws began. The analysis provides no support for the idea that the laws reduced homicides; instead, it finds evidence of an increase in firearm murders.

THE LAWS

On October 1, 1987, Florida adopted a shall issue law that greatly expanded eligibility to carry a concealed weapon.[8] The new statute required the state to grant a concealed weapon license to any qualified adult who had taken a firearms safety course. Those persons with a history of drug or alcohol abuse, a felony conviction, mental illness, physical inability, or who were not Florida residents were disqualified from obtaining a license.

Prior to the passage of the Florida shall issue law, county officials set their own standards for concealed carrying. Throughout the state, about 17,000 persons held permits, including 1,300 in Dade county (Miami) and 25 in Hillsborough county (Tampa).[9] The number of licenses rose steadily after the passage of the new law, reaching 141,000 in September 1994.[10]

Mississippi adopted a shall issue law on July 1, 1990.[11] The Mississippi law was similar to the Florida law, except that it did not require firearms safety training. Mississippi's earlier law was highly restrictive, generally allowing only security guards to have concealed weapons.[12] In contrast, the new law is more lenient; by November 1992, the state had issued 5,136 new licenses.[13]

Oregon adopted a shall issue law on January 1, 1990, in a compromise between supporters and opponents of stricter gun control measures.[14] Oregon's new law required county sheriffs to provide a concealed handgun license to any qualified adult who had taken a firearms safety course. People who could not obtain a license included: those with outstanding arrest warrants, those on pretrial release, those with a history of mental illness, or those with a felony or recent misdemeanor conviction.

In addition to easing laws on concealed carrying, Oregon's new law also tightened standards for buying a gun. While the old law barred convicted felons from owning handguns, the new law prohibited convicted felons from owning any type of firearm. Oregon's new law also lengthened the waiting period for handgun purchases and required more detailed background checks. It further prohibited most persons ineligible for a concealed handgun license from obtaining any firearm.

Before the passage of the new law in 1991, Oregon's sheriffs issued concealed handgun licenses at their discretion. In 1989, there were fewer than 500 licensed carriers in Clackamas, Multnomah, and Washington counties, the core of the Portland metropolitan area.[15] By October 1993, the number of licenses in these counties grew to 16,000.[16]

POSSIBLE EFFECTS OF SHALL ISSUE LICENSING ON CRIME

While the shall issue policies clearly increased the number of persons licensed to carry concealed weapons in Florida, Mississippi, and Oregon, their effects on crime are less obvious. There are grounds to believe that crime might increase, decrease, or remain the same after a shall issue law is passed.

Shall issue licensing might reduce crime by deterring criminal offenders. Criminals generally wish to avoid victims who may be carrying guns.[17] Knowledge that many citizens have concealed weapons could discourage attempts at crime, especially crimes against strangers and crimes in public areas.

On the other hand, shall issue licensing also might raise levels of criminal violence. This is so because shall issue laws increase the number of persons with easy access to guns. Zimring and Cook argue that assaults are often impulsive acts involving the most readily available weapons.[18] As guns are especially deadly weapons, more firearm carriers might result in more homicides.

Advocates of shall issue licensing cite figures showing that few legal carriers misuse their guns.[19] Yet greater tolerance for legal carrying may increase levels of illegal carrying as well. For example, criminals have more reason to carry firearms—and to use them—when their victims might be armed.[20] Further, if permission to carry a concealed weapon is easy to obtain, citizens and law enforcement officials may be less apt to view illegal carrying as a serious offense.

Still, shall issue licensing may be irrelevant to crime. Even in areas with shall issue policies, only a small fraction of adults have licenses to carry guns. Many citizens keep guns in their homes, and police officers often carry guns when off-duty and in plain clothes. The increase in available firearms due to shall issue licensing may be of little consequence.

EXISTING EVIDENCE ON THE EFFECTS OF SHALL ISSUE LICENSING

Most empirical discussions of shall issue licensing compare homicides in Florida before and after the beginning of its law. Homicide is the most accurately recorded crime, reducing the influence of measurement error on the comparison. Florida adopted its law earlier than did the other states, providing more time to study the effects.

All existing comparisons of Florida homicide rates before and after the passage of the Florida shall issue law found that Florida homicides decreased after the shall issue law. The National Rifle Association, for example, notes that Florida's homicide rate fell by 21 percent when comparing 1987 with 1992.[21]

Although the Florida experience appears to support a deterrent effect, the existing comparisons suffer from several weaknesses. First, these studies all use Uniform Crime Report data compiled by the Federal Bureau of Investigation

(FBI). In 1988, the FBI did not publish crime counts for Florida. Evaluations based on the FBI data thus must ignore 1988 or use estimates of the 1988 total. This is important because 1988 was the first full year after the law's passage.[22]

Second, the existing evaluations use short time series of annual data. Even in Florida, there are few annual observations after the law began, and most comparisons only include those years immediately prior to the law's passage. Because crime increases and decreases over time due to the operation of many factors, comparisons using short time series are highly prone to the influence of chance events that briefly push homicides above or below their average levels.

Third, the existing comparisons examine total homicide rates for the entire state. If some areas respond differently to the laws than do others, a statewide analysis may miss important effects. For example, the influence of shall issue laws may be greatest in urban settings where crime is most prevalent. If this is true, including rural areas in an analysis would make it more difficult to detect changes in violence. Similarly, combining firearms and other weapon homicides might mask effects unique to one type of murder.

Fourth, most existing studies compare homicide levels before the shall issue law only with levels in 1991 or later. In February 1991, Florida adopted background checks of handgun buyers, and in October 1991, it began a waiting period for handgun purchases.[23] Comparisons that use only 1991 or later years cannot separate the effects of the shall issue law from those of the other two laws. The reductions in homicides that these studies claim may as easily be due to the other policies as to shall issue licensing.

In short, current evaluations leave much room for doubt about the effects of the Florida law. The shall issue laws in Mississippi and in Oregon have not received even this limited attention. A more detailed analysis using data from all three states would allow stronger inferences about the impact of the policies.

RESEARCH DESIGN

Study Design and Data

Similar to existing evaluations of shall issue licensing, this study used an interrupted time series design to estimate average homicide levels before and after shall issue policies began.[24] We studied patterns in Florida, Mississippi, and Oregon. In addition, we analyzed monthly homicide counts and examined only large urban areas within the three states. To find if the laws influenced gun deaths differently, firearm homicides were separated from homicides by other means.

We conducted analyses for Dade (Miami), Duval (Jacksonville), and Hillsborough (Tampa) counties in Florida, and for Hinds (Jackson) county in Mississippi. Because there were relatively few homicides in Multnomah county (Portland), we combined Clackamas, Multnomah, and Washington counties in Oregon. For each area, we used death certificate data compiled by the National

Center for Health Statistics (NCHS) to count monthly homicides through December 1990.[25] Health departments in Florida, Mississippi, and Oregon provided additional cases from January 1991, to December 1992.

For all areas except Miami, we studied the period between January 1973 and December 1992 (240 months). We confined our Miami analysis to January 1983 through December 1992 (120 months) because of an unusually sharp increase in homicide rates in May 1980 after an influx of Cuban refugees. In late 1982 the rates appeared to stabilize.[26]

In total, there were 177 months before the shall issue law in Jacksonville and Tampa, and 57 months before the shall issue law in Miami. For all three Florida cities there were 63 months after the law. In Mississippi there were 210 prelaw months and 30 postlaw months. In Oregon there were 204 prelaw months and 36 postlaw months.

To remove the effects of systematic variation from each time series, we developed autoregressive integrated moving average (ARIMA) noise models.[27] The noise models allow for variables, such as poverty or age structure, which influenced homicides both before and after the legal changes. If not controlled, these variables may bias inferences about the laws.

After developing suitable noise models, we added intervention models to measure changes in homicides following the shall issue laws.[28] We considered three intervention models: an abrupt permanent change model, a gradual permanent change model, and an abrupt temporary change model.[29] For each series, the abrupt permanent change model provided the best fit to the data.[30]

Our analysis avoids the major problems of previous comparisons. The NCHS data collection system is independent of the FBI, allowing us to use 1988 Florida homicide counts.[31] The long monthly time series provides more stable estimates of homicide patterns before and after the shall issue laws began. By studying firearms and other weapon murders separately in several areas, we can more precisely isolate any changes due to the laws.

Threats to Validity and Supplementary Analysis

Interrupted time series studies are among the strongest nonexperimental research designs.[32] Still, as is true with any design, time series studies do not eliminate all threats to valid inference.

Perhaps the most important threat to the design's validity is "history the possibility that a permanent change in another variable produced an observed effect.[33] For example, suppose that each area adopted other policies that influenced crime when they began their shall issue laws. These policies then would be confounded with the laws, and they would be historical threats to validity.

The major method we used to avoid historical threats was replication of the analysis in five metropolitan areas. An unnoticed historical event may have increased or decreased homicides in any single area after its shall issue law began. Yet if similar outcomes occur in several different places after the laws, historical events become a less plausible explanation of the change.[34] With a consistent set of results, an historical explanation would require that each area witness permanent changes in other causes of homicide at about the time its law began. These changes would have to influence homicides in the same way in each area, increasing them in all five areas or decreasing them in all five areas.

The areas in our study are geographically separated and demographically diverse, and they adopted their laws at three different times. While the replications cannot entirely rule out history, a consistent set of results would greatly narrow the range of historical events that could account for an effect. On the other hand, a varied pattern of results, with large increases or decreases in only one or two areas, would support an historical explanation.

Beyond replication, we used two additional methods to assess historical threats. First, we searched for other legal changes, especially changes in firearms laws, which might affect homicides. The most significant laws we found were Florida's background check, adopted in February 1991, and waiting period, adopted in October 1991.[35]

Florida's waiting period and background check laws began more than three years after shall issue licensing, leaving little data to estimate their effects. Still, we included these laws in a supplementary analysis to verify that they were not confounded with the licensing policy. Because the waiting period followed the background checks closely in time, we considered them as a single law that began in February 1991.

As a second check on historical threats, we estimated models that included homicide counts for the entire United States as an additional independent variable. This analysis studied whether homicide changes in the five areas simply mirrored national patterns; that is, homicide levels may have changed after the laws only because of events common to the nation as a whole. If this were true, the shall issue laws would not influence homicides net of the national counts.

We could obtain national homicide counts only through the end of 1991.[36] This limits the amount of data after the shall issue laws, especially in Mississippi and Oregon. Still, the national analysis provides an idea of whether broad historical events can explain any observed local changes.

Besides considering historical threats, we also conducted a supplementary analysis that used homicide rates instead of homicide counts. The population of all five areas grew over the study period, especially in the Florida cities. Homicide counts thus may have changed after the laws in part because of increases in the populations at risk.

To remove the influence of population, we estimated models for homicide rates per 100,000 persons. Only annual population figures were available, so we aggregated homicides in each area by year.[37] Because the annual data provided few cases to study changes in rates, we next pooled all five areas using a fixed effects analysis of variance model.[38] This created a single set of data, with seventy observations before the laws and twenty after the laws.[39] As in the main analysis, we then estimated separate equations for firearm homicides and for homicides by other methods.

Table 1. Mean Numbers of Homicies Per Month, by Jurisdiction and Method, Before and After Implementation of Shall Issue Licensing

Type of Homicide and Location	Before the Shall Issue Law no./mo.	Change After the Shall Issue Law*			
		no./mo.	SE	%	t-Statistic
Firearm					
Miami	25.88	0.79	1.09	+3	0.73
Jacksonville	6.24	4.78	0.61	+75	7.84
Tampa	4.91	1.10	0.44	22	2.50
Portland area	2.79	−0.34	0.35	−12	−0.98
Jackson	3.64	1.57	0.47	+43	3.34
	Mean change +26.2%	Inverse normal combined Z = −6.01, p < .0001			
Other Methods					
Miami	9.58	−0.73	0.63	−8	−1.16
Jacksonville	2.83	1.03	0.32	+36	3.22
Tampa	2.74	0.48	0.42	+17	1.14
Portland area	2.46	−0.58	0.38	−24	−1.53
Jackson	1.34	−0.30	0.27	−22	−1.11
	Mean change = −0.2%	Inverse normal combined Z = +0.25, p = .8023			

*Difference between the mean number of homicides per month before implementation of the shall issue law and the mean number after its implementation.

In the pooled equations we first removed the mean homicide rates for each area and year. This controls for constant rate differences between the areas and for events that similarly influenced rates across all areas in a given year.[40] We then included intervention variables to measure the effects of the shall issue and (for the Florida cities) background check and waiting period laws.

RESULTS

Estimates of the effects of the shall issue laws on the monthly homicide counts appear in table 1. To simplify the presentation, we report only the means before the laws and the changes in homicides after the laws began.[41]

The results in table I show that firearms homicides increased in four of the five areas in the postlaw period. Except the increase in Miami and the decrease in Portland, these changes were statistically significant (p < .05). Expressed as percentages, the changes varied from a decrease of 12 percent (Portland) to an increase of 75 percent (Jacksonville).[42] Considering each area as a replication of the same experiment, gun homicides increased by an average of 26 percent. An inverse normal combined test of statistical significance easily rejected the null hypothesis of zero overall change.[43]

In contrast to gun homicides, homicides by other means did not show a consistent pattern of effects. Homicides without firearms increased in Tampa and Jacksonville, but they fell in the other three areas. Across all five areas, the

Table 2. Mean Numbers of Homicides Per Month in Florida Areas, by Jurisdiction and Method, Before and After Implementation of Shall Issue Licensing and Waiting Period and Background Check Laws

Type of Homicide and Location	Before the Laws no./mo.	Change After the Shall Issue Law*			Change After the Waiting Period and Background Check Laws**		
		no./mo.	SE	t-Statistic	no./mo.	SE	t-Statistic
Firearm							
Miami	25.88	2.25	1.19	1.89	−3.99	1.51	−2.64
Jacksonville	6.21	6.10	0.61	10.00	−3.11	0.86	−3.62
Tampa	4.91	1.35	0.52	2.60	−0.68	0.77	−0.88
Other Methods							
Miami	9.60	0.11	0.53	0.21	−2.48	0.68	−3.65
Jacksonville	2.86	1.25	0.38	3.29	−0.60	0.56	−1.07
Tampa	2.74	0.42	0.49	0.86	0.17	0.72	0.24

*Difference between the mean number of homicides per month before implementation of the shall issue law and the mean number after its implementation, controlling for the waiting period and background check laws.

**Difference between the mean number of homicides per month before implementation of the waiting period and background check laws and the mean number after their implementation, controlling for the shall issue law.

average change in homicides without guns was an increase of less than 1 percent. In combination, this change was statistically insignificant.

Table 2 contains the analysis for the Florida cities that includes the state's waiting period and background check laws. These results provide no evidence that the original estimates were due to confounding between the other laws and shall issue licensing. Adding the other laws slightly increased the coefficients for the shall issue policy, but it did not alter their statistical significance.

Although not central to our study, it is worth noting that the levels of each Florida firearms series decreased after the waiting period and background checks began. Yet homicides without guns also fell in two cities, and the policies should influence only firearm crimes. The results do not point to any strong conclusions about the waiting period and background check laws.

Table 3 presents the analysis that adds national homicide counts to control for patterns in the United States as a whole.[44] In each area, there was a positive relationship between local homicide patterns and patterns in the nation. Still, including the national counts only modestly changed the estimates for shall issue licensing.

Finally, table 4 reports the results for the annual homicide rates. Here the coefficient for the shall issue policies is the average effect across all five cities. Gun homicides increased on average by 4.5 per 100,000 persons, a value significantly different from zero. In contrast, murders without guns decreased insignificantly. Gun homicides fell insignificantly following Florida's waiting period and background check laws, while other weapon homicides increased.

Table 3. Mean Numbers of Homicides Per Month, by Jurisdiction and Method, Before and After Implementation of Shall Issue Licensing, Controlling for National Homicide Counts

Type of Homicide and Location	Constant no./mo.	Change After the Shall Issue Law*			Coefficient for National Homicide Counts**		
		no./mo.	SE	t-Statistic	slope	SE	t-Statistic
Firearm							
Miami	25.86	1.55	1.12	1.38	0.0144	0.0063	2.29
Jacksonville	6.23	5.36	0.64	8.37	0.0015	0.0019	0.79
Tampa	4.91	1.17	0.49	2.39	0.0014	0.0015	0.93
Portland area	2.80	−0.44	0.42	−1.05	0.0015	0.0014	1.07
Jackson	3.62	1.61	0.57	2.82	0.0011	0.0013	0.85
Other Methods							
Miami	9.62	−0.43	0.55	−0.78	0.0010	0.0051	0.20
Jacksonville	2.86	0.96	0.35	2.74	0.0181	0.0214	0.85
Tampa	2.75	0.81	0.45	1.80	0.0077	0.0205	0.38
Portland area	2.46	−0.28	0.43	−0.65	0.0039	0.0019	2.05
Jackson	1.35	0.22	0.27	0.81	0.0027	0.0013	2.08

*Difference between the mean number of homicides per month before implementation of the shall issue law and the mean number after its implementation, controlling for national homicide counts.
**Slope estimate for influence of national homicide counts, controlling for the shall issue law.

DISCUSSION

Across the five areas, firearms homicides increased in the aftermath of the shall issue laws. In contrast, homicides without guns remained steady. These findings were little altered when we considered other laws, controlled for variations in national homicide counts, and allowed for population change.

The pattern of results leads us to two conclusions, one stronger than the other. The stronger conclusion is that shall issue laws do not reduce homicides, at least in large urban areas. If there were such a decrease, other events would have to push murders up strongly enough to mask it in all five areas that we studied. Such events are possible, of course, but we believe that they are extremely unlikely.

The weaker conclusion is that shall issue laws raise levels of firearms murders. Coupled with a lack of influence on murders by other means, the laws thus increase the frequency of homicide. This interpretation is consistent with other work showing that policies to *discourage* firearms in public may help prevent violence. For example, studies by Pierce and Bowers and by O'Carroll et al. found that laws providing mandatory sentences for illegal gun carrying reduced firearms crimes in Boston and Detroit.[45] Similarly, Sherman et al. found that gun crimes fell during a Kansas City program that confiscated firearms from people who carried them outside their homes.[46]

Despite this evidence, we do not firmly conclude that shall issue licensing

Table 4. Pooled Annual Homicide Rates, Before and After Implementation of Shall Issue Licensing and Waiting Period and Background Check Laws

Firearms Homicide Rate Per 100,000			
	Coefficient Estimate	SE	t-Statistic
Shall Issue Licensing	4.52	1.75	2.58
Waiting Period and Background Check	−3.25	2.09	−1.55
Constant	11.20	0.53	21.13
Other Methods Homicide Rate Per 100,000			
	Coefficient Estimate	SE	t-stausfic
Shall Issue Licensing	−0.16	0.75	−0.21
Waiting Period and Background Check	1.81	0.90	2.01
Constant	5.02	0.23	21.83

leads to more firearms murders. This is so because the effects varied over the study areas. Firearms homicides significantly increased in only three areas, and one area witnessed an insignificant decrease. In combination, the increase in gun homicides was large and statistically significant. Yet we have only five replications, and two of these do not clearly fit the pattern.

The statistical significance of the combined results aside, the analysis implies that shall issue policies do not *always* raise levels of gun murder. Sometimes, at least, local conditions operate to blunt any effects. The areas without significant increases, Portland and Miami, may be unusual, but we lack the data to examine whether this is true.

Stated in another way, we cannot completely dismiss historical events as an explanation of the increases in firearms murders. One would need a complex theory to explain how history could mask a *decrease* in homicides after the laws. Historical accounts of the apparent *increase* might be much simpler. One would then be left with the hypothesis that the effects of the laws are nil.

A more definitive analysis should be possible in the future. Besides Mississippi and Oregon, six other states have adopted shall issue laws based on the Florida model. Four of these—Alaska, Idaho, Montana, and Wyoming—have small populations and low levels of criminal violence.[47] As a result, it would be difficult to perform a statistically meaningful analysis of changes in homicides after their laws began.

Yet, two more populous states, Arizona and Tennessee, enacted shall issue licensing in 1994.[48] Given several years of experience with the laws in these areas, future research could provide more certain estimates of the effects on firearms violence.

Between January 1995 and March 1995, the legislatures of Arkansas, Utah, and Virginia sent shall issue laws to their governors for signature.[49] Similar laws were pending in an additional fourteen states, including California, Illinois, and

Texas.[50] Given this level of interest, it is likely that shall issue licensing will continue to receive attention in the future.

While our analysis does not allow a firm conclusion that shall issue licensing increases firearms homicides, it does suggest caution about these laws. Some observers consider strict limits on firearms outside the home to be among the most effective forms of gun control.[51] Beyond any influence on violence, the policies are easy to enforce and they do not inconvenience most gun owners. When states weaken limits on concealed weapons, they may be giving up a simple and effective method of preventing firearms deaths.

NOTES

1. See James D. Wright et al., *Under the Gun: Weapons, Crime, and Violence in America* (New York: Aldine Pub. Co., 1983), pp. 243–72; Gary Kleck and E. Britt Patterson, "The Impact of Gun Control and Gun Ownership Levels on Violence Rates," *Journal of Quantitative Criminology* 9 (1993): 249.

2. See, eg., Franklin E. Zimring, "Firearms, Violence, and Public Policy," *Scientific American* 265 (1991): 48.

3. Gary Kleck, *Point Blank: Guns and Violence in America* (Hawthorne, N.Y.: Aldine de Gruyter, 1991), pp. 411–14.

4. Ibid.

5. Paul H. Blackman, "Carrying Handguns for Personal Protection: Issues of Research and and Public Policy" (presented at the Annual Meeting of the American Society of Criminology [November 1985]).

6. Ibid.; see also G. Ray Arnett, "Sincerely, GRA," *American Rifleman* 133 (1985): 7.

7. See, e.g., Wayne LaPierre, *Guns, Crime, and Freedom* (New York: Harper Perennial, 1994): 29–39; David B. Kopel, "Hold Your Fire: Gun Gontrol Won't Stop Rising Violence," *Policy Review* 63 (1993): 58.

8. Fla. Stat. ch. 790.06 (1992). See Richard Getchell, "Carrying Concealed Weapons in Self Defenses: Florida Adopts Uniform Regulations for the Issuance of Concealed Weapon Permits, *Florida State University Law Review* 15 (1987): 751.

9. See Lisa Getter, "Accused Criminals Get Gun Permits," *Miami Herald*, 15 May 1988, p. 1A; Stephen Koff and Bob Port, "Gun Permits Soar Through Loopholes," *St. Petersburg Times*, 7 January 1988, p. A1.

10. Florida Department of State, Division of Licensing, Concealed Weapons/Firearm License Statistical Report for Period 10/01/87 TO 09/30/94 (1994).

11. Miss. Code Ann. § 45-9-101 (1991).

12. David Snyder, "New Miss. Gun-Permit Law Raises Visions of Old West," *Times-Picayune* (New Orleans), 13 August 1990, p. A1.

13. Grace Simmons, "Police Want Concealed Guns Banned From Cars," *Clarion-Ledger* (Jackson), 11 November 1992, p. A1.

14. Or. Rev. Stat. § 166.291-§166.295 (1991). See also Rhonda Canby, "1989 Oregon Gun Control Legislation, *Willamette Law Review* 26 (1990): 565.

15. Bill MacKenzie, "Packin' the Heat," *Oregonian* (Portland), 4 November 1993, p. A1.

16. Ibid.

17. See, eg., James D. Wright and Peter H. Rossi, *Armed and Considered Dangerous: A Survey of Felons and their Firearms* (Hawthorne, N.Y.: Aldine de Gruyter, 1986), pp. 141–59.

18. Franklin Zimring, "Is Gun Control Likely to Reduce Violent Killings?" *University of Chicago Law Reveiw* 35 (1968): 721; Philip J. Cook, "The Technology of Personal Violence," *Crime and Justice*, vol. 14, ed. Michael Tonry (Chicago: University of Chicago Press, 1991).

19. See, e.g., LaPierre, *Guns, Crime, and Freedom*, pp. 36–38; Jeffrey R. Snyder, "A Nation of Cowards," *Public Interest* 13 (1993): 40. See also Florida Department of State, Concealed Weapons/Firearm License Statistical Report.

20. In a survey of prison inmates, Wright and Rossi found that a majority of gun-carrying criminals cited armed victims as an important motivation for their actions. Wright and Rossi, *Armed and Considered Dangerous*, p. 150. Of course, criminals rarely will know with certainty if a potential victim has a concealed gun. Even unarmed victims may therefore be more vulnerable to harm.

21. National Rifle Association, Institute for Legislative Action, *Fact Sheet: Carrying Concealed Firearms (CCW) Statistics* (1994). See also LaPierre, *Guns, Crime, and Freedom*, p. 33; Kopel, "Hold Your Fire," p. 63; George F. Will, "Are We 'A Nation of Cowards'?" *Newsweek*, 15 November 1993, pp. 92–93.

22. In addition, from 1988 through 1991 Florida did not report data to the FBI that distinguished firearms homicides from homicides by other means. Existing comparisons use only total homicide counts.

23. Fla. Stat. chs. 790.065, 790.0655 (1992).

24. See Thomas D. Cook and Donald T. Campbell, *Quasi-Experimentation: Design and Analysis Issues for Field Settings* (Chicago: Rand McNally College Pub. Co., 1979), pp. 207–32.

25. Department of Health and Human Services, National Center for Health Statistics, Inter-University Consortium for Political and Social Research, Mortality Detail Files, 1968 to 1990 (1993).

26. Still, we reached similar conclusions when we analyzed all 240 months of Miami data.

27. George, E. P. Box et al., *Time Series Analysis: Forecasting and Control*, 3d ed. (Englewood Cliffs, N.J.: Prentice Hall, 1994).

28. Ibid., pp. 462–69.

29. See David McDowall et al., *Interrupted Time Series Analysis* (Beverly Hills: Sage Publications, 1980), pp. 83–85.

30. Ibid., pp. 83–85 (discussing criteria for selecting the best-fitting model).

31. For a description of the FBI and NCHS data collection systems, see Marc Riedel, "Nationwide Homicide Data Sets An Evaluation of the Uniform Crime Reports and the National Center for Health Statistics Data," in *Measuring Crime: Large-Scale, Long-Range Efforts*, ed. Doris Layton MacKenzie et al. (Albany: State University of New York Press, 1990), p. 175.

32. See Donald T. Campbell and Julian C. Stanley, *Experimental and Quasi-Experimental Designs for Research* (Boston: Houghten Mifflin, 1963), pp. 37–43.

33. Cook and Campbell, "Quasi-Experimentation," p. 211.

34. Campbell and Stanley, *Experimental and Quasi-Experimental Designs for Research*, p. 42 (pointing out that the natural sciences heavily rely on time series designs, and use replications to rule out rival hypotheses).

35. Fla. Stat. chs. 790.065, 790.065 (1992). As we noted earlier, Oregon changed several other features of its firearms laws when it adopted shall issue licensing. Because these other changes began with the shall issue policy we cannot separately estimate their effects.

36. Department of Health and Human Services, National Center for Health Statistics, Inter-University Consortium for Political and Social Research, Mortality Detail Files, 1968 to 1991 (1994).

37. For 1973–1978 we used county-level population estimates from U.S. Department of Commerce Bureau of the Census, *Statistical Abstract of the United States* (various years). For 1980-1992 we used unpublished Census Bureau estimates. The Census Bureau did not estimate county populations in 1979, and we interpolated values for that year.

38. See Cheng Hsiao, *Analysis of Panel Data* (New York: Cambridge Univeristy Press, 1986).

39. Florida and Mississippi began their laws in the middle of the year. In the annual analysis we placed the interventions for these states at the first full year after the laws, 1988 for the Florida cities and 1991 for Jackson. Oregon's law began in January 1990, so we placed Portland's intervention at 1990.

40. Hsiao, *Analysis of Panel Data*, pp. 138–40.

41. An appendix that describes the analysis in more detail is available from the authors.

42. The NCHS dam include civilian justifiable homicides, in which private citizens killed crim-

inals during attempted felonies. We thus cannot dismiss the possibility that part of the rise in firearms murders was due to permit holders who shot offenders in self-defense. Still, justifiable homicides are rare, and it is not plausible that they could account for the bulk of the increase. According to FBI data for 1992, there were 262 justifiable handgun homicides in the entire United States, 1.7 percent of the 15,377 firearm murders. See Federal Bureau of Investigation, *Crime in the United States, 1992* (1993), pp. 15–22.

43. See Larry V. Hedges and Ingram Olking, *Statistical Methods For Meta-Analysis* (Orlando: Academic Press, 1985), p. 39–40. The test assumes that the replications are independent. Because we include three cities from the same state in the analysis, this is probably only approximately correct.

44. Because the national counts were not stationary in level, we used their first differences in this analsis. See Box, *Time Series Analysis:* pp. 89–130 for a discussion of nonstationary time series models.

45. Glenn L Pierce and William J. Bowers, "The Bartley-Fox Gun Law's Short-Term Impact an Crime in Boston," *American Academy of Political and Social Science* 455 (1981): 120–37; Patrick W. O'Carroll et al., "Preventing Homicide: An Evaluation of the Efficacy of a Detroit Gun Ordinance," *American Journal of Public Health* 81 (1991): 576.

46. Lawrence W. Sherman et al., "The Kansas City Gun Experiment," *National Institute of Justice Research in Brief* (January 1995). Sherman and associates note that about 20 precent of the seized firearms were legally carried.

47. Alaska Stat. §§ 18.65.700-8.65.720 (1994); Idaho Code § 18-3302 (1993); Mont. Code Ann. § 45–321 (1993); Wyo. Stat. § 6-8-104 (1994).

48. Ariz. Rev. Stat. Ann. § 13-3112 (1994); Tenn. Code Ann. § 39-17-1315 (1994).

49. Roger Worthington, "Support Mounting for Concealed Guns," *Chicago Tribune*, 6 March 1995, p. A1.

50. Sam Howe Verhovek, "States Seek to Let Citizens Carry Concealed Weapons," *New York Times*, 6 March 1995, p. A1.

51. See Mark H. Moore, "The Bird in Hand: A Feasible Strategy for Gun Control," *Journal of Policy Analysis and Management* 2(1983): 185; Samuel Walker, *Sense and Nonsense about Crime: A Policy Guide* 2d ed. (Monterey, Calif.: Brooks/Cole, 1989), 179–98.

30

GUN DECONTROL
WHEN FLORIDA MADE IT EASIER TO GET CARRY PERMITS

GARY KLECK

Most case studies of changes in gun law are studies of increases in gun control restrictiveness. However, there is as much to be learned about the efficacy of gun controls from decreases in strictness as there is from increases. The following describes Florida's experience with easing access to permits to carry guns in public places.

Prior to 1987, Florida had a county-administered, highly discretionary, "may issue" carry permit system. Each county commission *could* issue a carry license to any adult "of good moral character," but was not required by law to do so; the permit was also good only for carrying in the county in which it was issued (Florida 1976). County commissions (or their designees, such as sheriffs) were free to interpret "good moral character" as liberally or restrictively as they wished, so there was considerable room for variation across counties in permit issuance. In most urban counties, where the bulk of the crime was committed, permits were almost never issued. For example, in Hillsborough (Tampa) County, only twenty-five permits were in effect before the law was changed, while there were only thirty-one in Pinellas (St. Petersburg) County (*St. Petersburg Times*, 17 January 1988, p. 1A), and just twenty-three in Broward (Ft. Lauderdale) County (*Miami Herald*, 15 May 1988, p. 14A). On the other hand, if Florida's experience followed that of California, which had a similar county-administered discretionary permit system (*San Francisco Examiner*, 25 September 1986), rural counties probably issued permits at a much higher per capita rate.

As of October 1, 1987, the state law was changed to a uniform, stateadministered, largely nondiscretionary, "shall issue" permit system, with permits usable statewide. Unless applicants had disqualifying attributes, the state was required to issue a license to adult residents who submitted the $125 licensing fee (for a three-year license), got themselves fingerprinted, completed a gun safety program, and properly filled out the required forms. A license could be denied if the applicant was a minor, convicted felon, drug addict, alcoholic, mental incompetent, or had been committed to a mental institution, but in practice applications were rarely denied for any reason other than a criminal history or incomplete application forms. Likewise, once granted, licenses were rarely revoked for any reason other than criminal convictions. The permits did not authorize carrying in bars or other similar "places of nuisance," courtrooms, jails, government meeting places, schools, or colleges (Florida 1987, 1996). By October 31, 1996, 376,921 permits had been issued, including 239,666 initial permits and 137,255 renewals. On that date there were 194,356 valid concealed weapons licenses in Florida, representing 1.3 percent of Florida's population (Florida 1996). Thus, although millions of Floridians were eligible for permits, apparently relatively few wanted one badly enough to go through the required trouble and expense of applying.

Critics of the law had feared that the increase in legally authorized gun carriers would result in increased acts of violence involving permit holders, with angry motorists shooting it out over fender-benders on the freeway and the like. It is important to emphasize that critics specifically feared that *permit holders* would commit acts of criminal violence with their guns, in a return to the days of the Wild West (*St. Petersburg Times*, 17 January 1988, p. 1A; *Miami Herald*, 15 May 1988, p. 14A; Chicago Tribune, 4 January 1987, p. 6; *New York Times*, 6 March 1995, p. Al; *Christian Science Monitor*, 9 March 1995, p. 1). Prior to release of a report by David McDowall and his colleagues (McDowall et al. 1995a), the possibility that increased permit holder carrying might stimulate increased gun carrying by permitless criminals, thereby *in*directly increasing violence, was not even part of the public debate about these laws.

Detailed individual-level data allow us to assess problems among permit holders: gun violence in this group is virtually nonexistent. The most valuable data available pertain to Dade (Miami) County and are superior to any available statewide. The Metro-Dade Police Department gathered unusually comprehensive data because its director was especially worried about the impact of the new law. Officers were required to fill out a form every time they were involved in an incident involving a carry permit holder in any way, even if it involved neither an arrest nor a violent act. Dade County provides an especially strong test case of the proposition that permit holders would significantly contribute to an increase in criminal violence. It had the highest violence rate of any Florida county in 1987 (Florida 1988:58–82) and experienced the biggest absolute increase in the number of permits (Metro-Dade Police Department 1992). The number of permits in Dade County jumped from about 1,200 before the new law to 21,092 by August 31, 1992. Therefore, if increasing the legal carrying of guns was going to have an adverse impact anywhere, it should have done so in Dade.

Over a five-year period from September 30, 1987, through August 31, 1992, only twenty-two carry permit holders were arrested, eight of them involving a violent crime committed with a gun (Metro-Dade Police Department 1992). Thus, over a four-year, ten-month period, in the most violent county in the state, after an eighteenfold increase in the number of carry permit holders, there were only 1.7 arrests per year of a permit holder committing a violent act with a gun.

Balancing out these eight gun crime cases were nineteen incidents where permit holders reported that they used guns for self-protection against humans. In nine cases, the use was successful, in another two it may have been successful, and in five cases it was irrelevant to the outcome of the incident (e.g., the gun was used as the offender was leaving the scene). In two cases the gun use was unsuccessful and in one case the outcome was unknown (assessment of scenarios in Metro-Dade Police Department 1992).

Less detailed statewide data on permit revocations tell the same story. Permit holders convicted of a crime must have their permits revoked. Of 239,666 persons granted permits by October 31, 1996, only 408 had been revoked for conviction for any kind of crime committed after licensure, and only seventy-two of these involved the use of a gun, for an average of eight gun crime convictions per year (Florida 1996). Thus, only 0.03 percent of persons who ever obtained permits (1 in 3329) were convicted of crimes committed with a gun. Compared to the 194,356 people holding permits on September 30, 1995, this is an annual average of 4.18 gun crime convictions per hundred thousand current permit holders, or 1 in 24,519 permit holders per year. Even taking into account the fact that many crimes do not result in conviction, it is fair to say that criminal misuse of guns was extremely rare among Florida permit holders. There is only one known case of a Florida permit holder committing a criminal homicide with a gun (*Tallahassee Democrat*, 29 July 1989, p. 2C), and there is no basis for believing that this person would have refrained from carrying a gun had he not possessed a carry permit.

An initial report by McDowall et al. (1995a)* indicated that gun homicide had significantly increased in two high-crime Florida cities (Tampa and Jacksonville) following enactment of the new law. A critic, writing in the same issue of the journal that published this report, questioned why the authors had analyzed only three of Florida's sixty-seven counties, even though the law obviously applied statewide (Polsby 1995a). In response to the criticism, McDowall et al. finally analyzed data for the entire state. Their analysis of annual homicide rates for the state as a whole indicated that, as critics had suspected, the total homicide rate in Florida

---

*See David McDowall, Colin Loftin, and Brian Wiersema, "Easing Concealed Firearm Laws," in Part Four of this volume.—Ed.

declined after access to carry permits was eased. More specifically, the second panel of their table 2 indicated that, while the annual rate of *gun* homicides per hundred thousand population increased by 0.88 after the new law, the rate of *non*gun homicides *de*creased by the even larger amount of 1.11 (McDowall et al. 1995b:226). Thus, although the authors devoted not a word to this finding, the net change in statewide homicide rates was a decrease in total homicides of 0.23 per 100,000, a statistically insignificant decline of 2.9 percent over the 1987 statewide homicide rate. The results confirmed critics' suspicions that the authors had selected a seriously unrepresentative subset of Florida's counties to study, creating the misleading impression that the new carry law had caused an increase in homicide. In all likelihood the Tampa and Jacksonville increases in gun homicides were at least partly due to the increase in violence linked with the crack epidemic, which hit those cities at the same time as the new carry law.

It is not hard to imagine why liberalizing Florida's carry law did not increase violence. First, few people wanted to get carry permits. Second, people who were carrying illegally before the change presumably continued to carry, legally or not, after the change. The only people who are likely to have changed their rate of carrying were those who were unwilling to carry illegally before the change, but who were willing and able to get carry permits after the change. This would be some subset of the 1.3 percent of Floridians possessing permits. Third, among this "affected" group, there were evidently very few who were willing to commit acts of criminal violence. This is presumably because most violent people were either disqualified from getting permits under the new law, by virtue of having a felony conviction or falling into one of the other forbidden categories, or because they voluntarily refrained from applying for a permit. Although one newspaper proclaimed in a headline, "Gun Permits Soar Through Loopholes," the text of the article indicated that only sixty-eight of 1981 permit applicants in a five-county area had ever been even arrested for a crime, and only fifty had been found guilty of any crime (including twenty-five who had "final judgment withheld"). The article documented only six cases (one-third of 1 percent of the applicants) in which the applicant had been found guilty of a crime involving use or even threat of force, and only three of these (one-sixth of 1 percent) involved a gun. And of these three applicants, only one had actually been granted a permit (the other two applications were still being processed) (*St. Petersburg Times*, 17 January 1988, p. 1-A). In sum, very few people officially known to be violent got permits, so the law did not change the legal status of gun carrying for more than a handful of people likely to use their guns for an unlawful violent purpose.

After Florida's experience with relaxed carry permit laws, many other states followed suit, so that by November 1995, at least twenty-eight states had "shall issue" nondiscretionary carry laws on the books (*New York Times*, 2 November 1995), most of them modeled after the Florida statute. The most authoritative study of the impact of these laws was conducted by John Lott and David Mustard (1997). In contrast to McDowall et al. (1995a), Lott and Mustard did not confine their analysis to a handful of nonrandomly selected local areas, but instead analyzed all counties in the nation for which requisite data were available: over three thousand of them. Further, instead of assessing just three state laws, as did McDowall et al., they studied *every* "shall issue" carry law passed between 1977 and 1992. In addition, Lott and Mustard explicitly controlled for dozens of other possible causes of changes in crime rates, besides carry laws, allowing them to rule out the effects of many confounding variables and better isolate the effects of the carry laws, in contrast to McDowall et al., who did not explicitly control for *any* other known crime determinants. Also, by using a pooled time seriescrosssectional design, Lott and Mustard were able to take account of crime variation across areas as well as across time. Finally, Lott and Mustard evaluated the laws' impact on *all* forms of violence for which data were available, while McDowall et al. studied only homicide.

Lott and Mustard's results indicated that, contrary to the conclusions of their predecessors, homicide rates did *not* generally increase following liberalized carry laws. Once the full set of areas subject to the laws was systematically compared to areas without changes in carry laws, the data indicated that violence rates, including gun homicide rates, declined after these laws went into effect, a pattern that was especially pronounced in larger urban counties, where the increase in legally permitted carrying was greatest.

Lott and Mustard argued that their results indicated that the laws caused substantial reductions in violence rates by deterring prospective criminals afraid of encountering an armed victim. This conclusion could be challenged, in light of how modest the intervention was. The 1.3 percent of the population in places like Florida who obtained permits would represent at best only a slight increase in the share of potential crime victims who carry guns in public places. And if those who got permits were merely legitimating what they were already doing before the new laws, it would mean there was no increase at all in carrying or in actual risks to criminals. One can always speculate that criminals' perceptions of risk outran reality, but that is all this is—a speculation. More likely, the declines in crime coinciding with relaxation of carry laws were largely attributable to other factors not controlled in the Lott and Mustard analysis.

Nevertheless, the Lott and Mustard results decisively established that the McDowall et al. findings were the eccentric result of analysis of a tiny, unrepresentative set of local areas. Leaving aside issues of causation, the general statistical pattern was clearly that homicide and other violence rates declined after states made it easier for noncriminals to get carry permits. While it is debatable whether the laws reduce violence, the best available evidence indicates that they do not increase it. Since they may modestly increase defensive carrying and defensive use of guns in public places, and such use reduces the likelihood of injury or property loss in criminal attempts, the laws should increase the rate at which armed victims disrupt crimes even if they had no effect on the number of crimes attempted. Further, if the laws really do increase carrying, they probably make some people less fearful when out in public.

REFERENCES

Florida. 1976. *Florida Statutes Annotated.* St. Paul: West.

———. 1988. *Crime in Florida. 1987 Annual Report.* Tallahassee: Florida Department of Law Enforcement.

———. 1990. *Florida Assault Weapons Commission Report.* May 18, 1990. Tallahassee: Florida Department of State.

———. 1996. "Concealed Weapons/Firearms License Statistical Report for Period 10/01/87–10/31/96." Tallahassee: Florida Department of State, Division of Licensing.

Lott, John, and David B. M. Mustard. 1997. "Crime, deterrence and right-to-carry concealed handguns." *Journal of Legal Studies* 26:1–68.

McDowall, David, Colin Loftin, and Brian Wiersema. 1992. "A comparative study of the preventive effects of mandatory sentencing laws for gun crimes." *Journal of Criminal Law and Criminology* 83:378–94.

———. 1995a. "Easing concealed firearms laws." *Journal of Criminal Law and Criminology* 86:193–206.

McDowall, et al. 1995b. "Additional discussion about easing concealed firearms laws." *Journal of Criminal Law and Criminology* 86:221–27.

31

MORE GUNS, LESS CRIME

JOHN LOTT

AN OVERVIEW*

Does gun ownership save or cost lives, and how do the various gun laws affect this outcome?

To answer these questions I use a wide array of data. For instance, I have employed polls that allow us to track how gun ownership has changed over time in different states, as well as the massive FBI yearly crime rate data for all 3,054 U.S. counties from 1977 to 1992. I use additional, more recently available data for 1993 and 1994 later to check my results. Over the last decade, gun ownership has been growing for virtually all demographic groups, though the fastest growing group of gun owners is Republican women, thirty to forty-four years of age, who live in rural areas. National crime rates have been falling at the same time as gun ownership has been rising. Likewise, states experiencing the greatest reductions in crime are also the ones with the fastest growing percentages of gun ownership.

Overall, my conclusion is that criminals as a group tend to behave rationally—when crime becomes more difficult, less crime is committed. Higher arrest and conviction rates dramatically reduce crime. Criminals also move out of jurisdictions in which criminal deterrence increases. Yet criminals respond to more than just the actions taken by the police and the courts. Citizens can take private actions that also deter crime. Allowing citizens to carry concealed hand-

---

*From John Lott, *More Guns, Less Crime* (Chicago: University of Chicago Press, 1998), pp. 19–20. Reprinted with permission.

guns reduces violent crimes, and the reductions coincide very closely with the number of concealed handgun permits issued. Mass shootings in public places are reduced when law-abiding citizens are allowed to carry concealed handguns.

Not all crime categories showed reductions, however. Allowing concealed handguns might cause small increases in larceny and auto theft. When potential victims are able to arm themselves, some criminals turn away from crimes like robbery that require direct attacks and turn instead to such crimes as auto theft, where the probability of direct contact with victims is small.

There were other surprises as well. While the support for the strictest gun control laws is usually strongest in large cities, the largest drops in violent crime from legalized concealed handguns occurred in the most urban counties with the greatest populations and the highest crime rates. Given the limited resources available to law enforcement and our desire to spend those resources wisely to reduce crime, the results of my studies have implications for where police should concentrate their efforts. For example, I found that increasing arrest rates in the most crime-prone areas led to the greatest reductions in crime. Comparisons can also be made across different methods of fighting crime. Of all the methods studied so far by economists, the carrying of concealed handguns appears to be the most cost-effective method for reducing crime. Accident and suicide rates were unaltered by the presence of concealed handguns.

Guns also appear to be the great equalizer among the sexes. Murder rates decline when either more women or more men carry concealed handguns, but the effect is especially pronounced for women. One additional woman carrying a concealed handgun reduces the murder rate for women by about three to four times more than one additional man carrying a concealed handgun reduces the murder rate for men. This occurs because allowing a woman to defend herself with a concealed handgun produces a much larger change in her ability to defend herself than the change created by providing a man with a handgun.

While some evidence indicates that increased penalties for using a gun in the commission of a crime reduce crime, the effect is small. Furthermore, I find no crime-reduction benefits from state-mandated waiting periods and background checks before people are allowed to purchase guns. At the federal level, the Brady law has proven to be no more effective. Surprisingly, there is also little benefit from training requirements or age restrictions for concealed-handgun permits.

HOW TO TEST THE EFFECTS OF GUN CONTROL*

The Existing Literature

Despite intense feelings on both sides of the gun debate, I believe everyone is at heart motivated by the same concerns: Will gun control increase or decrease the

*From John Lott, *More Guns, Less Crime* (Chicago: University of Chicago Press, 1998), pp. 21–25. Reprinted with permission.

number of lives lost? Will these laws improve or degrade the quality of life when it comes to violent crime? The common fears we all share with regard to murders, rapes, robberies, and aggravated assaults motivate this discussion. Even those who debate the meaning of the Constitution's Second Amendment cannot help but be influenced by the answers to these questions.[1]

While anecdotal evidence is undoubtedly useful in understanding the issues at hand, it has definite limits in developing public policy. Good arguments exist on both sides, and neither side has a monopoly on stories. of tragedies that might have been avoided if the law had only been different. While one side presents the details of a loved one senselessly murdered in a massacre like the December 1993 Colin Ferguson shooting on the Long Island Railroad, the other side points to claims that if only Texas had allowed concealed handguns, the twenty-two lives lost in Luby's restaurant in Killeen in October 1991 could have been saved. Less publicized but equally tragic stories have been just as moving.

Surveys have filled many important gaps in our knowledge; nevertheless, they suffer from many inherent problems. For example, how accurately can a person judge whether the presence of a gun actually saved her life or whether it really prevented a criminal from attacking? Might people's policy preferences influence how they answer the pollster's questions? Other serious concerns arise with survey data. Does a criminal who is thwarted from committing one particular crime merely substitute another victim or another type of crime? Or might this general deterrence raise the costs of these undesirable activities enough so that some criminals stop committing crimes? Survey data just has not been able to answer such questions.

To study these issues more effectively, academics have turned to statistics on crime. Depending on what one counts as academic research, there are at least two hundred studies on gun control. The existing work falls into two categories, using either "timeseries" or "cross-sectional" data. Time-series data deal with one particular area (a city, county, or state) over many years; cross-sectional data look across many different geographic areas within the same year. The vast majority of gun control studies that examine time-series data present a comparison of the average murder rates before and after the change in laws; those that examine cross-sectional data compare murder rates across places with and without certain laws. Unfortunately, these studies make no attempt to relate fluctuations in crime rates to changing law-enforcement factors like arrest or conviction rates, prison-sentence lengths, or other obvious variables.

Both time-series and cross-sectional analyses have their limitations. Let us first examine the cross-sectional studies. Suppose, as happens to be true, that areas with the highest crime rates are the ones that most frequently adopt the most stringent gun control laws. Even if restrictions on guns were to lower the crime rates, it might appear otherwise. Suppose crime rates were lowered, but not by enough to reach the level of rates in low-crime areas that did not adopt the laws. In that case, looking across areas would make it appear that stricter gun control produced higher crime. Would this be proof that stricter gun control caused higher crime? Hardly. Ideally, one should examine how the high-crime areas that adopted the controls changed over time-not only relative to their past levels but also relative to areas without the controls. Economists refer to this as an "endogeneity" problem. The adoption of the policy is a reaction (that is, "endogenous") to other events, in this case crime.[2] To correctly estimate the impact of a law on crime, one must be able to distinguish and isolate the influence of crime on the adoption of the law.

For time-series data, other problems arise. For example, while the ideal study accounts for other factors that may help explain changing crime rates, a pure time-series study complicates such a task. Many potential causes of crime might fluctuate in any one jurisdiction over time, and it is very difficult to know which one of those changes might be responsible for the shifting crime rate. If two or more events occur at the same time in a particular jurisdiction, examining only that jurisdiction will not help us distinguish which event was responsible for the change in crime. Evidence is usually much stronger if a law changes in many different places at different times, and one can see whether similar crime patterns exist before and after such changes.

The solution to these problems is to combine both time-series and cross-sectional evidence and then allow separate variables, so that each year the national or regional changes in crime rates can be separated out and distinguished from any local deviations.[3] For example, crime may have fallen nationally between 1991 and 1992, but what this study is able to examine is whether there is an additional decline over and above that national drop in states that have adopted concealed-handgun laws. I also use a set of measures that control for the average differences in crime rates across places even after demographic, income, and other factors have been accounted for. No previous gun control studies have taken this approach.

The largest cross-sectional gun control study examined 170 cities in 1980.[4] While this study controlled for many differences across cities, no variables were used to deal with issues of deterrence (such as arrest or conviction rates or prison-sentence lengths). It also suffered from the bias discussed above that these cross-sectional studies face in showing a positive relationship between gun control and crime.

The time-series work on gun control that has been most heavily cited by the media was done by three criminologists at the University of Maryland* who looked at five different counties (one at a time) from three different states (three counties from Florida, one county from Mississippi, and one from Oregon) from 1973 to 1992 (though a different time period was used for Miami).[5] While this study has received a great deal of Media attention, it suffers from serious problems. Even though these concealed handgun laws were state laws, the authors say that they were primarily interested in studying the effect in urban areas. Yet they do not explain how they chose the particular counties used in their study.

---

*See "Easing Concealed Firearms Laws," in Part Four of this volume.—Ed.

For example, why examine Tampa but not Fort Lauderdale, or Jacksonville but not Orlando? Like most previous studies, their research does not account for any other variables that might also help explain the crime rates.

Some cross-sectional studies have taken a different approach and used the types of statistical techniques found in medical case studies. Possibly the best known paper was done by Arthur Kellermann and his many coauthors,[6] who purport to show that "keeping a gun in the home was strongly and independently associated with an increased risk of homicide."[7]* The data for this test consists of a "case sample" (444 homicides that occurred in the victim's homes in three counties) and a "control" group (388 "matched" individuals who lived near the deceased and were the same sex and race as well as the same age range). After information was obtained from relatives of the homicide victim or the control subjects regarding such things as whether they owned a gun or had a drug or alcohol problem, these authors attempted to see if the probability of a homicide was correlated with the ownership of a gun.

There are many problems with Kellermann et al.'s paper that undercut the misleading impression that victims were killed by the gun in the home. For example, they fail to report that in only 8 of these 444 homicide cases could it be established that the "gun involved had been kept in the home."[8] More important, the question posed by the authors cannot be tested properly using their chosen methodology because of the endogeneity problem discussed earlier with respect to cross-sectional data.

To demonstrate this, suppose that the same statistical method—with a matching control group—was used to do an analogous study on the efficacy of hospital care. Assume that we collected data just as these authors did; that is, we got a list of all the people who died in a particular county over the period of a year, and we asked their relatives whether they had been admitted to a hospital during the previous year. We would also put together a control sample with people of similar ages, sex, race, and neighborhoods, and ask these men and women whether they had been in a hospital during the past year. My bet is that we would find a very strong positive relationship between those who spent time in hospitals and those who died, quite probably a stronger relationship than in Kellermann's study on homicides and gun ownership. If so, would we take that as evidence that hospitals kill people? I would hope not. We would understand that, although our methods controlled for age, sex, race, and neighborhood, the people who had visited a hospital during the past year and the people in the "control" sample who did not visit a hospital were really not the same types of people. The difference is pretty obvious: those hospitalized were undoubtedly sick, and thus it should come as no surprise that they would face a higher probability of dying.

The relationship between homicides and gun ownership is no different. The

---

*See Arthur L. Kellermann et al., "Gun Ownership as a Risk Factor for Homicide in the Home," in Part Four of this volume.—Ed.

finding that those who are more likely to own guns suffer a higher homicide rate makes us ask, Why were they more likely to own guns? Could it be that they were at greater risk of being attacked? Is it possible that this difference arose because of a higher rate of illegal activities among those in the case study group than among those in the control group? Owning a gun could lower the probability of attack but still leave it higher than the probability faced by those who never felt the need to buy a gun to begin with. The fact that all or virtually all the homicide victims were killed by weapons brought into their homes by intruders makes this all the more plausible.

Unfortunately, the case study method was not designed for studying these types of social issues. Compare these endogeneity concerns with a laboratory experiment to test the effectiveness of a new drug. Some patients with the disease are provided with the drug, while others are given a placebo. The random assignment of who gets the drug and who receives the placebo is extremely important. A comparable approach to the link between homicide and guns would have researchers randomly place guns inside certain households and also randomly determine in which households guns would be forbidden. Who receives a gun would not be determined by other factors that might themselves be related to whether a person faces a high probability of being killed.

So how does one solve this causation problem? Think for a moment about the preceding hospital example. One approach would be to examine a change in something like the cost of going to hospitals. For example, if the cost of going to hospitals fell, one could see whether some people who would otherwise not have gone to the hospital would now seek help there. As we observed an increase in the number of people going to hospitals, we could then check to see whether this was associated with an increase or decrease in the number of deaths. By examining changes in hospital care prices, we could see what happens to people who now choose to go to the hospital and who were otherwise similar in terms of characteristics that would determine their probability of living.

Obviously, despite these concerns over previous work, only statistical evidence can reveal the net effect of gun laws on crimes and accidental deaths. The laws being studied here range from those that allow concealed-handgun permits to those demanding waiting periods or setting mandatory minimum sentences for using a gun in the commission of a crime. Instead of just examining how crime changes in a particular city or state, I analyze the first systematic national evidence for all 3,054 counties in the United States over the sixteen years from 1977 to 1992 and ask whether these rules saved or cost lives. I attempt to control for a change in the price people face in defending themselves by looking at the change in the laws regarding the carrying of concealed handguns. I will also use the data to examine why certain states have adopted concealed-handgun laws while others have not.

This effort is the first to study the questions of deterrence using these data. While many recent studies employ proxies for deterrence—such as police expenditures or general levels of imprisonment—I am able to use arrest rates by type of crime and also, for a subset of the data, conviction rates and sentence lengths by type of crime.[9] I also attempt to analyze a question noted but not empirically addressed in this literature: the concern over causality related to increases in both handgun use and crime rates. Do higher crime rates lead to increased handgun ownership or the reverse? The issue is more complicated than simply whether carrying concealed firearms reduces murders, because questions arise about whether criminals might substitute one type of crime for another as well as the extent to which accidental handgun deaths might increase. . . .

CONCEALED-HANDGUN LAWS AND CRIME RATES: THE EMPIRICAL EVIDENCE*

. . . The following discussion provides information on a wide range of law-enforcement activities, but the primary focus is on the link between the private ownership of guns and crime. What gun laws affect crime? Does increased gun ownership cause an increase or a decrease in murders? What is the impact of more lenient laws regarding gun ownership on accidental deaths and suicide?

The analysis begins by examining both county- and state-level crime data and then turns to evidence on the benefits of gun ownership for different groups, such as women and minorities. To test whether crime rate changes are a result of concealed-handgun laws, it is not enough simply to see whether these laws lower crime rates; changes in crime rates must also be linked to the changes in the number of concealed-handgun permits. We must remember also that the laws are not all the same: different states adopt different training and age requirements for obtaining a permit. These differences allow us to investigate whether the form of the concealed-handgun law matters as well as to test the importance of other gun control laws. Finally, evidence is provided on whether criminals move to other places when concealed-handgun laws are passed.

[My discussion] is organized to examine the simplest evidence first and then gradually considers more complicated issues. The first estimates measure whether the average crime rate falls in counties when they adopt concealed-handgun laws. By looking across counties or states at the same time that we examine them over time, we can test not only whether places with the most permits have the greatest reductions in crime, but also whether those with the greatest *increases* in permits have the greatest reductions in crime. Similarly, we can investigate how total gun ownership is related to the level of crime. Tracking gun ownership in individual states over time allows us to investigate how a crime in a state changes as its gun-ownership rates change.

---

*From John Lott, *More Guns, Less Crime* (Chicago: University of Chicago Press, 1998), pp. 50–96. Reprinted with permission.

Using County and State Data for the United States

The first group of estimates reported in table 1 attempts to explain the crime rates for nine different categories of crime. Each column in the table presents the changes in the crime rate for the crime described in the column heading. The numbers in each row represent the impact that a particular explanatory variable has on each crime rate. Three pieces of information are provided for most of the explanatory variables: (1) the percent change in the crime rate attributed to a particular change in the explanatory variable; (2) the percentage of the variation in the crime rate that can be explained by the variation in the explanatory variable;[10] and (3) one, two, or three asterisks denote whether a particular effect is statistically significant at least at the 1, 5, or 10 percent level, where the I percent level represents the most reliable result.[11]

While I am primarily interested in the impact of nondiscretionary laws, the estimates also account for many other variables: the arrest rate for each type of crime; population density and the number of people living in a county; measures of income, unemployment, and poverty; the percentage of the population that is a certain sex and race by ten-year age groupings (10 to 19 years of age, 20 to 29 years of age); and the set of variables described in the previous section to control for other county and year differences. The results clearly imply that nondiscretionary laws coincide with fewer murders, aggravated assaults, and rapes.[12] On the other hand, auto theft and larceny rates rise. Both changes are consistent with my discussion of the direct and substitution effects produced by concealed weapons.[13]

The results are also large, indicating how important the laws can be. When state concealed-handgun laws went into effect in a county, murders fell by about 8 percent, rapes fell by 5 percent, and aggravated assaults fell by 7 percent.[14] In 1992 the following numbers were reported: 18,469 murders; 79,272 rapes; 538,368 robberies; and 861,103 aggravated assaults in counties without nondiscretionary laws. The estimated coefficients suggest that if these counties had been subject to state concealed handgun laws and had thus been forced to issue handgun permits, murders in the United States would have declined by about 1,400.

Given the concern raised about increased accidental deaths from concealed weapons, it is interesting to note that the entire number of accidental handgun deaths in the United States in 1988 was only 200 (the last year for which these data are available for the entire United States).[15] Of this total, 22 accidental deaths were in states with concealed-handgun laws, while 178 occurred in states without these laws. The reduction in murders is as much as eight times greater than the total number of accidental deaths in concealed-handgun states. . . . If these initial results are accurate, the net effect of allowing concealed handguns is clearly to save lives, even in the implausible case that concealed handguns were somehow responsible for all accidental handgun deaths.[16]

As with murders, the results indicate that the number of rapes in states without nondiscretionary laws would have declined by 4,200, aggravated assaults by 60,000, and robberies by 12,000.[17]

Table 1. The effect of nondiscretionory concealed-handgun laws on crime rates: National, County-Level, Cross-Sectional, Time-Series Evidence

	Percent change in various crime rates for changes in explanatory variables								
Change in explanatory variable	Violent crime	Murder	Rape	Aggravated assault	Robbery	Property crime	Burglary	Larceny	Auto theft
Nondiscretionary law adopted	−4.9%* (1%)	−7.7%* (2%)	−5.3%* (1%)	− 7.0159 (1%)	−2.2%* (.3%)	2.7%* (1%)	.05% (.02%)	3.3%* (1%)	7.1%* (1%)
Arrest rate for the crime category (e.g., violent crime, murder, etc.) increased by 100 percentage points	−0.48%* (9%)	− 1.39%* (7%)	−0.81%* (4%)	−0.896%* (9%)	−0.57%* (4%)	−0.76%* (10%)	−2.4%* (11%)	−0.18%* (4%)	−0.18%* (3%)
Population per square mile increased by 1,000	6%* (5%)	−2% (1%)	−2% (1%)	0.58% (.4%)	31.6%* (17%)	0.48% (1%)	−7%* (9%)	3.7%* (4%)	48%* (36%)
Real per-capita personal income increased by $1,000	0.79%* (1%)	1.63%* (2%)	−0.59%*** (1%)	0.47% (1%)	0.47% (1%)	− 1.02%* (3%)	− 1.84%* (4%)	− 1.23%* (2%)	1.5%* (2%)
Real per-capita unemployment Ins. increased by $100	−2.2%* (.07%)	−4.6%* (1%)	−4.7%* (1%)	− 1.9%* (.05%)	0.7% (.01%)	3.8%* (2%)	6.0%* (3%)	1.9%* (.08%)	2..1% (.06%)
Real per-capita income maintenance increased by $100	−0.7% (.3%)	2.5%** (1%)	−1.7% (.7%)	1.39% (.77.)	−3.2%* (1%)	1.917.* (27.)	3.9%* (4%)	0.2% (.1%)	3.3% (2%)
Real per-capita retirement payments per person over 65 increased by $1,000	−0.197% (.5%)	−1.3% (3%)	−0.24% (.4%)	−0.68% (2%)	−0.55% (1%)	−0.87% (4%)	−1.06% (7%)	−0.63% (2%)	−0.93% (2%)
Population increased by 100,000	0.86% (1%)	−0.34%* (.4%)	−2.94% (3%)	0.45%* (.06%)	−0.61%*** (.06%)	−2.18%* (6%)	−2.14%* (5%)	−3.10%* (6%)	−0.04%* (.05%)

Note: The percentage reported in parentheses is the percent of a standard deviation change in the endogenous variable that can be explained by one-standard-deviation change in the exogenous variable. Year and county dummies are not shown, and the results for demographic variables are shown in appendix. All regressions use weighted least squares, where the weighting is each county's population. Entire sample used for all counties over the 1977–1992 period.

*The result is statistically significant at the 1 percent level for a two-tailed t-test.
**The result is statistically significant at the 5 percent level for a two-tailed t-test.
***The result is statistically significant at the 10 percent level for a two-tailed t-test.

On the other hand, property-crime rates increased after nondiscretionary laws were implemented. If states without concealed-handgun laws had passed such laws, there would have been 247,000 more property crimes in 1992 (a 2.7 percent increase). The increase is small compared to the changes that we observed for murder, rape, and aggravated assault, though it is about the same size as the change for robbery. Criminals respond to the threat of being shot while committing such crimes as robbery by choosing to commit less risky crimes that involve minimal contact with the victim.[18]

It is possible to put a rough dollar value on the losses from crime in the United States and thus on the potential gains from nondiscretionary laws. A recent National Institute of Justice study estimates the costs to victims of different types of crime by measuring lost productivity; out-of-pocket expenses,

Table 2. The effect of nondiscretionary concealed-handgun laws on victims' costs:
What if all states had adopted nondiscretionary laws?

	Change in number of crimes if states without nondiscretionary laws in 1992 had adopted them			Change in victims' costs if states without nondiscretionary laws in 1992 had adopted them		
Crime category	Estimates using county-level data	Estimates using county-level data and state time trends	Estimates using state-level data	Estimates using county-level data	Estimates using county-level data and state time trends	Estimates using state-level data
Murder	−1,410	−1,840	−1,590	−$4.2 billion	−5.57 billion	−$4.8 billion
Rape	−4,200	−3,700	−4,800	−$374 million	−$334 million	−$431 million
Aggravated assault	−60,400	−61,100	−93,900	−$1.4 billion	−$1.4 billion	−$2.2 billion
Robbery	−11,900	−10,990	−62,900	−$98 million	−$90 million	$518 million
Burglary	1,100	−112,700	−180,800	$1.5 million	−$162 million	−$261 million
Larceny	191,700	−93,300	−180,300	$73 million	−$35 million	−$69 million
Auto theft	89,900	−41,500	−11,100	$343 million	−$2 million	−$42 million
Total change in victims' costs				−$5.7 billion	−$7.6 billion	−$8.3 billion

Note: Estimates of the costs of crime are in 1992 dollars, from the National institute of Justice's study.

such as those for medical bills and property losses; and losses from fear, pain, suffering, and lost quality of life.[19] While the use of jury awards to measure losses such as fear, pain, suffering, and lost quality of life may be questioned, the estimates provide us with one method of comparing the reduction in violent crimes with the increase in property crimes.

By combining the estimated reduction in crime from table 1 with the National Institute of Justice's estimates of what these crimes would have cost victims had they occurred, table 2 reports the gain from allowing concealed handguns to be $5.7 billion in 1992 dollars. The reduction in violent crimes represents a gain of $6.2 billion ($4.2 billion from murder, $1.4 billion from aggravated assault, $374 million from rape, and $98 million from robbery), while the increase in property crimes represents a loss of $417 million ($343 million from auto theft, $73 million from larceny, and $1.5 million from burglary). However, while $5.7 billion is substantial, to put it into perspective, it equals only about 1.23 percent of the total losses to victims from these crime categories. These estimates are probably most sensitive to the value of life used (in the National Institute of Justice Study this was set at $1.84 million in 1992 dollars). Higher estimated values of life would obviously increase the net gains from the passage of concealed-handgun laws, while lower values would reduce the gains. To the extent that people are taking greater risks regarding crime because of any increased sense of safety produced by concealed-handgun laws,[20] the preceding numbers underestimate the total savings from allowing concealed handguns.

The arrest rate produces the most consistent effect on crime. Higher arrest rates are associated with lower crime rates for all categories of crime. Variation in the probability of arrest accounts for 3 to 11 percent of the variation in the various crime rates.[21] Again, the way to think about this is that the typical observed change in the arrest rate explains up to about 11 percent of the typical change in the crime rate. The crime most responsive to the arrest rate is burglary (11 percent), followed by property crimes (10 percent); aggravated assault and violent crimes more generally (9 percent); murder (7 percent); rape, robbery, and larceny (4 percent); and auto theft (3 percent).

For property crimes, the variation in the percentage of the population that is black, male, and between 10 and 19 years of age explains 22 percent of the ups and downs in the property-crime rate.[22] For violent crimes, the same number is 5 percent. Other patterns also show up in the data. Not surprisingly, a higher percentage of young females is positively and significantly associated with the occurrence of a greater number of rapes.[23] Population density appears to be most important in explaining robbery, burglary, and auto theft rates, with the typical variation in population density explaining 36 percent of the typical change across observations in auto theft.

Perhaps most surprising is the relatively small, even if frequently significant, effect of a county's per-capita income on crime rates. Changes in real per-capita income account for no more than 4 percent of the (changes in crime, and in seven of the specifications it explains at most 2 percent of the change. It is *not* safer to live in a high-income neighborhood if other characteristics (for example, demographics) are the same. Generally, high-income areas experience more violent crimes but fewer property crimes. The two notable exceptions to this rule are rape and auto theft: high-income areas experience fewer rapes and more auto theft. If the race, sex, and age variables are replaced with separate variables showing the percentage of the population that is black and white, 50 percent of the variation in the murder rate is explained by variations in the percentage of the population that is black. Yet because of the high rates at which blacks are arrested and incarcerated or are victims of crimes (for example, 38 percent of all murder victims in 1992 were black), this is not unexpected.

One general caveat should be made in evaluating the coefficients involving the demographic variables. Given the very small portions of the total populations that are in some of these narrow categories (this is particularly true for minority populations), the effect on the crime rate from a one-percentage-point increase in the percentage of the population in that category greatly overstates the true importance of that age, sex, or race grouping. The assumption of a one-percentage-point change is arbitrary and is only provided to give the reader a rough idea of what these coefficients mean. For a better understanding of the impact of these variables, relatively more weight should be placed on the second number, which shows how much of the variation in the various crime rates can be explained by the normal changes in each explanatory variable.[24]

We can take another look at the sensitivity of the results from table 1 and examine the impact of different subsets of the following variables: the nondiscretionary law, the nondiscretionary law and the arrest rates, and the nondiscretionary law and the variables that account for the national changes in crime rates across years. Each specification yields results that show even more significant effects from the nondiscretionary law, though when results exclude variables that measure how crime rates differ across counties, they are likely to tell us more about which states adopt these laws than about the impact of these laws on crime.[25] The low-crime states are the most likely to pass these laws, and their crime rates become even lower after their passage. . . .

In further attempts to test the sensitivity of the results to the various control variables used, I reestimated the specifications in table 1 without using either the percentages of the populations that fall into the different sex, race, and age categories or the measures of income; this tended to produce similar though somewhat more significant results with respect to concealed-handgun laws. The estimated gains from passing concealed-handgun laws were also larger.

While these regressions account for nationwide changes in crime rates on average over time, one concern is that individual states are likely to have their own unique time trends. The question here is whether the states adopting nondiscretionary concealed-handgun laws experienced falling crime rates over the entire time period. This cannot be true for all states as a whole, because . . . violent crimes have definitely not been diminishing during the entire period. However, if this downward trend existed for the states that adopted nondiscretionary laws, the variables shown in table 1 could indicate that the average crime rate was lower after the laws were passed, even though the drop in the average level was due merely to a continuation of a downward trend that began before the law took effect. To address this issue, I reestimated the specifications shown in table 1 by including state dummy variables that were each interacted with a time-trend variable.[26] This makes it possible to account not only for the national changes in crime rates with the individual year variables but also for any differences in state-specific trends.

When these individual state time trends were included, all results indicated that the concealed-handgun laws lowered crime, though the coefficients were not statistically significant for aggravated assault and larceny. Under this specification, the passage of nondiscretionary concealed-handgun laws in states that did not have them in 1992 would have reduced murders in that year by 1,839; rapes by 3,727; aggravated assaults by 10,990; robberies by 61,064; burglaries by 112,665; larcenies by 93,274; and auto thefts by 41,512. The total value of this reduction in crime in 1992 dollars would have been $7.6 billion. With the exceptions of aggravated assault and burglary, violent-crime rates still experienced larger drops from the adoption of concealed-handgun laws than did property crimes.

Despite the concerns over the aggregation issues discussed earlier, economists have relied on state-level data in analyzing crime primarily because of the difficulty and extra time required to assemble county-level data. . . . The large within-state heterogeneity raises significant concerns about relying too heavily on state-level data.

To provide a comparison with other crime studies relying on state-level data, table 3 reestimates the specifications reported in table 1 using state-level rather

Table 3. Aggregating the data: state-level, cross-sectional, time-series evidence

Change in explanatory variable	Percent change in various crime rates for changes in explanatory variables								
	Violent crime	Murder	Rape	Aggravated assault	Robbery	Property crime	Burglary	Larceny	Auto theft
Nondiscretionary law adopted	−10.1%* (5.8%)	−8.62%* (5%)	−6.07%* (4.7%)	−10.9% (6.5%)	−14.21%* (5.7%)	−4.19%* (4.8%)	−0.88% (.43%)	−8.25%* (7.6%)	−3.14% (3.8%)
Arrest rate for the crime category increased by 100 percentage points	−8.02%* (1.5%)	−7.3%* (5.3%)	−2.05%* (.69%)	−15.3%* (3.9%)	−10.5%* (14.4%)	−59.9%* (8.1%)	−14.5%* (6.5%)	−71.5%* (7.6%)	−.65.7%* (10.4%)

Note: Except for the use of state dummies in place of county dummies, the control variables are the same as those used in table 1 including year dummies, though they are not all reported. The percent reported in parentheses is the percent of a stardard deviation change in the endogenous variable that can be explained by a one-standard-deviation change in the exogenous variable. All regressions use weighted least squares, where the weighting is according to each state's population. Entire sample used over the 1977 to 1992 period.
*The result is statistically significant at the 1 percent level for a two-tailed t-test.
**The result is statistically significant at the 5 percent level for a two-tailed t-test.
***The result is statistically significant at the 10 percent level for a two-tailed t-test.

than county-level data. While the results in these two tables are generally similar, two differences immediately manifest themselves: (1) the specifications now imply that nondiscretionary concealed-handgun laws lower all types of crime, and (2) concealed-handgun laws explain much more of the variation in crime rates, while arrest rates (with the exception of robbery) explain much less of the variation.[27] While concealed-handgun laws lower both violent- and property-crime rates, the rates for violent crimes are still much more sensitive to the introduction of concealed handguns, falling two-and-one-half times more than those for property crimes.

Suppose we rely on the state-level results rather than the county-level estimates. We would then conclude that if all states had adopted nondiscretionary concealed-handgun laws in 1992, about 1,600 fewer murders and 4,800 fewer rapes would have been committed.[28] Overall, table 3 allows us to calculate that the estimated monetary gain from reductions in crime produced by nondiscretionary concealed-handgun laws was $8.3 billion in 1992 dollars (again, see table 2 for the precise breakdown). Yet, at least in the case of property crimes, the concealed-handgun law coefficients are sensitive to whether the regressions are run at the state or county level. This suggests that aggregating observations into units as large as states is a bad idea. . . . [29]

Differential Effects Across Counties, Between Men and Women, and By Race and Income

Let us now return to other issues concerning the county-level data. Criminal deterrence is unlikely to have the same impact across all counties. For instance, increasing the number of arrests can have different effects on crime in different areas, depending on the stigma attached to arrest. In areas where crime is rampant, the stigma of being arrested may be small, so that the impact of a change

Table 4. Aggregating the data: Do law-enforcement and nondiscretionary laws have the same effects in high- and low-crime areas?

Change in explanatory variable	Percent change in various crime rates for changes in explanatory variables								
	Violent crime	Murder	Rape	Aggravated assault	Robbery	Property crime	Burglary	Larceny	Auto theft
	Sample where country crime rates are above the median								
Nondiscretionary law adopted	−6.0*	−9.9%*	−7.2%*	−4.5%	−3.4%*	1.6%*	0.4%	3.0%*	5.2%
Arrest rate for the crime category increased by 100 percentage points	−5.2%*	−12.3%*	−3.3%*	−6.3%*	−29.4%*	−53.5%*	−56.5%*	−59.6%*	−.13.3%*
	Sample where country crime rates are below the median								
Nondiscretionary law adopted	−3.7**	−4.4%**	−3.0%*	−0.3%	−7.9%*	8.8%*	−3%	8.7%*	7.2%
Arrest rate for the crime category increased by 100 percentage points	−5.2%*	−4.9%*	−6.6%*	−6.8%*	−3.7%*	−13.5%*	−27.1%*	−10%*	−1.4%*

Note: The control variables are the same as those used in table 1, including year and country dummies, though they are not reported. All regressions use weighted least squares, where the weighting is each country's population. Entire sample used over the 1977 to 1992 period.
*The result is statistically significant at the 1 percent level for a two-tailed t-test.
**The result is statistically significant at the 5 percent level for a two-tailed t-test.
***The result is statistically significant at the 10 percent level for a two-tailed t-test.

in arrest rates is correspondingly small.[30] To test this, the specifications shown in table 1 were reestimated by breaking down the sample into two groups: (1) counties with above-median crime rates and (2) counties with below-median crime rates. Each set of data was reexamined separately.

As table 4 shows, concealed-handgun laws do indeed affect high- and low-crime counties similarly. The coefficient signs are consistently the same for both low- and high-crime counties, though for two of the crime categories—rape and aggravated assault—concealed-handgun laws have statistically significant effects only in the relatively high-crime counties. For most violent crimes—such as murder, rape, and aggravated assault—concealed-weapons laws have much greater deterrent effects in high-crime counties. In contrast, for robbery, property crimes, auto theft, burglary, and larceny, the effect appears to be greatest in low-crime counties.

Table 4 also shows that the deterrent effect of arrests is significantly different, at least at the 5 percent level, between high- and low-crime counties for eight of the nine crime categories (the one exception being violent crimes). The results further reject the hypothesis that arrests would be associated with greater stigma in low-crime areas. Additional arrests in low- and high-crime counties generate extremely similar changes in the aggregate category of violent crime, but the arrest-rate coefficient for murder is almost three times greater in high-crime counties than in lowcrime counties. If these results suggest any conclusion, it is that for most crimes, tougher measures have more of an impact in high-crime areas.

The effect of gun ownership by women deserves a special comment. Despite the relatively small number of women who obtain concealed-handgun permits, the concealed-handgun coefficient for explaining rapes in the first three sets of results is consistently similar in size to the effect that this variable has on other violent crime. January 1996 data for Washington and Oregon reveal that women constituted 18.6 and 22.9 percent, respectively, of those with concealed-handgun permits.[31] The set of women who were the most likely targets of rape probably chose to carry concealed handguns at much higher rates than women in general. The preceding results show that rapists are particularly deterred by handguns. As mentioned earlier, the National Crime Victimization Survey data show that providing a woman with a gun has a much greater effect on her ability to defend herself against a crime than providing a gun to a man. Thus, even if few women carry handguns, the change in the "cost" of attacking women could still be as great as the change in the "cost" of attacking men, despite the much higher number of men who are becoming armed. To phrase this differently, if one more woman carries a handgun, the extra protection for women in general is greater than the extra protection for men if one more man carries a handgun.[32]

These results raise a possible concern as to whether women have the right incentive to carry concealed handguns. Despite the fact that women who carry concealed handguns make other women so much safer, it is possible that women might decide not to carry them because they see their own personal gain as much smaller than the total benefit to all women that carrying a concealed handgun produces. While the problem is particularly pronounced for women, people in general often take into account only the benefits that they individually receive from carrying a gun and not the crime-reduction benefits that they are generating for others.[33]

An important concern is that passing a nondiscretionary concealed-handgun law should not affect all counties equally. In particular, when states had discretionary laws, counties with the highest populations were also those that most severely restricted people's ability to carry concealed weapons. Adopting nondiscretionary laws therefore produced the greatest change in the number of permits in the more populous counties. Thus, a significant advantage of using this county data is that it allows us to take advantage of county-level variation in the impact of nondiscretionary concealed-handgun laws. To test this variation across counties, figures 1 and 2 repeat all the specifications in table 1 but examine instead whether the effect of the nondiscretionary law varies with county population or population density. (The simplest way to do this is to multiply the nondiscretionary-law variable by either the county population or population density.) While all the other coefficients remain virtually unchanged, this new interaction implies the same crime-reducing effects from the nondiscretionary law as reported earlier. In all but one case the coefficients are more significant and larger.

The coefficients are consistent with the hypothesis that the new laws induce the greatest changes in the largest counties, which have a much greater response in both directions to changes in the laws. Violent crimes fall more and property crimes rise more in the largest counties. The figures indicate how these effects vary for counties of different sizes. For example, when counties with almost 600,000 people (two standard deviations above the mean population) pass a concealed-handgun law, the murder rate falls by 12 percent. That is 7.4 times more than it was reduced for the average county (75,773 people).

Although the law-enforcement officials that I talked to continually mentioned population as being the key variable, I also reexamined whether the laws had different effects in more densely populated counties. Given the close relationship between county population and population density, it is not too surprising to find that the impact of concealed handguns in more densely populated areas is similar to their impact in more populous counties. The most densely populated areas are the ones most helped by concealed-handgun laws. Passing a concealed-handgun law lowers the murder rate in counties with about 3,000 people per square mile (the levels found in Fairfax, Virginia; Orleans, Louisiana, which contains New Orleans; and Ramsey, Minnesota, which contains St. Paul) by 8.5 percent, 12 times more than it lowers murders in the average county. The only real difference between the results for population and population density occur for the burglary rate, where concealed-handgun laws are associated with a small reduction in burglaries for the most densely populated areas.

Figures 3 and 4 provide a similar breakdown by income and by the percentage of the population that is black. Higher-income areas and counties with relatively more blacks both have particularly large drops in crime associated with concealed-handgun laws. Counties with a 37 percent black population experienced 11 percent declines in both murder and aggravated assaults. The differences with respect to income were not as large.[34]

With the extremely high rates of murder and other crimes committed against blacks, it is understandable why so many blacks are concerned about gun control. University of Florida criminologist Gary Kleck says, "Blacks are more likely to have been victims of crime or to live in neighborhoods where there's a lot of crime involving guns. So, generally, blacks are more procontrol than whites are." Nationally, polls indicate that 83 percent of blacks support police permits for all gun purchases.[35] While many blacks want to make guns harder to get, the irony is that blacks benefit more than other groups from concealed-handgun laws. Allowing potential victims a means for self-defense is more important in crime-prone neighborhoods. Even more strikingly, the history of gun control (in the United States has often been a series of attempts to disarm blacks.[36] In explaining the urgency of adopting the U.S. Constitution's Fourteenth Amendment, Duke University Law Professor William Van Alstyne writes,

> It was, after all, the defenselessness of the Negroes (denied legal rights to keep and bear arms by state law) from attack by night riders—even to protect their own lives, their own families, and their own homes—that made it imperative that they, as citizens, could no longer be kept defenseless by a regime of state law denying them the common right to keep and bear arms.[37]

Indeed, even in the 1960s much of the increased regulation of firearms stemmed from the fear generated by Black Panthers who openly carried guns.

Alexis Herman, the current Secretary of Labor, experienced firsthand the physical risks of growing up black in Alabama. Describing her difficult confirmation hearings, an Associated Press story included the following story:

> Anyone who thought the frustrations of waiting for confirmation would discourage her knew nothing about the lessons Herman learned from her father. They forgot that he sued to integrate the Democratic Party in Alabama, and later became the state's first black ward leader. They never heard about the night he put a pistol in his young daughter's hands and stepped out of the car to confront the Ku Klux Klan.
>
> "He taught me that you have to face adversity. He taught me to stand by my principles," Herman said in the interview. "He also taught me how to work within the system for change."
>
> Herman said her father never raised his voice, but he always kept a small silver pistol under the driver's seat of his DeSoto as he drove from community meeting to community meeting around Mobile. She always sat close by his side, unless the pistol was out. "The only way that I ever knew trouble was around was that the gun would come out from under the driver's seat and he'd put it by his side," she said.
>
> As they left the home of a minister one Christmas Eve, the pistol was on the car seat. She was 5. "It was a dark road, a dirt road to get back to the main highway," she recalled. "We were driven off the road by another car, and they were Klansmen."
>
> She hid on the floor and her father pressed the pistol's white handle into her palm. "He told me, 'If anybody opens this door, I want you to pull this trigger.' " He locked the door behind him and walked ahead to keep them away from the car. She crouched in the dark, listening until the shouts and scuffling died down.
>
> Eventually, the minister came to the car to drive Herman home. Her father, who had been beaten, rode in another car.[38]

Recently, after testifying before the Illinois state House of Representatives on whether to pass a concealed-handgun bill, I was approached by a black representative from Chicago who supported the bill.[39] He told me that, at least for Illinois, he was not surprised by my finding that areas with large minority populations gained the most from these laws. Noting the high rate at which young, black males are stopped by police and the fact that it is currently a felony to possess a concealed handgun, he said that an honest, law-abiding, young, black male would be "nuts" to carry a concealed handgun in Illinois. He mentioned a case that had occurred just a week earlier: Alonzo Spellman—a black professional football player for the Chicago Bears—had been arrested in Chicago after a routine traffic violation revealed that he had a handgun in his car.[40] Noting the inability of the police to protect people in heavily black areas when "bad guys" already had illegal guns, the representative said he believed that the current power imbalance between law-abiding people and criminals was greatest in black areas.

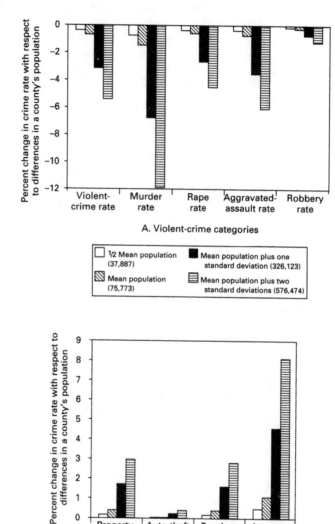

A. Violent-crime categories

B. Property-crime categories

Figure 1.   Do larger changes in crime rates from nondiscretionary concealed-handgun laws occur in more populous counties?

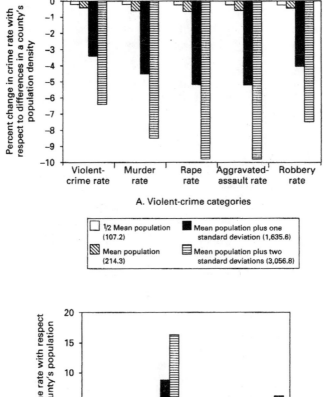

A. Violent-crime categories

| ☐ ½ Mean population (107.2) | ■ Mean population plus one standard deviation (1,635.6) |
| ▨ Mean population (214.3) | ▤ Mean population plus two standard deviations (3,056.8) |

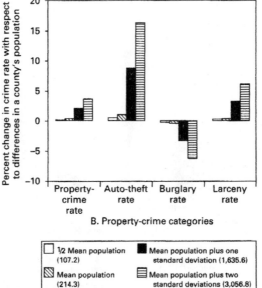

B. Property-crime categories

| ☐ ½ Mean population (107.2) | ■ Mean population plus one standard deviation (1,635.6) |
| ▨ Mean population (214.3) | ▤ Mean population plus two standard deviations (3,056.8) |

Figure 2.   Do larger changes in crime rates from nondiscretionary concealed-handgun laws occur in more densely populated counties?

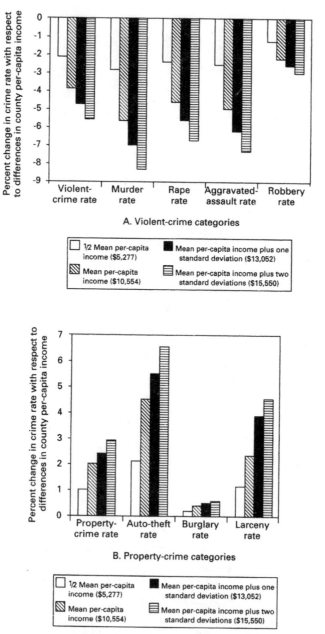

A. Violent-crime categories

□ ½ Mean per-capita income ($5,277)

■ Mean per-capita income plus one standard deviation ($13,052)

▨ Mean per-capita income ($10,554)

▤ Mean per-capita income plus two standard deviations ($15,550)

B. Property-crime categories

□ ½ Mean per-capita income ($5,277)

■ Mean per-capita income plus one standard deviation ($13,052)

▨ Mean per-capita income ($10,554)

▤ Mean per-capita income plus two standard deviations ($15,550)

Figure 3. How does the change in crime from nondiscretionary concealed-handgun laws vary with county per-capita income?

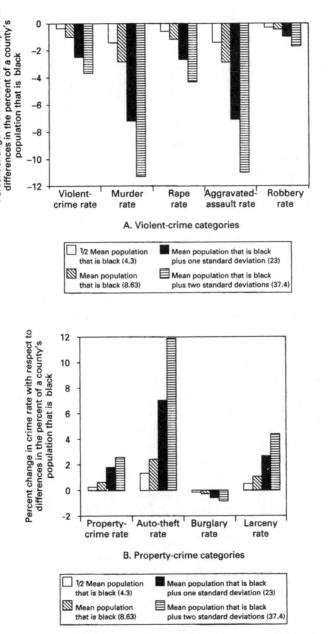

A. Violent-crime categories

| ☐ 1/2 Mean population that is black (4.3) | ■ Mean population that is black plus one standard deviation (23) |
| ▨ Mean population that is black (8.63) | ▤ Mean population that is black plus two standard deviations (37.4) |

B. Property-crime categories

| ☐ 1/2 Mean population that is black (4.3) | ■ Mean population that is black plus one standard deviation (23) |
| ▨ Mean population that is black (8.63) | ▤ Mean population that is black plus two standard deviations (37.4) |

Figure 4.   How does the change in crime from nondiscretionary concealed-handgun laws vary with the percent of a county's population that is black?

Perhaps it is not too surprising that blacks and those living in urban areas gain the most from being able to defend themselves with concealed handguns, since the absence of police appears most acute in black, central-city neighborhoods. Until 1983, the American Housing Survey annually asked sixty thousand households whether their neighborhoods had adequate police protection. Black, central-city residents were about twice as likely as whites generally to report that they did not have adequate protection, and six times more likely to say that they had considered moving because of an insufficient police presence in their neighborhoods.[41]

These results should at least give pause to the recent rush in California to pass city ordinances and state laws banning low-cost, Saturday night specials. Indeed, the results have implications for many gun control rules that raise gun prices. Law-abiding minorities in the most crimeprone areas produced the greatest crime reductions from being able to defend themselves. Unfortunately, however unintentionally, California's new laws risk disarming precisely these poor minorities.

Using Other Crime Rates to Explain the Changes in the Crime Rates Being Studied

Other questions still exist regarding the specifications employed here. Admittedly, although arrest rates and average differences in individual counties are controlled for, more can be done to account for the changing environments that determine the level of crime. One method is to use changes in other crime rates to help us understand why the crime rates that we are studying are changing over time. Table 5 reruns the specifications used to generate figure 1A but includes either the burglary or robbery rates as proxies for other changes in the criminal justice system. Robbery and burglary are the violent- and property-crime categories that are the least related to changes in concealed-handgun laws, but they still tend to move up and down together with all the other types of crimes.[42]

Some evidence that burglary or robbery rates will measure other changes in the criminal justice system or other omitted factors that explain changing crime rates can be seen in their correlations with other crime categories. Indeed, the robbery and burglary rates are very highly correlated with the other crime rates.[43] The two sets of specifications reported in table 5 closely bound the earlier estimates, and the estimates continue to imply that the introduction of concealed-handgun laws coincided with similarly large drops in violent crimes and increases in property crimes. These results differ from the preceding results in that the nondiscretionary laws are not significant related to robberies. The estimates on the other control variables also remain essentially unchanged.[44]

Crime: Changes in Levels Versus Changes in Trends

The preceding results in this chapter examined whether the average crime rate fell after the nondiscretionary laws went into effect. If changes in the law affect

Table 5. Using crime rates that are relatively unrelated to changes in nondiscretionary laws as a method of controlling for other changes in the legal environment: controlling for robbery and burglary rates

Change in explanatory variable	Percent change in various crime rates for changes in explanatory variables								
	Violent crime	Murder	Rape	Aggravated assault	Robbery	Property crime	Burglary	Larceny	Auto theft
	Controlling for robbery rates								
Nondiscretionary law adopted multiplied by county population (evaluated at mean country population)	−2.6%* 1%	−4.3%* 1.1%	−1.9%* 0.4%	−2.6% 0.4%	—	−1.4%* 0.5%	0.08% 0.04%	1.3%* 0.4%	3.7% 0.5%
Arrest rate for the crime category increased by 100 percentage points	−0.038%* 7%	−0.13%* 7%	−0.07%* 4%	−0.08%* 8%	—	−0.06%* 8%	−0.20%* 9%	−0.015%* 3%	−0.014%* 2%
	Controlling for burglary rates								
Change in explanatory variable	Violent crime	Murder	Rape	Aggravated assault	Robbery	Property crime	Burglary	Larceny	Auto theft
Nondiscretionary law adopted multiplied by county population (evaluated at mean country population)	−2.4%* 1%	−4.3%* 1.1%	−2.0%* 0.4%	−2.6% 0.4%	0.4% 0.04%	1.8%* 0.7%	—	1.4%* 0.4%	3.6% 0.5%
Arrest rate for the crime category increased by 100 percentage points	−0.026%* 5%	−0.13%* 6%	−0.05%* 3%	−0.05%* 5%	−0.043* 3%	−0.06%* 8%	—	−0.01%* 2%	−0.01%* 2%

Note: While not all the coefficient estimates are reported, all the control variables are the same as those used in table 1, including year and country dummies. All regressions use weighted least squares, where the weighting is each country's population. Net violent and property-crime rates are respectively net of robbery and burglary rates to avoid producing any artificial collinearity. Likewise, the arrest rates for those values omit the portion of the corresponding arrest rates due to arrests for robbergy and burglarly. While not reported, the coefficients for the robbery and burglary rates were extremely statistically significant and positive. Entire sample used over the 1977 to 1992 period.
   *The result is statistically significant at the 1 percent level for a two-tailed t-test.

behavior with a lag, changes in the trend are probably more relevant; therefore, a more important question is, How has the crime trend changed with the change in laws? Examining whether there is a change in levels or a change in whether the crime rate is rising or falling could yield very different results. For example, if the crime rate was rising right up until the law was adopted but falling thereafter, some values that appeared while crime rate was rising could equal some that appeared as it was falling. In other words, deceptively similar levels can represent dramatically different trends over time.

I used several methods to examine changes in the trends exhibited over time in crime rates. First, I reestimated the regressions in table 1, using year-to-year changes on all explanatory variables (see table 6). These regressions were run using both a variable that equals I when a nondiscretionary law is in effect as well as the change in that variable (called "differencing" the variable) to see if the initial passage of the law had an impact. The results consistently indicate that the law lowered the rates of violent crime, rape, and aggravated assault. Nondiscre-

Table 6. Results of rerunning the regressions on differences

Exogenous variables	Δln(violent-crime rate)	Δln (Murder rate)	Δln (Rape rate)	Δln(Aggravated assault rate)	Δln (Robbery rate)	Δln(Property crime rate)	Δln (Burglary rate)	Δln (Larceny rate)	Δln(Auto-theft rate)
	Percent change in various crime rates for changes in explanatory variables								
	All variables except for the nondiscretionary dummy differentiated								
Nondiscretionary law adopted	−2.2%***	−2.6%	−5.2%*	−4.6%	−3.3%****	5.2%*	3.5%*	5.2%*	12.8%*
First differences in the arrest rate for the crime category	−0.05%*	−0.15%*	−0.09%*	−0.09%*	−0.06%*	−0.08%*	−0.24%*	−0.02%*	−0.02%*
	All variables differenced								
First differences in the dummy for nondiscretionary law adopted ·	−2.7%*	−3.6%***	−3.9%*	−5.4%*	−0.7%	−4.8%*	0.7%	6.2%*	−24.2%*
First differences in the arrest rate for the crime category	−0.05%*	−0.15%*	−0.09%*	−0.09%*	−0.06%*	−0.08%*	−.24%*	−0.02%*	−0.02%*

Note: The variables for income; population; race, sex, and age of the population; and density are all in terms of first differences. While not all the coefficient estimates are reported, all the control variables used in table 1 are used here, including year and county dummies. All regressions use weighted least squares, where the weighting is each county's population. Entire sample used over the 1977 to 1992 period.
*The result is statistically significant at the 1 percent level for a two-tailed t-test.
***The result is statistically significant at the 10 percent level for a two-tailed t-test.
****The result is statistically significant at the 11 percent level for a two-tailed t-test.

tionary laws discourage murder in both specifications, but the effect is only statistically significant when the nondiscretionary variable is also differenced. The property-crime results are in line with those of earlier tables, showing that nondiscretionary laws produce increases in property crime. Violent crimes decreased by an average of about 2 percent annually, whereas property crimes increased by an average of about 5 percent.

As one might expect, the nondiscretionary laws affected crime immediately, with an additional change spread out over time. Why would the entire effect not be immediate? An obvious explanation is that not everyone who would eventually obtain a permit to carry a concealed handgun did so right away. For instance, as shown by the data in table 7, the number of permits granted in Florida, Oregon, and Pennsylvania was still increasing substantially long after the nondiscretionary law was put into effect. Florida's law was passed in 1987, Oregon's in 1990, and Pennsylvania's in 1989.

Reestimating the regression results from table 1 to account for different time trends in the crime rates before and after the passage of the law provides consistent strong evidence that the deterrent impact of concealed handguns increases with time. For most violent crimes, the time trend prior to the passage of the law indicates that crime was rising. The results using the simple time trends for these violent-crime categories are reported in table 8. Figures 5

Table 7. Permits granted by state: Florida, Oregon, and Pennsylvania

Year	Florida	Oregon	Pennsylvania
1987	17,000[a]	N.A.	N.A.
1988	33,451	N.A.	267,335[c]
1989	51,335	N.A.	314,925
1990	65,636	N.A.	360,649
1991	67,043	N.A.	399,428
1992	75,578	22,197[b]	360,919
1993	95,187	32,049	426,011
1994	134,008	43,216	492,421
1995	163,757	65,394	571,208
1996	192,016	78,258	N.A.

[a]Estimate of the number of concealed-handgun permits issued immediately before Florida's law went into effect from David McDowall, Colin Loftin, and Brian Wiersema, "Easing Concealed Firearms Laws: Effects on Homicide in Three States," *Journal of Criminal Law and Criminology* 86 (fall 1995): 194.
[b]December 31, 1991.
[c]Number of permits issued under discretionary law.

through 9 illustrate how the violent-crime rate varies before and after the implementation of nondiscretionary concealed-handgun laws when both the linear and squared time trends are employed. Comparing the slopes of the crime trends before and after the enactment of the laws shows that the trends become more negative to a degree that is statistically significant after the laws were passed.[45]

These results answer another possible objection: whether the findings are simply a result of so-called crime cycles. Crime rates rise or fall over time. If concealed-handgun laws were adopted at the peaks of these cycles (say, because concern over crime is great), the ensuing decline in crime might have occurred anyway without any help from the new laws. To deal with this, I controlled not only for national crime patterns but also for individual county patterns by employing burglary or robbery rates to explain the movement in the other crime rates. I even tried to control for individual state trends. Yet the simplest way of concisely illustrating that my results are not merely a product of the "normal" ups and downs in crime rates is to look again at the graphs in figures 5 to 9. With the exception of aggravated assault, the drops not only begin right when the laws pass but also take the crime rates well below what they had been before the passage of the laws. It is difficult to believe that, on the average, state legislatures could have timed the passage of these laws so accurately as to coincide with the peaks of crime waves; nor can the resulting declines be explained simply as reversions to normal levels.

Table 8. Change in time trends for crime rates before and after the adoption of nondiscretionary laws

Change in explanatory variable	Percent change in various crime rates for changes in explanatory variables								
	Violent crime	Murder	Rape	Aggravated assault	Robbery	Property crime	Auto theft	Burglary	Larceny
Change in crime rate from the difference in the annual change in crime rates in the years before and after the change in the law (annual rate after the law —annual rate before the law)	–0.9%*	–3%*	–1.4%*	–0.5%*	–2.7%*	–0.6%*	–0.3%**	–1.5%*	–0.1%

Note: The control variables are the same as those used in table 1, including year and county dummies, though they are not reported, because the coefficient estimates are very similar to those reported earlier. All regressions use weighted least squares, where the weighting is each county's population. Entire sample used over the 1977 to 1992 period.
*The result is statistically significant at the 1 percent level for a two-tailed t-test.
**The result is statistically significant at the 5 percent level for a two-tailed t-test.

Was the Impact of Nondiscretionary Concealed Handgun Laws the Same Everywhere?

Just as we found that the impact of nondiscretionary laws changed over time, we expect to find differences across states. The reason is the same in both cases: deterrence increases with the number of permits. While the information obtained from state government officials only pertained to why permits were issued at different rates across counties within a given state, the rate at which new permits are issued at the state level may also vary based upon population and population density. If this is true, then it should be possible to explain the differential effect that nondiscretionary laws have on crime in each of the states that passed such laws in the same way that we examined differences across counties.

Table 9 reexamines my earlier regressions, where I took into account that concealed-handgun laws have different effects across counties, depending upon how lenient officials had been in issuing permits under a previously discretionary system. The one change from earlier tables is that a different coefficient is used for the counties in each of the ten states that changed their laws during the 1977 to 1992 period. At least for violent crimes, the results indicate a very consistent effect of nondiscretionary concealed-handgun laws across states. Nine of the ten states experienced declines in violent-crime rates as a result of these laws, and eight of the ten states experienced declines in murder rates; in the states where violent crimes, murders, or robberies rose, the increases were very small. In fact, the largest increases were smaller than the smallest declines in the states where those crime rates fell.

Generally, the states with the largest decreases in any one category tended to have relatively large decreases across all the violent-crime categories, although the "leader" in each category varied across all the violent-crime categories.[46] Likewise, the states with relatively small crime decreases (for example, Georgia,

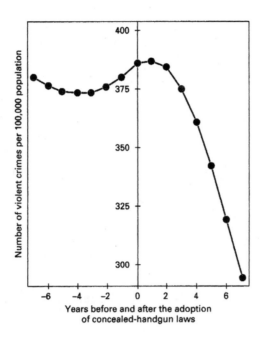

Figure 5. The effect of concealed-handgun laws on violent crimes

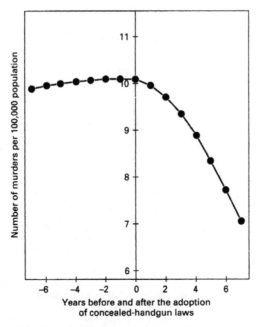

Figure 6. The effect of concealed-handgun laws on murders

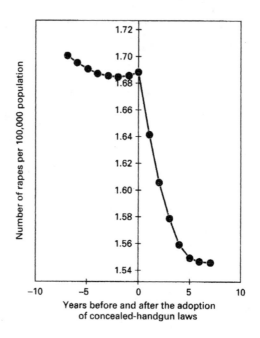

Figure 7. The effect of concealed-handgun laws on rapes

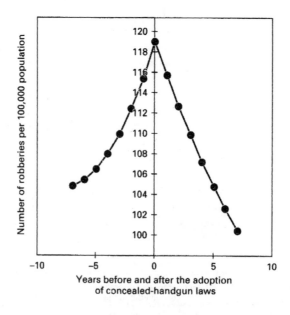

Figure 8. The effect of concealed-handgun laws on robbery rates

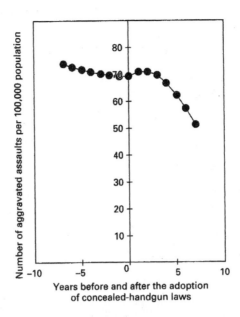

Figure 9. The effect of concealed-handgun laws on aggravated assaults

Oregon, Pennsylvania, and Virginia) tended to exhibit little change across all the categories.

Property crimes, on the other hand, exhibited no clear pattern. Property crimes fell in five states and increased in five states, and the size of any decrease or increase was quite small and unsystematic.

Ideally, any comparison across states would be based on changes in the number of permits issued rather than simply the enactment of the nondiscretionary law. States with the largest increases in permits should show the largest decreases in crime rates. Unfortunately, only a few states have recorded time-series data on the number of permits issued. . . . It is still useful to see whether the patterns in crime-rate changes found earlier across counties are also found across states. In particular, we would like to know whether the largest declines occurred in states with the largest or most dense populations, which we believed had the greatest increase in permits. The justification for the county-level differences was very strong because it was based on conversations with individual state officials, but those officials were not asked to make judgments across states (nor was it likely that they could do so). Further, there is much more heterogeneity across counties, and a greater number of observations. The relationship posited earlier for county populations also seems particularly tenuous when dealing with state-level data because a state with a large population could be made up of a large number of counties with small populations.

With this list of reservations in mind, let us look at the results we get by using state-level density data. Table 10 provides the results with respect to population

Table 9. State-specific impact of nondiscretionary concealed-handgun laws

	Violent crime	Murder	Rape	Aggravated assault	Robbery	Property crime	Auto theft	Burglary	Larceny
Florida	− 4 %	−10 %	− 8 %	− 4 %	0.3%	1 %	2 %	−0.3%	2 %
Georgia	− 0.2	− 2	0.5	− 0.2	0	1	1	1	1
Idaho	− 3	− 1	0.1	− 3	− 7	− 1	− 3	− 3	− 1
Maine	−17	− 5	1	−24	− 8	1	− 4	− 2	2
Mississippi	− 3	0.6	3	− 8	0	− 0.2	3	2	− 1
Montana	−10	− 5	−10	−12	− 6	− 4	− 5	5	− 4
Oregon	− 3	− 1	− 1	− 3	− 4	− 2	3	− 4	− 2
Pennsylvania	− 1	− 3	− 1	1	− 2	1	3	− 1	3
Virginia	− 2	1	− 1	− 2	− 2	− 1	− 2	− 2	− 1
West Virginia	− 1	11	− 5	− 1	1	3	0	4	2
Summary of the coeffieients' signs									
Negative	9	8	6	9	6	5	4	5	5
Positive	1	2	4	1	4	5	6	5	5

Note: The table uses arrest rates adjusted for counties wherein the adoption of nondiscreationary concealed-handgun laws was most likely to represent a real change from past practice by multiplying the nondiscretionary-law variables by the population in each country. The percents are evaluated at the mean county population.

density, and we find that, just as in the case of counties, larger declines in crime were recorded in the most densely populated states. The differences are quite large: the most densely populated states experienced decreases in violent crimes that were about three times greater than the decreases in states with the average density. The results were similar when state populations were taken into account.

Other Gun Control Laws and Different Types of Concealed-Handgun Laws

Two common restrictions on handguns arise from (1) increased sentencing penalties for crimes involving the use of a gun and (2) waiting periods required before a citizen can obtain a permit for a gun. How did these two types of laws affect crime rates? Could it be that these laws—rather than concealed-handgun laws—explain the deterrent effects? To answer this question, I reestimated the regressions in tables 1 and 3 by (1) adding a variable to control for state laws that increase sentencing penalties when crimes involve guns and (2) adding variables to measure the impact of waiting periods.[47] It is not clear whether adding an extra day to a waiting period had much of an effect; therefore, I included a variable for when the waiting period went into effect along with variables for the length of the waiting period in days and the length in days squared to pick up any differential impact from longer lengths. In both sets of regressions, the variable for nondiscretionary concealed-handgun laws remains generally consistent with the earlier results.[48] While the coefficients for arrest rates are not reported here, they also remain very similar to those shown previously.

So what about these other gun laws? The pattern that emerges from table 11 is much more ambiguous. The results for county-level data suggest that harsher

Table 10. Effects of concealed-handgun laws across states
related to differences in state population density

State population density	Violent crime	Murder	Rape	Aggravated assault	Robbery	Property crime	Auto theft	Burglary	Larceny
½ Mean 179 per square mile	− 2.7%	− 3.2%	− 5%	−1%	− 7 %	−1%	3%	− 5%	1%
Mean 358 per square mile	− 5.4	− 6.3	−10	−2	−14	−1	6	−10	2
Plus 1 standard deviation 778 per square mile	−11.8	−13.7	−21	−4	−29	−3	12	−22	4
Plus 2 standard deviations 1,197 per square mile	−18.2	−21.1	−32	−5	−45	−5	19	−33	7

Note: The The regressions used for this table multiplied the variable for whether the law was enacted by that state's population density. The control variables used to generate these estimates are the same as those used in table 1, including year and county dummies, though they are not reported, because the coefficient estimates are very similar to those reported earlier. All regressions use weighted least squares, where the weighting is each state's population.

sentences for the use of deadly weapons reduce violent crimes, especially crimes of aggravated assault and robbery. While the same county-level data frequently imply an impact on murder, rape, aggravated assault, and robbery, the effects are quite inconsistent. For example, simply requiring the waiting period appears to raise murder and rape rates but lower the rates for aggravated assault and robbery. The lengths of waiting periods also result in inconsistent patterns: longer periods at first lower and then raise the murder and rape rates, with the reverse occurring for aggravated assault. Using state-level data fails to confirm any statistically significant effects for the violent-crime categories. First, it reveals no statistically significant or economically consistent relationship between either the presence of waiting periods or their length and violent-crime rates. The directions of the effects also differ from those found using county data. Taken together, the results make it very difficult to argue that waiting periods (particularly long ones) have an overall beneficial effect on crime rates. In addition, one other finding is clear: laws involving sentence length and waiting periods do not alter my earlier findings with respect to nondiscretionary laws; that is, the earlier results for nondiscretionary laws cannot merely be reflecting the impact of other gun laws.

The Importance of the Types of Concealed Handgun Laws Adopted: Training and Age Requirements

Finally, we need to consider how concealed-handgun laws vary across states and whether the exact rules matter much. Several obvious differences exist: whether a training period is required, and if so, how long that period is; whether any minimum age limits are imposed; the number of years for which the permit is valid; where people are allowed to carry the gun (for example, whether schools, bars, and government buildings are excluded); residency requirements; and how much the permit costs. Six of these characteristics are reported in table 12 for the thirty-one states with nondiscretionary laws.

Table 11. Controlling for other gun laws

Exogenous variables	Violent crime	Murder	Rape	Aggravated assault	Robbery	Property crime	Burglary	Larceny	Auto theft
	County-level regressions								
Nondiscretionary law adopted	−4.2%*	−8.6%*	−6%	−5.5%*	−2%	−3.6%*	1%	−4.5%	8.2%
Enhanced sentencing law adopted	−4%	−0.3%	−1.1%	−1.5%***	−2.9%***	−0.001%	−2%	−1.2%***	−1.8%**
Waiting law adopted	−2.3%	23%*	25%*	−9.4%**	−9%***	2%	2%	−0.3%	−8%
Percent change in crime by increasing the waiting period by one day: linear effect	−0.08%	−9.4%*	−13.6%*	−6.5%*	−11%*	−1.5%***	−4.5%*	1.2%	−1%
Percent change in crime by increasing the waiting period by one day: squared effect	−0.08%	−0.55%*	0.8%*	−0.5%*	0.73%*	0.019%	0.23%*	−0.17%*	0.099%
	State-level regressions								
Nondiscretionary law adopted	−10.1%*	−8.1%**	−5.7%***	−10.2%*	−13.3%*	−3.4%	−7.6%*	−2.2%	−1%
Enhanced sentencing law adopted	3.5%	3%	3%	−2.8%	1%	3%***	−0.5%	3.7%**	2%
Waiting law adopted	10%	6.8%	22%*	−2.6%	15%	3.3%	6.5%	2.3%	−3.1%
Percent change in crime by increasing the waiting period by one day: linear effect	−3%	−3%	−10%*	−06.5%	−10%**	−0.95	−2.2%	−0.53%	−2.4%
Percent change in crime by increasing the waiting period by one day: squared effect	0.12%	−0.13%	0.13%	−0.041%	0.59%**	0.021%	0.05%	−0.06%	−0.25%

Note: The control variables are the same as those used in table 1, including year and county dummies, though they are not reported, because the coefficient estimates are very similar to those reported earlier. All regressions use weighted least squares, where the weighting is each state's population.

*The result is statistically significant at the 1 percent level for a two-tailed t-test.

**The result is statistically significant at the 5 percent level for a two-tailed t-test.

***The result is statistically significant at the 10 percent level for a two-tailed t-test.

A major issue in legislative debates on concealed-handgun laws is whether citizens will receive sufficient training to cope with situations that can require difficult, split-second decisions. Steve Grabowski, president of the Nebraska state chapter of the Fraternal Order of Police, notes that "police training is much more extensive than that required for concealed-handgun permits. The few hours of firearms instruction won't prepare a citizen to use the gun efficiently in a stress situation, which is a challenge even for professionals."[49] Others respond that significantly more training is required to use a gun offensively, as a police officer may be called on to do, than defensively. Law-abiding citizens appear reticent to use their guns and, as noted earlier, in the majority of cases simply brandishing the gun is sufficient to deter an attack.

Reestimating the earlier regressions, I included measures for whether a training period was required, for the length of the training period, and for the

Table 12. Current characteristics of different nondiscretionary concealed-handgun laws

State with nondiscretionary law	Last significant modification	Permit duration (years)	Training length (hours)	Age Requirement	Initial Fee	Renewal fee	Issuing Agency
Alabama	1936	1	None	21	$15–25	$6	Sheriff
Alaska	1994	5	12	21	$123	$57	Dept. of Public Safety
Arizona	1995	4	16	21	$50	?	Dept. of Public Safety
Arkansas	1995	4	5	21	$100	?	State Police
Connecticut	1986	5	5	21	$35	$35	State Police
Florida	1995	3	5	21	$85	$70	Dept. of State
Georgia	1996	5	None	21	$32		Judge of Probate Court
Idaho	1996	4	7	21	$56	$24	Sheriff
Indiana	1980	4	None	18	$25	$15	Chief of Police or Sheriff
Kentucky	1996	3	8 hrs classroom + firing range training	21	$60	$60	Sheriff
Louisiana	1996	4	9[a]	21	$100	?	Dept. of Public Safety
Maine	1985	4	5	21	$35	$20	Chief of Police or Sheriff
Mississippi	1990	4	None	21	$100	$50	Dept. of Public Safety
Montana	1991	4	None	18	$50	$25	Sheriff
Nevada	1995	5		21	$60	$25	Sheriff
New Hampshire	1923	2	None	21	$4		Chief of Police or Sheriff
North Carolina	1995	4	5	21	$90	$80	Sheriff
North Dakota	1985	3	None	21	$25		Bureau of Criminal Investigation
Oklahoma	1995	4	8	23	$125	$125	State Bureau of Criminal Investigation
Oregon	1993	4	5	21	$65	$50	Sheriff
Pennsylvania	1995	5	None	21	$17.50	$17.50	Chief of Police or Sheriff
South Carolina	1996	4		21	$50	$50	State Law Enforcement Division
South Dakota	1986	4	None	18	$6		Chief of Police or Sheriff
Tennessee	1996	4		21	$100		Dept. of Public Safety
Texas	1995	4	10–15	21	$140[b]	Set by dept.	Dept. of Public Safety
Utah	1995	2		21	$64		Dept. of Public Safety
Vermont (unregulated)	None	None	None	None	None	None	None
Virginia	1995	2	5	21	<$50	<$50	Clerk of Circuit Court
Washington	1995	5	None	21	$36 + 24 FBI fee	$33	Judge; Chief of Police, or Sheriff
West Virginia	1996	5	5	18	$50	$50	Sheriff
Wyoming	1994	5	–5	21	$50	$50	Attorney General

[a]This training period is waived for those who receive a permit directly from their local sheriff.
[b]The fee is reduced to $70 for those who are over 60 years of age.

age limit.[50] The presence or length of the training periods typically show no effect on crime, and although the effects are significant for robbery, the size of the effect is very small. On the other hand, age limits display quite different and statistically significant coefficients for different crimes. The twenty-one-year-old age limit appears to lower murder rates, but it tends to reduce the decline in rape and overall violent-crime rates that is normally associated with nondiscretionary concealed-handgun laws. Because of these different effects, it is difficult to draw firm conclusions regarding the effect of age limits.

Table 13. Earlier results reexamined using additional data for 1993 and 1994

Change in explanatory variable	Percent change in various crime rates for changes in explanatory variables				
	Violent crime	Murder	Rape	Aggravated assault	Robbery
Section A: Nondiscretionary law adopted	−4.4%*	−10.0%*	−3.0%*	−5.7%*	0.6%
Section B: The difference in the annual change in crime rates in the years before and after the change in the law (annual rate after the law minus annual rate before the law)	−0.5%*	−2.9%*	−1.7%*	−0.3%*	−2.2%
Section C: Brady law adopted	3%	−2.3%	3.9%**	3.7%**	−3.9%

Note: This table uses county-level, violent-crime data from the Uniform Crime Report that were not available until the rest of the book was written. Here I was not able to control for all the variables used in table 1. All regressions use weighted least squares, where the weighting is each county's population. Section C also controls for the other variables that were included in table 11 to account for changes in other gun laws. Section A corresponds to the regressions in table 1, section B to those in table 8, and section C to those in table 11, except that a dummy variable for the Brady law was added for those states that did not previously have at least a five-day waiting period.

*The result is statistically significant at the 1 percent level for a two-tailed t-test.
**The result is statistically significant at the 10 percent level for a two-tailed t-test.

Recent Data On Crime Rates

After I originally put the data together for this study . . . additional county-level data became available for 1993 and 1994 from the FBI's Uniform Crime Reports. These data allow us to evaluate the impact of the Brady law, which went into effect in 1994. They also allow us to doublecheck whether the results shown earlier were mere aberrations.

Table 13 reexamines the results from tables 1, 8, and 11 with these new data, and the findings are generally very similar to those already reported. The results in section A that correspond to table 4.1 imply an even larger drop in murder rates related to the passage of concealed-handgun laws (10 percent versus 7.7 percent previously), though the declines in the rates for overall violent crime as well as rape and aggravated assault are smaller. Robbery is also no longer statistically significant, and the point estimate is even positive. Given the inverted V shape of crime-rate trends over time, comparing the average crime rates before and after the passage of these laws is not enough, since crime rates that are rising before the law and falling afterward can produce similar average crime rates in the two periods. To deal with this, section B of table 13 corresponds to the results reported earlier in table 8. The estimates are again quite similar to those reported earlier. The effect on rape is larger than those previously reported, while the effects for aggravated assault and robbery are somewhat smaller. All the results indicate that concealed-handgun laws reduce crime, and all the findings are statistically significant.

Finally, section C of table 13 provides some very interesting estimates of the Brady law's impact by using a variable that equals 1 only for those states that did not previously have at least a five-day waiting period. The claims about the criminals who have been denied access to guns as a result of this law are not necessarily evidence that the Brady law lowers crime rates. Unfortunately, these claims tell us nothing about whether criminals are ultimately able to obtain guns illegally. In addition, to the extent that law-abiding citizens find it more difficult to obtain guns, they may be less able to defend themselves. For example, a woman who is being stalked may no longer be able to obtain a gun quickly to scare off an attacker. Numerous newspaper accounts tell of women who were attempting to buy guns because of threats by former lovers and were murdered or raped during the required waiting period.[51]

The evidence from 1994 indicates that the Brady law has been associated with significant increases in rapes and aggravated assaults, and the declines in murder and robbery have been statistically insignificant. All the other gun-control laws examined in table 11 were also controlled for here, but because their estimated impacts were essentially unchanged, they are not reported.

What Happens to Neighboring Counties in Adjacent States When Nondiscretionary Handgun Laws Are Adopted?

Up to this point we have asked what happens to crime rates in places that have adopted nondiscretionar. laws. If these laws do discourage criminals, however, they may react in several ways. We already have discussed two: criminals could stop committing crimes, or they could commit other, less dangerous crimes like those involving property, where the probability of contact with armed victims is low. A third possibility is that criminals may commit crimes in other areas where potential victims are not armed. A fourth outcome is also possible: eliminating crime in one area can help eliminate crime in other areas as well. This last outcome may occur if criminals had been using the county that adopted the law as a staging area. Crime-prone, poverty-stricken areas of cities may find that some of their crime spills over to adjacent areas.

This section seeks to test what effect concealed-handgun laws and higher arrest rates have on crime rates in adjacent counties in neighboring states. Since concealed-handgun laws are almost always passed at the state level, comparing adjacent counties in neighboring states allows us to examine the differential effect of concealed-handgun laws. Evidence that changes in a state's laws coincide with changes in crime rates in neighboring states will support the claim that the laws affect criminals. If these laws do not affect criminals, neighboring states should experience no changes in their crime rates.

Although any findings that nondiscretionary concealed-handgun laws cause criminals to leave the jurisdictions that adopt these laws would provide additional evidence of deterrence, such findings would also imply that simply looking at the direct effect of concealed-handgun laws on crime overestimates the total gain to society from these laws. In the extreme, if the entire reduction in crime from concealed-handgun laws was simply transferred to other areas, society as a whole would be no better off with these laws, even if individual jurisdictions benefited. While the evidence would confirm the importance of deterrence, adopting such a law in a single state might have a greater deterrent impact than if the entire nation adopted the law. The deterrent effect of adopting nondiscretionary concealed-handgun laws in additional states could also decline as more states adopted the laws.

To investigate these issues, I reran the regressions reported in table 1, using only those counties that were within fifty miles of counties in neighboring states. In addition to the variable that examines whether your own state has a nondiscretionary concealed-handgun law, I added three new variables. One variable averages the dummy variables for whether adjacent counties in neighboring counties have such laws. A second variable examines what happens when your county and your neighboring county adopt these laws. Finally, the neighboring counties' arrest rates are added, though I do not bother reporting them, because the evidence indicates that only the arrest rates in your own county, not your neighboring counties, matter in determining your crime rate.

The results reported in table 14 confirm that deterrent effects do spill over into neighboring areas. For all the violent-crime categories, adopting a concealed-handgun law reduces the number of violent crimes in your county, but these results also show that criminals who commit murder, rape, and robbery apparently move to adjacent states without the laws. The one violent-crime category that does not fit this pattern is aggravated assault: adopting a nondiscretionary concealed-handgun law lowers the number of aggravated assaults in neighboring counties. With respect to the benefits of all counties adopting the laws, the last column shows that all categories of violent crime are reduced the most when all counties adopt such laws. The results imply that murder rates decline by over 8 percent and aggravated assaults by around 21 percent when a county and its neighbors adopt concealed-handgun laws.

As a final test, I generated the figures showing crime trends before and after a neighbor's adoption of the law by the method previously used, in addition to the time trends for before and after one's own adoption of the concealed-handgun laws. The use of an additional squared term allows us to see if the effect on crime is not linear. . . . In all violent-crime categories, the adoption of concealed-handgun laws produces an immediate and large increase in violent-crime rates for neighboring counties, though unlike the direct effect of these laws on the crime rate in one's own county, the spillover effect in neighboring counties is relatively short-lived.

Overall, these results provide strong additional evidence for the deterrent effect of nondiscretionary concealed-handgun laws. They imply that the earlier estimate of the total social benefit from these laws may have overestimated the ini-

Table 14. Estimates of the impact of nondiscretionary concealed handgun laws on neighboring counties

	Percent change in own crime rate		
Type of crime	Own county has nondiscretionary law	Average neighbor has nondiscretionary law	Average neighbor and own county have nondiscretionary law
Violent crime	−5.5%	0	−5.7%
Murder	−7.6%	3.5%	−4.1%
Rape	−6.2%	6%	0
Robbery	−4%	2.8%	−1.1%
Aggravated assault	−7.4%	−3.3%	- 10.7%.
Property crime	1%	1%	2%
Auto theft	−1.3%	2%	3.4%
Burglary	1%	4.7%	−1%
Larceny	9%	−2%	10.8%

tial benefits, but underestimated the long-term benefits as more states adopt these laws. In the long run, the negative spillover effect subsides, and the adoption of these laws in all neighboring states has the greatest deterrent effect on crime.

Conclusions

The empirical work provides strong evidence that concealed-handgun laws reduce violent crime and that higher arrest rates deter all types of crime. The results confirm what law-enforcement officials have said—that nondiscretionary laws cause [the] greatest change in the number of permits issued for concealed handguns in the most populous, urbanized counties. This provides additional support for the claim that the greatest declines in crime rates are related to the greatest increases in concealed-handgun permits. The impact of concealed-handgun laws varies with a county's level of crime, its population and population density, its per capita income, and the percentage of the population that is black. Despite the opposition to these laws in large, urban, densely populated areas, those are the areas that benefit the most from the laws. Minorities and women tend to be the ones with the most to gain from being allowed to protect themselves.

Some of the broader issues concerning criminal deterrence were evaluated, and the hypotheses used produced information about the locations where increased police efforts had the most significant deterrent effects on crime. Splitting the data set into high-and low-crime counties shows that arrest rates do not affect crime rates equally in all counties: the greatest return to increasing arrest rates is in the most crime-prone areas.

The results also confirm some of the potential aggregation problems with state-level data. The county-level data explain about six times more variation in violent-crime rates and eight times more variation in property-crime rates than do state-level data. Generally, the effect of concealed-handgun laws on crime appeared much greater when state-level regressions were estimated. However, one conclusion is clear: the very different results for state and county-level data should make us very cautious in aggregating crime data. The differences in county characteristics show that dramatically greater differences exist among counties within any state than among different states. Whether increased arrest rates are concentrated in the highest-crime counties in a state or spread out equally across all counties makes a big difference in their impact on crime. Likewise, it is a mistake to think that concealed-handgun laws change crime rates in all counties in a state equally.

The three sets of estimates that rely on county-level data, state-level data, or county-level data that accounts for how the law affected different counties have their own strengths and weaknesses. While using countylevel data avoids the aggregation problems present with state-level data, the initial county-level regressions rely heavily on variation in state laws and thus are limited to comparing the variation in these fifty jurisdictions. If weight is thus given to any of the results, it would appear that the greatest weight should be given to the county-level regressions that interact the nondiscretionary-law variable with measures of how liberally different counties issued permits under the preexisting discretionary systems. These regressions not only avoid the aggregation problems but also take fullest advantage of the relationship between county-level variations in crime rates and the impact of nondiscretionary laws. They provide the strongest evidence that concealed-handgun laws reduce all types of crime. Despite these different approaches, one result is clear: the results are remarkably consistent with respect to the deterrent effect of nondiscretionary concealed-handgun laws on violent crime. Two of these three sets of estimates imply that concealed-handgun laws also result in lower property-crime rates, although these rates decline less than the rates for violent crimes.

This study represents a significant change in the general approach to crime studies. This is the first study to use cross-sectional time-series evidence at both the county and state levels. Instead of simply using either cross-sectional state- or city-level data, this study has made use of the much larger variations in arrest rates and crime rates between rural and urban areas, and it has been possible to control for whether the lower crime rates resulted from the gun laws themselves or from other differences in these areas (for example, low crime rates) that lead to the adoption of these laws.

THE POLITICAL PROCESS AND ACADEMIC DEBATE*

When my original study was released, many commentators were ready to attack it. Anyone who had shown any interest in looking at the article was given a copy

---

*From John Lott, *More Guns, Less Crime* (Chicago: University of Chicago Press, 1998), pp. 122–57. Reprinted with permission.

while I was in the process of revising it for the *Journal of Legal Studies*, although I quickly learned that it was not common practice to circulate studies to groups on both sides of the gun debate. Few comments were offered privately, but once the paper began to receive national press coverage, the attacks came very quickly.

Before the press coverage started, it was extremely difficult to get even a proponent of gun control to provide critical comments on the paper when I presented it at the Cato Institute in early August 1996. I approached twenty-two procontrol people before Jens Ludwig, a young assistant professor at Georgetown University, accepted my request to comment on the paper.

One of the more interesting experiences occurred when I asked Susan Glick, of the Violence Policy Center, to participate.[52] Glick, whom I called during June 1996, was one of the last people that I approached. She was unwilling to comment on my talk at Cato because she didn't want to "help give any publicity to the paper." Glick said that her appearance might help bring media attention to the paper that it wouldn't otherwise have gotten. When I pointed out that C-SPAN was likely to cover the event, she said she didn't care because "we can get good media whenever we want." When I asked her if I could at least send her a copy of the paper because I would appreciate any comments that she might have, she said, "Forget it, there is no way that I am going to look at it. Don't send it."[53]

However, when the publicity broke on the story with an article in *USA Today* on August 2, she was among the many people who left telephone messages immediately asking for a copy of the paper. In her case, the media were calling, and she "need[ed] [my] paper to be able to criticize it." Because of all the commotion that day, I was unable to get back to her right away. ABC National Television News was doing a story on my study for that day and when at around 3:00 P.M. the ABC reporter doing the story, Barry Serafin, called saying that certain objections had been raised about my paper, he mentioned that one of those who had criticized it was Ms. Glick. After talking to Mr. Serafin, I gave Glick a call to ask her if she still wanted a copy of my paper. She said that she wanted it sent to her right away and wondered if I could fax it to her. I then noted that her request seemed strange because I had just gotten off the telephone with Mr. Serafin at ABC News, who had told me that she had been very critical of the study, saying that it was "flawed." I asked how she could have said that there were flaws in the paper without even having looked at it yet. At that point Ms. Glick hung up the telephone.[54]

Many of the attacks from groups like Handgun Control, Inc. and the Violence Policy Center focused on claims that my study had been paid for by gun manufacturers or that the *Journal of Legal Studies* was not a peer-reviewed journal and that I had chosen to publish the study in a "student-edited journal" to avoid the close scrutiny that such a review would provide.[55] These attacks were completely false, and I believe that those making the charges knew them to be false. At least they had been told by all the relevant parties here at the University of Chicago and at the Olin Foundation that the funding issues were false, and the questions about publishing in a "student-edited journal" or one that was not peer reviewed were well known to be false because of the prominence of the journal. Some statements involved claims that my work was inferior to an earlier study by three criminologists at the University of Maryland who had examined five counties.

Other statements, like those in the *Los Angeles Times*, tried to discredit the scholarliness of the study by claiming that "in academic circles, meanwhile, scholars found it curious that he would publicize his findings before they were subjected to peer review."[56] In fact, the paper was reviewed and accepted months before media stories started discussing it in August 1996.

The attacks claiming that this work had been paid for by gun manufacturers have been unrelenting. Congressman Charles Schumer (D–N.Y.) wrote as follows in the *Wall Street Journal*: "I'd like to point out one other 'association.' The Associated Press reports that Prof. Lott's fellowship at the University of Chicago is funded by the Olin Foundation, which is 'associated with the Olin Corporation,' one of the nation's largest gun manufacturers. Maybe that's a coincidence, too. But it's also a fact."[57] Others were even more direct. In a letter that the Violence Policy Center mass-mailed to newspapers around the country, M. Kristen Rand, the center's federal policy director, wrote,

> Lott's work was, in essence, funded by the firearms industry—the primary beneficiary of increased handgun sales. Lott is the John M. Olin fellow at the University of Chicago law school, a position founded by the Olin Foundation. The foundation was established by John Olin of the Olin Corp., manufacturer of Winchester ammunition and maker of the infamous "Black Talon" bullet. Lott's study of concealed handgun laws is the product of gun-industry funding. . . . (See, as one of many examples, "Gun Industry Paid," *Omaha World Herald*, March 10, 1997, p. 8)[58]

Dan Kotowski, executive director of the Illinois Council Against Handgun Violence, said that "the study was biased because it was funded by the parent company of Winchester, Inc., a firearms manufacturer."[59] Kotowski is also quoted as saying that the claimed link between Winchester and my study's conclusions was "enough to call into question the study's legitimacy. It's more than a coincidence."[60] Similar claims have been made by employees of Handgun Control, Inc. and other gun control organizations.

Indeed, gun control groups that were unwilling to comment publicly on my study at the Cato Institute forum had time to arrange press conferences that were held exactly at the time that I was presenting my paper in Washington. Their claims were widely reported by the press in the initial news reports on my findings. A typical story stated that "Lott's academic position is funded by a grant from the Olin Foundation, which is associated with the Olin Corp. Olins Winchester division manufactures rifles and bullets,"[61] and it was covered in newspapers from the *Chicago Tribune* to the *Houston Chronicle* and the *Des Moines Register*, as well as in "highbrow" publications like the *National Journal*. The Associated Press released a partial correction stating that the Olin Foundation and Olin Corporation are separate organizations and that the Winchester subsidiary of the Olin Corporation makes ammunition, not guns, but a Nexis search of news stories revealed that only one newspaper in the entire country that had published the original report carried the Associated Press correction.[62]

Congressman Schumer's letter did produce a strong response from William Simon, the Olin Foundations president and former U.S. Secretary of the Treasury, in the *Wall Street Journal* for September 6, 1996:

An Insult to our Foundation

As president of the John M. Olin Foundation, I take great umbrage at Rep. Charles Schumer's scurrilous charge (Letters to the Editor, Sept. 4) that our foundation underwrites bogus research to advance the interests of companies that manufacture guns and ammunition. He asserts (falsely) that the John M. Olin Foundation is "associated" with the Olin Corp. and (falsely again) that the Olin Corp. is one of the nation's largest gun manufacturers. Mr. Schumer then suggests on the basis of these premises that Prof. John Lott's article on gun-control legislation (editorial page, Aug. 28) must have been fabricated because his research fellowship at the University of Chicago was funded by the John M. Olin Foundation.

This is an outrageous slander against our foundation, the Olin Corp., and the scholarly integrity of Prof. Lott. Mr. Schumer would have known that his charges were false if he had taken a little time to check his facts before rushing into print. Others have taken the trouble to do so. For example, Stephen Chapman of the *Chicago Trubune* looked into the charges surrounding Mr. Lotts study, and published an informative story in the Aug. 15 issue of that paper, which concluded that, in conducting his research, Prof. Lott was not influenced either by the John M. Olin Foundation or by the Olin Corp. Anyone wishing to comment on this controversy ought first to consult Mr. Chapman's article and, more importantly should follow his example of sifting the facts before reaching a conclusion. For readers of the journal, here are the key facts.

The John M. Olin Foundation, of which I have been president for nearly 20 years, is an independent foundation whose purpose is to support individuals and institutions working to strengthen the free enterprise system stem. We support academic programs at the finest institutions in the nation, including the University of Chicago, Harvard, Yale, Stanford, Columbia, the University of Virginia, and many others. We do not tell scholars what to write or what to say.

The foundation was created by the personal fortune of the late John M. Olin, and is not associated with the Olin Corp. The Olin Corp. has never sought to influence our deliberations. Our trustees have never taken into account the corporate interests of the Olin Corp. or any other company when reviewing grant proposals. We are as independent of the Olin Corp. as the Ford Foundation is of the Ford Motor Co.

The John M. Olin Foundation has supported for many years a program in law and economics at the University of Chicago Law School. This program is administered and directed by a committee of faculty members in the law school. This committee, after reviewing many applications in a very competitive process, awarded a research fellowship to Mr. Lott. We at the foundation had no knowledge of who applied for these fellowships, nor did we ever suggest that Mr. Lott should be awarded one of them. We did not commission his study, nor, indeed, did we even know of it until last month, when Mr. Lott presented his findings at a conference sponsored by a Washington think tank.

As a general rule, criticism of research studies should be based on factual grounds rather than on careless and irresponsible charges about the motives of the researcher. Mr. Lott's study should be evaluated on its own merits without imputing motives to him that do not exist. I urge Mr. Schumer to check his facts more carefully in the future.

Finally, it was incorrectly reported in the *Journal* (Sept. 5) that the John M. Olin Foundation is "headed by members of the family that founded the Olin Corp." This is untrue. The trustees and officers of the foundation have been selected by virtue of their devotion to John Olin's principles, not by virtue of family connections. Of our seven board members, only one is a member of the Olin family. None of our officers is a member of the Olin family—neither myself as president, nor our secretary-treasurer, nor our executive director.

This letter, I think, clarifies the funding issue, and I would only like to add that while the faculty at the law school chose to award me this fellowship, even they did not inquire into the specific research I planned to undertake.[63] The judgment was made solely on the quality and quantity of my past research, and while much of my work has dealt with crime, this was my first project involving gun control. No one other than myself had any idea what research I was planning to do. However, even if one somehow believed that Olin were trying to buy research, it must be getting a very poor return on its money. Given the hundreds of people at the different universities who have received the same type of fellowship, I have been the only one to work on the issue of gun control.

Unfortunately, as the quote from Ms. Rand's letter and statements by many other gun control advocates—made long after Simon's explanation—indicates, the facts about funding did little to curtail the comments of those spreading the false rumors.[64]

After these attacks on my funding, the gun control organizations brought up new issues. For example, during the spring of 1997 the Violence Policy Center sent out a press release entitled "Who Is John Lott?" that claimed, among other things, "Lott believes that some crime is good for society, that wealthy criminals should not be punished as harshly as poor convicts." I had in fact been arguing that "individuals guilty of the same crime should face the same expected level of punishment" and that with limited resources to fight crime, it is not possible to eliminate all of it.[65] I would have thought that most people would recognize these silly assertions for what they were, but they were picked up and republished by publications such as the *New Republic*.[66]

The aversion to honest public debate has been demonstrated to me over and over again since my study first received attention. Recently, for example, Randy Roth, a visiting colleague at the University of Chicago Law School, asked me to appear on a radio program that he does from the University of Hawaii on a public radio station. I had almost completely stopped doing radio interviews a few months before because they were too much of an interruption to my work, but Randy, whom I have known only very briefly from lunch-table conversation, seemed like a very interesting person, and I thought that it would be fun to do the show with him. I can only trust that he doesn't normally have as much trouble as he had this time in getting an opposing viewpoint for his program. In a note that Randy shared with me, he described a conversation that he had with Brandon Stone, of the Honolulu Police Department, whom he had been trying for a while to get to participate. Randy wrote as follows on March 3, 1997:

> Brandon called to say he had not changed his mind—he will not participate in any gun-control radio show involving John Lott. Furthermore, he said he had discussed this with all the others who are active in this area (the Hawaii Firearms Coalition, I think he called it), and that they have "banded together"—none will participate in such a show.
>
> He said he didn't want to "impugn" John's character . . . [and] then he went on to talk about all the money involved in this issue, the fact that [the] Olin Corp. is in the firearm business and financing John's chair, etc. He said John's study had been given to the media before experts first could discredit it, implying that this "tactic" was used because the study could not withstand the scrutiny of objective scholars.
>
> He said the ideas promoted by John's study are "fringe ideas" and that they are "dangerous." When I pointed out that such ideas not only have been publicly debated in other states, but that some of those states actually have enacted legislation, he basically just said that Hawaii is a special place and other states have sometimes been adversely affected by unfair tactics by the pro-gun lobby.
>
> I kept coming back to my belief that public debate is good and that my show would give him an opportunity to point out anything about John's study that he believes to be incorrect, irrelevant, distorted, or whatever. He kept saying that public debate does more harm than good when others misuse the forum. When he specifically mentions the firearm industry ("follow the money" was his suggestion, to understand what John's study is all about), I reminded him of John's association with the University of Chicago and his outstanding reputation, both for scholarship and integrity. He then said he realized John was "my friend," as though I couldn't be expected to be objective. He also said that John was "out of his field" in this area.
>
> My hunch is that its going to he extremely difficult finding a studio guest with the credentials and ability to do a good job on the pro-gun control side.
>
> After talking with Randy and in an attempt to create a balanced program, I also telephoned Mr. Stone. While we did not get into the detail that he went into with Randy, I did try to address his concerns over my funding and my own background in criminal justice as chief economist at the U.S. Sentencing Commission during the late 1980s. Stone also expressed his concerns to me that Hawaiians would not be best served by our debating the issue and that Hawaiians had already made up their minds on this topic. I said that he seemed like an articulate person and that it would be good to have a lively discussion on the

subject, but he said that the program "could only do more harm than good" and that any pro-gun-control participation would only lend "credibility" to the discussion.[67]

Before I did my original study, I would never have expected it to receive the attention that it did. None of the refereed journal articles that I have produced has received so much attention. Many people have told me that it was politically naive. That may be, but this much is clear: I never would have guessed how much people fear discussion of these issues. I never would have known how much effort goes into deliberately ignoring certain findings in order to deny them news coverage. Nor would I have seen, after news coverage did occur, how much energy goes into attacking the integrity of those who present such findings, with such slight reference—or no reference at all—to the actual merits of the research. I was also surprised by the absolute confidence shown by gun-control advocates that they could garner extensive news coverage whenever they wanted.

Criticisms of the Original Study

A second line of attack came from academic, quasi-academic, and gun control advocacy groups concerning the competence with which the study was conducted. Many of these objections were dealt with somewhere in the original study, which admittedly is very long. Yet it should have been easy enough for critics—especially academics—to check.

The attacks have been fairly harsh, especially by the standards of academic discourse. For example,

"They highlight things that support their hypothesis while they ignore things contrary to their hypothesis," said Daniel Webster, an assistant professor at Johns Hopkins University Center for Gun Policy and Research.

"We think the study falls far short of any reasonable standard of good social science research in making [their] case," said economist Daniel Nagin of Carnegie-Mellon University, who has analyzed Lott's data with colleague Dan Black.[68]

I have made the data I used available to all academics who have requested them, and so far professors at twenty-four universities have taken advantage of that. Of those who have made the effort to use the extensive data set, Dan Black and Daniel Nagin have been the only ones to publicly criticize the study.

The response from some academics, particularly those at the Johns Hopkins Center for Gun Policy and Research, has been highly unusual in many ways. For instance, who has ever heard of academics mounting an attack on a scholarly study by engaging in a systematic letter-writing campaign to local newspapers around the country?[69] One letter from a citizen to the *Springfield (Illinois) State Journal-Register* noted, "Dear Editor: Golly, I'm impressed that the staff at Johns Hopkins University reads our local *State Journal-Register*. I wonder if they subscribe to it."[70]

The rest of this paper briefly reviews the critiques and then provides my responses to their concerns. I discuss a number of issues below that represent criticisms raised in a variety of published or unpublished research papers as well as in the popular press:

Is the scale of the effect realistic?

> Large reductions in violence are quite unlikely because they would be out of pro-
> portion to the small scale of the change in carrying firearms that the legislation
> produced. (Franklin Zimring and Gordon Hawkins, "Concealed-Handgun Per-
> mits: The Case of the Counterfeit Deterrent," *The Responsive Community* [spring
> 1997]: 59, cited hereafter as Zimring and Hawkins, "Counterfeit Deterrent")

In some states, like Pennsylvania, almost 5 percent of the population has con-cealed-handgun permits. In others, like Florida, the portion is about 2 percent and growing quickly. The question here is whether these percentages of the pop-ulation are sufficient to generate 8 percent reductions in murders or 5 percent reductions in rapes. One important point to take into account is that applicants for permits do not constitute a random sample of the population. Applicants are likely to be those most at risk. The relevant comparison is not between the per-centage of the population being attacked and the percentage of the entire pop-ulation holding permits, but between the percentage of the population most vul-nerable to attack and the percentage of that population holding permits.

Let us consider some numbers from the sample to see how believable these results are. The yearly murder rate for the average county is 5.65 murders per 100,000 people, that is, .00565 percent of the people in the average county are murdered each year. An 8 percent change in this murder rate amounts to a reduction of 0.0005 percent. Obviously, even if only 2 percent of the population have handgun permits, that 2 percent is a huge number relative to the 0.0005 percent reduction in the murder rate. Even the largest category of violent crimes, aggravated assault, involves 180 cases per 100,000 people in the average county per year (that is, 0.18 percent of the people are victims of this crime in the typical year). A 7 percent change in this number implies that the assault rate declines from 0.18 percent of the population to 0.167 percent of the popula-tion. Again, this 0.013 percent change in the assault rate is quite small compared to the observed changes in the number of concealed-handgun permits.

Even if those who carry concealed handguns face exactly the same risk of being attacked as everyone else, a 2 percent increase in the portion of the pop-ulation carrying concealed handguns seems comparable to the percentage-point reductions in crime. Bearing in mind that those carrying guns are most likely to be at risk, the drop in crime rates correlated with the presence of these guns even begins to seem relatively small. Assuming that just 2 percent of the population carries concealed handguns, the drop in the murder rate only requires that 0.025 percent of those with concealed-handgun permits successfully ward off a life-threatening attack to achieve the 0.0005 percent reduction in the murder rate.

The analogous percentage for aggravated assaults is only 0.65 percent. In other words, if less than seven-tenths of one percent of those with concealed handguns successfully ward off an assault, that would account for the observed drop in the assault rate.

The importance of "crime cycles"

> Crime rates tend to be cyclical with somewhat predictable declines following several years of increases. . . . Shall-issue laws, as well as a number of other measures intended to reduce crime, tend to be enacted during periods of rising crime. Therefore, the reductions in violent crime . . . attribute[d] to the implementation of shall-issue laws may be due to the variety of other crime-fighting measures, or to a commonly observed downward drift in crime levels towards some long-term average. (Daniel W. Webster, "The Claims That Right-to-Carry Laws Reduce Violent Crime Are Unsubstantiated," The Johns Hopkins Center for Gun Policy and Research, copy obtained March 6, 1997, p. 1; cited hereafter as Webster, "Claims")

Despite claims to the contrary, the regressions do control for national and state crime trends in several different ways. At the national level, I use a separate variable for each year, a technique that allows me to account for the changes in average national crime rates from one year to another. Any national cycles in crime rates should be accounted for by this method. At the state level, some of the estimates use a separate time trend for each state, and the results with this method generally yielded even larger drops in violent-crime rates associated with nondiscretionary (shall-issue) laws.

To illustrate that the results are not merely due to the "normal" ups and downs for crime, we can look again at . . . crime patterns before and after the adoption of the nondiscretionary laws. The declines not only begin right when the concealed-handgun laws pass, but the crime rates end up well below their levels prior to the law. Even if laws to combat crime are passed when crime is rising, why would one believe that they happened to be passed right at the peak of any crime cycle?

As to the concern that other changes in law enforcement may have been occurring at the same time, the estimates account for changes in other gun control laws and changes in law enforcement as measured by arrest and conviction rates as well as by prison terms. No previous study of crime has attempted to control for as many different factors that might explain changes in the crime rate.

Did I assume that there was an immediate and constant effect from these laws and that the effect should be the same everywhere?

> The "statistical models assumed: (1) an immediate and constant effect of shall-issue laws, and (2) similar effects across different states and counties." (Webster, "Claims," p. 2; see also Dan Black and Daniel Nagin, "Do 'Right to-Carry' Laws Deter Violent Crime?" *Journal of Legal Studies* 27 [January 1998], p. 213)

One of the central arguments both in the original paper and here is that the size of the deterrent effect is related to the number of permits issued, and it takes many years before states reach their long-run level of permits.

I did not expect the number of permits to change equally across either counties or states. A major reason for the larger effect on crime in the more urban counties was that in rural areas, permit requests already were being approved; hence it was in urban areas that the number of permitted concealed handguns increased the most.

A week later, in response to a column that I published in the *Omaha World-Herald*,[71] Mr. Webster modified this claim somewhat:

> Lott claims that his analysis did not assume an immediate and constant effect, but that is contrary to his published article, in which the vast majority of the statistical models assume such an effect. (Daniel W. Webster, "Concealed-Gun Research Flawed," *Omaha World-Herald*, March 12, 1997; emphasis added)

When one does research, it is most appropriate to take the simplest specifications first and then gradually make things more complicated. The simplest way of doing this is to examine the mean crime rates before and after the change in a law. Then one would examine the trends that existed before and after the law. This is the pattern that I followed in my earlier work, and I have followed the same pattern here. The bottom line should be, How did the different ways of examining the data affect the results? What occurs here is that (1) the average crime rate falls after the nondiscretionary concealed-handgun laws are adopted; (2) violent-crime rates were rising until these laws were adopted, and they fell dramatically after that; and (3) the magnitude of the drops, both across counties and states and over time, corresponds to the number of permits issued. . . .

*Should robbery be the crime most affected by the
adoption of the nondiscretionary law?*

> Shall-issue laws were adopted principally to deter predatory street crime, the most common example of which is robbery by a stranger. But [the] results indicate that shall-issue laws had little or no effect on robbery rates. Instead the strongest deterrent effects estimated were for rape, aggravated assault, and murder. (Webster, "Claims," p. 3)

> Is it credible that laws that allow citizens to carry guns in public appear to have almost no effect on robberies, most of which occur in public spaces, yet do reduce the number of rapes, most of which occur outside of public spaces within someone's home? (Jens Ludwig, speaking on *Morning Edition*, National Public Radio, 10:00 A.M. ET December 10, 1996)

I have two responses. First, as anyone who has carefully read [my discussion] will know, it is simply not true that the results show "little or no effect on robbery rates." Whether the effect was greater for robbery or other violent crimes depends on whether one simply compares the mean crime rates before and after the laws (in which case the effect is relatively small for robbery) or compares the slopes before and after the law (in which case the effect for robbery is the largest).

Second, it is not clear that robbery should exhibit the largest impacts, primarily because the term *robbery* encompasses many crimes that are not street robberies. For instance, we do not expect bank or residential robberies to decrease; in fact, they could even rise. Allowing law-abiding citizens to carry concealed handguns makes street robberies more difficult, and thus may make other crimes like residential robbery *relatively* more attractive. Yet not only is it possible that these two different components of robbery could move in opposite directions, but to rank some of these different crimes, one requires information on how sensitive different types of criminals are to the increased threat.

Making claims about what will happen to different types of violent crimes is much more difficult than predicting the relative differences between, say, crimes that involve no contact with victims and crimes that do. Even here, however, some of these questions cannot be settled a priori, For example, when violent crimes decline, more people may feel free to walk around in neighborhoods, which implies that they are more likely to observe the illegal actions of strangers.[72] Criminals who commit violent crimes are also likely to commit some property crimes, and anything that can make an area unattractive to them will reduce both types of crime.

*Do concealed-handgun laws cause criminals
to substitute property crimes for rape?*

> Lott and Mustard argue that criminals, in response to shall-issue laws, substitute property crimes unlikely to involve contact with victims. But their theory and findings do not comport with any credible criminological theory because theft is the motive for only a small fraction of the violent crimes for which Lott and Mustard find shall-issue effects. It is difficult to rationalize why a criminal would, for example, steal a car because he felt deterred from raping or assaulting someone. (Webster, "Claims," p. 4. See also Jens Ludwig, "Do Permissive Concealed-Carry Laws Reduce Violent Crime?" Georgetown University working paper, October 8, 1996, p. 19, hereafter cited as Ludwig, "Permissive Concealed-Carry Laws.")

No one believes that hardcore rapists who are committing their crimes only for sexual gratification will turn into auto thieves, though some thefts do also involve aggravated assault, rape, or murder.[73] Indeed, 16 percent of murders in Chicago from 1990 to 1995 occurred in the process of a robbery.[74] What is most likely to happen, however, is that robbers will try to obtain money by other means such as auto theft or larceny. Although it is not unusual for rape victims to be robbed, the decline in rape most likely reflects the would-be rapist's fear of being shot.

I am also not completely clear on what Webster means when he says that "theft is the motive for only a small fraction of violent crimes," since robbery accounted for as much as 34 percent of all violent crimes committed during the sample between 1977 and 1992 (and this excludes robberies that were committed when other more serious crimes like murder or rape occurred in connection with the robbery). . . .

The impact of including Florida in the sample

> Our concern is particularly severe for the state of Florida. With the Mariel boat lift of 1980 and the thriving drug trade, Florida's crime rates are quite volatile. Moreover, four years after the passage of the right-to-carry law in 1987, Florida passed several gun-related measures, including background checks of handgun buyers and a waiting period for handgun purchases. To test the sensitivity of the results to the inclusion of Florida, we reestimated the model . . . without Florida. Only in the robbery equation can we reject the hypothesis that the crime rate two and three years after adoptions is different than the crime rate two and three years prior to adoption. (Dan Black and Daniel Nagin, "Do 'Right-to-Carry' Laws Deter Violent Crime?" Carnegie-Mellon University working paper, October 16, 1996, p. 9)

> In fact, Nagin and Black said they found that virtually all of the claimed benefits of carry laws were attributable to changes in the crime rate in just one state: Florida. (Richard Morin, "Unconventional Wisdom: New facts and Hot Stats from the Social Sciences," *Washington Post*, March 23, 1997, p. C5)

This particular suggestion—that we should throw out the data for Florida because the drop in violent crimes is so large that it affects the results—is very ironic. Handgun Control, Inc. and other gun control groups continue, as of this writing, to cite the 1995 University of Maryland study, which claimed that if evidence existed of a detrimental impact of concealed handguns, it was for Florida.[75] If the Maryland study is to be believed, the inclusion of Florida must have biased my results in the opposite direction.[76]

More important, as we shall see below, the reasons given by Black and Nagin for dropping Florida from the sample are simply not valid. Furthermore, the impact of excluding Florida is different from what they claim. Figure 10 shows the murder rate in Florida from the early 1980s until 1992. The Mariel boat lift did dramatically raise violent-crime rates like murder, but these rates had returned to their pre-Mariel levels by 1982. For murder, the rate was extremely stable until the nondiscretionary concealed-handgun law passed there in 1987, when it began to drop dramatically.

The claim that Florida should be removed from the data because a waiting period and a background check went into effect in 1992 is even weaker. If this were a valid reason for exclusion, why not exclude other states with these laws as well? Why only remove Florida? Seventeen other states had waiting periods in

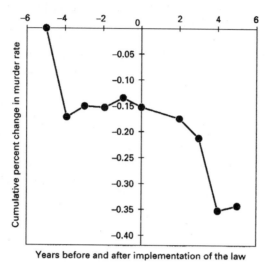

Figure 10. Florida's murder rates

1992. A more valid response would be to try to account for the impact of these other laws Indeed, accounting for these other laws slightly strengthens the evidence that concealed handguns deter crime.

The graph for Florida in figure 10 produces other interesting results. The murder rate declined in each consecutive year following the implementation of the concealed-handgun law until 1992, the first year that these other, much-touted, gun control laws went into effect. I am not claiming that these laws caused murder rates to rise, but this graph surely makes it more difficult to argue that laws restricting the ability of law-abiding citizens to obtain guns would reduce crime. . . .

Black and Nagin seem to feel that their role in this debate is to see if they can find some specification using any combination of the data that weakens the results.[77] But traditional statistical tests of significance are based on the assumption that the researcher is not deliberately choosing which results to present. Even if a result is statistically significant at the 1 percent level, one would expect that one out of every one hundred regressions would not yield a statistically significant result; in other words, out of one thousand regressions, one would expect to find at least ten for which the impact of nondiscretionary concealed-handgun laws was not statistically significant.

Lott's claims that Florida's concealed-carry law was responsible for lower murder rates in that state is questionable. Florida did not experience reductions in murders and rapes until four or five years after the law was liberalized. Lott attributes this "delayed effect" to the cumulative influence of increases in carrying permits. Other research attributes Florida's declines in murders in the 1990s to laws requiring background checks and waiting periods for handgun purchases that were implemented several years after gun-carrying laws were liberalized. (Webster, "Flawed")

Much of Webster's comment echoes the issues raised previously by Black and Nagin—indeed, I assume that he is referring to their piece when he mentions "other research." However, while I have tested whether other gun control laws might explain these declines in crime, Black and Nagin did not do so, but merely appealed to "other research" to support their affirmation. The preceding quotation seems to imply that my argument involved some sort of "tipping" point: as the number of permits rose, the murder rate eventually declined. Florida's decline in murder rates corresponded closely with the rise in concealed-handgun permits: no lag appears in the decline; rather, the decline begins as soon as the law goes into effect. . . .

How much does the impact of these laws vary across states?

[Dan Black and Dan Nagin] found the annual murder rate did go down in six of the ten states—but it went up in the other four, including a 100 percent increase in West Virginia. Rape dropped in five states-but increased in the other five. And the robbery rate went down in six statesbut went up in four. "That's curious," Black said. If concealed weapons laws were really so beneficial, their impact should not be so "wildly" different from state to state. (Richard Morin, "Unconventional Wisdom: New Facts and Hot Stats from the Social Sciences," Washington Post, March 23, 1997, p. C5)

Unfortunately, Black's and Nagin's evidence was not based on statewide crime rates but on the crime rates for counties with over 100,000 people. This fact is important, for instance, in West Virginia, where it means that only one single county—Kanawha—was examined. The other fifty-four counties in West Virginia, which include 89 percent of the states population, were excluded from their estimates. They used only one county for three of the ten states, and only three counties for another state. In fact, Black and Nagin managed to eliminate 85 percent of all counties in the nation in their analysis.

. . . My estimates using all the counties certainly did not yield "wildly" different estimates across states. Violent-crime rates fell in nine of the ten states enacting new nondiscretionary concealed-handgun laws between 1977 and 1992. The differences that did exist across states can be explained by differences in the rates at which concealed-handgun permits were issued. . . . States that issued more permits experienced greater reductions in crime. . . .

Should concealed-handgun laws have differential effects
on the murder rates of youths and adults?

Ludwig points out that in many states only adults may carry concealed weapons. So, according to Lott's deterrence theory, adults should be safer than young

> people. But this hasn't happened, Ludwig says. (Kathleen Schalch describing Jens Ludwig's arguments on *Morning Edition*, National Public Radio, 10:00 A.M. ET Tuesday, December 10, 1996.)

[Elsewhere] I tested the hypothesis that murder rates would be lower for adults than for adolescents under nondiscretionary concealed-handgun laws, and reported the results in the original paper. However, the results did not bear out this possibility. Concealed-handgun laws reduce murder rates for both adults and for adolescents. One explanation may simply be that young people also benefited from the carrying of concealed handguns by adults. Several plausible scenarios may explain this. First, criminals may well tend to leave an area where law-abiding adults carry concealed handguns, and since all age groups live in the same neighborhood, this lowers crime rates for all population groups. Second, when gun-carrying adults are physically present, they may able to protect some youngsters in threatening situations.

Could some other factor be lowering the juvenile murder rate—something that is unrelated to concealed handguns? Certainly, the results of any research may be affected by unknown factors. But until such a factor has been found, it is premature to conclude, as Ludwig does, that "these findings are not consistent with the hypothesis that shall-issue laws decrease crime through a deterrence effect."[78]

Are changes in the characteristics of victims consistent with the theory?

> Lott and Mustard offer data on the character of victims in homicide cases. They report (astonishingly) that the proportion of stranger killings increases following the enactment of right-to-carry laws, while the proportion of intrafamily killings declines. That right-to-carry laws deter intrafamily homicides more than they deter stranger homicides is inconceivable. (Albert W Alschuler, "Two Guns, Four Guns, Six Guns, More: Does Arming the Public Reduce Crime?" *Valparaiso University Law Review* 31 (1997):369)

> Josh Sugarmann of the Violence Prevention Center noted that most murders are committed by people who know each other. "Concealed-weapons laws are not passed to protect people from people they know," Sugarmann said. (Doug Finke, "Sides Stick to Their Guns, Concealed-Carry Bill Set for Showdown in General Assembly," *Springfield State Journal-Register*, March 31, 1997, p. 1)

As noted, . . . the category of acquaintance murder is extremely broad (encompassing shootings of cab drivers, gang members, drug dealers or buyers, and prostitutes or their clients). For the Chicago data that we discussed, the number of acquaintance murders involving friends was actually only a small percentage of the total number of acquaintance murders. If the breakdown found for Chicago provides even the remotest proxy for the national data, it is not particularly surprising that the relative share of acquaintance murders involving friends should rise, because we expect that many of the murders in this category are unlikely to be affected by law-abiding citizens carrying concealed handguns. Family members may also find that concealed handguns protect them from other estranged family members. A wife seeking a divorce may find that a concealed handgun provides her protection against a husband who is unwilling to let go of the relationship, and attacks by such people do not always take place in a home. Surely there are many cases of spousal abuse where women fear for their lives and find that a handgun provides them with a significant degree of protection.

A recent case involving a woman who used a handgun to protect herself from an abusive husband created an important new legal precedent in California: for the first time, women are now allowed to use self-defense before they suffer serious blows. The *San Francisco Examiner* reported as follows:

> [Fay] Johnson, a 47-year-old mother of four, said that on July 2, 1995, she feared her 62-year-old husband, Clarence, would beat her as he always did after a weekend of drinking and hanging out with his motorcycle buddies.
>
> She had overspent her budget on supplies for a Fourth of July barbecue and didn't have dinner ready, and the house was not clean—so when she heard her husband's motorcycle pull into the driveway, she decided to take matters into her own hands.
>
> Johnson said she grabbed a loaded gun . . . [and fired,] hitting her husband five times. He survived and testified against her. She was arrested and spent 21 months in prison until her acquittal.
>
> "I regret being in jail, but I just wouldn't tolerate it anymore," said Johnson, a friendly, articulate woman who is celebrating her freedom with her children and six grandchildren. "It would have been suicide."
>
> Johnson said she had endured nearly 25 years of mental and physical abuse at the hands of her husband, whose usual form of punishment was slamming her head into a wall. The beatings got so bad, she said, that she had to be hospitalized twice and tried getting counseling until he found out and forced her to stop. She said the pressure of the abuse had culminated that fateful day.[79]

Pointing to women who use handguns to protect themselves from abusive husbands or boyfriends in no way proves that the primary effects of concealed-handgun laws will involve such uses of guns, but these cases should keep us from concluding that significant benefits for these women are "inconceivable."

With reference to Alschuler's discussion, however, two points must be made clear. First, the diverse breakdown of these groupings makes it difficult to predict on theoretical grounds how the number of murders among family members, acquaintances, strangers, or unknown cases should necessarily change relative to each other. Second, as Alschuler himself has noted, these estimates are suggestive; they are not statistically significant, in that we cannot say with much certainty how concealed-handgun laws have affected the proportions of victims across the categories mentioned above.

An additional response should be made to Sugarmann's claims. Even if one accepts the claim that nondiscretionary concealed-handgun laws do not reduce the number of murders against people who know each other (and I do not concede this), what about other types of murders, such as those arising from street robbery? For Chicago during the period from 1990 to 1995, 16 percent of all murders involved nonacquaintance robbery. Moreover, one must ask about non-friend acquaintance murders (excluding prostitution, gang, and drug cases), murders by complete strangers, and at least some of those murders still classified as mysteries (an additional 22 to 46 percent of all murders). Since permitted handguns are virtually never used in crimes against others and they do not produce accidental deaths, should not the reduction of these other types of murders still be deemed important?[80]

Do nondiscretionary concealed-handgun laws
only affect crimes that occur in public places?

> Handguns were freely available for home and business use in all the "shall-issue" jurisdictions prior to the new laws. The new carrying privilege would thus not affect home or business self-defense but should have most of its preventive impact on street crime and offenses occurring in other public places. But the study contains no qualitative analysis of different patterns within crime categories to corroborate the right-to-carry prevention hypothesis. (Zimring and Hawkins, "Counterfeit Deterrent," p. 54)

Contrary to the claim of Zimring and Hawkins, concealed handguns may very well affect crime in homes and businesses in several ways. First, being allowed to carry a concealed gun outside is likely to increase the number of guns owned by law-abiding citizens. Since these guns will be kept at least part of the time in the home, this should have a deterrent effect on crimes committed at home and also at one's business. Second, as some of the evidence suggests, nondiscretionary laws could even increase the number of crimes that occur in the home as criminals turn away from other crimes, like street robbery, for which the risks that criminals face have gone up. These two effects would thus work in opposite directions. Finally, to the extent that nondiscretionary handgun laws drive criminals out of a certain geographical area, rates for all types of crimes could fall.

Aggregation of the crime categories makes it difficult to separate all the different substitution effects. Still, the results presented here are very consistent with the two primary dimensions that we focused on: whether there is contact between the criminal and the victim, and whether the crime occurs where law-abiding citizens could already legally carry a gun.

Is it reasonable to make comparisons across states?

> The sort of state that passes a "shall-issue" law in the 1980s is apt to be the same kind of place where ordinary citizens carrying concealed firearms might not be regarded as a major problem even before the law changed. . . . Idaho is not the

same sort of place that New York is, and there seem to be systematic differences between states that change standards for concealed weapons and those that do not. (Zimring and Hawkins, "Counterfeit Deterrent," pp. 50–51)

The observed drop in crime rates in states that have enacted nondiscretionary concealed-handgun laws does not by itself imply that we will observe the same effect in other states that adopt such laws later. Several different issues arise here. First, the regressions used [here] have attempted to control for many differences that can explain the level of crime (for example, income, poverty, unemployment, population and population density, demographic characteristics, law enforcement, other gun laws). Admittedly, even my long list of variables does not pick up all the differences between states, which is the reason that a variable is added for each county or state to pick up the average differences in crime rates across places. Individual time trends are also allowed for each state.

Yet despite all these attempts to control for variables, some caution is still in order—especially when dealing with areas that are particularly extreme along dimensions that do not have obvious counterparts in areas with nondiscretionary laws. One obvious example would be New York City. While the regression results show that areas with the largest and most dense populations gain the most from nondiscretionary laws, there is always the possibility that the relationship changes for values of population and density that are different from those in places where we have been able to study the effects of these laws. To date, the fourth and fifth largest cities in the country have passed nondiscretionary laws (Houston and Philadelphia), and additional experience with large cities may help determine whether these laws would be equally useful in a city like New York. If one were skeptical about the effects in large cities, the laws should first be changed in Los Angeles and Chicago.

A second issue is whether there is something unique about states that have adopted nondiscretionary laws, and whether that characteristic caused them not only to adopt the laws but also reduced the potential problems resulting from adoption. For example, if local legislators in a few states had special information confirming that the citizens in their state were uniquely trustworthy with regard to concealed handguns, that might have led these few states to pass the laws and have little difficulty with them. It could then "falsely" appear that nondiscretionary laws are generally successful. Such an argument may have been plausible at one time, but its force has declined now that such large and varied areas are covered by these laws. Equally important is the fact that not all jurisdictions have willingly adopted these laws. Many urban areas, such as Atlanta and Philadelphia, fought strongly against them, but lost out to coalitions of rural and suburban representatives. Philadelphias opposition was so strong that when Pennsylvania's nondiscretionary law was first passed, Philadelphia was partially exempted.

Does my discussion provide a "theory" linking concealed-handgun ownership to reductions in crime? Do the data allow me to link the passage of these laws with the reduction in crime?

> Two idiosyncratic aspects of the Lott and Mustard analysis deserve special mention. . . . In the first place, there is very little in the way of explicit theory advanced to explain where and when right-to-carry laws should operate as deterrents to the types of crime that can be frustrated by citizens carrying concealed handguns. . . . They have no data to measure the critical intermediate steps between passing the legislation and reductions in crime rates. This is the second important failing. . . . that is not a recurrent feature in econometric studies. (Zimring and Hawkins, "Counterfeit Deterrent," pp. 52, 54)

This set of complaints is difficult to understand. The theory is obvious: A would-be criminal act is deterred by the risk of being shot. Many different tests described [here] support this theory. Not only does the drop in crime begin when nondiscretionary laws are adopted, but the extent of the decline is related to the number of permits issued in a state. Nondiscretionary laws reduce crime the most in areas with the greatest increases in the number of permits. As expected, crimes that involve criminals and victims in direct contact and crimes occurring in places where the victim was previously unable to carry a gun are the ones that consistently decrease the most.

What can we infer about causality?

> Anyone who has taken a course in logical thinking has been exposed to the fallacy of arguing that because A happened (in this case, passage of a concealed-weapon law) and then B happened (the slowing of the rate of violent crime), A must surely have caused B. You can speculate that the passage of concealed-gun legislation caused a subsequent slowing of the rate of violent crime in various states, but you certainly can't prove it, despite the repeated claims that a University of Chicago law professor's "study" has offered "definitive scholarly proof." (Harold W. Andersen, "Gun Study Akin to Numbers Game," *Omaha World Herald*, April 3, 1997, p. 15)

An obvious danger arises in inferring causality because two events may coincide in time simply by chance, or some unknown factor may be the cause of both events. Random chance is a frequent concern with pure time-series data when there is just one change in a law. It is not hard to believe that when one is examining a single state, unrelated events A and B just happened to occur at the same time. Yet the data examined here involve many different states that changed their laws in many different years. The odds that one might falsely attribute the changes in the crime rate to changes in the concealed-handgun laws decline as one examines more experiences. The measures of statistical significance are in fact designed to tell us the likelihood that two events may have occurred randomly together.

The more serious possibility is that some other factor may have caused both the reduction in crime rates and the passage of the law to occur at the same time. For example, concern over crime might result in the passage of both concealed-handgun laws and tougher law-enforcement measures. Thus, if the arrest rate rose at the same time that the concealed-handgun law passed, not accounting for changes in the arrest rate might result in falsely attributing some of the reduction in crime rates to the concealed-handgun law. For a critic to attack the paper, the correct approach would have been to state what variables were not included in the analysis. Indeed, it is possible that the regressions do not control for some important factor. However, this study uses the most comprehensive set of control variables yet used in a study of crime, let alone any previous study on gun control. The vast majority of gun-control studies do not take any other factors that may influence crime into account, and no previous study has included such variables as the arrest or conviction rate or sentence length.

Other pieces of evidence also help to tie together cause and effect. For example, the adoption of nondiscretionary concealed-handgun laws has not produced equal effects in all counties in a state. Since counties with easily identifiable characteristics (such as rural location and small population) tended to be much more liberal in granting permits prior to the change in the law, we would expect them to experience the smallest changes in crime rates, and this is in fact what we observe. States that were expected to issue the greatest number of new permits and did so after passing nondiscretionary laws observed the largest declines in crime. We know that the number of concealed-handgun permits in a state rises over time, so we expect to see a greater reduction in crime after a nondiscretionary law has been in effect for several years than right after it has passed. Again, this is what we observe. Finally, where data on the actual number of permits at the county level are available, we find that the number of murders declines as the number of permits increases.

The notion of statistical significance and the number of different specifications examined [here] are also important. Even if a relationship is false, it might be possible to find a few specifications out of a hundred that show a statistically significant relationship. Here we have presented over a thousand specifications that together provide an extremely consistent and statistically significant pattern about the relationship between nondiscretionary concealedhandgun laws and crime.

Concerns about the arrest rates due to missing observations

To control for variation in the probability of apprehension, the [Lott and Mustard] model specification includes the arrest ratio, which is the number of arrests per reported crime. Our replication analysis shows that the inclusion of this variable materially affects the size and composition of the estimation data set. Specifically, division by zero forces all counties with no reported crimes of a particular type in a given year to be dropped from the sample for that year. [Lott's and Mustard's] sample contains all counties, regardless of size, and this problem of dropping counties with no reported crimes is particularly severe in small counties with few crimes. The frequencies of missing data are 46.6 percent for homicide, 30.5 percent for rape, 12.2 percent for aggravated assault, and 29.5 percent for robbery. Thus, the [Lott and Mustard] model excludes observations based on the realization of the dependent variable, potentially creating a substantial selection bias. Our strategy for finessing the missing data problem is to analyze only counties maintaining populations of at least 100,000 during the period 1977 to 1992. . . . Compared to the sample [comprising] all counties, the missing data rate in the large-county sample is low: 3.82 percent for homicide, 1.08 percent for rape, 1.18 percent for assault, and 1.09 percent for robberies. (Dan Black and Daniel Nagin, "Do 'Right-to-Carry' Laws Deter Violent Crime?" *Journal of Legal Studies* 27 [January 1998])

The arguments made by Black and Nagin have changed over time, and some of their statements are not consistent.[81] In part because of the public nature of their attacks, I have tried to deal with all of the different attacks, so that those who have heard them may hear my responses. The problem described immediately above by Black and Nagin is indeed something one should be concerned about, but I had already dealt with the problem of missing observations. . . . The discussion by Black and Nagin exaggerates the extent of the problem and, depending on the crime category being examined, quite amazingly proposes to solve the missing data problem by throwing out data for between 77 and 87 percent of the counties.

Black and Nagin present a very misleading picture of the trade-offs involved with the solution that examined the more populous counties.[82] The relevant comparison is between weighted numbers of missing observations, not the total number of missing observations, since the regressions are weighted by county population and the missing observations tend to be from relatively small counties, which are given a smaller weight.[83] When this is done, the benefits obtained by excluding all counties with fewer than 100,000 people become much more questionable. The most extreme case is for aggravated assault, where Black and Nagin eliminate 86 percent of the sample (a 29 percent drop in the weighted frequency) in order to reduce weighted missing values from 2.8 to 1.5 percent. Even for murder, 77 percent of the sample is dropped, so that the weighted missing data declines from 11.7 to 1.9 percent. The rape and robbery categories lie between these two cases, both in terms of the number of counties with fewer than 100,000 people and in terms of the change in the amount of weighted missing data.[84]

Why they choose to emphasize the cut-off that they did is neither explained nor obvious. The current cost-benefit ratio is rather lopsided. For example, eliminating counties with fewer than 20,000 people would have removed 70 percent of the missing arrest ratios for murder and lost only 20 percent of the observations (the weighted frequencies are 23 and 6 percent respectively). There is nothing wrong with seeing whether the estimates provide the same results over counties of various sizes, but if that is their true motivation for excluding portions of the data, it should be clearly stated.

Despite ignoring all these observations, it is only when they *also* remove the data for Florida that they weaken my results for murder and rape (though the results for aggravated assault and robbery are even larger and more statistically significant). Only eighty-six counties with more than 100,000 people adopted nondiscretionary concealed-handgun laws between 1977 and 1992, and twenty of these counties are in Florida. Yet after all this exclusion of data, Black and Nagin still find no evidence that allowing law-abiding citizens to carry concealed handguns increases crime, and two violent-crime categories show a statistically significant drop in crime. The difference between their approach and mine is rather stark: I did not select which observations to include; I used all the data for all the counties over the entire period for which observations were available.

What can we learn about the deterrent effect
of concealed handguns from this study?

> The regression study [that Lott and Mustard] report is an all-or-nothing proposition as far as knowledge of legal impact is concerned. If the model is wrong, if their bottom-line estimates of impact cannot withstand scrutiny, there is no intermediate knowledge of the law's effects on behavior that can help us sort out the manifold effects of such legislation. As soon as we find flaws in the major conclusions, the regression analyses tell us nothing. What we know from this study about the effects of "shall-carry" laws is, therefore, nothing at all. (Zimring and Hawkins, "Counterfeit Deterrent," p. 59)

Academics can reasonably differ about what factors account for changes in crime. Sociologists and criminologists, for example, have examined gun control without trying to control for changes in arrest or conviction rates. Others might be particularly concerned about the impact of drugs on crime. Economists such as myself try to include measures of deterrence, though I am also sympathetic to other concerns. [Here] and in my other research, my approach has not been to say that only one set of variables or even one specification can explain the crime rate. My attitude has been that if someone believes that a variable is important and has any plausible reason for including it, I have made an effort to include it. [I] report many different approaches and specifications—all of which support the conclusion that allowing law-abiding citizens to carry concealed handguns reduces crime. I believe that no other study on crime has used as extensive a data set as was used here, and no previous study has attempted to control for as many different specifications.

Summarizing the concerns about the evidence that
concealed-handgun laws deter crime

> The gun lobby claims to have a new weapon in its arsenal this year-a study by economist John Lott. But the Lott study shoots blanks. In reviewing Lott's research and methodology, Carnegie-Mellon University Profs. Daniel Nagin and

Dan Black, and Georgetown University's Prof. Jens Ludwig corrected for the many fatal flaws in Lott's original analysis and found no evidence of his claim that easing restrictions on carrying concealed handguns leads to a decrease in violent crime. Nagin, Black, and Ludwig recently concluded in a televised debate with Lott that "there is absolutely no credible evidence to support the idea that permissive concealed-carry laws reduce violent crime," and that "it would be a mistake to formulate policy based on the findings from Dr. Lott's study." (James Brady, "Concealed Handguns; Putting More Guns on Streets Won't Make America Safer," *Minneapolis Star Tribune*, March 21, 1997, p. 21A)

Unlike the authors of past papers on gun control such as Arthur Kellermann and the authors of the 1995 University of Maryland study, I immediately made my data available to all academics who requested it.[85] To date, my data have been supplied to academics at twenty-four universities, including Harvard, Stanford, the University of Pennsylvania, Emory, Vanderbilt, Louisiana State, Michigan State, Florida State, the University of Texas, the University of Houston, the University of Maryland, Georgetown, and William and Mary College.

James Brady's op-ed piece ignores the fact that some of these academics from Vanderbilt, Emory, and Texas paid their own way to attend the December 9, 1996, debate sponsored by his organization—Handgun Control. While Handgun Control insisted on rules that did not allow these academics to participate, I am sure that they would have spoken out to support the integrity of my original study.

Those who have attempted to replicate the findings in the original *Journal of Legal Studies* paper have been able to do so, and many have gone beyond this to provide additional support for the basic findings. For example, economists at Vanderbilt University have estimated over 10,000 regressions attempting to see whether the deterrent effects of nondiscretionary laws are at all sensitive to all possible combinations of the various data sets on demographics, income, population, arrest rates, and so on. Their results are consistent with those reported [here].[86]

I have tried to examine the critiques leveled against my work. In many cases, the concerns they describe were addressed in the original paper. In others, I believe that relatively simple responses exist to the complaints. However, even taking these critics at their worst, I still believe that a comment that I made at the December 9 discussion sponsored by Handgun Control still holds:

Six months ago, who would have thought that Handgun Control would be rushing out studies to argue that allowing law-abiding citizens to carry concealed handguns would have no effect, or might have a delayed impact, in terms of dropping crimes? (*Morning Edition*, National Public Radio, 10:00 A.M. ET, December 10, 1996)

NOTES

1. The Supreme Court justices would not uphold broad protections for gun ownership "if they thought blood would flow in the streets." This point was made by Professor Daniel Polsby in a talk given at the University of Chicago, February 20, 1997. As he points out, the Supreme Court would not have allowed the publication of the Pentagon Papers', despite the arguments about the freedom of the press, if it had posed a severe military risk to the United States. It is not the role of this book to debate the purpose of the Second Amendment. However, the argument that the Second Amendment implies broad protection of gun ownership seems quite strong. William Van Alstyne argues that the reference to a "well-regulated Militia" refers to the "ordinary citizen" and that it was emphatically not an allusion to "regular armed soldiers." It was ordinary citizens who were to bring their own arms to form an army, when the Republic was in danger. The amendment was viewed as the ultimate limit on a government's turning against the will of the people. See William Van Alstyne, "The Second Amendment Right to Arms," *Duke Law Review* 43 (April 1994): 1236–55.

2. The opposite of endogenous is exogenous. An exogenous change in something is an independent change, not a response to something else. In reality, almost everything is to some extent related to something else, so the distinction between exogenous and endogenous is a matter of degree. Since models and statistical methods must put a limit on how much to include, some variables will always be treated as "exogenously given," rather than dependent on other variables. For the social sciences, this is a constant headache. Virtually any study is open to the criticism that "if variable X depends upon variable Y, your results are not necessarily valid." In general, larger studies that rely on more data have better chances of reliably incorporating more relationships. Part of the process of doing research is determining which relationships may raise important concerns for readers and then attempting to test for those concerns.

3. With purely cross-sectional data, if one recognizes that differences may exist in crime rates even after all the demographic and criminal-punishment variables are accounted for, there are simply not enough observations to take these regional differences into account. One cannot control for more variables than one has observations to explain.

The problem with time-series data is the same. Time-series studies typically assume that crime follows a particular type of time trend (for example, they may simply assume that crime rises at a constant rate over time, or they may assume more complicated growth rates involving squared or cubic relationships). Yet almost any crime pattern over time is possible, and, as with cross-sectional data, unexplained differences over time will persist even after all the demographic and criminal-punishment variables are accounted for. Ideally, one could allow each year to have a different effect, but with time-series data we would again find that we had more variables with which to explain changes than we had observations to explain.

4. Gary Kleck and E. Britt Patterson, "The Impact of Gun Control and Gun Ownership Levels on Violence Rates," *Journal of Quantitative Criminology* 9 (1993): 249–87.

5. David McDowall, Colin Loftin, and Brian Wiersema, "Easing Concealed Firearm Laws: Effects on Homicide in Three States," *Journal of Criminal Law and Criminology* 86 (fall 1995): 193–206.

6. Arthur L. Kellermann, et al., "Gun Ownership as a Risk Factor for Homicide in the Home," *New England Journal of Medicine* (October 7, 1993): 1084–91.

7. Ibid., p. 1084.

8. The interesting letter that provoked this response from Kellermann et at. was written by students in a graduate statistics class at St. Louis University. See the *New England Journal of Medicine* (February 3, 1994): 366, 368.

9. Recent attempts to relate the crime rate to the prison population concern me. Besides difficulties in relating the total prison population to any particular type of crime, I think it is problematic to compare a stock (the prison population) with a flow (the crime rate). See, for example, Steven Levitt, "The Effect of Prison Population Size on Crime Rates: Evidence from Prison Overcrowding Litigation," *Quarterly Journal of Economics* 111 (1996): 144–67.

10. More precisely, it is the percentage of a one-standard-deviation change in the crime rate that can be explained by a one-standard-deviation change in the endogenous variable.

11. All the results are reported for the higher threshold required with a two-tailed t-test.

12. One possible concern with these initial results arises from my use of an aggregate public-policy variable (state right-to-carry laws) on county-level data. See Bruce C. Greenwald, "A General Analysis of the Bias in the Estimated Standard Errors of Least Squares Coefficients," *Journal of Econometrics* 22 (Aug. 1983): 323–38; and Brent R. Moulton, "An Illustration of a Pitfall in Estimating the Effects of Aggregate Variables on Micro Units," *Review of Economics and Statistics* 72 (1990): 334. Moulton writes, "If disturbances are correlated within the groupings that are used to merge aggregate with micro data, however then even small levels of correlation can cause the standard errors from the ordinary least squares (OLS) to be seriously biased downward." Yet this should not really be a concern here because of my use of dummy variables for all the counties, which is equivalent to using state dummies as well as county dummies for all but one of the counties within each state. Using these dummy variables thus allows us to control for any disturbances that are correlated within any individual state. The regressions discussed in table 2 reestimate the specifications shown in table 1 but also include state dummies that are interacted with a time trend. This should thus not only control for any disturbances that are correlated with the states, but also for any disturbances that are correlated within a state over time. Finally, while right-to-carry laws are almost always statewide laws, there is one exception. Pennsylvania partially exempted its largest county (Philadelphia) from the law when it was passed in 1989, and it remained exempt from the law during the rest of the sample period. However, permits granted in the counties surrounding Philadelphia were valid for use in the city.

13. However, the increase in the number of property crimes is larger than the decrease in the number of robberies.

14. While I adopt the classifications used by Cramer and Kopel in "'Shall Issue': The New Wave of Concealed- Handgun Permit Laws," *Tennessee Law Review* 62 (spring 1995), some are more convinced by other classifications of states (for example, see Doug Weil, "Response to John Lott's Study on the Impact of 'Carry-Concealed' Laws on Crime Rates," *U.S. Newswire*, August 8, 1996; and Stephen P. Teret, "Critical Comments on a Paper by Lott and Mustard," School of Hygiene and Public Health, Johns Hopkins University, mimeo, August 7, 1996). Setting the "shall-issue" dummy for Maine to zero and rerunning the regressions shown in table 1 results in the "shall issue" coefficient equaling –3 percent for violent crimes, –8 percent for murder, –6 percent for rape, –4.5 for aggravated assault, –1 percent for robbery, 3 percent for property crimes, 8.1 percent for automobile theft, -0.4 percent for burglary, and 3 percent. for larceny. Similarly, setting the "shall-issue" dummy for Virginia to zero results in the "shall-issue" coefficient equaling –4 percent for violent crimes, –9 percent for murder, –5 percent for rape, –5 percent for aggravated assault, –0.11 percent for robbery, 3 percent for property crimes, 9 percent. for automobile theft, 2 percent for burglary, and 3 percent for larceny. As a final test, dropping both Maine and Virginia from the data set results in the "shall-issue" coefficient equaling –2 percent for violent crimes, –10 percent for murder, –6 percent for rape, –3 percent for aggravated assault, 0.6 percent for robber, 3.6 percent for property crimes, 10 percent for automobile theft, 2 percent for burglary, and 4 percent for larceny.

15. This information is obtained from Mortality Detail Records provided by the U.S. Department of Health and Human Services.

16. This assumption is implausible for many reasons. One reason is that accidental handgun deaths occur in states without concealed handgun laws.

17. Given the possible relationship between drug prices and crime, I reran the regressions in table 1 and included an additional variable for cocaine prices. One argument linking drug prices and crime is that if the demand for drugs is inelastic and if people commit crimes in order to finance their habits, higher drug prices might lead to increased levels of crime. Using the Drug Enforcement Administrations STRIDE data set from 1977 to 1992 (with the exceptions of 1988 and 1989), Michael Grossman, Frank J. Chaloupka, and Charles C. Brown, ("The Demand for Cocaine by Young Adults: A Rational Addiction Approach," NBER working paper, July 1996), estimate the price of cocaine as a function of its purity, weight, year dummies, year dummies interacted with eight

regional dummies, and individual city dummies. There are two problems with this measure of pre-dicted prices: (1) it removes observations during a couple of important years during which changes were occurring in concealed-handgun laws, and (2) the predicted values that I obtained ignored the city-level observations. The reduced number of observations provides an important reason why I do not include this variable in the regressions shown in table 1. However, the primary impact of including this new variable is to make the "shall-issue" coefficients in the violent-crime regressions even more negative and more significant (for example, the coefficient for the violent-crime regression becomes –7.5 percent, –10 percent for the murder regression, –7.7 percent for rape, and –11 percent for aggravated assault, with all of them significant at more than the 0.01 level). Only for the burglary regression does the "shall-issue" coefficient change appreciably: it becomes negative and insignificant. The variable for drug prices itself is negatively related to murders and rapes and posi-tively and significantly related, at least at the 0.01 level for a one-tailed t-test, to all the other cate-gories of crime. I would like to thank Michael Grossman for providing me with the original regres-sions on drug prices from his paper.

18. In contrast, if we had instead inquired what difference it would make in crime rates if either all states or no states adopted right-to-carry concealed-handgun laws, the case of all states adopting concealed-handgun laws would have produced 2,000 fewer murders; 5,700 fewer rapes; 79,000 fewer aggravated assaults; and 14,900 fewer robberies. In contrast, property crimes would have risen by 336,410.

19. Ted R. Miller, Mark A. Cohen, and Brian Wierserna, *Victim Costs and Consequences: A New Look* (Washington, D.C.: National Institute of Justice, February 1996).

20. See Sam Peltzman, "The Effects of Automobile Safety Regulation," *Journal of Political Economy* 83 (Aug. 1975): 677–725.

21. To be more precise, a one-standard-deviation change in the probability of arrest accounts for 3 to I I percent of a one-standard-deviation change in the various crime rates.

22. Translating this into statistical terms, a one-standard-deviation change in the percentage of the population that is black, male, and between 10 and 19 years of age explains 22 percent of the ups and downs in the crime rate.

23. This is particularly observed when there are more black females between the ages of 20 and 39, more white females between the ages of 10 and 39 and over 65, and females of other races between 20 and 29.

24. In other words, the second number shows how a one-standard-deviation change in an explanatory variable explains a certain percent of a one-standard-deviation change in the various crime rates.

25. While I believe that such variables as the arrest rate should be included in any regressions on crime, one concern with the results reported in the various tables is over whether the relationship between the "shall-issue" variable and the crime rates occurs, even when all the other variables are not controlled for. Using weighted least squares and reporting only the "shall-issue" coefficients, I estimated the following regression coefficients.

How do average crime rates differ among states with and without nondiscretionary laws?

Crime rates	Crime rates in states with nondiscretionary concealed-handgun laws compared to those without the law (regressing the crime rate only on thevariable for the law)	Crime rates in states with nondiscretionary concealed-handgun laws compared to those without the law after adjusting for national trends (regressing the crime rate on the variable for the law and year dummy variables)
Violent crimes	–40%	–57%
Murder	–48	–52
Rape	–16	–28
Aggravated assault	–38	–57

Crime rates	Crime rates in states with nondiscretionary concealed-handgun laws compared to those without the law (regressing the crime rate the law)	Crime rates in states with nondiscretionary concealed-handgun laws compared to those without the law after adjusting for national trends (regressing the crime rate on the variable for the law and year dummy variables)
Robbery	-62	-75
Property crime	-17	-20
Auto theft	-31	-43
Burglary	-28	-24
Larceny	-11	-15

Note: The only factors included are the presence of the law and/or year-specific effects. All these differences are statistically significant at least at the 1 percent level for a two-tailed t-test. To calculate these percentages, I used the approximation 100 [exp(coefficient) −1).

26. The time-trend variable ranges from 1 to 16: for the first year in the sample, it equals 1; for the last year it is 16.

27. Other differences arise in the other control variables, such as those relating to the portion of the population of a certain race, sex, and age. For example, the percent of black males in the population between 10 and 19 is no longer statistically significant.

28. If the task instead had been to determine the difference in crime rates when either all states or no states adopt the right-to-carry handgun laws, the case of all states adopting concealed-handgun laws would have produced 2,048 fewer murders, 6,618 fewer rapes, 129,114 fewer aggravated assaults, and 86,459 fewer robberies. Non-arson property crimes also would have fallen by 511,940.

29. Generally, aggregation is frowned on in statistics anyway as it reduces the amount of information yielded by the data set. Lumping data together into a group cannot yield any new information that did not exist before; it only reduces the richness of the data.

30. Eric Rasmusen, "Stigma and Self-Fulfilling Expectations of Criminality," *Journal of Law and Economics* 39 (October 1996): 519–44.

31. In January 1996, women held 118,728 permits in Washington and 17,930 permits in Oregon. The time-series data available for Oregon during the sample period even indicate that 17.6 percent of all permit holders were women in 1991. The Washington state data were obtained from Joe Vincent of the Department of Licensing Firearms Unit in Olympia Washington. The Oregon state data were obtained from Mike Woodward of the Law Enforcement Data System, Department of State Police, Salem, Oregon. Recent evidence from Texas indicates that about 28 percent of applicants were women ("NRA poll: Sales people No. 1 for Permit Applications," *Dallas Morning News*, 19 April 1996, p. 32A).

32. For an interesting discussion of the benefits to -women of owning guns, see Paxton Quigley, *Armed and Female* (New York: E. P. Dutton, 1989).

33. Unpublished information obtained by Kleck and Gertz in their 1995 National Self-Defense Survey implies that women were as likely as men to use handguns in self-defense in or near their homes (defined as in the yard, carport, apartment hall, street adjacent to home, detached garage, etc.), but that women were less than half as likely to use a gun in self-defense away from home. See Gary Kleck and Marc Gertz, "Armed Resistance to Crime: The Prevalence and Nature of Self-Defense with a Gun," *Journal of Criminal Law and Criminology* 86 (fall 1995): 249–87.

34. Counties with real personal income of about $15,000 in real 1983 dollars experienced 8 percent drops in murder, while mean-income counties experienced a 5.5 percent drop.

35. Lori Montgomery, "More Blacks Say Guns Are Answer to Urban Violence," *Houston Chronicle*, 9 July 1995, p. Al. This article argues that while the opposition to guns in the black community is strong, more people are coming to understand the benefits of self-protection.

36. For an excellent overview of the role of race in gun control, see Robert J. Cottrol and Ray-

mond T. Diamond, "The Second Amendment: Toward an Afro-Americanist Reconsideration," *Georgetown Law Review* 80 (Dec. 1991): 309.

37. See William Van Alstyne, "The Second Amendment Right to Arms," *Duke Law Review* 43 (April 1994): 1236–55. In slave states prior to the Civil War, the freedoms guaranteed under the Bill of Rights were regularly restricted by states because of the fear that free reign might lead to an insurrection. As Akhil Reed Amar writes, "In a society that saw itself under siege after Nat Turner's rebellion, access to firearms had to be strictly restricted, especially to free blacks." See Akhil Reed Amar, "The Bill of Rights and the Fourteenth Amendment," *Yale Law Journal* 101 (April 1992): 1193.

38. *Associated Press Newswire*, 9 May 1997, 4:37 P.M. EDT. As the *Washington Times* recently noted, this story "comes at an awkward time for the administration, since President Clinton has spent the last week or two berating Republicans for failing to include in anticrime legislation a provision requiring that child safety locks be sold with guns to keep children from hurting themselves" (Editorial, "The Story of a Gun and a Kid," *Washington Times*, 22 May 1997, p. A18).

39. The conversation took place on March 18, 1997, though regrettably I have misplaced the note containing the representative's name.

40. John Carpenter, "Six Other States Have Same Law," *Chicago Sun-Times*, 11 March 1997, p. 8.

41. John J. Dilutio Jr., "The Question of Black Crime," *The Public Interest* 117 (fall 1994): 3–24. Similar concerns about the inability of minorities to rely on the police was also expressed to me by Assemblyman Rod Wright (D-Los Angeles) during testimony before the California Assembly's Public Safety Committee on November 18, 1997.

42. One additional minor change is made in two of the earlier specifications. In order to avoid any artificial collinearity either between violent crime and robbery or between property crimes and burglars, violent crimes net of robbery and property crimes net of burglary are used as the endogenous variables when robbery or burglary are controlled for.

43. The Pearson correlation coefficient between robbery and the other crime categories ranges between .49 and .80, and all are so statistically significant that a negative correlation would only appear randomly once out of every ten thousand times. For burglary, the correlations range from 0.45 to 0.68, and they are also equally statistically significant.

44. All the results in tables 1 and 4 as well as the regressions related to both parts of figure 1 were reestimated to deal with the concerns raised in chapter 3 over the "noise" in arrest rates arising from the timing of offenses and arrests and the possibility of multiple offenders. I reran all the regressions in this section by limiting the sample to those counties with populations over 10,000, over 100,000, and then over 200,000 people. The more the sample was restricted to larger-population counties, the stronger and more statistically significant was the relationship between concealed-handgun laws and the previously reported effects on crime. This is consistent with the evidence reported in figure 1. The arrest-rate results also tended to be stronger and more significant. I further reestimated all the regressions by redefining the arrest rate as the number of arrests over the last three years divided by the total number of offenses over the last three years. Despite the reduced sample size, the results remained similar to those already reported.

45. More formally, by using restricted least squares, we can test whether constraining the coefficients for the period before the law produces results that yield the same pattern after the passage of the law. Using both the time-trend and the time-trend-squared relationships, the F-tests reject the hypothesis that the before and after relationships are the same, at least at the 10 percent level, for all the crime categories except aggravated assault and larceny, for which the F-tests are only significant at the 20 percent level, Using only the time-trend relationship, the F-tests reject the hypothesis in all the cases.

46. The main exception was West Virginia, which showed large drops in murder but not in other crime categories.

47. See Thomas B. Marvell and Carlisle E. Moody, "The Impact of Enhanced Prison Terms for Felonies Committed with Guns," *Criminology* 33 (May 1995): 259–60.

48. I should note, however, that the "nondiscretionary" coefficients for robbery in the county-level regressions and for property crimes using the state levels are no longer statistically significant.

49. Toni Heinzl, "Police Groups Oppose Concealed-Weapons Bill," *Omaha World-Herald*, 18 March 1997, p. 9SF.

50. A simple dummy variable is used for whether the limit was 18 or 21 years of age.

51. Here is one example: "Mrs. Elmasri, a Wisconsin woman whose estranged husband had threatened her and her children, called a firearms instructor for advice on how to buy a gun for self-defense. She was advised that, under Wisconsin's progressive handgun law, she would have to wait 48 hours so that the police could perform the required background check.

"Twenty-four hours later, . . . Mrs. Elmasri's husband murdered the defenseless woman and her two children" (William P. Cheshire, "Gun Laws No Answer for Crime," *Arizona Republic*, 10 January 1993, p. Cl.) Other examples can be found in David B. Kopel, "Background Checks and Waiting Periods," in *Guns: Who Should Have Them*, ed. David B. Kopel (Amherst, N.Y.: Prometheus Books, 1995.) Other examples tell of women who successfully evaded these restrictions to obtain guns.

In September 1990, mail carrier Catherine Latta of Charlotte, N.C., went to the police to obtain permission to buy a handgun. Her ex-boyfriend had previously robbed her, assaulted her several times, and raped her. The clerk at the sheriffs office informed her that processing a gun permit would take two to four weeks. "I told her I'd be dead by then," Latta recalled.

> That afternoon, Latta bought an illegal $20 semiautomatic pistol on the street. Five hours later, her ex-boyfriend attacked her outside her house. She shot him dead. The county prosecutor decided not to prosecute Latta for either the self-defense homicide or the illegal gun. (Quoted from David B. Kopel, "Guns and Crime: Does Restricting Firearms Really Reduce Violence?" *San Diego Union-Tribune*, 9 May 1993, p. G4.)

For another example where a woman's ability. to defend herself would have been impaired by a waiting period, see "Waiting Period Law Might Have Cost Mother's Life," *USA Today*, 27 May 1994, p. 10A.

52. The Violence Policy Center grew out of the National Coalition to Ban Handguns.

53. Douglas Weil, the research director for Handgun Control, Inc., has publicly disagreed with the claim that most gun-control advocates initially refused to comment on my study. In a letter to the *Washington Times*, Weil wrote,

> The *Washington Times* editorial ("Armed and Safer," Aug. 14) is misinformed and misguided. The *Times* falsely claims that gun-control proponents "initially refused to read" John Lott's and David Mustard's study of the impact of laws regarding the right to carry concealed guns, and that I attacked the researchers' motivations rather than challenge the study "on the merits." This charge is untrue.
>
> One look at the study would prove the *Times* wrong. On the title page of the study, several pro–gun-control researchers are credited for their comments "on the merits" of the study. Included in this list are David McDowall, a criminologist at the University of Maryland; Philip Cook, an economist at Duke University; and myself, research director for the Center to Prevent Handgun Violence.
>
> Upon reviewing the study, I found Mr. Lott's methodology to be seriously flawed. I told Mr. Lott that his study did not adequately control for the whole range of ways that state and local governments attempt to lower the crime rate. In Oregon, for example, the same legislation that made it easier to carry a concealed handgun included one of the toughest new, handgun-purchase laws in the country—a 15-day waiting period and fingerprint-background check on all purchases. . . .
>
> I gladly shared my critique of this study with Mr. Lott and will now reiterate it here; as someone fully credentialed to evaluate Mr. Lott's and Mr. Mustard's work, I would have recommended that the paper he rejected. (See Douglas Weil, "A Few Thoughts on the Study of Handgun Violence and Gun Control," *Washington Times*, 22 August 1996, p. A16.)

While it is true that I thanked Mr. Weil in my paper for a comment that he made, his single comment was nothing like what his letter to the *Times* claimed. Before he explained his concerns to the press, he and I had no discussions about whether I had controlled for "ways that state and local governments attempt to lower the crime rate," possibly because my study not only controls for arrest and conviction rates, prison sentences, the number of police officers and police payroll, but also waiting periods and criminal penalties for using a gun in the commission of a crime.

Mr. Weil's sole comment to me came after two previous telephone calls over a month and a half in which Mr. Weil had said that he was too busy to give me any comments. His sole comment on August 1 was that he was upset that I had cited a study by a professor, Gary Kleck, with whom Weil disagreed. I attempted to meet this unusual but minor criticism by rewriting the relevant sentence on the first page in a further attempt to dispassionately state the alternative hypotheses.

Mr. Weil's claims are particularly difficult to understand in light of a conversation that I had with him on August 5. After hearing him discuss my paper on the news, I called him to say how, surprised I was to hear about his telling the press that the paper was "fundamentally flawed" when the only comment that he had given me was on the reference to Kleck. Mr. Weil then immediately demanded to know whether it was true that I had thanked him for giving comments on the paper. He had heard from people in the news media who had seen a draft with his name listed among those thanked. (On August 1, I had added his name to the list of people who had given comments, and when the news of the paper suddenly broke on August 2 with the story, in USA Today, it was this new version that had been faxed to the news media.) He wanted to know if I was trying to "embarrass" him with others in the gun control community, and he insisted that had not given me any comments. I said that I had only done it to be nice, and I mentioned the concern that he raised about the reference to Kleck. Weil then demanded that I "immediately remove [his] name" from the paper.

54. This was not my only experience with Ms. Glick. On August 8, 1996, six days after the events of August 2 described above, I appeared with her on MSNBC. After I tried to make an introductory statement setting out my findings, Ms. Glick attacked me for having my study funded by "gun manufacturers." She claimed that I was a "shill" for the gun manufactures and that it was important that I be properly identified as not being an objective academic. She also claimed that there were many serious problems with the paper. Referring to the study she asserted that it was a fraud.

I responded by saying that these were very serious charges and that if she had some evidence, she should say what it was. I told her that I didn't think she had any such evidence, and that if she didn't, we should talk about the issues involved in the study.

At this point the moderator broke in and said to Ms. Glick that he agreed that these were very serious charges, and he asked her what evidence she had for her statements. Glick responded by saying that she had lots of evidence and that it was quite obvious to her that this study had been done to benefit gun manufacturers.

The moderator then asked her to comment further on her claim that there were serious problems with the study, and she stated that one only had to go to page 2 before finding a problem. Her concern was that I had used data for Florida that was a year and a half old. The moderator then asked her why this was a problem, since I couldn't be expected to use data that was, say, as recent as last week. Ms. Glick responded by saying that a lot of things could have changed since the most recent data were available. I then mentioned that I had obtained more recent data since the study had been written and that the pattern of people not using permitted guns improperly had held true from October 1987 to December 31, 1995.

A more recent exchange that I had with the Violence Policy Center's President, Josh Sugarmann, on MSNBC on February 24, 1997, involved the same accusations.

55. Douglas Weil, from the Center to Prevent Handgun Violence, a division of Handgun Control, wrote the following to the *Washington Times*: "Given that Mr. Lott has published 70 papers in peer-reviewed journals, it is curious that he has chosen a law review for his research on concealed-gun-carrying laws" (*Washington Times*, 22 August 1996, p. A16).

56. Scott Harris, "To Build a Better America, Pack Heat," *Los Angeles Times*, 9 January 1997, p. Bl. In many ways, my study was indeed fortunate for the coverage that it received. It appears that no other study documenting the ability of guns to deter crime has received the same level of coverage. MediaWatch, a conservative organization tracking the content of television news programs,

reviewed every gun-control story on four evening shows (ABC's *World News Tonight*, CBS's *Evening News*, CNN's *The World Today*, and NBCs *Nightly News*) and three morning broadcasts (ABCs *Good Morning America*, CBS's *This Morning*, and NBC's *Today*) from July 1, 1995 through June 30, 1997. MediaWatch categorized news stories in the following way: "Analysts counted the number of pro– and anti–gun control statements by reporters in each story. Pieces with a disparity of greater than 1.5 to 1 were categorized as either for or against gun control. Stories closer than the ratio were deemed neutral. Among statements recorded as pro–gun control: violent crime occurs because of guns, not criminals, and gun control prevents crime. Categorized as arguments against gun control: gun control would not reduce crime; that criminals, not guns are the problem; Americans have a constitutional right to keep and bear arms; right-to-carry concealed weapons laws caused a drop in crime." MediaWatch concluded that "in 244 gun policy stories, those favoring gun control outnumbered stories opposing gun control by 157 to 10, or a ratio of almost 16 to 1 (77 were neutral). Talking heads were slightly more balanced: gun control advocates outnumbered gun-rights spokesmen 165 to 110 (40 were neutral)." The news coverage of my study apparently accounted for 4 of the 10 "anti-gun control" news reports. (*Networks Use First Amendment Rights to Promote Opponents of Second Amendment Rights: Gun Rights Forces Outgunned on TV*, MediaWatch, July 1997.)

57. One of the unfortunate consequences of such attacks is the anger that they generate among the audience. For example, after Congressman Schumer's letter to the *Wall Street Journal*, I received dozens of angry telephone calls denouncing me for publishing my *Wall Street Journal* op-ed piece on concealed-handgun laws without first publicly stating that the research had been paid for by gun manufacturers. Other letters from the Violence Policy Center making these funding claims produced similar results.

Understandably, given the seriousness of the charges, this matter has been brought up by legislators in every state in which I have testified before the state legislature. Other politicians have also taken up these charges. Minnesota State Rep. Wes Skoglund (DFL–Minneapolis) provided one of the milder statements of these charges in the *Minneapolis Star Tribune* (29 March 1997, p. A13): "Betterman [a Minnesota state representative] uses a much-publicized study by John Lott Jr., of the University of Chicago, to back up her claims about the benefits of her radical gun-carry law. . . . But what no one has told you about Lott's study is that it has been found to be inaccurate and flawed. And Betterman didn't tell you that the study was funded by the Olin Foundation, which was created by the founder of Winchester Arms."

58. I telephoned Ms. Rand to ask her what evidence she had for her claim that the study was "the product of gun-industry funding" and reminded her that the public relations office at the University of Chicago had already explained the funding issue to her boss, Josh Sugarmann, but Ms. Rand hung up on me within about a minute.

59. Alex Rodriquez, "Gun Debate Flares; Study: Concealed Weapons Deter Crime," *Chicago Sun-Times*, 9 August 1996, p. 2. Kotowski made his remark at a press conference organized by the Violence Policy Center, whose president, Josh Sugarmann, had been clearly told by the press office at the University of Chicago on August 6 that these charges were not true (as the letter by William E. Simon shown later will explain). Catherine Behan in the press office spent an hour trying to explain to him how funding works at Universities.

60. *Chicago Tribune*, 15 August 1996.

61. "Study: Concealed Guns Deterring Violent Crime," *Austin American Statesman*, 9 August 1996, p. A12.

62. The brief correction ran in the *Austin American Statesman*, 10 August 1996.

63. As Mr. Simon mentions, one journalist who looked into these charges was Stephen Chapman of the *Chicago Tribune*. One part of his article that is particularly relevant follows:

Another problem is that the [Olin] foundation didn't (1) choose Lott as a fellow, (2) give him money, or (3) approve his topic. It made a grant to the law school's law and economics program (one of many grants it makes to top universities around the country). A committee at the law school then awarded the fellowship to Lott, one of many applicants in a highly competitive process.

Even the committee had nothing to do with his choice of topics. The fellowship was to allow Lott—a prolific scholar who has published some 75 academic articles—to do research on whatever subject he chose. . . .

To accept their conspiracy theory, you have to believe the following: A company that derives a small share of its earnings from sporting ammunition somehow prevailed on an independent family foundation to funnel money to a scholar who was willing to risk his academic reputation (and, since he does not yet have tenure, his future employment) by fudging data to serve the interests of the firearms lobby—and one of the premier research universities in the world cooperated in the fraud. (See Stephen Chapman, "A Gun Study and a Conspiracy Theory," *Chicago Tribune*, 15 August 1996, p. 31)

64. A Gannett Newswire story quoted a spokeswoman for the Coalition to Stop Gun Violence who made similar statements: "But Katcher said the study . . . was funded by the Olin Foundation, which has strong ties to the gun industry. The study has 'been proven by a series of well-known, well-respected researchers to be inaccurate, false, junk science,' she said." (Dennis Camire, "Legislation before Congress Would Allow Concealed Weapons Nationwide," Gannett News Service, 6 June 1997.)

65. John R. Lott Jr., "Should the Wealthy Be Able to 'Buy Justice'?" *Journal of Political Economy* 95 (December 1987): 1307.

66. "Notebook," *The New Republic*, 14 April 1997, p. 10.

67. After much effort, Randy was eventually able to get Cynthia Henry Thielen, a Hawaiian State Representative, to participate in the radio program.

68. Richard Morin, "Unconventional Wisdom: New Facts and Hot Stats from the Social Sciences," *Washington Post*, 23 March 1997, p. C5.

69. It is surely not uncommon for academics to write letters to their local newspapers or to national or international publications, and indeed such letters were also written (see, for example, *The Economist*, 7 December 1996, p. 8). But to track down the letters of everyday citizens to local newspapers and send replies is unusual.

70. The *Springfield State Journal-Register*, 26 November 1996. Steven Teret, director of the Center for Gun Policy and Research wrote dozens of letters to newspapers across the country. They usually began with statements like the following: "Recently in a letter to the editor dated October 19, Kurt Amebury cited the work of two University of Chicago professors" (*Orlando Sentinel*, 16 November 1996, p. A18); "Recently the *Dispatch* published a letter to the editor citing the work of two researchers" (*Columbus Dispatch*, 16 November 1996, p. A11); "The *State Journal-Register* October 28 published two letters citing research by the University of Chicago's John Lott" (*Springfield State Journal-Register*, 13 November 1996, p. 6); or "A recent letter to the editor . . ." (*Buffalo News*, 17 November 1996, p. H3). In late November, I asked Stephen Teret how many newspapers he had sent letters to. He would not give me an exact count, but he said "dozens" and then listed the names of some major newspapers to which they had written. It is curious that none of the effort put into responding to my paper by the Center has gone into writing a comment for submission to the *Journal of Legal Studies*, where my original paper was published. Nor has the Center prepared a response for any other scholarly journal.

71. My opinion piece appeared in the *Omaha World-Herald*, 9 March 1997, p. B9.

72. This point is similar to the "broken-window" argument made by Wilson and Kelling; see James Q Wilson and George L. Kelling, "Making Neighborhoods Safe," *Atlantic Monthly*, February 1989.

73. Some robberies also involve rape. While I am not taking a stand on whether rape or robbery is the primary motivation for the attack, there might be cases where robbery was the primary motive.

74. Information obtained from Kathy O'Connell at the Illinois Criminal Justice Information Authority.

75. For example, see Douglas Weil, "A Few Thoughts on the Study of Handgun Violence and Gun Control," *Washington Times*, 22 August 1996, p. A16.

76. The durability of these initial false claims about Florida's crime rates can be seen in more recent popular publications. For example, William Tucker, writing in the *Weekly Standard*, claims that "Florida crime rates remained level from 1988 to 1990, then took a big dive. As with all social phenomena, though, it is difficult to isolate cause and effect." See William Tucker, "Maybe You Should Carry a Handgun," *Weekly Standard*, 16 December 1996, p. 30.

77. In an attempt to facilitate Black's and Nagin's research, I provided them not only with all the data that they used but also computer files containing the regressions, in order to facilitate the replication of each of my regressions. It was thus very easy for them to try all possible permutations of my regressions, doing such things as excluding one state at a time or excluding data based on other criteria.

78. Jens Ludwig, "Do Permissive Concealed-Carry Laws Reduce Violent Crime?" Georgetown University working paper (October 8, 1996), p. 12.

79. "Battered Woman Found Not Guilty for Shooting Her Husband Five Times," *San Francisco Examiner*, 9 April 1997.

80. In Chicago from 1990 to 1995, 383 murders (or 7.2 percent of all murders) were committed by a spouse.

81. For a detailed discussion of how Black's and Nagin's arguments have changed over time, see my paper entitled "If at First You Don't Succeed . . ." : The Perils of Data Mining When There Is a Paper (and Video) Trail: The Concealed-Handgun Debate," *Journal of Legal Studies* 27 (January 1998).

82. Black and Nagin. "Do 'Right-to-Carry' Laws Deter Violent Crime," Carnegie-Mellon working paper, version of December 18, p. 5n. 4.

83. The December 18, 1996, version of their paper included a footnote admitting this point:

> Lott and Mustard weight their regression by the county's population, and smaller counties are much more likely to have missing data than larger counties. When we weight the data by population, the frequencies of missing data are 11.7 percent for homicides, 5.6 percent, for rapes, 2.8 percent for assaults, and 5 percent for robberies.

In discussing the sample comprising only counties with more than 100,000 people, they write in the same paper that "the (weighted) frequencies of missing arrest ratios are 1.9 percent for homicides, 0.9 percent for rapes, 1.5 percent for assaults, and 0.9 percent for robberies."

84. For rape, 82 percent of the counties are deleted to reduce the weighted frequencies of missing data from 5.6 to 0.9 percent. Finally, for robbery (the only other category that they examine), 82 percent of the observations are removed to reduce the weighted missing data from 5 to 0.9 percent.

85. The reluctance of gun control advocates to share their data is quite widespread. In May 1997 I tried to obtain data from the Police Foundation about a study that they had recently released by Philip Cook and Jens Ludwig, but after many telephone calls I was told by Earl Hamilton on May 27, "Well, lots of other researchers like Arthur Kellermann do not release their data." I responded by saying that was true, but that it was not something other researchers approved of, nor did it give people much confidence in his results.

86. See William Alan Bartley, Mark Cohen, and Luke Froeb, "The Effect of Concealed Weapon Laws: Estimating Misspecification Uncertainty," Vanderbilt University working paper (1997).

PART FIVE

THE SECOND AMENDMENT

THE AMERICAN CULTURE WARS REVISITED

I cannot help but suspect that the best explanation for the absence of the Second Amendment from the legal consciousness of the elite bar, including the component found in the legal academy, is derived from a mixture of sheer opposition to the idea of private ownership of guns and perhaps subconscious fear that altogether plausible, perhaps even "winning" interpretations of the Second Amendment would present real hurdles to those of us supporting prohibitionary regulation.

Sanford Levinson—"The Embarrassing Second Amendment"
Yale Law Journal, 1989

A well regulated militia, being necessary to the security of a Free State, the right of the people to keep and bear Arms, shall not be infringed.

Second Amendment
U.S. Constitution

What does the Second Amendment mean? Historian Joyce Lee Malcolm, tracing the origins of the amendment both in English history and law as well the American historical and constitutional experience supports the view that:

> The Second Amendment was meant to accomplish two distinct goals each perceived as crucial to the maintenance of liberty. First, it was meant to guarantee the right to have arms for self-defense and self-preservation. Such an individual right was the legacy of the English Bill of Rights. . . . The second and related objective concerned the militia. . . . Madison's original version of the amend-

541

ment as well as those suggested by the states, described the militia as either "composed of" or "including" the body of people (therefore) . . . the peoples' right to have weapons was to be sacrosanct.

Historian Gary Wills will disagree with virtually all of Professor Malcolm's historical and constitutional assertions and interpretations regarding the amendment as well as those of constitutional scholars who support her point of view.

These selections serve the following purposes: to present important historical and constitutional issues bearing upon interpreting the meanings of the amendment, to pinpoint key issues of controversy, to explain the contemporary significance contending parties in the gun debate attach to the amendment, to enable the reader to consider the degree to which either or both selections are two-sided or the degree to which history is one-sidedly utilized to pursue the agendas of Americas' culture wars.

32

TO KEEP AND BEAR ARMS

THE ORIGINS OF AN ANGLO-AMERICAN RIGHT

JOYCE LEE MALCOLM

THE SECOND AMENDMENT AND THE ENGLISH LEGACY*

According to an American Bar Association report of 1975 there is less agreement, more misinformation, and less understanding of the right of citizens to keep and bear arms than on any other current controversial constitutional issue.[1] "The crux of the controversy," the report points out, "is the construction of the Second Amendment to the Constitution." Yet its authors find little point in dwelling on that construction since they conclude, "It is doubtful that the Founding Fathers had any intent in mind with regard to the meaning of this Amendment.[2]

. . . [I] start from the premise that James Madison and his associates took seriously the task of selecting and defining the liberties that constitute the American Bill of Rights; that they had a specific intention in each instance; and that in this particular instance their views were profoundly, albeit not exclusively, shaped by the British model. If this is correct, then the attitudes embodied in the English right to have arms and the intent behind it can offer some badly needed insight into the meaning of the Second Amendment.

Whatever the merits of the Bar Association report, the authors did not exaggerate the wholesale confusion about the intent of the Second Amendment. The

---

543

amendment reads: "A well-regulated militia being necessary to the security of a free State, the right of the people to keep and bear arms shall not be infringed." Although the amendment's drafters presumably believed it quite clear, the shared understandings upon which it was based have vanished and this single sentence has proven capable of an amazing range of interpretations. Its most troublesome aspect is the purpose of its pronouncement "a well-regulated Militia being necessary to the security of a free state." Two hundred years after its passage there is no agreement why it is there or what it means. Was it meant to restrict the right to have arms to militia members; to indicate *the* most pressing reason for an armed citizenry; or simply to proclaim the need for a free people to have a conscript, rather than a professional, army? And what sort of militia did the framers have in mind—a select group of citizen-soldiers, every able-bodied male citizen, or didn't it matter? Emphasis on the militia clause has been proffered as evidence that the right to have arms was only a "collective right" to defend the state, not an individual right to defend oneself. Emphasis on the main clause with its assertion of the inviolability of the people's right to have weapons has been cited as proof of an individual right to have arms.

Since 1975, the bar report notwithstanding, there has been an increasingly impressive debate over interpretation.[3] In an effort to understand the amendment's meaning, authors have stressed the philosophical impact on the founders of classical and enlightenment views of armed citizens and citizen-armies and the practical effect of the wilderness, egalitarianism, and individuality on American thought and practice. The significance of English common law and English liberties has received less attention. When Americans have turned to the English tradition for guidance their efforts have been hampered by the absence of studies of the Englishman's right to have weapons or of the place of firearms in English society. Little wonder that American legal scholars have often misunderstood the English right, English practice, and sometimes English history as well.[4]

There are legitimate reasons to approach the English legacy warily. More than a century elapsed between passage of the English and American bills of rights with important repercussions for both nations. Moreover, there are obvious differences of setting and political philosophy. And while American drafters adopted some English rights verbatim, the language of the two pronouncements on arms differs markedly and importantly. The English drafters claimed for Protestants a right to "have arms for their defence," provided that these were "suitable to their condition and as allowed by law." These restrictions have led some American scholars to conclude that any traditional right of Englishmen to own weapons was "more nominal than real."[5] By contrast, the American right claims for "the people"—presumably regardless of their religion, state, or condition—a right to keep and carry weapons that the government, or at least the federal government, must not breach. The American language is much broader, unless one restricts the entire right to members of a well-regulated militia. Yet if colonial Americans regarded their right to be armed as one of their rights as Englishmen, they are unlikely to have narrowed it.

In a second departure the militia, so prominent a focus of the American right, isn't mentioned in the English right or in later justifications of it. Yet such is the zeal of some American scholars seeking to confine a right to bear arms to members of the militia that they have attempted to graft a nonexistent militia clause onto the English right. Roy Weatherup, for instance, insists the English guarantee that "the Subjects which are Protestants may have arms for their defence" actually meant: "Protestant members of the militia might keep and bear arms in accordance with their militia duties for the defense of the realm.[6] Notwithstanding the fact that the Convention which drafted the English Declaration of Rights explicitly rejected the phrase "their common defence" in favor of "their defence," Weatherup found "no recognition of any personal right to bear arms.[7] . . .

When Alexis de Tocqueville visited the young American republic he was struck by the pervasive English influence. To his mind there was "not an opinion, custom, or law . . . which the point of departure will not easily explain."[8] De Tocqueville's otherwise sharp eyes picked out the broad pattern but obviously missed importance differences; yet his impression is an important reminder that the colonists were men and women steeped in English laws, English customs, English prejudices, and English habits of mind. Indeed, the transplantation of an English legal framework was official policy. The entire body of the common law was to be applied in the new setting except where circumstances made it impracticable. "Let an Englishman go where he will," Richard West, counsel to the Board of Trade, explained in 1720, "he carries as much of law and liberty with him as the nature of things will bear."[9] To this English base colonists speedily added their own laws and regulations. While Kermit Hall sees this as an active process by which "informed persons made choices that were always important under often novel, and invariably difficult circumstances," he finds that "English law remained the source of authority" and that "this transatlantic connection persisted even after the colonies achieved independence."[10]

This continuity, especially of rights, was significant. The English government's great success in luring Englishmen to America's wild shores was due in part to pledges that the emigrants and their children would continue to possess "all the rights of natural subjects, as if born and abiding in England."[11] A guarantee of these rights, for example, was incorporated into the charters of Virginia, Connecticut, and Massachusetts, and fundamental principles of English jurisprudence, with their protection of personal liberty and private property, were specifically incorporated into the laws of the Maryland General Assembly in 1639, the Massachusetts Body of Liberties in 1641, the West New Jersey Charter of Fundamental Laws in 1676, and the New York "Charter of Libertyes and Privilidges" in 1683.[12]

As English imperial policy evolved and the rights of Englishmen were refined and expanded in the wake of the Glorious Revolution, shrewd observers wondered how fully Americans would or could enjoy these rights. In his study of the effects of the Glorious Revolution on the colonies, David Lovejoy contends that "despite significant changes won by Englishmen in England, the lesson the Revolution taught colonies was that they were dominions of the Crown to be dealt with as the King wished, with no assurance of Englishmen's rights on permanent bases."[13] If Americans did learn this lesson before the eighteenth century, they nevertheless continued to believe that they were entitled to the rights of native-born Englishmen, as their charters and their laws proclaimed. Since 1689 these rights included the right of Protestants to keep and use weapons. Unlike the thorny problem of colonial representation in Parliament, nothing stood in the way of the transmission of this right to the New World. In fact, circumstances in the colonies ensured that both the right and the duty to be armed were broader than the English original.

Despite a diversity of colonial settings, each with its "richly textured pattern of legal institutions and activity," the approach to private arms ownership and the employment of an armed citizenry was remarkably uniform from colony to colony.[14] The perils of frontier life did have an impact on the colonists' retention of an armed citizenry, but the effect was to modify an old tradition rather than to create a new one.[15] Every colony passed legislation to establish the familiar institutions of the militia and watch and ward.[16] Like the English militia, the colonial militia played a primarily defensive role, with armies of volunteers organized whenever an offensive campaign was planned.[17] All men between the ages of sixteen and sixty were liable for militia service, with some exceptions for clergy, religious objectors, and Negroes.

The dangers all the colonies faced, however, were so great that not only militia members but all householders were ordered to be armed. A 1623 law of Plymouth colony, for example, stipulated that "in regard of our dispersion so far asunder and the inconvenience that may befall, it is further ordered that every freeman or other inhabitant of this colony provide for himselfe and each under him able to beare armes a sufficient musket and other serviceable peece for war . . . with what speede may be."[18] A similar Virginia statute of 164 required "all masters of families" to furnish themselves and "all those of their families which shall be capable of arms (excepting negroes) with arms both offensive and defensive."[19]

Colonial law went another step beyond English law and required colonists to carry weapons. A Newport law of 1639 provided that "noe man shall go two miles from the Towne unarmed, eyther with Gunn or Sword; and that none shall come to any public Meeting without his weapon."[20] Early Virginia laws required "that no man go or send abroad without a sufficient partie well armed," and "that men go not to worke in the ground without their arms (and a centinell upon them)." They even specified that "all men that are fitting to beare armes, shall bring their pieces to the church uppon payne of every offence, if the mayster allow not thereof to pay 2 lb of tobacco."[21]

It is scarcely surprising that settlers living in the wilderness would enact measures for their individual and mutual protection; a century later, however, Connecticut's revised militia act still ordered all citizens, both "listed" soldiers of the militia and every other householder, to "always be provided with and have in continual readiness, a well-fixed firelock . . . or other good firearms . . . a good sword, or cutlass . . . one pound of good powder, four pounds of bullets fit for his gun, and twelve flints."[22] And in 1770, not long before the Revolution, the colony of Georgia felt it necessary "for the better security of the inhabitants" to require every white male resident "to carry firearms to places of public worship."[23] In this instance the purpose was to defend colonists "from internal dangers and insurrections." But whether the threat came from foreigners, Indians, or slaves the means of defense was the same—the arming of the citizenry.

The emphasis of the colonial governments was on ensuring that the populace was well armed, not on restricting individual stocks of weapons. They had neither the incentive nor the ability to replicate common law restrictions on the type or quantity of arms a citizen owned based upon his condition or religion. Nor was the protection of game a consideration in America. Game was plentiful and prospective emigrants were guaranteed the "liberty of fishing and fowling."[24] The usual restrictions on the use of firearms in crowded areas or with intention to terrify were put in place, but the emphasis was on the duty to be armed and a freer use of private firearms than existed in England. This was true even in the aftermath of insurrection. An act passed in 1676 after Bacon's Rebellion against the colonial administration in Virginia forbade five or more armed persons to assemble without authorization, but was careful to affirm that "liberty is granted to all persons to carry their arms wheresoever they go."[25]

This liberality did not extend to all New World residents. Just as the English regarded Catholics as potential subversives who were permitted the use of firearms only on sufferance, Indians and black slaves were the suspect populations of the New World. With certain exceptions both groups were barred from owning firearms. The authors of a recent study of the right of blacks to have firearms argue that the need for racial control was instrumental in the transformation of the English right to have arms into a broader right for white Americans.[26]

Efforts were made to prevent Indians from acquiring firearms. The Massachusetts general laws of 1648, the Commonwealth's first legal code, made it a crime for anyone to "directly or indirectly amend, repair . . . any gun, small or great, belonging to any Indian. . . . Nor shall [he] sell or give to any Indian, directly or indirectly, any such gun, or ally gun-powder upon payn of ten pounds fine."[27] Yet in 1675–1676, during the great Indian uprising in New England known as King Philip's War, the Indians were "well supplied with muskets, bullets, and powder" and described as "dead shots."[28] No wonder a Virginia statute that same year made selling arms or ammunition to Indians a crime for which the culprit was to die "without benefit of clergy" and to forfeit his estate.[29] As noncitizens Indians were neither expected, nor usually allowed, to participate in the militia.[30]

The second group forbidden to possess weapons were black slaves, with restrictions sometimes extended to free blacks. These restrictions varied with the particular colony's degree of reliance upon slave labor and the state of its internal and external security. Northern colonies were ambivalent about blacks possessing firearms. The policy they adopted was similar to that applied to Catholics in England. Blacks in Massachusetts and Connecticut were permitted to keep private firearms but did not serve in the militia. New Jersey excluded blacks from militia service but permitted free Negroes to have firearms.[31] A Virginia statute of 1639 that required white men to be armed at public expense did not require, but did not specifically prohibit, black men from having arms.[32] The following year, however, Virginia passed "An Act Preventing Negroes from Bearing Arms" directed against slaves, and in 1680 a further statute forbade all Negroes, slave and free, from carrying weapons.[33] Free Negroes in Virginia could keep one gun in their home, however, and blacks living on frontier plantations, whether slave or free, were permitted to have firearms. South Carolina at first permitted free blacks to be armed and serve in the militia, but during the eighteenth century reversed the policy.[34] Georgia insisted upon a license for even temporary use of a gun by a slave.[35]

Neither the Indian nor the slave was a citizen, therefore neither was entitled to the rights of English subjects. Both were, like English Catholics, also regarded as a threat to the established order, and even free blacks were treated with caution. Their inability to legally own weapons merely confirmed their status as outsiders and inferiors.

If the development of an armed citizenry in the American colonies was influenced by English law, liberty, and custom and enhanced by the perils of the wilderness and racial tensions, it was undergirded by an antigovernment and antiarmy legacy from seventeenth- and eighteenth-century England. English theory on the respective merits and hazards of armies and militia remained unshaken during the late seventeenth and eighteenth centuries, even when English practice diverged from English professions and when the much-eulogized English militia failed to live up to its billing and become an effective or reliable substitute for the army." The issue of the incompatibility of freedom and standing armies was kept in the public eye by domestic alarms, such as King William's plan to maintain a large peacetime army, and continental events, and remained a favourite theme of pamphleteers. The dilemma of how to ensure the security of the realm while preserving the liberty of its people was made more formidable by the so-called military revolution on the Continent.[37] But as an island nation England could more easily afford to cling to principle for the sake of individual liberties. An ocean and vast wilderness offered a similar luxury to its American colonies. In addition there were legal protections. When large armies were necessary during wartime, or when the army began to take over the militia's domestic peacekeeping duties, Englishmen counted upon the stipulations in the Bill of Rights that no standing army could be maintained in time of peace without consent of Parliament, that Protestant subjects had the right to have arms, and the annual Mutiny Act to protect their civil liberties.[38] Even as the role and size of the English army increased, therefore, Englishmen on both sides of the Atlantic remained highly skeptical of that institution and looked to their legal protections up to the eve of the American Revolution. . . .

The Second Amendment was meant to accomplish two distinct goals, each perceived as crucial to the maintenance of liberty. First, it was meant to guarantee the individual's right to have arms for self defense and self-preservation. Such an individual right was a legacy of the English Bill of Rights. This is also plain from American colonial practice, the debates over the Constitution, and state proposals for what was to become the Second Amendment. In keeping with colonial precedent, the American article broadened the English protection. English restrictions had limited the right to have arms to Protestants and made the type and quantity of such weapons dependent upon what was deemed "suitable" to a person's "condition." The English also included the proviso that the right to have arms was to be "as allowed by law." Americans swept aside these limitations and forbade any "infringement" upon the right of the people to keep and bear arms.

These privately owned arms were meant to serve a larger purpose as well, albeit the American framers of the Second Amendment, like their English predecessors, rejected language linking their right to "the common defense." When, as Blackstone phrased it, "the sanctions of society and laws are found insufficient to restrain the violence of oppression," these private weapons would afford the people the means to vindicate their liberties.[39]

The second and related objective concerned the militia, and it is the coupling of these two objectives that has caused the most confusion. The customary American militia necessitated an armed public, and Madison's original version of the amendment, as well as those suggested by the states, described the militia as either "composed of" or "including" the body of the people.[40] A select militia was regarded as little better than a standing army.[41] The argument that today's National Guardsmen, members of a select militia, would constitute the *only* persons entitled to keep and bear arms has no historical foundation. Indeed, it would seem redundant to specify that members of a militia had the right to be armed. A militia could scarcely function otherwise. But the argument that this constitutional right to have weapons was exclusively for members of a militia falters on another ground. The House committee eliminated the stipulation that the militia be "well-armed," and the Senate, in what became the final version of the amendment, eliminated the description of the militia as composed of the "body of the people." These changes left open the possibility of a poorly armed and narrowly based militia that many Americans feared might be the result of federal control. Yet the amendment guaranteed that the right of "the people" to have arms not be infringed. Whatever the future composition of the militia, therefore, however well or ill armed, was not crucial because the people's right to have weapons was to be sacrosanct. As was the case in the English tradition, the arms in the hands of the people, not the militia, are relied upon "to restrain the violence of oppression."

The Constitution gave to the federal government broad authority over state militia. Was the Second Amendment meant to placate states fearful about this loss of control? In fact not one of the ninety-seven distinct amendments pro-posed by state ratifying conventions asked for a *return* of any control that had been allocated to the federal government over the militia. In any event, the Second Amendment does nothing to alter the situation. Indeed, that was pre-cisely the complaint of the anti-Federalist *Centinel* in a discussion of the House version of the arms article. The *Centinel* found that "the absolute command vested by other sections in Congress over the militia, are [*sic*] not in the least abridged by this amendment."[42] Had the intent been to reapportion this power some diminution of federal control would have been mandated. None was.

The clause concerning the militia was not intended to limit ownership of arms to militia members, or return control of the militia to the states, but rather to express the preference for a militia over a standing army. The army had been written into the Constitution. Despite checks within the Constitution to make it responsive to civil authority, the army was considered a threat to liberty. State constitutions that had a bill of rights had copied the English model and prohib-ited a standing army in time of peace without the consent of their state legisla-tures. Five states hid urged such an amendment for the federal constitution. Some had suggested that a two-thirds or even a three-fourths vote of members of each house be required to approve a standing army in time of peace.[43] Indeed, George Mason had attempted to add such a proviso during the con-vention when he moved to preface the clause granting Congress authority to organize, arm, and discipline the militia with the words "And that the liberties of the people may be better secured against the danger of standing armies in time of peace.[44] A strong statement of preference for a militia must have seemed more tactful than an expression of distrust of the army. The Second Amend-ment, therefore, stated that it was the militia, not the army, that was necessary to the security of a free state. The reference to a "well-regulated" militia was meant to encourage the federal government to keep the militia in good order.

The position of this amendment, second among the ten amendments added to the Constitution as a Bill of Rights, underscored its importance to contem-poraries. It was no less than the safety valve of the Constitution. It afforded the means whereby, if parchment barriers proved inadequate, the people could pro-tect their liberties or alter their government. It gave to the people the ultimate power of the sword. The *Philadelphia Federal Gazette* and *Philadelphia Evening Post* of Thursday, June 18, 1789, in an article later reprinted in New York and Boston, explained each of the proposed amendments to be sent to the states for ratification. The aim of the article that became the Second Amendment was explained this way: "As civil rulers, not having their duty to the people duly before them, may attempt to tyrannize, and as the military forces which must be occasionally raised to defend our country, might pervert their power to the injury of their fellow-citizens, the people are confirmed . . . in their right to keep and bear their private arms.[45]

The protection it granted was a blanket one. William Rawle, George Wash-ington's candidate for the nation's first attorney general, described the scope of

the Second Amendment's guarantee. "The prohibition," hewrote, "is general."
"No clause in the constitution could by any rule of construction be conceived
to give congress a power to disarm the people. Such a flagitious attempt could
only be made under some general pretence by a state legislature. But if in any
blind pursuit of inordinate power, either should attempt it, this amendment may
be appealed to as a restraint on both."[46]

The Second Amendment brought the American Constitution into closer
conformity with its English predecessor. In both cases, the intention was to
guarantee citizens the means for self-defense and to ensure that when, in the
course of time, it was necessary to raise standing armies, they would never pose
a danger to the liberties of the people.

AFTERWORD*

The right to be armed has not worn well, despite its enshrinement in the English and American bills of rights.[47] It is no longer a right of Englishmen.[48] The
curious will still find it in the English Bill of Rights, but it has been so gently
teased from public use that most Britons have no notion of when or how it came
to be withdrawn. The American Second Amendment, on the other hand, is at
the center of a noisy and emotional debate. It has been "infringed" by numerous
laws and is under fierce assault. Many who believe it guarantees an individual
right regard it as a dangerous anachronism, others insist that no individual right
was ever intended. Two recent law review articles characterize it, respectively, as
"embarrassing" and "terrifying," adjectives unlikely to be ascribed to any other
right.[49] Given new historical evidence of the Second Amendment's original
intent, it is reasonable to ask how, if at all, this information should be applied.
Americans, unsure whether banning weapons will make their lives more or less
dangerous, can certainly question whether the purpose of its eighteenth-century
authors is of other than academic interest. Although the demise of the English
right and the significance of the Second Amendment's original intent are outside the scope of this essay, they deserve to be addressed. . . .

From the expiration of the Seizure of Arms Act to the twentieth century,
"any person could purchase and keep in his possession a firearm without any
restriction."[50] Belief in its utility for individual and constitutional defence
remained firm, even after the creation of a professional police force in 1839. In
1850 the great Whig historian Thomas Macaulay maintained that it was "the
security without which every other is insufficient."[51] Nearly forty years later
James Paterson, in *Commentaries on the Liberty of the Subject and the Laws of
England Relating to the Security of the Person*, was emphatic that "in all countries
where personal freedom is valued, however much each individual may rely on
legal redress, the right of each to carry arms—and these the best and the

*From Joyce Lee Malcolm, *To Keep and Bear Arms: The Origins of a Anglo-American Right*
(Cambridge, Mass.: Harvard University Press, 1994), pp. 165–77.

sharpest—for his own protection in case of extremity, is a right of nature indelible and irrepressible, and the more it is sought to be repressed the more it will recur.[52]

By the mid-twentieth century this right had vanished, and with it the attitude that undergirded it. Compare Paterson's stance with the sanctimonious tone of "America's Vigilante Values," a recent article in the *Economist*. The author, ignorant of his own nation's history, is astonished that "out of reverence for the constitution, America has always refused to countenance effective national controls on the possession of guns: a restraint on personal liberty that seems, in most civilised countries, essential to the happiness of others."[53] Or consider *Freedom, the Individual, and the Law*, purportedly the first book to "survey comprehensively" the state of civil liberties in Britain, which fails to mention any right to be armed or even a right to self-defense.[54] For its author, Harris Street, security means only national security, and disarmament, military disarmament.[55] Between Paterson and Street lay the First World War. While the reverberations of the French Revolution left the English right to keep arms intact, the repercussions of World War I and the Bolshevik Revolution did not.

The Englishman's right to have weapons had always depended upon what was "allowed by law." As long as Parliament refused to intrude upon that right, legal restrictions were minor.[56] At the beginning of the twentieth century, the only important firearms law was the Gun Licence Act of 1870 which required anyone who wished to carry a gun outside his home to purchase an excise licence for 10s. at a post office. This was actually a revenue measure. In 1893 and again in 1895 the House of Commons decisively rejected a stringent pistol control bill as "grandmotherly, unnecessary and futile."[57] The Pistols Act that eventually passed in 1903 merely prohibited the sale of pistols to minors and felons.[58] But in 1920, a century after passage of the Seizure of Arms Act, Parliament approved a comprehensive arms control measure that effectively repealed the right to be armed by requiring a firearm certificate for anyone wishing to "purchase, possess, use or carry any description of firearm or ammunition for the weapon.[59] The local chief of police was to decide who could obtain a certificate and to exclude anyone of intemperate habits, unsound mind, or "for any reason unfitted to be trusted with firearms." Beyond the latitude provided by the exclusion of anyone "for any reason unfitted to be trusted," the applicant had to convince the officer that he had a "good reason for requiring such a certificate." In the House of Lords the government spokesman conceded that "good reason" would be "determined by practice."[60] An Englishman refused a certificate could appeal to a court, but Irishmen were denied any appeal.

A firearms certificate specified not only the weapon but the precise quantity of ammunition an individual could purchase and hold at any one time. Each certificate was renewable every three years for a fee. The penalty for a violation of the act was a fine not exceeding £50—a substantial sum in 1919—or imprisonment with or without hard labour for a term not exceeding three months, or both.[61] While fitness requirements for pistol and rifle certificates were strict, those for shotguns for the English, though not the Irish, were more perfunctory. The act also included sweeping controls over the manufacture, import, transportation, and sale of weapons and ammunition.

The announced rationale for the dramatic shift in firearms policy was an increase in armed crime. Yet statistics for London show no such increase. True, guns were freely available and crime common. But the rate of *armed* crime was extraordinarily low.[62] Between 1878 and 1886, for instance, the average number of burglaries in London in which firearms were used was two cases per year. From 1887 to 1891 this had risen to 3.6 cases per year. Between 1911 and 1913 the average number of crimes of all types involving any sort of firearm in London—then the largest city in the world—was 45. And between 1915 and 1917 the average number of crimes in which firearms were used actually fell from 45 to 15, though this decline may be attributable to the government's extensive controls over firearms under the Defence of the Realm Act, and to many potential criminals being off in the war. But if an increase in armed crime was not the motive for the act, what was?

Confidential cabinet papers point to government fears not of crime but of disorder and even revolution. Reading these papers today, one finds the tone of Cabinet meetings in January and February of 1920 almost hysterical. The Cabinet secretary left one such meeting with his "head fairly reeling. I felt I had been in Bedlam. Red revolution and blood and war at home and abroad!"[63] He was skeptical about the danger and believed that the prime minister was as well, but some of the ministers were deeply concerned about sabotage and revolution.[64] There were real, if exaggerated, reasons for alarm. The Great War had been preceded by industrial unrest and had been waged with appalling ferocity. Demobilization brought back to Britain thousands of soldiers brutalized in a savage and senseless conflict.[65] The Bolshevik Revolution was in full swing, and 1920 would see the creation of the Communist Party of Great Britain and the Trades Union Congress. Wages were extremely low, and, in the midst of a rash of strikes, the government was threatened with a general strike.[66] Ireland was in a state of virtual civil war. Regulation 40B of the Defence of the Realm Act—the emergency measure which had given the government the power to impose stringent restrictions upon the manufacture, sale, and possession of firearms and ammunition—was due to expire on August 31, 1920.

The government laid out a strategy to protect itself. The home secretary had plans to raise a temporary force of 10,000 soldiers but was assured by the prime minister that they would be "of little use," and ministers discussed making weapons available "for distribution to friends of the Government."[67] At the same time, it was suggested that a bill was needed "for licensing persons to bear arms," a strategy which "has been useful in Ireland because the authorities know who were possessed of arms." In 1918 a secret Home Office committee had drafted legislation to control firearms and had urged its adoption before demobilization: "It is desirable that the arms which are being dispersed over the country by soldiers returning from the Front should be brought without delay under the system of control which we recommend." [68] The proposed legislation would help ensure order, but Shortt, the home secretary, warned the Cabinet that "there had always been objections" to control of firearms.[69] The government had little need for the act during the war, but its substantial powers under the Defence of the Realm Act were now due to expire.

The reaction of Parliament in 1920 to the government's arms control bill is in sharp contrast to the behaviour of Parliament a century earlier when the Seizure of Arms Act was passed. Both were postwar eras with social and industrial violence and the fear of revolution. But whereas in 1820 the government's harsh measures were hotly contested, limited in area, and temporary, the new bill was sweeping, permanent, and exposed a sea change in attitude. It is well beyond the scope of this study to pin down, if that is possible, the reason for this change of attitude. On the traditional litmus test of faith in the public—their right to be armed—the governors of the twentieth century betrayed an embarrassing loss of confidence. Or perhaps modern Britain had, as the author of the article in the *Economist* suggests, merely wished to become a more "civilized nation." The incredible loss of life in the Great War had led to a revulsion against violence. It is ironic but understandable that the very purpose of the right to be armed that Blackstone and generations after him had considered crucial to the maintenance of limited government—the ability of the people to rebel—had caused the government and the governing classes to lose their nerve and remove the right. They claimed, however, that in 1920 there were other, safer means to preserve popular control. Little thought was given to individual defense.

The manner in which the government attempted to slip its arms bill by Parliament betrays its anxiety about the reception it would receive, and how recent the shift in attitude toward the old right was. It was introduced to the House of Lords on March 31 where it met with no objections. The bill emerged somewhat strengthened and was sent on to the Commons. After its first reading in the Commons on June 1, 1920, it was scheduled for a second reading and full debate the following day. This was cancelled. Then, at 10:40 on the evening of June 8, the bill was brought back without warning and with two other bills scheduled for consideration in the few minutes remaining before adjournment.[70] Only a handful of those members present were given copies of the text. The home secretary, Mr. Shortt, introduced it as "quite a short Bill . . . which in all probability will commend itself to the House and be regarded as noncontroversial."[71] The aim, he assured members, was to keep weapons from criminals and other dangerous persons, not to hamper "legitimate sport."[72] Shortt apparently left the impression that the bill would help deal with soldiers "who had become used to violence in the War" and threatened to become "a menace to the public."[73] The point was not lost. "After any great war," Major Barnes pointed out later in the debate, "there is a certain callousness with regard to life that needs to be dealt with." He noted that the previous firearms bill, the Pistols Act, was introduced in 1903 "after the South African War, and arose out of the necessities of the time."[74]

Shortt's point may have hit home but his strategy had failed. There was anger at the timing and manner of the debate and a variety of objections to the bill's contents. Interestingly, evidence of a new attitude toward the "ancient, indubitable right" on the part of both opponents and defenders of the bill surfaced in the debate. At the outset the government's motives were questioned. James Hogge suggested that the act might be applied to "grant the use of firearms to one class of people and absolutely deny it to another class."[75] James Kiley voiced the perennial argument that it would not reduce armed crime: "So far as burglars are concerned it will really have no effect. These men are dangerous, but there is nothing in this Bill which will adequately deal with them."[56] Only one member, Mr. Jameson, argued that ordinary people needed firearms for their personal protection. He took exception to the clause relating to Ireland because "for very many peaceful, law-abiding people it is a necessity of life almost that, if they are to remain in life, they shall have firearms with which to defend themselves against murderers and rebels. . . . The danger is that if you pass a law like this it will be obeyed by the peaceable subject, but not by the murderers and criminals. Therefore, the latter will retain their arms while the murderee, if I may use the word, will be deprived of his arms."[77]

Lieutenant-Commander Kenworthy had a series of objections.[78] He found himself in agreement with "older" MPs that the new legislation was redundant; they need only enforce the 1903 Pistols Act. Then Kenworthy addressed the deeper issue: "There is a much greater principle involved than the mere prevention of discharged convicts having weapons. In the past one of the most jealously guarded rights of the English was that of carrying arms. For long our people fought with great tenacity for the right of carrying the weapon of the day . . . and it was only in quite recent times that was given up. It has been a well-known object of the Central Government in this country to deprive people of their weapons."[79] He pointed out that Henry VII managed to break the power of the nobility by gaining control of England's artillery. Kenworthy continued:

> I do not know whether this Bill is aimed at any such goal as that but, if so, I would point out to the right hon. Gentleman that if he deprives private citizens in this country of every sort of weapon they could possibly use, he will not have deprived them of their power, because the great weapon of democracy to-day is not the halberd or the sword or firearms, but the power of withholding their]about I am sure that the power of withholding his labour is one of which certain Members of our Executive would very much like to deprive him. But it is our last line of defence against tyranny.[80]

He balked at granting the police the right to determine fitness for a certificate, considering it "contrary to English practice." The Pistols Act had placed that authority in the hands of a magistrate.

Major Earl Winterton leapt to the bill's defense and charged Kenworthy with holding "the most extraordinary theories of constitutional history and law."

His idea is that the State is an aggressive body, which is endeavouring to deprive the private individual of the weapons which Heaven has given into his hands to fight against the State. . . . Holding those views, and believing that it is desirable or legitimate or justifiable for private individuals to arm themselves, with . . . the ultimate intention of using their arms against the forces of the State, he objects to this Bill. There are other people who hold those views in this country, and it is because of the existence of people of that type that the Government has introduced this Bill.[81]

Kenworthy interrupted, "I do not think the Noble Lord wishes to misrepresent me . . . surely he understands that the very foundation of the liberty of the subject in this country is that he can, if driven to do so, resist, and I hope he will always be able to resist. You can only govern with the consent of the people."[82] The Earl refused to be drawn into "a long constitutional argument" but judged it "intolerable that, at this time, such a doctrine should be preached in this House as that it is desirable that people should arm themselves against the State."[83] He maintained that before the war the majority of Englishmen "had almost forgotten that there were such things as firearms and it was not necessary that the Home Secretary or the police should possess the powers which are necessary to-day." He backed away from the suggestion that "any attempt at armed insurrection is likely on the part of the great mass of the people of this country," but insisted that those "who wish to overthrow the State by violent means" must not be allowed to obtain firearms.[84]

Barnes then returned to the constitutional argument on behalf of the government. He judged "nothing more dangerous at the present time, or indeed at any time, than to lead the people of the country to believe that their method of redress was in the direction of armed resistance to the State."[85] "The time for that," he continued, "has gone."

We have in our methods of election, in our access to Parliament, and in other ways, means of redress against the action of the State which in times past were not afforded, and some of us, looking back into history, may believe it was because at one time people were able to carry weapons and use them against the State that we are in the happy position in which we find ourselves to-day. We certainly owe much of our liberty to-day, and the fact that we do not need, and I hope never will need, to resort to armed resistance, to the fact that some 200 or 300 years ago there were people who found it necessary to take up arms against the State.[86]

Neither side argued against the need for popular control, although they found that control in different expedients. But Barnes seems to have been correct that there was "unanimous agreement on both sides of the House" that whenever the Executive tends to aggression, "whether it be against life and liberty or against property," the subject should have "free appeal to the Courts . . . and it is by giving him opportunity through Parliament and through the Courts to find redress that we shall most effectively turn his attention away from using weapons."[87] When the question was put the House divided, with 254 voting in favour of the bill and only 6 against.

For many years the legislation was liberally enforced. Perhaps for that reason Britons had little sense of its potential. It was refined in 1937 and in 1968 extended to include shotguns. Police policies and massive increases in fees in recent years have combined to reduce sharply the number of those holding firearms certificates. At the same time, however, armed crime has increased. The Firearms Control Act was not really necessary to prevent revolution and has failed to stop armed crime or eliminate illegally owned weapons.[88] But that is not really the point. The point is that a British parliament, fearful of mayhem and social upheaval, deprived the public of a right to be armed, hoping that the people's other rights—to petition Parliament and the courts and to strike— would prevent tyranny. One wonders what Blackstone would think. He took account of recourse to the courts and the right to petition Parliament, and still believed a right to be armed essential. Or Macaulay, who, writing after the Reform Act made elections more equitable and professional police had been established, still insisted that the right to be armed was the "security without which every other is insufficient."

Are Britons sufficiently protected without the dangerous option of armed insurrection? Are individual Britons able to defend themselves and their families without recourse to firearms? Great Britain's modest level of violent crime has not skyrocketed and, since 1920, things have remained "in their legal and set-tled course." In DeLolme's words, the people have not needed "to move." Let us hope the decision taken in 1920 is never put to the test, and that other "democratic contrivances," other "quarantine Measures against that ancient plague, the lust for power," can achieve the same end.[89]

Should the Second Amendment to the American Constitution be permitted to go the way of the English right to be armed, as a dangerous relic of another era? In fact, it cannot be legislated out of existence in the same way. The American Congress is not sovereign, our Constitution is. The Constitution has a clear pro-cedure for altering its contents-amenclinent. If the government and people in their wisdom come to the conclusion that no need for the right of the people to be armed exists, or that such a right does more harm than good, then amend-ment is the course that should be followed. While it is unconstitutional to legis-late a right out of existence, this particular right is threatened with misinterpre-tation to the point of meaninglessness.[90] Granted, this is a far easier method of elimination than amendment, being much quicker and not requiring the same rigid consensus or forthright discussion of its constitutional relevancy. But it is also the way of danger. For to ignore all evidence of the meaning and intent of one of those rights included in the Bill of Rights is to create the most dangerous sort of precedent, one whose consequences could flow far beyond this one issue and endanger the fabric of liberty.

Should the Second Amendment be altered or eliminated through amendment? Before that is considered it is imperative to grant the founders of the American Constitution, whose wisdom in so much else has borne the test of time, the courtesy of considering why they included this right. Their original intent is of not only academic but immediate interest. What does the right actually mean, and why did they consider it essential? Are standing armies still a threat to a twentieth-century world? Do the people need a right and a means to revolution? Will other rights suffice? Are individuals still in need of personal weapons, "and these the best and the sharpest," for protection "in case of extremity?[91] I am not an advocate but a historian and ask merely for a decent respect for the past. We are not forced into lockstep with our forefathers. But we owe them our considered attention before we disregard a right they felt it imperative to bestow upon us.

NOTES

1. Ben R. Miller, sec.3, "The Legal Basis for Firearms Controls," *Report to the American Bar Association*, 22 (1975), p. 22.

2. Ibid., p. 26.

3. See Joyce Lee Malcolm, "The Right of the People to Keep and Bear Arms: The Common Law Tradition," *The Hastings Constitutional Law Quarterly* 10, no. 2 (winter 1983), especially pp. 286–289; Sanford Levinson, "The Embarrassing Second Amendment," *The Yale Law Journal* 99 (1989); Don B. Kates Jr., "Handgun Prohibition and the Original Meaning of the Second Amendment," *Michigan Law Review* 82, no. 2 (November 1983); Robert E. Shalhope, "The Ideological Origins of the Second Amendment," *The Journal of American History* 69, no. 1 (December, 1982); David T. Hardy, "The Second Amendment and the Bill of Rights," *The Journal of Law and Politics* 4, no. 1 (summer 1987); Lawrence Cress, "An Armed Community: The Origins and Meaning of the Right to Bear Arms," *The journal of American History* 71, no. 1 (June 1984); Shathope and Cress, "The Second Amendment and the Right to Bear Arms: An Exchange," *The Journal of American History* 71, no. 3 (December 1984). Stephen P. Halbrook, *That Every Man Be Armed. The Evolution of a Constitutional Right* (Albuquerque, 1984), a survey of Second Amendment history, particularly of value for the period after the ratification of the Second Amendment, should be used with caution for English common law history. See Joyce Lee Malcolm, "That Every Man Be Armed," *The George Washington Law Review* 54, nos. 2 and 3 (January and March 1986): 452–464. Also see Stephen P. Halbrook, *A Right to Bear Arms: State and Federal Bills of Rights and Constitutional Guarantees* (Westport, Conn., 1989); Lee Kenner and James Anderson, *The Gun in America* (Westport, 1975). Earlier works of interest are George D. Newton and Franklin E. Zimring, "Firearms and Violence in American Life: A Staff Report Submitted to the National Commission on the Causes and Prevention of Violence" (Washington, 1969); John Levin, "The Right to Bear Arms: The Development of the American Experience," *Chicago-Kent Law Review* 148 (1971); Roy Weatherup, "Standing Armies and Armed Citizens: An Historical Analysis of the Second Amendment," *Hastings Constitutional Law Quarterly* 2 (1975).

4. See, for example, Malcolm, "Right of the People to Keep and Bear Arms," pp. 285–89.

5. Newton and Zimring, "Firearms and Violence in American Life," p. 255; Kenner and Anderson, *The Gun in America*, pp. 25–27.

6. Weatherup, "Standing Armies and Armed Citizens," pp. 973–74.

7. Ibid. Weatherup also denied that the complaints in the Declaration of Rights that James II had disarmed Protestants were to be taken literally.

8. Alexis de Tocqueville, *Democracy in America*, ed. J. P. Mayer, trans. George Lawrence (Garden City, 1969), p. 32.

9. Cited by Weatherup, "Standing Armies and Armed Citizens," p. 975n. 33; *Blankand* v *Galdy*, 1693, discussed by Thomas Barnes in *English Legal System Carryover to the Colonies*, p. 16. And see George Lee Haskins, *Law and Authority in Early Massachusetts: A Study in Tradition and Design* (New York, 1960), pp. 4–8. More specifically, English law was applicable either as it existed on the date of settlement in settled colonies or as it existed on the date the first colonial assembly met in the case of conquered colonies. See *Cambell* v. *Hall*. In the first volume of *Commentaries*, Blackstone distinguished between uninhabited countries where "all the English laws are immediately there in force" once Englishmen settle, and conquered countries that have laws of their own. In this last case the King may alter or change those laws. He placed "our American plantations" in the latter category. See William Blackstone, *Commentaries on the Laws of England*, 4 vols., 1st ed., repr. (Chicago, 1979), 1:304–305. Colonial charters that provided for common law include the charters of Massachusetts (1626); Rhode Island (1663); Connecticut (1662); New York (1664); New Jersey (charter date unknown); Pennsylvania (1681); Delaware (1701); Maryland (1701; Virginia (1606); North Carolina (1663); South Carolina (1712); and Georgia (1732)

10. See Kermit Hall, *The Magic Mirror: Law in American History* (Oxford, 1989), pp. 11–12.

11. The growth of the population in England's American colonies was phenomenal. The population in 1670 of approximately 85,000 persons had quadrupled by 1713 and quadrupled again by 1754 to some 1,500,000 persons. See Samuel Eliot Morison, *The Oxford History of the American People*, 3 vols. (New York, 1972), 1:196. On the charters see, for example, the Charter of Virginia, 1606, *The Federal and State Constitutions, Colonial Charters, and Other Organic Laws of the States, Territories, and Colonies*, ed. F. Thorpe (1909); Charter of Connecticut, Charles II, *The Public Records of the Colony of Connecticut*, ed. J. Hammond Trumbull et al., 15 vols. (Hartford, 1852–1890), 1:7.; Charter of Massachusetts Bay, William & Mary, *Acts and Resolves of the Province of Massachuetts Bay* (Boston, 1869), vol. 1, p. 14.

12. See McDonald, *Novus Ordo Seclorum*, pp. 12–13.

13. David S. Lovejoy, *The Glorious Revolution in America* (New York, 1972), p. 378.

14. Hall, *Magic Mirror*, p. 13

15. Part of the impetus to limit slavery in Georgia, for example, was the need to increase the number of armed free men in the frontier population.

16. See, for example, *The Book of the General Lawes and Libertyes Concerning the Inhabitants of the Massachusetts Bay* (1st ed. Boston, 1648; photo. repr. 1975), pp. 39–42; *The Public Records of the Colony of Connecticut; Records of the Colony of Rhode Island and Providence Plantations in New England*, ed. J. Bartlett, 10 vols. (Providence, 1856–1865).

17. Fred Anderson compares the Massachusetts militia to "an all-purpose military infrastructure: a combination of home guard, draft board, and rearechelon supply network." Fred Anderson, *A People's Army: Massachusetts Soldiers and Society in the Seven Years' War* (Chapel Hill, 1984), p. 27.

18. *Laws of Colony of New Plymouth, 1623*, repr. in *The Compact with the Charter and Laws of the Colony of New Plymouth* (Boston, 1836), p. 31.

19. "An Act Preventing Negroes from Bearing Arms" (1640), *The Old Dominion in the Seventeenth Century: A Documentary History of Virginia, 1606–1689*, ed. W. Billings (Chapel Hill, 1975), p. 172.

20. *Records of Colony of Rhode Island*, 1:94.

21. *The Statutes at Large: Being A Collection of All the Laws of Virginia from the First Session of the Legislature, in the Year 1619*, ed. William Waller Hening (New York, 1823), 1:127, nos. 24, 25, 27, 28; 1:174, Act 51 (1631–1632).

22. *Records of Colony of Connecticut*, 8:380.

23. *The Colonial Records of the State of Georgia* (Atlanta, 1904–1910), vol. I, XIX, pt. I, pp. 137–39.

24. See "Governor Nicholls' Answer to the Severall Queries Relative to the Planters in the Territories of His Royal Highness the Duke of Yorke in America," *Documents Relative to the Colonial History of the State of New York*, ed. E. B. O'Callaghan and B. Fernow, 15 vols. (Albany, 1853–1887), 1:88; *Massachusetts General Laws*, p. 35.

25. See Halbrook, *That Every Man Be Armed*, pp. 56–57.

26. See Robert Cottrol and Raymond T. Diamond, "The Second Amendment: Toward an Afro-Americanist Reconsideration," *The Georgetown Law Journal* 80, no. 2 (December, 1990), pp. 323–24.

27. *Massachusetts General Laws*, p. 28. And see *Laws of Colony of New Plymouth*, p. 63.

28. Morison, *The Oxford History of the American People*, 1:159.

29. "An Act for the Safeguard and Defence of the Country against the Indians," 28 Car. II, cited by Halbrook, *That Every Man Be Armed*, p. 56.

30. There is an instance in 1652 where Massachusetts apparently did require such participation. See Winthrop Jordan, *White over Black. American Attitudes toward the Negro, 1550–1812* (Chapel Hill, 1968), p. 71.

31. Lorenzo J. Greene, *The Negro in Colonial New England* (New York, 1968), p. 127. Also see Jordan, *White over Black*, p. 71.

32. A. L. Higginbotham, *In the Matter of Color: Race and the American Legal Process: The Colonial Period* (New York, 1978), p. 32.

33. *Old Dominion in the Seventeenth Century*, p. 172; Higginbotham, *In the Matter of Color*, p. 32.

34. See Higginbotham, *In the Matter of Color*, pp. 201–215.

35. *Colonial Records of Georgia*, XIX, pt. I, pp. 76–77.

36. See J. R. Western, *The English Militia in the Eighteenth Century: The Story of a Political Issue, 1660–1802* (London, 1965), for a general discussion of the problems facing the English militia. The Mutiny Act remained of only twelve-month duration into the twentieth century.

37. See Michael Roberts, *The Military Revolution* (Belfast, 1956).

38. I Will. & Mar., sess. 2, c.2; I Will. & Mar., c.5. And see Thomas Alan Critchley, *The Conquest of Violence: Order and Liberty in Britain* (London, 1970), p. 68; Western, *English Militia*, p. 73. Reid finds English magistrates sometimes reluctant to use the army to quell riots. See Reid, *In Defiance of the Law*, pp. 233–134, app. p. 235.

39. Blackstone, *Commentaries*, 1:139.

40. See the proposals of Virginia, New York, North Carolina, and Rhode Island, in *Documentary History of the Constitution*, 2:380, 191, 269, 314.

41. See John Smiley, *Documentary History of the Ratification*, 2:509.

42. "Centinel, Revived," no. 24, *Independent Gazetteer*, September 9, 1789, p. 2, col. 2, and cited by Halbrook, *That Every Man Be Armed*, p. 80.

43. *Documentary History of the Constitution*, 2:143, 191, 269, 314; Elliot, *State Debates*, 2:406.

44. Madison, *Notes*, p. 639.

45. *Philadelphia Federal Gazette* and *Philadelphia Evening Post*, 18 June 1789, no. 68, vol. 2, p. 2, repr. by *New York Packet*, June 23, 1789, p. 2, col. 1–2, and by *Boston Centenial*, 4 July 1789, p. 1, col. 2.

46. William Rawle, *A View of the Constitution of the United States of America*, 2d ed. (Philadelphia, 1829), pp. 125–26.

47. Benjamin N. Cardozo, *The Nature of the Judicial Process* (New Haven, 1921), pp. 92–93.

48. This means not that firearms are unobtainable in Great Britain, but that there is no right to have them.

49. Sanford Levinson, "The Embarrassing Second Amendment," *The Yale Law Review* 99, no 3 (December 1989); David C. Williams, "Civic Republicanism and the Citizen Militia: The Terrifying Second Amendment," *The Yale Law Review* 101, no. 3 (December 1991).

50. This statement of fact was made by the Earl of Onslow in introducing the government's firearms bill in the House of Lords on April 27, 1920. See *Parliamentary Debates*, House of Lords, new series, 39:1025.

51. Thomas Macaulay, *Critical and Historical Essays, Contributed to the Edinburgh Review* (Leipzig, 1850), pp. 154, 162.

52. James Paterson, *Commentaries on the Liberty of the Subject and the Law of England Relating to the Security of the Person*, 2 vols. (London, 1877), 1:441.

53. *The Economist*, June 20–26, 1992, p. 17.

54. Harris Street, *Freedom, the Individual and the Law*, 2d ed. (Bristol, 1963), p. 10.

55. Ibid., pp. 191, 205.

56. "An Act to amend the Law relating to Firearms and other Weapons and Ammunition, and to amend the Unlawful Drilling Act, 1819," 10 & 11 Geo. V, c.43. And see Colin Greenwood, *Firearms Control: A Study of Armed Crime and Firearms Control in England and Wales* (London, 1972), p. 2 5.

57. Greenwood, *Firearms Control*, p. 25.

58. The Pistols Act of 1903, 3 Edward VII, c.18, did not apply to Ireland and, according to the Earl of Onslow, "A person there can purchase and keep in his possession any number of pistols of any size or description, without even going through the formality of buying a gun licence." See *Parliamentary Debates*, 39:1026. For a brief account of the parliamentary debates on the pistol control bills of 1893 and 1895, see Greenwood, *Firearms Control*, pp. 23–25.

59. "An Act to amend the Law relating to Firearms and other Weapons and Ammunition, and to amend the Unlawful Drilling Act, 1819," 10 & 11 Geo. V, c.43.

60. *Parliamentary Debates*, 39:1030.

61. These penalties were substantially greater in Ireland, which was in a virtual state of civil war at the time. Imprisonment could be for two years, there was no provision for appeal, and additional powers of arrest and search were conferred upon police constables in dealing with persons suspected of being in possession of firearms.

62. I am indebted to Colin Greenwood, author of *Firearms Control*, for the crime statistics that follow.

63. Thomas Jones, *Whitehall Diary*, ed. Keith Middlemas, 3 vols. (Oxford, 1969), 1:97.

64. The Cabinet discussions are from Jones, *Whitehall Diary*, I:97–102.

65. Prior to World War I there was growing anxiety about pistol-wielding anarchists and the dangers of rapid-firing revolvers, but the statistics fail to reflect any real increase in armed crime.

66. Of these strikes, the first was that of the metropolitan police in August 1918. Their wages had fallen so low that many officers' families were actually destitute.

67. According to Jones's notes, he believed that the Prime Minister merely "played the role of taking the revolution very seriously." There were suspicions that the panic "was a War Office dodge for increasing the number of army recruits." When the Prime Minister pointed out that the eight battalions intended for the plebiscitary areas had been detained at home, the Home Office secretary's demand for the 10,000 men was dropped. See Jones, *Whitehall Diary*, 1:99.

68. Indeed, their first recommendation was that military firearms and ammunition that belonged to the government should on demobilization be returned to store and remain under "*complete and permanent Government control.*" Military firearms that belonged to officers or enlisted men were to be prevented from being thrown upon the market. "Report of Committee on the Control of Firearms," #5514, 1918, par. 16, Cambridge Institute of Criminology.

69. The Committee was chaired by Sir Emley Blackwell, Under Secretary of State for the Home Department, and included the former Commissioner of the Prison Service and representatives from the metropolitan police, the county and borough police, the Board of Customs, the Board of Trade, the War Office, and the Irish Office. It met in secret and its reports were never published.

70. See *The Parliamentary Debates: Official Report*, House of Commons, 5th series, 1920, 130:361–370, 655–686.

71. Ibid., 130:361. When discussion resumed on the bill on June 10, the government was accused of having "attempted to force it through the House at a late hour." See 130:656–657.

72. Ibid., 130:361–62.

73. Ibid., p. 657.

74. Ibid., p. 672.

75. Ibid., pp. 364–65.

76. Ibid., p. 369.

77. Ibid., 133:86.

78. See Ibid., 130:656–65.

79. Ibid., p. 658.

80. Ibid., pp. 658–59.

81. Ibid., pp. 662–63.

82. Ibid., p. 663.

83. Ibid.

84. Ibid., pp. 664–65.

85. Ibid., p. 670.

86. Ibid., p. 671. And see p. 674.

87. Ibid., p. 671.

88. There are now fewer than 50,000 pistols in legitimate hands in England and Wales. According to Cohin Greenwood, since the end of World War II a quarter of a million illegally held pistols have been confiscated by the police, and the annual numbers confiscated continue to increase. The number of illegal pistols confiscated in London over a four-year period exceeded the number of legally held pistols. I wish to thank Mr. Greenwood for making the results of his studies available to me.

89. Friedrich Wilhelm Neitzsche, in *The Viking Book of Aphorisms*, ed. W. H. Auden and Louis Kronenberger (New York, 1966), p. 310.

90. See Levinson, "The Embarrassing Second Amendment."

91. Paterson, *Commentaries on the Liberty of the Subject*, 1:441.

33

"TO KEEP AND BEAR ARMS"

GARRY WILLS

Over the last decade, an industrious band of lawyers, historians, and criminologists has created a vast outpouring of articles justifying individual gun ownership on the basis of the Second Amendment: "A well regulated militia being necessary to the security of a free state, the right of the people to keep and bear arms shall not be infringed."

This body of commentary, much of it published in refereed law journals, has changed attitudes toward the Second Amendment. The National Rifle Association's lobbyists distribute it to legislators. Journalists like Michael Kinsley and George Will disseminate this school's views. Members of it now claim, on the basis of their work's quantity and what they believe is its quality, that scholarship on this subject is now all theirs—so that even to hold an opposing view is enough to "discredit its supporters," according to the historian Joyce Lee Malcolm.[1]

The *Tennessee Law Review* devotes most of its spring issue to a collection of articles by members of this school, including one that says its authors have created "the Standard Model" for interpreting the Second Amendment. To this mood of self-congratulation can be added the fact that a majority of Americans tell pollsters that they believe the Second Amendment protects private ownership of guns. So the defenders of that position feel they hold both the scholarly high ground and the popular consensus. The five who constitute a kind of inner circle of Standard Modelers—Robert J. Cottrol, Stephen E. Halbrook, Don B.

Reprinted with permission from the *New York Review of Books*, 21 September 1995. Copyright © 1995, NYREV, Inc.

Kates, Joyce Lee Malcolm, and Robert E. Shalhope—recycle each other's arguments energetically. Three of the five write in the *Tennessee Law Review* issue, one of them (Malcolm) devoting her essay to the fourth (Cottrol), while the fifth (Shalhope) is frequently cited.

Then why is there such an air of grievance, of positive victimhood, in the writings of the "Standard Model" school? They talk of the little honor they are given, of the "mendacious" attitude of the legal establishment, of a rigidity that refuses to recognize their triumph. Don Kates (with coauthors) sputters in mixed metaphors of an opposition that "exists in a vacuum of lock-step orthodoxy almost hermetically sealed from the existence of contrary data and scholarship."[2] Randy F. Barnett, introducing the *Tennessee Law Review* symposium predicts dire things if people do not "accord some respect to those citizens (and academics) whose views it [the Standard Model Scholarship] supports."[3] Glenn Harlan Reynolds, in the article stating the Standard Model thesis, argues that militia extremism may be fueled by the Model's opponents, who are "treating the Constitution, too, as a preserve of the elite."[4]

Their own reciprocating nods and citations of approval are apparently not enough for these authors. Nor is popular support enough. They still talk like Rodney Dangerfield, getting no respect. They should ask themselves more penetratingly why this should be. Perhaps it is the quality of their arguments that makes them hard to take seriously. . . .

Yet both the general public, which has a disposition to believe that the Second Amendment protects gun ownership, and the NRA lobby are holstered in that view by the sheer mass of the articles now being ground out and published in journals. It is difficult to sort out all the extraneous, irrelevant, and partial material daily thrown into the debate. Even to make a beginning is difficult. One must separate what the Second Amendment says from a whole list of other matters not immediately at issue. Some argue, for instance, that there is a natural right to own guns (Blackstone is often quoted here) antecedent to the right protected by the amendment, or that such a right may be protected in other places (common law, state constitutions, statute, custom, etc.). All that could be true without affecting the original scope of the Second Amendment. One could argue for instance, that owners of property have a right to charge rental on it—but that is not the point at issue in the Third Amendment (against quartering federal troops on private property).

In order to make any progress at all, we must restrict ourselves to what, precisely, is covered by the Second Amendment. That is not hard to determine, once the irrelevant debris adrift around its every term has been cleared away. Each term exists in a discernible historic context, as does the sentence structure of the amendment.

That amendment, as Madison first moved it, read:

The right of the people to keep and bear arms shall not be infringed; a well armed and well regulated militia being the best security of a free country; but no person religiously scrupulous of bearing arms shall be compelled to render military service in person.[5]

The whole sentence looks to military matters, the second clause giving the reason for the right's existence, and the third giving an exception to that right. The connection of the parts can be made obvious by using the same structure to describe other rights. One could say, for instance: "The right of free speech shall not be infringed; an open exchange of views giving the best security to intellectual liberty; but no person shall be free to commit libel." Every part is explained in relation to every other part. The third clause makes certain what Madison means *in this place* by "bear arms." He is not saying that Quakers, who oppose war, will not be allowed to use guns for hunting or sport.

Did the changes made to Madison's proposed amendment remove it from its original (solely military) context? Only two substitutions were made in the wording—"country" became "state" and "the best security of" became "necessary to." This latter change might demote the right to bear arms by comparison with other rights (perhaps, say, free speech is the very best security of freedom), but it does not alter the thing being discussed.[6] Beyond that, nothing was *added* to the text, so it could not be altered by addition. Was it altered by deletion? "Well armed and" was dropped, in drafting sessions that generally compressed the language, but "well regulated" includes "well armed." . . . Then the whole third clause was omitted—but for a reason that still dealt with the military consequences of the sentence.

Elbridge Gerry objected to the third clause on the grounds that rulers might *declare* some people "scrupulous" and then exclude them from service—as some tended to declare Quakers ineligible for office since they take no oaths; or as Catholics were once declared incapable, without scruple, of defending a Protestant government.[7] Gerry was clearly talking of public service, not whether Quakers should go hunting or target shooting. His objection resembles the one Samuel Johnson made to limiting militia service by the imposition of a religious oath.[8]

One transposition was made in Madison's sqntence, but it *strengthened* the military context, as even the Standard Modeler, Joyce Lee Malcolm, admits.[9] The basis for the asserted right was put first, as is normal in legal documents. The preamble, the "whereas," the context-establishing clause—these set the frame for what follows: "A well regulated militia being necessary to the security of a free State, the right of the people to keep and bear arms shall not be infringed." To use again the parallel sentence on free speech, transposition would produce: "An open exchange of views being necessary to the security of intellectual liberty, the right of free speech shall not be infringed." Such preceding declaration of intent is found, for example, in the Constitulion's copyright clause (Article I, Section 8, Clause 8), where the simple listing of granted powers "to coin money . . . to declare war," etc., is varied by a prior statement of purpose: "to promote the progress of science and useful arts by securing for limited times to authors and inventors." The prefixed words give the reason for, and scope of, what follows.

So nothing was added or changed that affected Madison's original subject matter. The things removed did not change the sentence's frame of reference. The transposition fixed the sentence even more precisely in a military context. How, then, did the ratification alter Madison's terms? The Standard Modelers draw on an argument made by Stephen Halbrook, an argument often cited by the NRA:

> The Senate specifically rejected a proposal to add "for the common defense" after "to keep and bear arms," thereby precluding any construction that the right was restricted to militia purposes and to common defense against foreign aggression or domestic tyranny.[10]

His proof of deliberate preclusion is this passage in the Senate records: "It was moved, to insert the words, 'for the common defence,' but the motion was not successful." We are not told why the motion failed. We know the Senate was mainly compressing and combining the amendments, not adding to the language. There are several possible reasons for the action, all more plausible than Halbrook's suggestion that "for the common defense" would have *imported* a military sense that is lacking without it. The military sense is the obvious sense. It does not cease to become the obvious sense if something that *might* have been added was not added.

The obvious reason for excluding the term "common defense" is that it could make the amendment seem to support only joint action of the state militias acting in common (shared) defense under federal control. The Articles of Confederation had used "common defense" to mean just that, and the defenders of state militias would not want to restrict themselves to that alone."[11] The likelihood that this is the proper reason is strengthened when it is considered in relation to another change the drafters made, in Madison's text, from "free country" to "free state." We are not expressly given the reason for that change, either; but most people (including Standard Modeler Malcolm) agree that the reason was to emphasize the state's separate militias, not the common defense of the country.[12] If that is the obvious reason there, it is also the obvious reason for omitting "common defense."

There are other possible (though less plausible) reasons for the omissions— e.g., to prevent tautology. What is neither warranted nor plausible is Halbrook's certitude that these words were omitted *deliberately* to *preclude* militia-language. The whole context of the amendment was always military. Halbrook cannot effect an alchemical change of substance by bringing two words, "common defense," near to, but not into, the amendment. . . .

The Standard Model finds, squirreled away in the Second Amendment, not only a private right to own guns for any purpose but a public right to oppose with arms the government of the United States. It grounds this claim in the right of insurrection, which clearly does exist whenever tyranny exists. Yet the right to *overthrow* government is not given by government. It arises when government no longer has authority. One cannot say one rebels by right of that nonexistent authority. Modern militias say the government itself instructs them to overthrow government—and wacky scholars endorse this view. They think the Constitution is so deranged a document that it brands as the greatest crime a war upon itself (in Article III: "Treason against the United States shall consist only in levying war against them") and then instructs its citizens to take this up (in the Second Amendment). According to this doctrine, a well-regulated group is meant to overthrow its own regulator, and a soldier swearing to obey orders is disqualified for true militia virtue.

Gun advocates claim that a militia is meant to oppose (not assist) the standing army. But even in England the militia's role was not to fight the king's army. The point of the militias was to make it unnecessary to establish a standing army. That no longer applied when the Second Amendment was adopted, since the Constitution had already provided Congress the powers to "raise and support armies" (Article I, Section 8, Clause 12), to "provide and maintain a navy" (Clause 13), and "to make rules for the government and regulation of the land and naval forces" (Clause 14). The battle against a standing army was lost when the Constitution was ratified, and nothing in the Second Amendment as it was proposed and passed altered that.[13] Nor did it change the Constitution's provision for using militias "to suppress insurrections" (Clause 15), not to foment them.

Yet gun advocates continue to quote from the ratification debates as if those arguments applied to the interpretation of the Second Amendment. They were aimed at the military clauses in the proposed Constitution. Patrick Henry and others did not want the Constitbtion to pass precisely because it would set up a standing army—and it did.

One of the Standard Modelers' favorite quotations, meant to prove that the militia was designed to fight against, not for, the federal government, is James Madison's argument, in *Federalist* No. 46, that any foreseeable national army could not conquer a militia of "half a million citizens with arms in their hands." But Madison says this while what he calls a "visionary supposition"—that the federal government has become a tyranny, overthrowing freedom.

> That the people and the States should for a sufficient period of time elect an uninterrupted succession of men ready to betray both; that the traitors should throughout this period, uniformly and systematically preserve some fixed plan for the extension of the military establishment; that the governments and the people of the States should silently and patiently behold the gathering storm, and continue to supply the materials, until it should be prepared to burst on their own heads, must appear to every one more like the incoherent dreams of a delirious jealousy, or the misjudged exaggeration of a counterfeit zeal, than like the sober apprehensions of genuine patriotism.[14]

Madison says he will grant, *per impossible*, such a hypothesis in order to consider the result:

> A correspondence would be opened. Plans of resistance would be concerted. One spirit would animate and conduct the whole. The same combination in short would result from an apprehension of the federal, as was produced by the dread of the foreign yoke.

Madison is describing the Revolution, when Committees of Correspondence, Minutemen, and other bodies of resistance to tyranny sprang into being. It is not the "well-regulated militia" under the Constitution that is being described, but the revolutionary effort of a people overthrowing any despotism that replaces the Constitution and makes it void. Tyrannicides do not take their warrant from the tyrant's writ. In Madison's dire hypothesis, all bets are off and the pre-government right of resistance replaces governmental regulations *including the Second Amendment*. He is not describing the militia as envisioned in the Second Amendment. To use his words as if they explained the amendment's proper functioning is absurd.

It is from such material that the Standard Model makes its case that militias are supposed to oppose the government that organizes, funds, and regulates them. They have been helped along by two frivolous but influential articles supposedly written "from the left," published in the *Yale Law Journal*. In 1989, Sanford Levinson found the idea of a right to revolution in the Second Amendment so "interesting" that it, along with other things in the text, could be "embarrassing" to liberals like himself.[14] One sign of this article's influence is that it dazzled the eminent constitutionalist George Will, whose praise for the article has been disseminated ever since by the National Rifle Association.[16] In 1991, David L. Williams upped Sanford Levinson's bid, calling the Second Amendment not only "embarrassing" but "terrifying" because it imports republican resistance into a merely liberal document.[17] If no modern militia meets the standards of republican virtue, then the courts should try to enforce the Second Amendment by other "republican" steps—like universal service, broader distribution of property, and other things Professor Williams agrees with. Any document would be terrifying if it mandates whatever a professor has on his wish list.

Both Levinson and Williams quote indiscriminately from republican literature and the ratification debates as if the question of a standing army were still "up" when the amendment was framed and ratified. With scholars like these, the NRA hardly needs to hire its own propagandists. They all agree, for their own circuitous reasons, that Second Amendment militias are organized, funded, and regulated by the federal government so that they may take arms against the federal government. It sometimes seems as if our law journals were being composed by Lewis Carroll using various other pseudonyms.

Gun advocates claim that the "right of the people" to keep and bear arms is distributive, the right of every individual taken singly. It has that sense in, for instance, the Fourth Amendment ("the right of the people to be secure in their persons"):But the militia as "the people" was always the *populus armatus*, in the corporate sense (one cannot be a one-person militia; one must be formed into groups). Thus Trenchard calls the militia "the people" even though as we have seen, the groups he thought of were far from universal.[18] The militia literature often refers to "the great body of the people" as forming the militia, and body (corpus) is a necessarily corporate term. The great body means "the larger portion or sector of" (OED, "great," 8:c). This usage came from concepts like "sovereignty is in the people." This does not mean that every individual is his or her own sovereign. When the American people revolted against England, there were loyalists, hold-outs, pacifists who did not join the revolution. Yet Americans claimed that the "whole people" rose, as Madison wrote in the *Federalist*, since the connection with body makes "whole" retain its original, its etymological sense—wholesome, hale, sound (*sanus*). The whole people is the *corpus sanum*, what Madison calls "the people at large."[19] Thus "the people" form militias though not every individual is included in them. The people as a popular body (*corpus*) was often contrasted with the rulers (*senatus populusque*), which is not a distributive sense (that would exclude senators from individual rights).

Gun advocates like to quote republican literature, based on classical history, to say that every citizen should be a soldier. That was true of Greece and Rome, where slaves gave citizens far greater freedom to be devoted to political and military life. But we should remember two things. Ancient citizens were not trained to be *militiamen*, a force supplementary to regular troops. Athenians were trained to *be* the regular troops (hoplites), as Romans trained to be legionaries. And, second, initiation into citizenship was part of the same process that inducted one into religious duties to the state.[20] No modern republic has contemplated such militarization and regimentation of political life, which is the very farthest thing from the individualism of those who would read the Second Amendment distributively. Political life was *corporate* life in antiquity.

A false universalism makes the Standard Modelers say that the militia mentioned in the Second Amendment is made up of the entire citizenry. Enrollment of a segment of the populace in the National Guard does not count, since that is what the British described negatively as a "select" militia.[21] The attempt to raise a volunteer force for royal use across local lines was seen, in the seventeenth century, as a step toward assembling the elements of a standing army. But that does not mean that the ordinary local militia was ever universal. No locale could empty out its fields and shops to train all males of the appropriate age. The militia was in fact "select" in that it represented the local squirearchy and its dependents. The very operation of the militia depended on some people continuing their ordinary work—civil officials, food suppliers, sowers and harvesters, ostlers, blacksmiths, and the like. The very term "trained bands" means that the militia was not universal: only those with the time, opportunity, acceptance, and will to be exercised in training were actual "bandsmen," on whose discipline depended the effectiveness of the trained bands in precluding the need for a standing army. Any break-down of order at the local level would destroy the argument that militias were a sufficient defense of the kingdom under ordinary circumstances.

It is true that Congress passed a militia law in 1792 providing that every able-bodied man should equip himself with a musket to serve in the militia—but it was a dead letter, since no organized training was provided for.[22] This was like defining the jury pool as the citizenry at large without providing for voir dires, so that no jury panels could be formed. Not until Congress passed the Dick Act in 1903 was the overall organization of a trained militia (the Guard) put on a regular basis. The gun advocates' talk of a time when the militia of the United States was universal is not nostalgia for a past reality, but a present dream about a past dream. The militia actions of the nineteenth century were sporadic, "select," and largely ineffectual.[23]

Adam Smith predicted in the eighteenth century, and Max Weber confirmed in this century, that modern principles of the division of labor, specialization of sci-entific warfare, and bureaucratization of responsibility would shift the functions of the eighteenth-century militia to professional armies and to local police forces, giving the state a *"monopoly on force"* as a matter of efficiency. George Washington, who had bitterly criticized the militias during the Revolution, tried to adhere to the Second Amendment by proposing what was known as the Knox Plan, for a small but well-trained militia. Congress, instead, gave him the Militia Act of 1792, which made of the militia a velleity.

Why, in fact, did Madison propose the Second Amendment? Not to prevent a standing army. That was already established by Article I, and the amendment did not overthrow it. Not to organize the militia. That, too, was mandated by Article I. Even a Standard Modeler like Joyce Lee Malcolm treats the amendment as, constitutionally, a gesture: "A strong statement of preference for a militia must have seemed more tactful than an expression of distrust of the army."[24] Consti-tutional law normally enacts more than "a strong statement of preference."

Why, then, did Madison propose the Second Amendment? For the same reason that he proposed the Third, against quartering troops on the civilian pop-ulation. That was a remnant of old royal attempts to create a standing army by requisition of civilian facilities. It had no real meaning in a government that is authorized to build barracks, forts, and camps. But it was part of the anti-royal rhetoric of freedom that had shown up, like the militia language, in state requests for amendments to the Constitution.

Madison knew that the best way to win acceptance of the new government was to accommodate its critics on the matter of a bill of rights. He had opposed that during the ratification debates, recognizing that people like Robert White-hill and Patrick Henry were using the demand to kill the document, not to improve it. His assessment was confirmed when Antifederalists like Henry and Whitehill changed their stance and *opposed* the amendments when Madison offered them. Henry thought that the amendments would "tend to injure rather than serve the cause of liberty" by lulling the suspicions of those who had demanded amendments in the first place. . . . The Antifederalist strategy, it seems, was to reject the most popular of the amendments, thus making it necessary for Congress to take up the whole matter again.[25]

Henry feared that Madison was doing in the Antifederalists with sweet talk, and he was right. Madison confided to a friend: "It will kill the opposition everywhere."[26] Sweet-talking the militia was a small price to pay for such a coup—and it had as much impact on real life as the anti-quartering provisions that arose from the same motive. Thus he crafted an amendment that did not prevent the standing army (and was not meant to) but drew on popular terms that were used for that purpose in the past. His sentence structure set as totally military a context for this amendment as for the Third. Every term in the Second Amendment, taken singly, has as its first and most obvious meaning a military meaning. Taken together, each strengthens the significance of all the others as part of a military rhetoric.

Against this body of evidence we have the linguistic tricks of the Standard Model which wrench terms from context and impose fanciful meanings on them. The Standard Model takes apart the joint phrasing of keep-and-bear arms to make "keep" mean only keep-in-the-home-for-private-use and "bear arms" mean carry-a-gun-in-the-hand. The ratification-debate attacks on the militia clause of the Constitution are illegitimately applied to the support of the later amendment. Madison is made to talk as if obliterating the government could be a way to obey the government. We are told that the Second Amendment is deliberately insurrectionary and proclaimed (in an absent-minded way) the right of armed rebellion as a method of regulating the military. We are told that arms, all the equipage of war, can be borne in a coat pocket. Heraldry is mixed with haberdashery, humbug with history, and scholarly looking footnotes with simple-minded literalism. By the methods used in the Standard Model, we could argue that a good eighteenth-century meaning for "quarter" shows that the Third Amendment was intended to prevent soldiers from having their limbs lopped off in private homes.

As I said at the beginning, my argument does not deny any private right to own and use firearms. Perhaps that can be defended on other grounds—natural law, common law, tradition, statute. It is certainly true that most people assumed such a right in the 1780s—so naturally, in fact, that the question was not "up" and calling for specific guarantees. All I maintain is that Madison did not address that question when drafting his amendment. When he excepted those with religious scruple, he made clear that "bear arms" meant wage war—no Quaker was to be deprived of his hunting gun.

The recent effort to find a new meaning for the Second Amendment comes from the failure of appeals to other sources as a warrant for the omnipresence of guns of all types in private hands. Easy access to all these guns is hard to justify in pragmatic terms, as a matter of social policy. Mere common law or statute may yield to common sense and specific cultural needs. That is why the gun advocates appeal, above pragmatism and common sense, to a supposed sacred right enshrined in a document Americans revere. Those advocates love to quote Sanford Levinson, who compares the admitted "social costs" of adhering to gun rights with the social costs of observing the First Amendment.[27] We have to put up with all kinds of bad talk in the name of free talk. So we must put up with our world-record rates of homicide, suicide, and accidental shootings because, whether we like it or not, the Constitution tells us to. Well, it doesn't.

NOTES

1. Joyce Lee Malcolm, "Gun Control and the Constitution: Sources and Explorations on the Second Amendment," *Tennessee Law Review* (spring 1995): 815.

2. Don B. Kates, Henry E. Schaffer, John K. Lattimer, George B. Murray, and Edwin H. Cassem, "Guns and Public Health: Epidemic of Violence or Pandemic of Propaganda?" *Tennessee Law Review* (spring 1995): 519.

3. Randy E. Barnett, "Guns, Militias, and Oklahoma City," *Tennessee Law Review* (spring 1995): 452.

4. Glenn Harlan Reynolds, "A Critical Guide to the Second Amendment," *Tennessee Law Review* (Spring 1995), p. 512.

5. Bernard Schwartz, *The Bill of Rights: A Documentary History*, vol. 2 (Chelsea House, 1971), p. 1026.

6. It was a commonplace that a proper militia was "the best security" to a state—meaning best physical guarantor of "national security." Adam Smith uses just those words in his *Lectures on Jurisprudence* (Oxford University Press, 1978), p. 543. But Madison broadened the issue by distinguishing a free country's protection.

7. Bernard Schwartz, *The Bill of Rights*, vol. 2, p. 1107; "They can declare who are religiously scrupulous, and prevent them from bearing arms."

8. "See Johnson's texts analyzed J. C. D. Clark, in *Samuel Johnson: Literature, Religion and English Cultural Politics From the Restoration to Romanticism* (Cambridge Univerity Press, 1994), pp. 120–26.

9. Joyce Lee Malcolm, *To Keep a Bear Arms: The Origins of an Anglo-American Right* (Harvard Univerity Press, 1994), pp. 160–61: "The language had also been tightened by reversing the reference to the military and the right of the people to bear arms, perhaps intentionally putting more emphasis on the militia."

10. Stephen P. Halbrook, *That Every Man Be Armed*. For the motion that failed, see Schwartz, *The Bill of Rights*, vol. 2, pp. 1143–54.

11. See Articles of Confederation, draft Articles X, XI, and XII, all of which used "common defence" for confederated action, and Articles VII and VIII as passed. See *The Documentary History of the Ratification of the Constitution*, ed. Merrill Jensen, vol. 1 (State Historical Society of Wisconsin, 1976), pp. 81, 89. Article VIII stated:

All charges of war, and all other expenses that shall be incurred for the common defence or general welfare, are allowed by the united states in congress assembled, shall be defrayed out of a common treasury . . . according to such mode as the united states in congress assembled shall from time to time direct and appoint. [italics added]

Alexander Hamilton used "common defence" in the same way, in *Federalist* No. 25 (Jacob E. Cooke, editor, Wesleyan University Press, 1961, p. 158).

12. Malcolm, *To Keep and Bear Arms*, p. 160: "In keeping with state proposals, the word 'state' had been substituted for Madison's 'country.' 'State' was a more precise term and, since a state was a polity, it could refer either to one state or to the United States."

13. Of course, the original point of British resistance to standing armies was lost in America. The militias were parliament's tool to keep the king from having a regular revenue for standing forces. in America, the parliament (Congress) had established itself as the organizer and founder of the military forces, a point made both by Hamilton in the *Federalist* (Nos. 24, 26, 28) and Madison (Elliot, *Debates in the Several States Conventions*, vol. 3, p. 383).

14. James Madison, *Federalist* No. 46, pp. 320–21.

15. Sanford Levinson, "The Embarrassing Second Amendment," *Yale Law Journal* (December 1989): 637–59.

16. See Wayne LaPierre, *Guns, Crime, and Freedom* (Regnery Publishing, 1994), pp. 12, 175. For the constitutionalism of George Will, see Garry Wills, "Undemocratic Vistas," *New York Review of Books*, 19 November 1992, pp. 28–34.

17. David C. Williams, "Civic Republicanism and the Second Amendment: The Terrifying Second Amendment," *Yale Law Journal* (December 1991): 551–615.

18. Trenchard, *An Argument*, p. 15.

19. Madison, *Federalist* No. 46, p. 316.

20. See for instance, S. D. Lambert, *The Phratries of Attica* (University of Michigan Press, 1993), pp. 25–58, 205–36.

21. Ironically, the private militias of our day like to compare themselves with the Minutemen of the Revolutionary era—yet those were volunteer forces joined only by the ideologically compatible, something far closer to the "select militia" of the eighteenth century than is the contemporary National Guard. For the lack of universal service in colonial militias, see John Shy, *A People Numerous and Armed* (Oxford University Press, 1976), pp. 21–33.

22. The best summary of this matter is by Frederick Bernays Wiener, "The Militia Clause of the Constitution," *Harvard Law Review* (December 1940): 181–219.

23. Wiener, "The Militia Clause," pp. 188–93.

24. Malcolm, *To Keep and Bear Arms*, p. 164.

25. Richard Beeman, Patrick Henry (McGraw-Hill, 1974), pp. 170–72. There is a good contemporary description of Henry's attempt to kill the Bill of Rights he had earlier demanded in *The Papers of James Madison*, vol. 12 (University Press of Virginia, 1979), pp. 463–65.

26. Madison, *Papers*, vol. 12, p. 347. Madison called the Bill of Rights "the nauseous project of amendments," which he considered unnecessary in a republic, but "not improper in itself," and useful for preempting a position it could be inconvenient to surrender to the Antifederalists (pp. 346–47). This is hardly the stubborn call to a last bastion of freedom that gun advocates find in the Second Amendment.

27. Levinson, "The Embarrassing Second Amendment," pp. 657–59.

SELECTED BIBLIOGRAPHY

Alba, Richard D., and Steven F. Messner. 1995a. "Point Blank against itself." *Journal of Quantitative Criminology* 11:391–410.

———. 1995b. "Point Blank and the evidence: A rejoinder to Gary Kleck." *Journal of Quantitative Criminology* 11:425–28.

Alvianti, Joseph D., and William R. Drake. 1975. *Handgun Control . . . Issues and Alternatives.* Washington, D.C.: U.S. Conference of Mayors.

Bakal, Carl. 1966. *The Right to Bear Arms.* New York: McGraw-Hill.

Bergstein, Jack M., David Hemenway, Bruce Kennedy, Sher Quaday, and Roseannna Ander. 1966. "Guns in young hands." *Journal of Trauma* 41:794–98.

Boyd, Jeffrey H., and E. K. Mowscicki. 1986 "Firearms and youth suicide." *American Journal of Public Health* 76:1240–42.

Britt, Chester, III, Gary Kleck, and David J. Bordua. 1996a. "A reassessment of the D.C. gun law: Some cautionary notes on the use of interrupted time series designs for policy impact assessment." *Law & Society Review* 30:361–80.

———. 1996b. "Avoidance and misunderstanding: A rejoinder to McDowall et al." *Law & Society Review* 30:393–97.

Cook, Philip. J. 1976. "A strategic choice analysis of robbery." In *Sample Surveys of the Victims of Crime.* Edited by Wesley Skogan. Cambridge: Ballinger, pp. 173–87.

———. 1985a. "The case of the missing victims: Gunshot woundings in the National Crime Survey." *Journal of Quantitative Criminology* 1:91–102.

Cook, Philip J., and Jens Ludwig. 1996a. "You got me: How many defensive gun users per year?" Paper presented at the annual meetings of the Homicide Research Working Group, Santa Monica, May 17.

Cook, Philip J., Stephanie Molliconi, and Thomas B. Cole. 1995. "Regulating gun markets." *Journal of Criminal Law & Criminology* 86:59–92.

Cook, Philip J., and Mark C. Moore. 1994. "Gun control." In *Crime.* Edited by James Q. Wilson and Joan Petersilia. San Francisco: Institute for Contemporary Studies, pp. 267–94, 566–71.

DeMaio, Vincent, S. Kalousdian, and J. M. Loeb. 1992. "Assault weapons as a public health hazard." *Journal of the American Medical Association* 286:3073.

Dixon, Jo, and Alan J. Lizotte. 1987. "Gun ownership and Southern Subculture of Violence." *American Journal of Sociology* 93:383–405.

Greenwood, Colin. 1972. *Firearms Control: A Study of Armed Crime and Firearms Control in England and Wales.* London: Routledge.

Hemenway, David. 1997. "Survey research and self-defense gun use." *Journal of Criminal Law & Criminology.*

Hemenway, David, Sara J. Solnick, and Deborah R. Azrael. 1995a. "Firearm training and storage." *Journal of the American Medical Association* 273:48–50.

Henigan, Dennis A., E. Bruce Nicholson, and David Hemenway. 1995. *Guns and the Constitution: The Myth of Second Amendment Protection for Firearms in America.* Northampton, Mass.: Aletheia.

Hill, Gary D., Frank M. Howell, and Ernest T. Driver. 1985. "Gender, fear, and protective handgun ownership." *Criminology* 23:541–52.

Kaplan, John, 1979. "Controlling firearms." *Cleveland State Law Review* 28:1–28.

Kates, Don B., Jr. 1979a. "Toward a history of handgun prohibition in the United States." In *Restricting Handguns: The Liberal Skeptics Speak Out.* Edited by Don B. Kates Jr. Croton-on-Hudson, N.Y.: North River, pp. 7–30.

———. 1983. "Handgun prohibition and the original meaning of the Second Amendment." *Michigan Law Review* 82:204–73.

———. 1984a. "Handgun banning in light of the prohibition experience." In *Firearms and Violence: Issues of Public Policy.* Edited by Don B. Kates Jr. Cambridge, Mass.: Ballinger, pp. 139–65.

———. 1986b. "Criminological perspectives on gun control and gun prohibition legislation." In *Why Handgun Bans Can't Work.* Edited by Don B. Kates Jr. Bellevue, Wash.: Second Amendment Foundation, pp. 3–76.

Kates, Don B., Jr. and Gary Kleck. 2000. *The Great American Gun Debate: Essays on Firearms and Violence.* Amherst, N.Y.: Prometheus Books.

Kates, Don B., Henry E. Schaffer, John K. Lattimer, George B. Murray, and Edwin H. Cassem, 1995. "Guns and public health: Epidemic of violence or pandemic of propaganda?" *Tennessee Law Review* 62:513–96.

Kellermann, Arthur L., and Donald T. Reay. 1986. "Protection or peril? An analysis of firearm-related deaths in the home." *New England Journal of Medicine* 355:1438–44.

Kellermann, Arthur L., Frederick P. Rivara, Roberta K. Lee, Joyce G. Banton, Peter Cummings, Bela B. Hackman, and Grant Somes, 1996. "Injuries due to firearms in three cities." *New England Journal of Medicine* 355:1438–44.

Kellermann, Arthur L., Frederick P. Rivara, Grant Somes, Donald T. Reay, Jerry Francisco, Joyce Gillentine Banton, Janice Prodzinski, Corinne Fligner, and Bela B. Hackman. 1992. "Suicide in the home in relation to gun ownership." *New England Journal of Medicine* 327:467–72.

Kennett, Lee, and James LaVerne Anderson. 1975. *The Gun in America: The Origins of a National Dilemma.* Westport, Conn.: Greenwood.

Kleck, Gary. 1979. "Capital punishment, gun ownership, and homicide." *American Journal of Sociology* 84:882–910.

———. 1984a "The relationship between gun ownership levels and rates of violence in the United States." In *Firearms and Violence: Issues of Public Policy.* Edited by Don B. Kates Jr. Cambridge, Mass.: Ballinger, pp. 99–135.

———. 1991. *Point Blank: Guns and Violence in America.* Hawthorne, N.Y.: Aldine de Gruyter.

———. 1997. *Targeting Guns.* Hawthorne, N.Y.: Aldine de Gruyter.

Kleck, Gary, and David J. Bordua. 1983. "The factual foundations for certain key assumptions of gun control." *Law & Policy* Quarterly 5:271–98.

Kleck, Gary, and Marc Gertz. 1995. "Armed resistance to crime: The prevalence and nature of self-defense with a gun." *Journal of Criminal Law and Criminology* 86:150–87.

Kleck, Gary, and Karen McElrath. 1990. "The impact of weaponry on human violence." *Social Forces* 69:669–92.

Kleck, Gary, and E. Britt Patterson. 1993. "The impact of gun control and gun ownership levels on violence rates." *Journal of Quantitative Criminology* 9:249–88.

Kopel, David. 1992. *The Samurai, the Mountie, and the Cowboy.* Amherst, N.Y.: Prometheus.

———. 1995. *Guns Who Should Have Them?* Edited by David B. Kopel. Amherst, N.Y.: Prometheus.

Loftin, Colin, and David McDowell, 1981. " 'One with a gun gets you two': mandatory sentencing and firearms violence in Detroit." *Annals* 455:150–67.

Lott, John. 1998. *More Guns, Less Crime.* Chicago: University of Chicago Press.

Lott, John, and David B. M. Mustard. 1997. "Crime deterrence and right-to-carry concealed hand-guns." *Journal of Legal Studies* 26:1–68.

Malcolm, Joyce Lee. 1994. *To Keep and Bear Arms: The Origins of an Anglo-American Right.* Cambridge, Mass: Harvard University Press.

McDowall, David, Alan Lizotte, and Brian Wiersema. 1991. "General deterrence through civilian gun ownership." *Criminology* 29:541–59.

McDowall, David, Colin Loftin, and Brian Wiersema. 1992. "A comparative study of the preventive effects of mandatory sentencing laws for gun crimes." *Journal of Criminal Law and Criminology* 83:378–94.

McDowall, David, and Brian Wiersema. 1994. "The incidence of defensive firearm use by U.S. crime victims, 1987 through 1990." *American Journal of Public Health* 84:1982–84.

McDowell, David, Brian Wiersema, and Colin Loftin. 1989. "Did mandatory firearm ownership in Kennesaw really prevent burglaries?" *Sociology and Social Research* 74:48–51.

National Research Council. 1993. *Understanding and Preventing Violence.* Washington, D.C.: National Academy Press.

Robin, Gerald D. 1991. *Violent Crime and Gun Control.* Cincinnati, Ohio: Anderson.

Roth, Jeffrey A. 1994. "Firearms and violence." National Institute of Justice. Research in Brief. Washington, D.C.: U.S. Government Printing Office.

Sheley, Joseph F., Charles J. Brody, and James D. Wright. 1994. "Women and handguns: Evidence from national surveys, 1973–1991." *Social Science Research* 23:219–35.

Shields, Pete. 1981. *Guns Don't Die—People Do.* New York: Arbor House.

Teret, Stephen P., Garen Wintemute, and P. L. Beilenson. 1992. "The Firearm Fatality Reporting System: A proposal." *Journal of the American Medical Association* 267:3073–74.

Weil, Douglas S., and David Hemenway. 1992. "Loaded guns in the home: Analysis of a national random survey of gun owners." *Journal of the American Medical Association* 267:3033–37.

Wilson, James Q. 1976. "Crime and punishment in England." *Public Interest* 43:3–25.

———. 1995. "Just take away their guns." *New York Times Magazine,* 20 March 1994, pp. 46–47.

Wintemute, Garen J. 1987. "Firearms as a cause of death in the United States, 1920–1982." *Journal of Trauma* 27:532–36.

———. 1996. "The relationship between firearm design and firearm violence." *Journal of the American Medical Association* 275:1749–53.

———. 1987. "When children shoot children: 88 unintended deaths in California." *Journal of the American Medical Association* 257:3107–9.

Wright, James D., and Peter H. Rossi. 1985. *The Armed Criminal in America: A Survey of Incarcerated Felons.* National Institute of Justice Research Report. Washington, D.C.: U.S. Government Printing Office.

Wright, James D., and Peter H. Rossi. 1986. *Armed and Considered Dangerous: A Survey of Felons and Their Firearms.* Hawthorne, N.Y.: Aldine de Gruyter.

Wright, James D., Peter H. Rossi, and Kathleen Daly. 1983. *Under the Gun: Weapons, Crime, and Violence in America.* Hawthorne, N.Y.: Aldine de Gruyter.

Yeager, Matthew G., Joseph D. Alviani, and Nancy Loving. 1976. *How Well Does the Handgun Protect You and Your Family?* Handgun Control Staff Technical Report 2. Washington, D.C.: United States Conference of Mayors.

Young, Robert L., David McDowall, and Colin Loftin. 1987. "Collective security and the ownership of firearms for protection." *Criminology* 25:47–62.

Zimring, Franklin E. 1968. "Is gun control likely to reduce violent killings?" *University of Chicago Law Review* 35:721–37.

———. 1991. "Firearms, violence, and public policy." *Scientific American* 265:48- 58.

———. 1993. "Policy research on firearms and violence." *Health Affairs* 12:109–22.

———. 1995. "Reflections on firearms and the criminal law." *Journal of Criminal Law and Criminology* 86:1–9.

Zimring, Franklin E., and Gordon Hawkins. 1987. *The Citizen's Guide to Gun Control.* New York: Macmillan.

———. 1997. *Crime Is Not the Problem: Lethal Violence in America.* New York: Oxford University Press.

CONTRIBUTORS

B. Bruce-Briggs, contributor to *Public Interest*.

Philip J. Cook, Professor of Public Policy and Economics, Duke University.

Mark Gertz, Professor, School of Criminology and Criminal Justice, Florida State University.

Barry Glassner, Professor of Sociology, University of Southern California.

Gordon Hawkins, Senior Fellow, Earl Warren Legal Institute at the University of California at Berkeley.

Richard Hofstadter, (deceased) American Historian, Pulitzer Prize Winner.

Barbara Kantrowicz, Journalist, *Newsweek* Magazine.

J. P. Kassirer, M.D., formerly Editor-in-chief, *New England Journal of Medicine*.

Don B. Kates, Criminologist and Attorney, Benenson and Kates, San Francisco, California.

Arthur L. Kellermann, M.D. M.P.H., Medical Director, Emergency Department, Regional Medical Center, Memphis, Tennessee.

Gary Kleck, Professor, School of Criminology and Criminal Justice, Florida State University.

David B. Kopel, Attorney and Research Director of the Independence Institute, Denver, Colorado.

John B. Lattimer, M.D., Professor Emeritus, Columbia Medical School.

Colin Loftin, Professor of Criminology, Institute of Criminal Justice and Criminology, University of Maryland.

John Lott, Professor of Economics, Yale University.

Joyce Lee Malcolm, Professor of History, Bentley College.

David McDowall, Violence Research Group and Department of Criminology and Criminal Justice, University of Maryland at College Park.

Albert J. Reiss Jr., Professor, Department of Sociology, Yale University.

Frederick P. Rivara, M.D., M.P.H., Department Preventative Medicine, University of Tennessee.

Roger Rosenblatt, Journalist, Newsweek Magazine.

Jeffrey A. Roth, Principal, Staff Officer, National Research Council of the National Academy of Sciences.

John Ruscio, Psychologist, Department of Psychology, Elizabethtown College.

Norman B. Rushford, Department of Biostatistics and Epidemiology, University of Tennessee, Memphis.

Henry E. Schaffer, Professor of Genetics and Mathematics, North Carolina State University.

William R. Tonso, Professor Emeritus, Sociology Department, Evansville University.

Brian Wiersema, Violence Research Group and Department of Criminology and Criminal Justice, University of Maryland at College Park.

Gary Wills, formerly Professor of American Culture and Public Policy, Northwestern University.

Marvin Wolfgang (deceased), Professor of Sociology, University of Pennsylvania.

Franklin E. Zimring, Director of the Earl Waren Legal Institute and William G. Simon, Professor of Law at the University of California at Berkeley.